THE ONLY GOOD DALEK & THE DALEK PROJECT

JUSTIN RICHARDS • MIKE COLLINS

BBC BOOKS

DOCTOR WHO

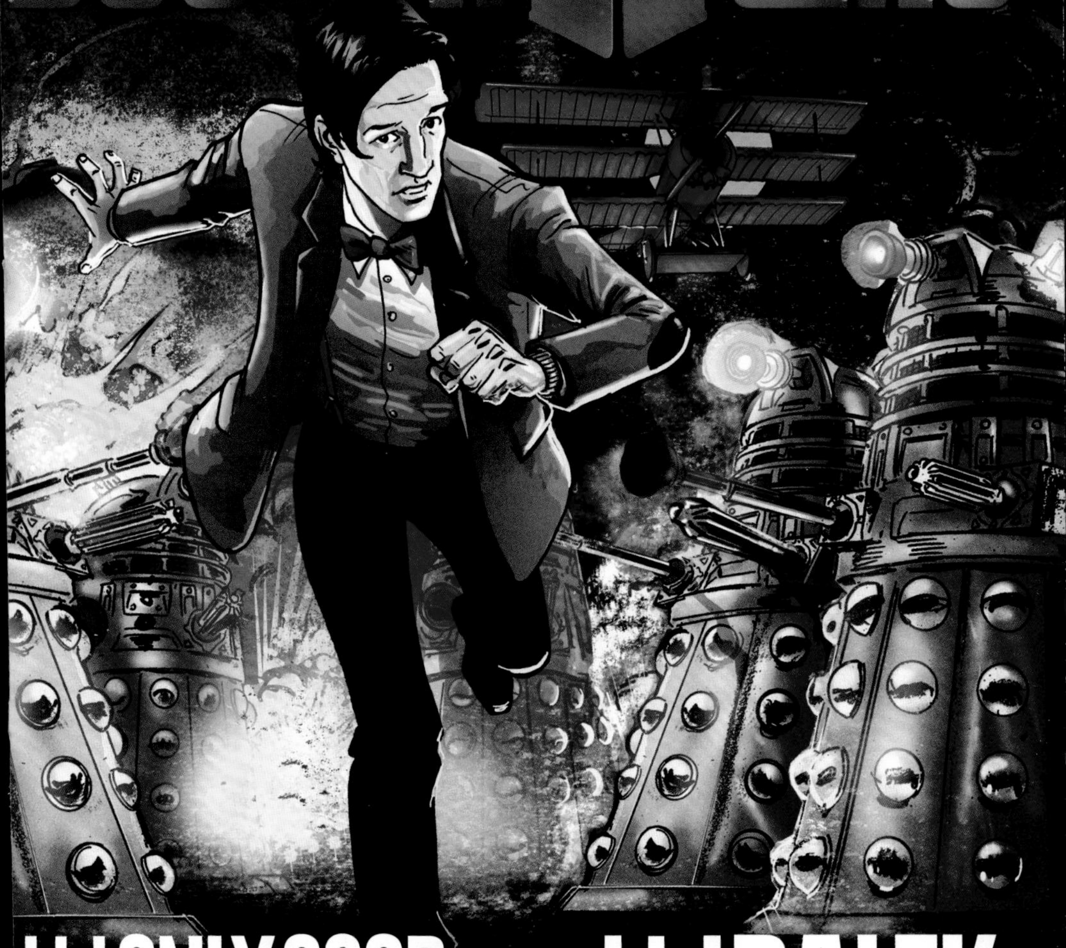

THE ONLY GOOD DALEK & THE DALEK PROJECT

JUSTIN RICHARDS • MIKE COLLINS

1 3 5 7 9 10 8 6 4 2

BBC Books, an imprint of Ebury Publishing
20 Vauxhall Bridge Road,
London SW1V 2SA

BBC Books is part of the Penguin Random House group of companies whose addresses can be found at global.penguinrandomhouse.com

Penguin Random House UK

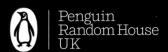

Executive producers: Steven Moffat and Brian Minchin

Doctor Who: The Only Good Dalek first published by BBC Books in 2010
Doctor Who: The Dalek Project first published by BBC Books in 2012

www.eburypublishing.co.uk

A CIP catalogue record for this book is available from the British Library

ISBN 9781785940781

Commissioning editor: Albert DePetrillo
Editorial Manager: Nicholas Payne
Series consultant: Justin Richards
Project editor: Steve Tribe
Cover design: Mike Collins, Lee Binding and Two Associates
Design: Lee Binding @ tea-lady.co.uk
Production: Phil Spencer and Alex Goddard

Printed and bound in China by C&C Offset Printing Co., Ltd

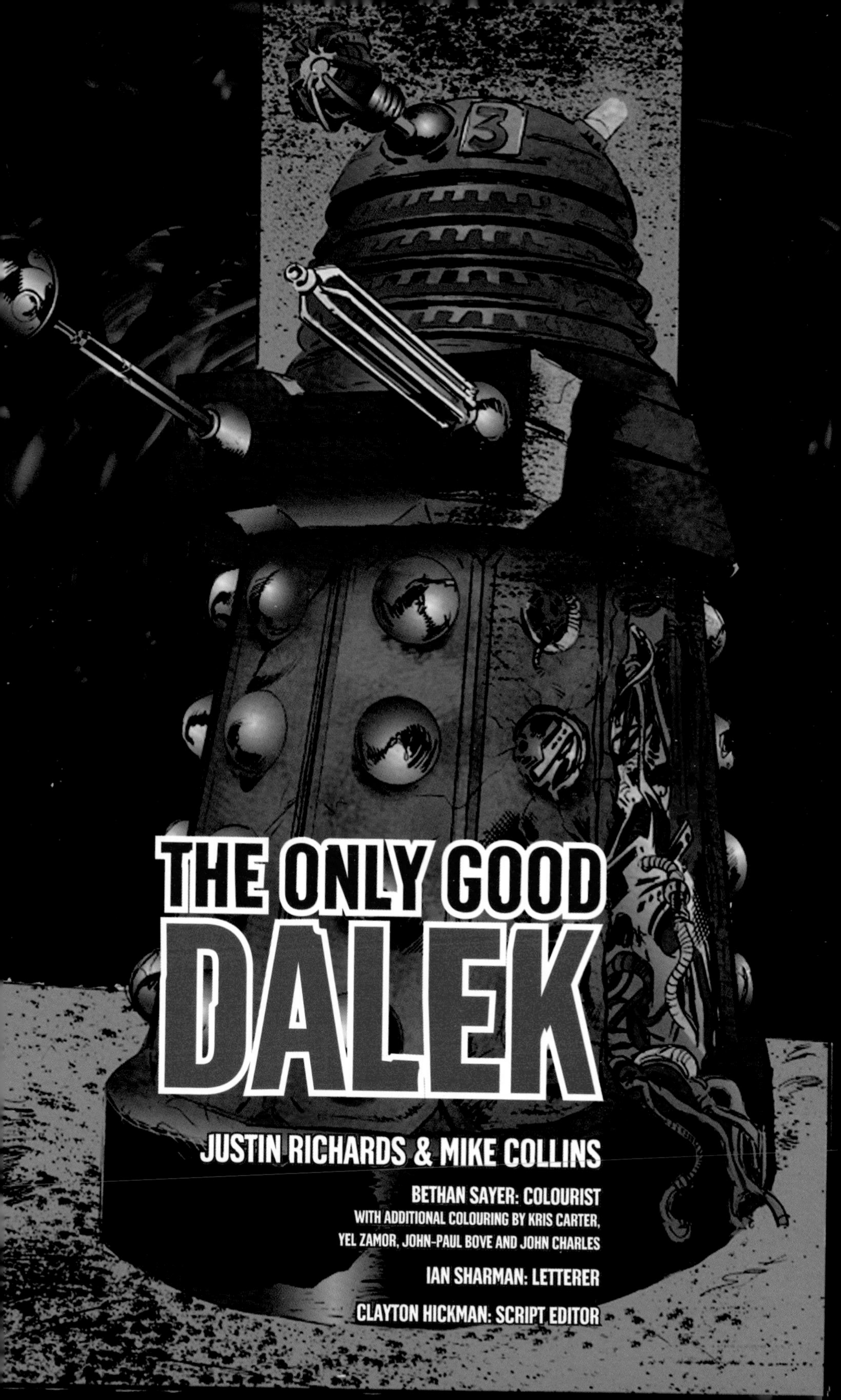

THE ONLY GOOD DALEK

JUSTIN RICHARDS & MIKE COLLINS

BETHAN SAYER: COLOURIST
WITH ADDITIONAL COLOURING BY KRIS CARTER,
YEL ZAMOR, JOHN-PAUL BOVE AND JOHN CHARLES

IAN SHARMAN: LETTERER

CLAYTON HICKMAN: SCRIPT EDITOR

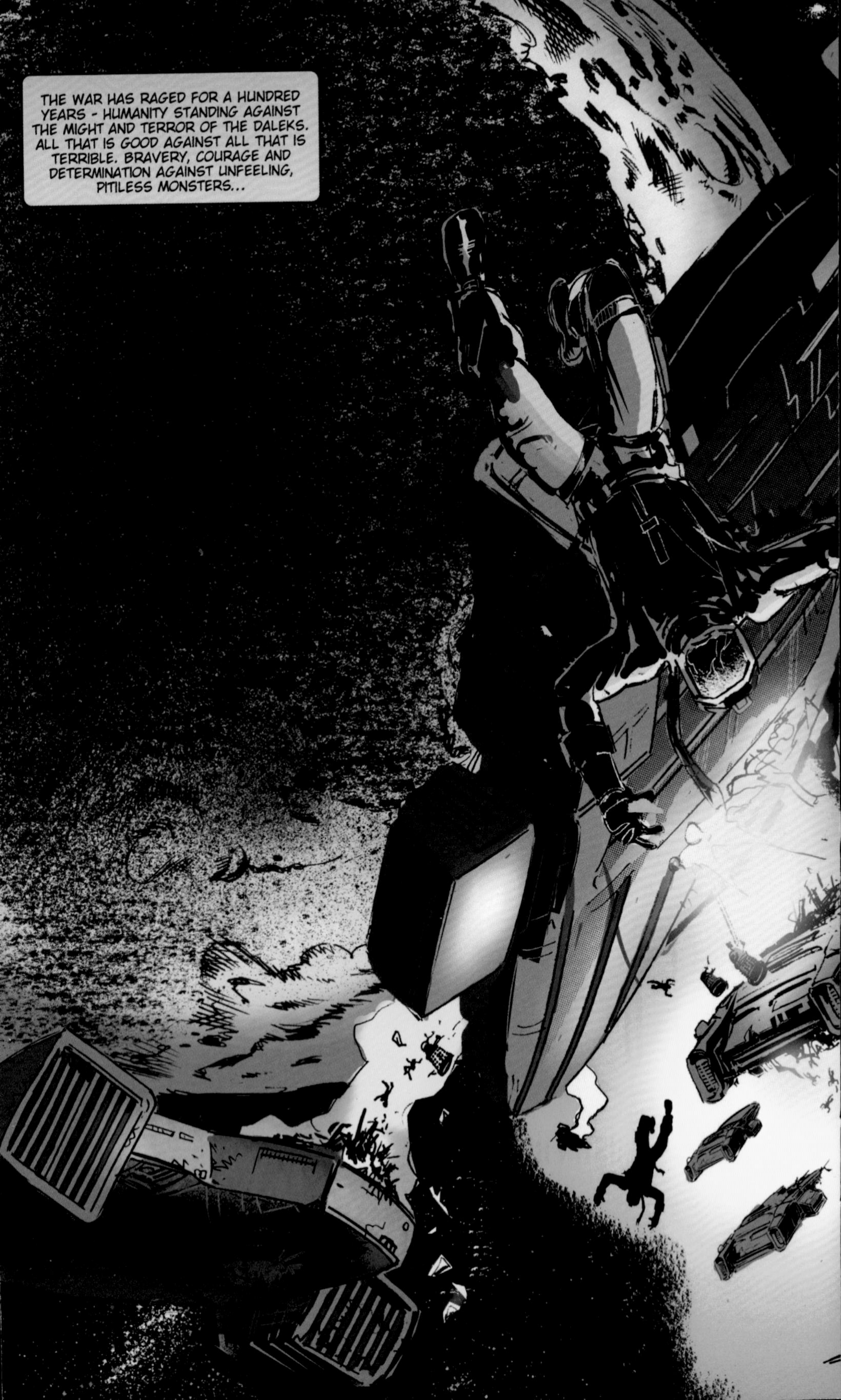
THE WAR HAS RAGED FOR A HUNDRED YEARS - HUMANITY STANDING AGAINST THE MIGHT AND TERROR OF THE DALEKS. ALL THAT IS GOOD AGAINST ALL THAT IS TERRIBLE. BRAVERY, COURAGE AND DETERMINATION AGAINST UNFEELING, PITILESS MONSTERS...

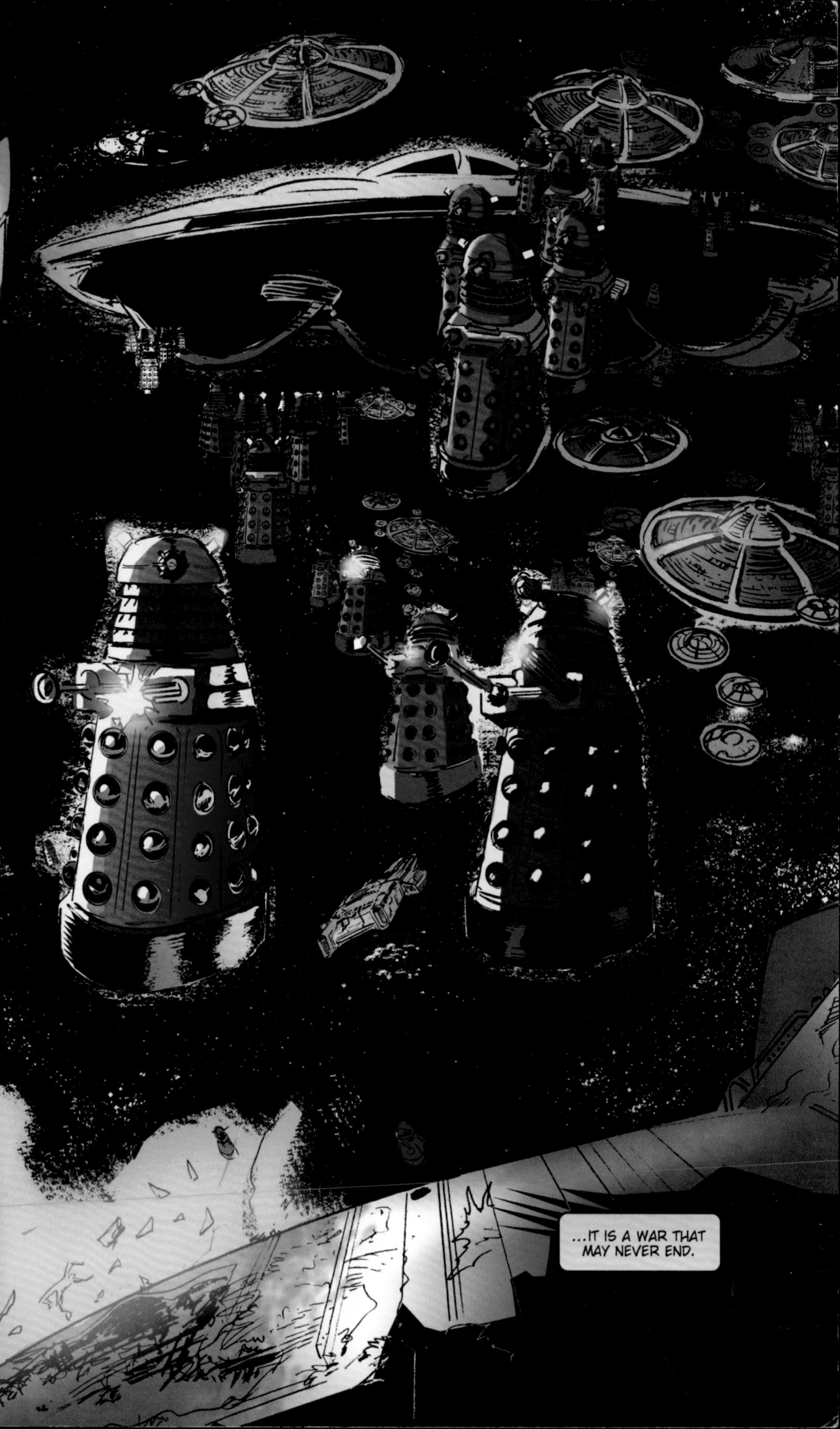
...IT IS A WAR THAT MAY NEVER END.

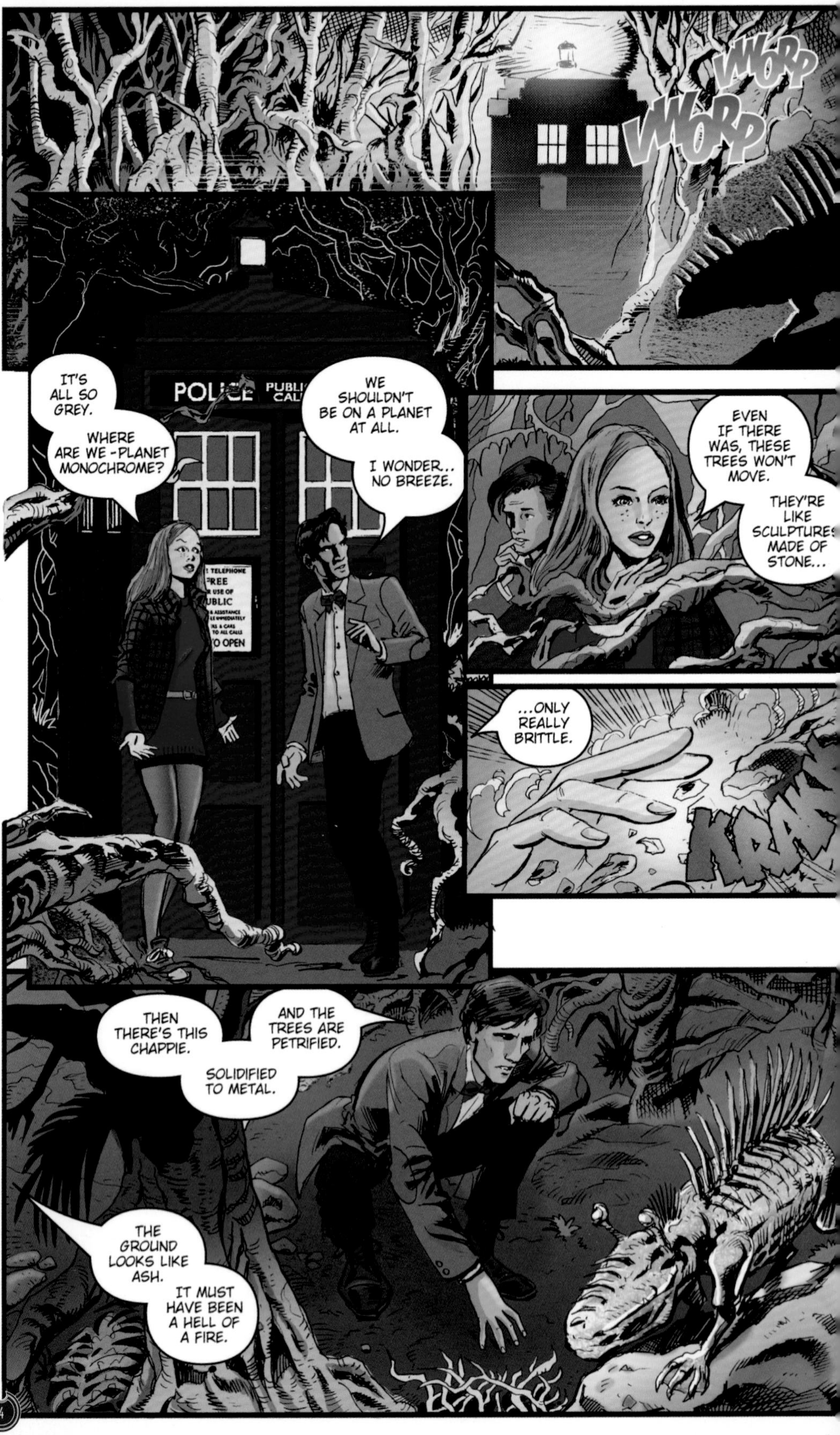
VWORP
VWORP
POLICE PUBLIC CALL
IT'S ALL SO GREY.
WHERE ARE WE - PLANET MONOCHROME?
WE SHOULDN'T BE ON A PLANET AT ALL.
I WONDER... NO BREEZE.
EVEN IF THERE WAS, THESE TREES WON'T MOVE.
THEY'RE LIKE SCULPTURES MADE OF STONE...
...ONLY REALLY BRITTLE.
THEN THERE'S THIS CHAPPIE.
AND THE TREES ARE PETRIFIED.
SOLIDIFIED TO METAL.
THE GROUND LOOKS LIKE ASH.
IT MUST HAVE BEEN A HELL OF A FIRE.

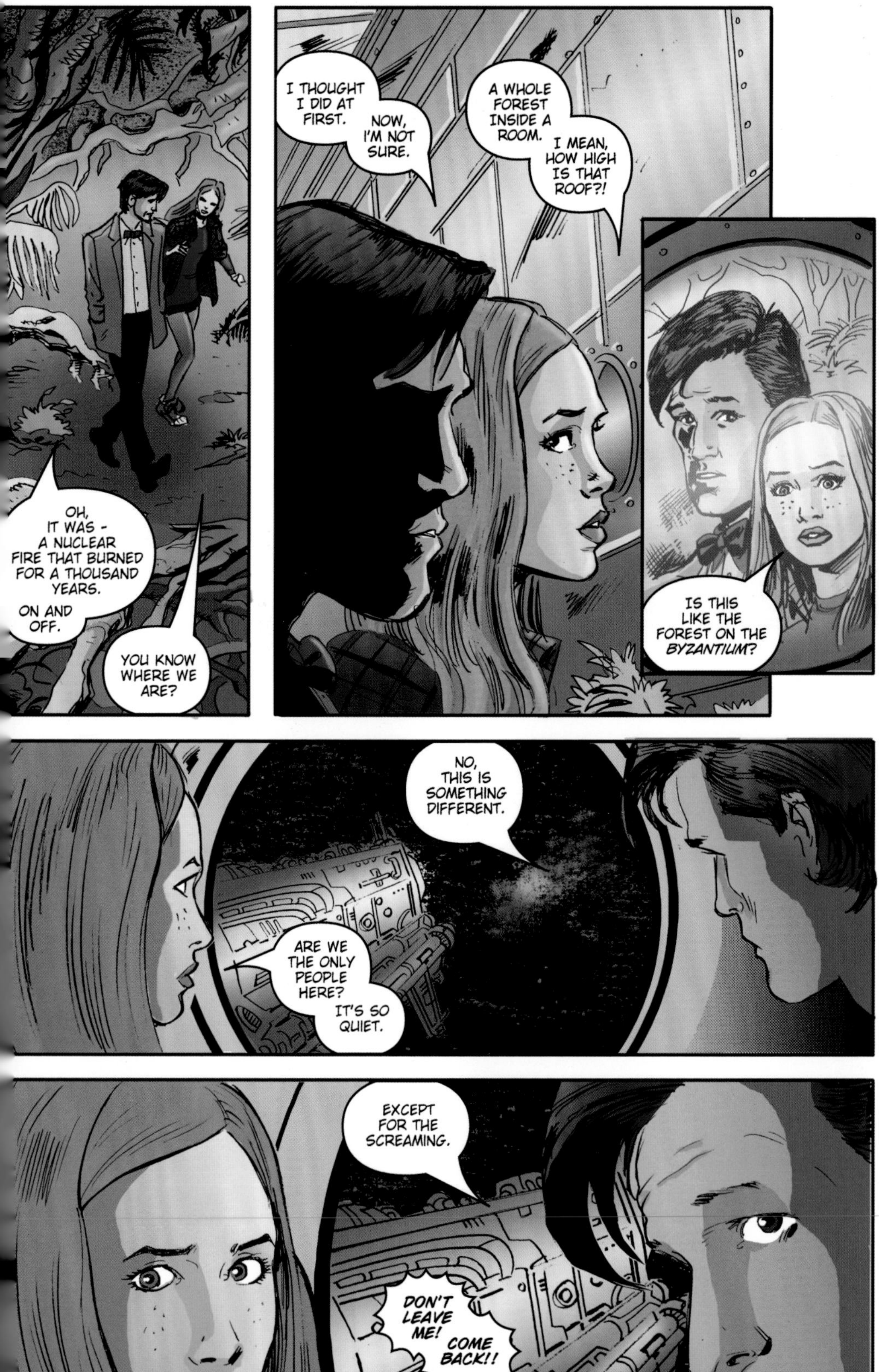

I THOUGHT I DID AT FIRST.
NOW, I'M NOT SURE.
A WHOLE FOREST INSIDE A ROOM.
I MEAN, HOW HIGH IS THAT ROOF?!
OH, IT WAS - A NUCLEAR FIRE THAT BURNED FOR A THOUSAND YEARS.
ON AND OFF.
YOU KNOW WHERE WE ARE?
IS THIS LIKE THE FOREST ON THE *BYZANTIUM*?
NO, THIS IS SOMETHING DIFFERENT.
ARE WE THE ONLY PEOPLE HERE?
IT'S SO QUIET.
EXCEPT FOR THE SCREAMING.
DON'T LEAVE ME!
COME BACK!!

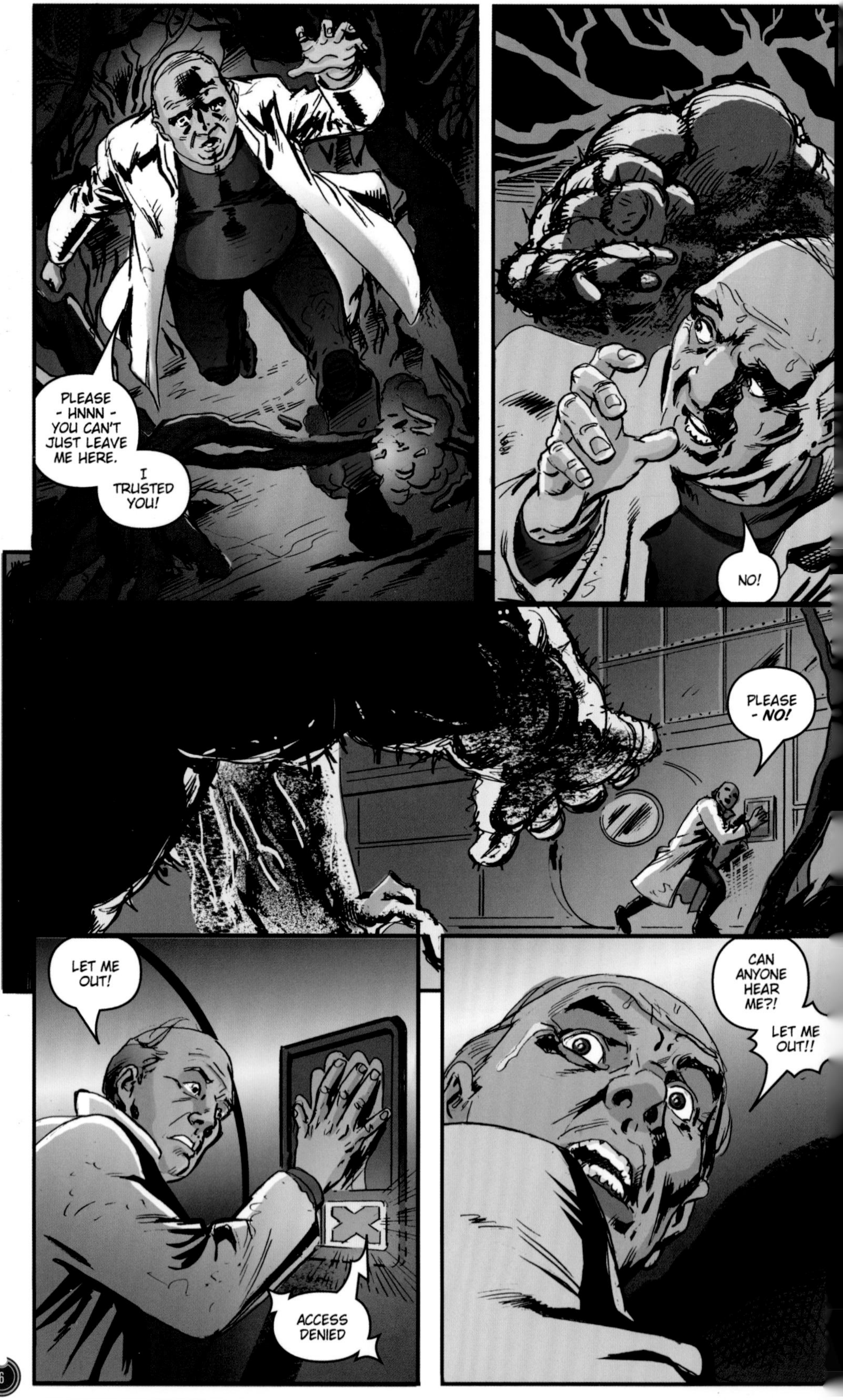
PLEASE - HNNN - YOU CAN'T JUST LEAVE ME HERE.
I TRUSTED YOU!
NO!
PLEASE - NO!
LET ME OUT!
ACCESS DENIED
CAN ANYONE HEAR ME?!
LET ME OUT!!

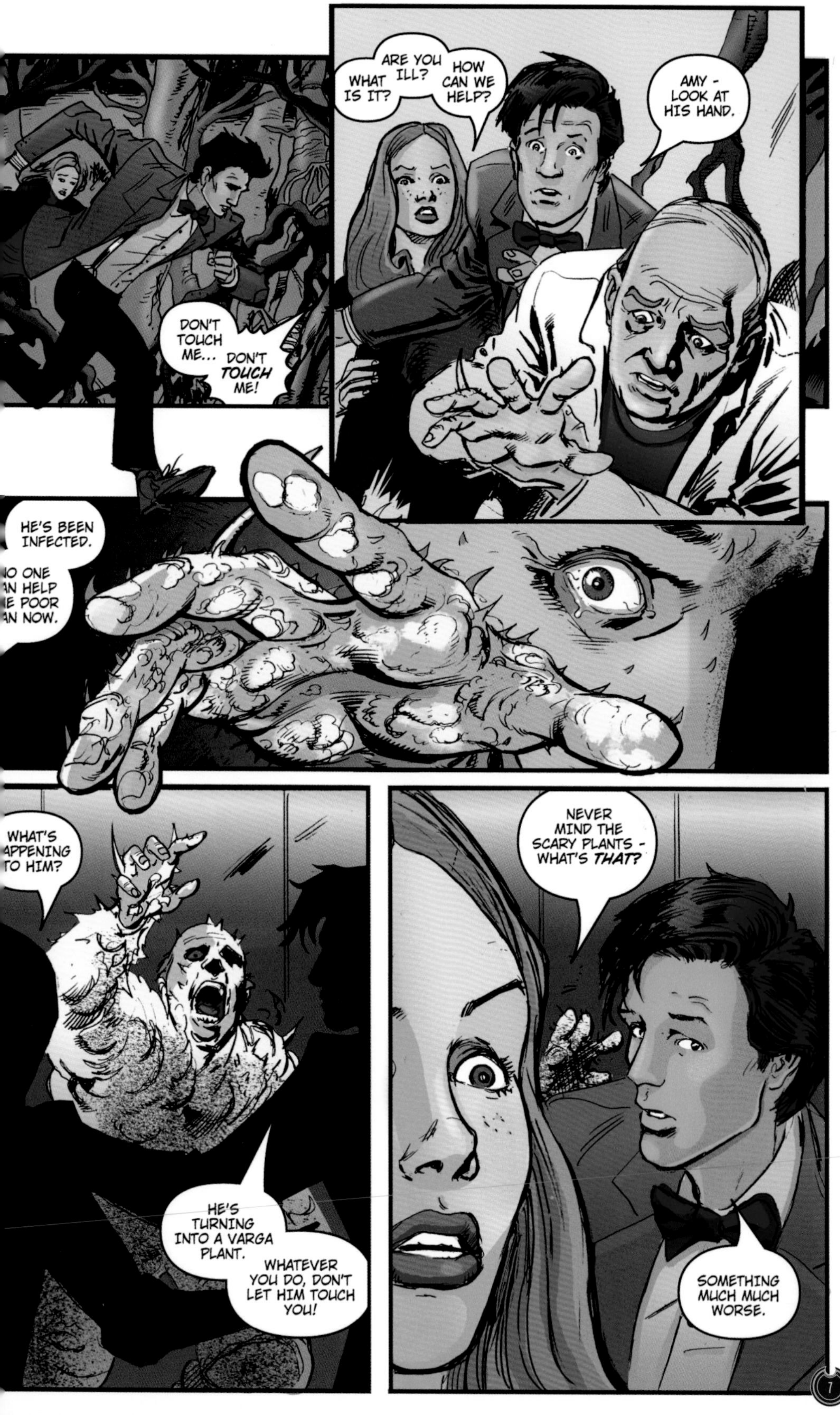

DON'T TOUCH ME... DON'T TOUCH ME!
WHAT IS IT?
ARE YOU ILL?
HOW CAN WE HELP?
AMY - LOOK AT HIS HAND.
HE'S BEEN INFECTED.
WHAT'S
TO HIM?
HE'S TURNING INTO A VARGA PLANT.
WHATEVER YOU DO, DON'T LET HIM TOUCH YOU!
NEVER MIND THE SCARY PLANTS - WHAT'S THAT?
SOMETHING MUCH MUCH WORSE.

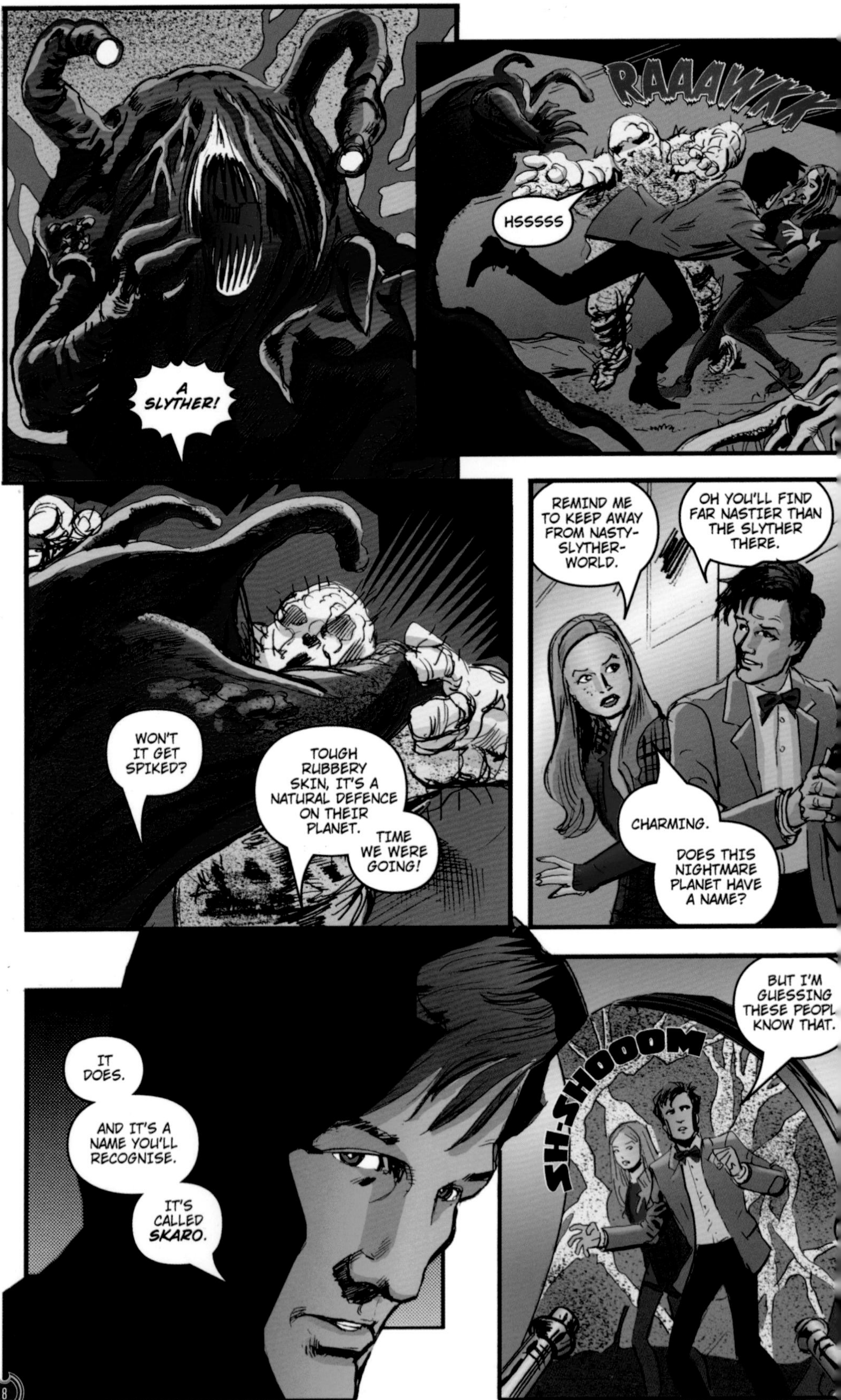

A SLYTHER!
RAAAWKK
HSSSSS
WON'T IT GET SPIKED?
TOUGH RUBBERY SKIN, IT'S A NATURAL DEFENCE ON THEIR PLANET.
TIME WE WERE GOING!
REMIND ME TO KEEP AWAY FROM NASTY-SLYTHER-WORLD.
OH YOU'LL FIND FAR NASTIER THAN THE SLYTHER THERE.
CHARMING.
DOES THIS NIGHTMARE PLANET HAVE A NAME?
IT DOES.
AND IT'S A NAME YOU'LL RECOGNISE.
IT'S CALLED SKARO.
SH-SHOOOM
BUT I'M GUESSING THESE PEOPL KNOW THAT.

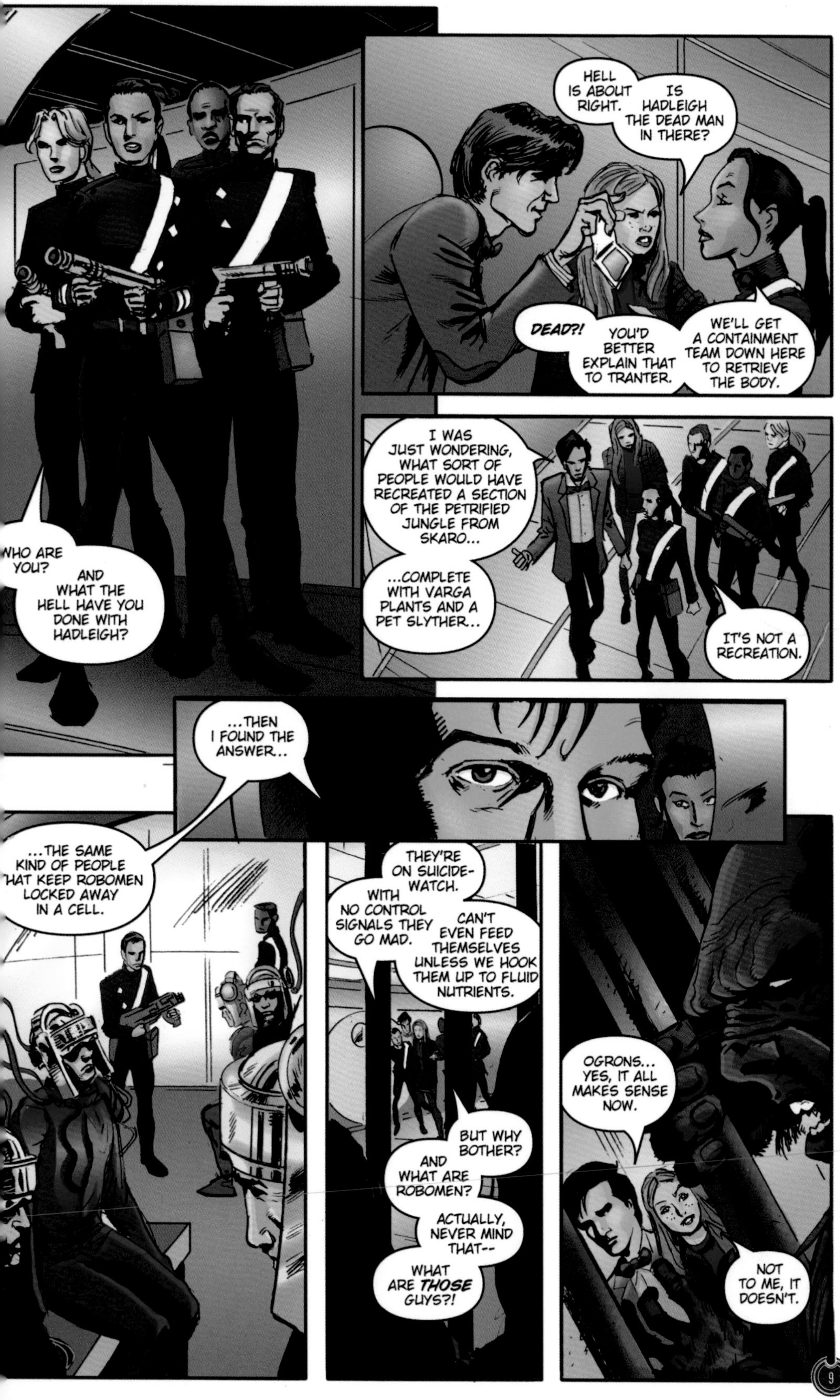
WHO ARE YOU?
AND WHAT THE HELL HAVE YOU DONE WITH HADLEIGH?
HELL IS ABOUT RIGHT.
IS HADLEIGH THE DEAD MAN IN THERE?
DEAD?!
YOU'D BETTER EXPLAIN THAT TO TRANTER.
WE'LL GET A CONTAINMENT TEAM DOWN HERE TO RETRIEVE THE BODY.
I WAS JUST WONDERING, WHAT SORT OF PEOPLE WOULD HAVE RECREATED A SECTION OF THE PETRIFIED JUNGLE FROM SKARO...
...COMPLETE WITH VARGA PLANTS AND A PET SLYTHER...
IT'S NOT A RECREATION.
...THEN I FOUND THE ANSWER...
...THE SAME KIND OF PEOPLE THAT KEEP ROBOMEN LOCKED AWAY IN A CELL.
THEY'RE ON SUICIDE-WATCH.
WITH NO CONTROL SIGNALS THEY GO MAD.
CAN'T EVEN FEED THEMSELVES UNLESS WE HOOK THEM UP TO FLUID NUTRIENTS.
BUT WHY BOTHER?
AND WHAT ARE ROBOMEN?
ACTUALLY, NEVER MIND THAT--
WHAT ARE THOSE GUYS?!
OGRONS... YES, IT ALL MAKES SENSE NOW.
NOT TO ME, IT DOESN'T.

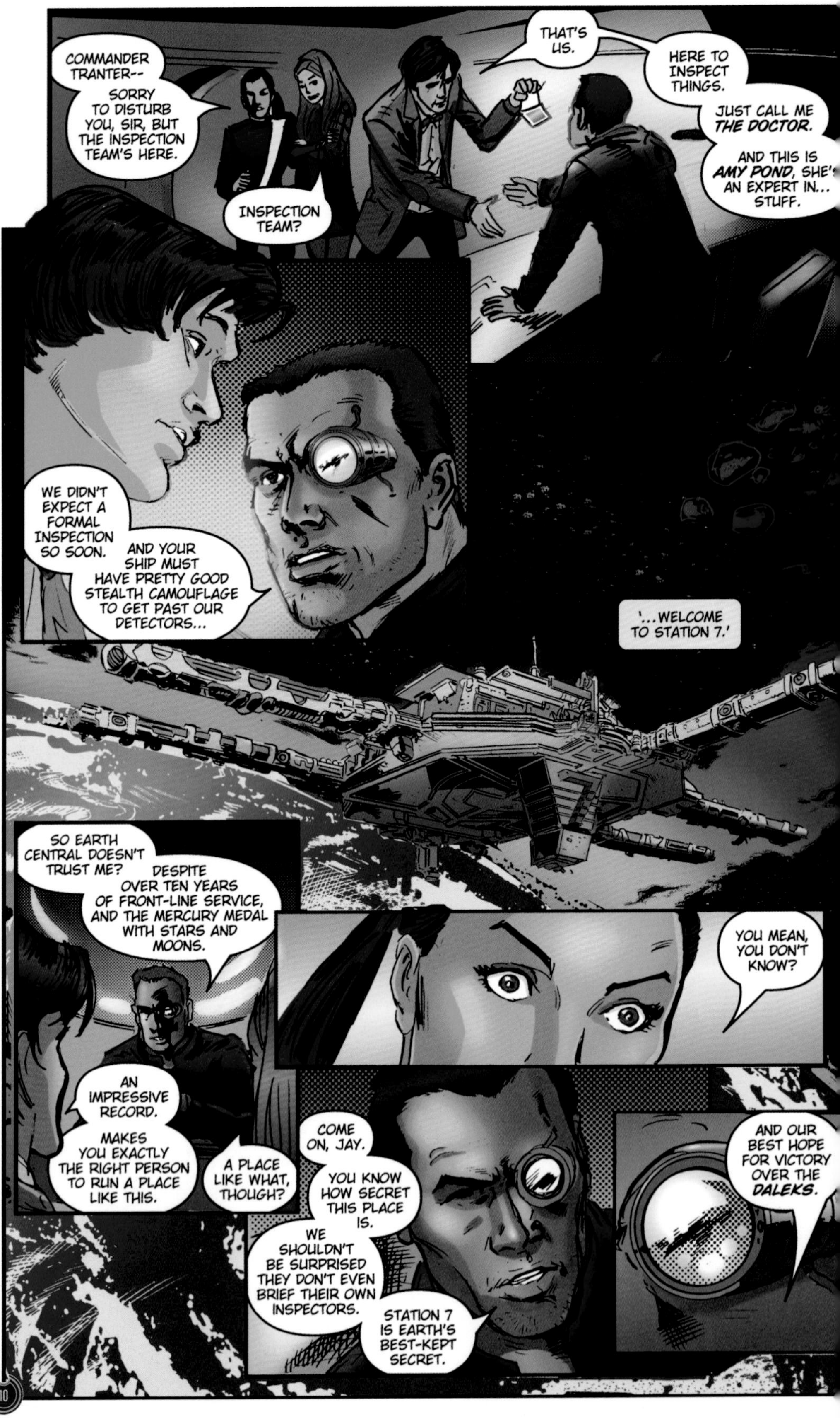
COMMANDER TRANTER--
SORRY TO DISTURB YOU, SIR, BUT THE INSPECTION TEAM'S HERE.
INSPECTION TEAM?
THAT'S US.
HERE TO INSPECT THINGS.
JUST CALL ME THE DOCTOR.
AND THIS IS AMY POND, SHE'S AN EXPERT IN... STUFF.
WE DIDN'T EXPECT A FORMAL INSPECTION SO SOON.
AND YOUR SHIP MUST HAVE PRETTY GOOD STEALTH CAMOUFLAGE TO GET PAST OUR DETECTORS...
'...WELCOME TO STATION 7.'
SO EARTH CENTRAL DOESN'T TRUST ME?
DESPITE OVER TEN YEARS OF FRONT-LINE SERVICE, AND THE MERCURY MEDAL WITH STARS AND MOONS.
YOU MEAN, YOU DON'T KNOW?
AN IMPRESSIVE RECORD.
MAKES YOU EXACTLY THE RIGHT PERSON TO RUN A PLACE LIKE THIS.
A PLACE LIKE WHAT, THOUGH?
COME ON, JAY.
YOU KNOW HOW SECRET THIS PLACE IS.
WE SHOULDN'T BE SURPRISED THEY DON'T EVEN BRIEF THEIR OWN INSPECTORS.
STATION 7 IS EARTH'S BEST-KEPT SECRET.
AND OUR BEST HOPE FOR VICTORY OVER THE DALEKS.

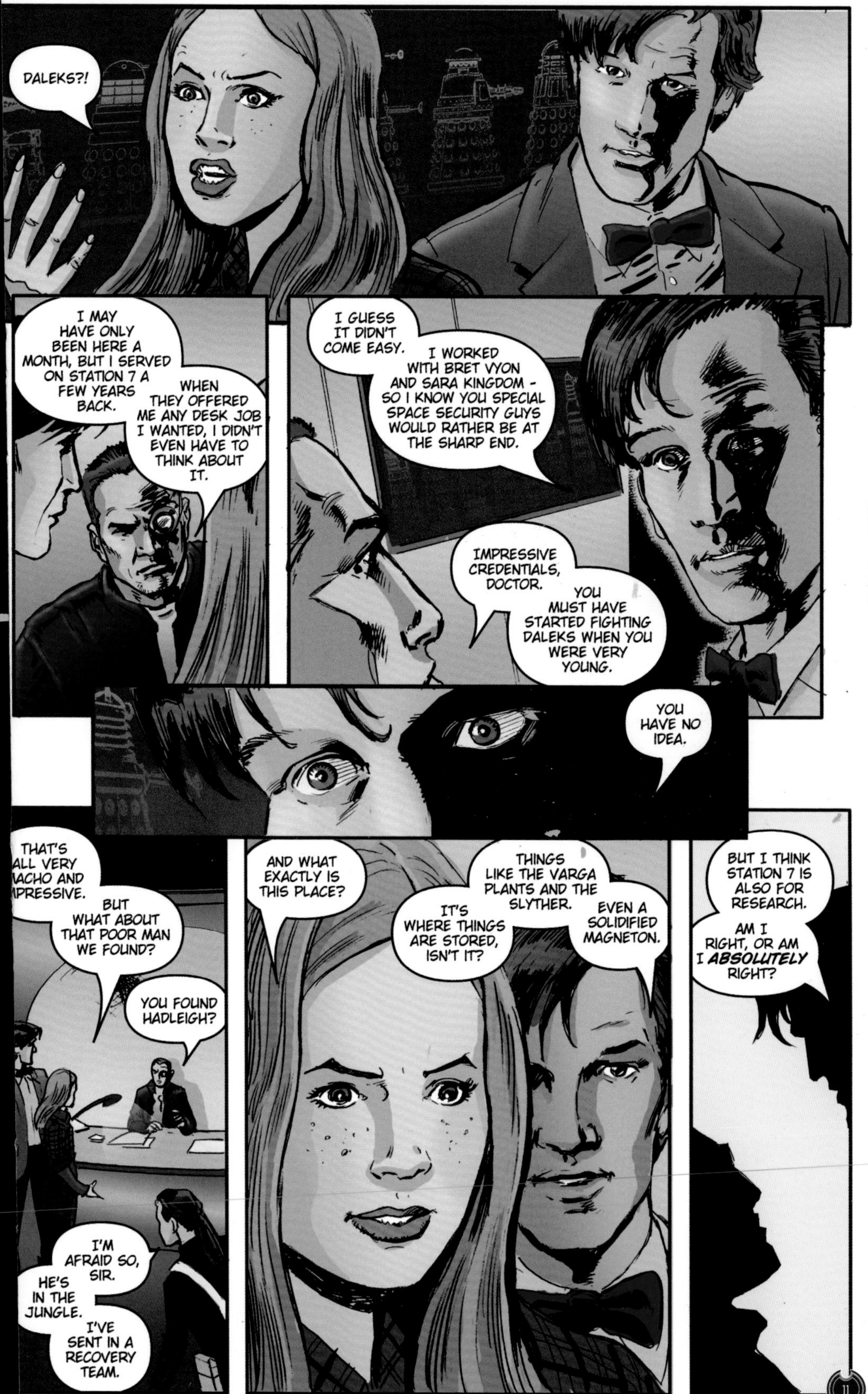

DALEKS?!
I MAY HAVE ONLY BEEN HERE A MONTH, BUT I SERVED ON STATION 7 A FEW YEARS BACK.
WHEN THEY OFFERED ME ANY DESK JOB I WANTED, I DIDN'T EVEN HAVE TO THINK ABOUT IT.
I GUESS IT DIDN'T COME EASY.
I WORKED WITH BRET VYON AND SARA KINGDOM - SO I KNOW YOU SPECIAL SPACE SECURITY GUYS WOULD RATHER BE AT THE SHARP END.
IMPRESSIVE CREDENTIALS, DOCTOR.
YOU MUST HAVE STARTED FIGHTING DALEKS WHEN YOU WERE VERY YOUNG.
YOU HAVE NO IDEA.
THAT'S ALL VERY MACHO AND MPRESSIVE.
BUT WHAT ABOUT THAT POOR MAN WE FOUND?
YOU FOUND HADLEIGH?
I'M AFRAID SO, SIR.
HE'S IN THE JUNGLE.
I'VE SENT IN A RECOVERY TEAM.
AND WHAT EXACTLY IS THIS PLACE?
IT'S WHERE THINGS ARE STORED, ISN'T IT?
THINGS LIKE THE VARGA PLANTS AND THE SLYTHER.
EVEN A SOLIDIFIED MAGNETON.
BUT I THINK STATION 7 IS ALSO FOR RESEARCH.
AM I RIGHT, OR AM I ***ABSOLUTELY*** RIGHT?

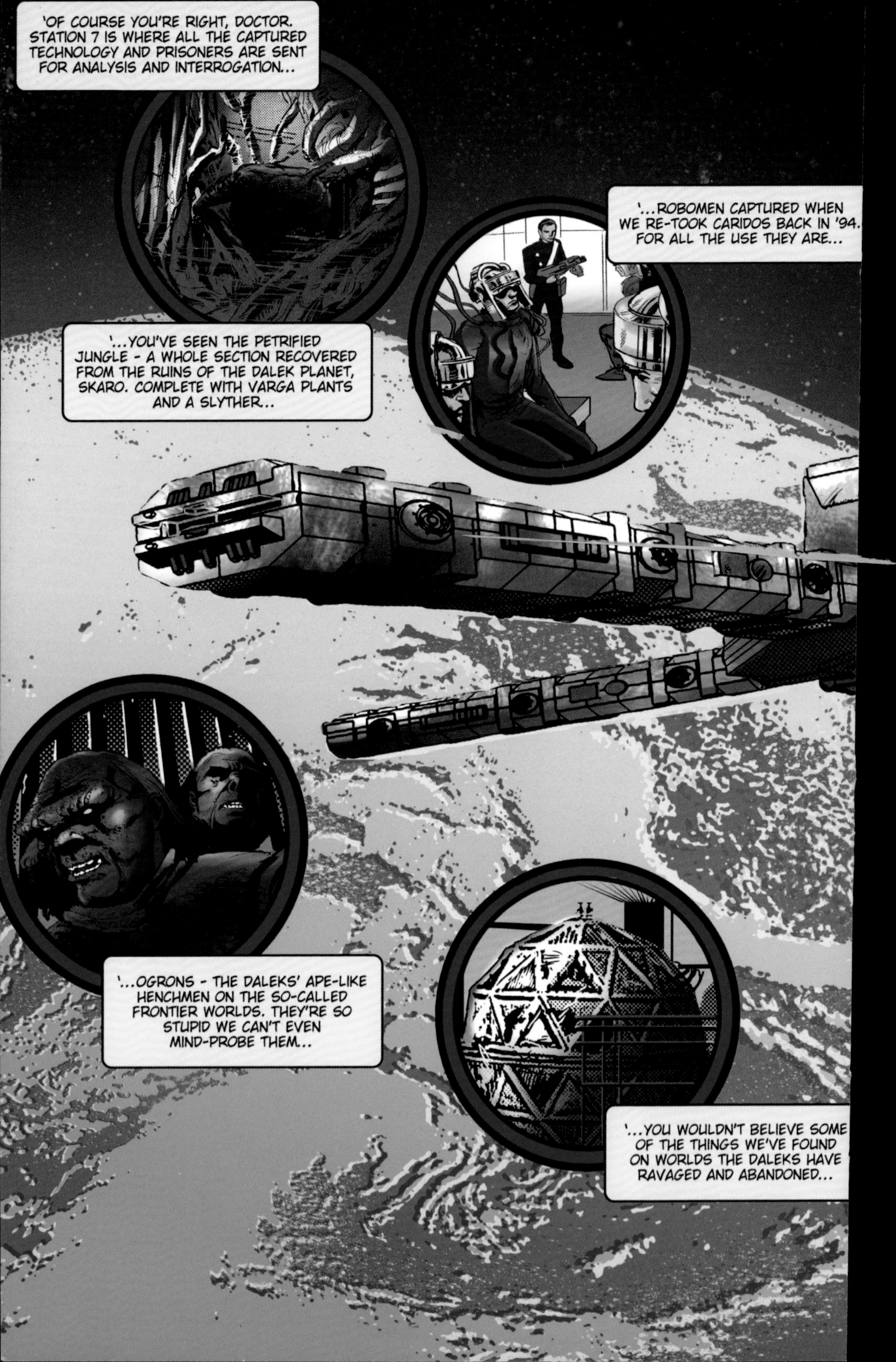

'OF COURSE YOU'RE RIGHT, DOCTOR. STATION 7 IS WHERE ALL THE CAPTURED TECHNOLOGY AND PRISONERS ARE SENT FOR ANALYSIS AND INTERROGATION...
'...YOU'VE SEEN THE PETRIFIED JUNGLE - A WHOLE SECTION RECOVERED FROM THE RUINS OF THE DALEK PLANET, SKARO. COMPLETE WITH VARGA PLANTS AND A SLYTHER...
'...ROBOMEN CAPTURED WHEN WE RE-TOOK CARIDOS BACK IN '94. FOR ALL THE USE THEY ARE...
'...OGRONS - THE DALEKS' APE-LIKE HENCHMEN ON THE SO-CALLED FRONTIER WORLDS. THEY'RE SO STUPID WE CAN'T EVEN MIND-PROBE THEM...
'...YOU WOULDN'T BELIEVE SOME OF THE THINGS WE'VE FOUND ON WORLDS THE DALEKS HAVE RAVAGED AND ABANDONED...

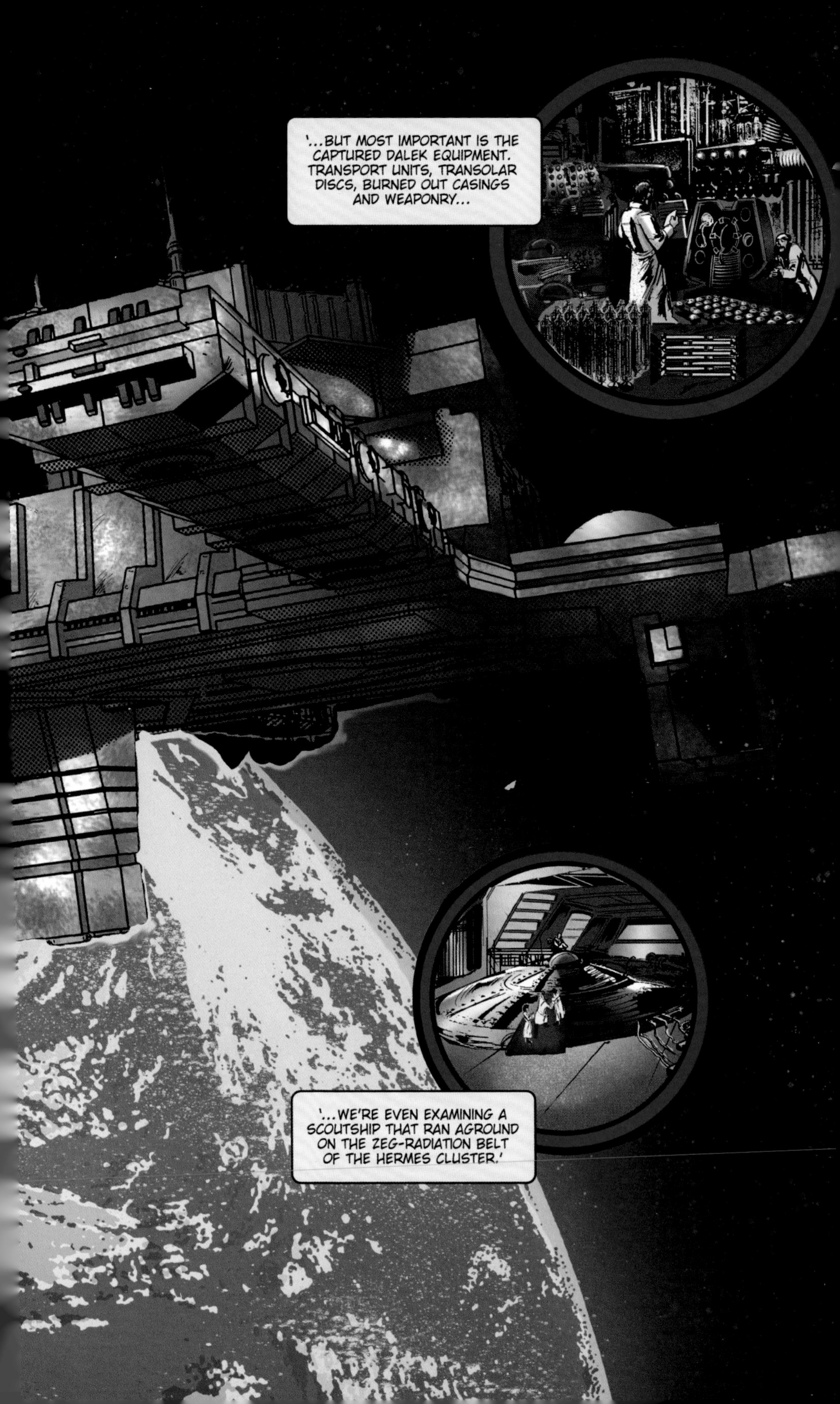
'...BUT MOST IMPORTANT IS THE CAPTURED DALEK EQUIPMENT. TRANSPORT UNITS, TRANSOLAR DISCS, BURNED OUT CASINGS AND WEAPONRY...
'...WE'RE EVEN EXAMINING A SCOUTSHIP THAT RAN AGROUND ON THE ZEG-RADIATION BELT OF THE HERMES CLUSTER.'

OF COURSE, NONE OF IT WORKS. THE SECRETS OF THE DALEKS CONTINUE TO ELUDE US.

ANY DALEK TECHNOLOGY WILL ONLY WORK FOR DALEKS. WHICH BRINGS ME NEATLY TO THE OBVIOUS QUESTION...

THERE'S ONE THING MISSING FROM YOUR COLLECTION.

SHOOO

COME HERE.

LET ME SHOW YOU SOMETHING.

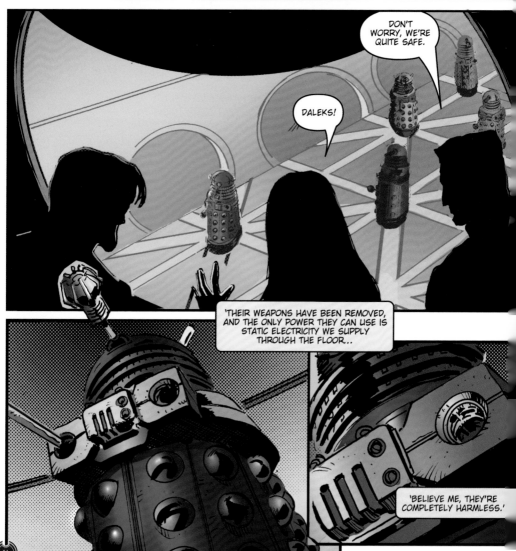

DON'T WORRY, WE'RE QUITE SAFE.

DALEKS!

'THEIR WEAPONS HAVE BEEN REMOVED, AND THE ONLY POWER THEY CAN USE IS STATIC ELECTRICITY WE SUPPLY THROUGH THE FLOOR...

'BELIEVE ME, THEY'RE COMPLETELY HARMLESS.'

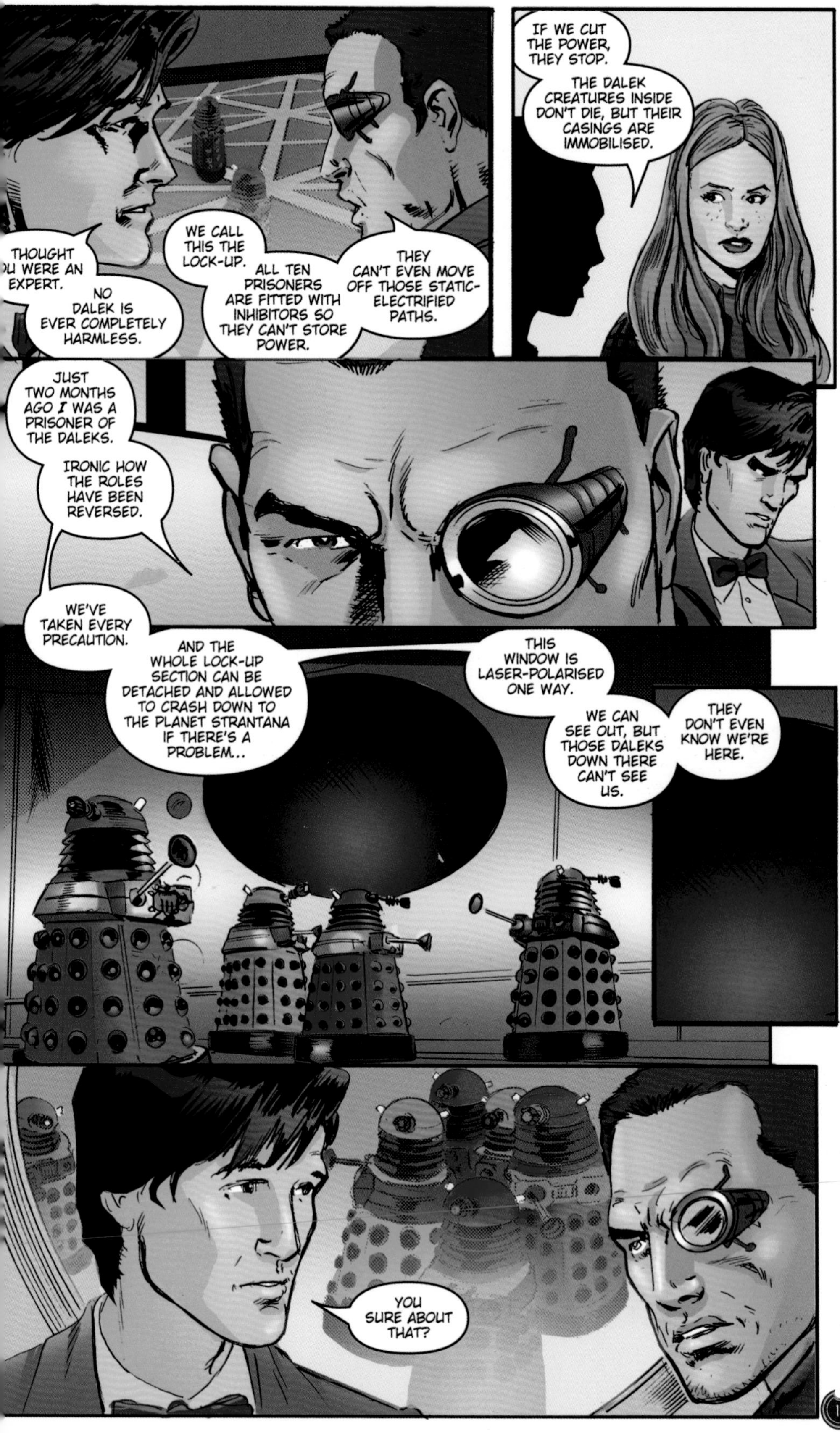

THOUGHT
OU WERE AN
EXPERT.
NO
DALEK IS
EVER COMPLETELY
HARMLESS.
WE CALL
THIS THE
LOCK-UP.
ALL TEN
PRISONERS
ARE FITTED WITH
INHIBITORS SO
THEY CAN'T STORE
POWER.
THEY
CAN'T EVEN MOVE
OFF THOSE STATIC-
ELECTRIFIED
PATHS.
IF WE CUT
THE POWER,
THEY STOP.
THE DALEK
CREATURES INSIDE
DON'T DIE, BUT THEIR
CASINGS ARE
IMMOBILISED.
JUST
TWO MONTHS
AGO *I* WAS A
PRISONER OF
THE DALEKS.
IRONIC HOW
THE ROLES
HAVE BEEN
REVERSED.
WE'VE
TAKEN EVERY
PRECAUTION.
AND THE
WHOLE LOCK-UP
SECTION CAN BE
DETACHED AND ALLOWED
TO CRASH DOWN TO
THE PLANET STRANTANA
IF THERE'S A
PROBLEM...
THIS
WINDOW IS
LASER-POLARISED
ONE WAY.
WE CAN
SEE OUT, BUT
THOSE DALEKS
DOWN THERE
CAN'T SEE
US.
THEY
DON'T EVEN
KNOW WE'RE
HERE.
YOU
SURE ABOUT
THAT?

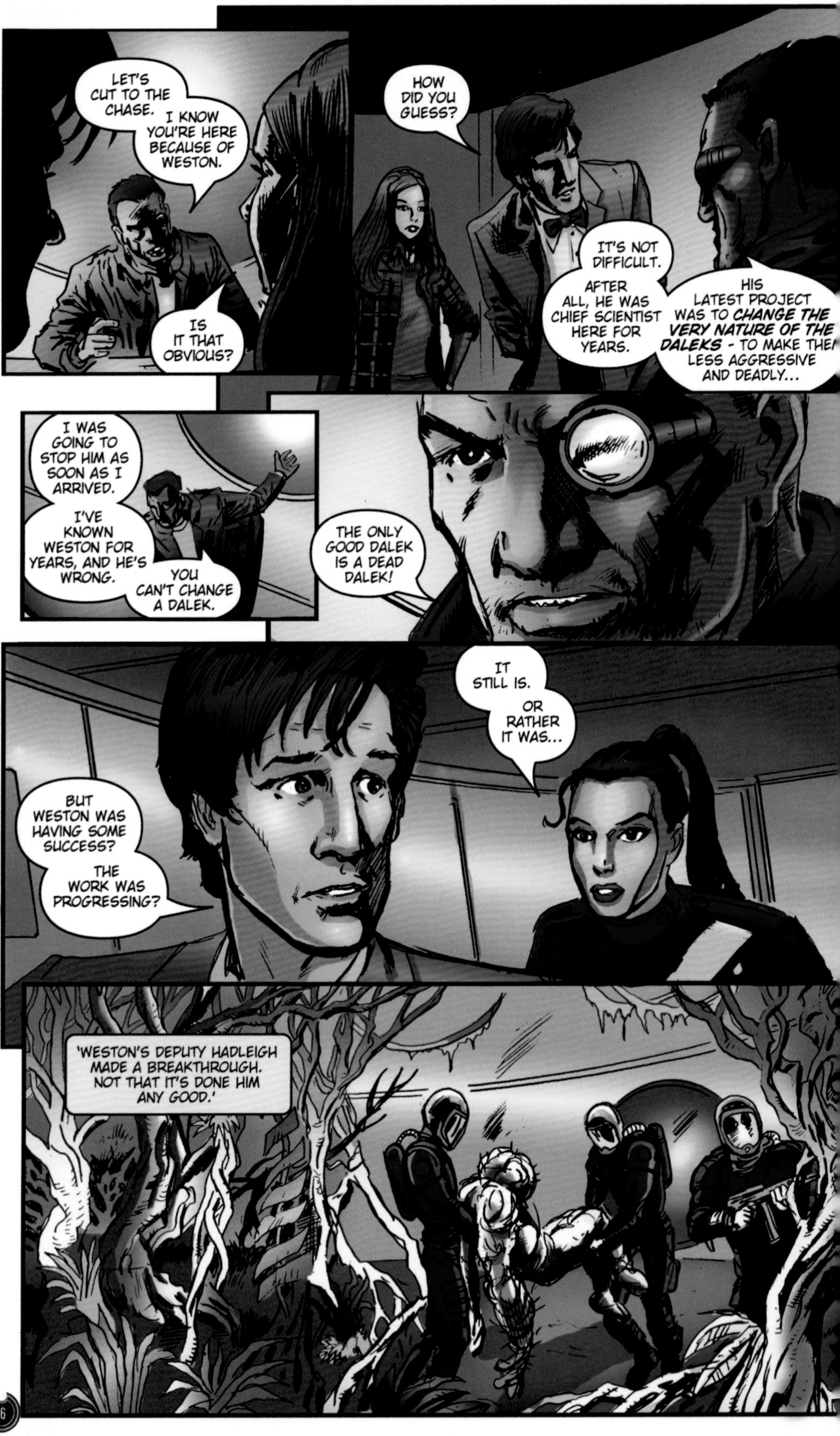
LET'S CUT TO THE CHASE.
I KNOW YOU'RE HERE BECAUSE OF WESTON.
IS IT THAT OBVIOUS?
HOW DID YOU GUESS?
IT'S NOT DIFFICULT.
AFTER ALL, HE WAS CHIEF SCIENTIST HERE FOR YEARS.
HIS LATEST PROJECT WAS TO CHANGE THE VERY NATURE OF THE DALEKS - TO MAKE THE LESS AGGRESSIVE AND DEADLY...
I WAS GOING TO STOP HIM AS SOON AS I ARRIVED.
I'VE KNOWN WESTON FOR YEARS, AND HE'S WRONG.
YOU CAN'T CHANGE A DALEK.
THE ONLY GOOD DALEK IS A DEAD DALEK!
BUT WESTON WAS HAVING SOME SUCCESS?
THE WORK WAS PROGRESSING?
IT STILL IS.
OR RATHER IT WAS...
'WESTON'S DEPUTY HADLEIGH MADE A BREAKTHROUGH. NOT THAT IT'S DONE HIM ANY GOOD.'

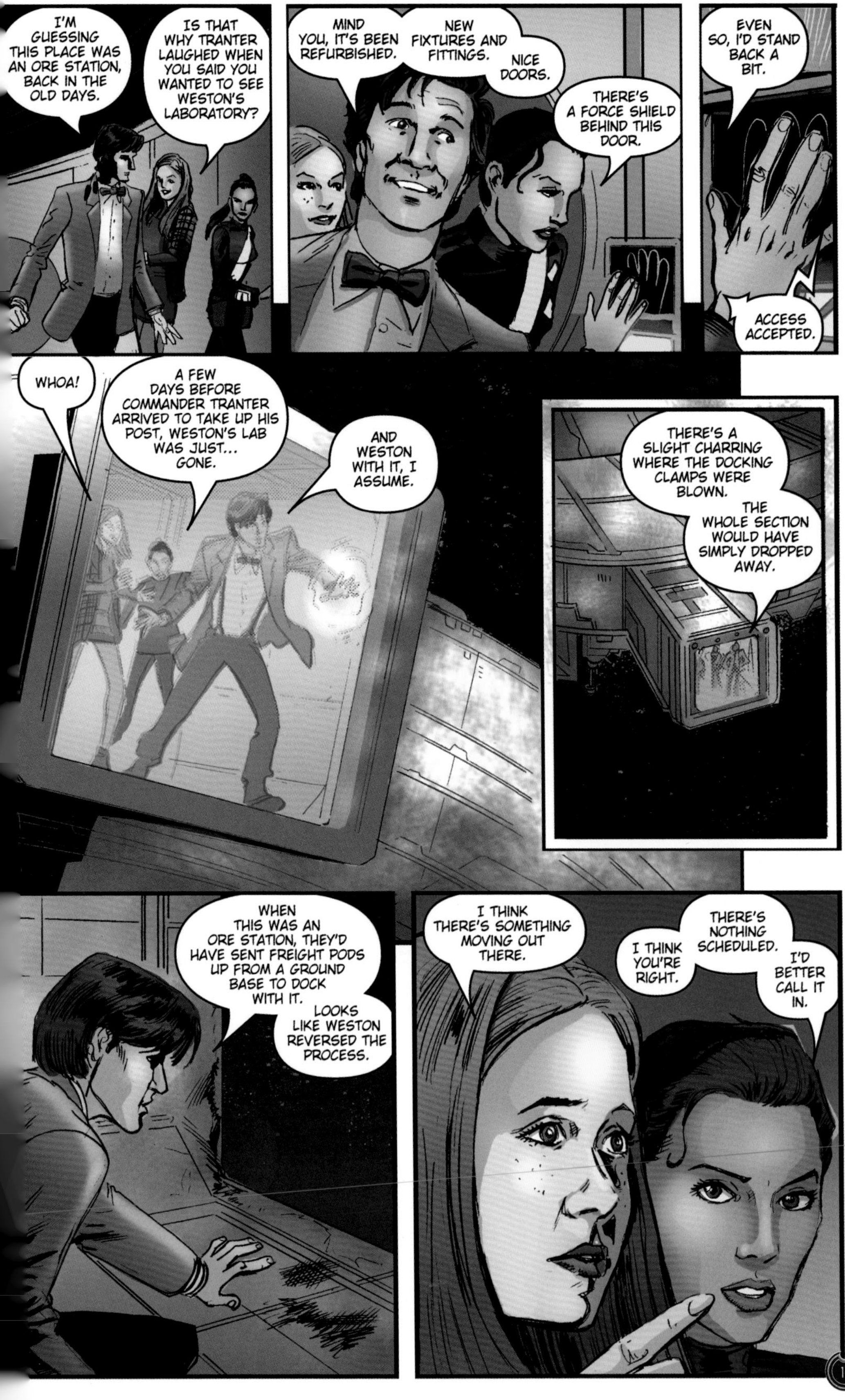
I'M GUESSING THIS PLACE WAS AN ORE STATION, BACK IN THE OLD DAYS.
IS THAT WHY TRANTER LAUGHED WHEN YOU SAID YOU WANTED TO SEE WESTON'S LABORATORY?
MIND YOU, IT'S BEEN REFURBISHED.
NEW FIXTURES AND FITTINGS.
NICE DOORS.
THERE'S A FORCE SHIELD BEHIND THIS DOOR.
EVEN SO, I'D STAND BACK A BIT.
ACCESS ACCEPTED.
WHOA!
A FEW DAYS BEFORE COMMANDER TRANTER ARRIVED TO TAKE UP HIS POST, WESTON'S LAB WAS JUST... GONE.
AND WESTON WITH IT, I ASSUME.
THERE'S A SLIGHT CHARRING WHERE THE DOCKING CLAMPS WERE BLOWN.
THE WHOLE SECTION WOULD HAVE SIMPLY DROPPED AWAY.
WHEN THIS WAS AN ORE STATION, THEY'D HAVE SENT FREIGHT PODS UP FROM A GROUND BASE TO DOCK WITH IT.
LOOKS LIKE WESTON REVERSED THE PROCESS.
I THINK THERE'S SOMETHING MOVING OUT THERE.
I THINK YOU'RE RIGHT.
THERE'S NOTHING SCHEDULED.
I'D BETTER CALL IT IN.

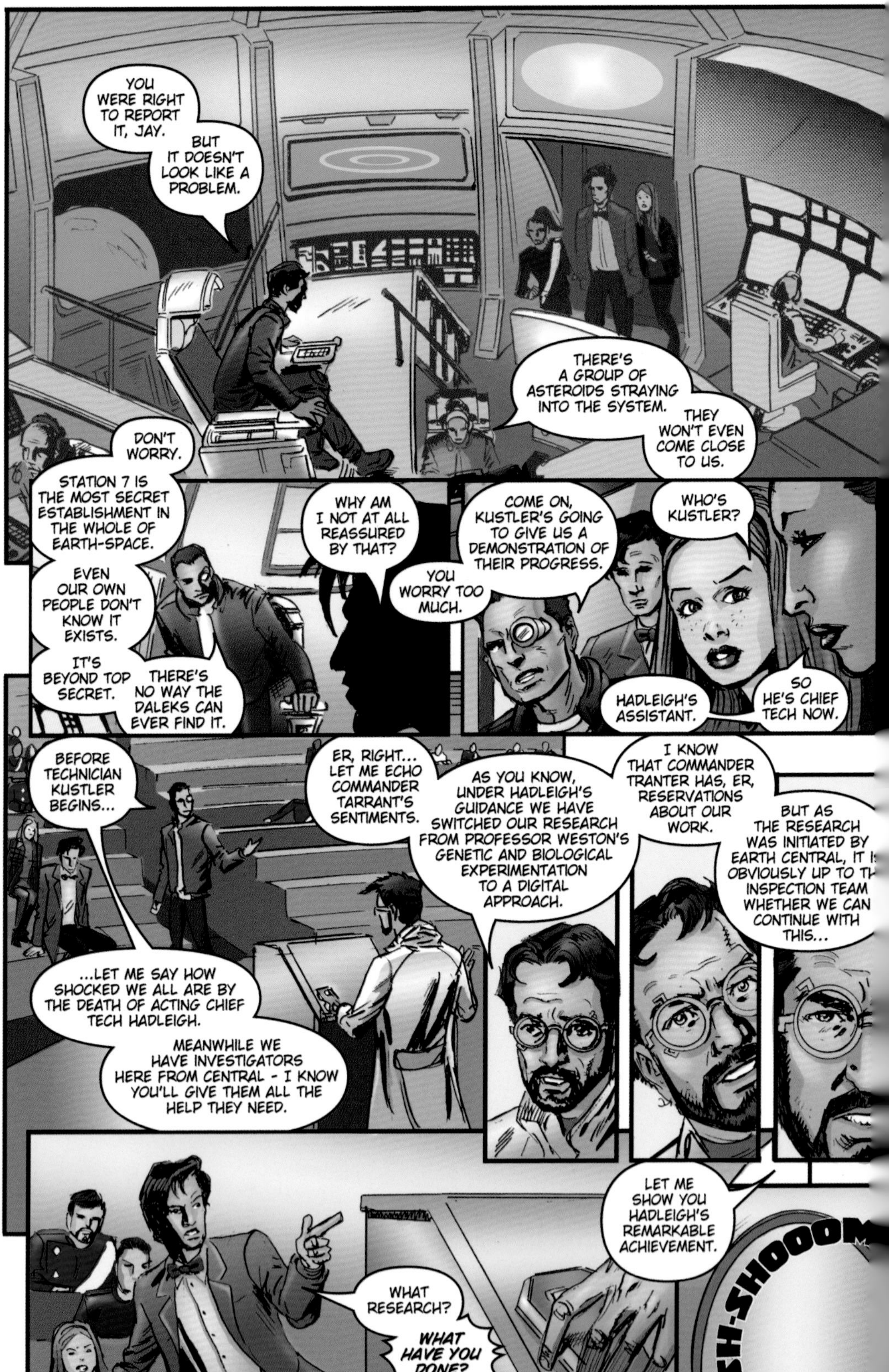
YOU WERE RIGHT TO REPORT IT, JAY.
BUT IT DOESN'T LOOK LIKE A PROBLEM.
THERE'S A GROUP OF ASTEROIDS STRAYING INTO THE SYSTEM.
THEY WON'T EVEN COME CLOSE TO US.
DON'T WORRY.
STATION 7 IS THE MOST SECRET ESTABLISHMENT IN THE WHOLE OF EARTH-SPACE.
EVEN OUR OWN PEOPLE DON'T KNOW IT EXISTS.
IT'S BEYOND TOP SECRET.
THERE'S NO WAY THE DALEKS CAN EVER FIND IT.
WHY AM I NOT AT ALL REASSURED BY THAT?
YOU WORRY TOO MUCH.
COME ON, KUSTLER'S GOING TO GIVE US A DEMONSTRATION OF THEIR PROGRESS.
WHO'S KUSTLER?
HADLEIGH'S ASSISTANT.
SO HE'S CHIEF TECH NOW.
BEFORE TECHNICIAN KUSTLER BEGINS...
...LET ME SAY HOW SHOCKED WE ALL ARE BY THE DEATH OF ACTING CHIEF TECH HADLEIGH.
MEANWHILE WE HAVE INVESTIGATORS HERE FROM CENTRAL - I KNOW YOU'LL GIVE THEM ALL THE HELP THEY NEED.
ER, RIGHT... LET ME ECHO COMMANDER TARRANT'S SENTIMENTS.
AS YOU KNOW, UNDER HADLEIGH'S GUIDANCE WE HAVE SWITCHED OUR RESEARCH FROM PROFESSOR WESTON'S GENETIC AND BIOLOGICAL EXPERIMENTATION TO A DIGITAL APPROACH.
I KNOW THAT COMMANDER TRANTER HAS, ER, RESERVATIONS ABOUT OUR WORK.
BUT AS THE RESEARCH WAS INITIATED BY EARTH CENTRAL, IT IS OBVIOUSLY UP TO THE INSPECTION TEAM WHETHER WE CAN CONTINUE WITH THIS...
LET ME SHOW YOU HADLEIGH'S REMARKABLE ACHIEVEMENT.
WHAT RESEARCH?
WHAT HAVE YOU DONE?
SH-SHOOOM

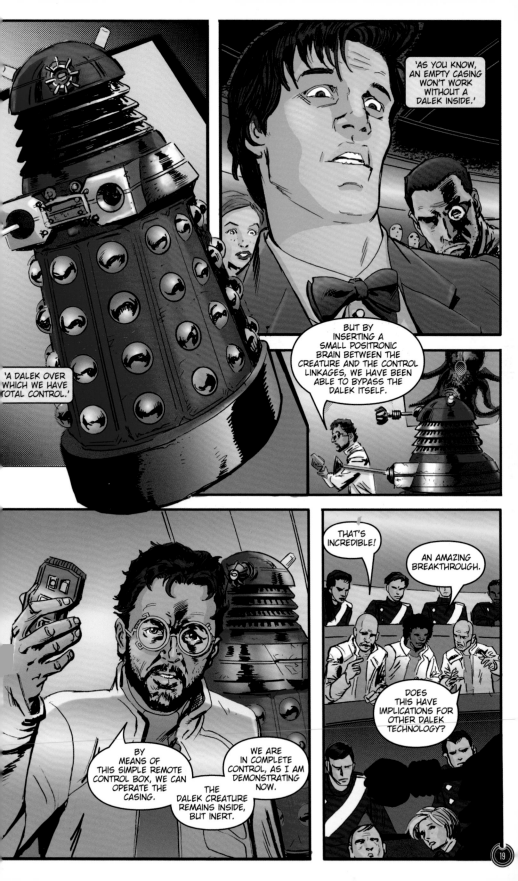

'AS YOU KNOW, AN EMPTY CASING WON'T WORK WITHOUT A DALEK INSIDE.'

'A DALEK OVER WHICH WE HAVE TOTAL CONTROL.'

BUT BY INSERTING A SMALL POSITRONIC BRAIN BETWEEN THE CREATURE AND THE CONTROL LINKAGES, WE HAVE BEEN ABLE TO BYPASS THE DALEK ITSELF.

THAT'S INCREDIBLE!

AN AMAZING BREAKTHROUGH.

DOES THIS HAVE IMPLICATIONS FOR OTHER DALEK TECHNOLOGY?

BY MEANS OF THIS SIMPLE REMOTE CONTROL BOX, WE CAN OPERATE THE CASING.

WE ARE IN COMPLETE CONTROL, AS I AM DEMONSTRATING NOW.

THE DALEK CREATURE REMAINS INSIDE, BUT INERT.

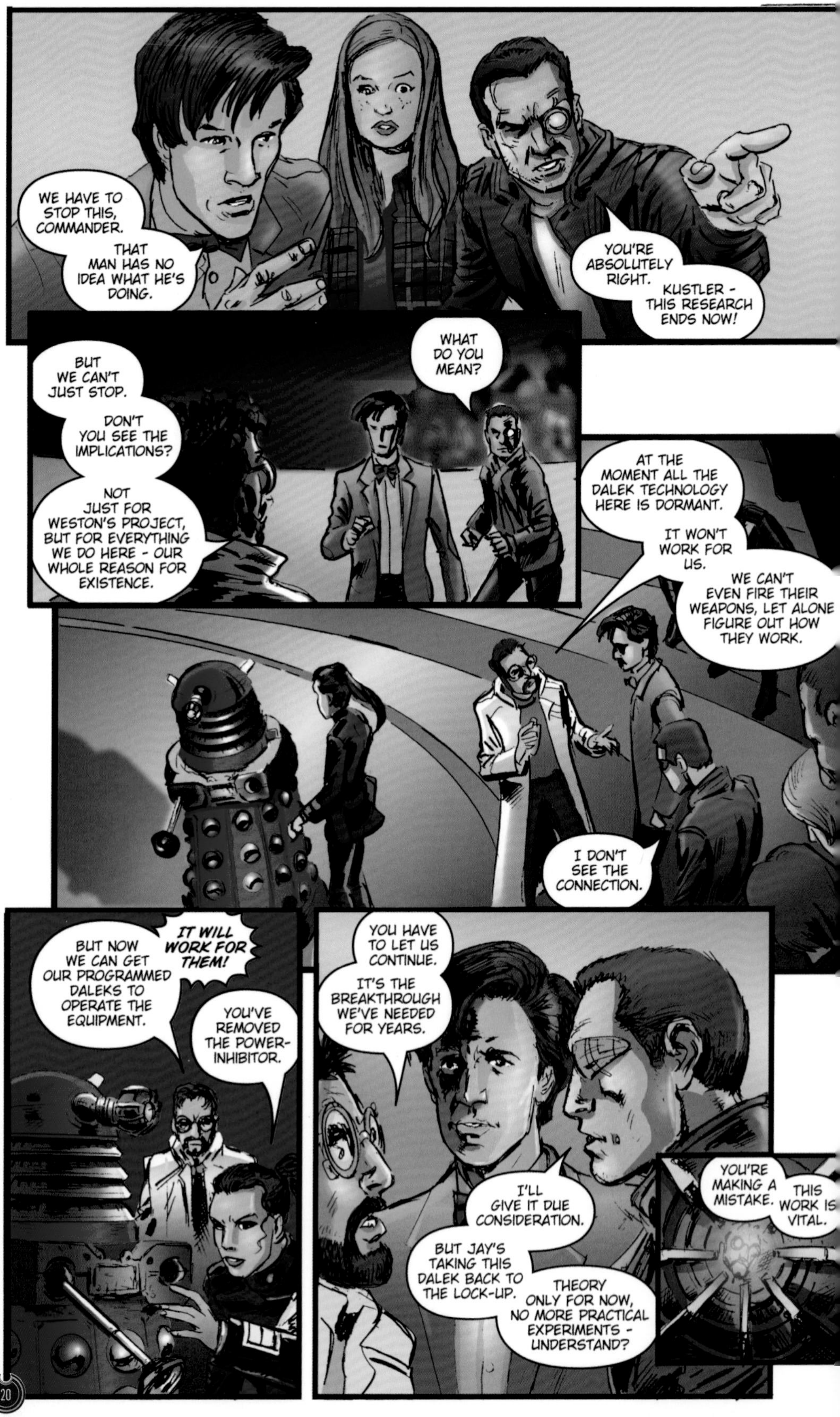
WE HAVE TO STOP THIS, COMMANDER.
THAT MAN HAS NO IDEA WHAT HE'S DOING.
YOU'RE ABSOLUTELY RIGHT.
KUSTLER - THIS RESEARCH ENDS NOW!
BUT WE CAN'T JUST STOP.
DON'T YOU SEE THE IMPLICATIONS?
NOT JUST FOR WESTON'S PROJECT, BUT FOR EVERYTHING WE DO HERE - OUR WHOLE REASON FOR EXISTENCE.
WHAT DO YOU MEAN?
AT THE MOMENT ALL THE DALEK TECHNOLOGY HERE IS DORMANT.
IT WON'T WORK FOR US.
WE CAN'T EVEN FIRE THEIR WEAPONS, LET ALONE FIGURE OUT HOW THEY WORK.
I DON'T SEE THE CONNECTION.
BUT NOW WE CAN GET OUR PROGRAMMED DALEKS TO OPERATE THE EQUIPMENT.
IT WILL WORK FOR THEM!
YOU'VE REMOVED THE POWER-INHIBITOR.
YOU HAVE TO LET US CONTINUE.
IT'S THE BREAKTHROUGH WE'VE NEEDED FOR YEARS.
I'LL GIVE IT DUE CONSIDERATION.
BUT JAY'S TAKING THIS DALEK BACK TO THE LOCK-UP.
THEORY ONLY FOR NOW, NO MORE PRACTICAL EXPERIMENTS - UNDERSTAND?
YOU'RE MAKING A MISTAKE.
THIS WORK IS VITAL.

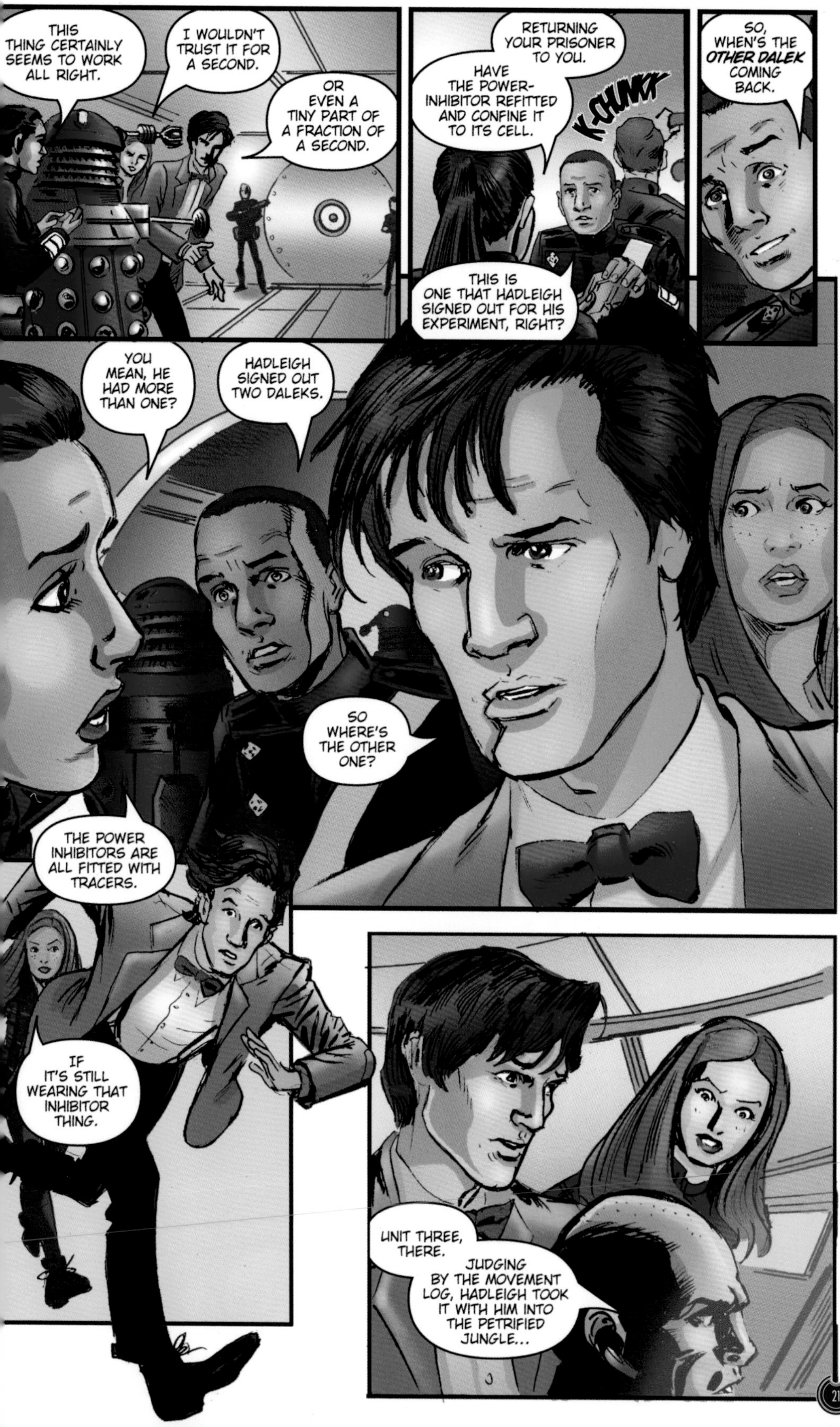

THIS THING CERTAINLY SEEMS TO WORK ALL RIGHT.
I WOULDN'T TRUST IT FOR A SECOND.
OR EVEN A TINY PART OF A FRACTION OF A SECOND.
RETURNING YOUR PRISONER TO YOU.
HAVE THE POWER-INHIBITOR REFITTED AND CONFINE IT TO ITS CELL.
K-CHUNKK
THIS IS ONE THAT HADLEIGH SIGNED OUT FOR HIS EXPERIMENT, RIGHT?
SO, WHEN'S THE OTHER DALEK COMING BACK.
YOU MEAN, HE HAD MORE THAN ONE?
HADLEIGH SIGNED OUT TWO DALEKS.
SO WHERE'S THE OTHER ONE?
THE POWER INHIBITORS ARE ALL FITTED WITH TRACERS.
IF IT'S STILL WEARING THAT INHIBITOR THING.
UNIT THREE, THERE.
JUDGING BY THE MOVEMENT LOG, HADLEIGH TOOK IT WITH HIM INTO THE PETRIFIED JUNGLE...

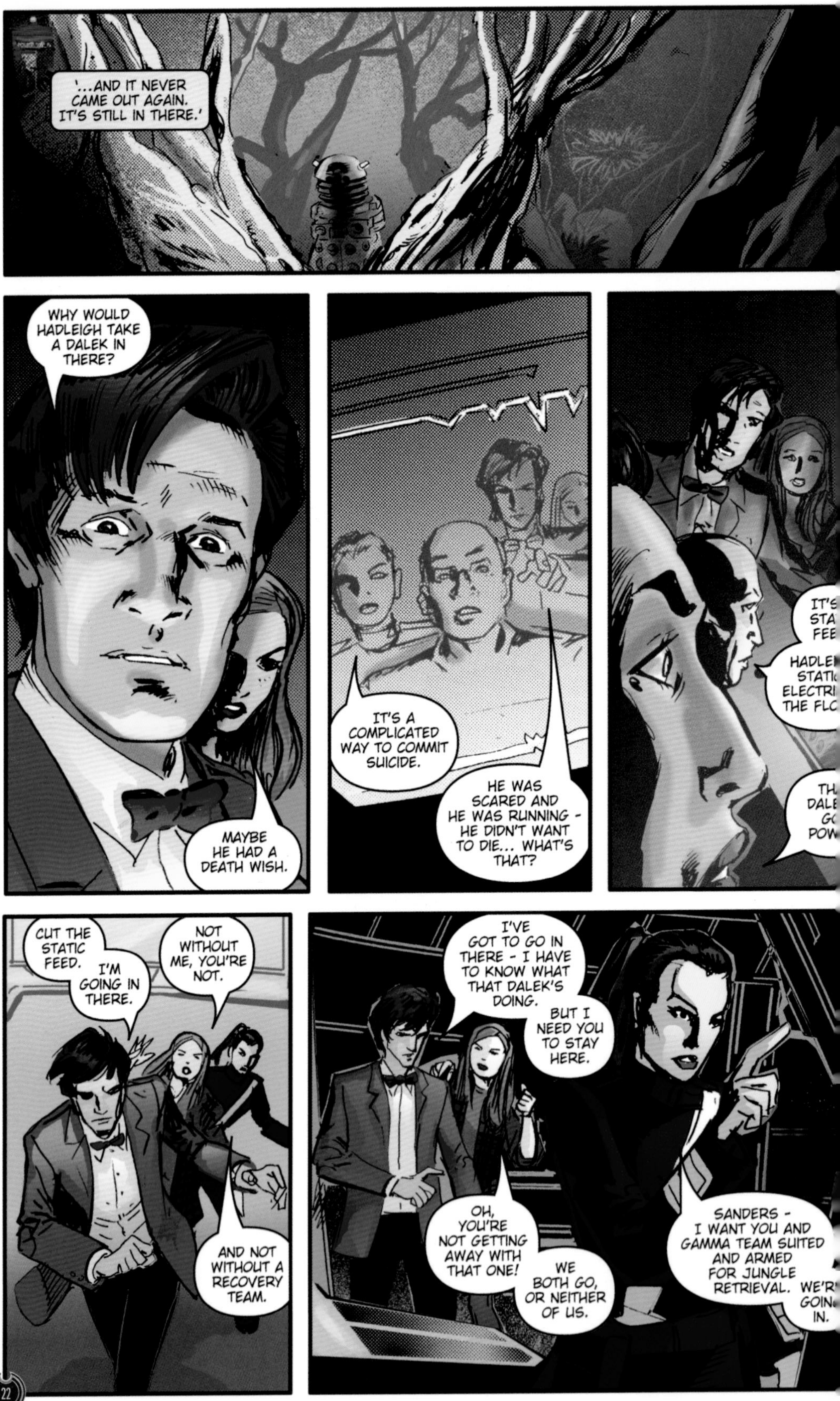
'...AND IT NEVER CAME OUT AGAIN. IT'S STILL IN THERE.'
WHY WOULD HADLEIGH TAKE A DALEK IN THERE?
MAYBE HE HAD A DEATH WISH.
IT'S A COMPLICATED WAY TO COMMIT SUICIDE.
HE WAS SCARED AND HE WAS RUNNING - HE DIDN'T WANT TO DIE... WHAT'S THAT?
IT'S STA FEE
HADLE STATI ELECTRI THE FL
TH DALE G POW
CUT THE STATIC FEED.
I'M GOING IN THERE.
NOT WITHOUT ME, YOU'RE NOT.
AND NOT WITHOUT A RECOVERY TEAM.
I'VE GOT TO GO IN THERE - I HAVE TO KNOW WHAT THAT DALEK'S DOING.
BUT I NEED YOU TO STAY HERE.
OH, YOU'RE NOT GETTING AWAY WITH THAT ONE!
WE BOTH GO, OR NEITHER OF US.
SANDERS - I WANT YOU AND GAMMA TEAM SUITED AND ARMED FOR JUNGLE RETRIEVAL.
WE'R GOIN IN.

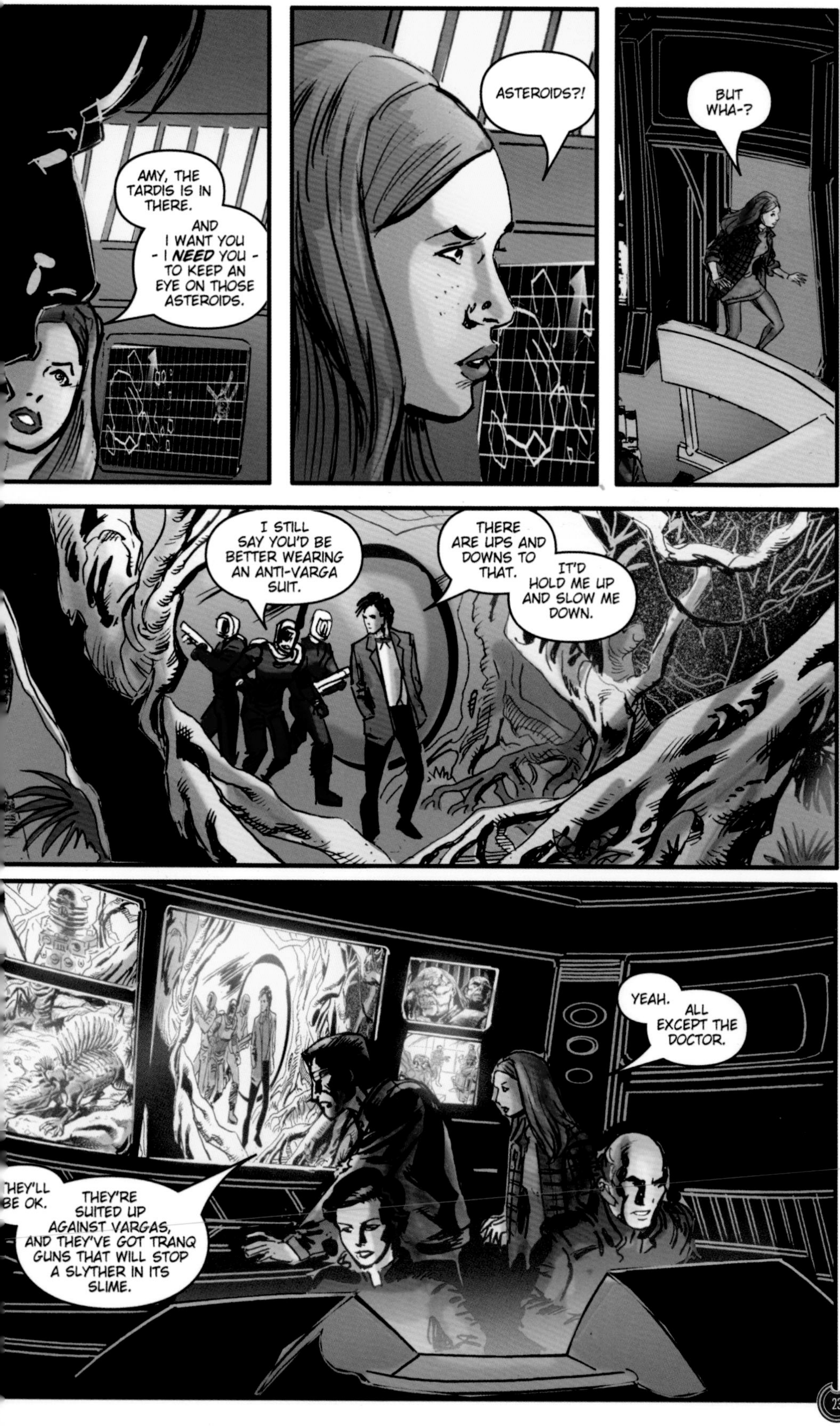
AMY, THE TARDIS IS IN THERE.
AND I WANT YOU - I NEED YOU - TO KEEP AN EYE ON THOSE ASTEROIDS.
ASTEROIDS?!
BUT WHA-?
I STILL SAY YOU'D BE BETTER WEARING AN ANTI-VARGA SUIT.
THERE ARE UPS AND DOWNS TO THAT.
IT'D HOLD ME UP AND SLOW ME DOWN.
THEY'LL BE OK.
THEY'RE SUITED UP AGAINST VARGAS, AND THEY'VE GOT TRANQ GUNS THAT WILL STOP A SLYTHER IN ITS SLIME.
YEAH.
ALL EXCEPT THE DOCTOR.

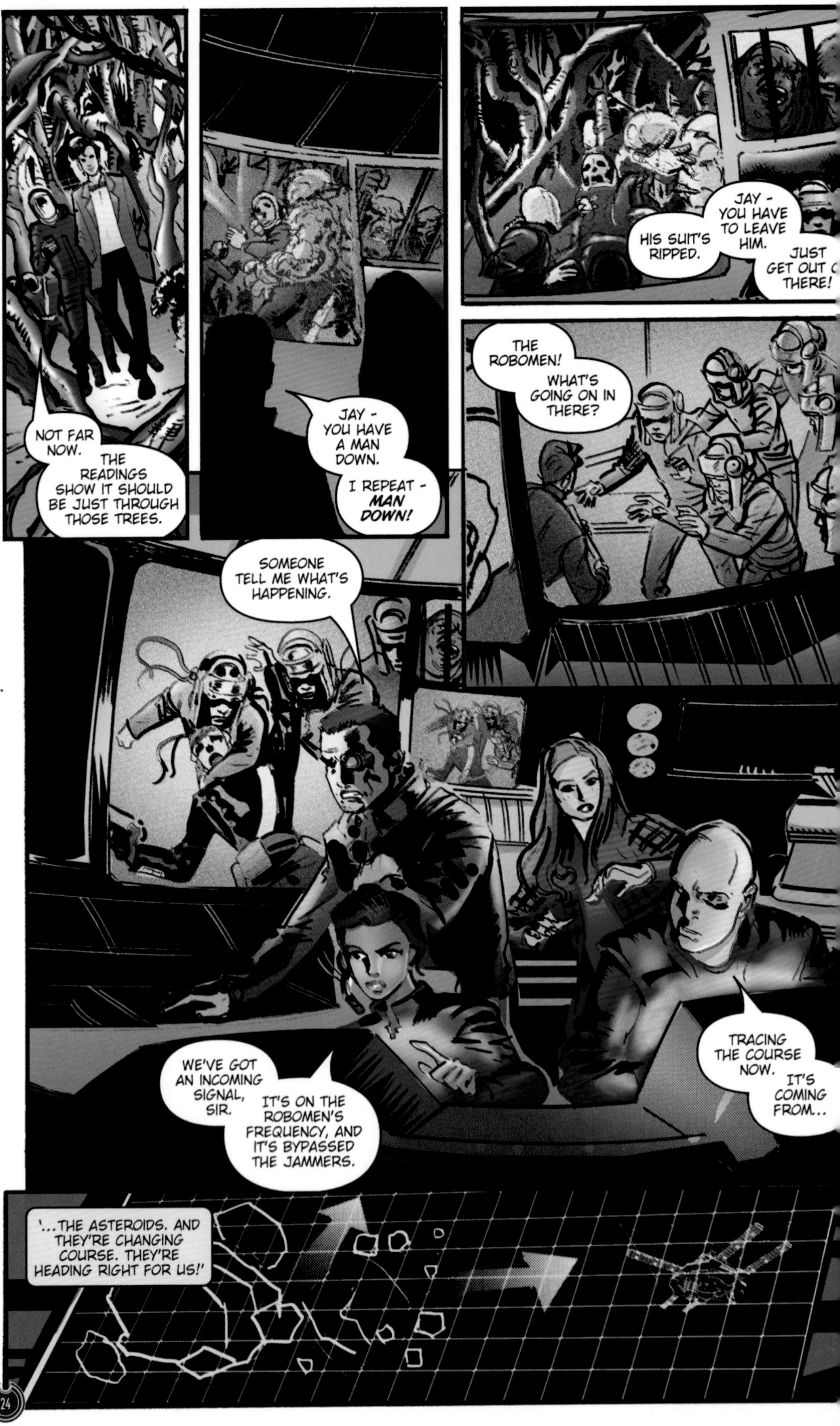
NOT FAR NOW.
THE READINGS SHOW IT SHOULD BE JUST THROUGH THOSE TREES.
JAY - YOU HAVE A MAN DOWN.
I REPEAT - MAN DOWN!
HIS SUIT'S RIPPED.
JAY - YOU HAVE TO LEAVE HIM.
JUST GET OUT OF THERE!
THE ROBOMEN!
WHAT'S GOING ON IN THERE?
SOMEONE TELL ME WHAT'S HAPPENING.
WE'VE GOT AN INCOMING SIGNAL, SIR.
IT'S ON THE ROBOMEN'S FREQUENCY, AND IT'S BYPASSED THE JAMMERS.
TRACING THE COURSE NOW.
IT'S COMING FROM...
'...THE ASTEROIDS. AND THEY'RE CHANGING COURSE. THEY'RE HEADING RIGHT FOR US!'

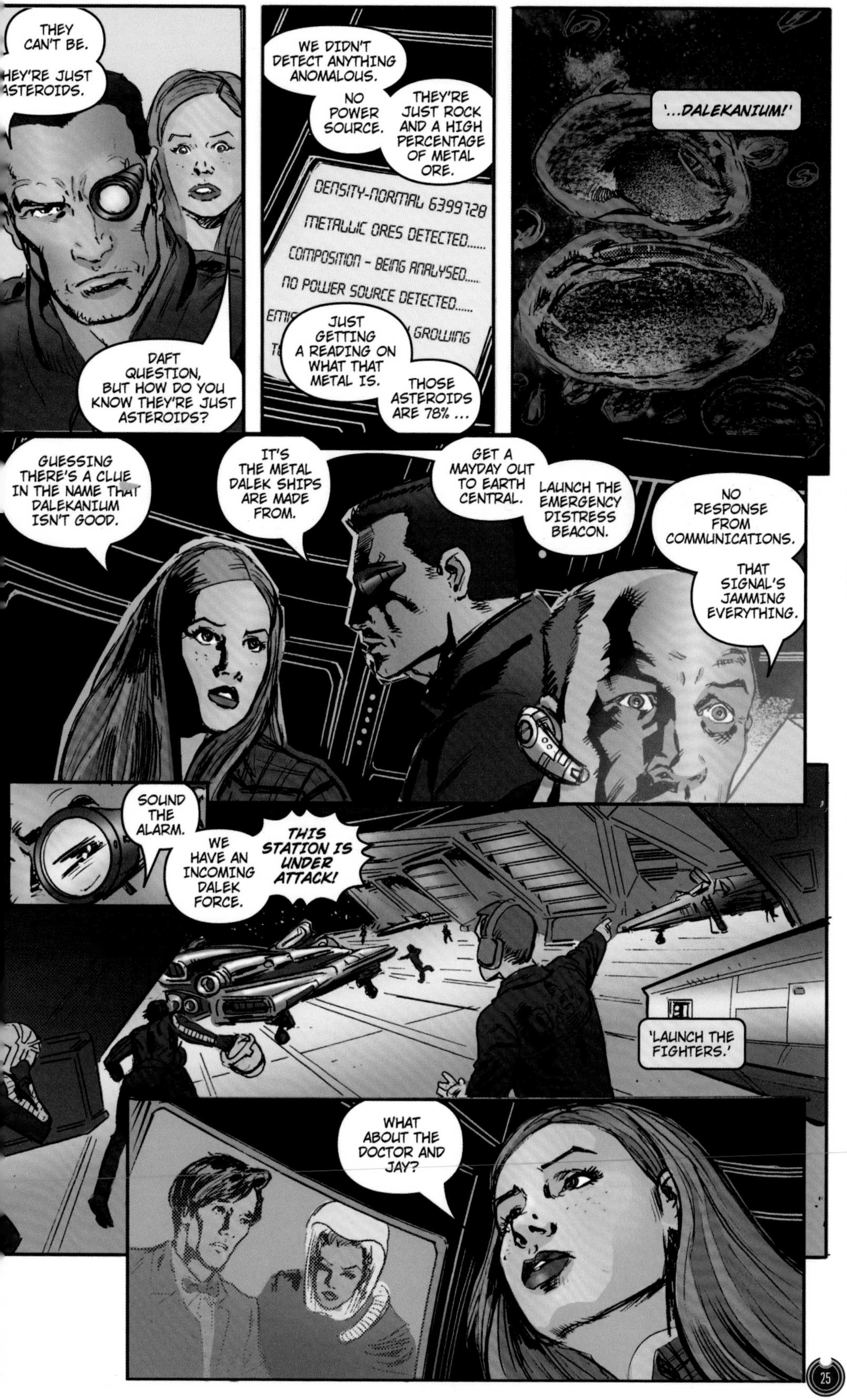

THEY CAN'T BE.
THEY'RE JUST ASTEROIDS.
WE DIDN'T DETECT ANYTHING ANOMALOUS.
NO POWER SOURCE.
THEY'RE JUST ROCK AND A HIGH PERCENTAGE OF METAL ORE.
DENSITY-NORMAL 6399728
METALLIC ORES DETECTED......
COMPOSITION - BEING ANALYSED.....
NO POWER SOURCE DETECTED......
DAFT QUESTION, BUT HOW DO YOU KNOW THEY'RE JUST ASTEROIDS?
JUST GETTING A READING ON WHAT THAT METAL IS.
THOSE ASTEROIDS ARE 78% ...
'...DALEKANIUM!'
GUESSING THERE'S A CLUE IN THE NAME THAT DALEKANIUM ISN'T GOOD.
IT'S THE METAL DALEK SHIPS ARE MADE FROM.
GET A MAYDAY OUT TO EARTH CENTRAL.
LAUNCH THE EMERGENCY DISTRESS BEACON.
NO RESPONSE FROM COMMUNICATIONS.
THAT SIGNAL'S JAMMING EVERYTHING.
SOUND THE ALARM.
WE HAVE AN INCOMING DALEK FORCE.
THIS STATION IS UNDER ATTACK!
'LAUNCH THE FIGHTERS.'
WHAT ABOUT THE DOCTOR AND JAY?

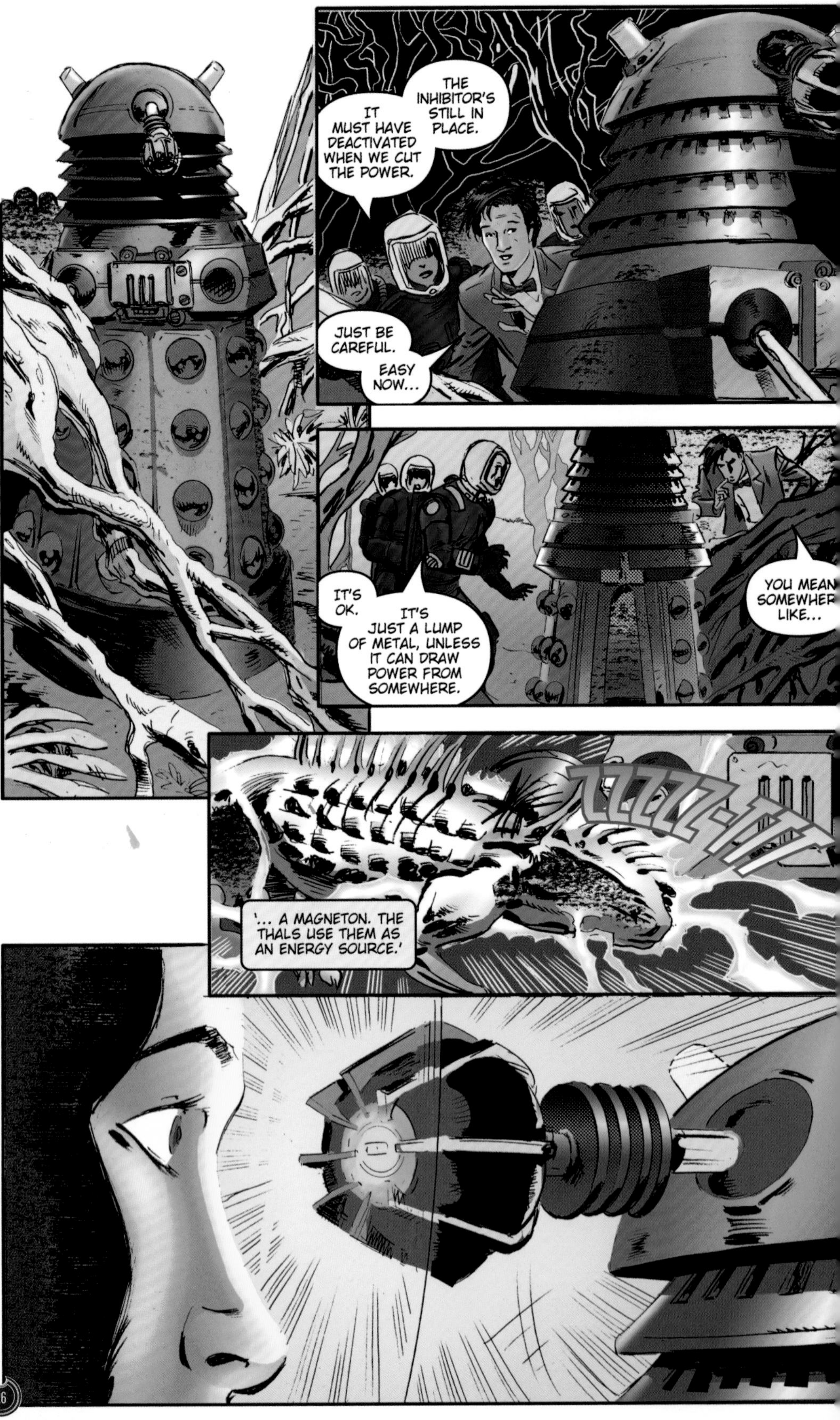
THE INHIBITOR'S STILL IN PLACE.
IT MUST HAVE DEACTIVATED WHEN WE CUT THE POWER.
JUST BE CAREFUL.
EASY NOW...
IT'S OK.
IT'S JUST A LUMP OF METAL, UNLESS IT CAN DRAW POWER FROM SOMEWHERE.
YOU MEAN SOMEWHER LIKE...
ZZZZZ-TTT
'... A MAGNETON. THE THALS USE THEM AS AN ENERGY SOURCE.'

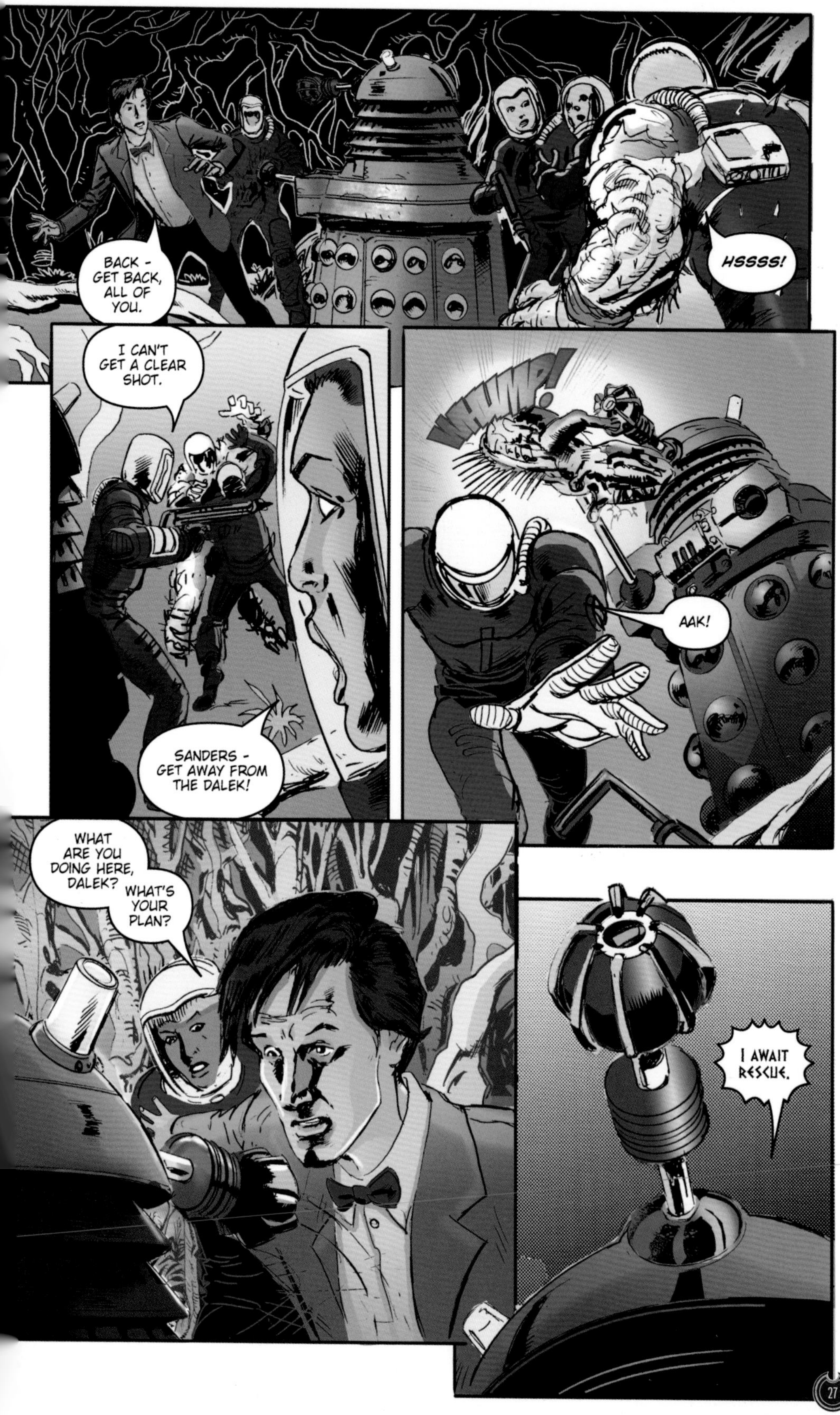

BACK - GET BACK, ALL OF YOU.
HSSSS!
I CAN'T GET A CLEAR SHOT.
SANDERS - GET AWAY FROM THE DALEK!
WHUMP!
AAK!
WHAT ARE YOU DOING HERE, DALEK?
WHAT'S YOUR PLAN?
I AWAIT RESCUE.

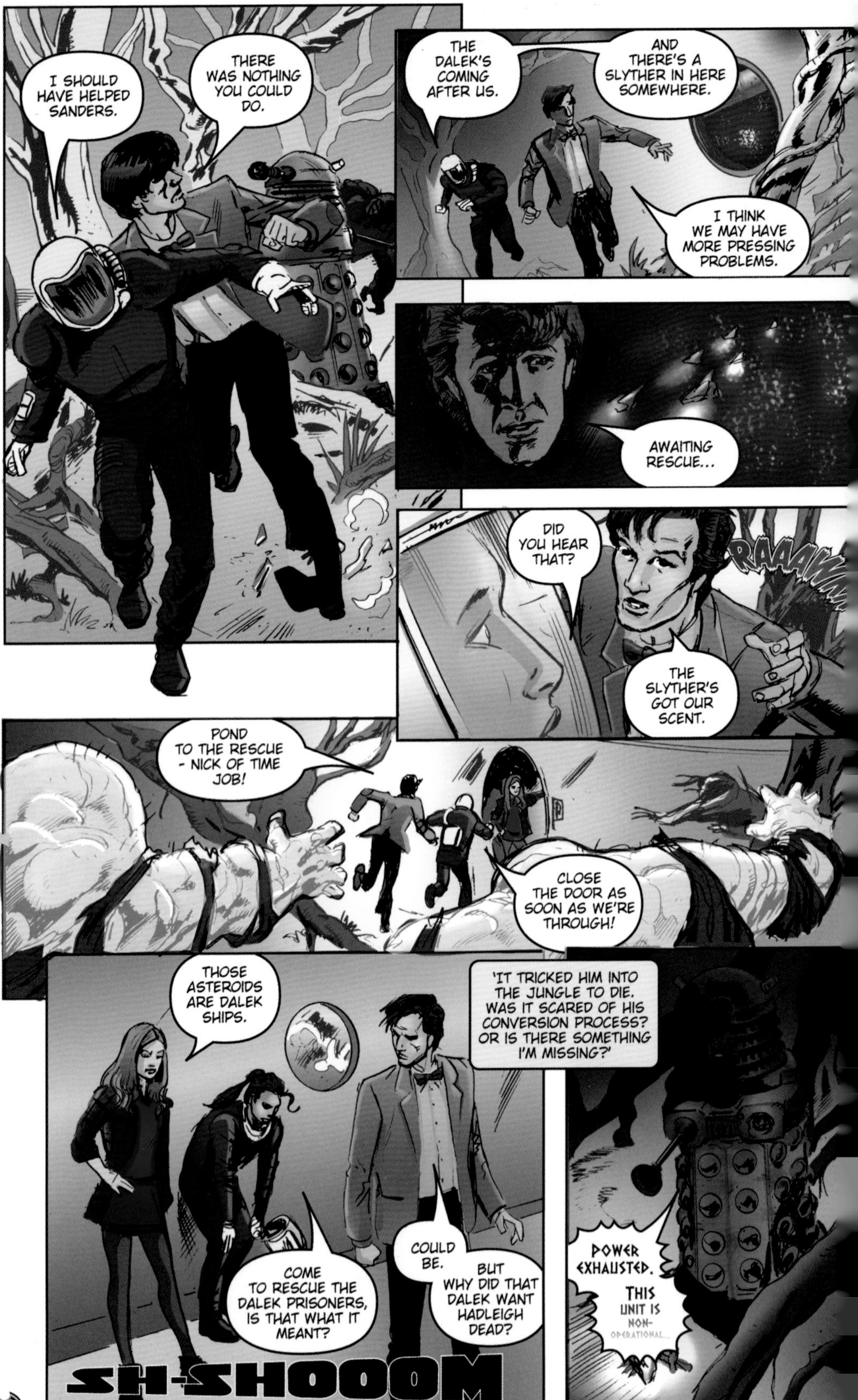
I SHOULD HAVE HELPED SANDERS.
THERE WAS NOTHING YOU COULD DO.
THE DALEK'S COMING AFTER US.
AND THERE'S A SLYTHER IN HERE SOMEWHERE.
I THINK WE MAY HAVE MORE PRESSING PROBLEMS.
AWAITING RESCUE...
DID YOU HEAR THAT?
RAAAWW
THE SLYTHER'S GOT OUR SCENT.
POND TO THE RESCUE - NICK OF TIME JOB!
CLOSE THE DOOR AS SOON AS WE'RE THROUGH!
THOSE ASTEROIDS ARE DALEK SHIPS.
COME TO RESCUE THE DALEK PRISONERS, IS THAT WHAT IT MEANT?
COULD BE.
BUT WHY DID THAT DALEK WANT HADLEIGH DEAD?
'IT TRICKED HIM INTO THE JUNGLE TO DIE. WAS IT SCARED OF HIS CONVERSION PROCESS? OR IS THERE SOMETHING I'M MISSING?'
POWER EXHAUSTED.
THIS UNIT IS NON-OPERATIONAL...
SH-SHOOOM

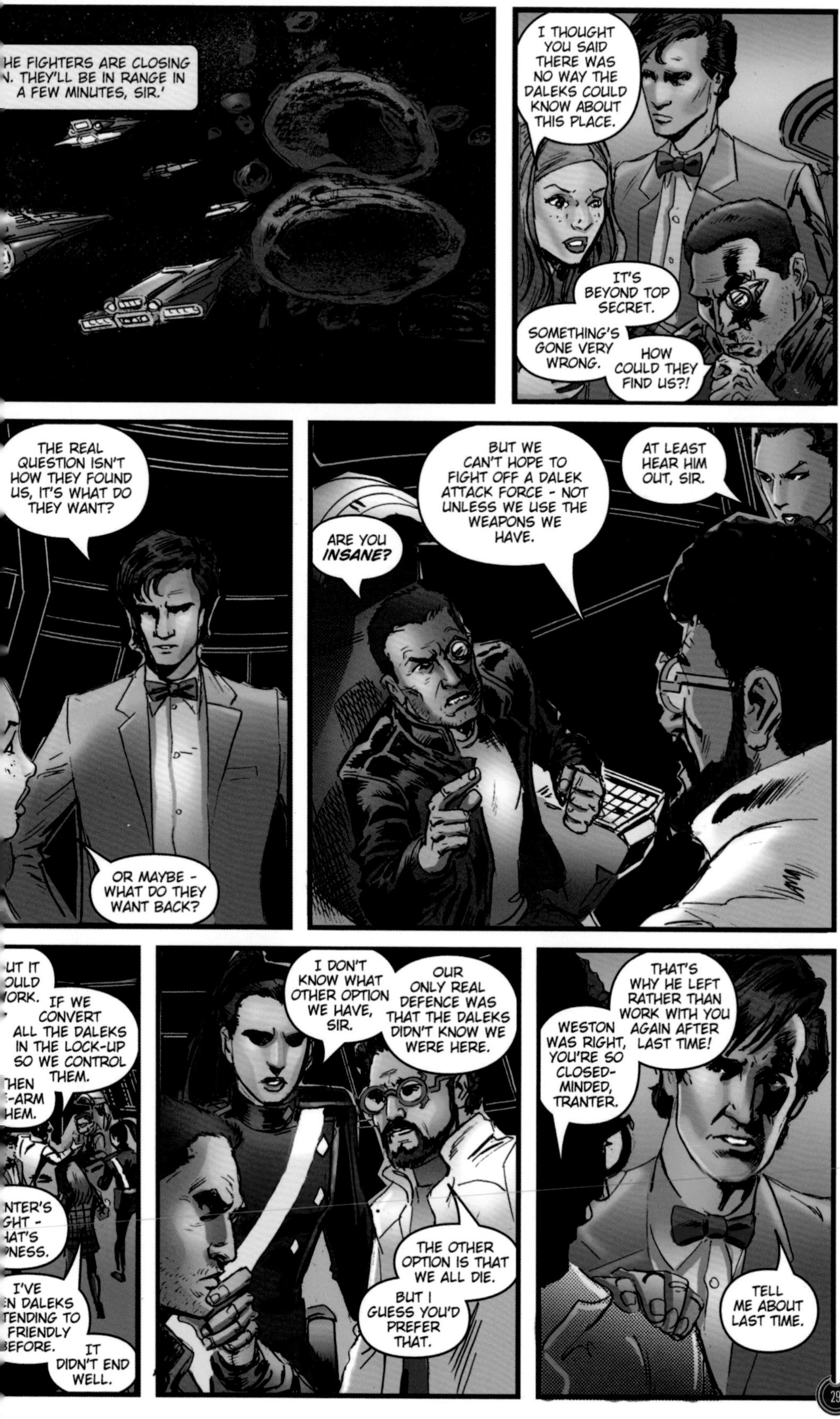

HE FIGHTERS ARE CLOSING N. THEY'LL BE IN RANGE IN A FEW MINUTES, SIR.'
I THOUGHT YOU SAID THERE WAS NO WAY THE DALEKS COULD KNOW ABOUT THIS PLACE.
IT'S BEYOND TOP SECRET.
SOMETHING'S GONE VERY WRONG.
HOW COULD THEY FIND US?!
THE REAL QUESTION ISN'T HOW THEY FOUND US, IT'S WHAT DO THEY WANT?
OR MAYBE - WHAT DO THEY WANT BACK?
BUT WE CAN'T HOPE TO FIGHT OFF A DALEK ATTACK FORCE - NOT UNLESS WE USE THE WEAPONS WE HAVE.
AT LEAST HEAR HIM OUT, SIR.
ARE YOU *INSANE?*
UT IT OULD ORK.
IF WE CONVERT ALL THE DALEKS IN THE LOCK-UP SO WE CONTROL THEM.
THEN -ARM HEM.
NTER'S GHT - HAT'S DNESS.
I'VE N DALEKS TENDING TO FRIENDLY BEFORE.
IT DIDN'T END WELL.
I DON'T KNOW WHAT OTHER OPTION WE HAVE, SIR.
OUR ONLY REAL DEFENCE WAS THAT THE DALEKS DIDN'T KNOW WE WERE HERE.
THE OTHER OPTION IS THAT WE ALL DIE.
BUT I GUESS YOU'D PREFER THAT.
WESTON WAS RIGHT, YOU'RE SO CLOSED-MINDED, TRANTER.
THAT'S WHY HE LEFT RATHER THAN WORK WITH YOU AGAIN AFTER LAST TIME!
TELL ME ABOUT LAST TIME.

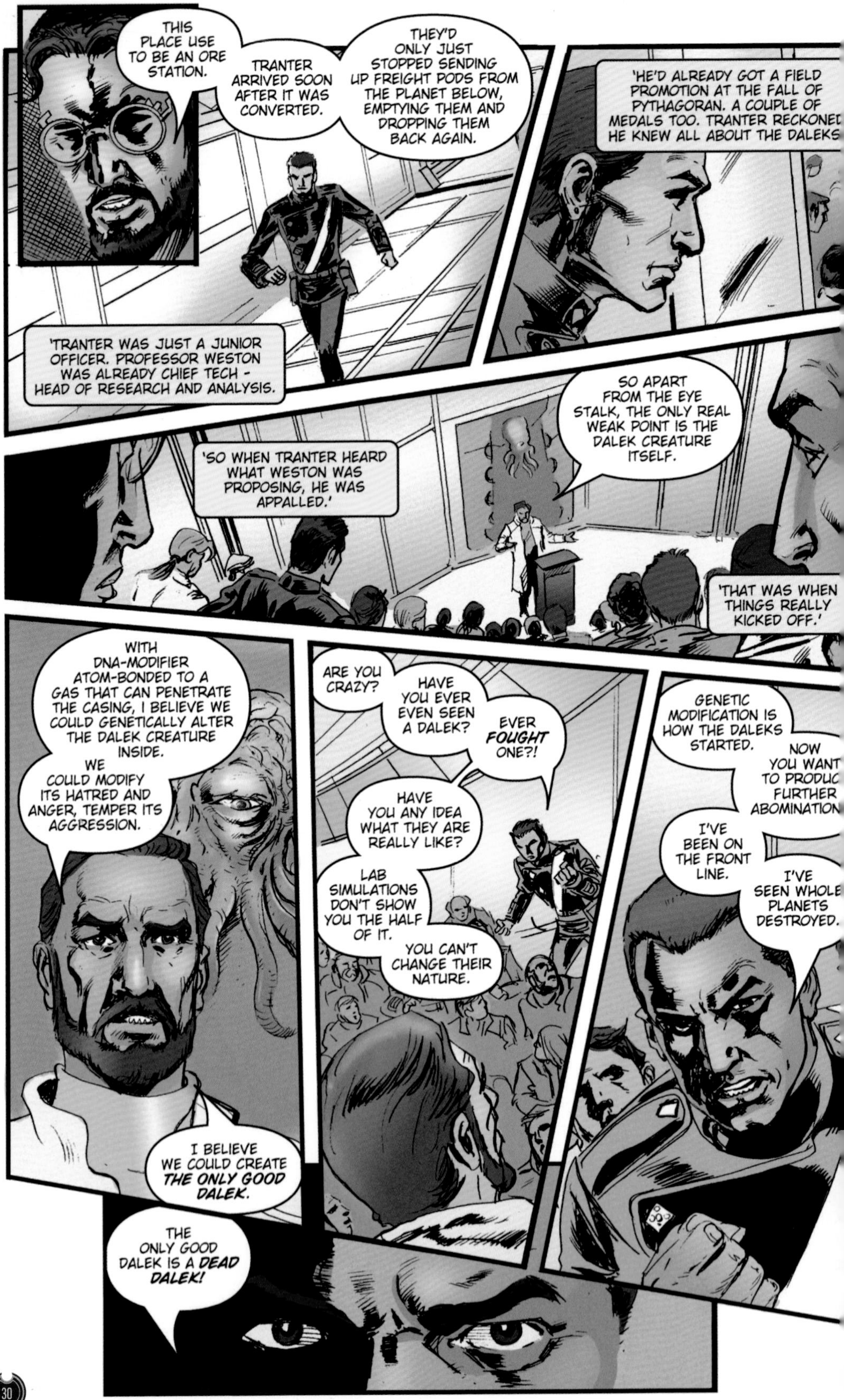

THIS PLACE USE TO BE AN ORE STATION.
TRANTER ARRIVED SOON AFTER IT WAS CONVERTED.
THEY'D ONLY JUST STOPPED SENDING UP FREIGHT PODS FROM THE PLANET BELOW, EMPTYING THEM AND DROPPING THEM BACK AGAIN.
'TRANTER WAS JUST A JUNIOR OFFICER. PROFESSOR WESTON WAS ALREADY CHIEF TECH - HEAD OF RESEARCH AND ANALYSIS.
'HE'D ALREADY GOT A FIELD PROMOTION AT THE FALL OF PYTHAGORAN. A COUPLE OF MEDALS TOO. TRANTER RECKONED HE KNEW ALL ABOUT THE DALEKS
'SO WHEN TRANTER HEARD WHAT WESTON WAS PROPOSING, HE WAS APPALLED.'
SO APART FROM THE EYE STALK, THE ONLY REAL WEAK POINT IS THE DALEK CREATURE ITSELF.
'THAT WAS WHEN THINGS REALLY KICKED OFF.'
WITH DNA-MODIFIER ATOM-BONDED TO A GAS THAT CAN PENETRATE THE CASING, I BELIEVE WE COULD GENETICALLY ALTER THE DALEK CREATURE INSIDE.
WE COULD MODIFY ITS HATRED AND ANGER, TEMPER ITS AGGRESSION.
I BELIEVE WE COULD CREATE *THE ONLY GOOD DALEK*.
ARE YOU CRAZY?
HAVE YOU EVER EVEN SEEN A DALEK?
EVER *FOUGHT* ONE?!
HAVE YOU ANY IDEA WHAT THEY ARE REALLY LIKE?
LAB SIMULATIONS DON'T SHOW YOU THE HALF OF IT.
YOU CAN'T CHANGE THEIR NATURE.
GENETIC MODIFICATION IS HOW THE DALEKS STARTED.
NOW YOU WANT TO PRODUC FURTHER ABOMINATION
I'VE BEEN ON THE FRONT LINE.
I'VE SEEN WHOLE PLANETS DESTROYED.
THE ONLY GOOD DALEK IS A *DEAD DALEK!*

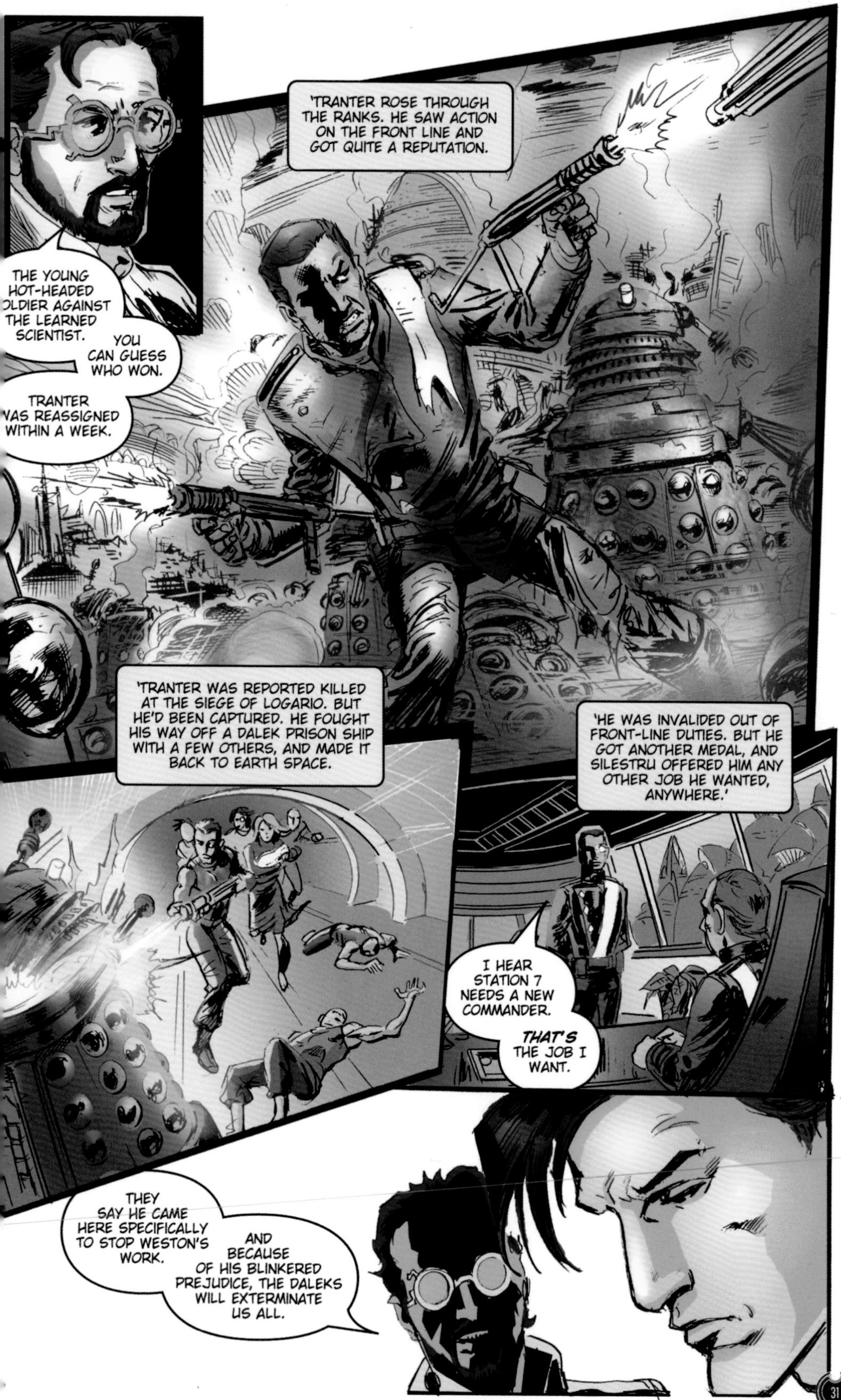
'TRANTER ROSE THROUGH THE RANKS. HE SAW ACTION ON THE FRONT LINE AND GOT QUITE A REPUTATION.
THE YOUNG HOT-HEADED OLDIER AGAINST THE LEARNED SCIENTIST.
YOU CAN GUESS WHO WON.
TRANTER VAS REASSIGNED WITHIN A WEEK.
'TRANTER WAS REPORTED KILLED AT THE SIEGE OF LOGARIO. BUT HE'D BEEN CAPTURED. HE FOUGHT HIS WAY OFF A DALEK PRISON SHIP WITH A FEW OTHERS, AND MADE IT BACK TO EARTH SPACE.
'HE WAS INVALIDED OUT OF FRONT-LINE DUTIES. BUT HE GOT ANOTHER MEDAL, AND SILESTRU OFFERED HIM ANY OTHER JOB HE WANTED, ANYWHERE.'
I HEAR STATION 7 NEEDS A NEW COMMANDER.
THAT'S THE JOB I WANT.
THEY SAY HE CAME HERE SPECIFICALLY TO STOP WESTON'S WORK.
AND BECAUSE OF HIS BLINKERED PREJUDICE, THE DALEKS WILL EXTERMINATE US ALL.

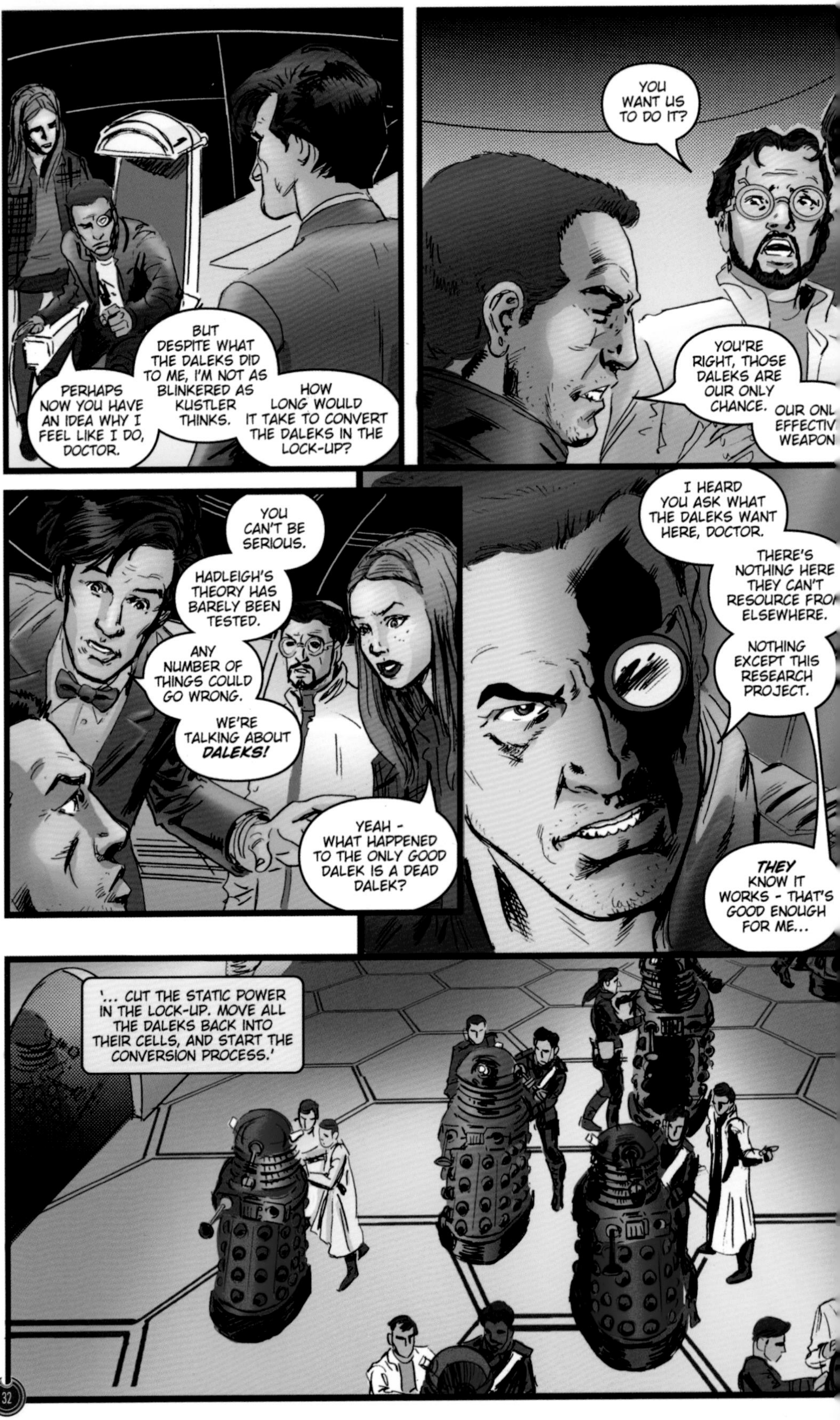
PERHAPS NOW YOU HAVE AN IDEA WHY I FEEL LIKE I DO, DOCTOR.
BUT DESPITE WHAT THE DALEKS DID TO ME, I'M NOT AS BLINKERED AS KUSTLER THINKS.
HOW LONG WOULD IT TAKE TO CONVERT THE DALEKS IN THE LOCK-UP?
YOU WANT US TO DO IT?
YOU'RE RIGHT, THOSE DALEKS ARE OUR ONLY CHANCE.
OUR ONL EFFECTIV WEAPON
YOU CAN'T BE SERIOUS.
HADLEIGH'S THEORY HAS BARELY BEEN TESTED.
ANY NUMBER OF THINGS COULD GO WRONG.
WE'RE TALKING ABOUT *DALEKS!*
YEAH - WHAT HAPPENED TO THE ONLY GOOD DALEK IS A DEAD DALEK?
I HEARD YOU ASK WHAT THE DALEKS WANT HERE, DOCTOR.
THERE'S NOTHING HERE THEY CAN'T RESOURCE FRO ELSEWHERE.
NOTHING EXCEPT THIS RESEARCH PROJECT.
THEY KNOW IT WORKS - THAT'S GOOD ENOUGH FOR ME...
'... CUT THE STATIC POWER IN THE LOCK-UP. MOVE ALL THE DALEKS BACK INTO THEIR CELLS, AND START THE CONVERSION PROCESS.'

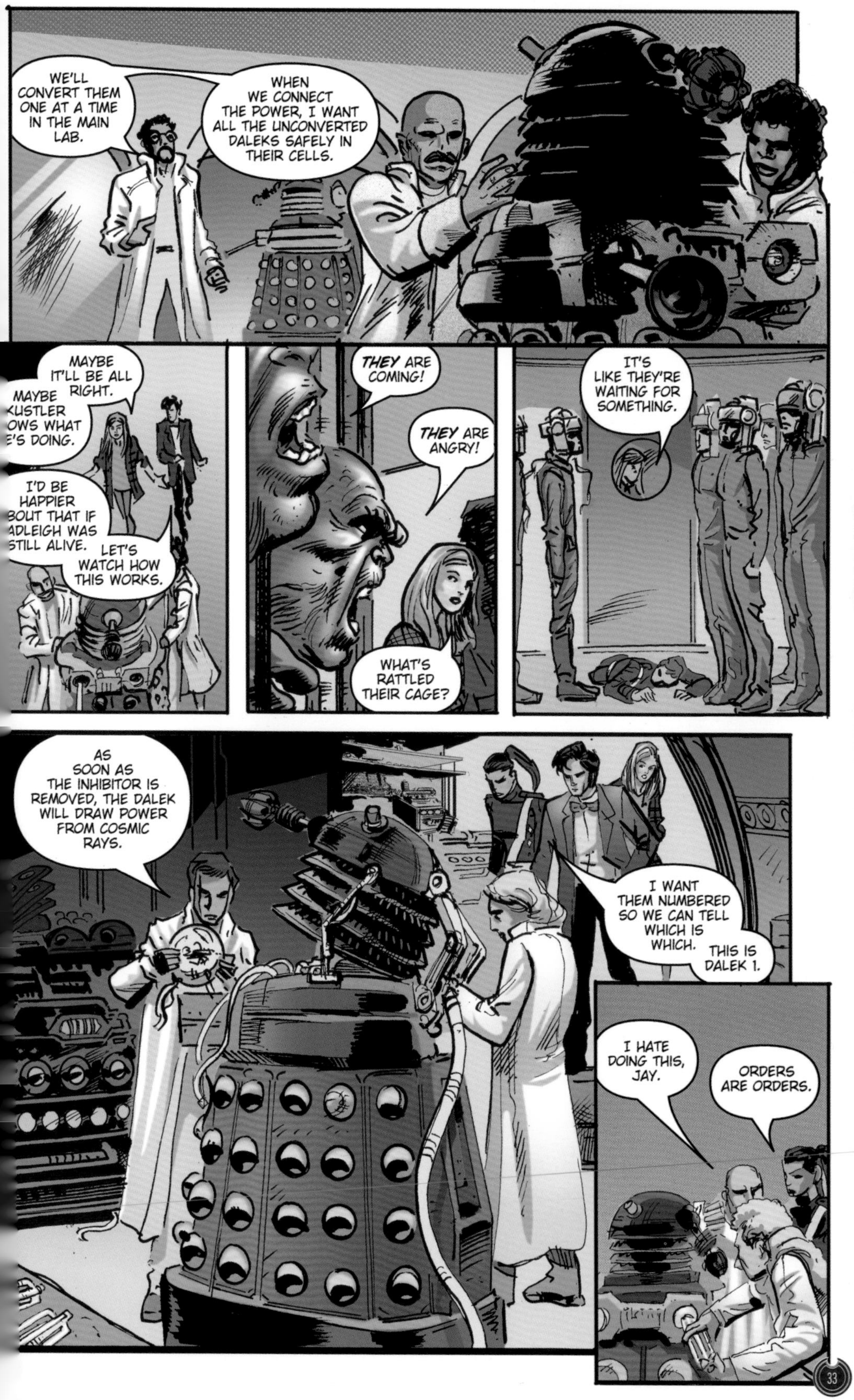

WE'LL CONVERT THEM ONE AT A TIME IN THE MAIN LAB.
WHEN WE CONNECT THE POWER, I WANT ALL THE UNCONVERTED DALEKS SAFELY IN THEIR CELLS.
MAYBE IT'LL BE ALL RIGHT.
MAYBE KUSTLER OWS WHAT E'S DOING.
I'D BE HAPPIER BOUT THAT IF ADLEIGH WAS STILL ALIVE.
LET'S WATCH HOW THIS WORKS.
THEY ARE COMING!
THEY ARE ANGRY!
WHAT'S RATTLED THEIR CAGE?
IT'S LIKE THEY'RE WAITING FOR SOMETHING.
AS SOON AS THE INHIBITOR IS REMOVED, THE DALEK WILL DRAW POWER FROM COSMIC RAYS.
I WANT THEM NUMBERED SO WE CAN TELL WHICH IS WHICH.
THIS IS DALEK 1.
I HATE DOING THIS, JAY.
ORDERS ARE ORDERS.

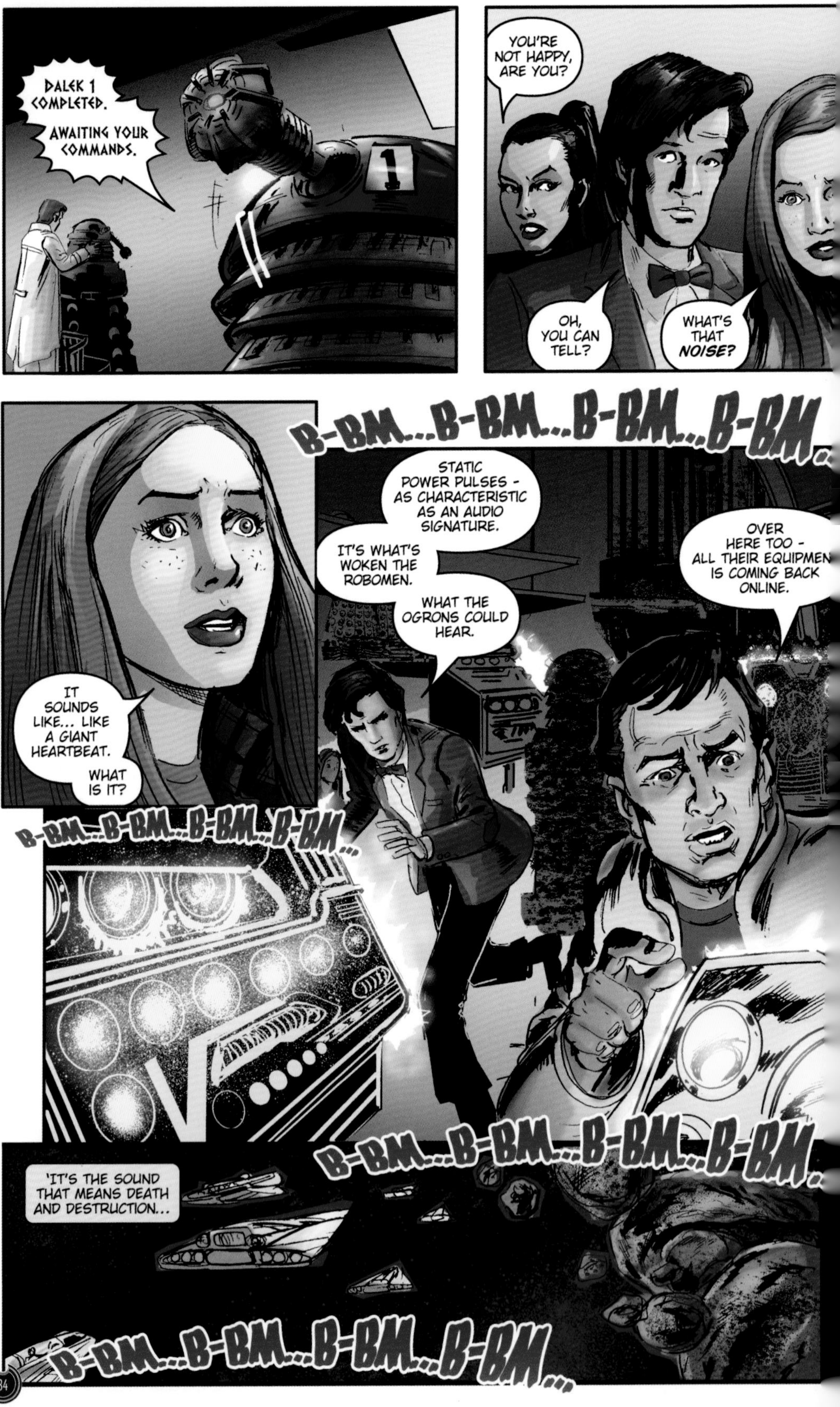
DALEK 1 COMPLETED.
AWAITING YOUR COMMANDS.
YOU'RE NOT HAPPY, ARE YOU?
OH, YOU CAN TELL?
WHAT'S THAT *NOISE?*
B-BM...B-BM...B-BM...B-BM...
IT SOUNDS LIKE... LIKE A GIANT HEARTBEAT.
WHAT IS IT?
STATIC POWER PULSES - AS CHARACTERISTIC AS AN AUDIO SIGNATURE.
IT'S WHAT'S WOKEN THE ROBOMEN.
WHAT THE OGRONS COULD HEAR.
OVER HERE TOO - ALL THEIR EQUIPMEN IS COMING BACK ONLINE.
B-BM...B-BM...B-BM...B-BM...
B-BM...B-BM...B-BM...B-BM...
'IT'S THE SOUND THAT MEANS DEATH AND DESTRUCTION...
B-BM...B-BM...B-BM...B-BM...

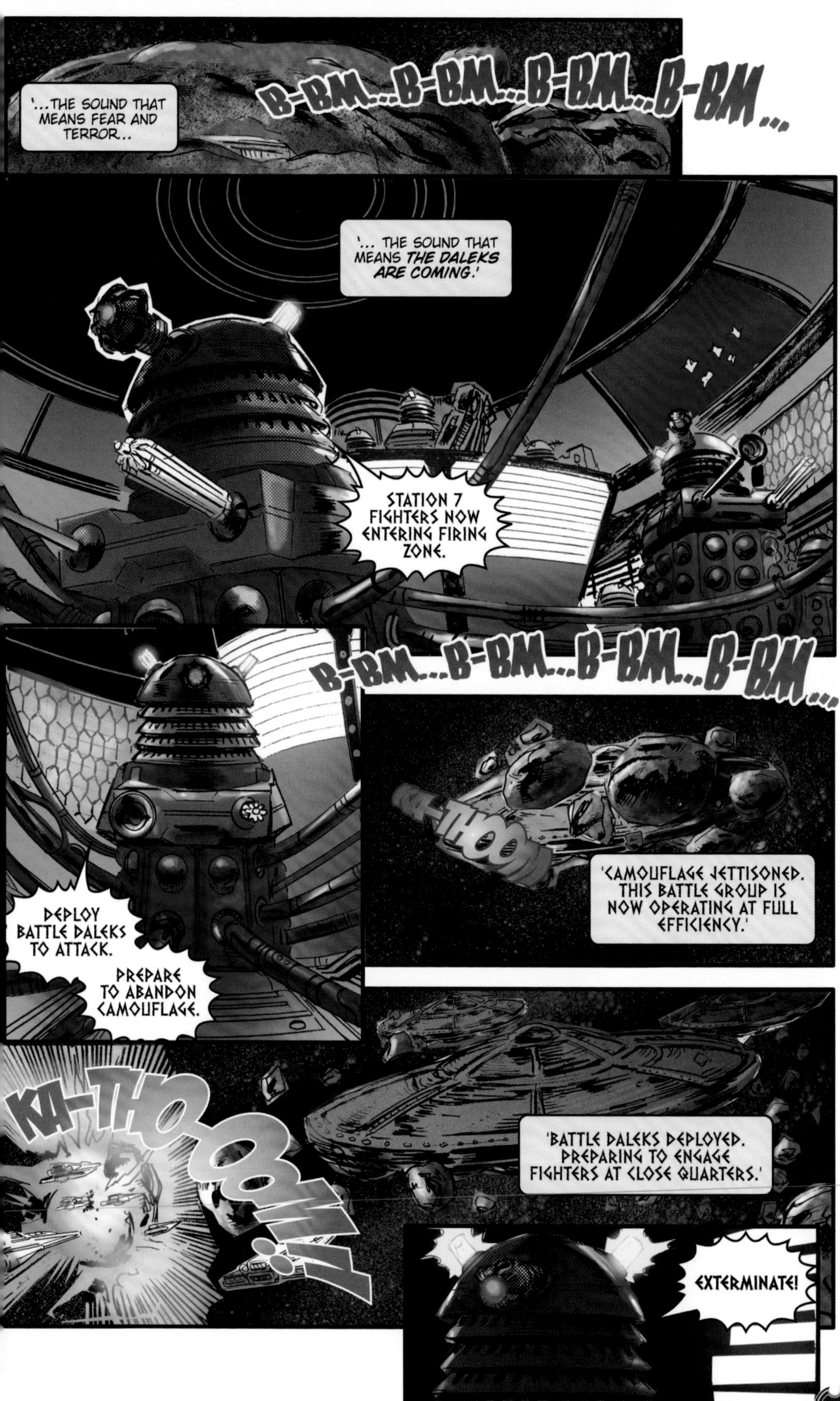
'...THE SOUND THAT MEANS FEAR AND TERROR..
B-BM...B-BM...B-BM...B-BM...
'... THE SOUND THAT MEANS THE DALEKS ARE COMING.'
STATION 7 FIGHTERS NOW ENTERING FIRING ZONE.
B-BM...B-BM...B-BM...B-BM...
DEPLOY BATTLE DALEKS TO ATTACK.
PREPARE TO ABANDON CAMOUFLAGE.
KA-THOOM
'CAMOUFLAGE JETTISONED. THIS BATTLE GROUP IS NOW OPERATING AT FULL EFFICIENCY.'
KA-THOOOOM!!!
'BATTLE DALEKS DEPLOYED. PREPARING TO ENGAGE FIGHTERS AT CLOSE QUARTERS.'
EXTERMINATE!

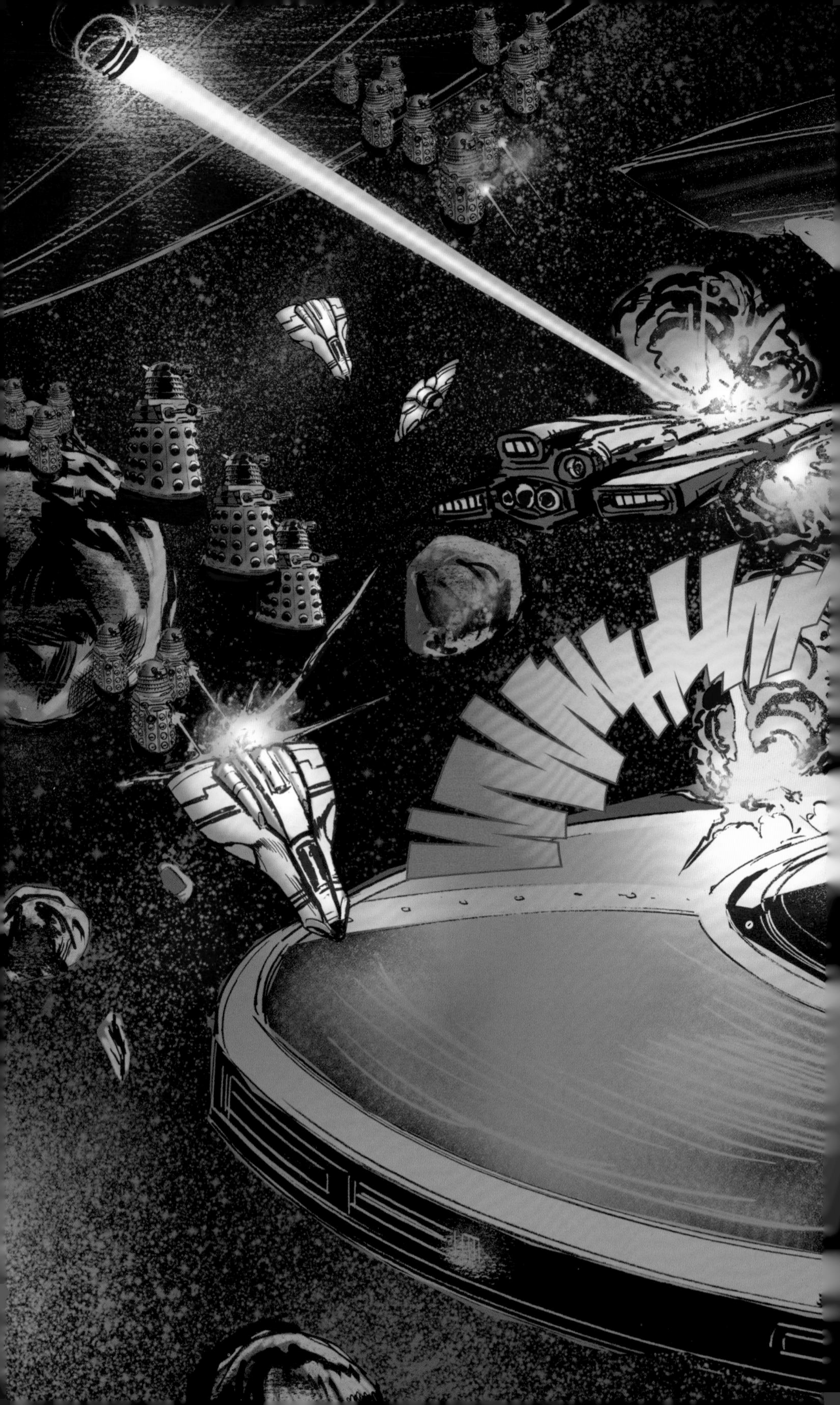

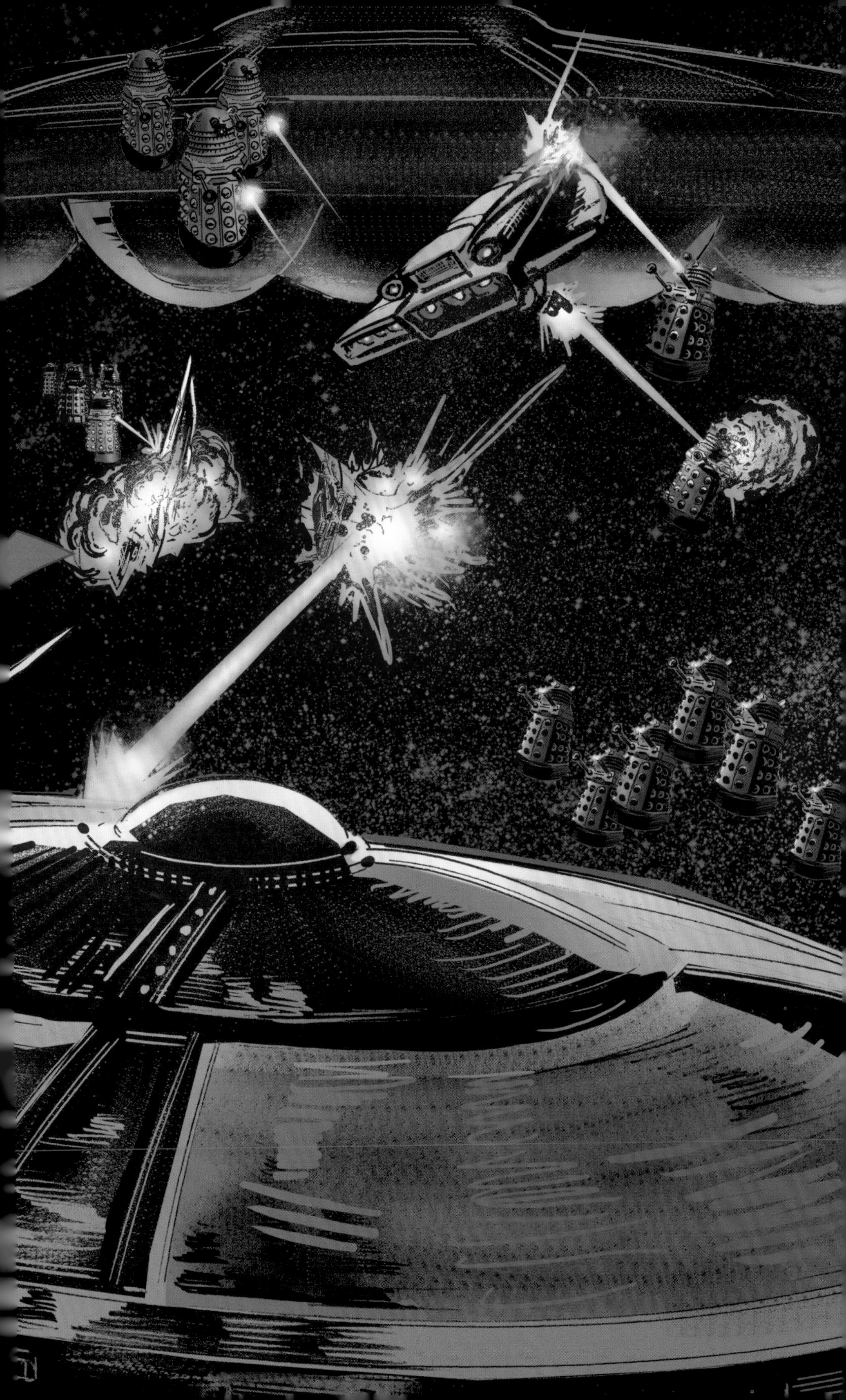

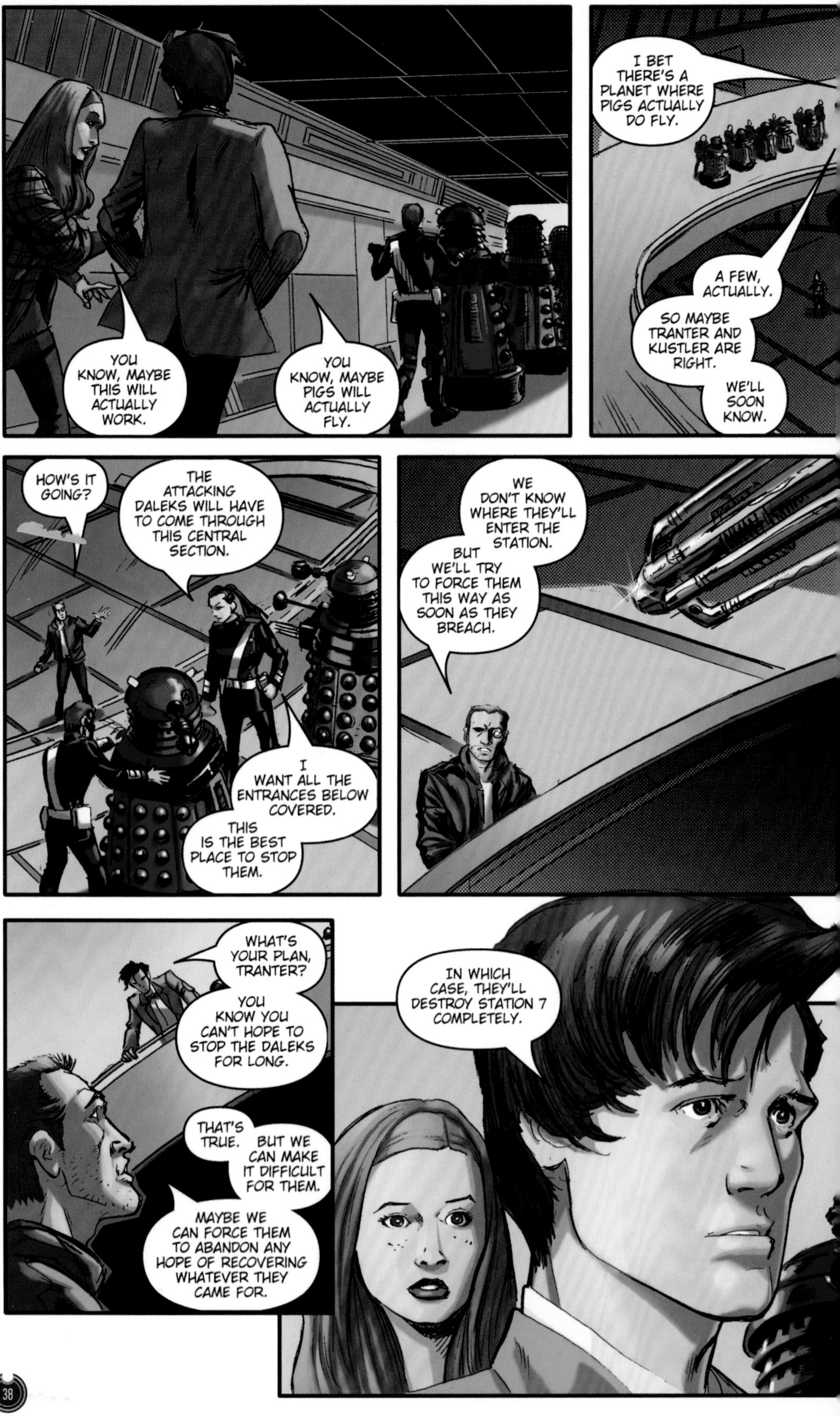
YOU KNOW, MAYBE THIS WILL ACTUALLY WORK.
YOU KNOW, MAYBE PIGS WILL ACTUALLY FLY.
I BET THERE'S A PLANET WHERE PIGS ACTUALLY DO FLY.
A FEW, ACTUALLY.
SO MAYBE TRANTER AND KUSTLER ARE RIGHT.
WE'LL SOON KNOW.
HOW'S IT GOING?
THE ATTACKING DALEKS WILL HAVE TO COME THROUGH THIS CENTRAL SECTION.
I WANT ALL THE ENTRANCES BELOW COVERED.
THIS IS THE BEST PLACE TO STOP THEM.
WE DON'T KNOW WHERE THEY'LL ENTER THE STATION.
BUT WE'LL TRY TO FORCE THEM THIS WAY AS SOON AS THEY BREACH.
WHAT'S YOUR PLAN, TRANTER?
YOU KNOW YOU CAN'T HOPE TO STOP THE DALEKS FOR LONG.
THAT'S TRUE.
BUT WE CAN MAKE IT DIFFICULT FOR THEM.
MAYBE WE CAN FORCE THEM TO ABANDON ANY HOPE OF RECOVERING WHATEVER THEY CAME FOR.
IN WHICH CASE, THEY'LL DESTROY STATION 7 COMPLETELY.

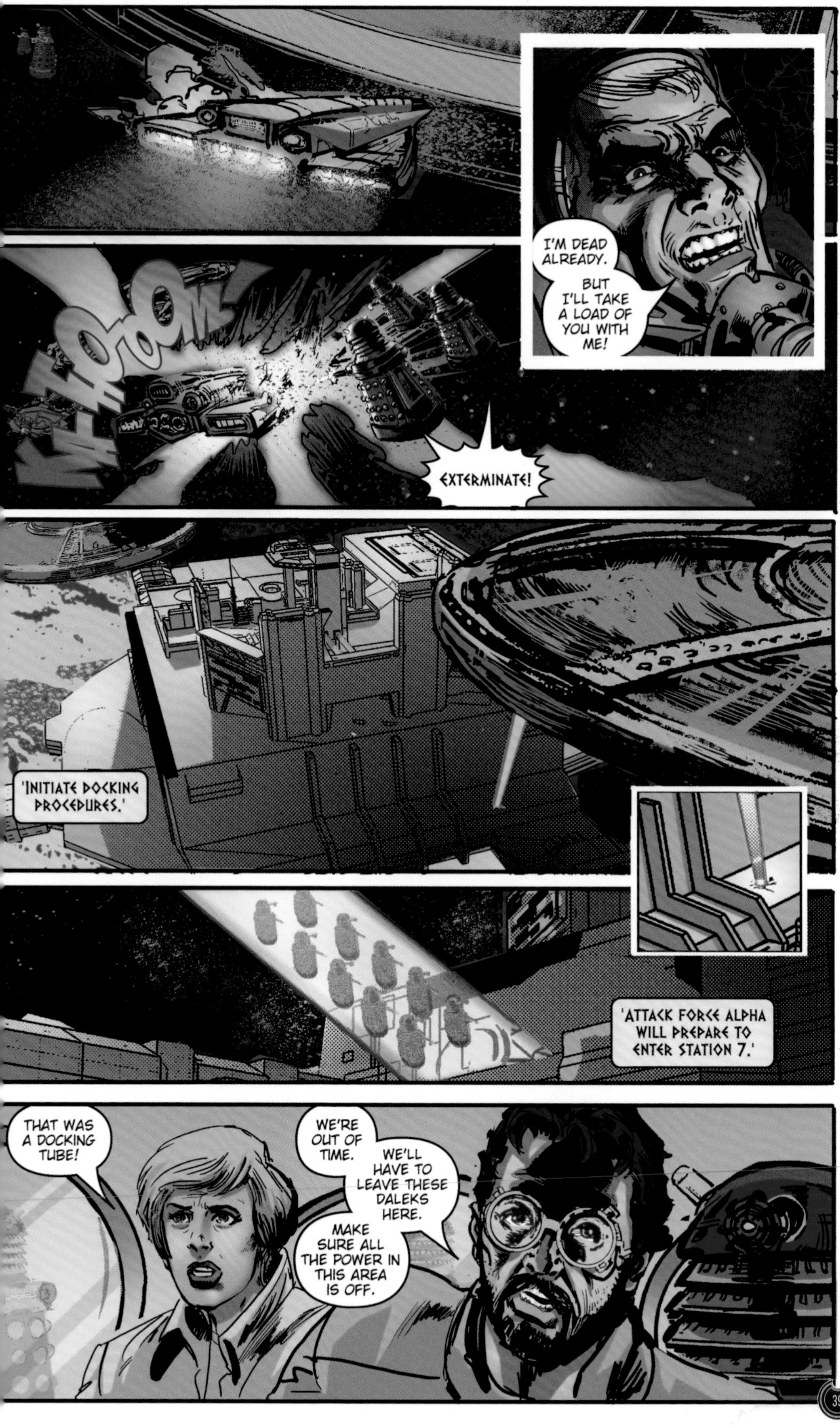

I'M DEAD ALREADY.
BUT I'LL TAKE A LOAD OF YOU WITH ME!
WHOOM!
EXTERMINATE!
'INITIATE DOCKING PROCEDURES.'
'ATTACK FORCE ALPHA WILL PREPARE TO ENTER STATION 7.'
THAT WAS A DOCKING TUBE!
WE'RE OUT OF TIME.
WE'LL HAVE TO LEAVE THESE DALEKS HERE.
MAKE SURE ALL THE POWER IN THIS AREA IS OFF.

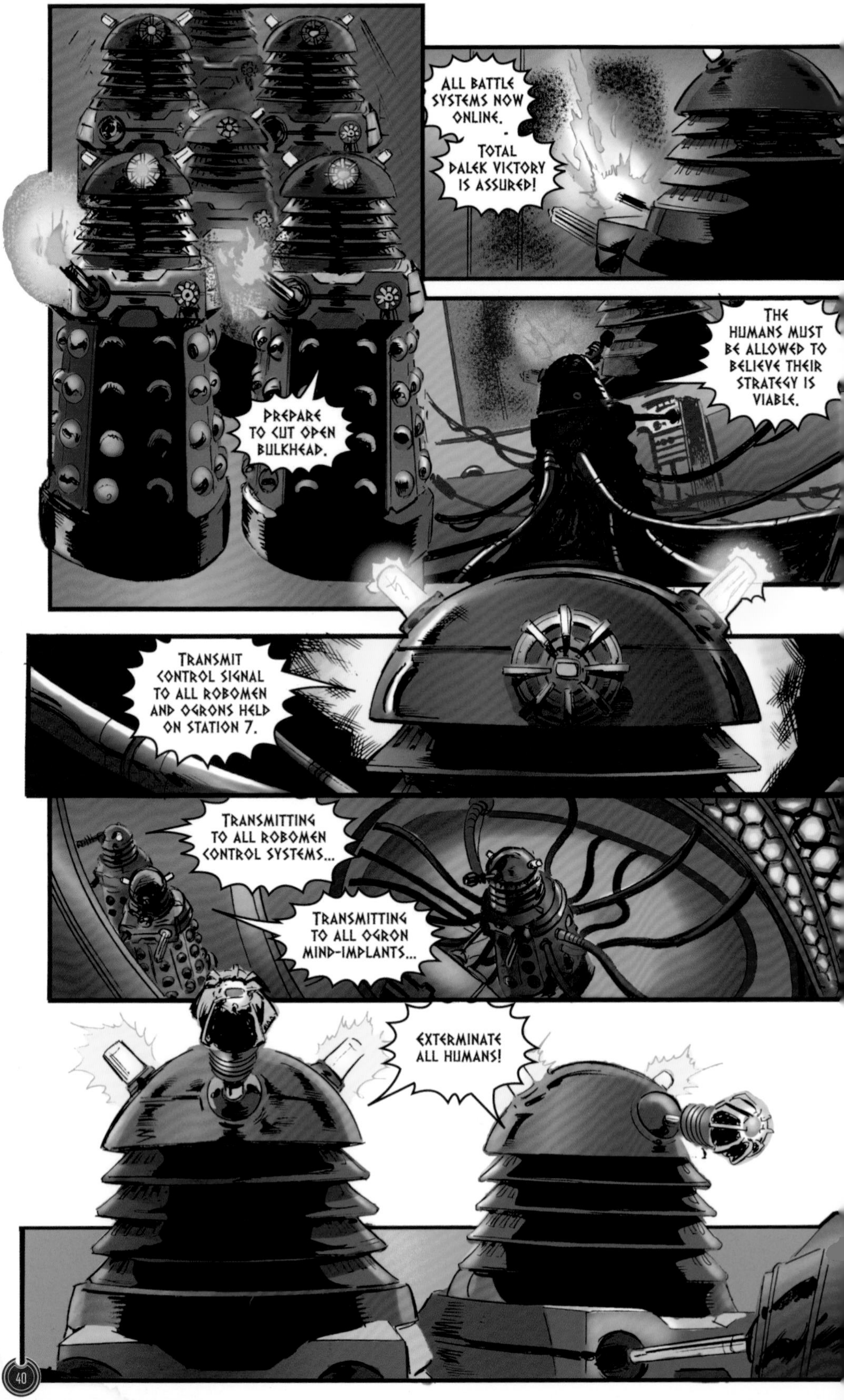
ALL BATTLE SYSTEMS NOW ONLINE.
TOTAL DALEK VICTORY IS ASSURED!
PREPARE TO CUT OPEN BULKHEAD.
THE HUMANS MUST BE ALLOWED TO BELIEVE THEIR STRATEGY IS VIABLE.
TRANSMIT CONTROL SIGNAL TO ALL ROBOMEN AND OGRONS HELD ON STATION 7.
TRANSMITTING TO ALL ROBOMEN CONTROL SYSTEMS...
TRANSMITTING TO ALL OGRON MIND-IMPLANTS...
EXTERMINATE ALL HUMANS!

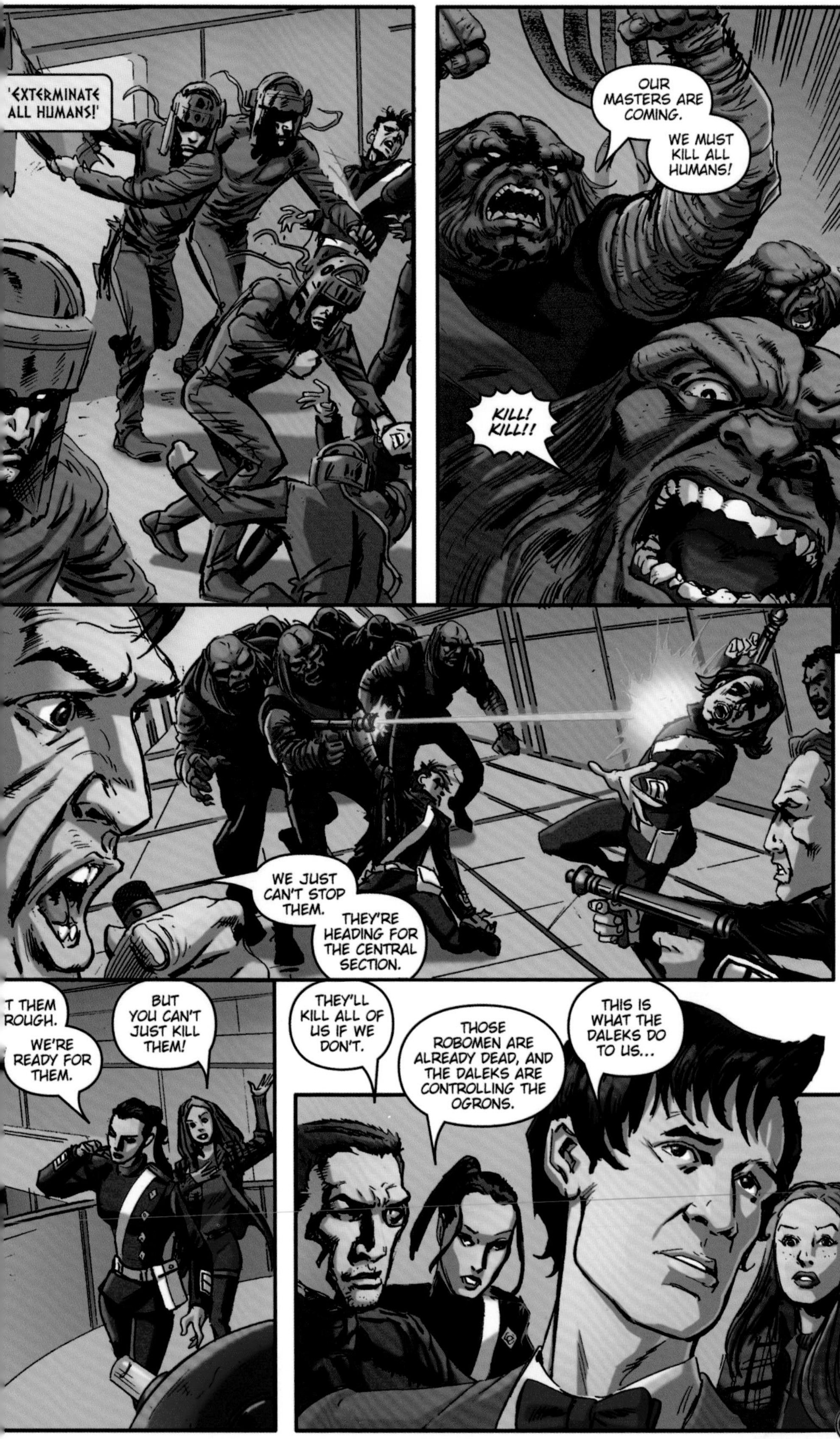
'EXTERMINATE ALL HUMANS!'
OUR MASTERS ARE COMING.
WE MUST KILL ALL HUMANS!
KILL! KILL!!
WE JUST CAN'T STOP THEM.
THEY'RE HEADING FOR THE CENTRAL SECTION.
T THEM ROUGH.
WE'RE READY FOR THEM.
BUT YOU CAN'T JUST KILL THEM!
THEY'LL KILL ALL OF US IF WE DON'T.
THOSE ROBOMEN ARE ALREADY DEAD, AND THE DALEKS ARE CONTROLLING THE OGRONS.
THIS IS WHAT THE DALEKS DO TO US...

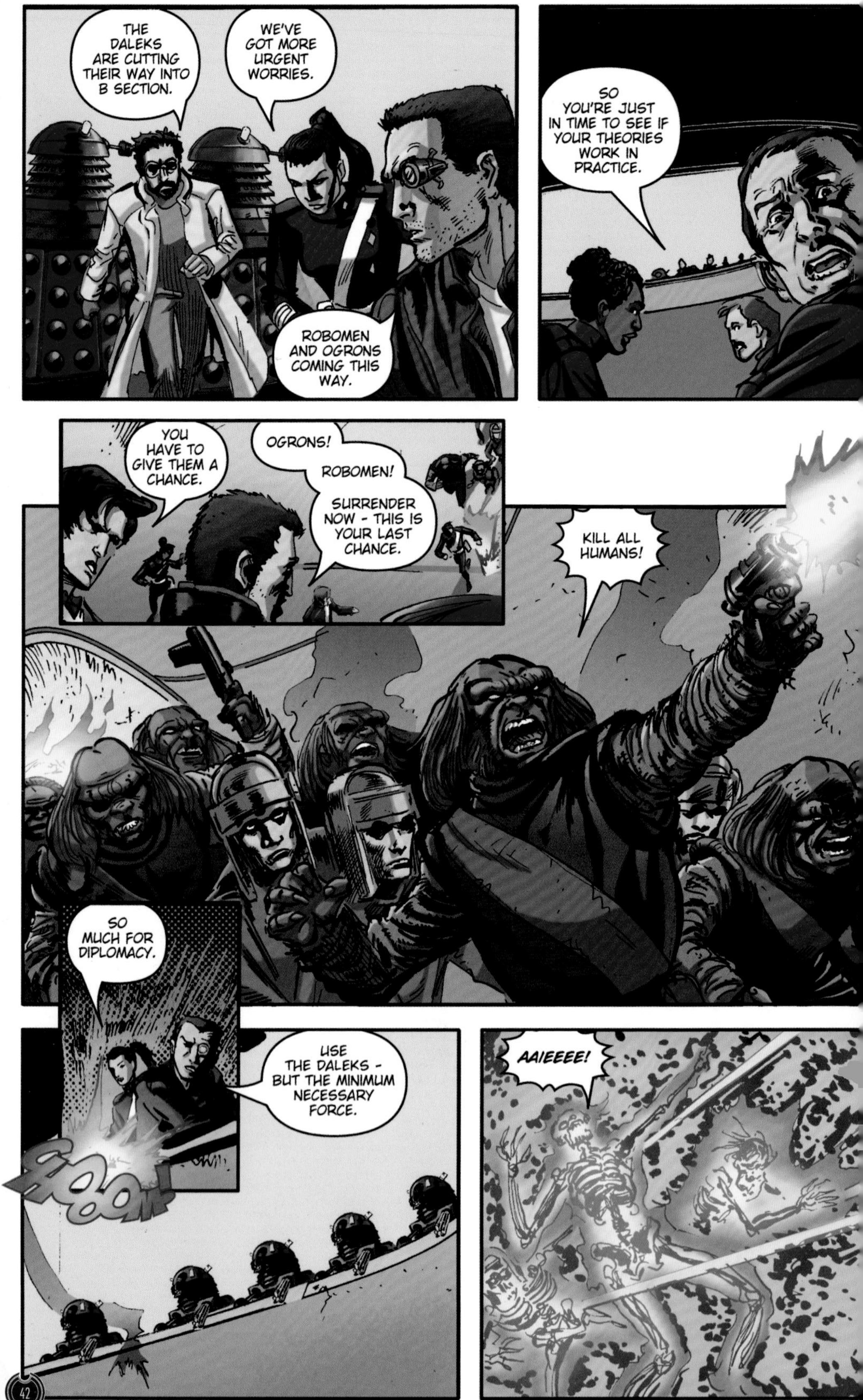
THE DALEKS ARE CUTTING THEIR WAY INTO B SECTION.
WE'VE GOT MORE URGENT WORRIES.
ROBOMEN AND OGRONS COMING THIS WAY.
SO YOU'RE JUST IN TIME TO SEE IF YOUR THEORIES WORK IN PRACTICE.
YOU HAVE TO GIVE THEM A CHANCE.
OGRONS!
ROBOMEN!
SURRENDER NOW - THIS IS YOUR LAST CHANCE.
KILL ALL HUMANS!
SO MUCH FOR DIPLOMACY.
USE THE DALEKS - BUT THE MINIMUM NECESSARY FORCE.
FOOM
AAIEEEE!

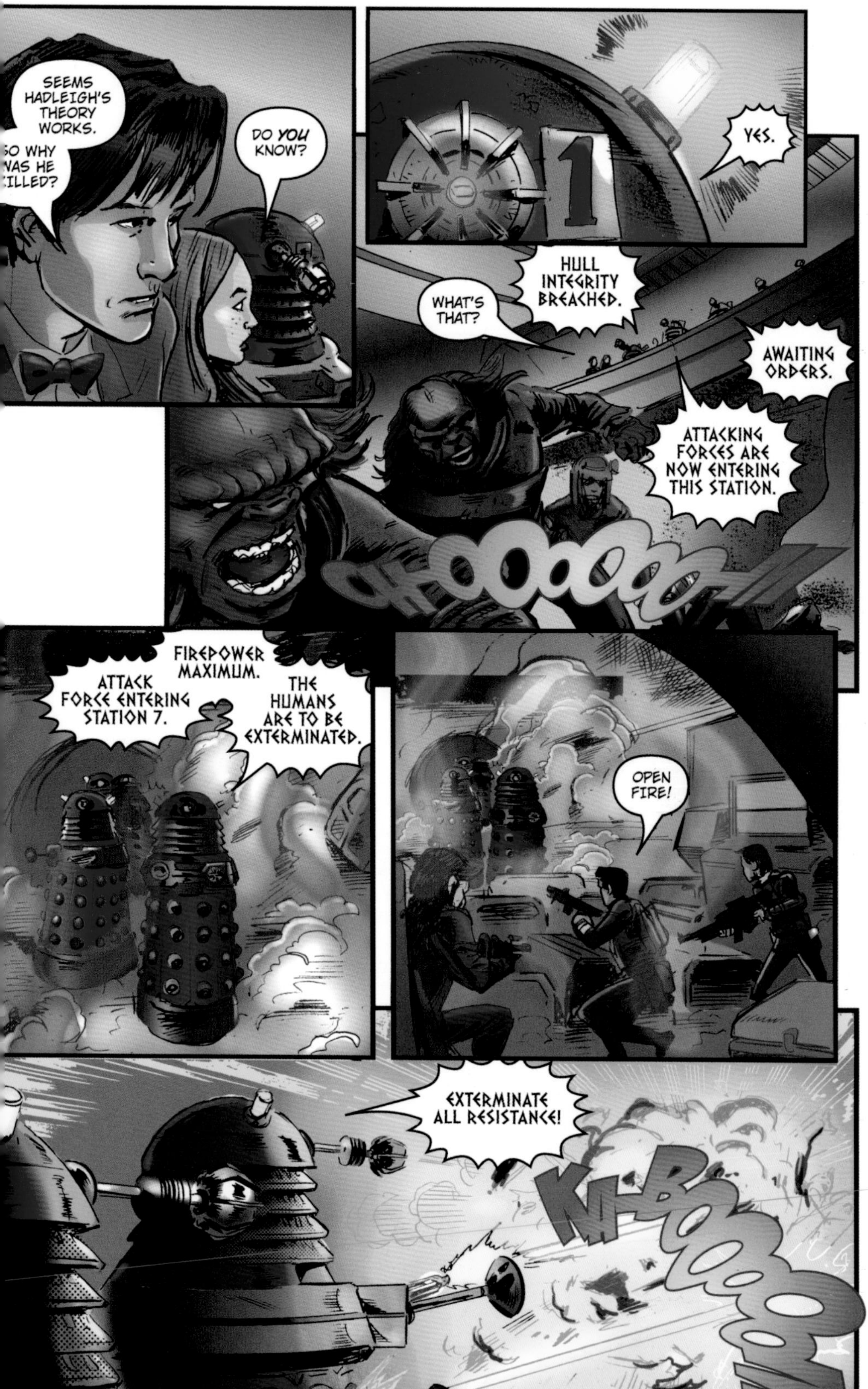
SEEMS HADLEIGH'S THEORY WORKS.
SO WHY WAS HE KILLED?
DO *YOU* KNOW?
YES.
HULL INTEGRITY BREACHED.
WHAT'S THAT?
AWAITING ORDERS.
ATTACKING FORCES ARE NOW ENTERING THIS STATION.
FIREPOWER MAXIMUM.
ATTACK FORCE ENTERING STATION 7.
THE HUMANS ARE TO BE EXTERMINATED.
OPEN FIRE!
EXTERMINATE ALL RESISTANCE!
KA-BOOOOOOM!

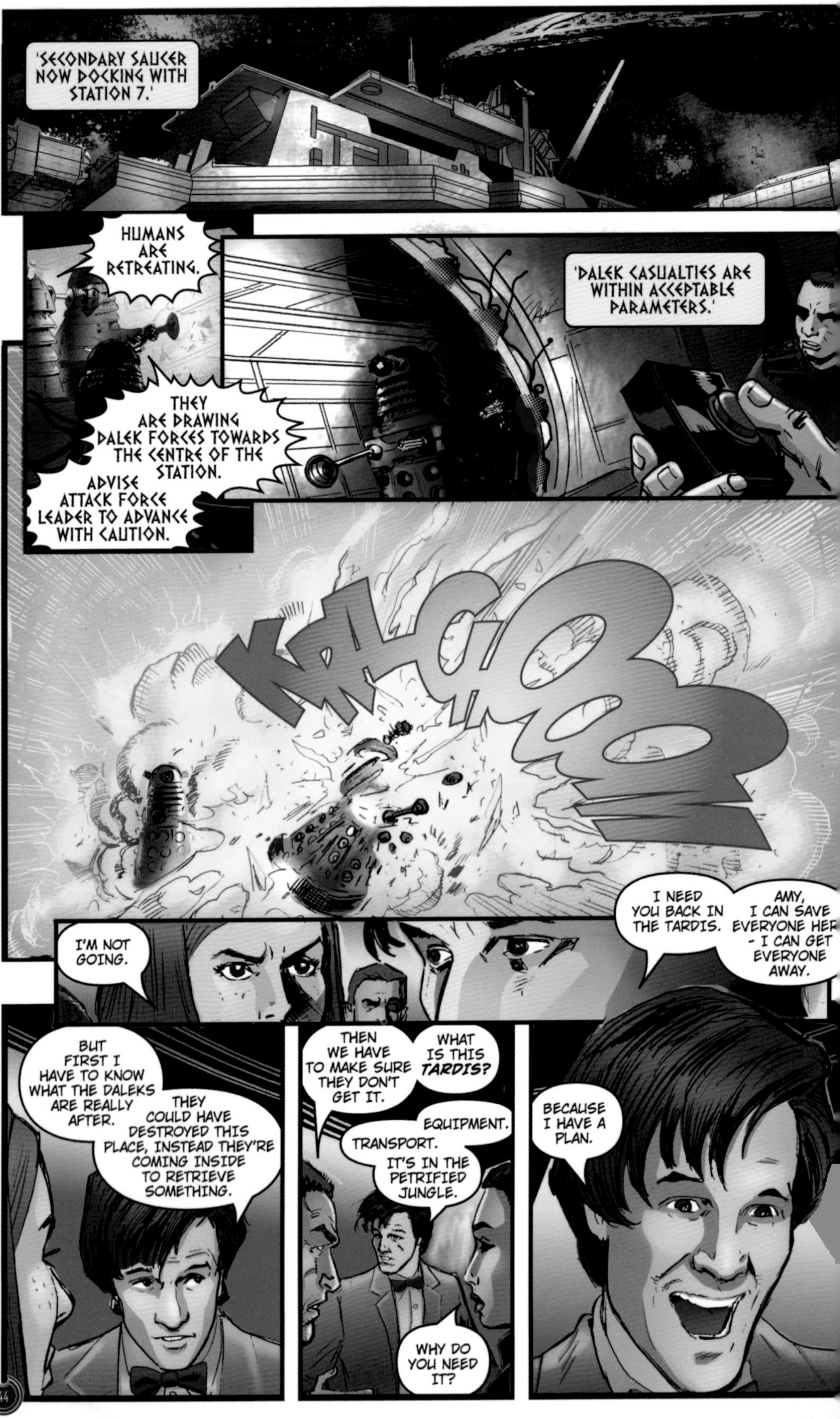
'SECONDARY SAUCER NOW DOCKING WITH STATION 7.'
HUMANS ARE RETREATING.
'DALEK CASUALTIES ARE WITHIN ACCEPTABLE PARAMETERS.'
THEY ARE DRAWING DALEK FORCES TOWARDS THE CENTRE OF THE STATION.
ADVISE ATTACK FORCE LEADER TO ADVANCE WITH CAUTION.
KA-BOOM
I NEED YOU BACK IN THE TARDIS.
AMY, I CAN SAVE EVERYONE HER - I CAN GET EVERYONE AWAY.
I'M NOT GOING.
BUT FIRST I HAVE TO KNOW WHAT THE DALEKS ARE REALLY AFTER.
THEY COULD HAVE DESTROYED THIS PLACE, INSTEAD THEY'RE COMING INSIDE TO RETRIEVE SOMETHING.
THEN WE HAVE TO MAKE SURE THEY DON'T GET IT.
WHAT IS THIS TARDIS?
EQUIPMENT.
TRANSPORT.
IT'S IN THE PETRIFIED JUNGLE.
WHY DO YOU NEED IT?
BECAUSE I HAVE A PLAN.

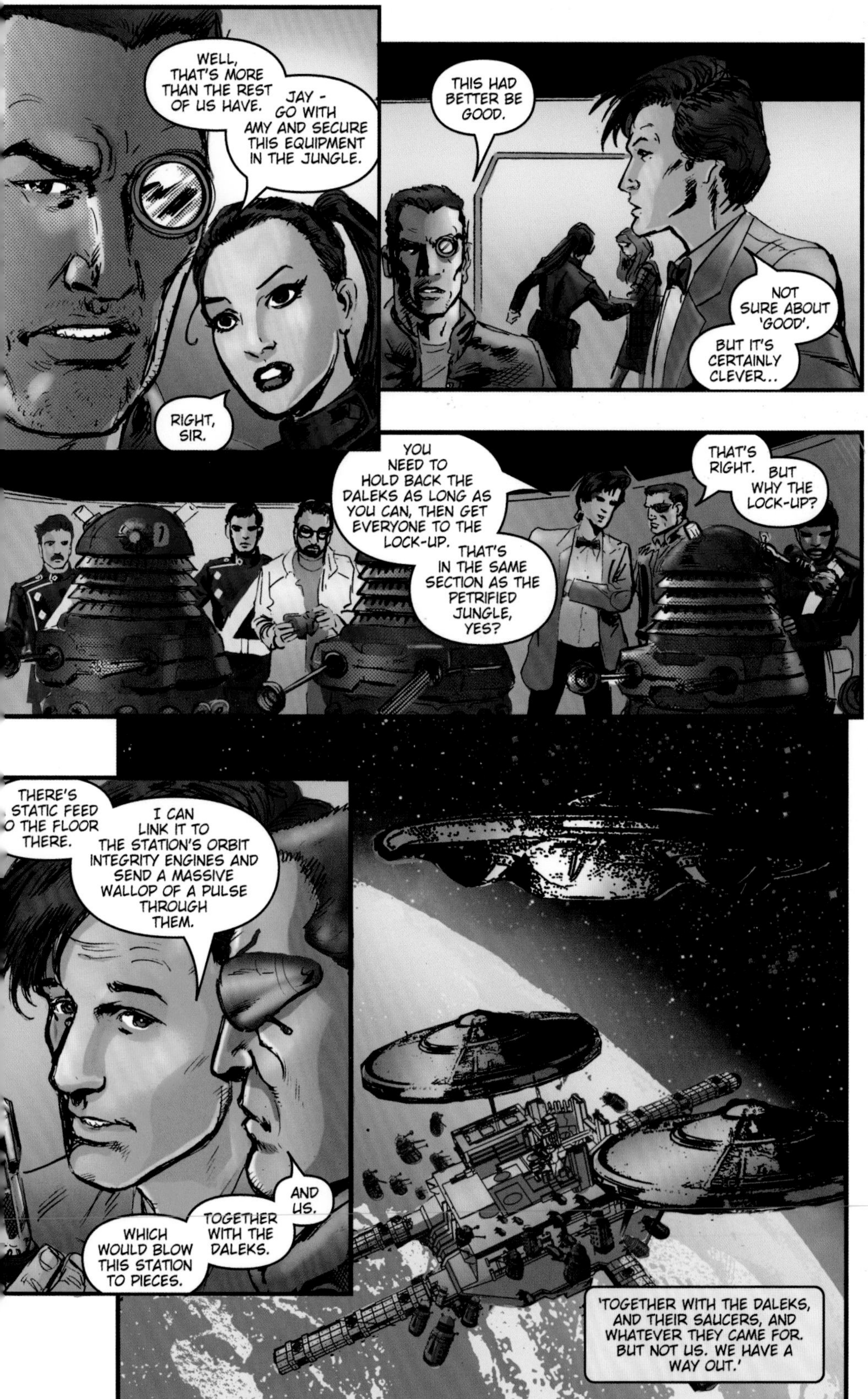
WELL, THAT'S MORE THAN THE REST OF US HAVE.
JAY - GO WITH AMY AND SECURE THIS EQUIPMENT IN THE JUNGLE.
RIGHT, SIR.
THIS HAD BETTER BE GOOD.
NOT SURE ABOUT 'GOOD'.
BUT IT'S CERTAINLY CLEVER..
YOU NEED TO HOLD BACK THE DALEKS AS LONG AS YOU CAN, THEN GET EVERYONE TO THE LOCK-UP.
THAT'S IN THE SAME SECTION AS THE PETRIFIED JUNGLE, YES?
THAT'S RIGHT.
BUT WHY THE LOCK-UP?
THERE'S STATIC FEED O THE FLOOR THERE.
I CAN LINK IT TO THE STATION'S ORBIT INTEGRITY ENGINES AND SEND A MASSIVE WALLOP OF A PULSE THROUGH THEM.
WHICH WOULD BLOW THIS STATION TO PIECES.
TOGETHER WITH THE DALEKS.
AND US.
'TOGETHER WITH THE DALEKS, AND THEIR SAUCERS, AND WHATEVER THEY CAME FOR. BUT NOT US. WE HAVE A WAY OUT.'

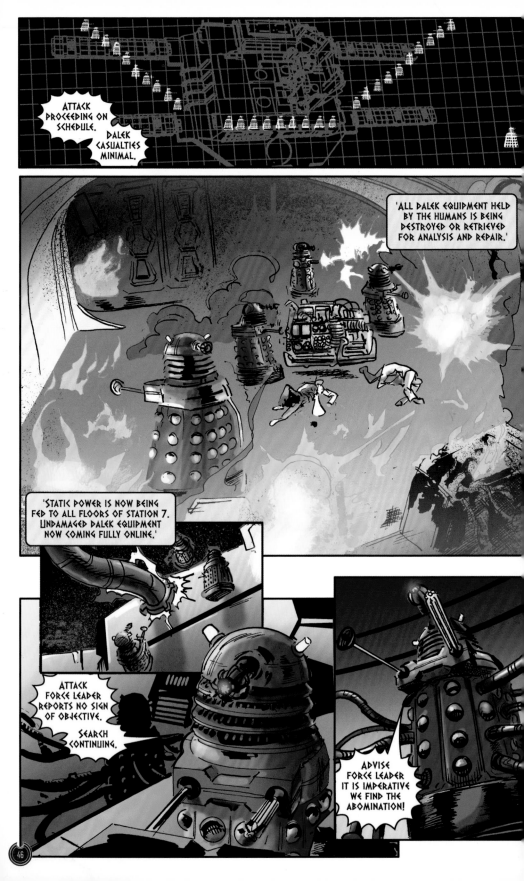

ATTACK PROCEEDING ON SCHEDULE. DALEK CASUALTIES MINIMAL.

'ALL DALEK EQUIPMENT HELD BY THE HUMANS IS BEING DESTROYED OR RETRIEVED FOR ANALYSIS AND REPAIR.'

'STATIC POWER IS NOW BEING FED TO ALL FLOORS OF STATION 7. UNDAMAGED DALEK EQUIPMENT NOW COMING FULLY ONLINE.'

ATTACK FORCE LEADER REPORTS NO SIGN OF OBJECTIVE.

SEARCH CONTINUING.

ADVISE FORCE LEADER IT IS IMPERATIVE WE FIND THE ABOMINATION!

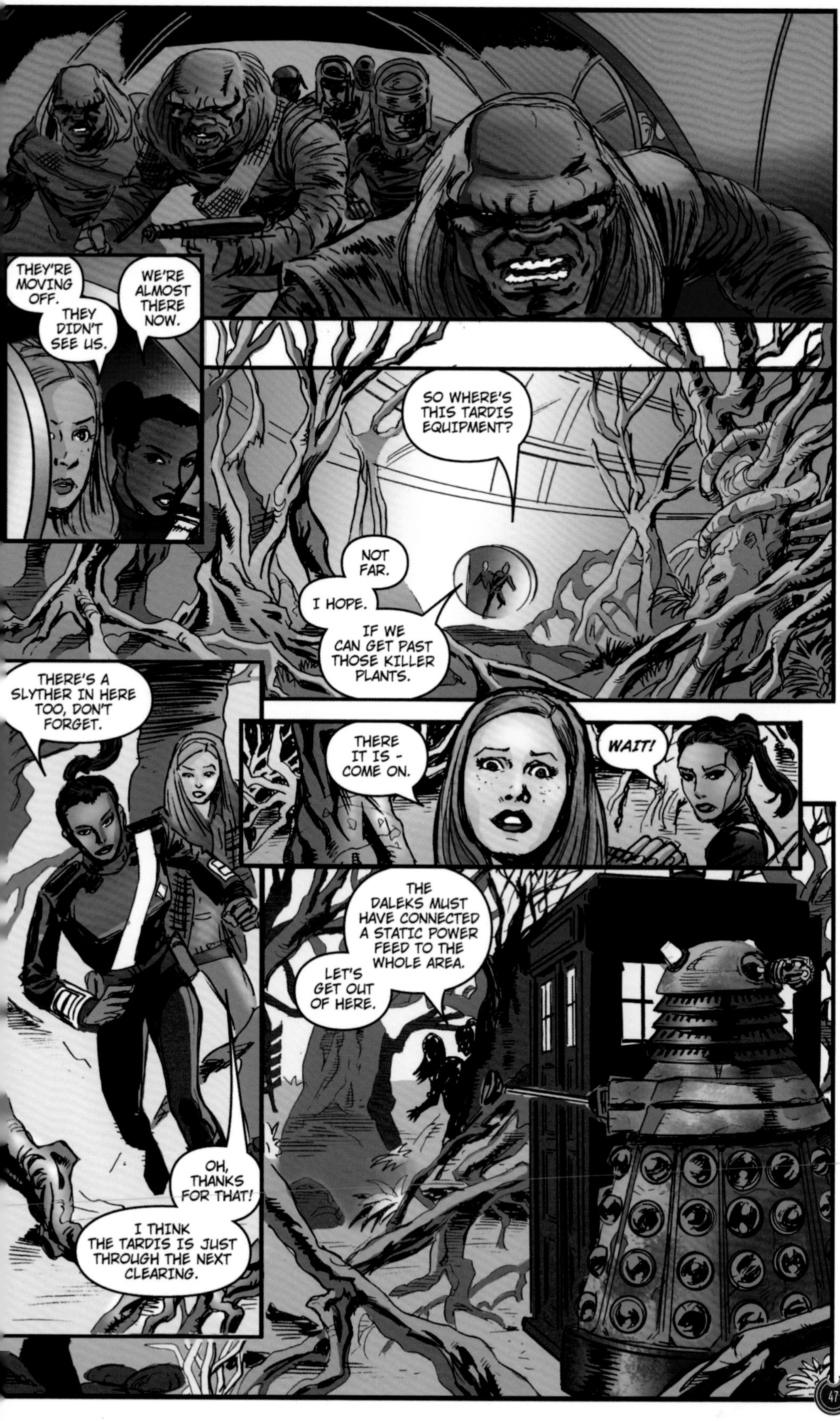
THEY'RE MOVING OFF.
THEY DIDN'T SEE US.
WE'RE ALMOST THERE NOW.
SO WHERE'S THIS TARDIS EQUIPMENT?
NOT FAR.
I HOPE.
IF WE CAN GET PAST THOSE KILLER PLANTS.
THERE'S A SLYTHER IN HERE TOO, DON'T FORGET.
OH, THANKS FOR THAT!
I THINK THE TARDIS IS JUST THROUGH THE NEXT CLEARING.
THERE IT IS - COME ON.
WAIT!
THE DALEKS MUST HAVE CONNECTED A STATIC POWER FEED TO THE WHOLE AREA.
LET'S GET OUT OF HERE.

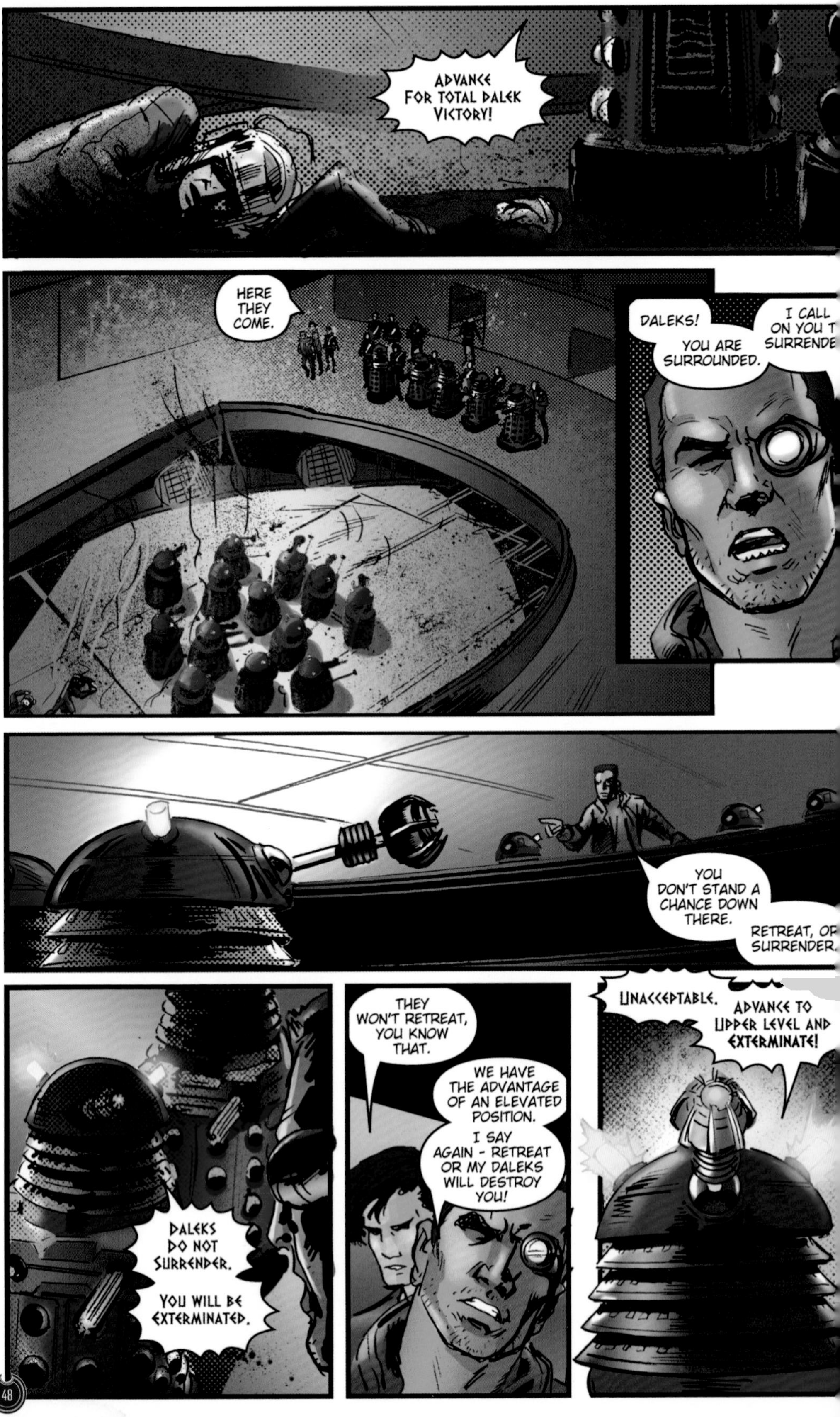

ADVANCE FOR TOTAL DALEK VICTORY!
HERE THEY COME.
DALEKS!
YOU ARE SURROUNDED.
I CALL ON YOU T SURRENDE
YOU DON'T STAND A CHANCE DOWN THERE.
RETREAT, OF SURRENDER.
DALEKS DO NOT SURRENDER.
YOU WILL BE EXTERMINATED.
THEY WON'T RETREAT, YOU KNOW THAT.
WE HAVE THE ADVANTAGE OF AN ELEVATED POSITION.
I SAY AGAIN - RETREAT OR MY DALEKS WILL DESTROY YOU!
UNACCEPTABLE.
ADVANCE TO UPPER LEVEL AND EXTERMINATE!

YOU HAVE NO CHOICE.

I KNOW, DOCTOR.

OPEN FIRE!

IT'S NOT WORKING.

NOTHING'S HAPPENING!

Klik-Klik-Klik

TRY AGAIN, IT HAS TO WORK.

WHAT'S HAPPENING?

THE CONVERSION PROCESS DOESN'T WORK.

IT'S ALL A TRICK.

EVERYONE OUT - BACK TO THE LOCK-UP, NOW!

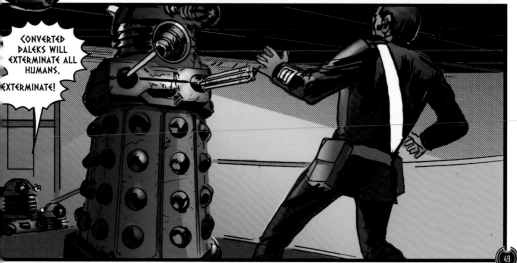

CONVERTED DALEKS WILL EXTERMINATE ALL HUMANS.

EXTERMINATE!

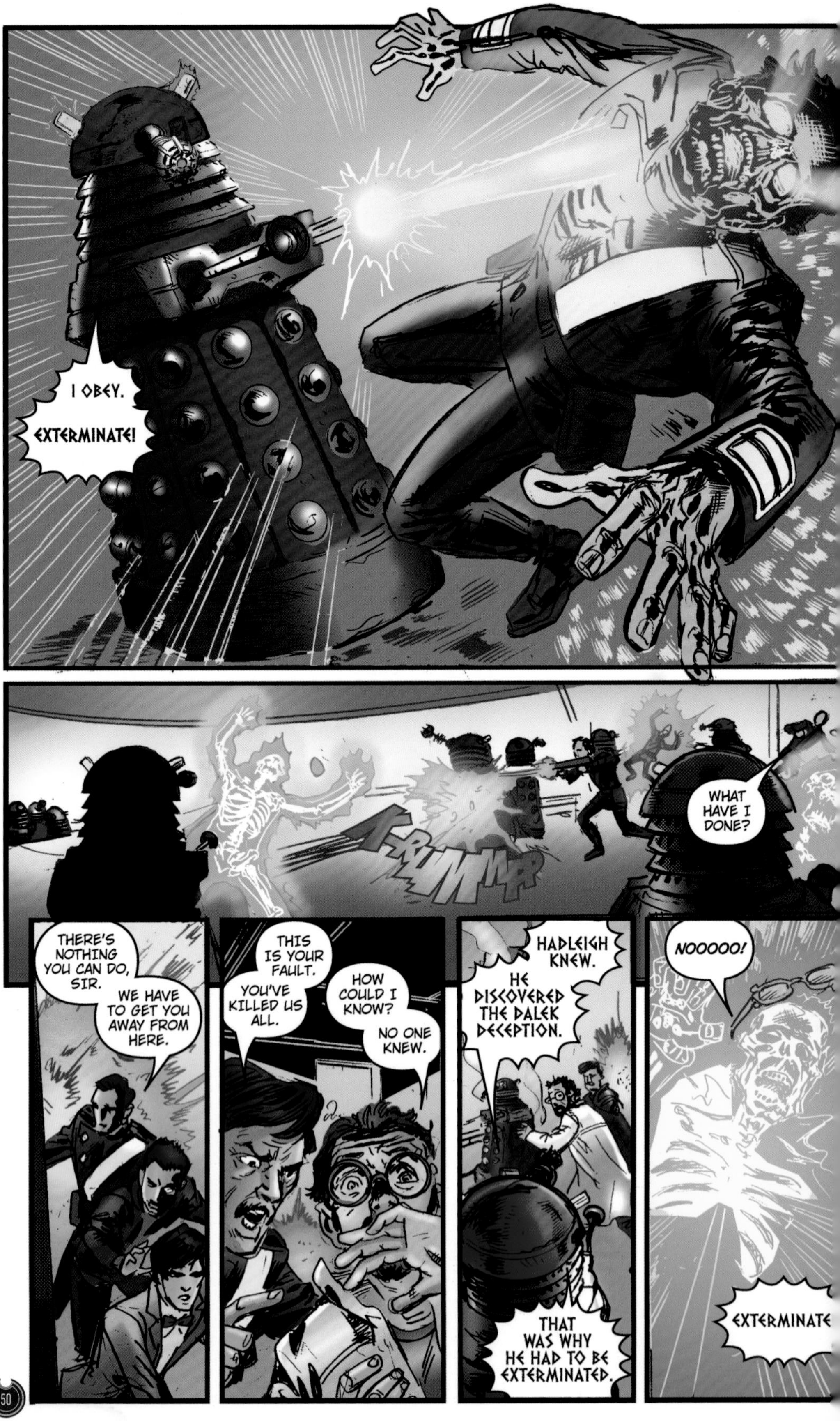
I OBEY.
EXTERMINATE!
WHAT HAVE I DONE?
THERE'S NOTHING YOU CAN DO, SIR.
WE HAVE TO GET YOU AWAY FROM HERE.
THIS IS YOUR FAULT.
YOU'VE KILLED US ALL.
HOW COULD I KNOW?
NO ONE KNEW.
HADLEIGH KNEW.
HE DISCOVERED THE DALEK DECEPTION.
THAT WAS WHY HE HAD TO BE EXTERMINATED.
NOOOOO!
EXTERMINATE

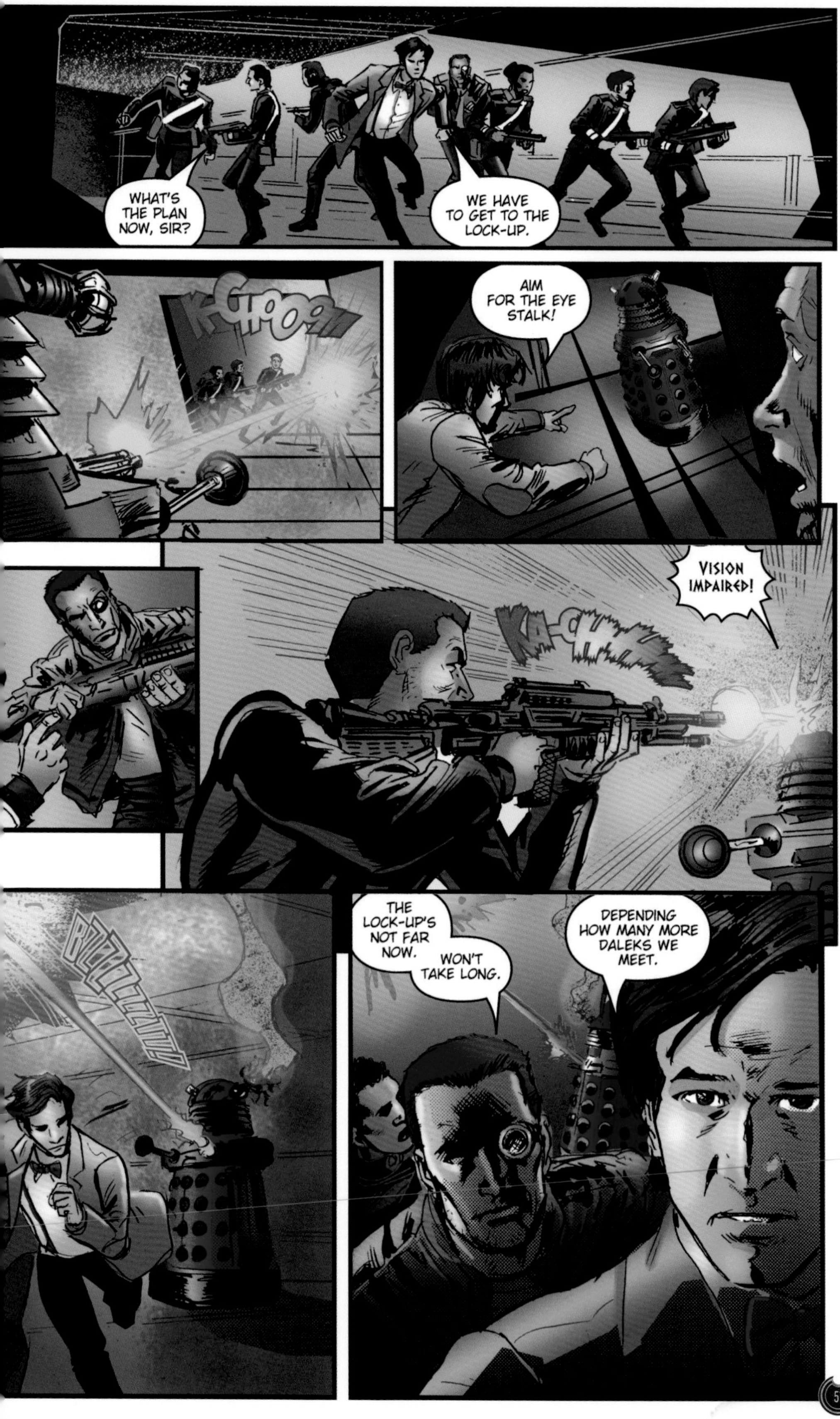
WHAT'S THE PLAN NOW, SIR?
WE HAVE TO GET TO THE LOCK-UP.
AIM FOR THE EYE STALK!
VISION IMPAIRED!
THE LOCK-UP'S NOT FAR NOW.
WON'T TAKE LONG.
DEPENDING HOW MANY MORE DALEKS WE MEET.

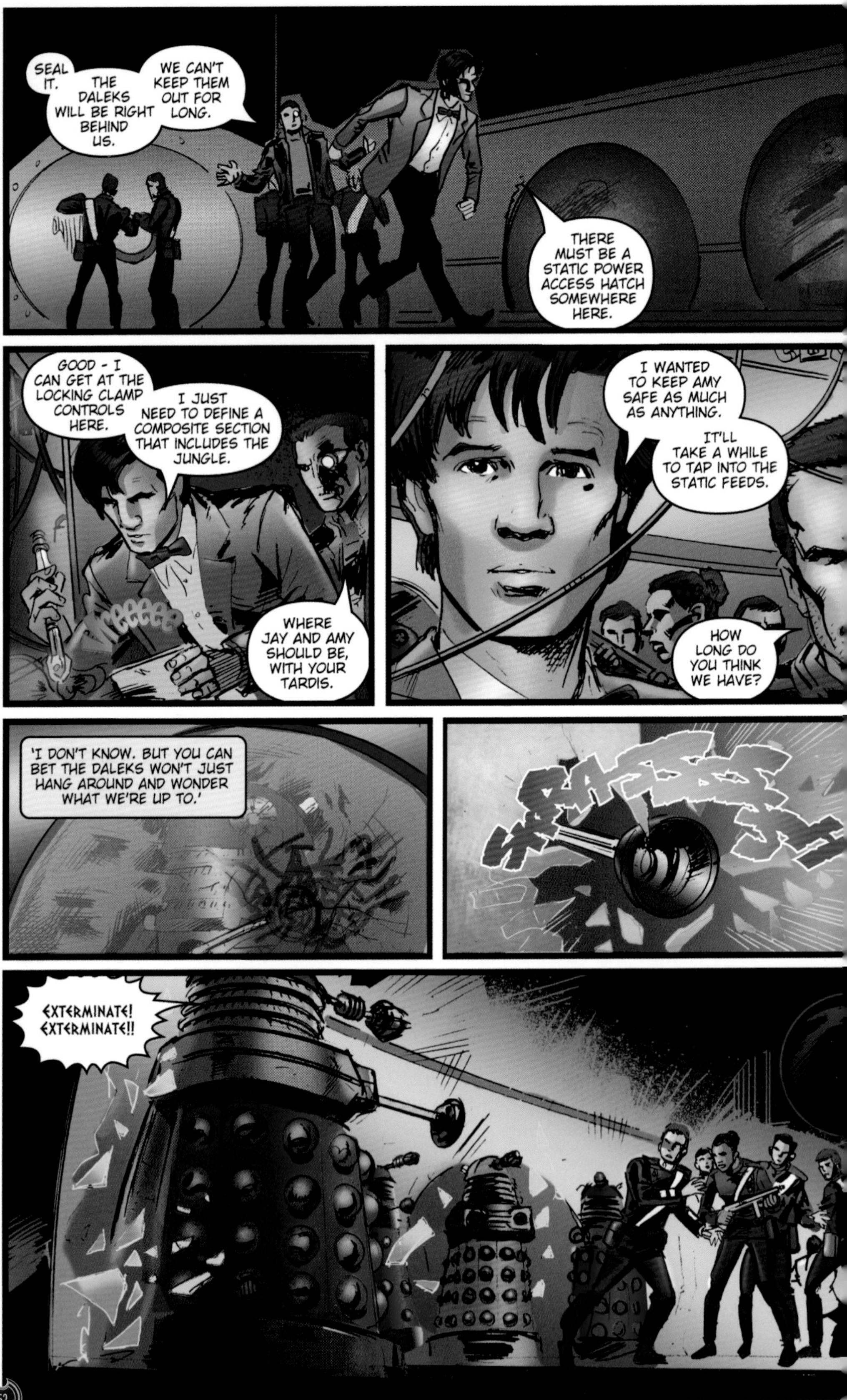
SEAL IT.
THE DALEKS WILL BE RIGHT BEHIND US.
WE CAN'T KEEP THEM OUT FOR LONG.
THERE MUST BE A STATIC POWER ACCESS HATCH SOMEWHERE HERE.
GOOD - I CAN GET AT THE LOCKING CLAMP CONTROLS HERE.
I JUST NEED TO DEFINE A COMPOSITE SECTION THAT INCLUDES THE JUNGLE.
WHERE JAY AND AMY SHOULD BE, WITH YOUR TARDIS.
I WANTED TO KEEP AMY SAFE AS MUCH AS ANYTHING.
IT'LL TAKE A WHILE TO TAP INTO THE STATIC FEEDS.
HOW LONG DO YOU THINK WE HAVE?
'I DON'T KNOW. BUT YOU CAN BET THE DALEKS WON'T JUST HANG AROUND AND WONDER WHAT WE'RE UP TO.'
EXTERMINATE! EXTERMINATE!!

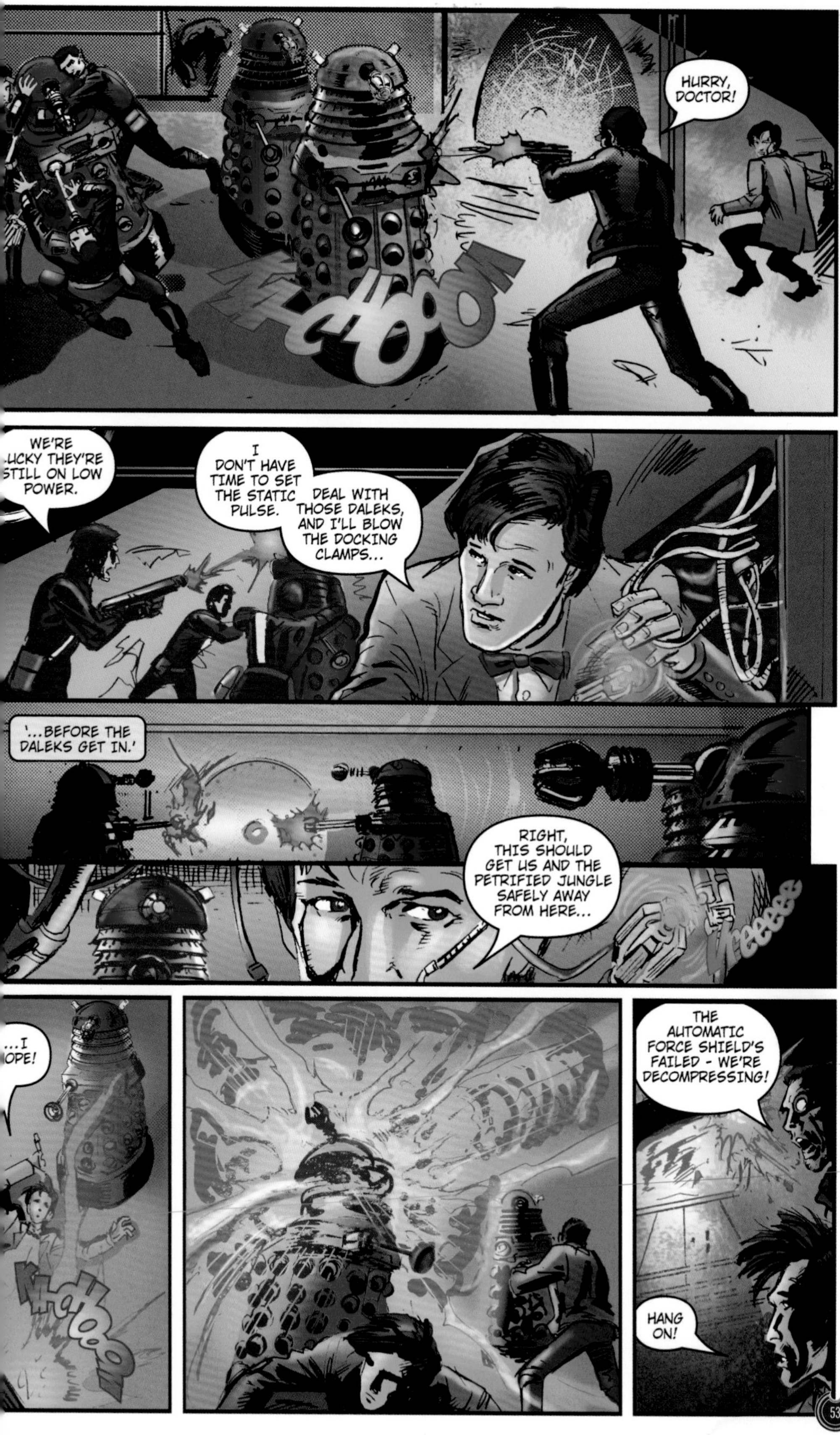
HURRY, DOCTOR!
TCHOOM
WE'RE LUCKY THEY'RE STILL ON LOW POWER.
I DON'T HAVE TIME TO SET THE STATIC PULSE.
DEAL WITH THOSE DALEKS, AND I'LL BLOW THE DOCKING CLAMPS...
'...BEFORE THE DALEKS GET IN.'
RIGHT, THIS SHOULD GET US AND THE PETRIFIED JUNGLE SAFELY AWAY FROM HERE...
...I HOPE!
THE AUTOMATIC FORCE SHIELD'S FAILED - WE'RE DECOMPRESSING!
HANG ON!

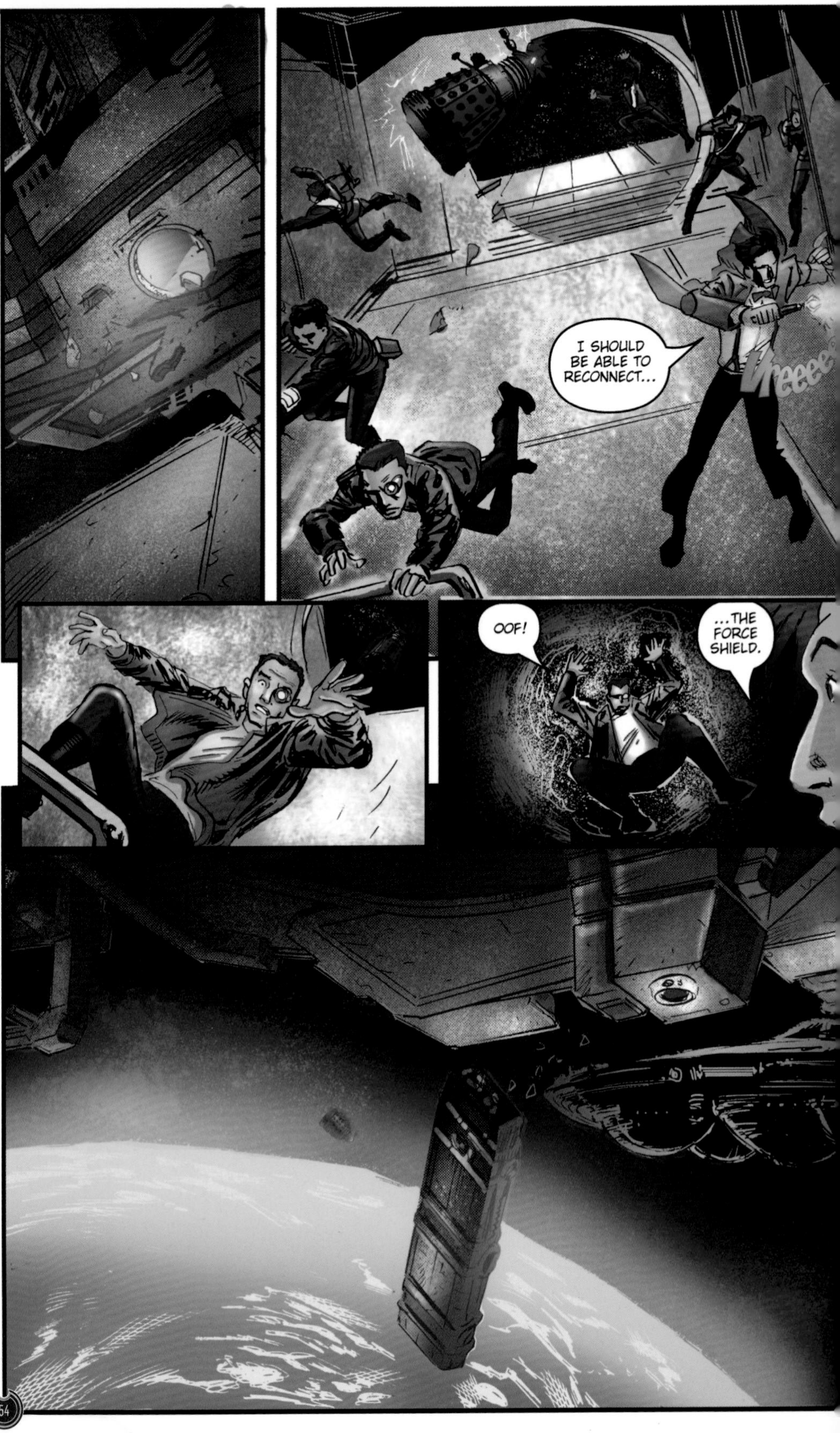
I SHOULD BE ABLE TO RECONNECT...
OOF!
...THE FORCE SHIELD.

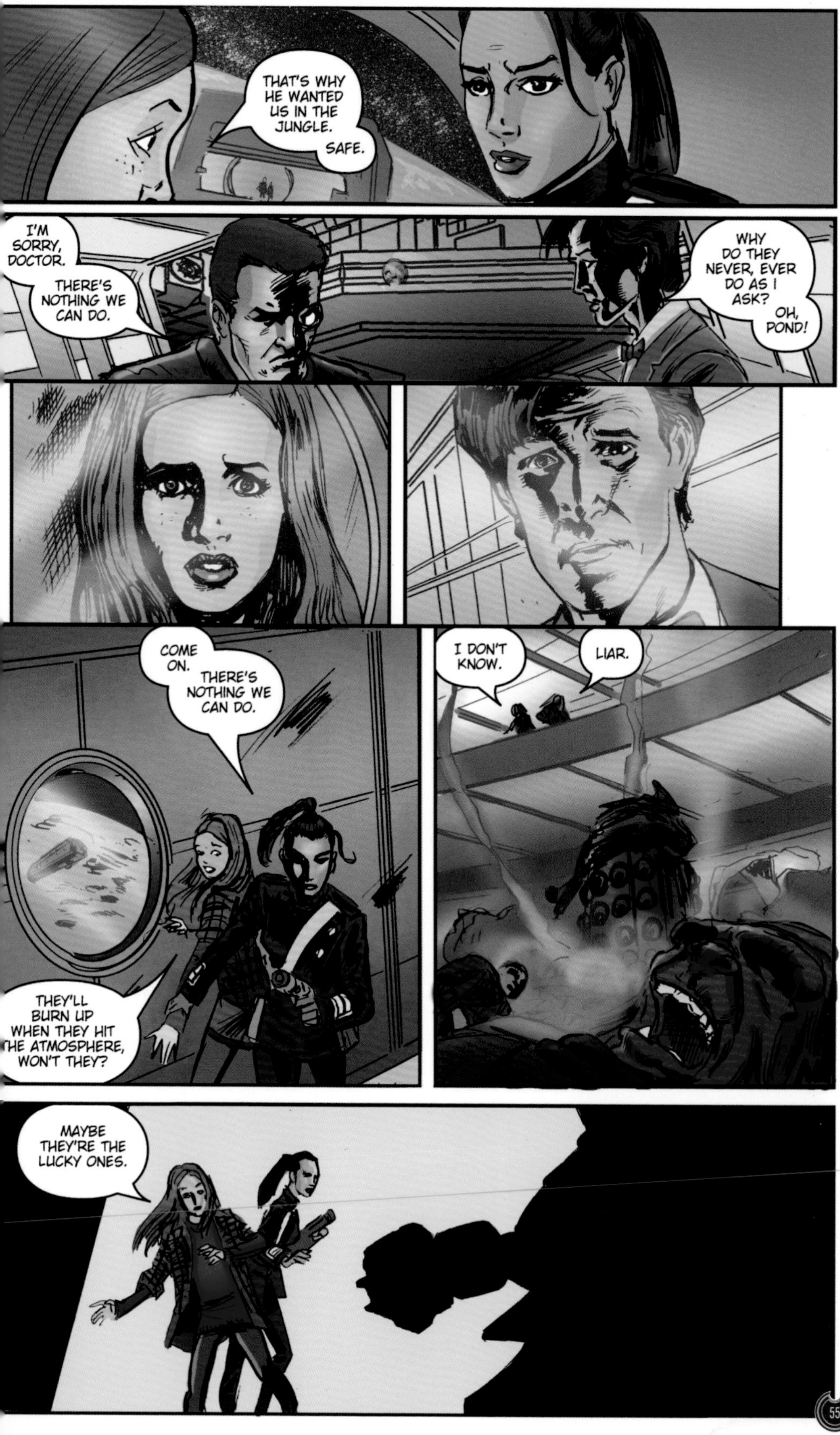
THAT'S WHY HE WANTED US IN THE JUNGLE.
SAFE.
I'M SORRY, DOCTOR.
THERE'S NOTHING WE CAN DO.
WHY DO THEY NEVER, EVER DO AS I ASK?
OH, POND!
COME ON.
THERE'S NOTHING WE CAN DO.
THEY'LL BURN UP WHEN THEY HIT THE ATMOSPHERE, WON'T THEY?
I DON'T KNOW.
LIAR.
MAYBE THEY'RE THE LUCKY ONES.

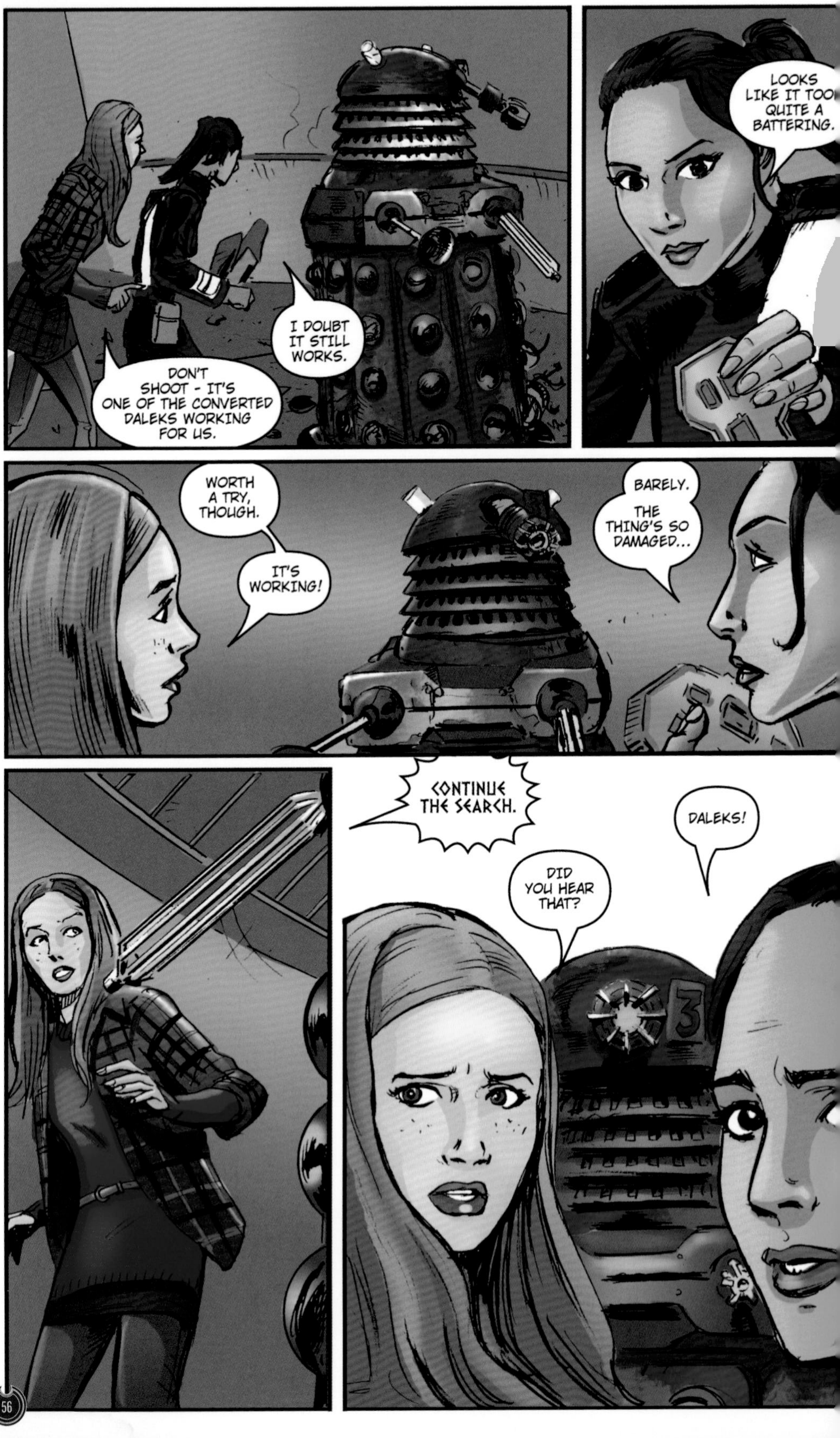
DON'T SHOOT - IT'S ONE OF THE CONVERTED DALEKS WORKING FOR US.
I DOUBT IT STILL WORKS.
LOOKS LIKE IT TOO QUITE A BATTERING.
WORTH A TRY, THOUGH.
IT'S WORKING!
BARELY.
THE THING'S SO DAMAGED...
CONTINUE THE SEARCH.
DALEKS!
DID YOU HEAR THAT?

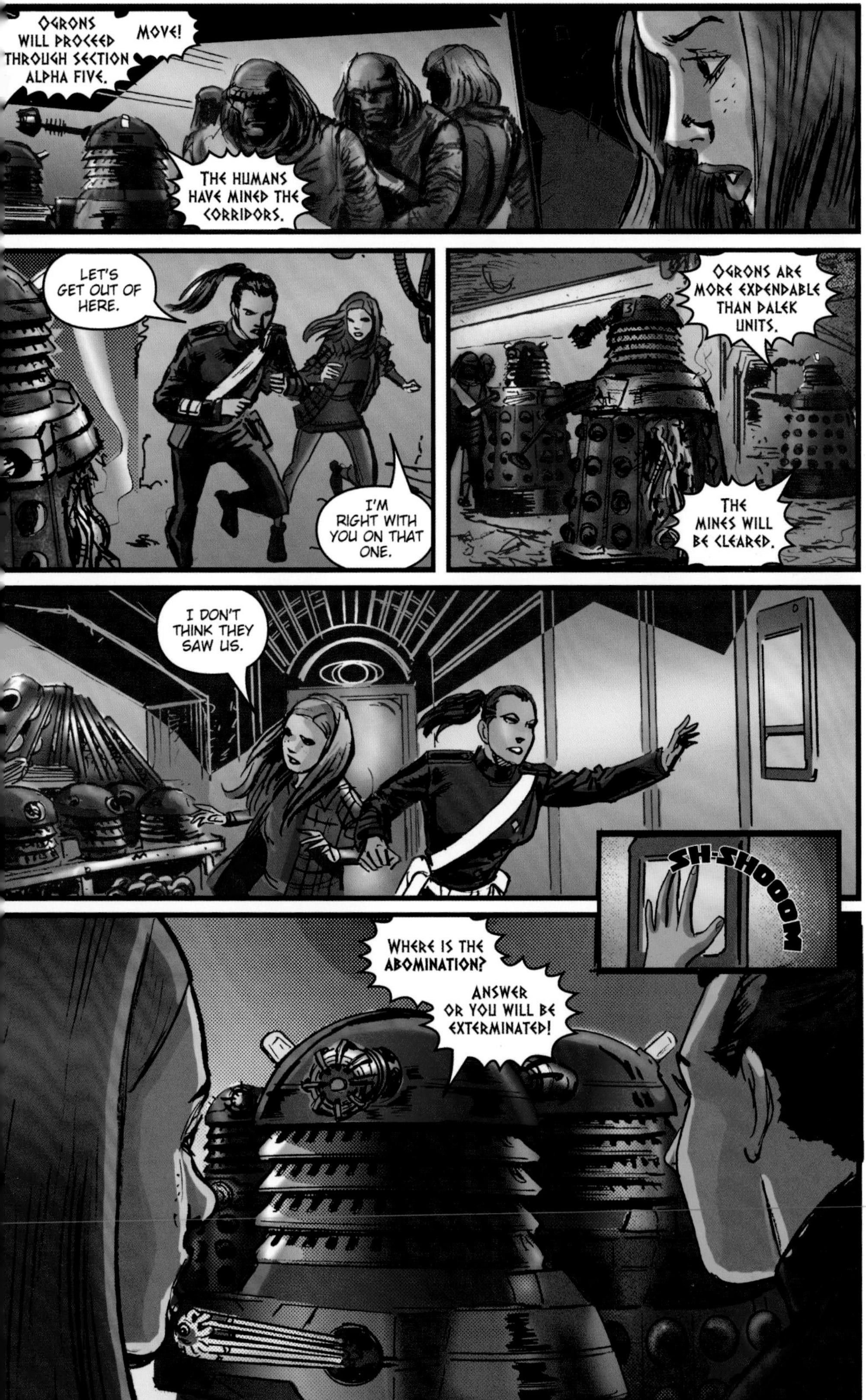
OGRONS WILL PROCEED THROUGH SECTION ALPHA FIVE.
MOVE!
THE HUMANS HAVE MINED THE CORRIDORS.
LET'S GET OUT OF HERE.
I'M RIGHT WITH YOU ON THAT ONE.
OGRONS ARE MORE EXPENDABLE THAN DALEK UNITS.
THE MINES WILL BE CLEARED.
I DON'T THINK THEY SAW US.
SH-SHOOOM
WHERE IS THE ABOMINATION?
ANSWER OR YOU WILL BE EXTERMINATED!

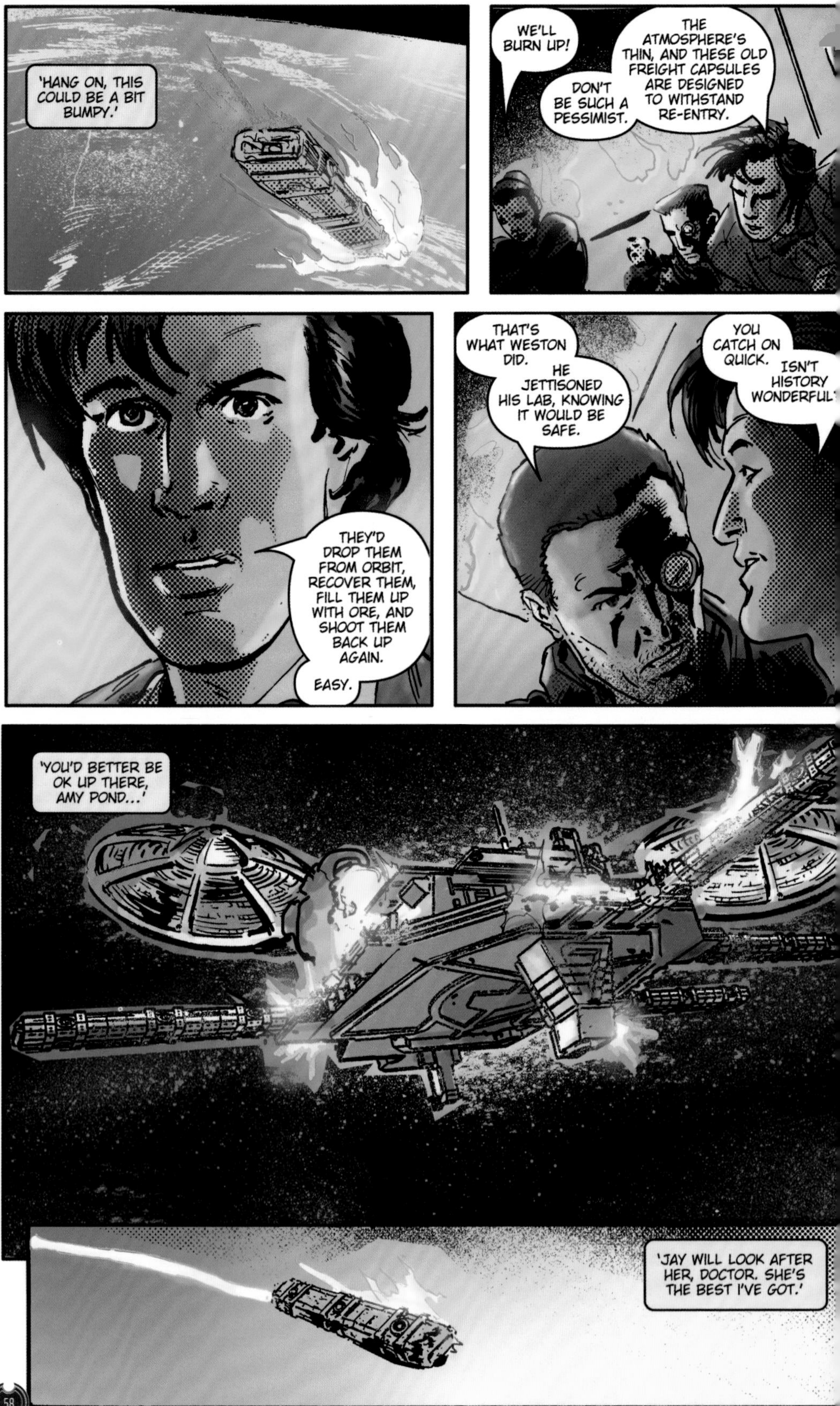

'HANG ON, THIS COULD BE A BIT BUMPY.'
WE'LL BURN UP!
DON'T BE SUCH A PESSIMIST.
THE ATMOSPHERE'S THIN, AND THESE OLD FREIGHT CAPSULES ARE DESIGNED TO WITHSTAND RE-ENTRY.
THEY'D DROP THEM FROM ORBIT, RECOVER THEM, FILL THEM UP WITH ORE, AND SHOOT THEM BACK UP AGAIN.
EASY.
THAT'S WHAT WESTON DID.
HE JETTISONED HIS LAB, KNOWING IT WOULD BE SAFE.
YOU CATCH ON QUICK.
ISN'T HISTORY WONDERFUL
'YOU'D BETTER BE OK UP THERE, AMY POND...'
'JAY WILL LOOK AFTER HER, DOCTOR. SHE'S THE BEST I'VE GOT.'

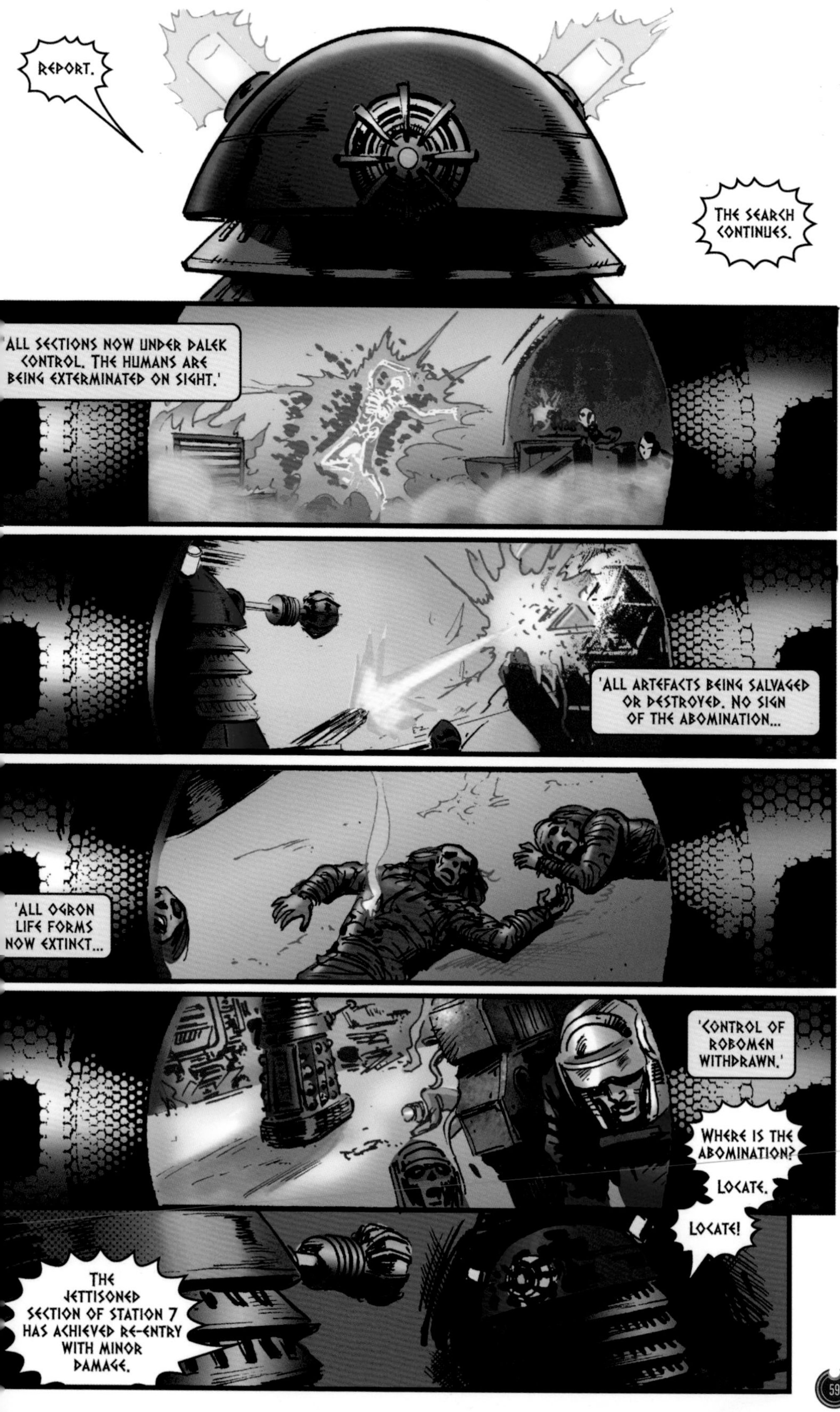
REPORT.
THE SEARCH CONTINUES.
'ALL SECTIONS NOW UNDER DALEK CONTROL. THE HUMANS ARE BEING EXTERMINATED ON SIGHT.'
'ALL ARTEFACTS BEING SALVAGED OR DESTROYED. NO SIGN OF THE ABOMINATION...
'ALL OGRON LIFE FORMS NOW EXTINCT...
'CONTROL OF ROBOMEN WITHDRAWN.'
WHERE IS THE ABOMINATION?
LOCATE.
LOCATE!
THE JETTISONED SECTION OF STATION 7 HAS ACHIEVED RE-ENTRY WITH MINOR DAMAGE.

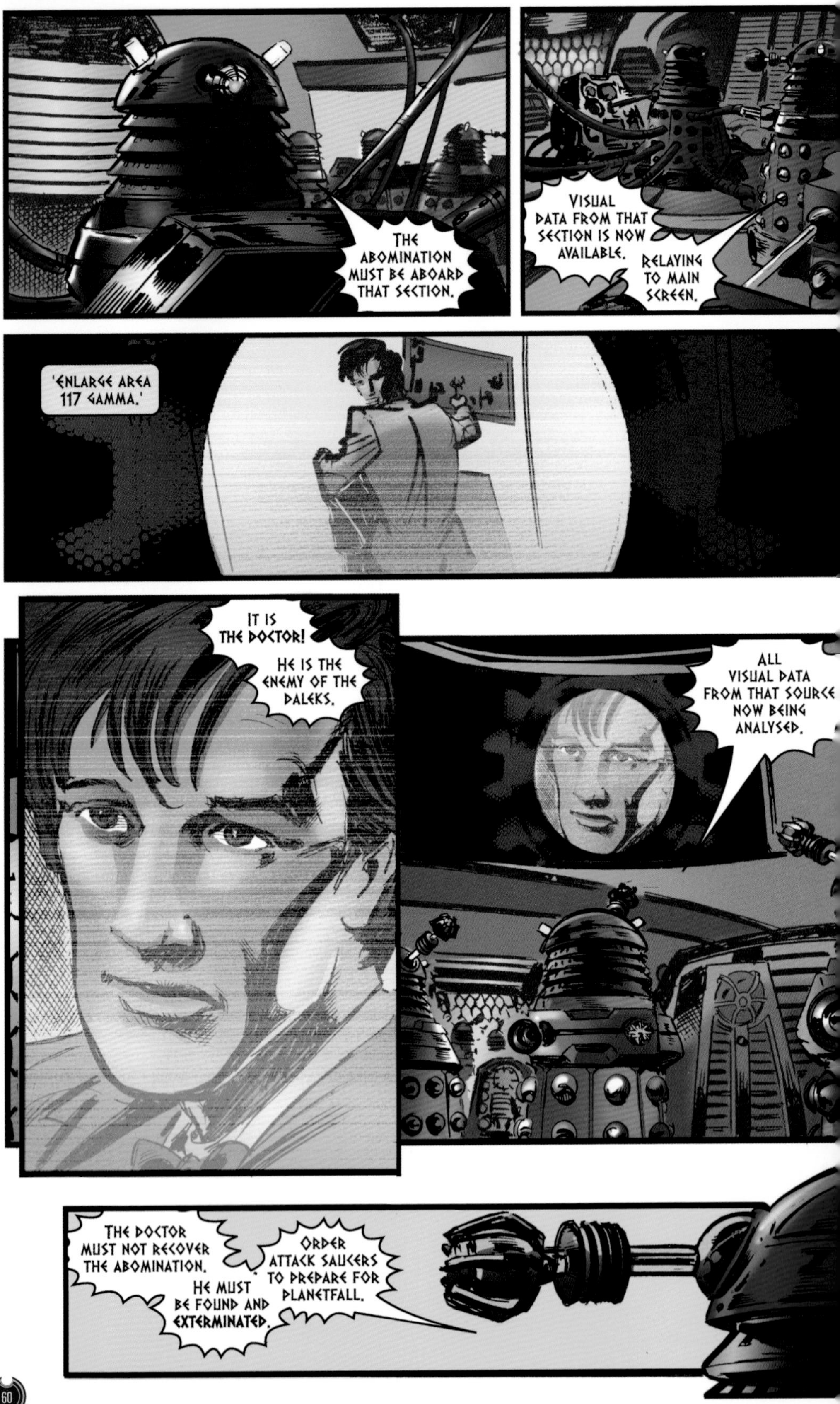
THE ABOMINATION MUST BE ABOARD THAT SECTION.
VISUAL DATA FROM THAT SECTION IS NOW AVAILABLE.
RELAYING TO MAIN SCREEN.
'ENLARGE AREA 117 GAMMA.'
IT IS THE DOCTOR!
HE IS THE ENEMY OF THE DALEKS.
ALL VISUAL DATA FROM THAT SOURCE NOW BEING ANALYSED.
THE DOCTOR MUST NOT RECOVER THE ABOMINATION.
HE MUST BE FOUND AND EXTERMINATED.
ORDER ATTACK SAUCERS TO PREPARE FOR PLANETFALL.

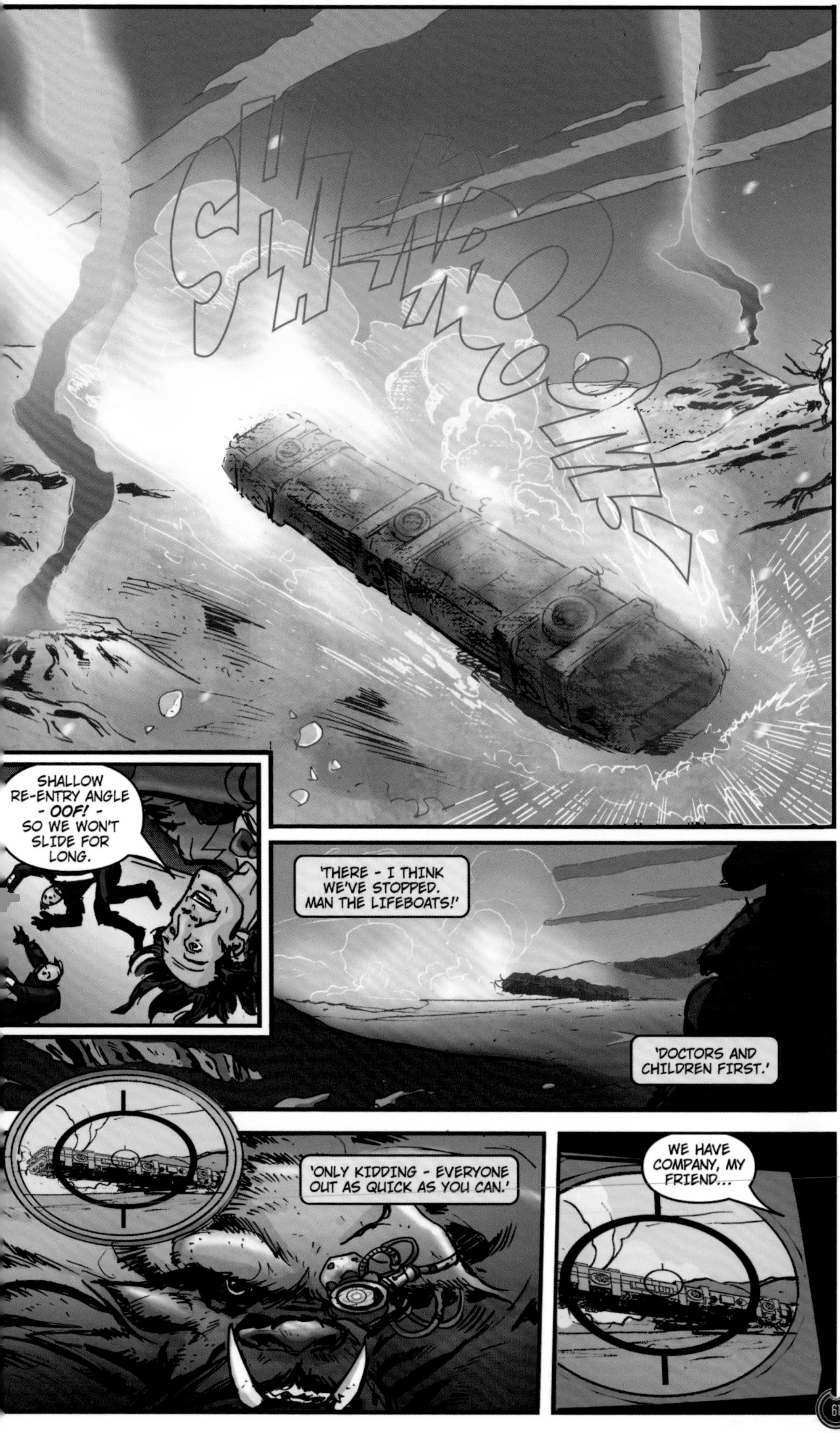
SHHAROOM!
SHALLOW RE-ENTRY ANGLE - OOF! - SO WE WON'T SLIDE FOR LONG.
'THERE - I THINK WE'VE STOPPED. MAN THE LIFEBOATS!'
'DOCTORS AND CHILDREN FIRST.'
'ONLY KIDDING - EVERYONE OUT AS QUICK AS YOU CAN.'
WE HAVE COMPANY, MY FRIEND...

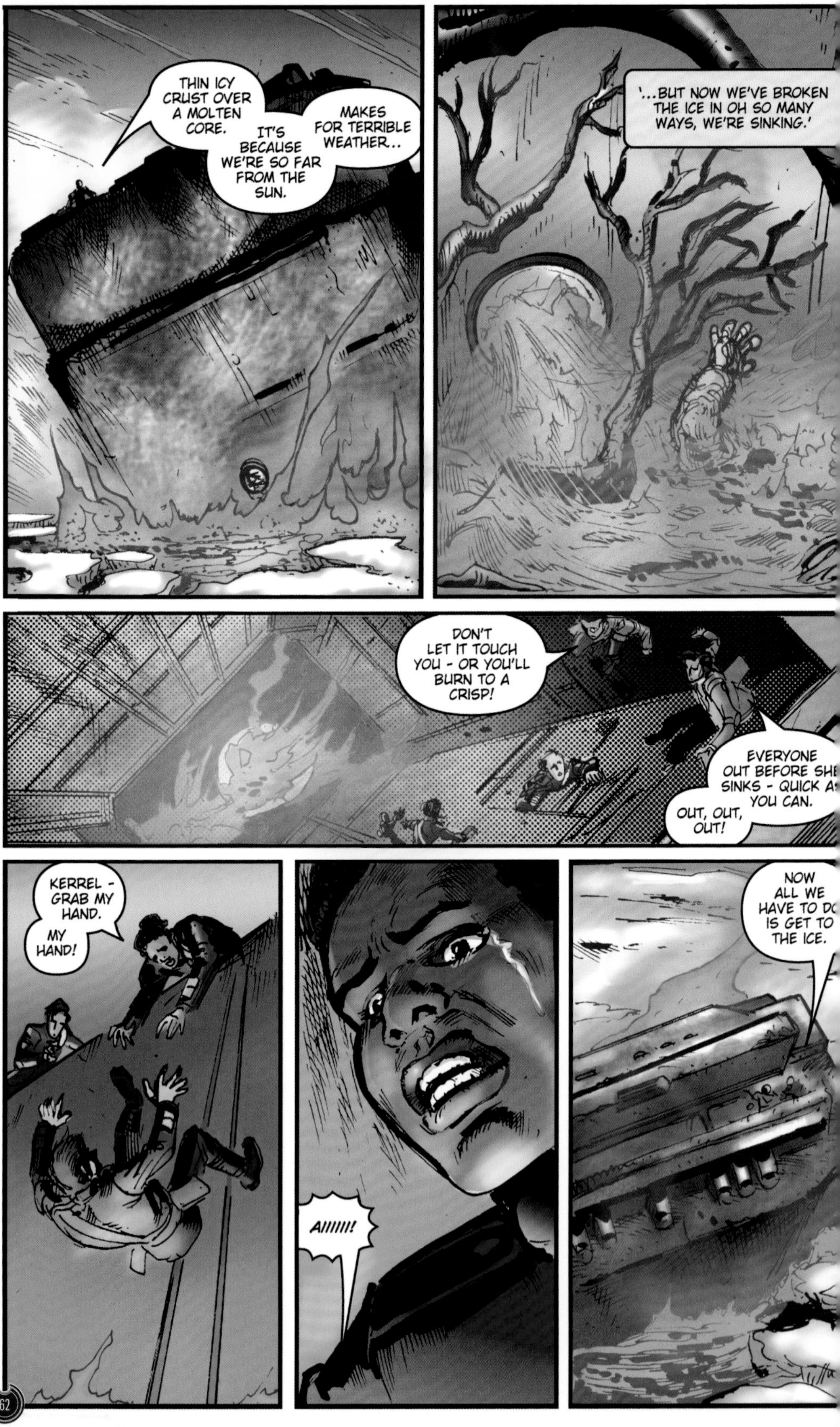
THIN ICY CRUST OVER A MOLTEN CORE.
IT'S BECAUSE WE'RE SO FAR FROM THE SUN.
MAKES FOR TERRIBLE WEATHER...
'...BUT NOW WE'VE BROKEN THE ICE IN OH SO MANY WAYS, WE'RE SINKING.'
DON'T LET IT TOUCH YOU - OR YOU'LL BURN TO A CRISP!
EVERYONE OUT BEFORE SHE SINKS - QUICK AS YOU CAN.
OUT, OUT, OUT!
KERREL - GRAB MY HAND.
MY HAND!
AIIIIII!
NOW ALL WE HAVE TO DO IS GET TO THE ICE.

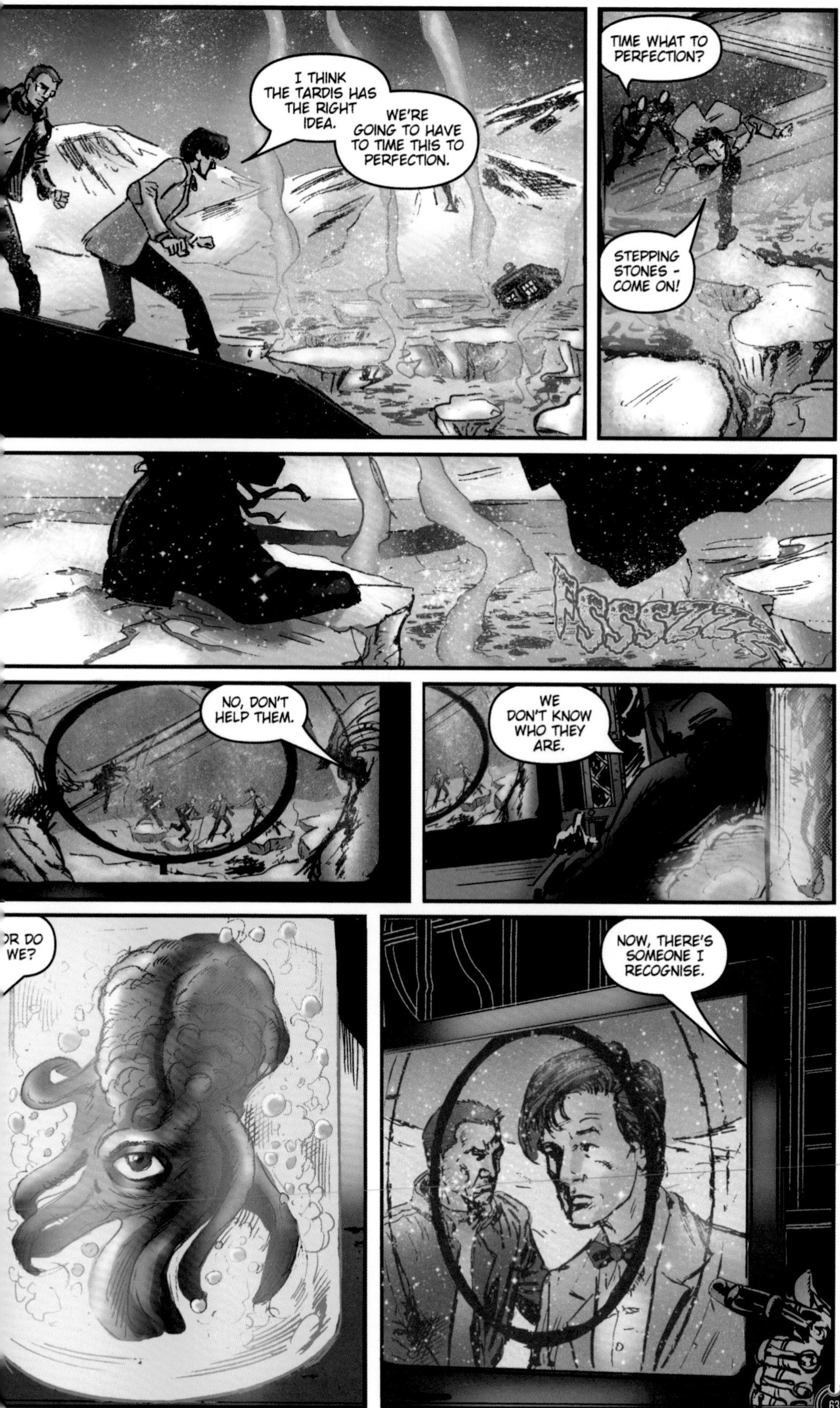
I THINK THE TARDIS HAS THE RIGHT IDEA.
WE'RE GOING TO HAVE TO TIME THIS TO PERFECTION.
TIME WHAT TO PERFECTION?
STEPPING STONES - COME ON!
NO, DON'T HELP THEM.
WE DON'T KNOW WHO THEY ARE.
OR DO WE?
NOW, THERE'S SOMEONE I RECOGNISE.

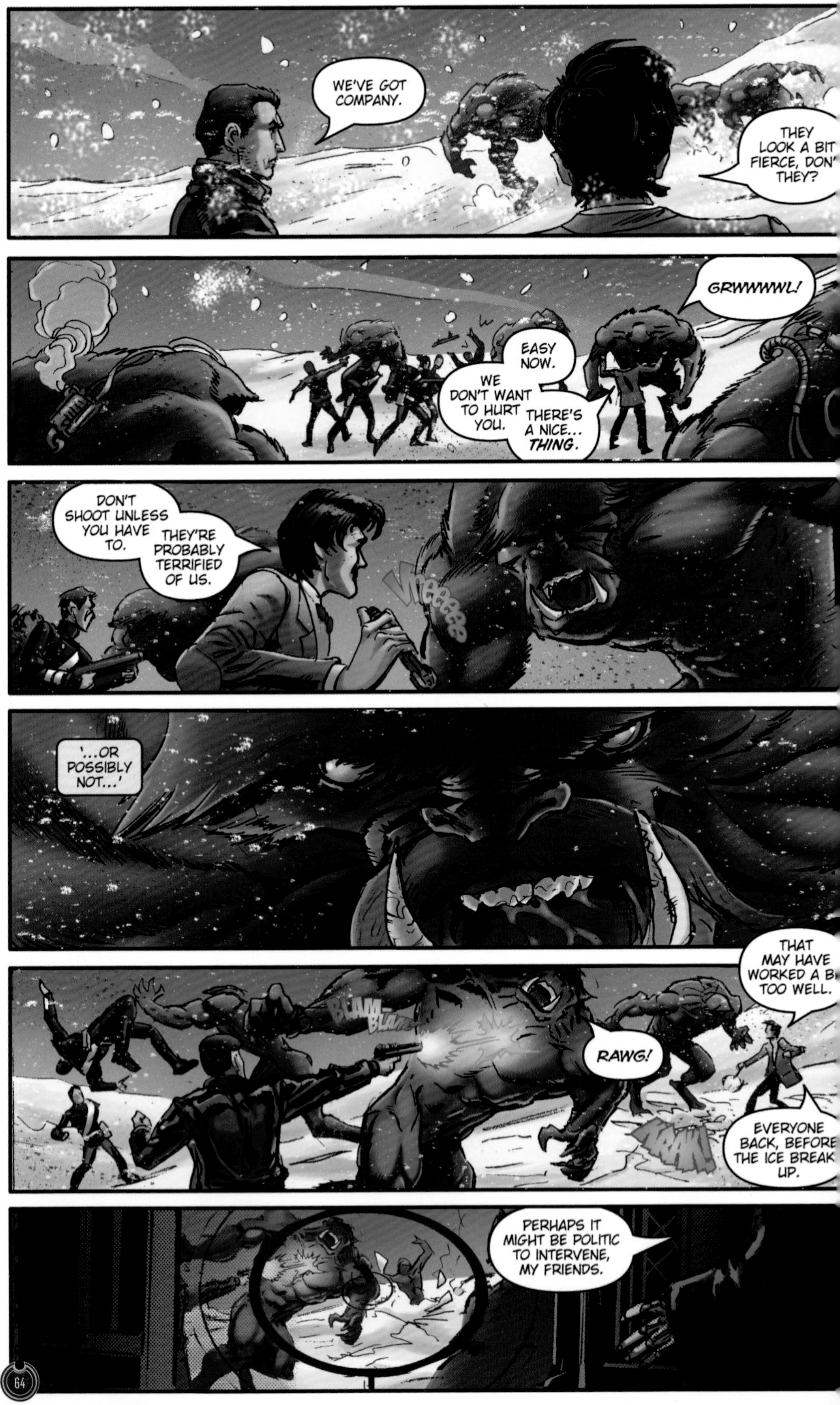
WE'VE GOT COMPANY.
THEY LOOK A BIT FIERCE, DON' THEY?
GRWWWWL!
EASY NOW.
WE DON'T WANT TO HURT YOU.
THERE'S A NICE... THING.
DON'T SHOOT UNLESS YOU HAVE TO.
THEY'RE PROBABLY TERRIFIED OF US.
'...OR POSSIBLY NOT...'
THAT MAY HAVE WORKED A B TOO WELL.
RAWG!
EVERYONE BACK, BEFORE THE ICE BREAK UP.
PERHAPS IT MIGHT BE POLITIC TO INTERVENE, MY FRIENDS.

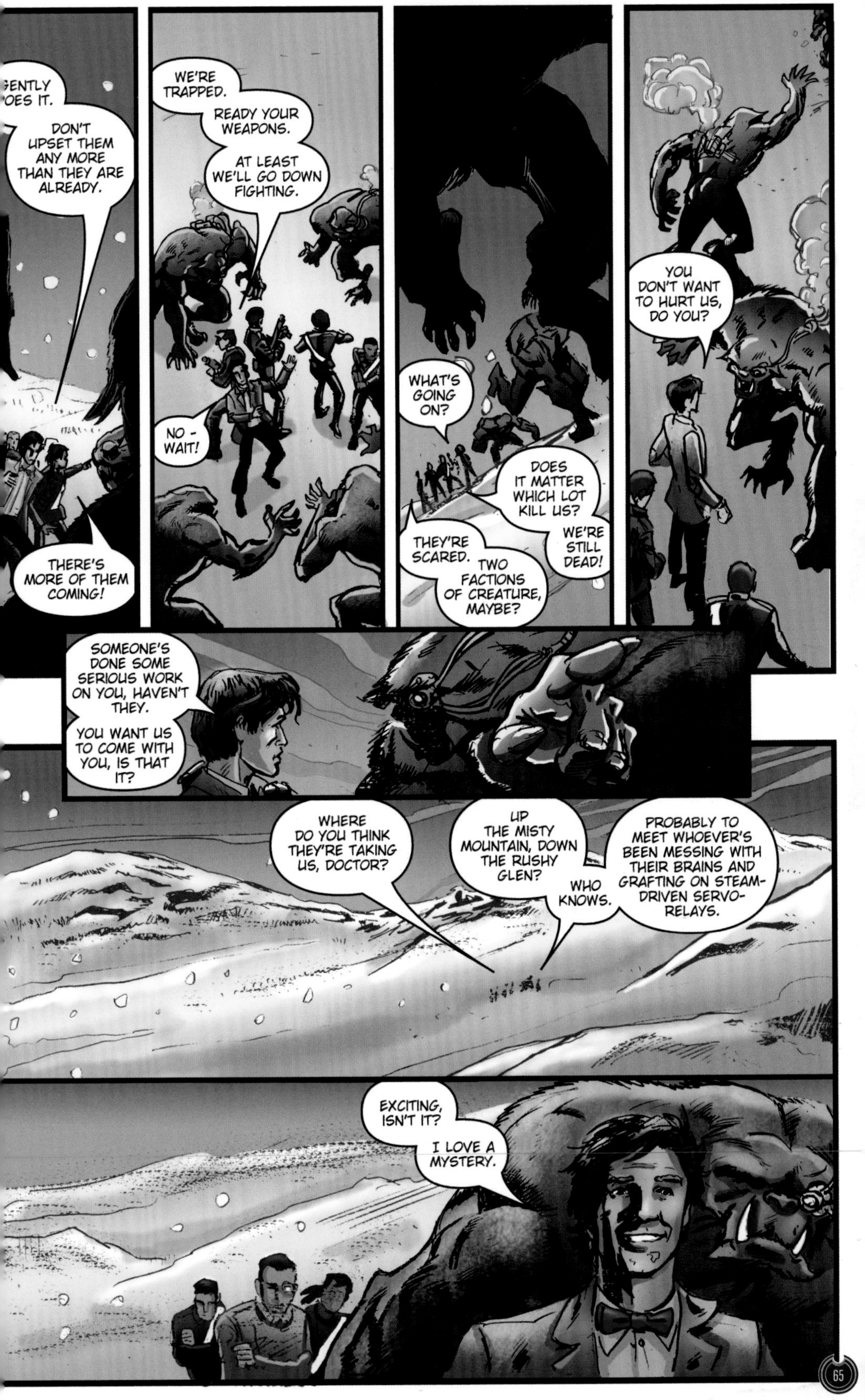
GENTLY DOES IT.
DON'T UPSET THEM ANY MORE THAN THEY ARE ALREADY.
THERE'S MORE OF THEM COMING!
WE'RE TRAPPED.
READY YOUR WEAPONS.
AT LEAST WE'LL GO DOWN FIGHTING.
NO - WAIT!
WHAT'S GOING ON?
THEY'RE SCARED.
TWO FACTIONS OF CREATURE, MAYBE?
DOES IT MATTER WHICH LOT KILL US?
WE'RE STILL DEAD!
YOU DON'T WANT TO HURT US, DO YOU?
SOMEONE'S DONE SOME SERIOUS WORK ON YOU, HAVEN'T THEY.
YOU WANT US TO COME WITH YOU, IS THAT IT?
WHERE DO YOU THINK THEY'RE TAKING US, DOCTOR?
UP THE MISTY MOUNTAIN, DOWN THE RUSHY GLEN?
WHO KNOWS.
PROBABLY TO MEET WHOEVER'S BEEN MESSING WITH THEIR BRAINS AND GRAFTING ON STEAM-DRIVEN SERVO-RELAYS.
EXCITING, ISN'T IT?
I LOVE A MYSTERY.

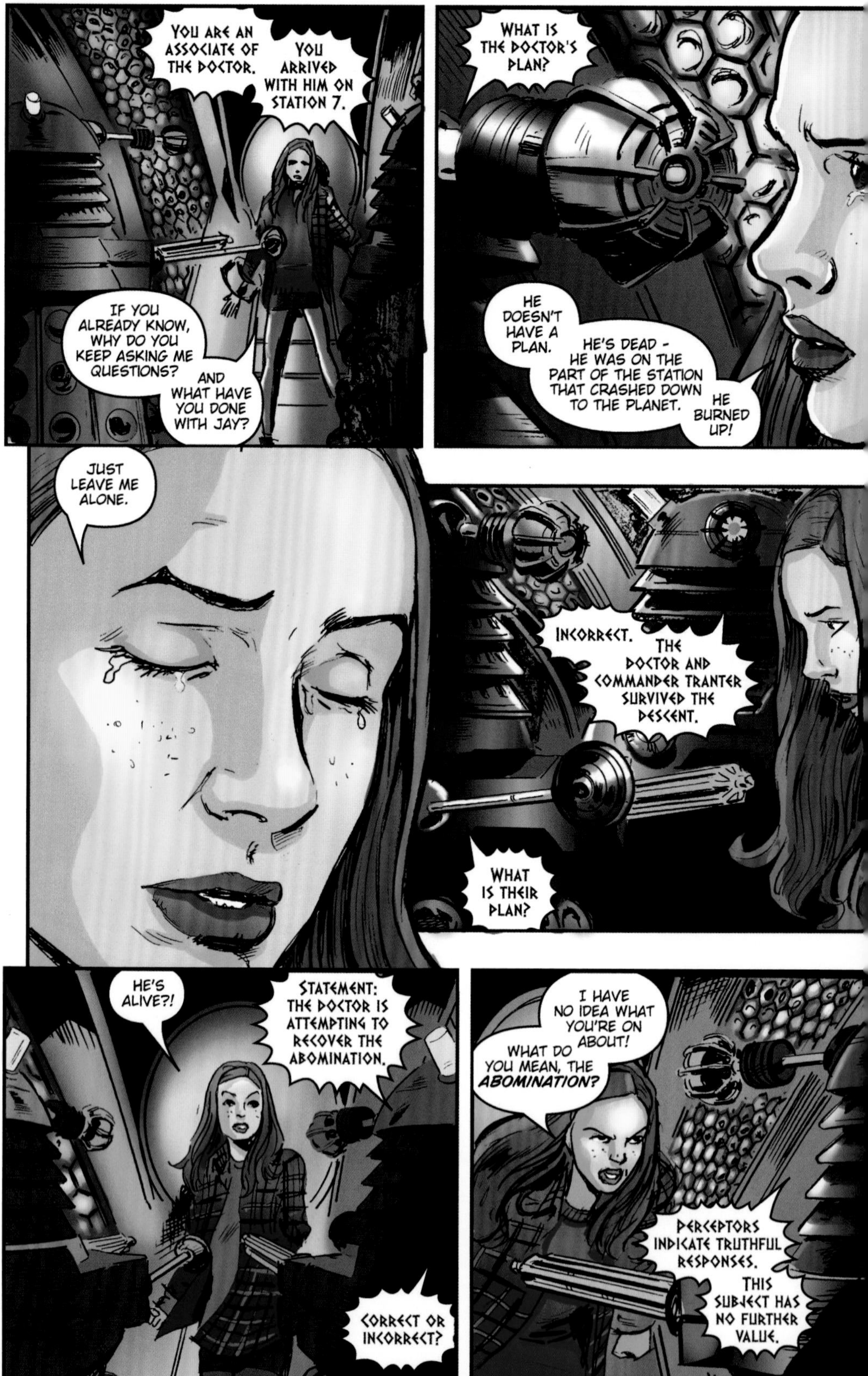
YOU ARE AN ASSOCIATE OF THE DOCTOR.
YOU ARRIVED WITH HIM ON STATION 7.
IF YOU ALREADY KNOW, WHY DO YOU KEEP ASKING ME QUESTIONS?
AND WHAT HAVE YOU DONE WITH JAY?
WHAT IS THE DOCTOR'S PLAN?
HE DOESN'T HAVE A PLAN.
HE'S DEAD - HE WAS ON THE PART OF THE STATION THAT CRASHED DOWN TO THE PLANET.
HE BURNED UP!
JUST LEAVE ME ALONE.
INCORRECT.
THE DOCTOR AND COMMANDER TRANTER SURVIVED THE DESCENT.
WHAT IS THEIR PLAN?
HE'S ALIVE?!
STATEMENT: THE DOCTOR IS ATTEMPTING TO RECOVER THE ABOMINATION.
CORRECT OR INCORRECT?
I HAVE NO IDEA WHAT YOU'RE ON ABOUT!
WHAT DO YOU MEAN, THE ABOMINATION?
PERCEPTORS INDICATE TRUTHFUL RESPONSES.
THIS SUBJECT HAS NO FURTHER VALUE.

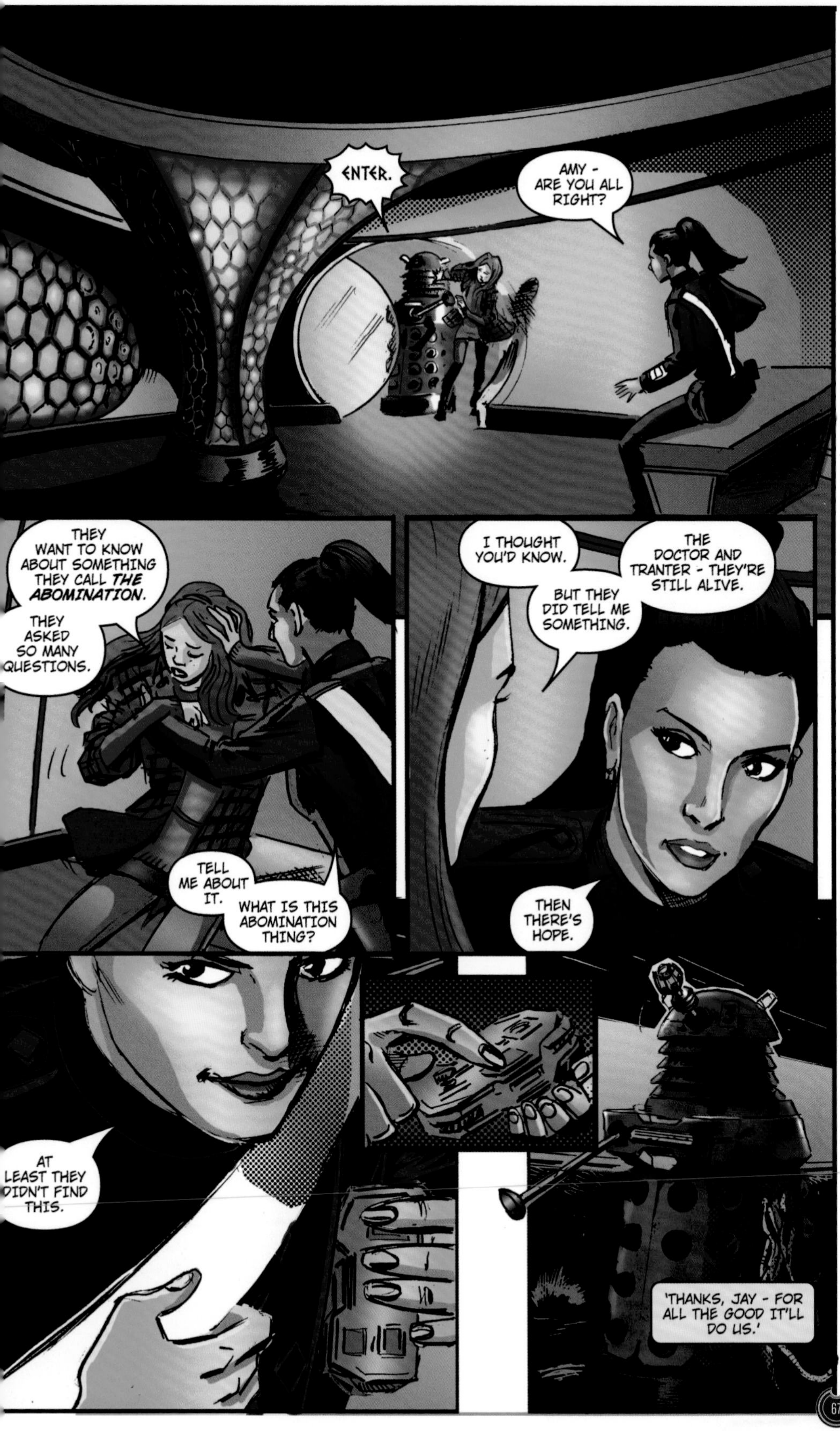
ENTER.
AMY - ARE YOU ALL RIGHT?
THEY WANT TO KNOW ABOUT SOMETHING THEY CALL ***THE ABOMINATION***.
THEY ASKED SO MANY QUESTIONS.
TELL ME ABOUT IT.
WHAT IS THIS ABOMINATION THING?
I THOUGHT YOU'D KNOW.
BUT THEY DID TELL ME SOMETHING.
THE DOCTOR AND TRANTER - THEY'RE STILL ALIVE.
THEN THERE'S HOPE.
AT LEAST THEY DIDN'T FIND THIS.
'THANKS, JAY - FOR ALL THE GOOD IT'LL DO US.'

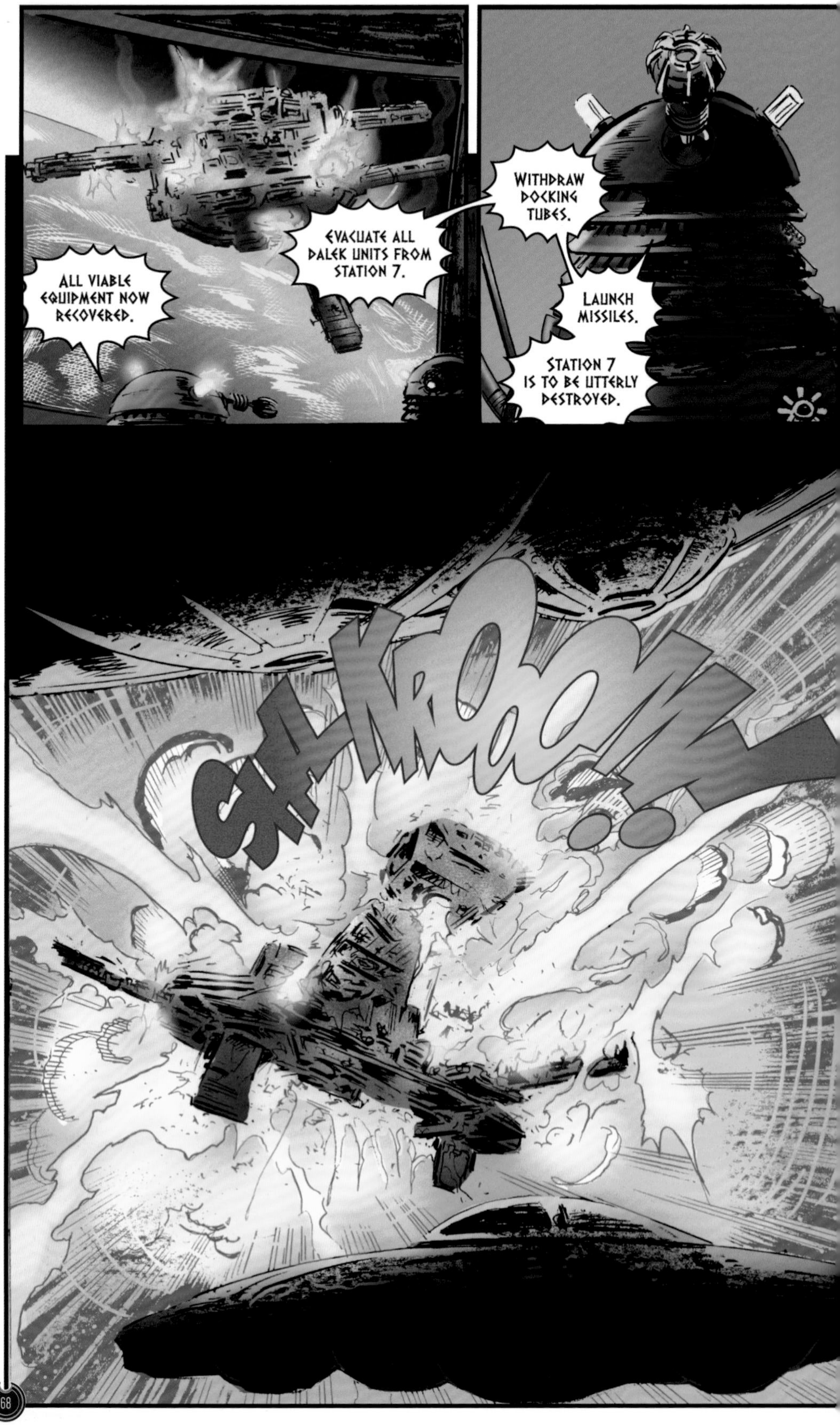
ALL VIABLE EQUIPMENT NOW RECOVERED.
EVACUATE ALL DALEK UNITS FROM STATION 7.
WITHDRAW DOCKING TUBES.
LAUNCH MISSILES.
STATION 7 IS TO BE UTTERLY DESTROYED.
SHHKROOOM...

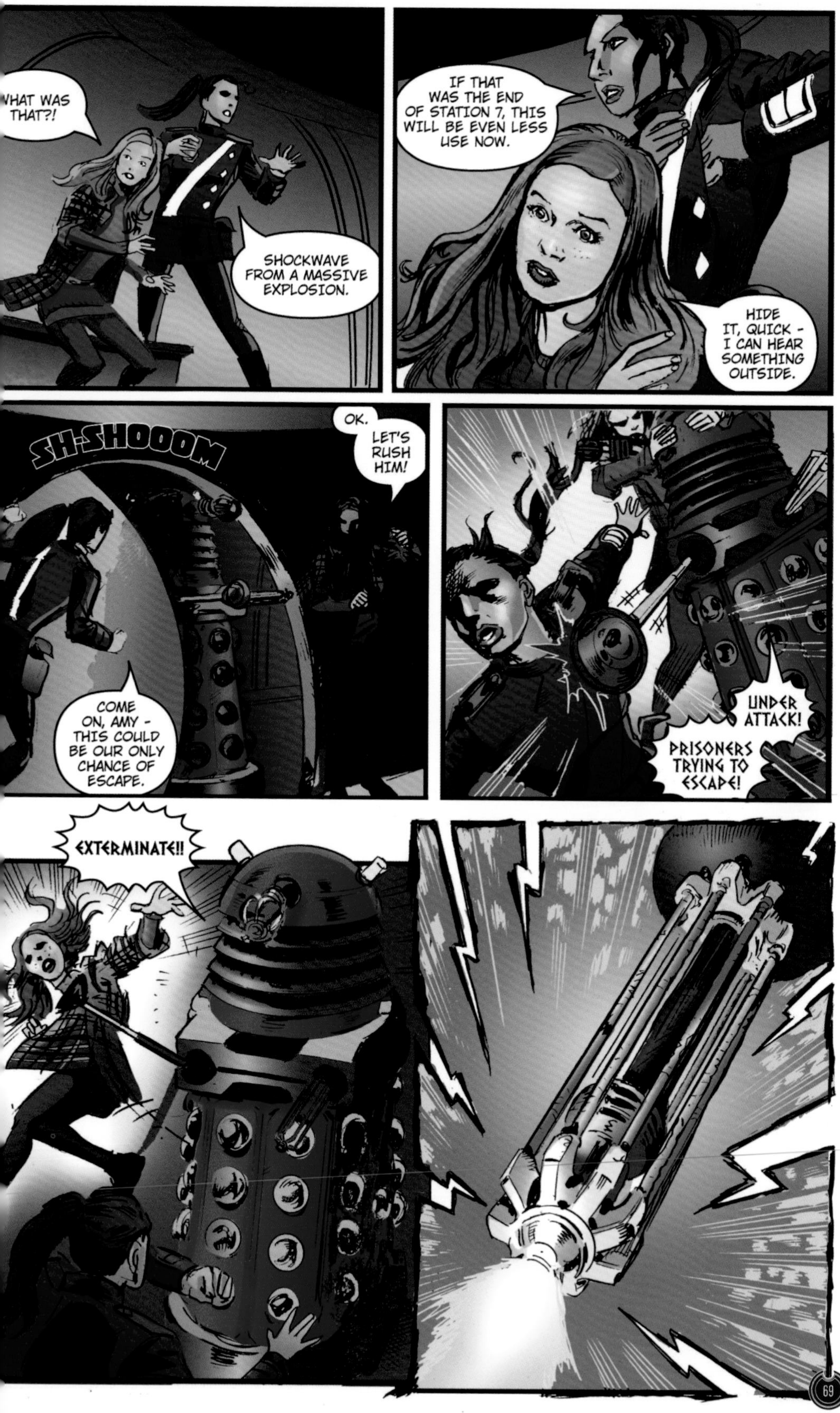
WHAT WAS THAT?!
SHOCKWAVE FROM A MASSIVE EXPLOSION.
IF THAT WAS THE END OF STATION 7, THIS WILL BE EVEN LESS USE NOW.
HIDE IT, QUICK - I CAN HEAR SOMETHING OUTSIDE.
SH-SHOOOM
OK.
LET'S RUSH HIM!
COME ON, AMY - THIS COULD BE OUR ONLY CHANCE OF ESCAPE.
UNDER ATTACK!
PRISONERS TRYING TO ESCAPE!
EXTERMINATE!!

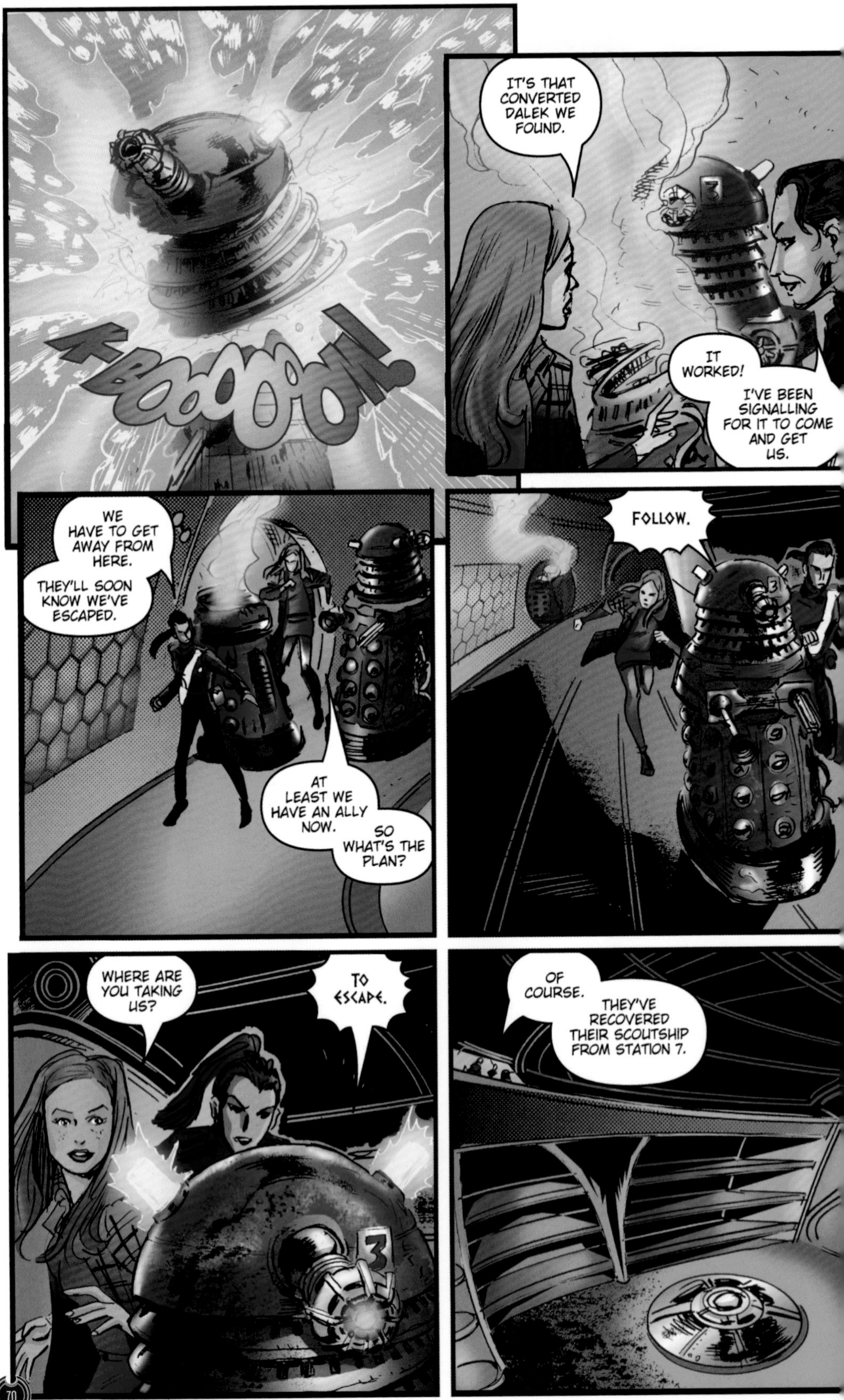
KBOOOOOM!
IT'S THAT CONVERTED DALEK WE FOUND.
IT WORKED!
I'VE BEEN SIGNALLING FOR IT TO COME AND GET US.
WE HAVE TO GET AWAY FROM HERE.
THEY'LL SOON KNOW WE'VE ESCAPED.
AT LEAST WE HAVE AN ALLY NOW.
SO WHAT'S THE PLAN?
FOLLOW.
WHERE ARE YOU TAKING US?
TO ESCAPE.
OF COURSE.
THEY'VE RECOVERED THEIR SCOUTSHIP FROM STATION 7.

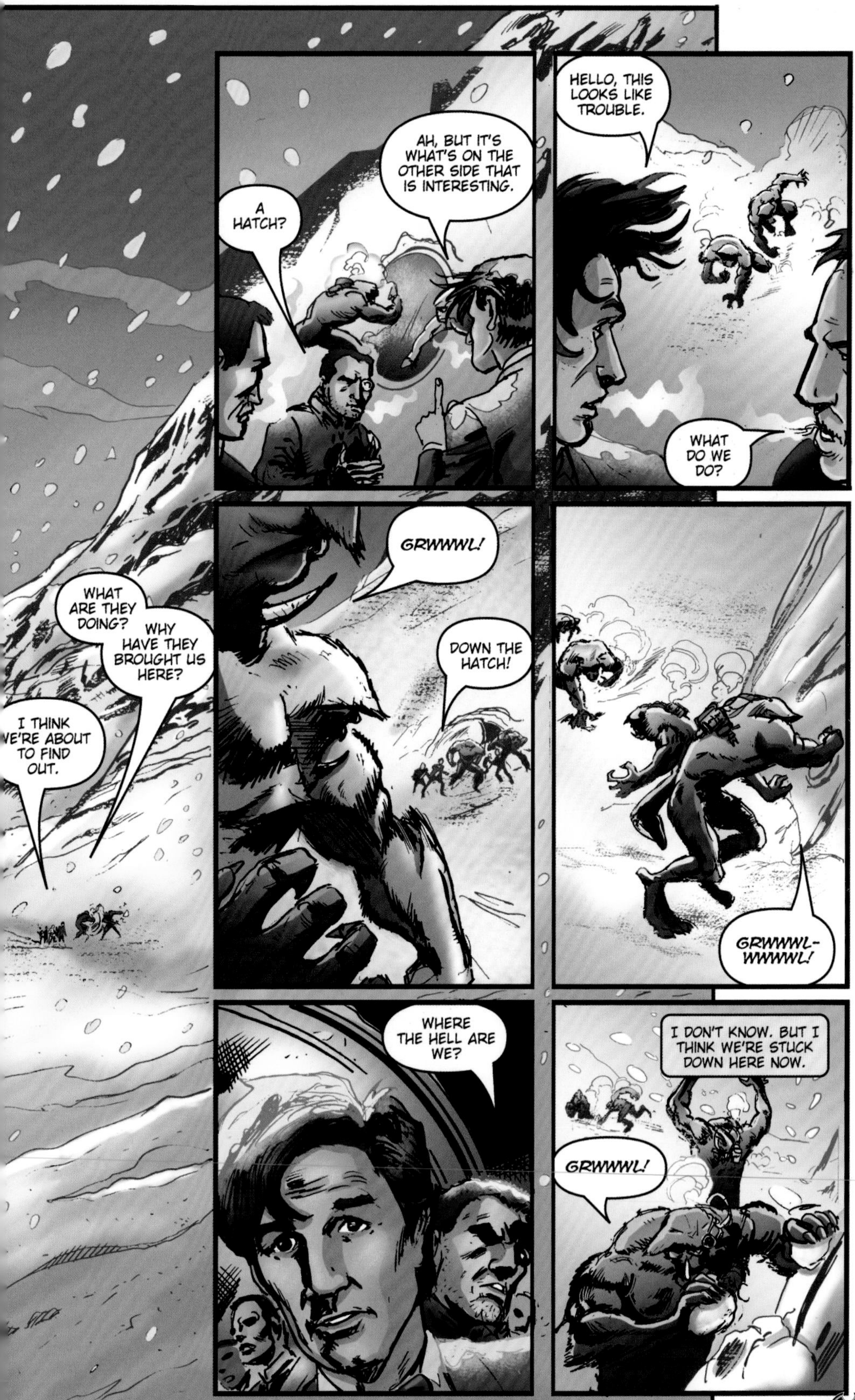

A HATCH?
AH, BUT IT'S WHAT'S ON THE OTHER SIDE THAT IS INTERESTING.
HELLO, THIS LOOKS LIKE TROUBLE.
WHAT DO WE DO?
WHAT ARE THEY DOING?
WHY HAVE THEY BROUGHT US HERE?
I THINK WE'RE ABOUT TO FIND OUT.
GRWWWL!
DOWN THE HATCH!
GRWWWL-WWWWL!
WHERE THE HELL ARE WE?
I DON'T KNOW. BUT I THINK WE'RE STUCK DOWN HERE NOW.
GRWWWL!

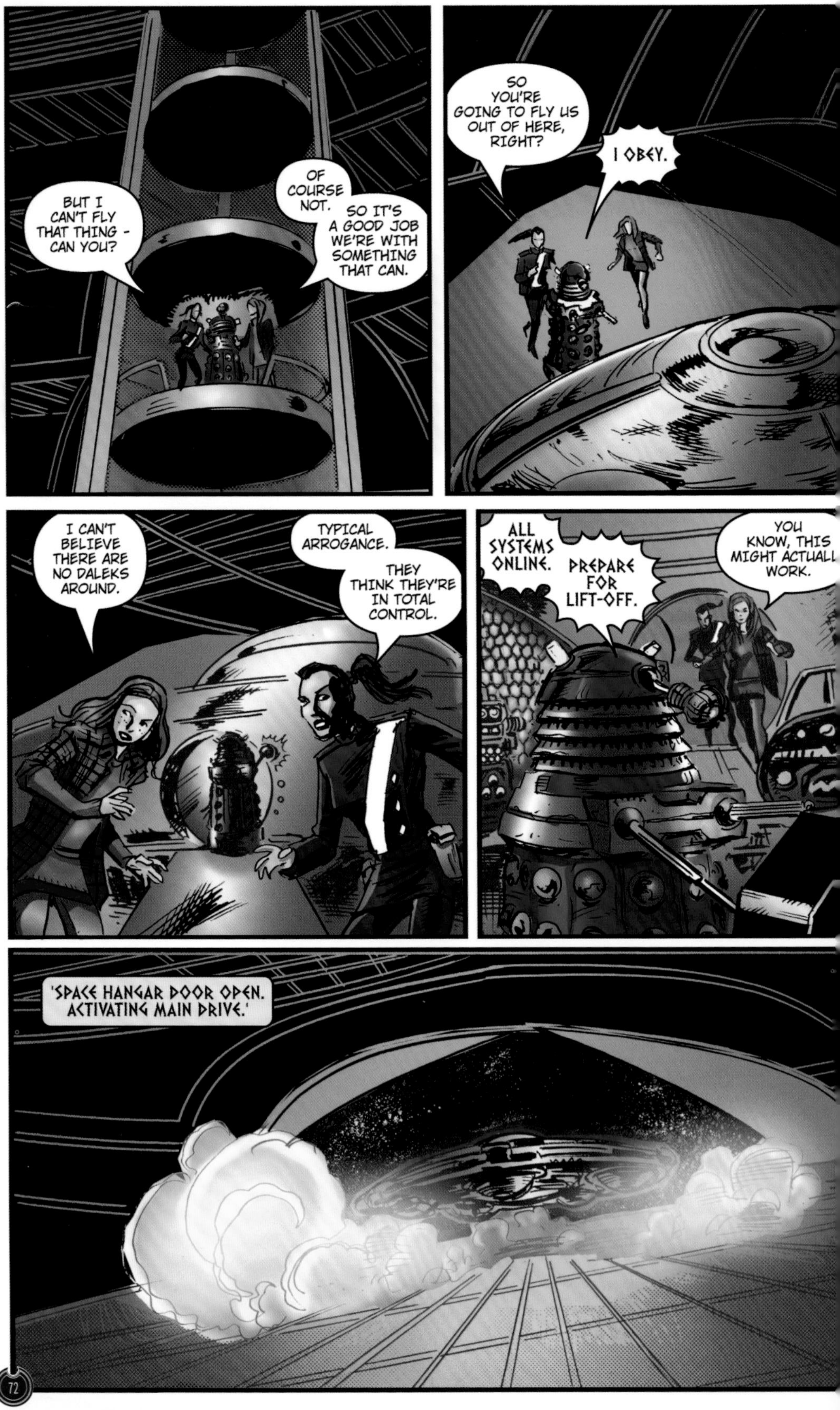

BUT I CAN'T FLY THAT THING - CAN YOU?
OF COURSE NOT.
SO IT'S A GOOD JOB WE'RE WITH SOMETHING THAT CAN.
SO YOU'RE GOING TO FLY US OUT OF HERE, RIGHT?
I OBEY.
I CAN'T BELIEVE THERE ARE NO DALEKS AROUND.
TYPICAL ARROGANCE.
THEY THINK THEY'RE IN TOTAL CONTROL.
ALL SYSTEMS ONLINE.
PREPARE FOR LIFT-OFF.
YOU KNOW, THIS MIGHT ACTUALL WORK.
'SPACE HANGAR DOOR OPEN. ACTIVATING MAIN DRIVE.'

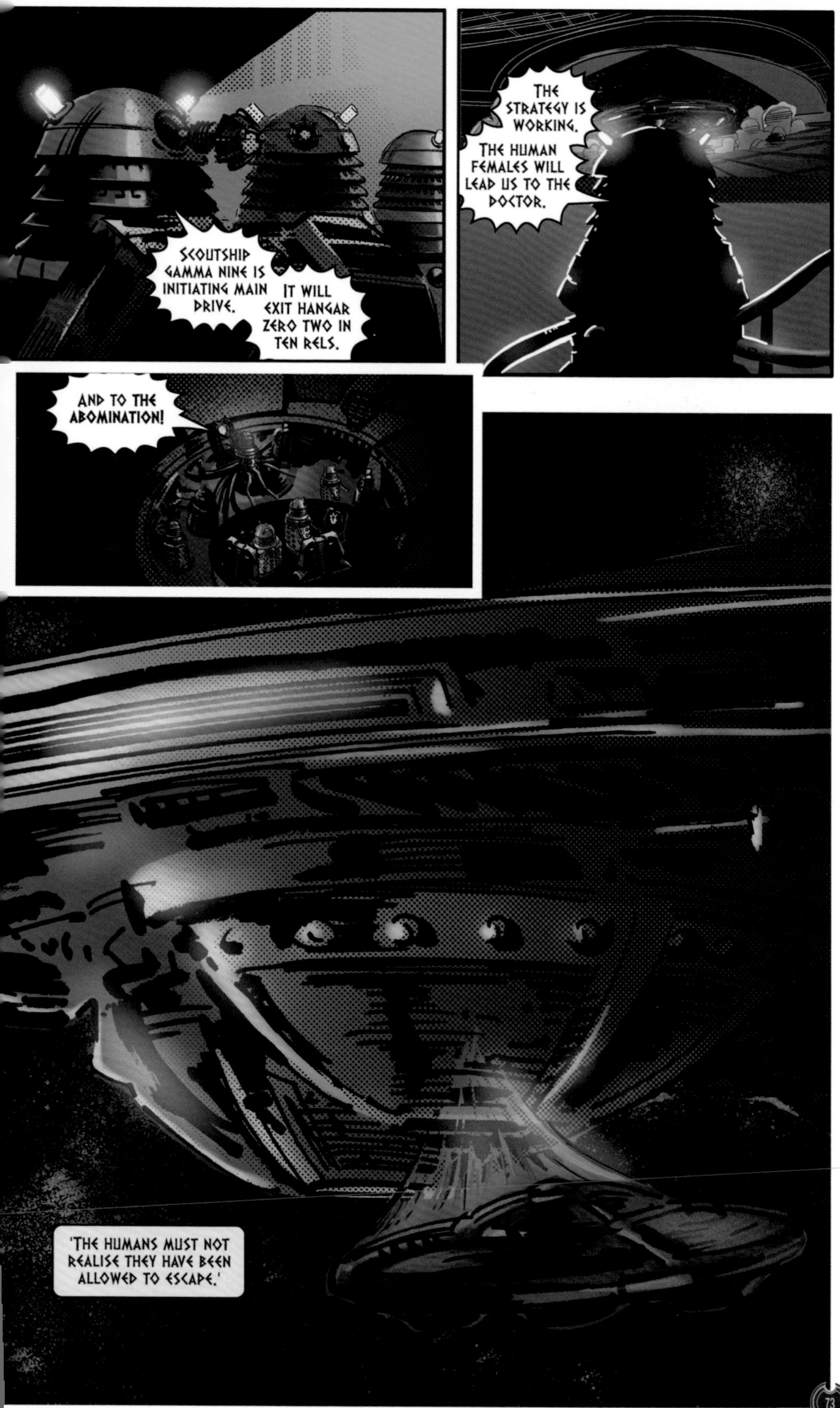
SCOUTSHIP GAMMA NINE IS INITIATING MAIN DRIVE.
IT WILL EXIT HANGAR ZERO TWO IN TEN RELS.
THE STRATEGY IS WORKING.
THE HUMAN FEMALES WILL LEAD US TO THE DOCTOR.
AND TO THE ABOMINATION!
'THE HUMANS MUST NOT REALISE THEY HAVE BEEN ALLOWED TO ESCAPE.'

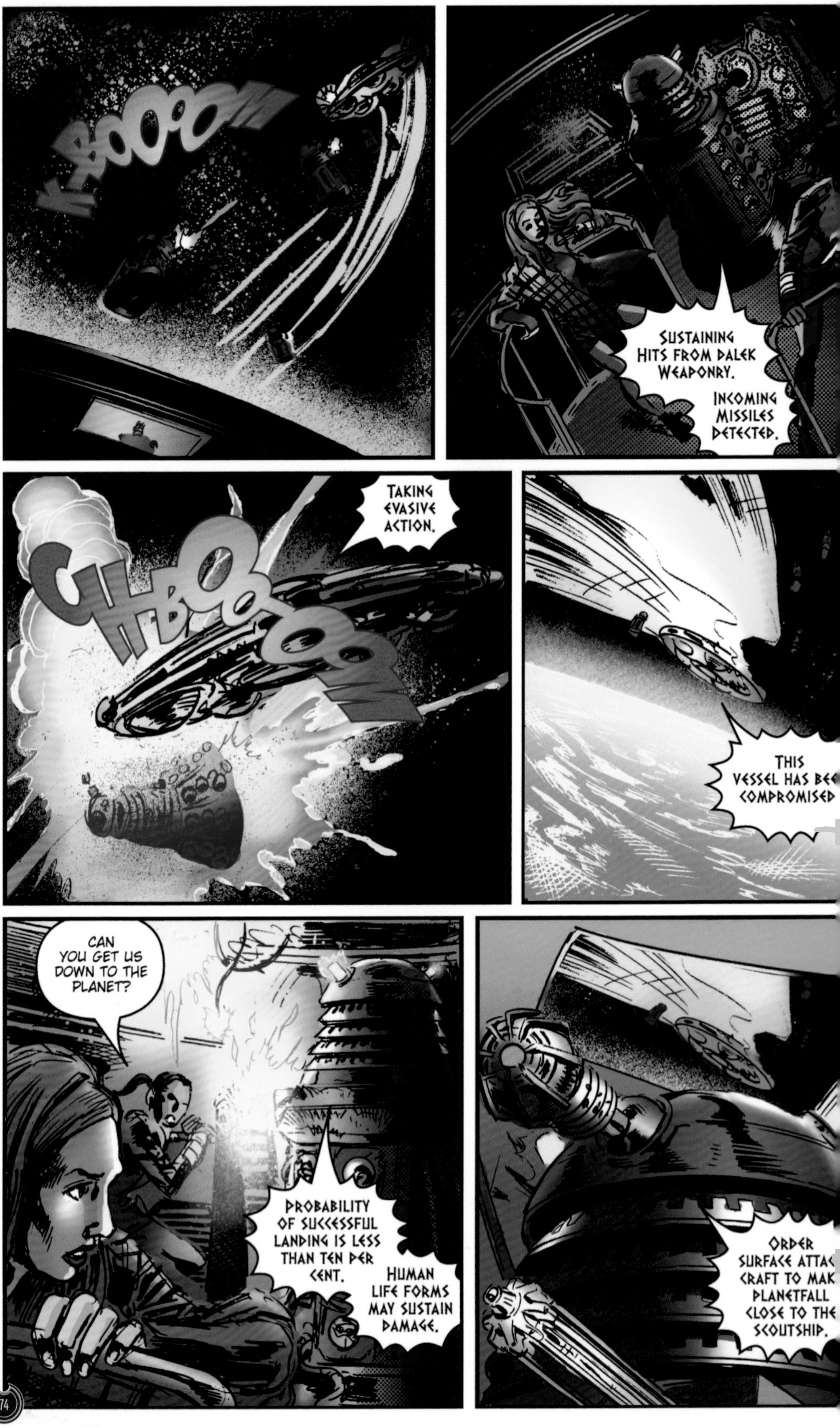
KABOOOM
SUSTAINING HITS FROM DALEK WEAPONRY.
INCOMING MISSILES DETECTED.
TAKING EVASIVE ACTION.
CHBOOOOM
THIS VESSEL HAS BEE COMPROMISED
CAN YOU GET US DOWN TO THE PLANET?
PROBABILITY OF SUCCESSFUL LANDING IS LESS THAN TEN PER CENT.
HUMAN LIFE FORMS MAY SUSTAIN DAMAGE.
ORDER SURFACE ATTAC CRAFT TO MAK PLANETFALL CLOSE TO THE SCOUTSHIP.

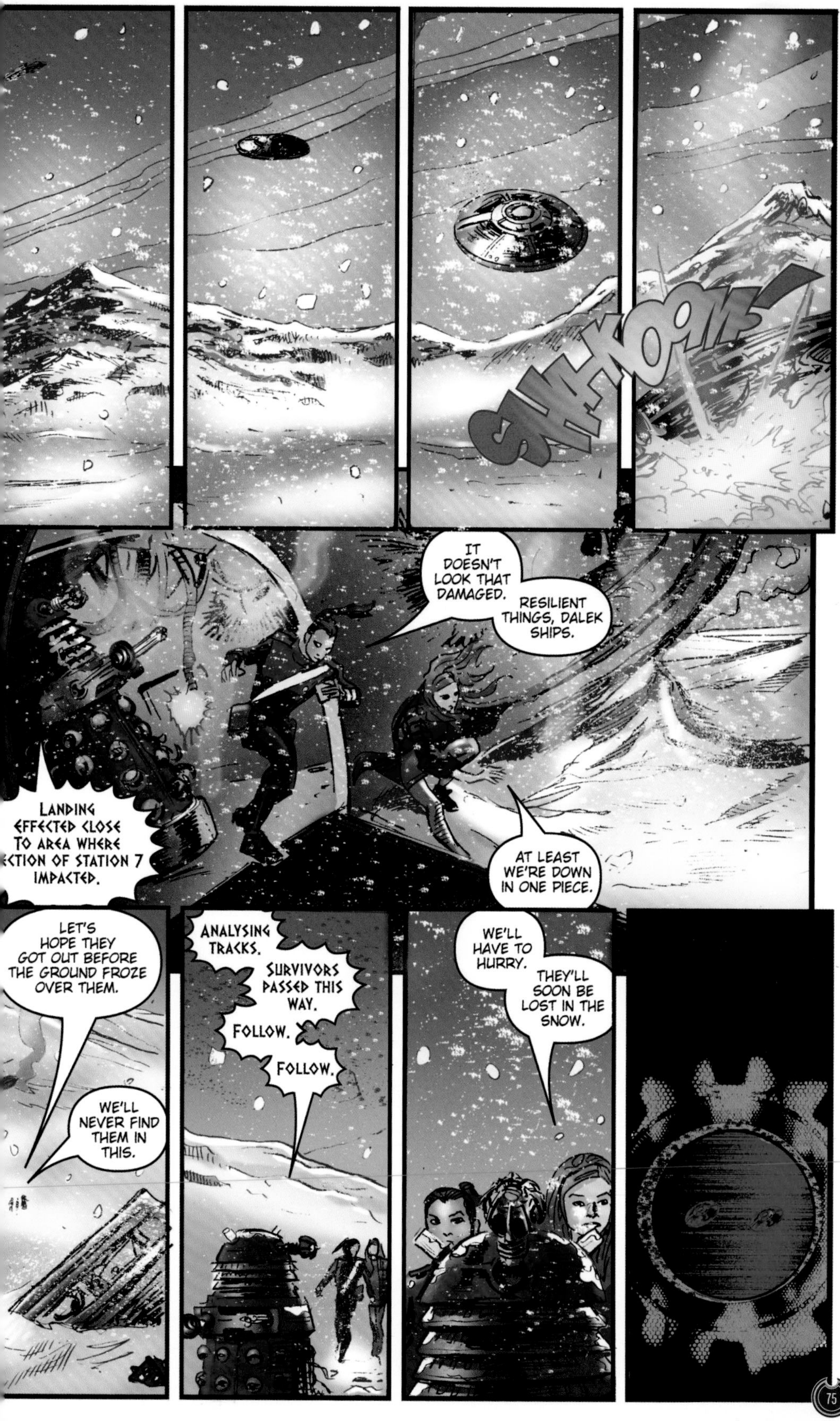
SHH-KOOM!
IT DOESN'T LOOK THAT DAMAGED.
RESILIENT THINGS, DALEK SHIPS.
LANDING EFFECTED CLOSE TO AREA WHERE ECTION OF STATION 7 IMPACTED.
AT LEAST WE'RE DOWN IN ONE PIECE.
LET'S HOPE THEY GOT OUT BEFORE THE GROUND FROZE OVER THEM.
WE'LL NEVER FIND THEM IN THIS.
ANALYSING TRACKS.
SURVIVORS PASSED THIS WAY.
FOLLOW.
FOLLOW.
WE'LL HAVE TO HURRY.
THEY'LL SOON BE LOST IN THE SNOW.

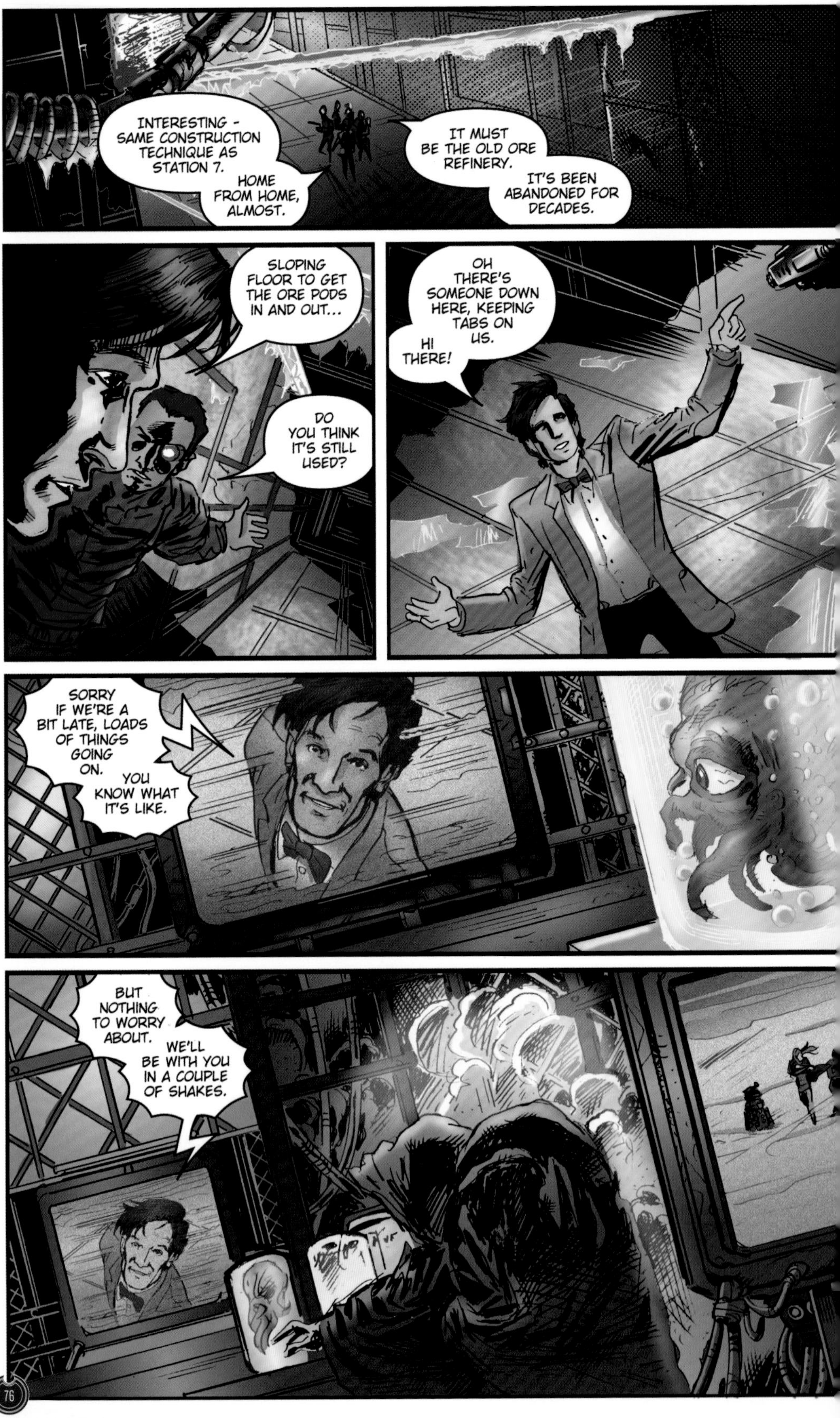
INTERESTING - SAME CONSTRUCTION TECHNIQUE AS STATION 7.
HOME FROM HOME, ALMOST.
IT MUST BE THE OLD ORE REFINERY.
IT'S BEEN ABANDONED FOR DECADES.
SLOPING FLOOR TO GET THE ORE PODS IN AND OUT...
DO YOU THINK IT'S STILL USED?
OH THERE'S SOMEONE DOWN HERE, KEEPING TABS ON US.
HI THERE!
SORRY IF WE'RE A BIT LATE, LOADS OF THINGS GOING ON.
YOU KNOW WHAT IT'S LIKE.
BUT NOTHING TO WORRY ABOUT.
WE'LL BE WITH YOU IN A COUPLE OF SHAKES.

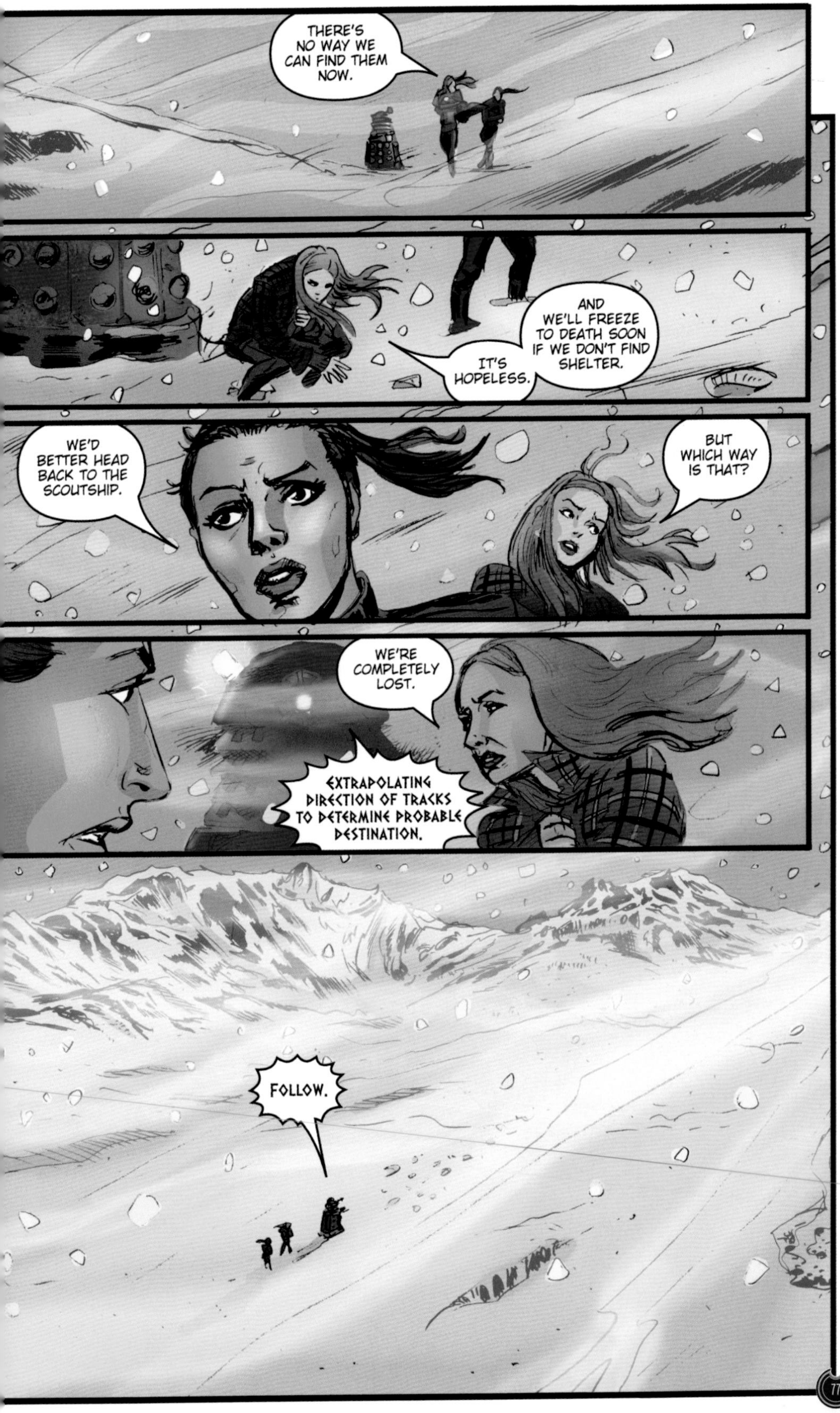
THERE'S NO WAY WE CAN FIND THEM NOW.
AND WE'LL FREEZE TO DEATH SOON IF WE DON'T FIND SHELTER.
IT'S HOPELESS.
WE'D BETTER HEAD BACK TO THE SCOUTSHIP.
BUT WHICH WAY IS THAT?
WE'RE COMPLETELY LOST.
EXTRAPOLATING DIRECTION OF TRACKS TO DETERMINE PROBABLE DESTINATION.
FOLLOW.

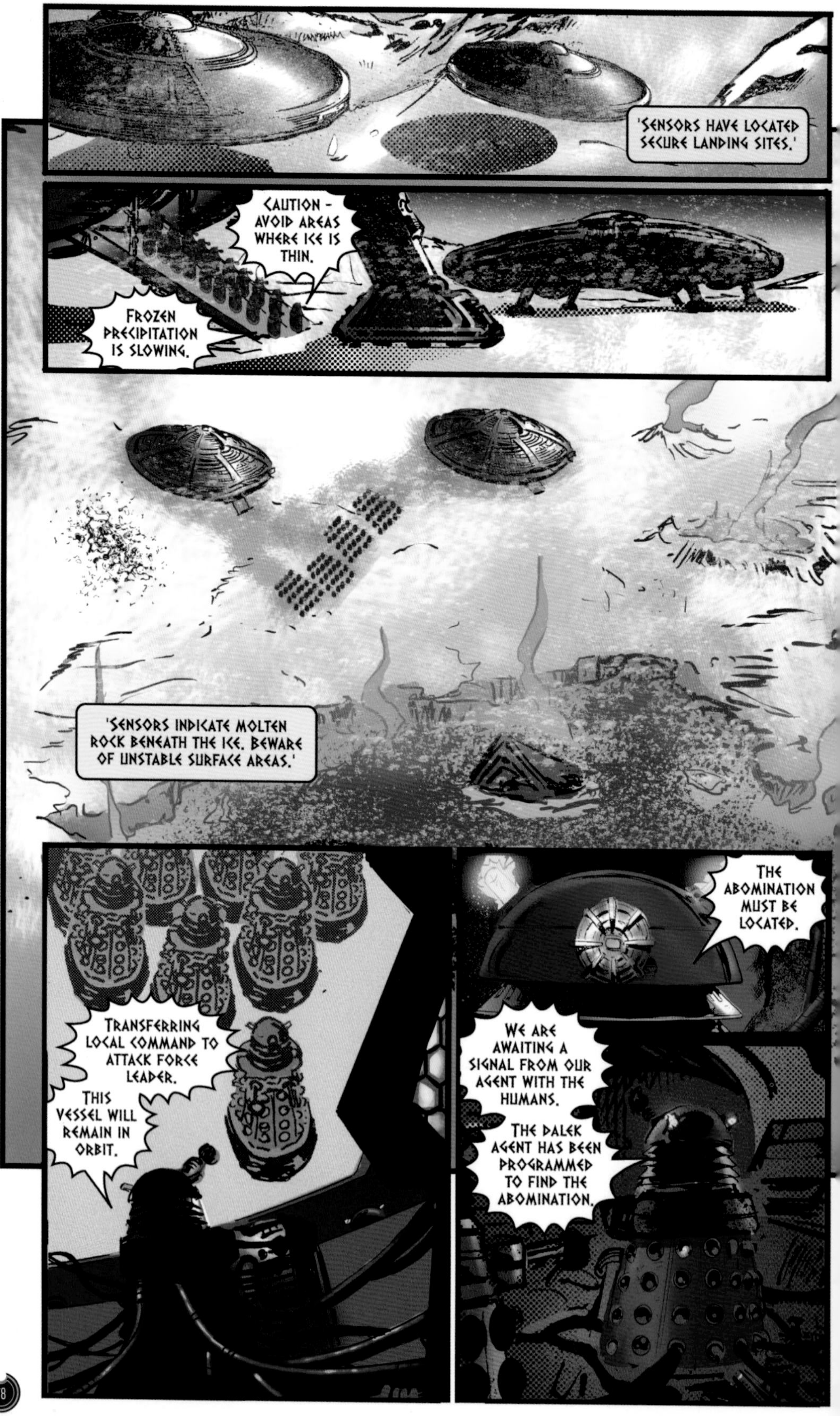
'Sensors have located secure landing sites.'
Caution - avoid areas where ice is thin.
Frozen precipitation is slowing.
'Sensors indicate molten rock beneath the ice. Beware of unstable surface areas.'
Transferring local command to attack force leader.
This vessel will remain in orbit.
The abomination must be located.
We are awaiting a signal from our agent with the humans.
The Dalek agent has been programmed to find the abomination.

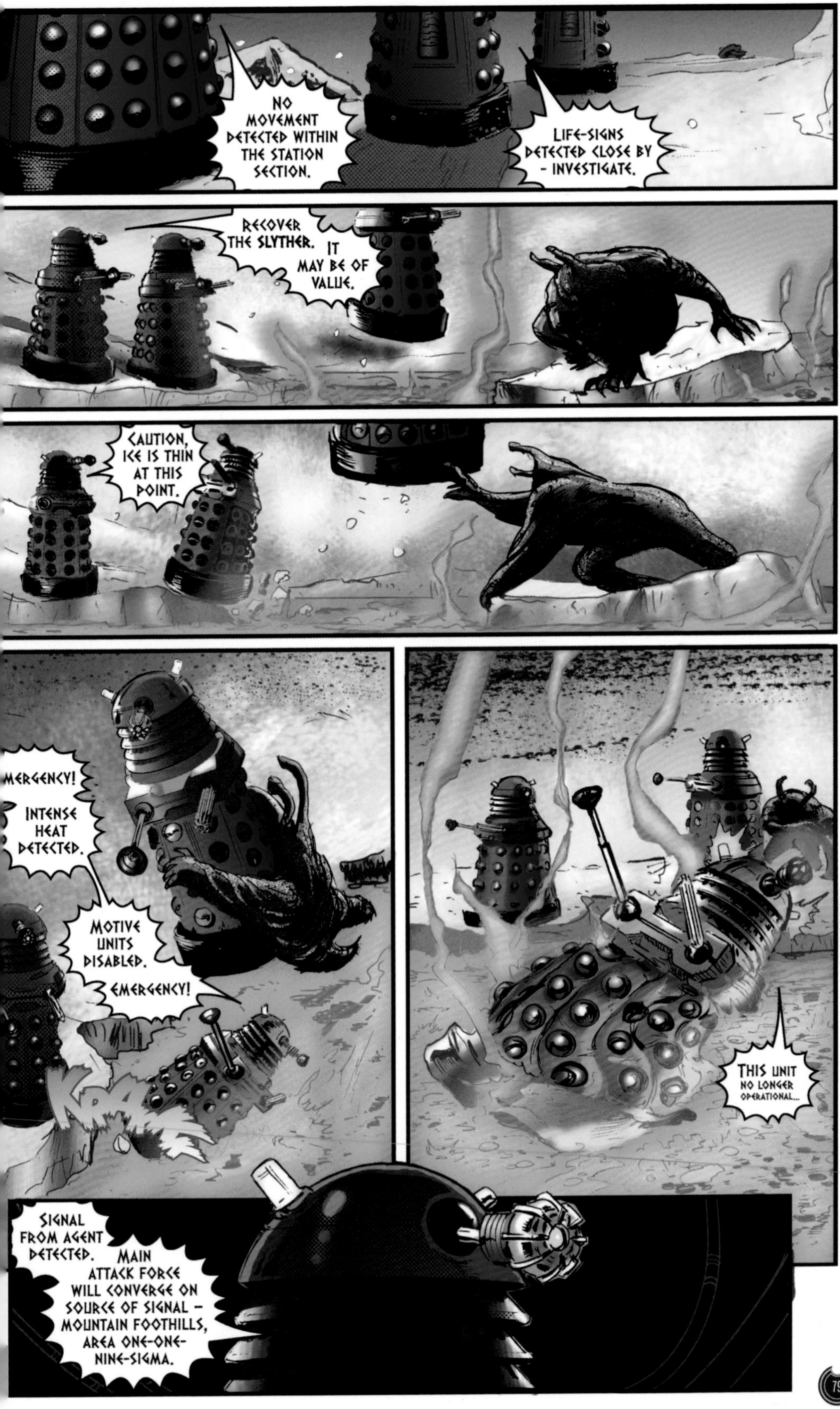
NO MOVEMENT DETECTED WITHIN THE STATION SECTION.
LIFE-SIGNS DETECTED CLOSE BY - INVESTIGATE.
RECOVER THE SLYTHER. IT MAY BE OF VALUE.
CAUTION, ICE IS THIN AT THIS POINT.
MERGENCY!
INTENSE HEAT DETECTED.
MOTIVE UNITS DISABLED.
EMERGENCY!
THIS UNIT NO LONGER OPERATIONAL...
SIGNAL FROM AGENT DETECTED.
MAIN ATTACK FORCE WILL CONVERGE ON SOURCE OF SIGNAL – MOUNTAIN FOOTHILLS, AREA ONE-ONE-NINE-SIGMA.

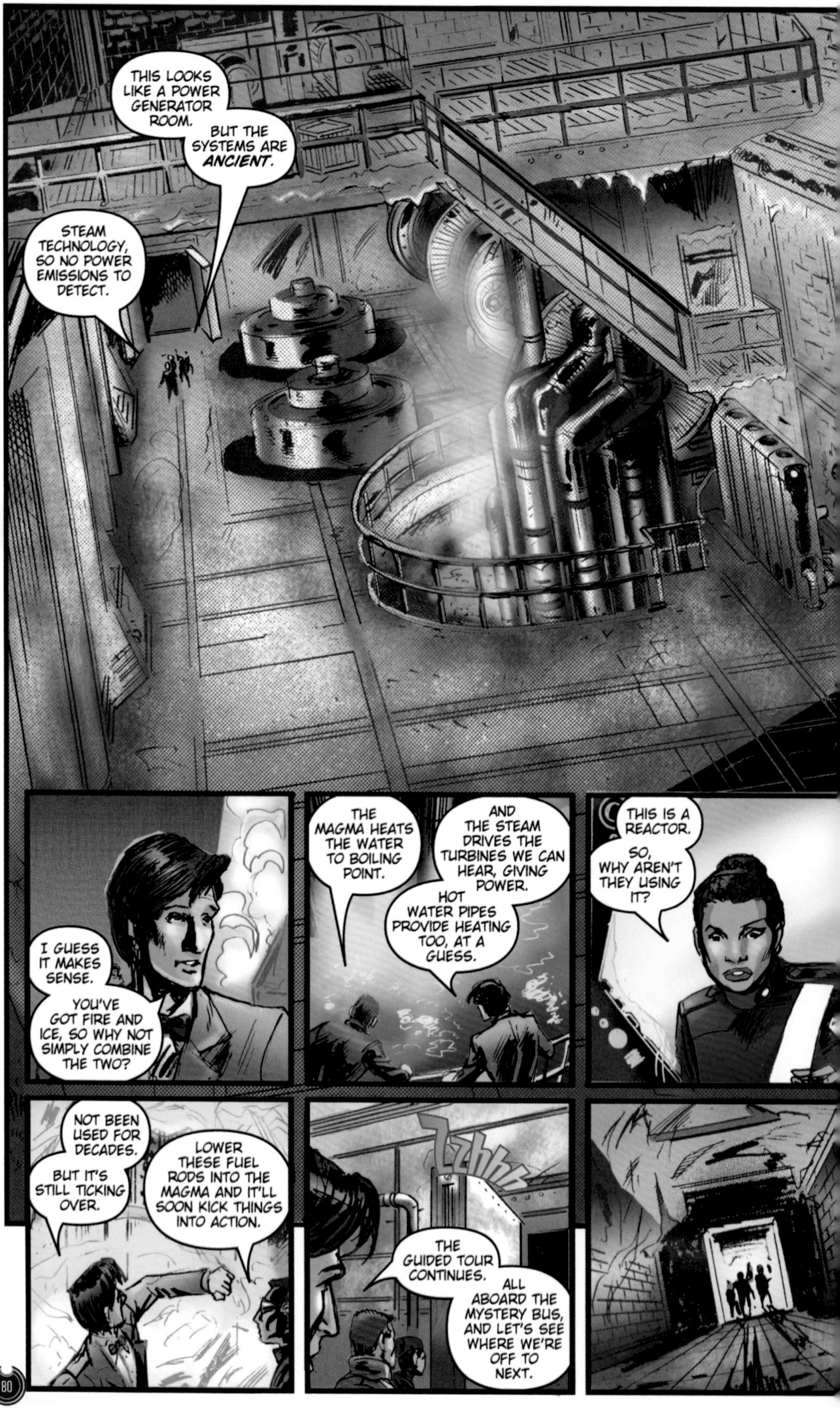
THIS LOOKS LIKE A POWER GENERATOR ROOM.
BUT THE SYSTEMS ARE *ANCIENT*.
STEAM TECHNOLOGY, SO NO POWER EMISSIONS TO DETECT.
I GUESS IT MAKES SENSE.
YOU'VE GOT FIRE AND ICE, SO WHY NOT SIMPLY COMBINE THE TWO?
THE MAGMA HEATS THE WATER TO BOILING POINT.
AND THE STEAM DRIVES THE TURBINES WE CAN HEAR, GIVING POWER.
HOT WATER PIPES PROVIDE HEATING TOO, AT A GUESS.
THIS IS A REACTOR.
SO, WHY AREN'T THEY USING IT?
NOT BEEN USED FOR DECADES.
BUT IT'S STILL TICKING OVER.
LOWER THESE FUEL RODS INTO THE MAGMA AND IT'LL SOON KICK THINGS INTO ACTION.
ZZHHH
THE GUIDED TOUR CONTINUES.
ALL ABOARD THE MYSTERY BUS, AND LET'S SEE WHERE WE'RE OFF TO NEXT.

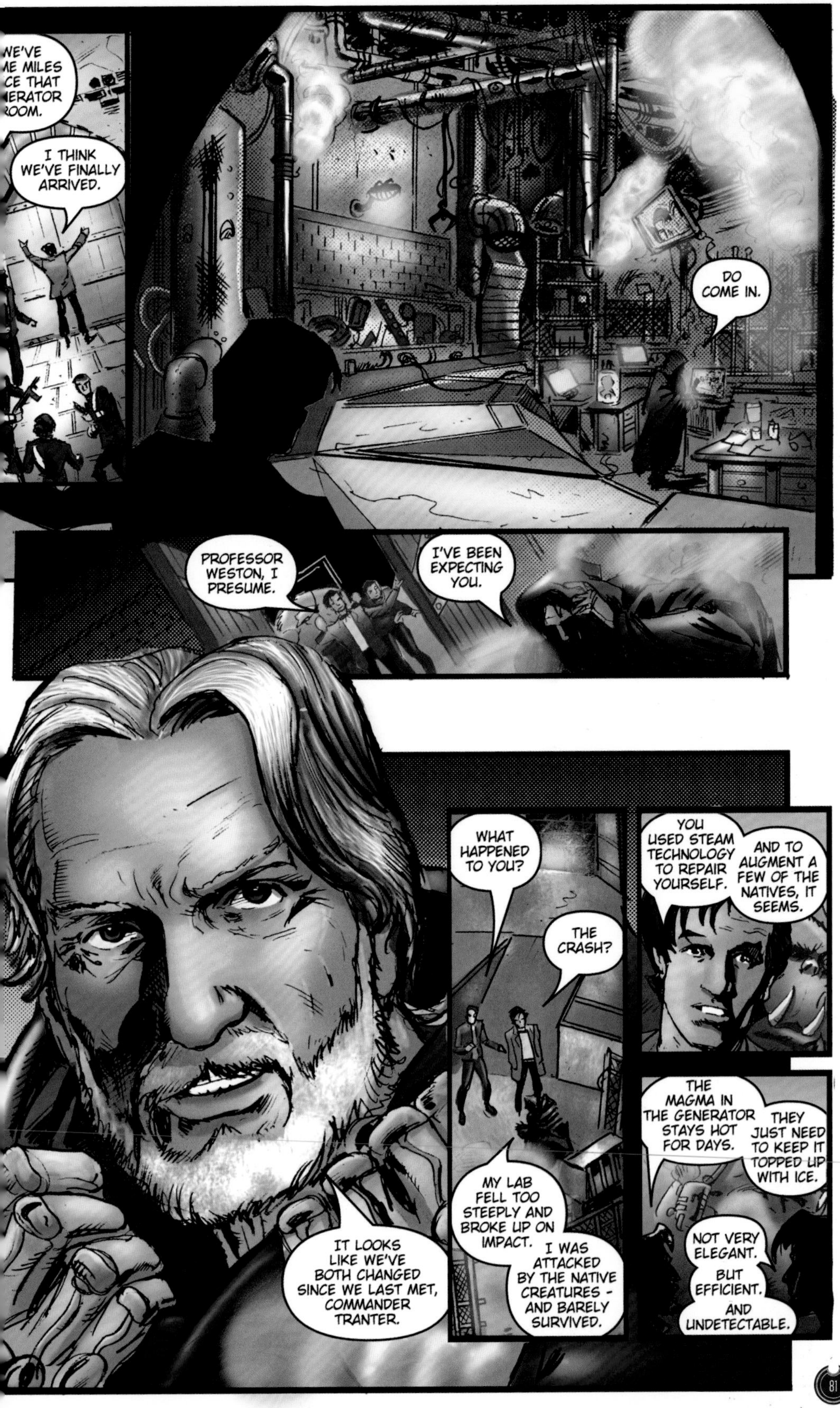
WE'VE
ME MILES
CE THAT
ERATOR
ROOM.
I THINK WE'VE FINALLY ARRIVED.
DO COME IN.
PROFESSOR WESTON, I PRESUME.
I'VE BEEN EXPECTING YOU.
IT LOOKS LIKE WE'VE BOTH CHANGED SINCE WE LAST MET, COMMANDER TRANTER.
WHAT HAPPENED TO YOU?
THE CRASH?
MY LAB FELL TOO STEEPLY AND BROKE UP ON IMPACT.
I WAS ATTACKED BY THE NATIVE CREATURES - AND BARELY SURVIVED.
YOU USED STEAM TECHNOLOGY TO REPAIR YOURSELF.
AND TO AUGMENT A FEW OF THE NATIVES, IT SEEMS.
THE MAGMA IN THE GENERATOR STAYS HOT FOR DAYS.
THEY JUST NEED TO KEEP IT TOPPED UP WITH ICE.
NOT VERY ELEGANT.
BUT EFFICIENT.
AND UNDETECTABLE.

AVERN, ISN'T IT?

AND GRIBBIN AND PHELPS.

YOU LOOK LIKE YOU'VE HAD A ROUGH TIME.

YOU COULD SAY THAT, PROFESSOR, SIR.

SHOW THEM WHERE THEY CAN GET SOME REST, AND BRING THEM FOOD AND DRINK.

THANK YOU.

YOU GOING WITH THEM, DOCTOR?

OH I'LL STAY HERE WITH YOU TWO. THIS IS ALL VERY... INTERESTING.

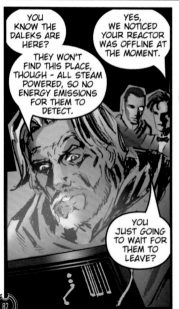

YOU KNOW THE DALEKS ARE HERE?

YES, WE NOTICED YOUR REACTOR WAS OFFLINE AT THE MOMENT.

THEY WON'T FIND THIS PLACE, THOUGH - ALL STEAM POWERED, SO NO ENERGY EMISSIONS FOR THEM TO DETECT.

YOU JUST GOING TO WAIT FOR THEM TO LEAVE?

OH NO, INDEED.

I SHALL SEND MY AUGMENTED CREATURES TO ATTACK THEM.

BUT - HANG ON...

STARTING WITH THESE HUMAN COLLABORATORS.

BUT THAT'S AMY.

AN JA

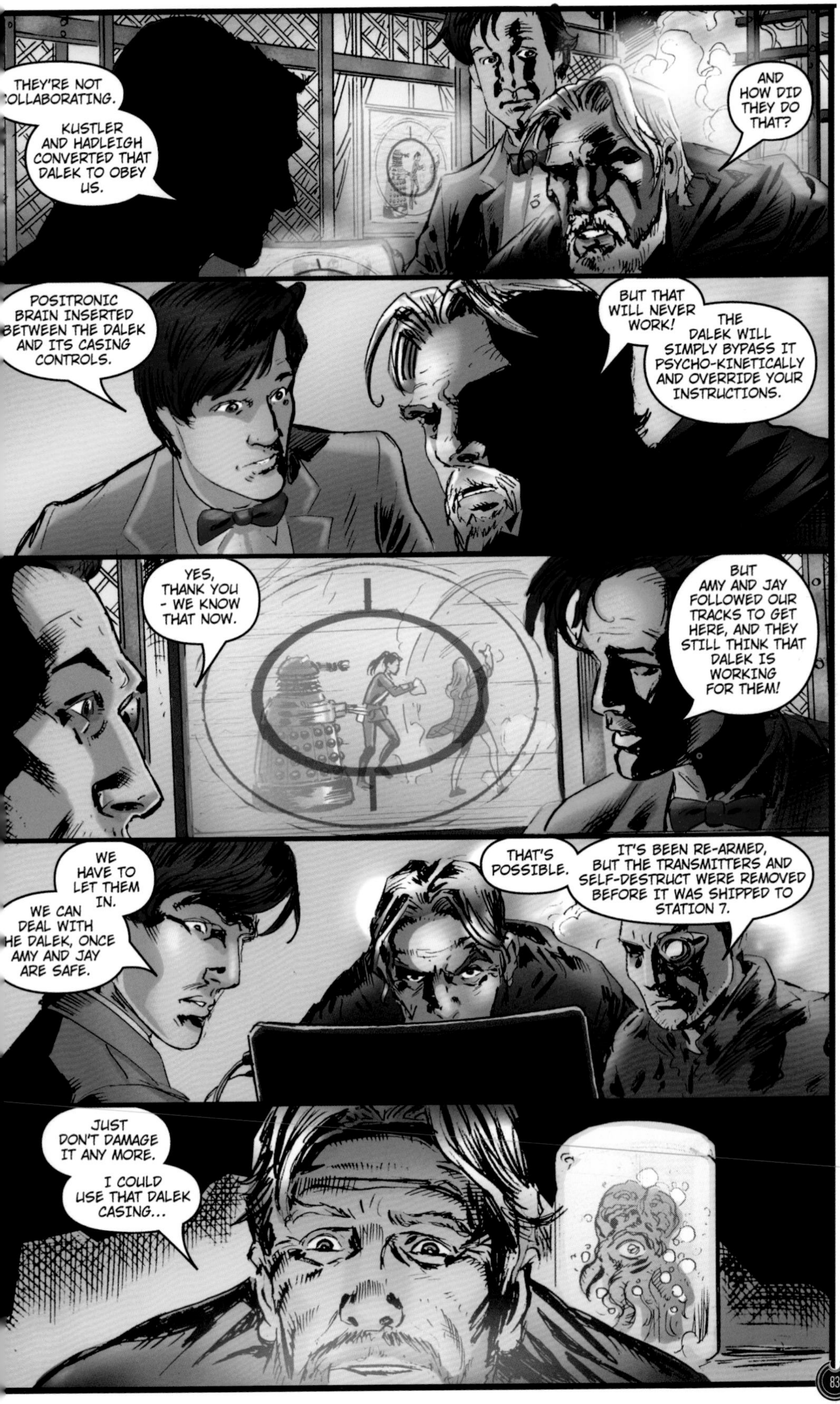
THEY'RE NOT COLLABORATING.
KUSTLER AND HADLEIGH CONVERTED THAT DALEK TO OBEY US.
AND HOW DID THEY DO THAT?
POSITRONIC BRAIN INSERTED BETWEEN THE DALEK AND ITS CASING CONTROLS.
BUT THAT WILL NEVER WORK!
THE DALEK WILL SIMPLY BYPASS IT PSYCHO-KINETICALLY AND OVERRIDE YOUR INSTRUCTIONS.
YES, THANK YOU - WE KNOW THAT NOW.
BUT AMY AND JAY FOLLOWED OUR TRACKS TO GET HERE, AND THEY STILL THINK THAT DALEK IS WORKING FOR THEM!
WE HAVE TO LET THEM IN.
WE CAN DEAL WITH THE DALEK, ONCE AMY AND JAY ARE SAFE.
THAT'S POSSIBLE.
IT'S BEEN RE-ARMED, BUT THE TRANSMITTERS AND SELF-DESTRUCT WERE REMOVED BEFORE IT WAS SHIPPED TO STATION 7.
JUST DON'T DAMAGE IT ANY MORE.
I COULD USE THAT DALEK CASING...

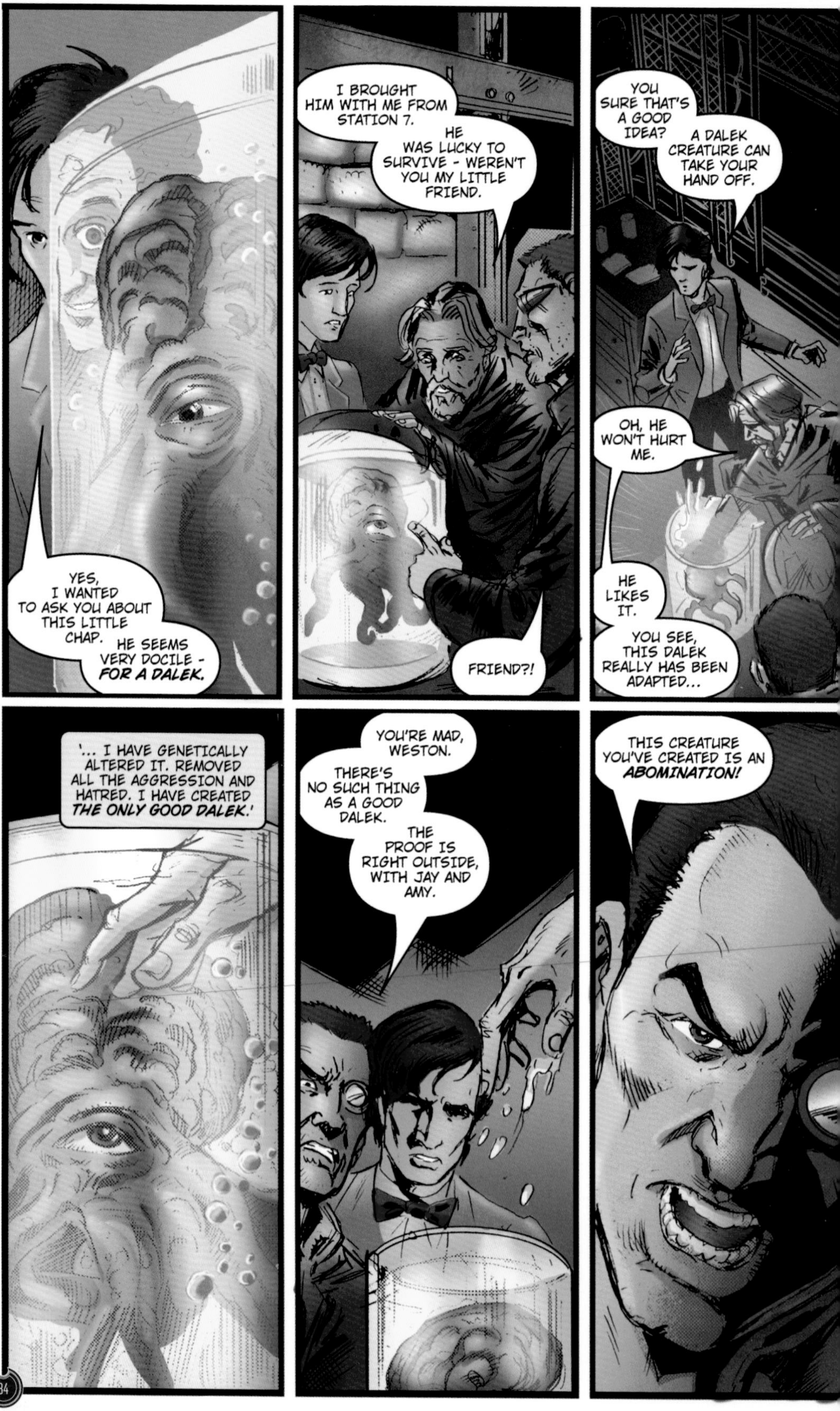

YES, I WANTED TO ASK YOU ABOUT THIS LITTLE CHAP.
HE SEEMS VERY DOCILE - FOR A DALEK.
I BROUGHT HIM WITH ME FROM STATION 7.
HE WAS LUCKY TO SURVIVE - WEREN'T YOU MY LITTLE FRIEND.
FRIEND?!
YOU SURE THAT'S A GOOD IDEA?
A DALEK CREATURE CAN TAKE YOUR HAND OFF.
OH, HE WON'T HURT ME.
HE LIKES IT.
YOU SEE, THIS DALEK REALLY HAS BEEN ADAPTED...
'... I HAVE GENETICALLY ALTERED IT. REMOVED ALL THE AGGRESSION AND HATRED. I HAVE CREATED THE ONLY GOOD DALEK.'
YOU'RE MAD, WESTON.
THERE'S NO SUCH THING AS A GOOD DALEK.
THE PROOF IS RIGHT OUTSIDE, WITH JAY AND AMY.
THIS CREATURE YOU'VE CREATED IS AN ABOMINATION!

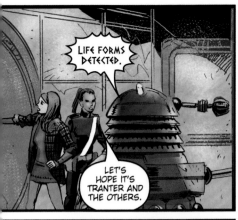

LIFE FORMS DETECTED.

LET'S HOPE IT'S TRANTER AND THE OTHERS.

SOMEONE'S GONE TO SOME SERIOUS TROUBLE DOWN HERE.

WHOEVER IT IS WANTS US TO FOLLOW A PARTICULAR ROUTE - OPENING BULKHEADS AND UNLOCKING DOORS FOR US.

SO FAR SO GOOD, THEY'RE HEADING THIS WAY.

I'M AFRAID THEY AREN'T THE ONLY ONES.

IT SEEMS THE DALEKS KNOW WHERE WE ARE.

BUT HOW IS THAT POSSIBLE? WE'RE HIDDEN HERE - NO EMISSIONS, NOTHING.

NEVER UNDERESTIMATE THE DALEKS. I'D HAVE THOUGHT YOU'D BOTH LEARNED THAT BY NOW.

WHERE ARE YOU GOING?

TO STOP THE DALEKS FINDING US.

YOU PROBABLY CAN'T STOP THEM, BUT DO YOUR BEST TO HOLD THE DALEKS BACK, MY FRIENDS.

WAIT - I'M GOING WITH THEM.

WE HAVE TO STOP THE DALEKS GETTING PROFESSOR WESTON'S WORK. YOU HAVE TO GET HIM AWAY.

WE'LL ALL GO. THAT'S WHAT STATION 7 WAS ABOUT. IT'S OUR JOB. WE'LL BUY YOU AS MUCH TIME AS WE CAN, SIR.

IT WAS A PRIVILEGE TO SERVE WITH YOU. A PRIVILEGE AND AN HONOUR.

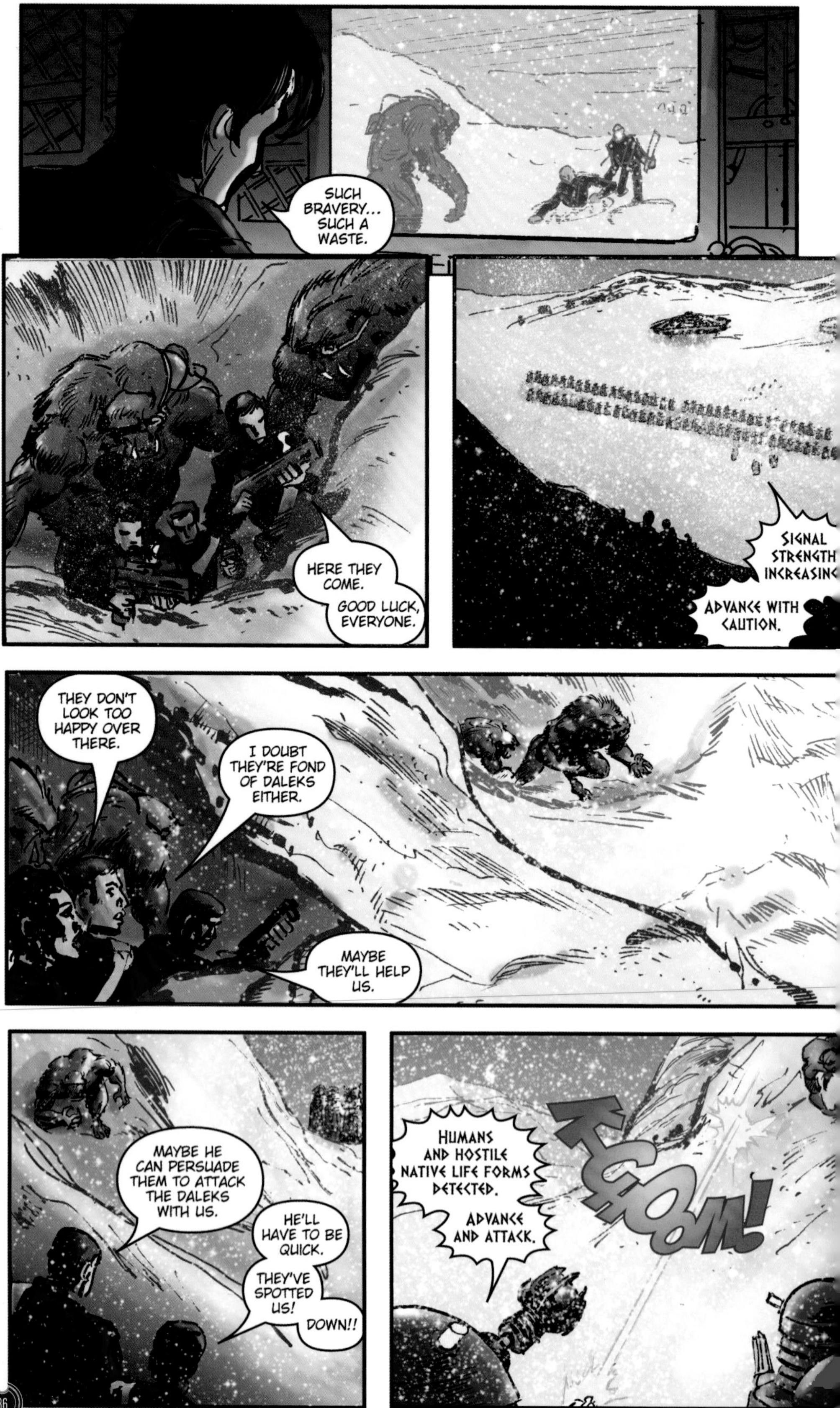
SUCH BRAVERY... SUCH A WASTE.
HERE THEY COME.
GOOD LUCK, EVERYONE.
SIGNAL STRENGTH INCREASING
ADVANCE WITH CAUTION.
THEY DON'T LOOK TOO HAPPY OVER THERE.
I DOUBT THEY'RE FOND OF DALEKS EITHER.
MAYBE THEY'LL HELP US.
MAYBE HE CAN PERSUADE THEM TO ATTACK THE DALEKS WITH US.
HE'LL HAVE TO BE QUICK.
THEY'VE SPOTTED US!
DOWN!!
HUMANS AND HOSTILE NATIVE LIFE FORMS DETECTED.
ADVANCE AND ATTACK.
KA-BOOM!

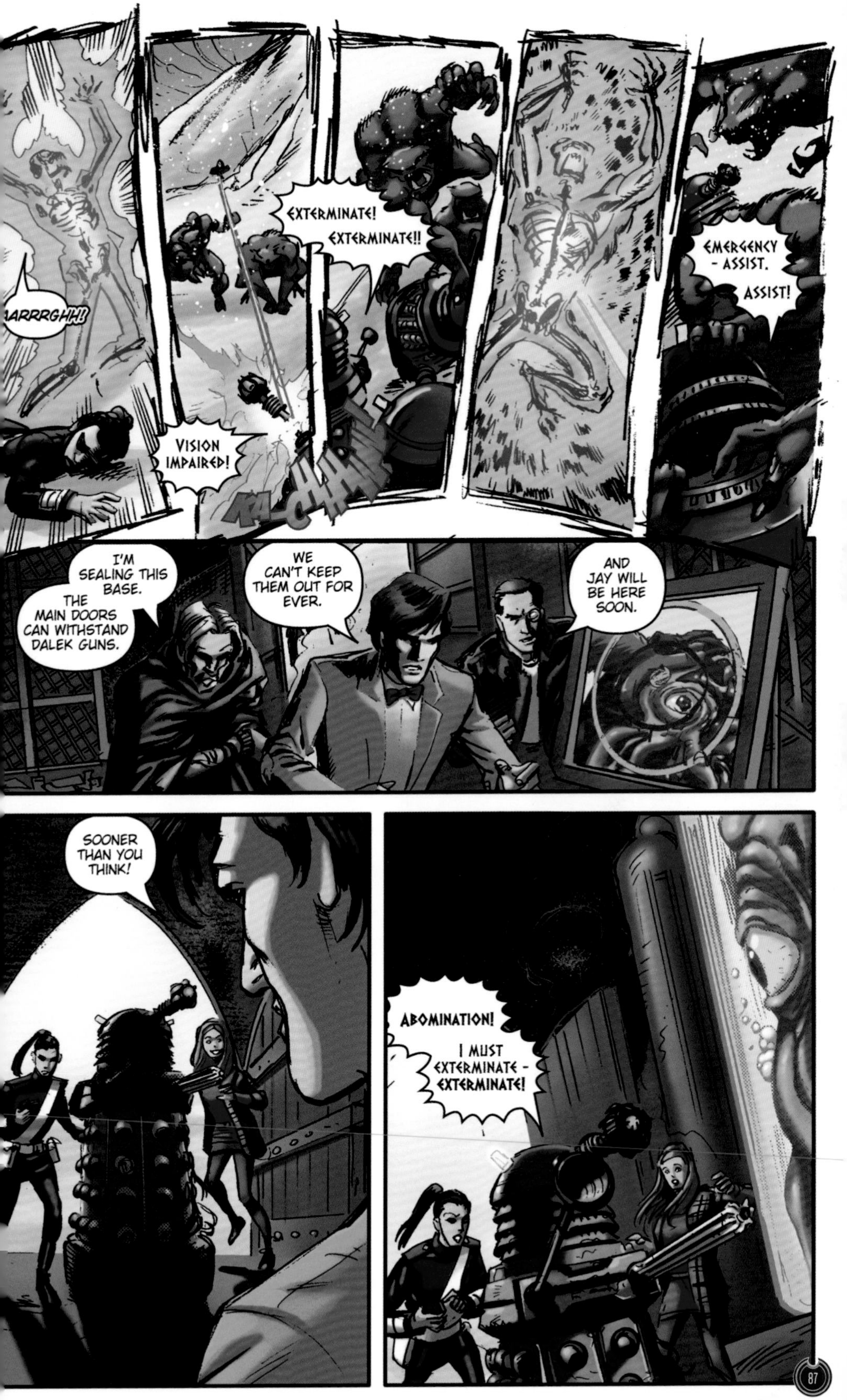
AARRRGHH!
VISION IMPAIRED!
EXTERMINATE!
EXTERMINATE!!
KA-CHAK
EMERGENCY - ASSIST.
ASSIST!
I'M SEALING THIS BASE.
THE MAIN DOORS CAN WITHSTAND DALEK GUNS.
WE CAN'T KEEP THEM OUT FOR EVER.
AND JAY WILL BE HERE SOON.
SOONER THAN YOU THINK!
ABOMINATION!
I MUST EXTERMINATE - EXTERMINATE!

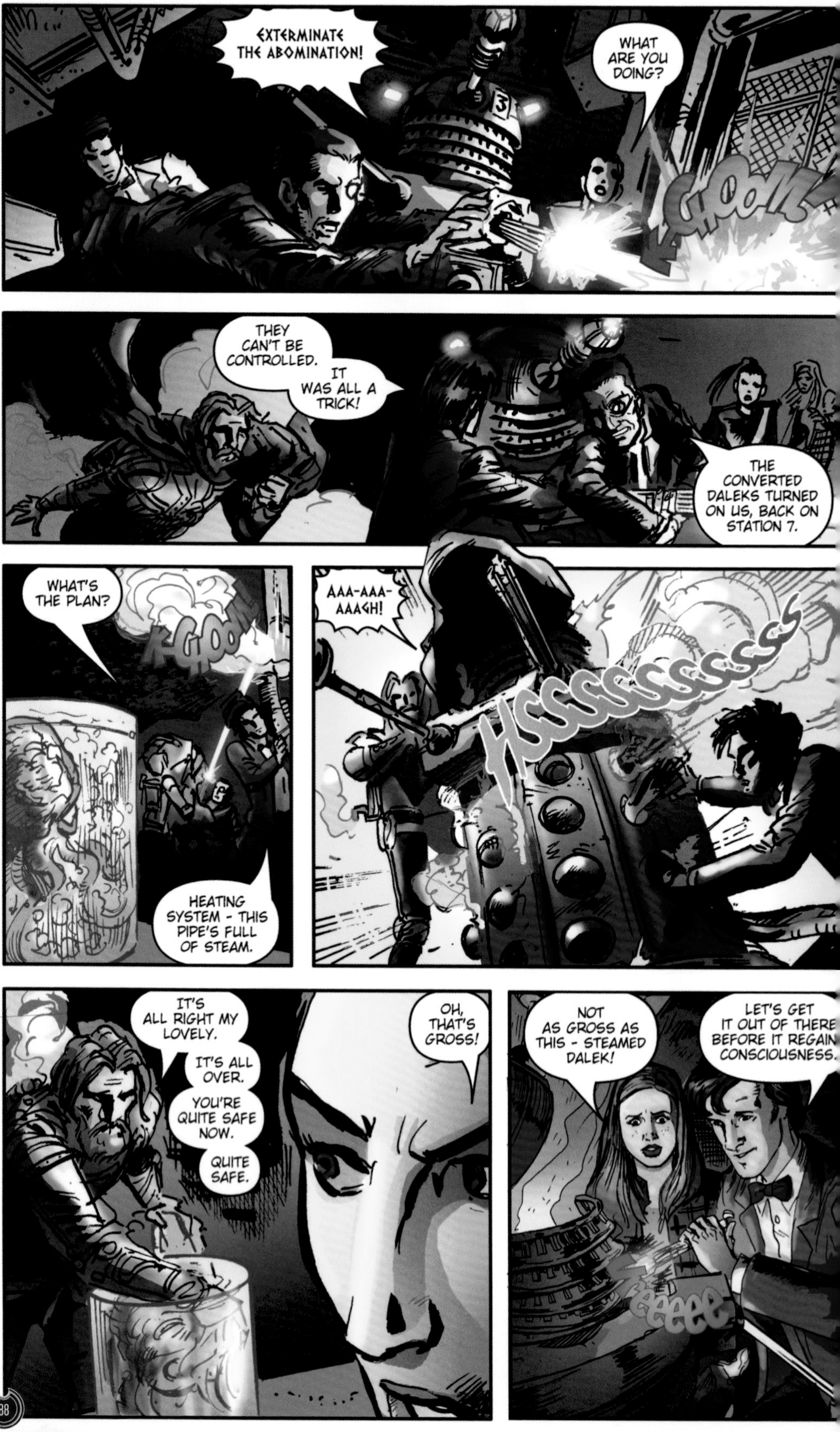
EXTERMINATE THE ABOMINATION!
WHAT ARE YOU DOING?
K-CHOOM!
THEY CAN'T BE CONTROLLED.
IT WAS ALL A TRICK!
THE CONVERTED DALEKS TURNED ON US, BACK ON STATION 7.
WHAT'S THE PLAN?
K-CHOO
HEATING SYSTEM - THIS PIPE'S FULL OF STEAM.
AAA-AAA-AAAGH!
HSSSSSSSSSS
IT'S ALL RIGHT MY LOVELY.
IT'S ALL OVER.
YOU'RE QUITE SAFE NOW.
QUITE SAFE.
OH, THAT'S GROSS!
NOT AS GROSS AS THIS - STEAMED DALEK!
LET'S GET IT OUT OF THERE BEFORE IT REGAIN CONSCIOUSNESS.
zeeeee

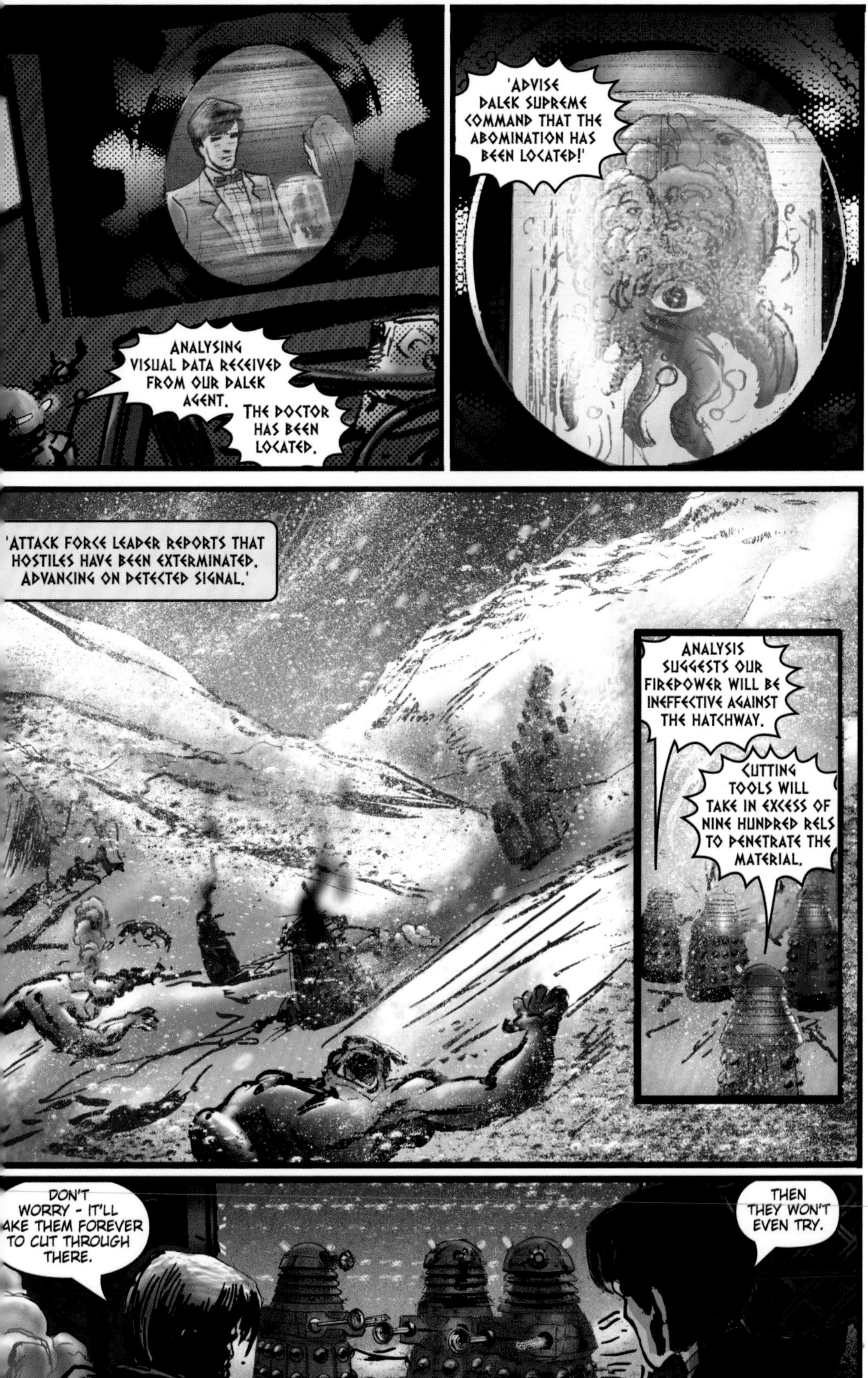
ANALYSING VISUAL DATA RECEIVED FROM OUR DALEK AGENT.
THE DOCTOR HAS BEEN LOCATED.
'ADVISE DALEK SUPREME COMMAND THAT THE ABOMINATION HAS BEEN LOCATED!'
'ATTACK FORCE LEADER REPORTS THAT HOSTILES HAVE BEEN EXTERMINATED. ADVANCING ON DETECTED SIGNAL.'
ANALYSIS SUGGESTS OUR FIREPOWER WILL BE INEFFECTIVE AGAINST THE HATCHWAY.
CUTTING TOOLS WILL TAKE IN EXCESS OF NINE HUNDRED RELS TO PENETRATE THE MATERIAL.
DON'T WORRY - IT'LL
AKE THEM FOREVER
TO CUT THROUGH THERE.
THEN THEY WON'T EVEN TRY.

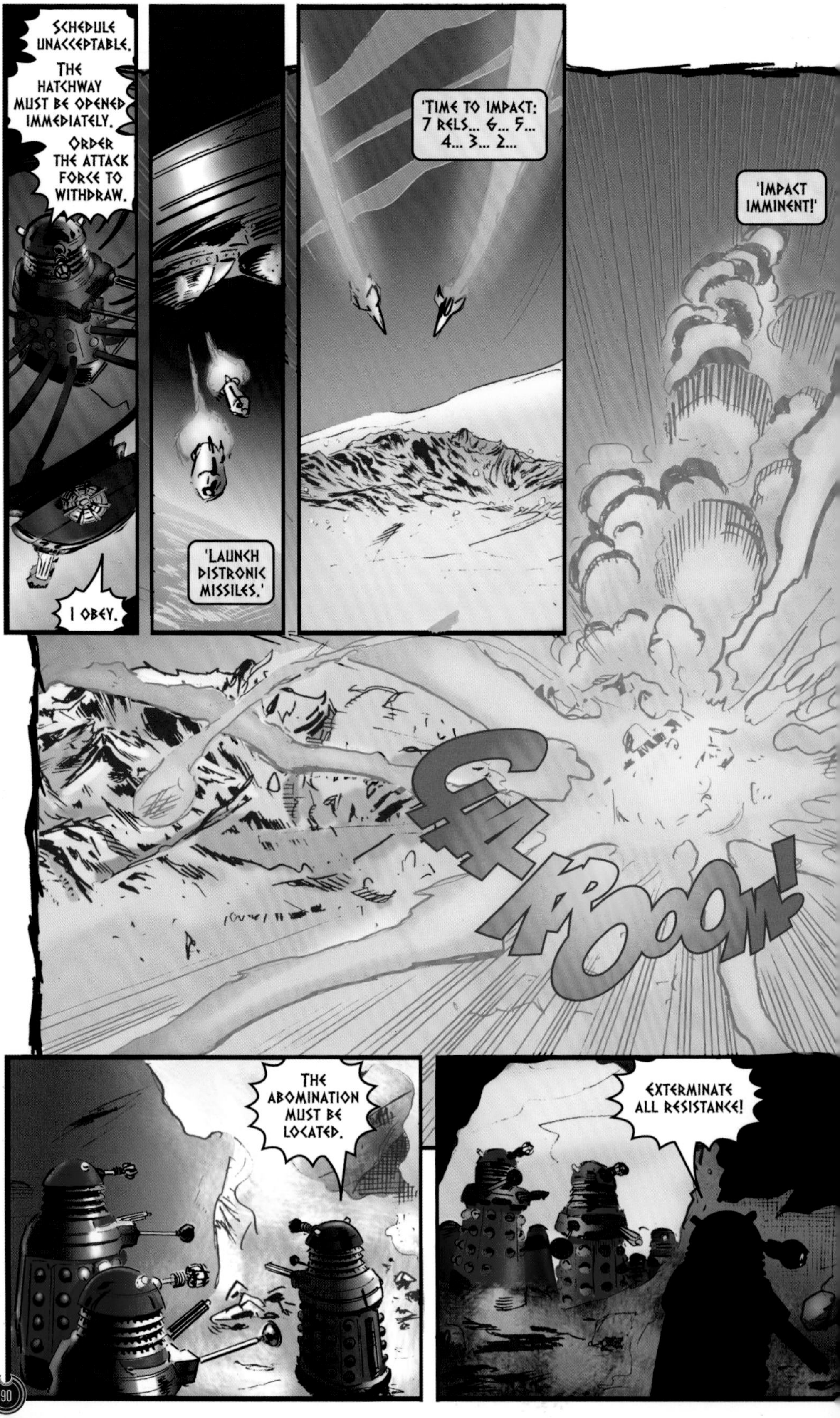
SCHEDULE UNACCEPTABLE.
THE HATCHWAY MUST BE OPENED IMMEDIATELY.
ORDER THE ATTACK FORCE TO WITHDRAW.
I OBEY.
'LAUNCH DISTRONIC MISSILES.'
'TIME TO IMPACT: 7 RELS... 6... 5... 4... 3... 2...
'IMPACT IMMINENT!'
CHAPOOOM!
THE ABOMINATION MUST BE LOCATED.
EXTERMINATE ALL RESISTANCE!

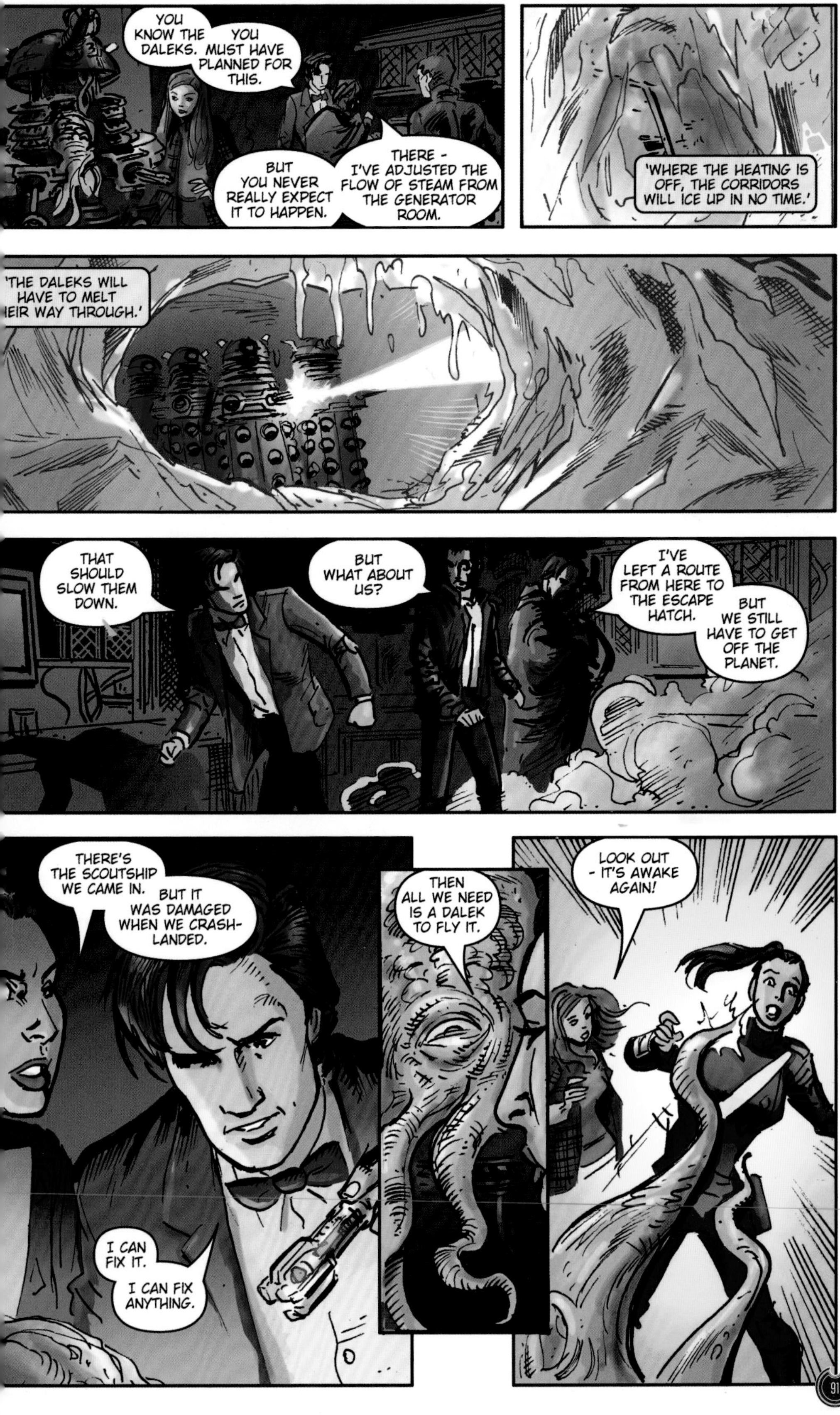
YOU KNOW THE DALEKS.
YOU MUST HAVE PLANNED FOR THIS.
BUT YOU NEVER REALLY EXPECT IT TO HAPPEN.
THERE - I'VE ADJUSTED THE FLOW OF STEAM FROM THE GENERATOR ROOM.
'WHERE THE HEATING IS OFF, THE CORRIDORS WILL ICE UP IN NO TIME.'
'THE DALEKS WILL HAVE TO MELT THEIR WAY THROUGH.'
THAT SHOULD SLOW THEM DOWN.
BUT WHAT ABOUT US?
I'VE LEFT A ROUTE FROM HERE TO THE ESCAPE HATCH.
BUT WE STILL HAVE TO GET OFF THE PLANET.
THERE'S THE SCOUTSHIP WE CAME IN.
BUT IT WAS DAMAGED WHEN WE CRASH-LANDED.
I CAN FIX IT.
I CAN FIX ANYTHING.
THEN ALL WE NEED IS A DALEK TO FLY IT.
LOOK OUT - IT'S AWAKE AGAIN!

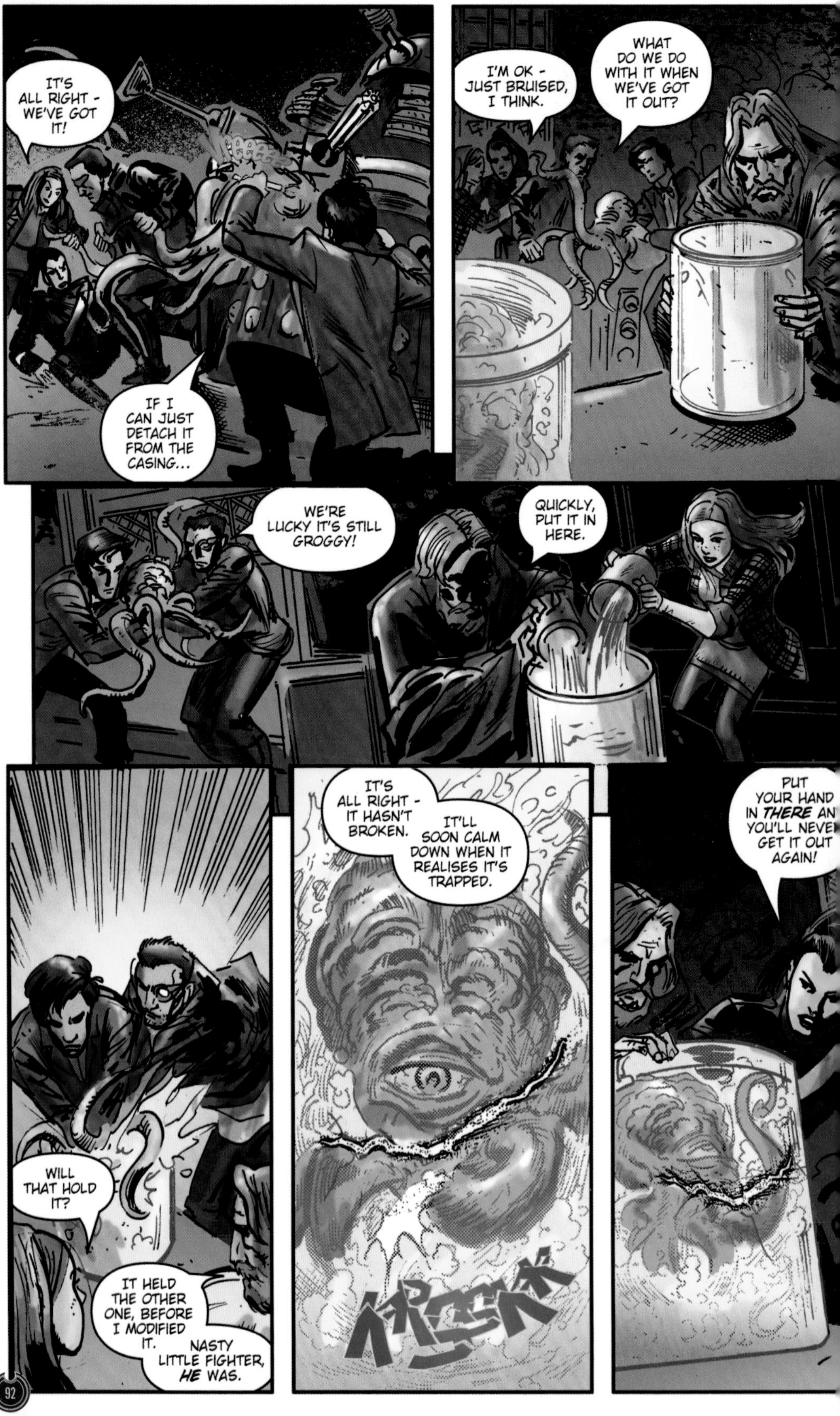
IT'S ALL RIGHT - WE'VE GOT IT!
IF I CAN JUST DETACH IT FROM THE CASING...
I'M OK - JUST BRUISED, I THINK.
WHAT DO WE DO WITH IT WHEN WE'VE GOT IT OUT?
WE'RE LUCKY IT'S STILL GROGGY!
QUICKLY, PUT IT IN HERE.
WILL THAT HOLD IT?
IT HELD THE OTHER ONE, BEFORE I MODIFIED IT.
NASTY LITTLE FIGHTER, HE WAS.
IT'S ALL RIGHT - IT HASN'T BROKEN.
IT'LL SOON CALM DOWN WHEN IT REALISES IT'S TRAPPED.
PUT YOUR HAND IN THERE AN YOU'LL NEVE GET IT OUT AGAIN!

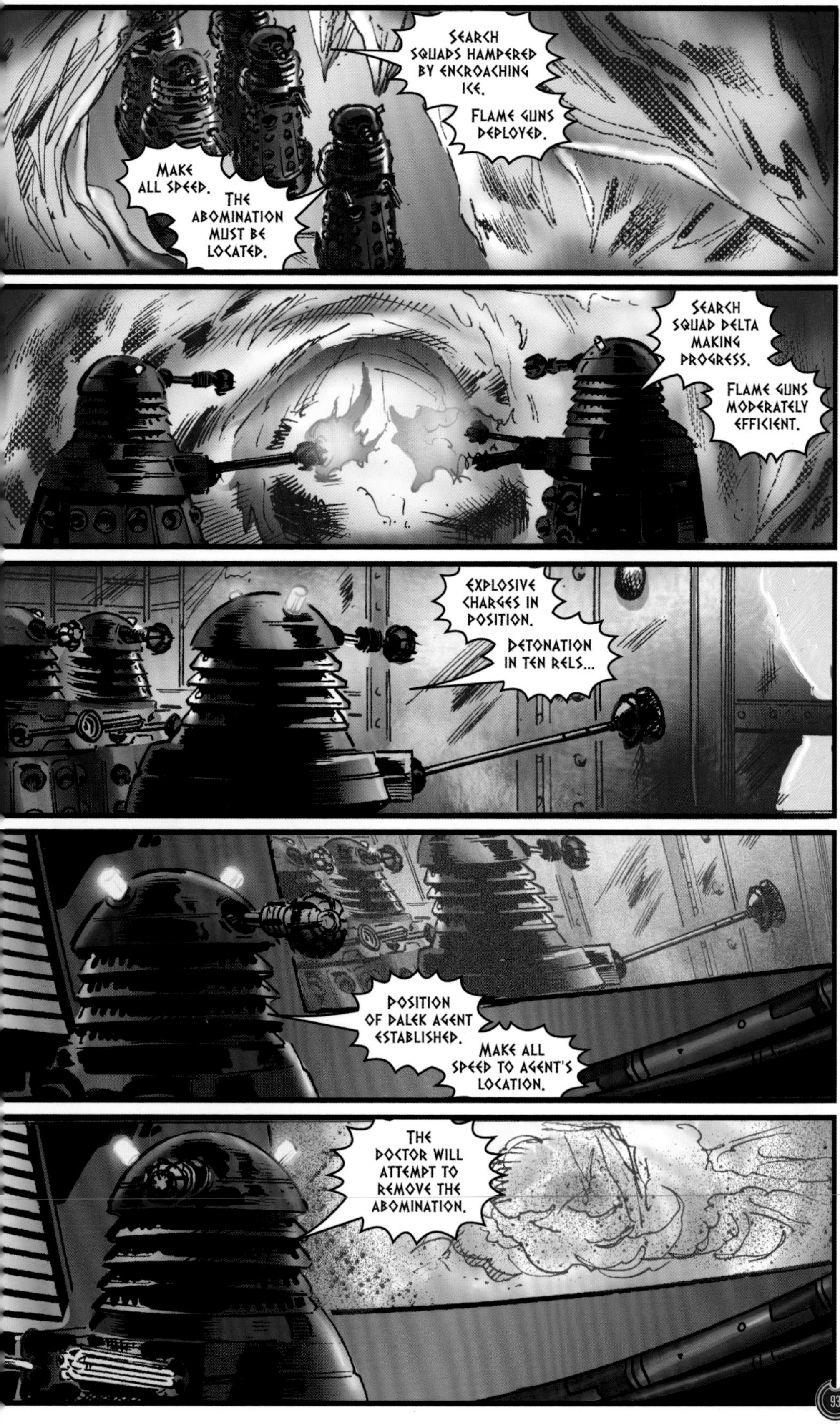
SEARCH SQUADS HAMPERED BY ENCROACHING ICE.
FLAME GUNS DEPLOYED.
MAKE ALL SPEED.
THE ABOMINATION MUST BE LOCATED.
SEARCH SQUAD DELTA MAKING PROGRESS.
FLAME GUNS MODERATELY EFFICIENT.
EXPLOSIVE CHARGES IN POSITION.
DETONATION IN TEN RELS...
POSITION OF DALEK AGENT ESTABLISHED.
MAKE ALL SPEED TO AGENT'S LOCATION.
THE DOCTOR WILL ATTEMPT TO REMOVE THE ABOMINATION.

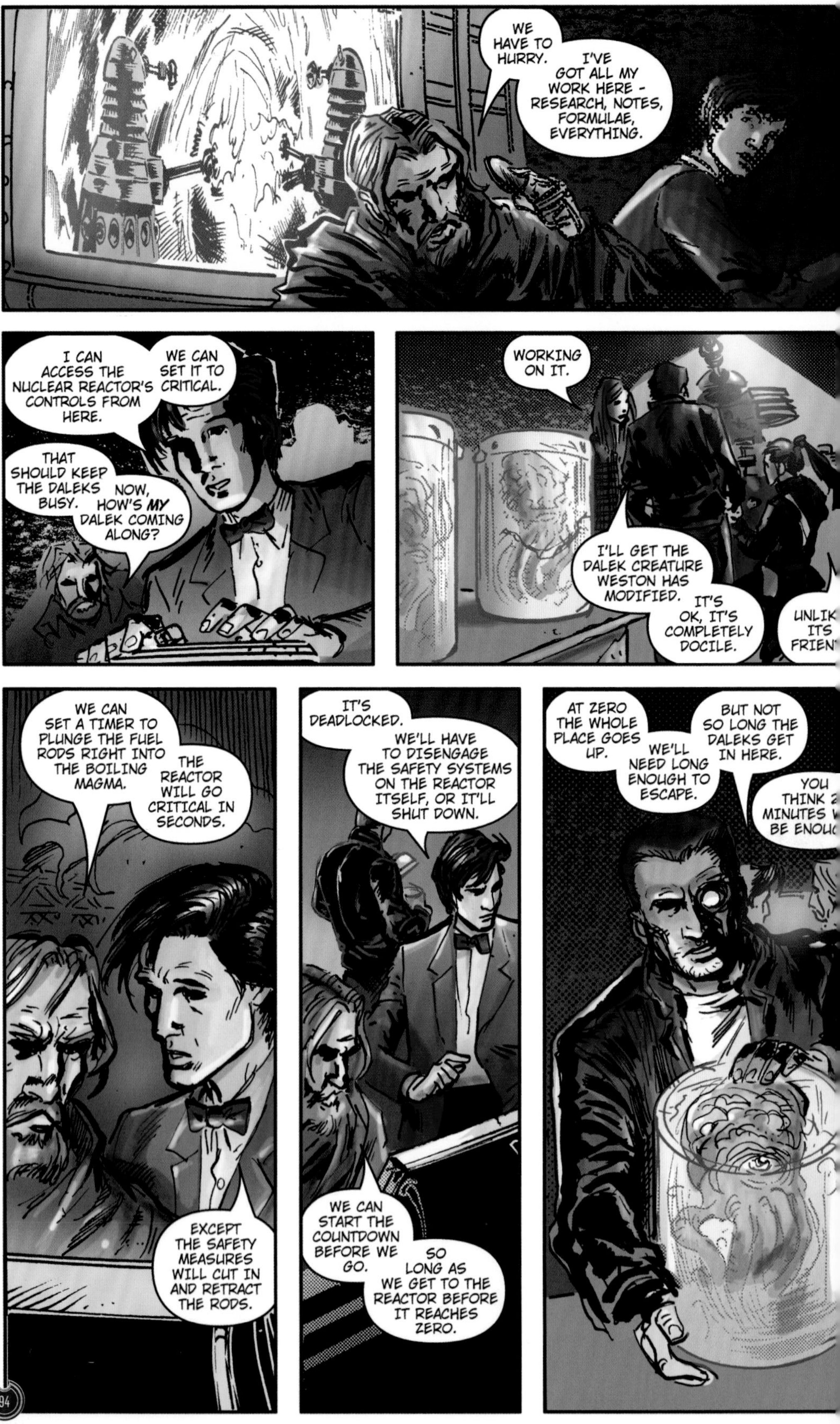

WE HAVE TO HURRY.
I'VE GOT ALL MY WORK HERE - RESEARCH, NOTES, FORMULAE, EVERYTHING.
I CAN ACCESS THE NUCLEAR REACTOR'S CONTROLS FROM HERE.
WE CAN SET IT TO CRITICAL.
THAT SHOULD KEEP THE DALEKS BUSY.
NOW, HOW'S *MY* DALEK COMING ALONG?
WORKING ON IT.
I'LL GET THE DALEK CREATURE WESTON HAS MODIFIED.
IT'S OK, IT'S COMPLETELY DOCILE.
UNLIK ITS FRIEN
WE CAN SET A TIMER TO PLUNGE THE FUEL RODS RIGHT INTO THE BOILING MAGMA.
THE REACTOR WILL GO CRITICAL IN SECONDS.
EXCEPT THE SAFETY MEASURES WILL CUT IN AND RETRACT THE RODS.
IT'S DEADLOCKED.
WE'LL HAVE TO DISENGAGE THE SAFETY SYSTEMS ON THE REACTOR ITSELF, OR IT'LL SHUT DOWN.
WE CAN START THE COUNTDOWN BEFORE WE GO.
SO LONG AS WE GET TO THE REACTOR BEFORE IT REACHES ZERO.
AT ZERO THE WHOLE PLACE GOES UP.
WE'LL NEED LONG ENOUGH TO ESCAPE.
BUT NOT SO LONG THE DALEKS GET IN HERE.
YOU THINK 2 MINUTES W BE ENOUG

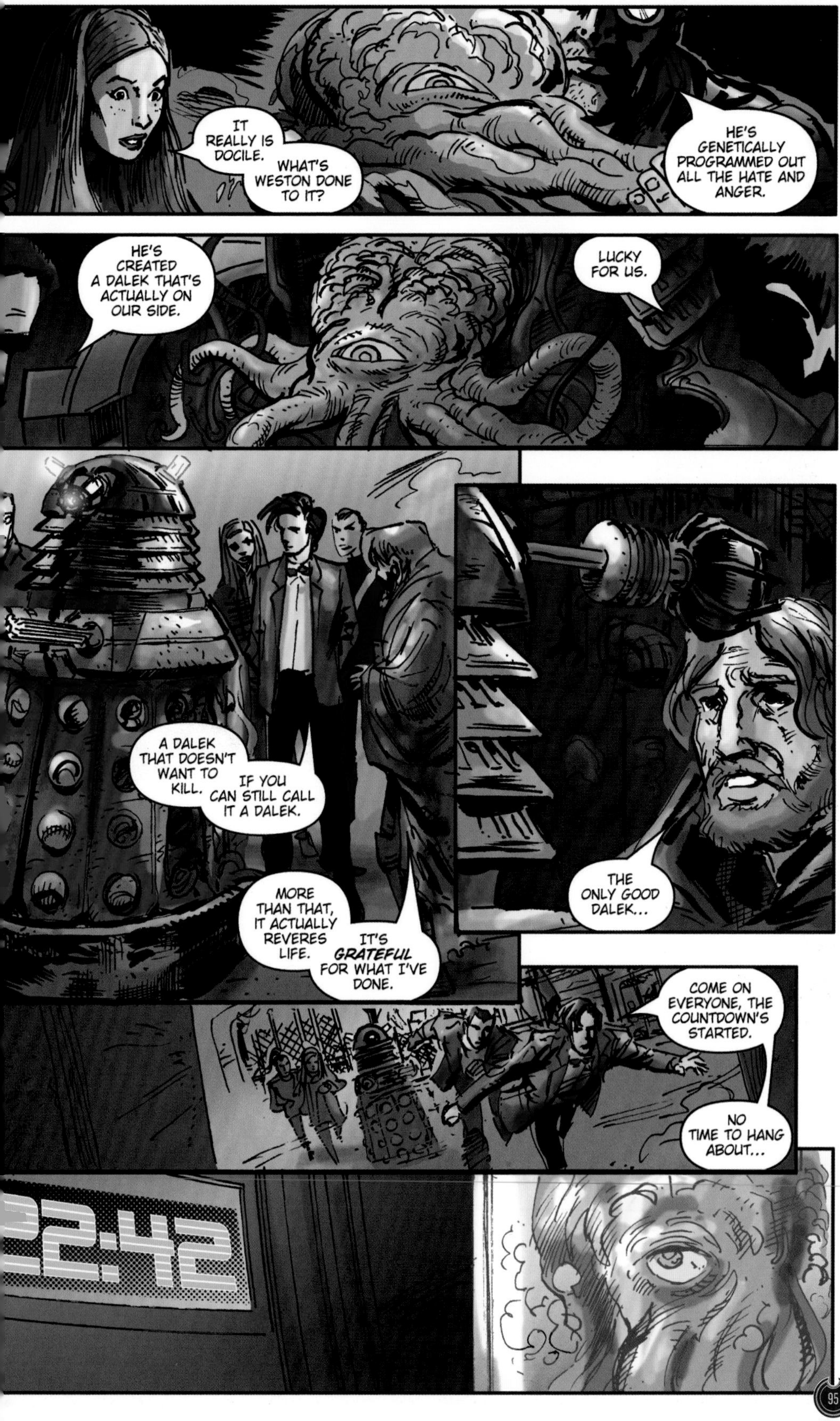
IT REALLY IS DOCILE.
WHAT'S WESTON DONE TO IT?
HE'S GENETICALLY PROGRAMMED OUT ALL THE HATE AND ANGER.
HE'S CREATED A DALEK THAT'S ACTUALLY ON OUR SIDE.
LUCKY FOR US.
A DALEK THAT DOESN'T WANT TO KILL.
IF YOU CAN STILL CALL IT A DALEK.
MORE THAN THAT, IT ACTUALLY REVERES LIFE.
IT'S *GRATEFUL* FOR WHAT I'VE DONE.
THE ONLY GOOD DALEK...
COME ON EVERYONE, THE COUNTDOWN'S STARTED.
NO TIME TO HANG ABOUT...
22:42

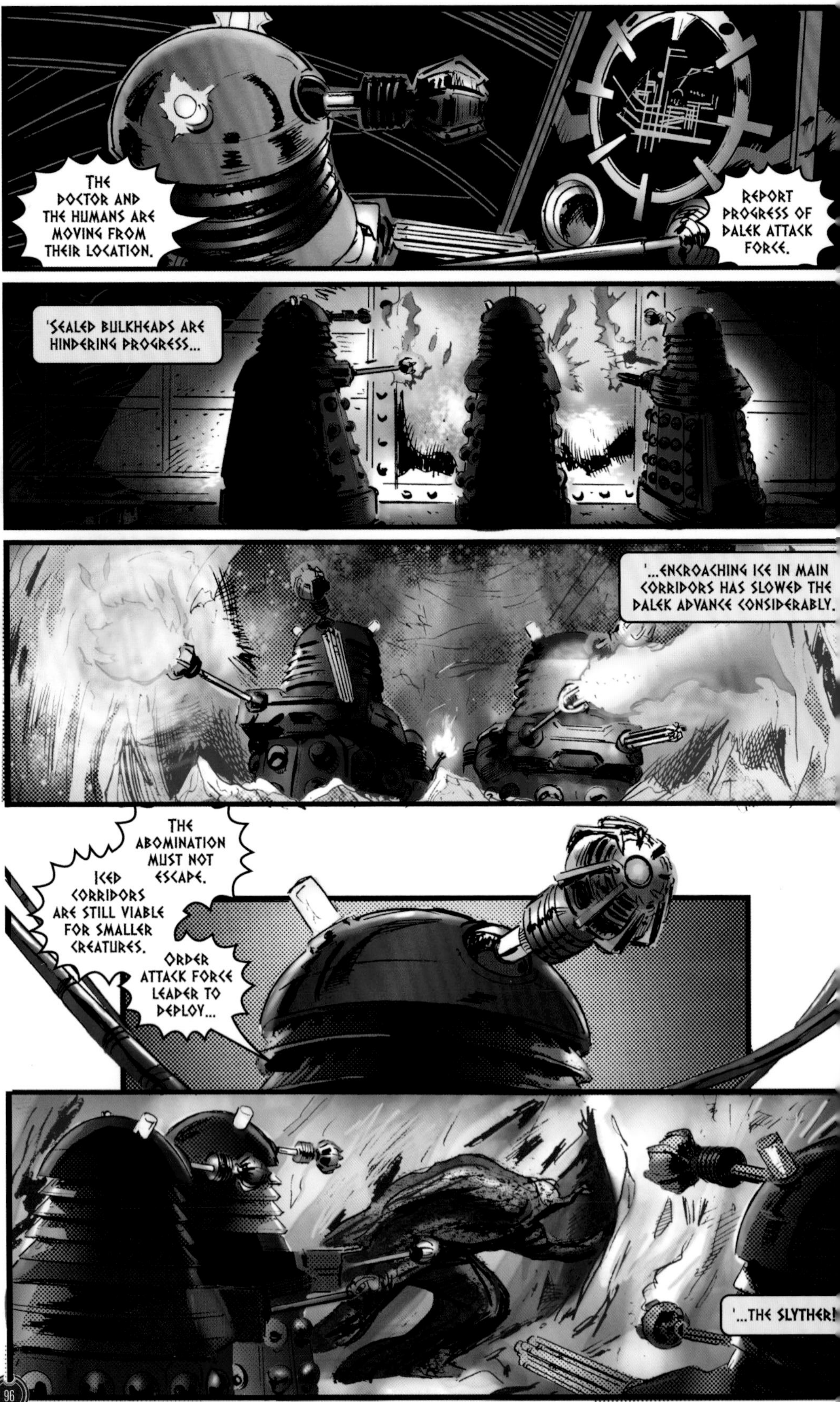
THE DOCTOR AND THE HUMANS ARE MOVING FROM THEIR LOCATION.
REPORT PROGRESS OF DALEK ATTACK FORCE.
'SEALED BULKHEADS ARE HINDERING PROGRESS...
'...ENCROACHING ICE IN MAIN CORRIDORS HAS SLOWED THE DALEK ADVANCE CONSIDERABLY.
THE ABOMINATION MUST NOT ESCAPE.
ICED CORRIDORS ARE STILL VIABLE FOR SMALLER CREATURES.
ORDER ATTACK FORCE LEADER TO DEPLOY...
'...THE SLYTHER!

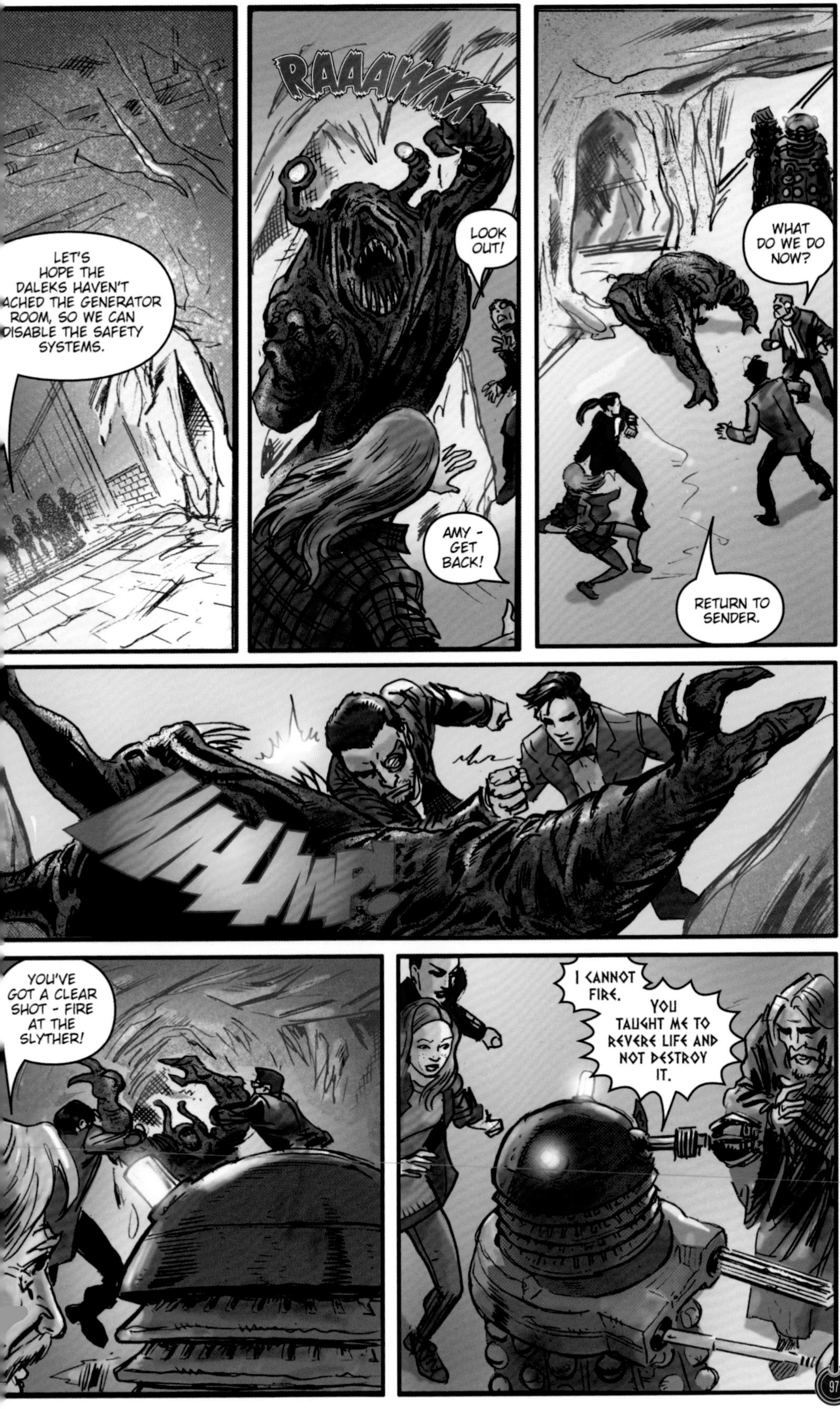
LET'S HOPE THE DALEKS HAVEN'T ACHED THE GENERATOR ROOM, SO WE CAN DISABLE THE SAFETY SYSTEMS.
RAAAWKK
LOOK OUT!
AMY - GET BACK!
WHAT DO WE DO NOW?
RETURN TO SENDER.
YOU'VE GOT A CLEAR SHOT - FIRE AT THE SLYTHER!
I CANNOT FIRE.
YOU TAUGHT ME TO REVERE LIFE AND NOT DESTROY IT.

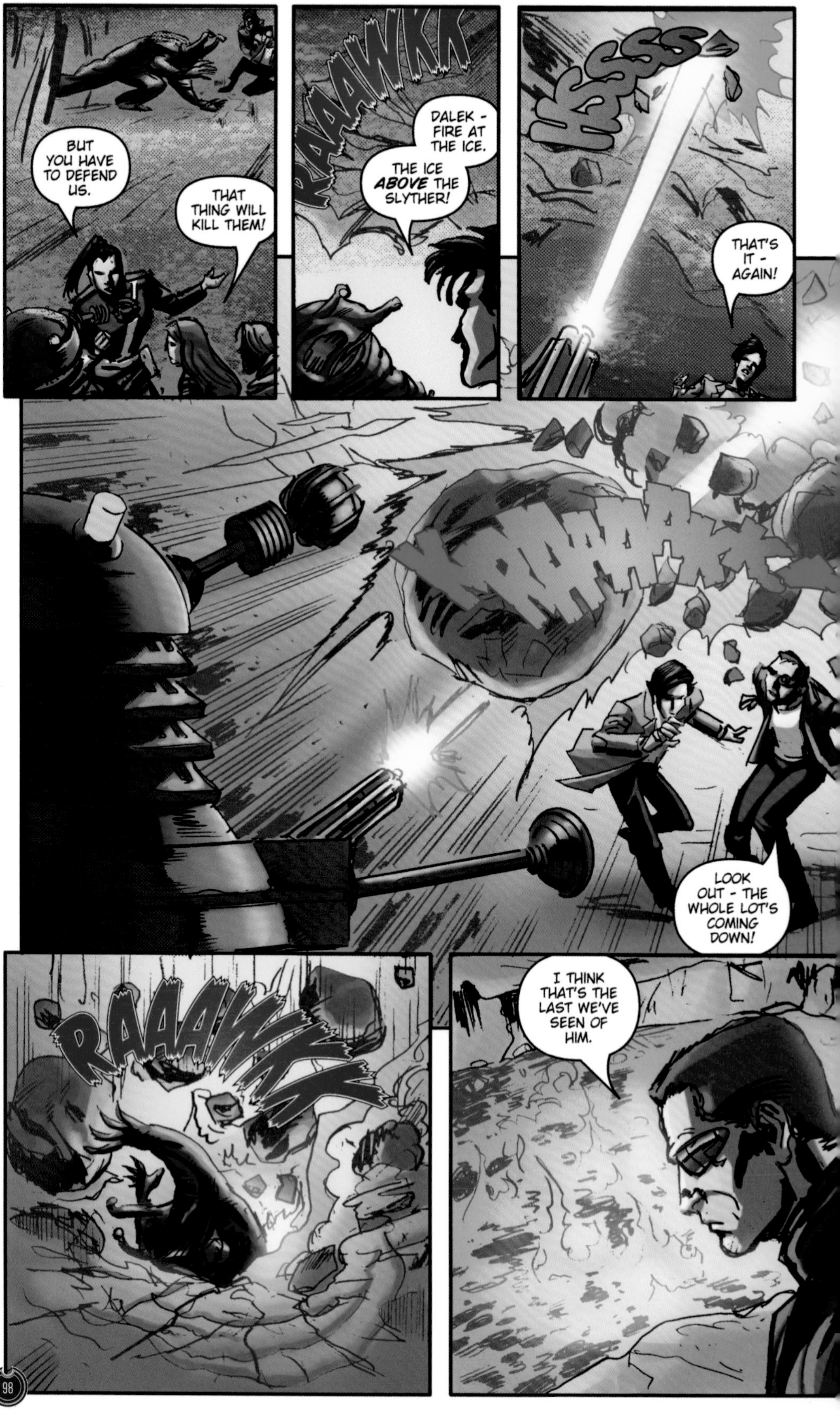
BUT YOU HAVE TO DEFEND US.
THAT THING WILL KILL THEM!
RAAAWKK
DALEK - FIRE AT THE ICE.
THE ICE ABOVE THE SLYTHER!
HSSSS
THAT'S IT - AGAIN!
LOOK OUT - THE WHOLE LOT'S COMING DOWN!
RAAAWKK
I THINK THAT'S THE LAST WE'VE SEEN OF HIM.

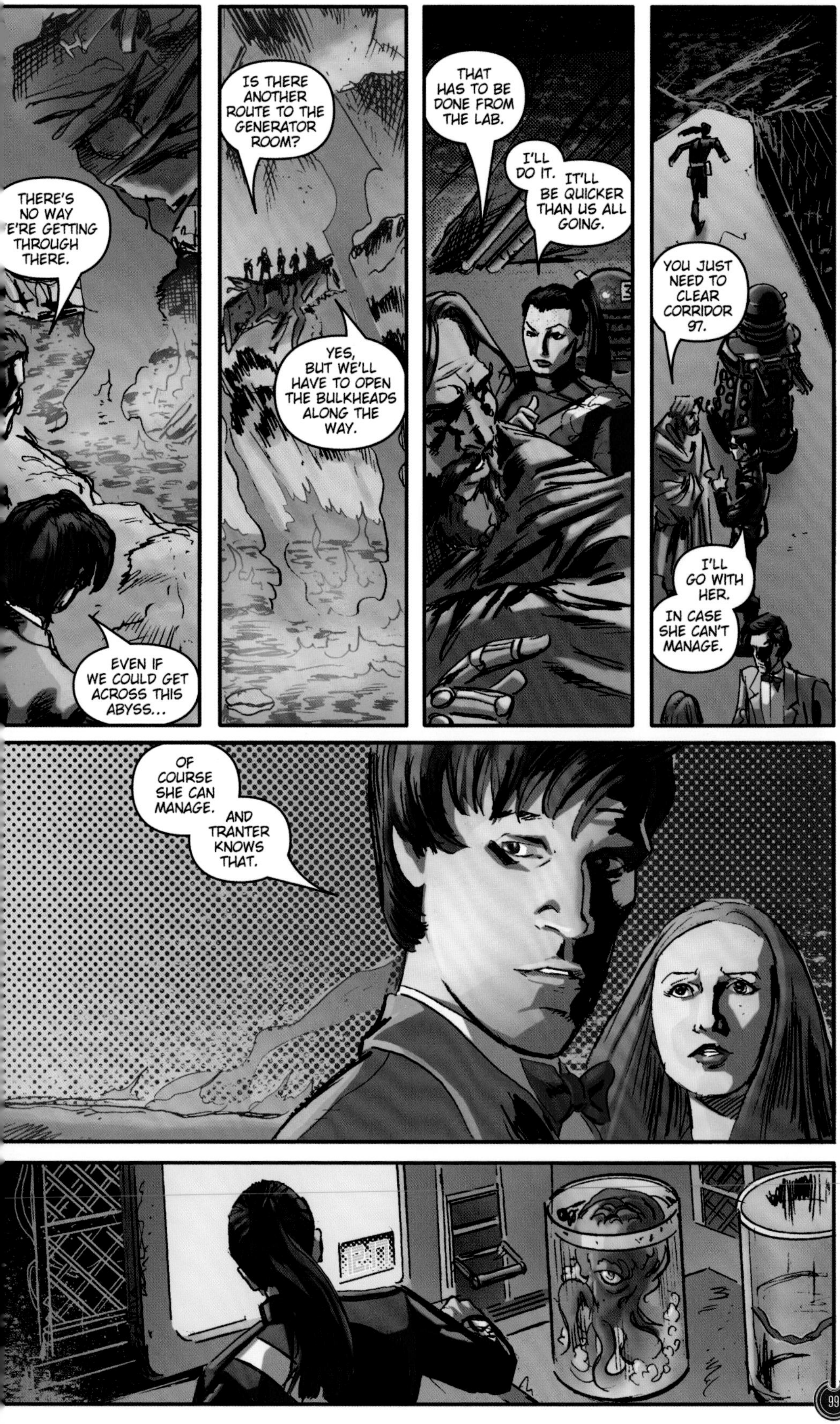

THERE'S NO WAY WE'RE GETTING THROUGH THERE.
EVEN IF WE COULD GET ACROSS THIS ABYSS...
IS THERE ANOTHER ROUTE TO THE GENERATOR ROOM?
YES, BUT WE'LL HAVE TO OPEN THE BULKHEADS ALONG THE WAY.
THAT HAS TO BE DONE FROM THE LAB.
I'LL DO IT.
IT'LL BE QUICKER THAN US ALL GOING.
YOU JUST NEED TO CLEAR CORRIDOR 97.
I'LL GO WITH HER.
IN CASE SHE CAN'T MANAGE.
OF COURSE SHE CAN MANAGE.
AND TRANTER KNOWS THAT.

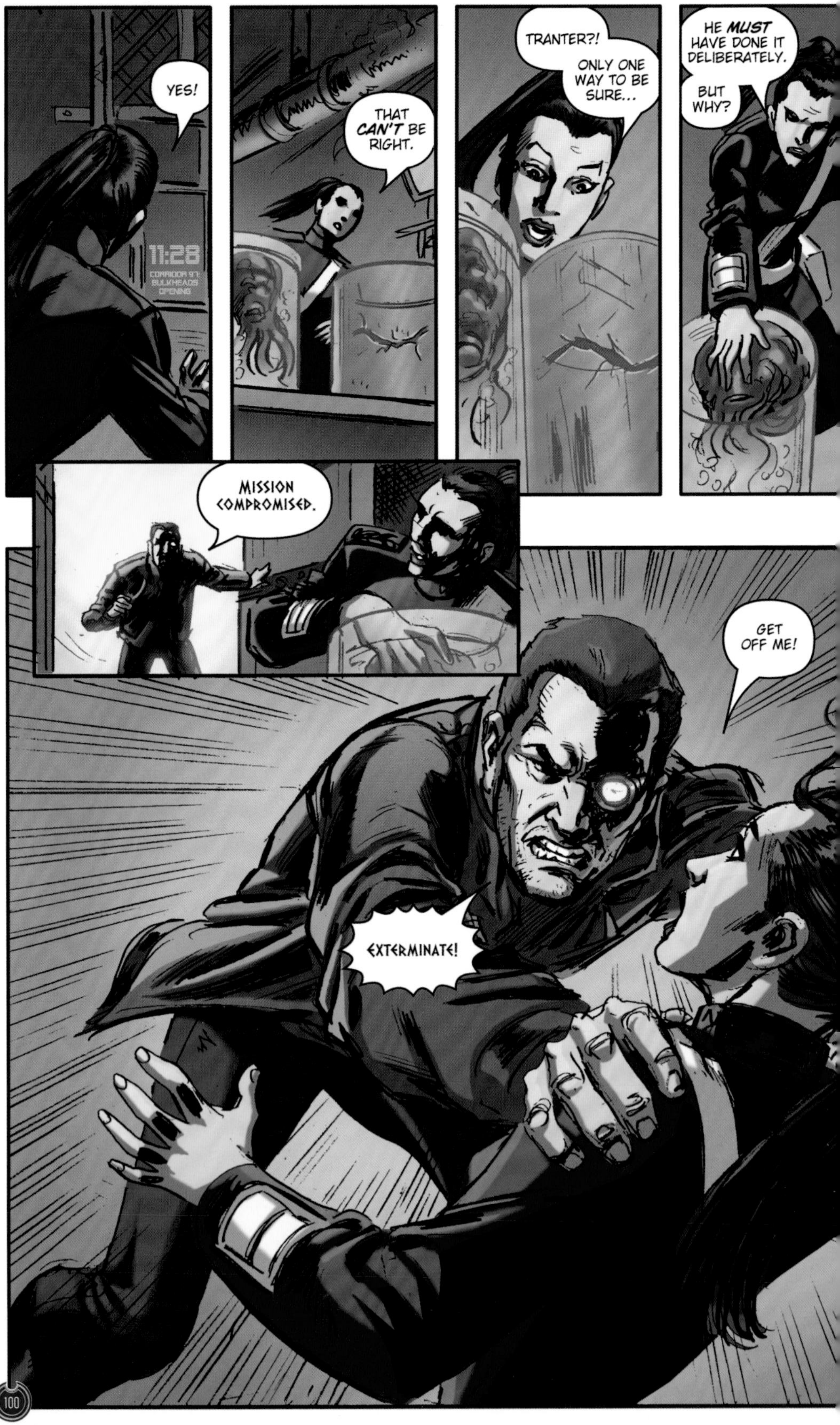
YES!
11:28
CORRIDOR 97: BULKHEADS OPENING
THAT CAN'T BE RIGHT.
TRANTER?!
ONLY ONE WAY TO BE SURE...
HE MUST HAVE DONE IT DELIBERATELY.
BUT WHY?
MISSION COMPROMISED.
GET OFF ME!
EXTERMINATE!

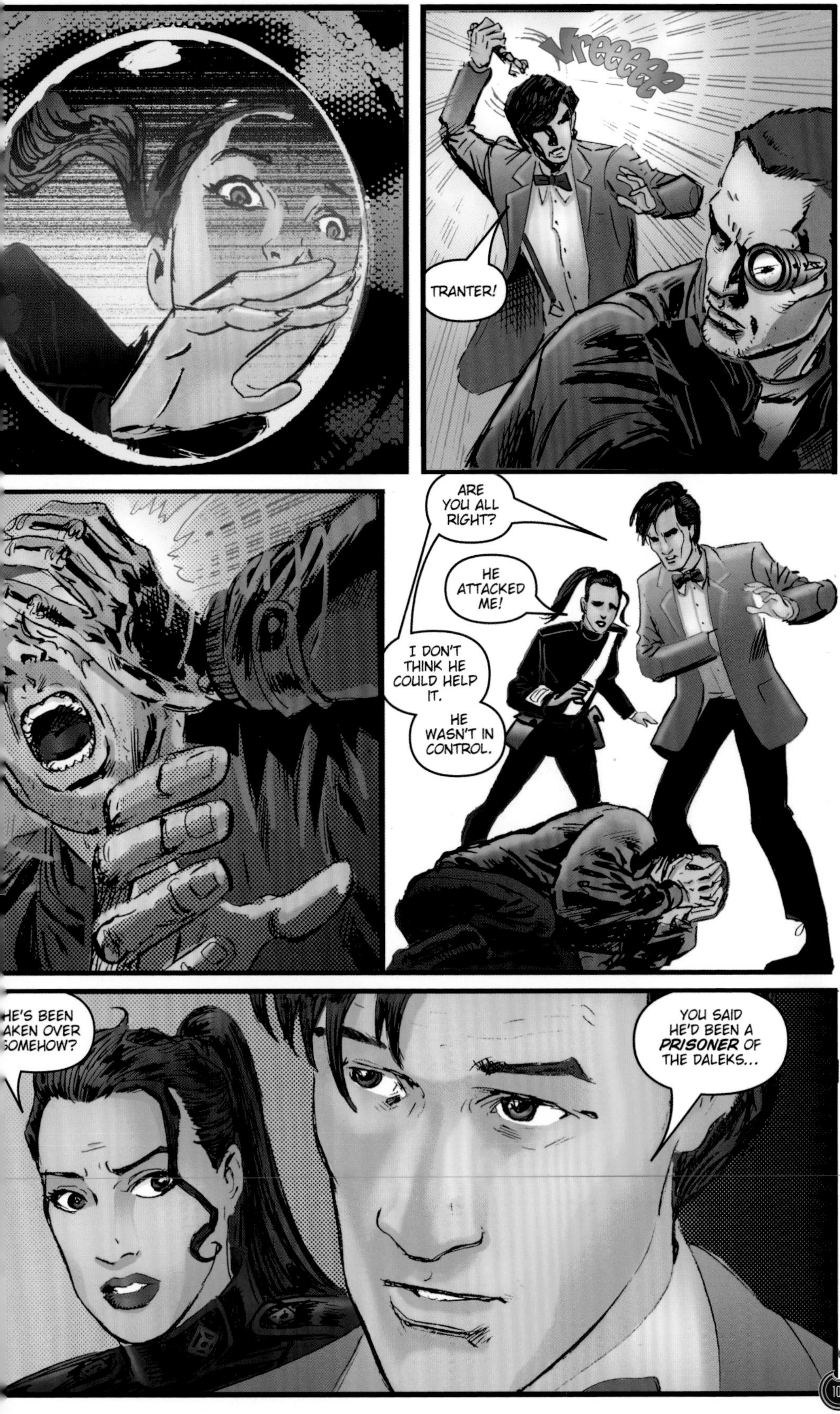
VREEEEEE
TRANTER!
ARE YOU ALL RIGHT?
HE ATTACKED ME!
I DON'T THINK HE COULD HELP IT.
HE WASN'T IN CONTROL.
HE'S BEEN AKEN OVER SOMEHOW?
YOU SAID HE'D BEEN A PRISONER OF THE DALEKS...

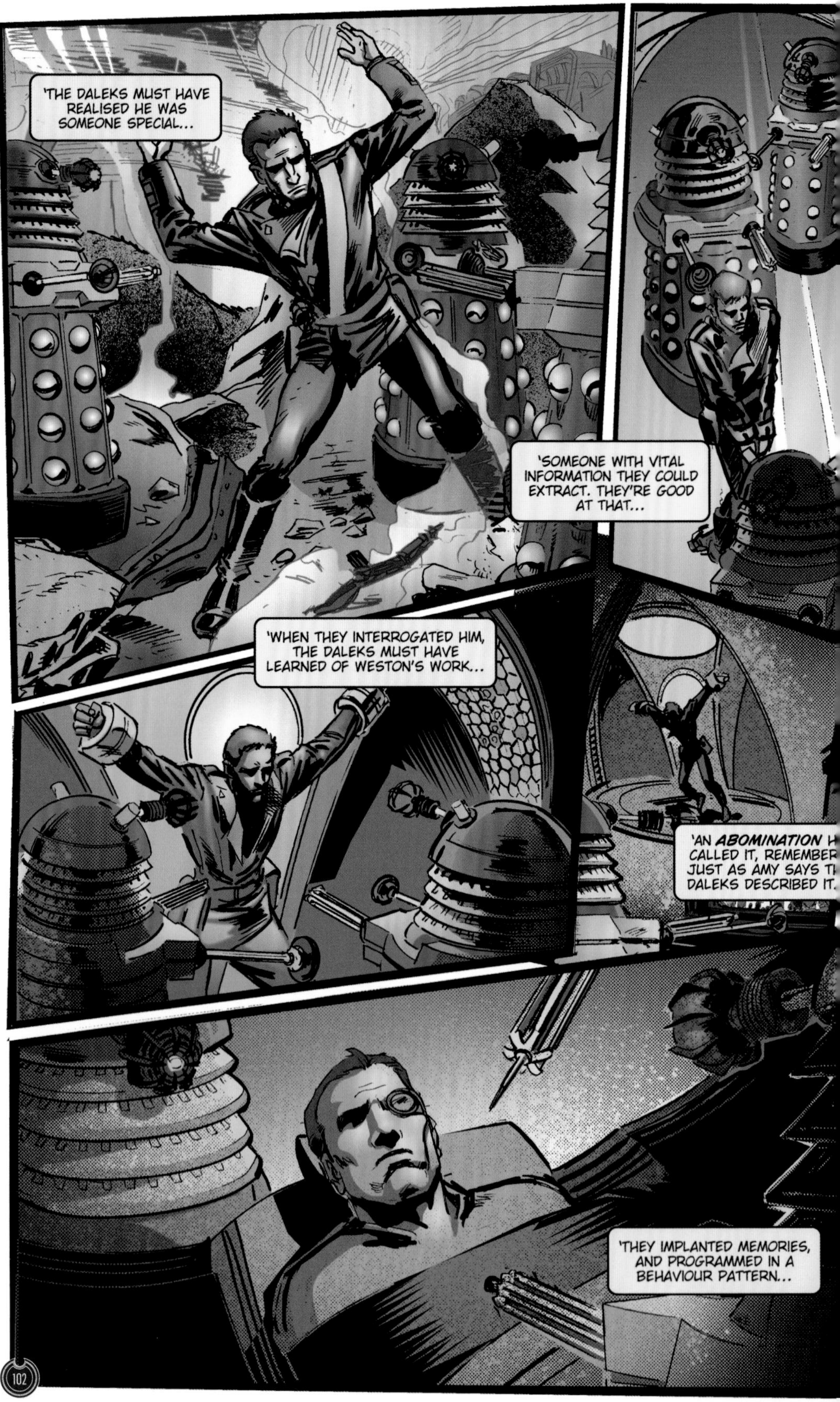
'THE DALEKS MUST HAVE REALISED HE WAS SOMEONE SPECIAL...
'SOMEONE WITH VITAL INFORMATION THEY COULD EXTRACT. THEY'RE GOOD AT THAT...
'WHEN THEY INTERROGATED HIM, THE DALEKS MUST HAVE LEARNED OF WESTON'S WORK...
'AN ABOMINATION H CALLED IT, REMEMBER JUST AS AMY SAYS T DALEKS DESCRIBED IT.
'THEY IMPLANTED MEMORIES, AND PROGRAMMED IN A BEHAVIOUR PATTERN...

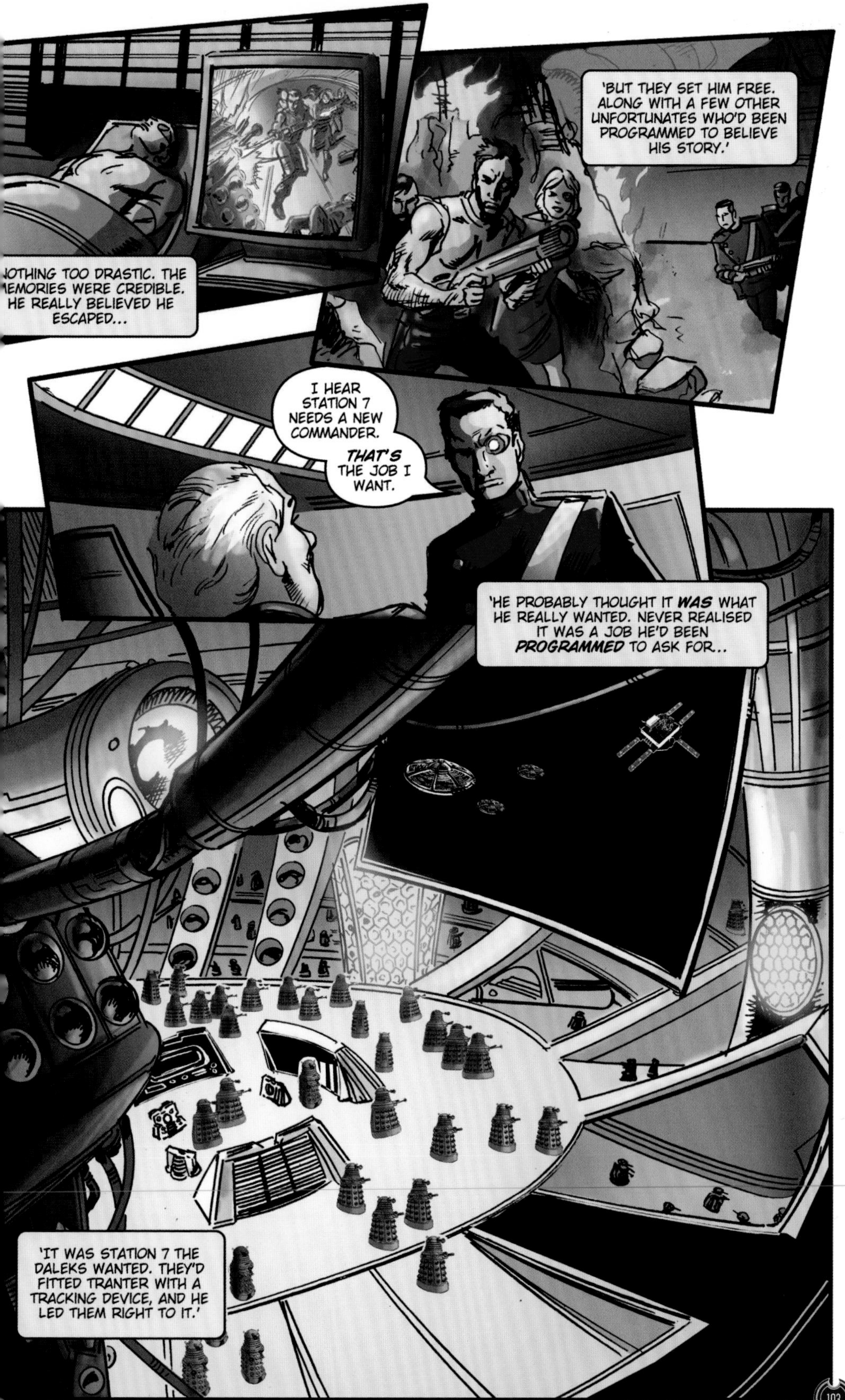

'BUT THEY SET HIM FREE. ALONG WITH A FEW OTHER UNFORTUNATES WHO'D BEEN PROGRAMMED TO BELIEVE HIS STORY.'
NOTHING TOO DRASTIC. THE MEMORIES WERE CREDIBLE. HE REALLY BELIEVED HE ESCAPED...
I HEAR STATION 7 NEEDS A NEW COMMANDER.
THAT'S THE JOB I WANT.
'HE PROBABLY THOUGHT IT WAS WHAT HE REALLY WANTED. NEVER REALISED IT WAS A JOB HE'D BEEN PROGRAMMED TO ASK FOR...
'IT WAS STATION 7 THE DALEKS WANTED. THEY'D FITTED TRANTER WITH A TRACKING DEVICE, AND HE LED THEM RIGHT TO IT.'

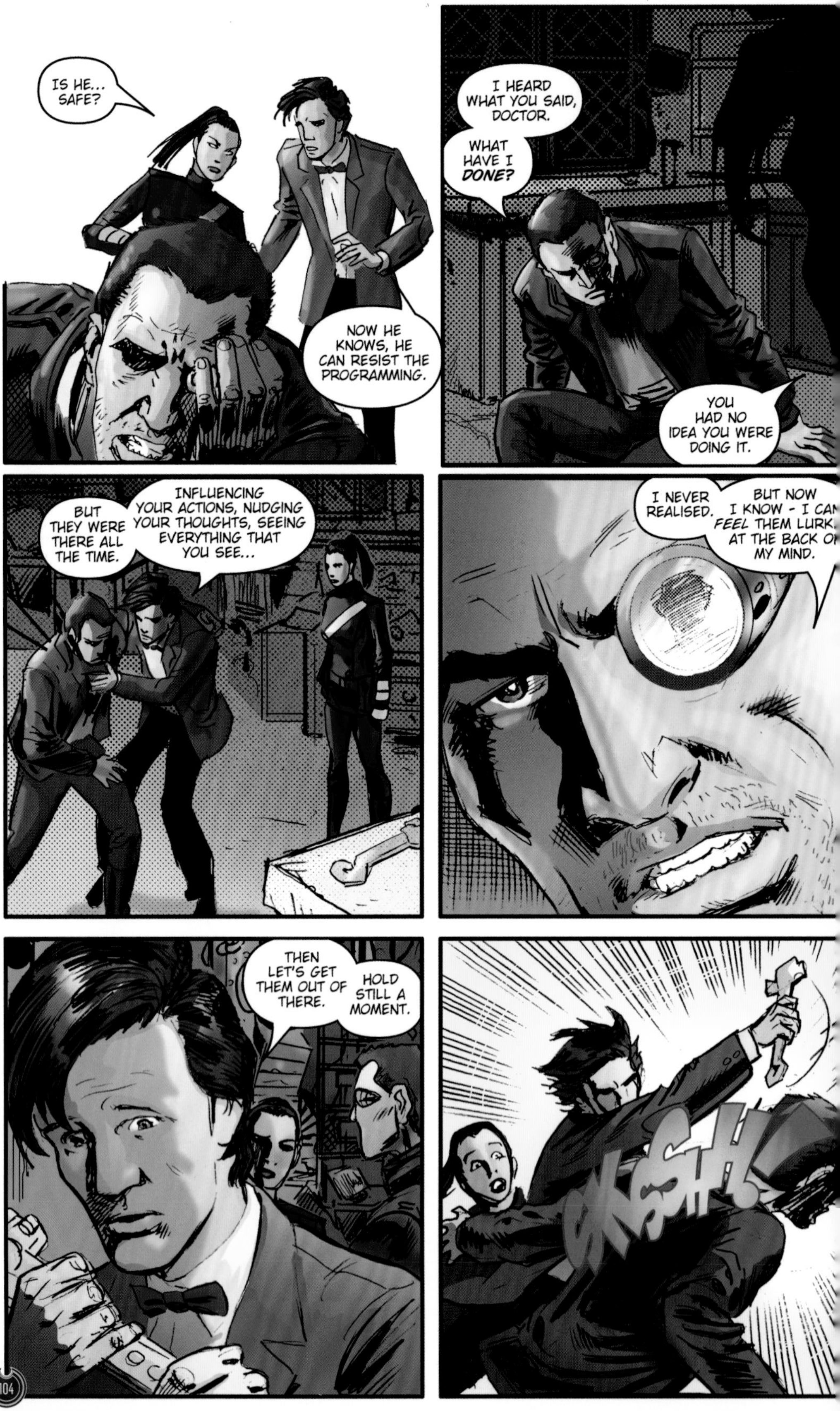
IS HE... SAFE?
NOW HE KNOWS, HE CAN RESIST THE PROGRAMMING.
I HEARD WHAT YOU SAID, DOCTOR.
WHAT HAVE I DONE?
YOU HAD NO IDEA YOU WERE DOING IT.
BUT THEY WERE THERE ALL THE TIME.
INFLUENCING YOUR ACTIONS, NUDGING YOUR THOUGHTS, SEEING EVERYTHING THAT YOU SEE...
I NEVER REALISED.
BUT NOW I KNOW - I CAN FEEL THEM LURK AT THE BACK OF MY MIND.
THEN LET'S GET THEM OUT OF THERE.
HOLD STILL A MOMENT.

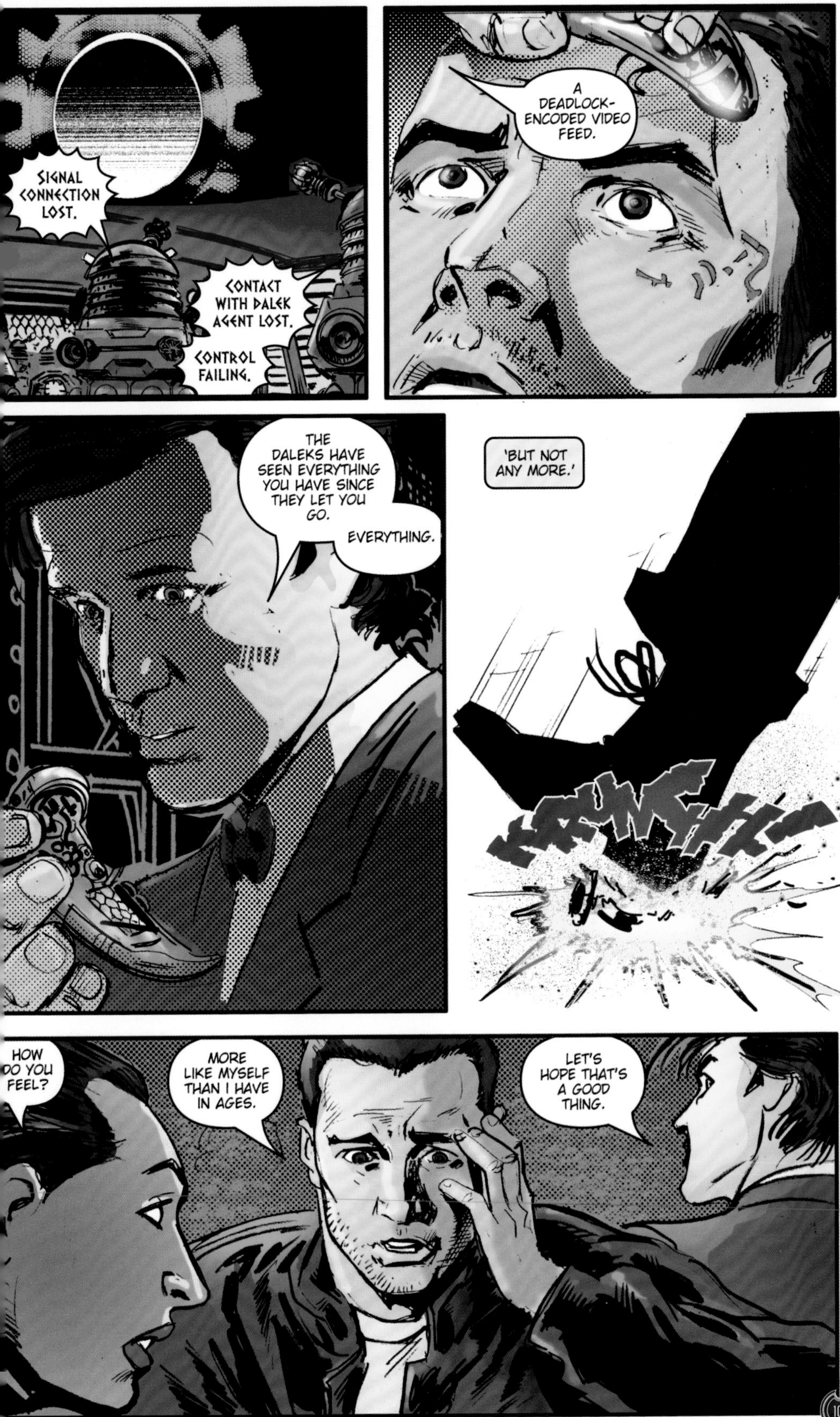
SIGNAL CONNECTION LOST.
CONTACT WITH DALEK AGENT LOST.
CONTROL FAILING.
A DEADLOCK-ENCODED VIDEO FEED.
THE DALEKS HAVE SEEN EVERYTHING YOU HAVE SINCE THEY LET YOU GO.
EVERYTHING.
'BUT NOT ANY MORE.'
HOW DO YOU FEEL?
MORE LIKE MYSELF THAN I HAVE IN AGES.
LET'S HOPE THAT'S A GOOD THING.

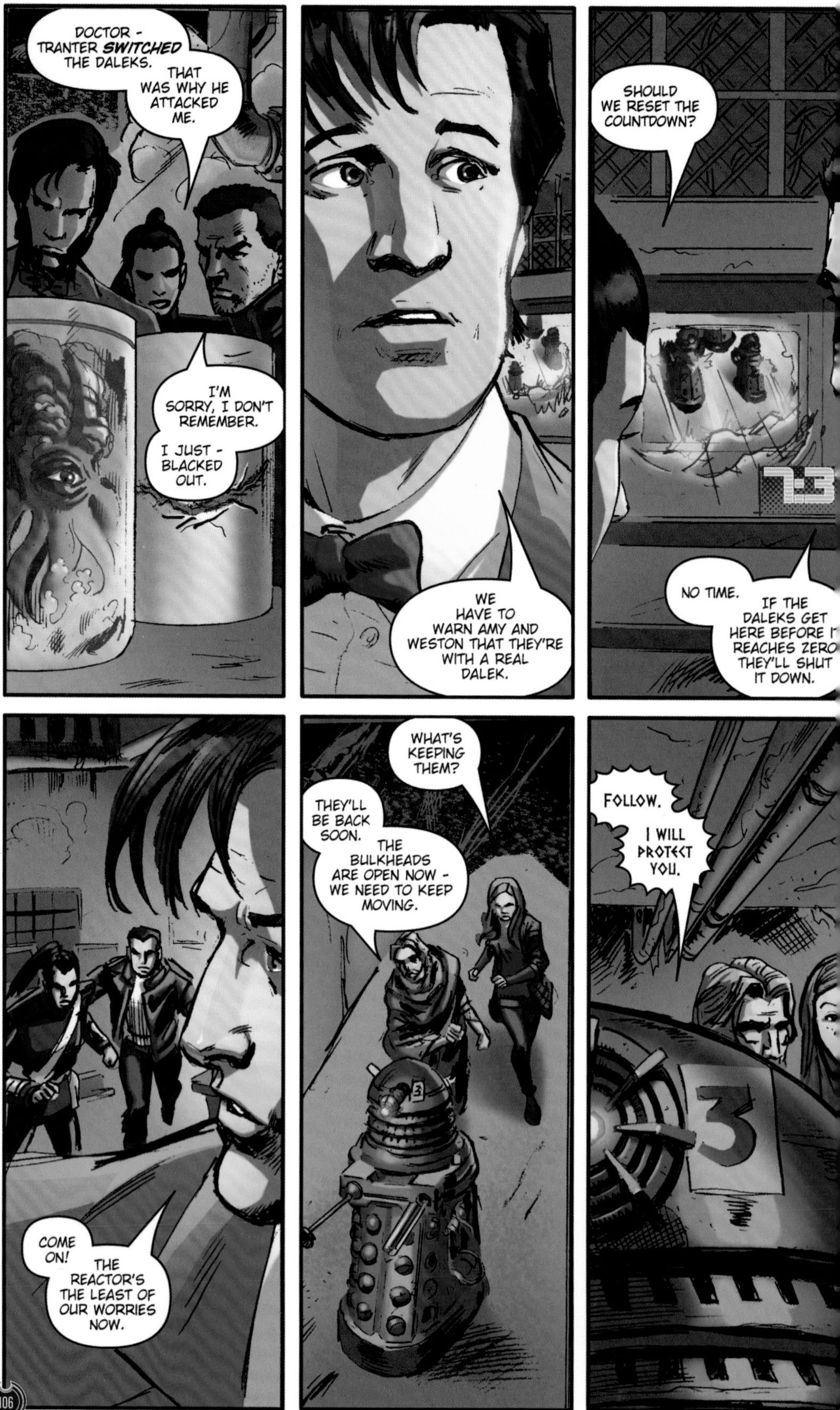
DOCTOR - TRANTER SWITCHED THE DALEKS.
THAT WAS WHY HE ATTACKED ME.
I'M SORRY, I DON'T REMEMBER.
I JUST - BLACKED OUT.
WE HAVE TO WARN AMY AND WESTON THAT THEY'RE WITH A REAL DALEK.
SHOULD WE RESET THE COUNTDOWN?
NO TIME.
IF THE DALEKS GET HERE BEFORE I' REACHES ZERO THEY'LL SHUT IT DOWN.
COME ON!
THE REACTOR'S THE LEAST OF OUR WORRIES NOW.
WHAT'S KEEPING THEM?
THEY'LL BE BACK SOON.
THE BULKHEADS ARE OPEN NOW - WE NEED TO KEEP MOVING.
FOLLOW.
I WILL PROTECT YOU.

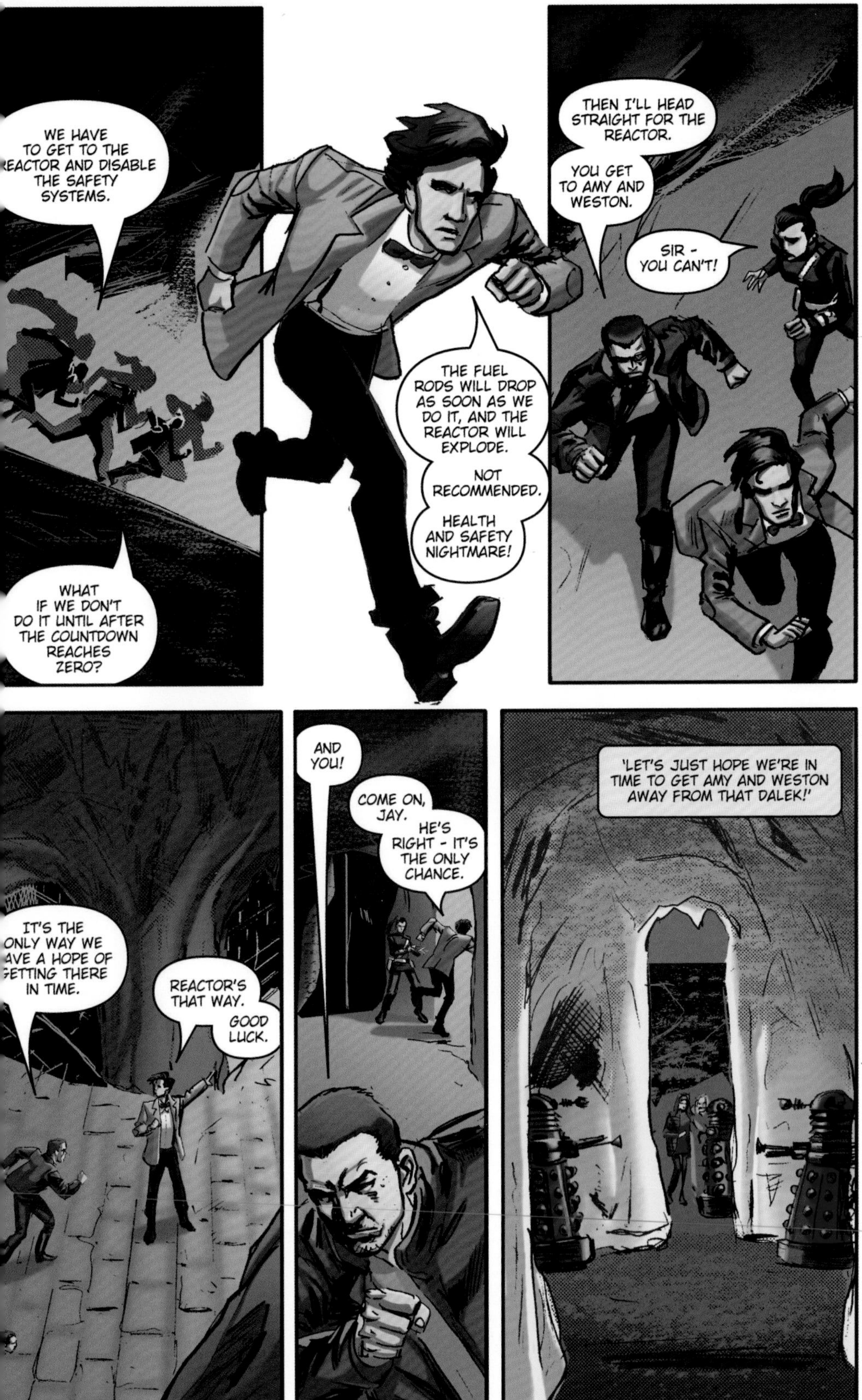
WE HAVE TO GET TO THE REACTOR AND DISABLE THE SAFETY SYSTEMS.
THE FUEL RODS WILL DROP AS SOON AS WE DO IT, AND THE REACTOR WILL EXPLODE.
NOT RECOMMENDED.
HEALTH AND SAFETY NIGHTMARE!
WHAT IF WE DON'T DO IT UNTIL AFTER THE COUNTDOWN REACHES ZERO?
THEN I'LL HEAD STRAIGHT FOR THE REACTOR.
YOU GET TO AMY AND WESTON.
SIR - YOU CAN'T!
IT'S THE ONLY WAY WE HAVE A HOPE OF GETTING THERE IN TIME.
REACTOR'S THAT WAY.
GOOD LUCK.
AND YOU!
COME ON, JAY.
HE'S RIGHT - IT'S THE ONLY CHANCE.
'LET'S JUST HOPE WE'RE IN TIME TO GET AMY AND WESTON AWAY FROM THAT DALEK!'

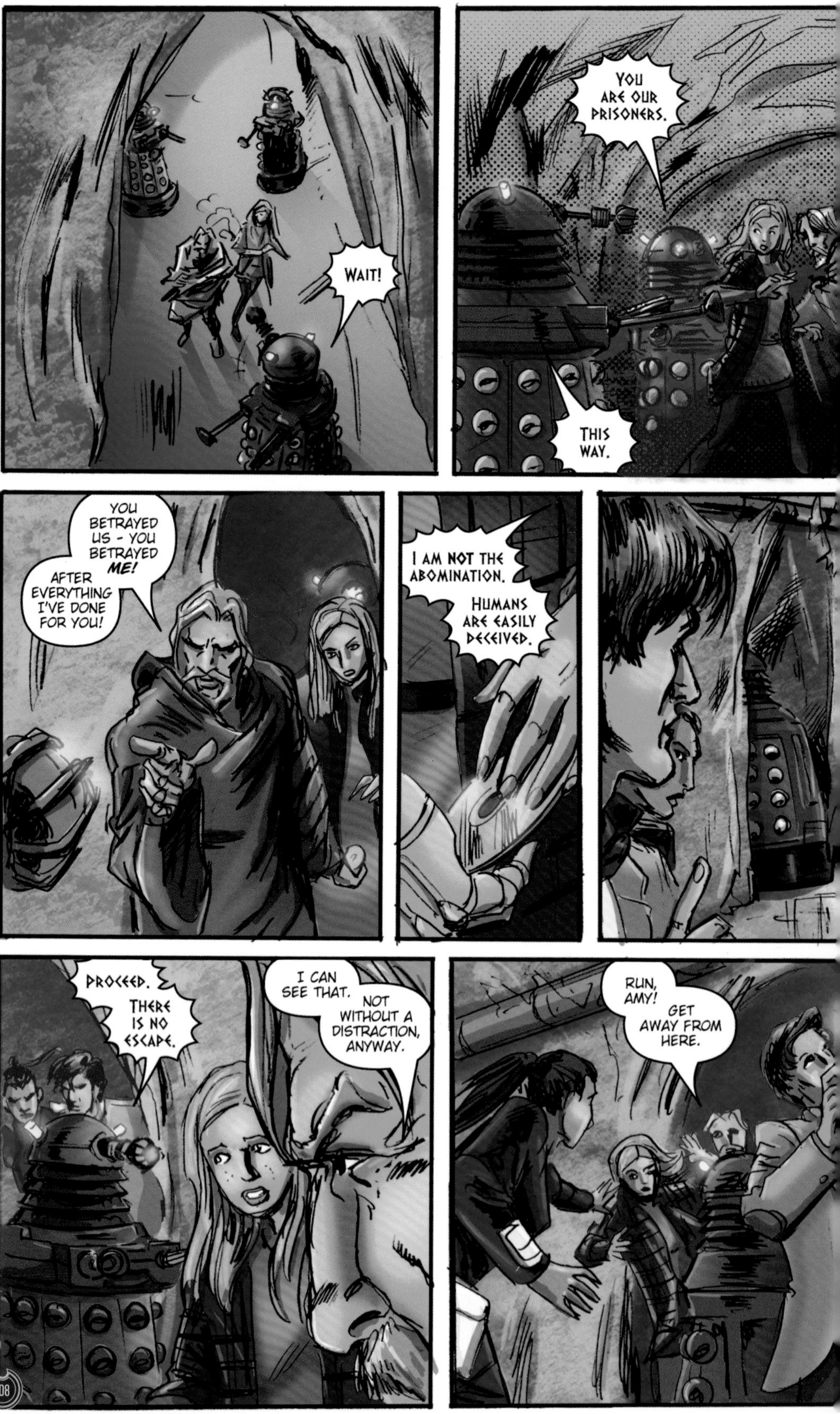
WAIT!
YOU ARE OUR PRISONERS.
THIS WAY.
YOU BETRAYED US - YOU BETRAYED ME!
AFTER EVERYTHING I'VE DONE FOR YOU!
I AM NOT THE ABOMINATION.
HUMANS ARE EASILY DECEIVED.
PROCEED.
THERE IS NO ESCAPE.
I CAN SEE THAT.
NOT WITHOUT A DISTRACTION, ANYWAY.
RUN, AMY!
GET AWAY FROM HERE.

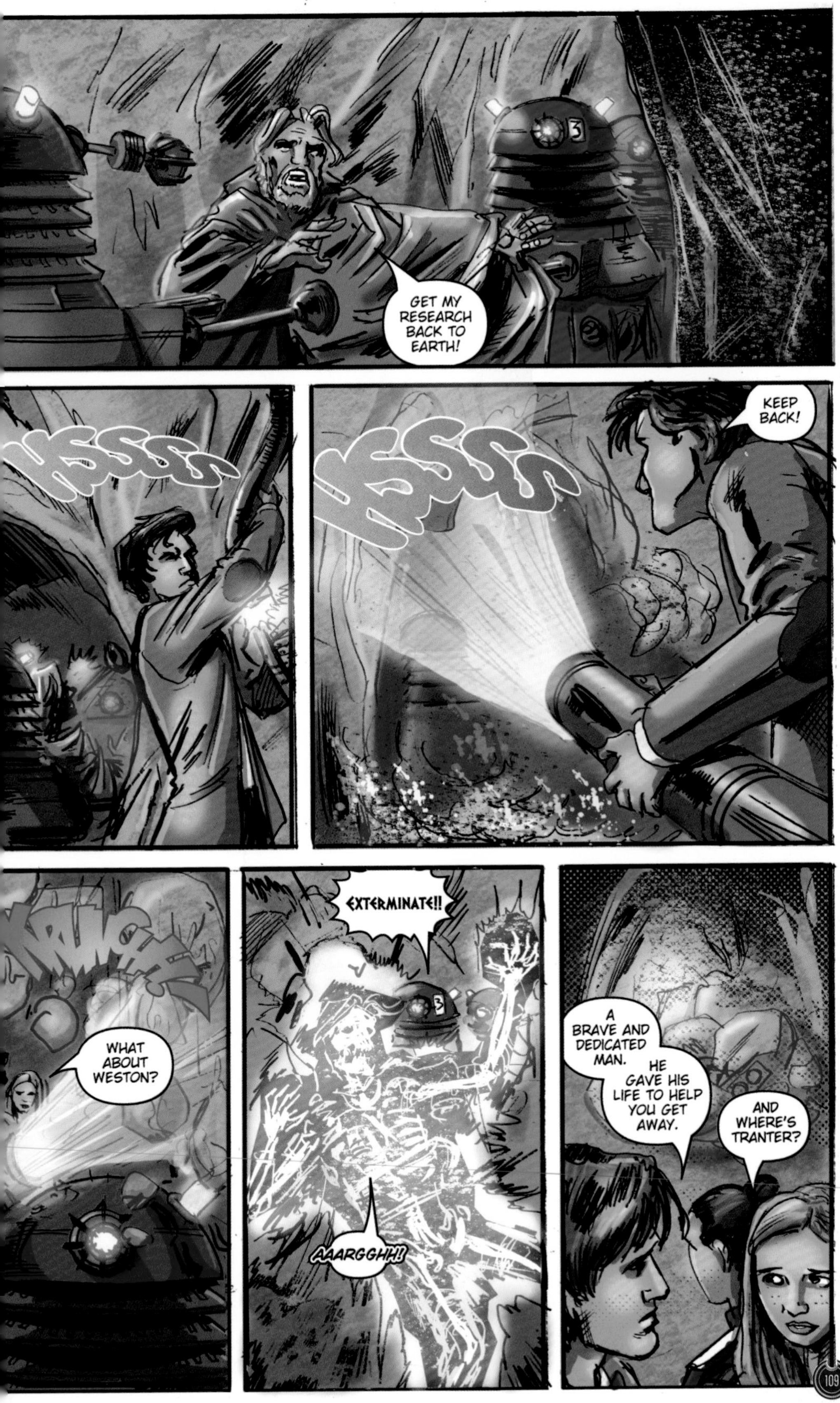
GET MY RESEARCH BACK TO EARTH!
KSSSS
KSSSS
KEEP BACK!
WHAT ABOUT WESTON?
EXTERMINATE!!
AAARGGHH!
A BRAVE AND DEDICATED MAN.
HE GAVE HIS LIFE TO HELP YOU GET AWAY.
AND WHERE'S TRANTER?

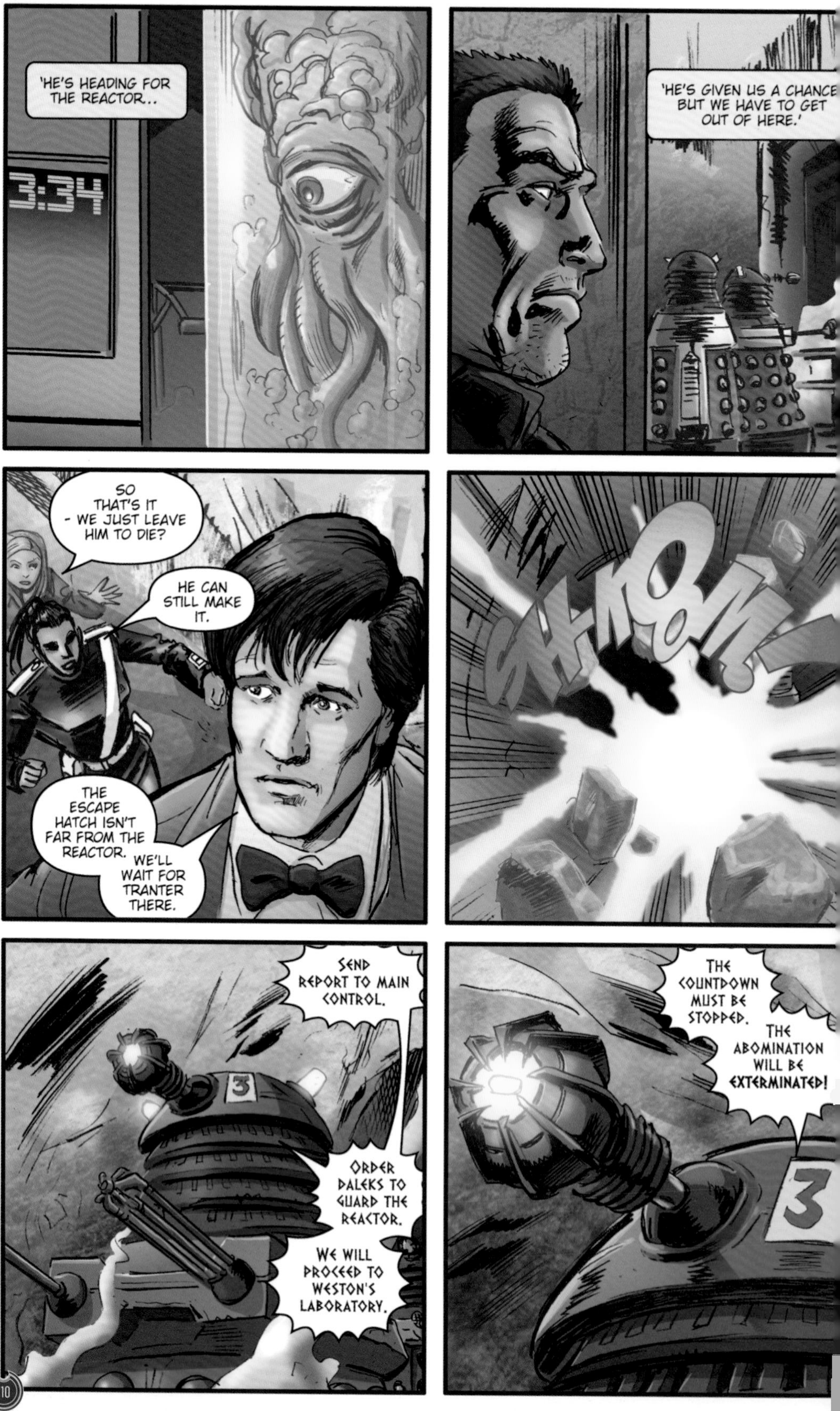

'HE'S HEADING FOR THE REACTOR..
3:34
'HE'S GIVEN US A CHANCE BUT WE HAVE TO GET OUT OF HERE.'
SO THAT'S IT - WE JUST LEAVE HIM TO DIE?
HE CAN STILL MAKE IT.
THE ESCAPE HATCH ISN'T FAR FROM THE REACTOR.
WE'LL WAIT FOR TRANTER THERE.
SEND REPORT TO MAIN CONTROL.
ORDER DALEKS TO GUARD THE REACTOR.
WE WILL PROCEED TO WESTON'S LABORATORY.
THE COUNTDOWN MUST BE STOPPED.
THE ABOMINATION WILL BE EXTERMINATED!

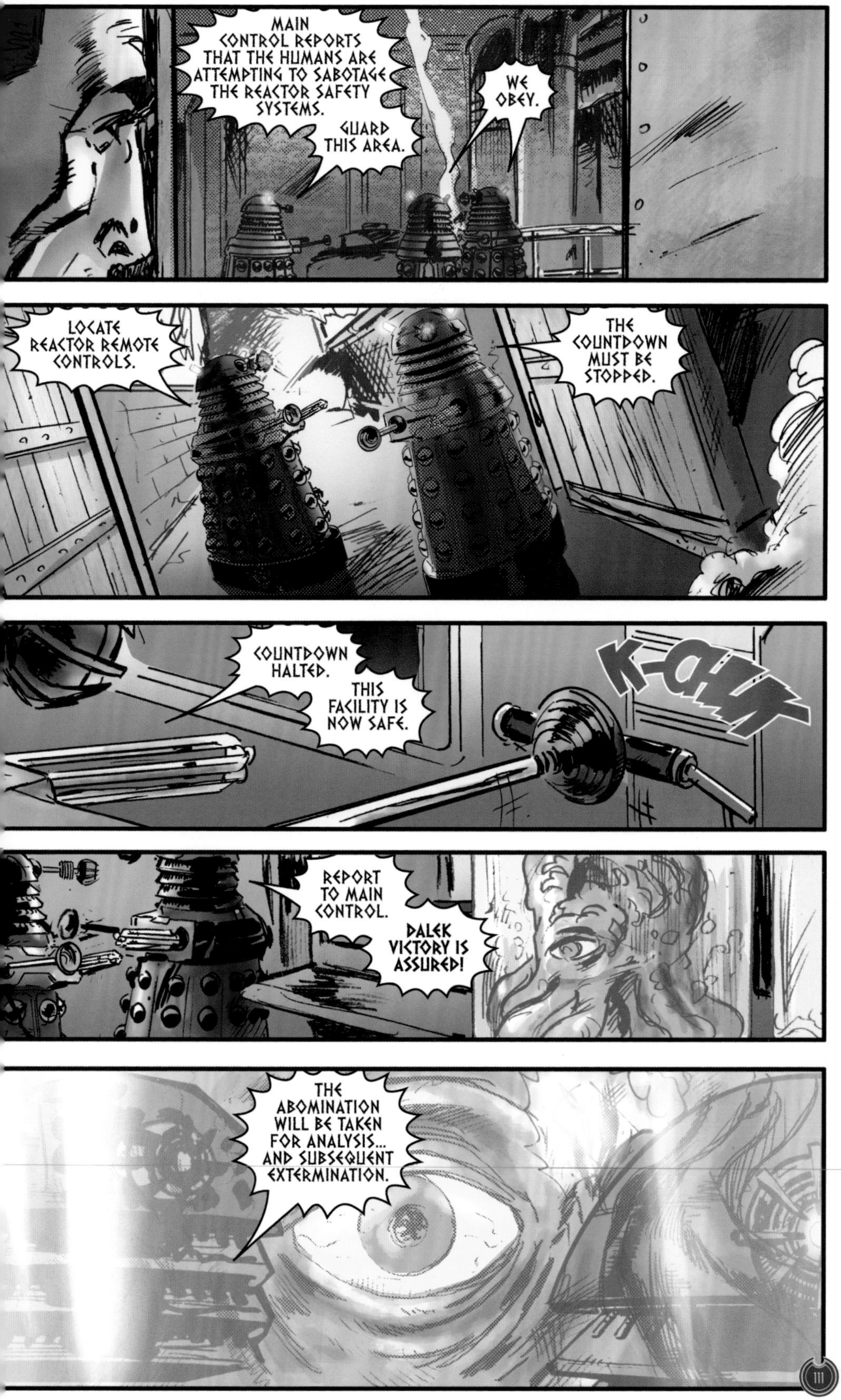
MAIN CONTROL REPORTS THAT THE HUMANS ARE ATTEMPTING TO SABOTAGE THE REACTOR SAFETY SYSTEMS.
GUARD THIS AREA.
WE OBEY.
LOCATE REACTOR REMOTE CONTROLS.
THE COUNTDOWN MUST BE STOPPED.
COUNTDOWN HALTED.
THIS FACILITY IS NOW SAFE.
K-CHUK
REPORT TO MAIN CONTROL.
DALEK VICTORY IS ASSURED!
THE ABOMINATION WILL BE TAKEN FOR ANALYSIS... AND SUBSEQUENT EXTERMINATION.

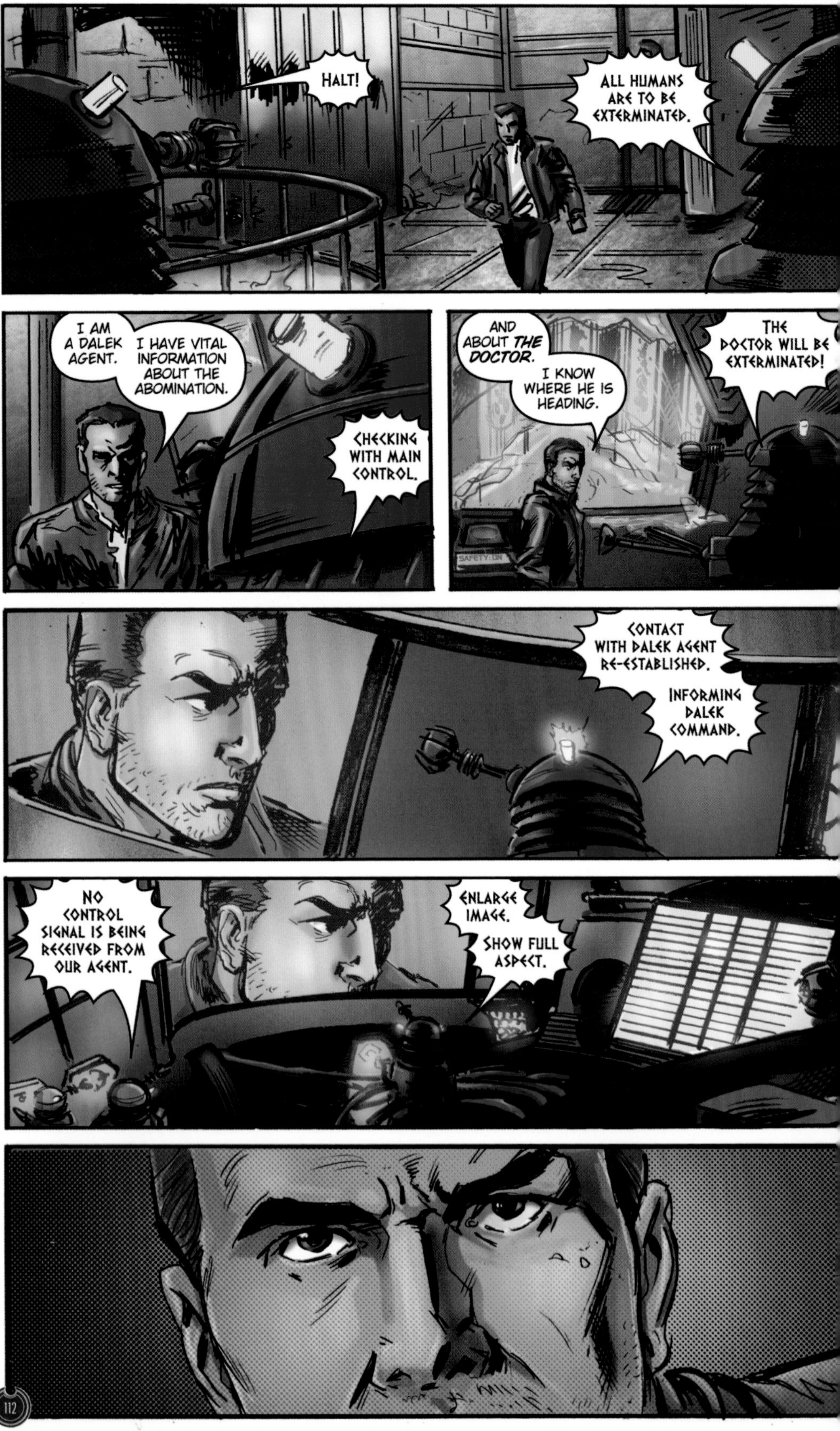
HALT!
ALL HUMANS ARE TO BE EXTERMINATED.
I AM A DALEK AGENT.
I HAVE VITAL INFORMATION ABOUT THE ABOMINATION.
CHECKING WITH MAIN CONTROL.
AND ABOUT THE DOCTOR.
I KNOW WHERE HE IS HEADING.
THE DOCTOR WILL BE EXTERMINATED!
SAFETY: ON
CONTACT WITH DALEK AGENT RE-ESTABLISHED.
INFORMING DALEK COMMAND.
NO CONTROL SIGNAL IS BEING RECEIVED FROM OUR AGENT.
ENLARGE IMAGE.
SHOW FULL ASPECT.

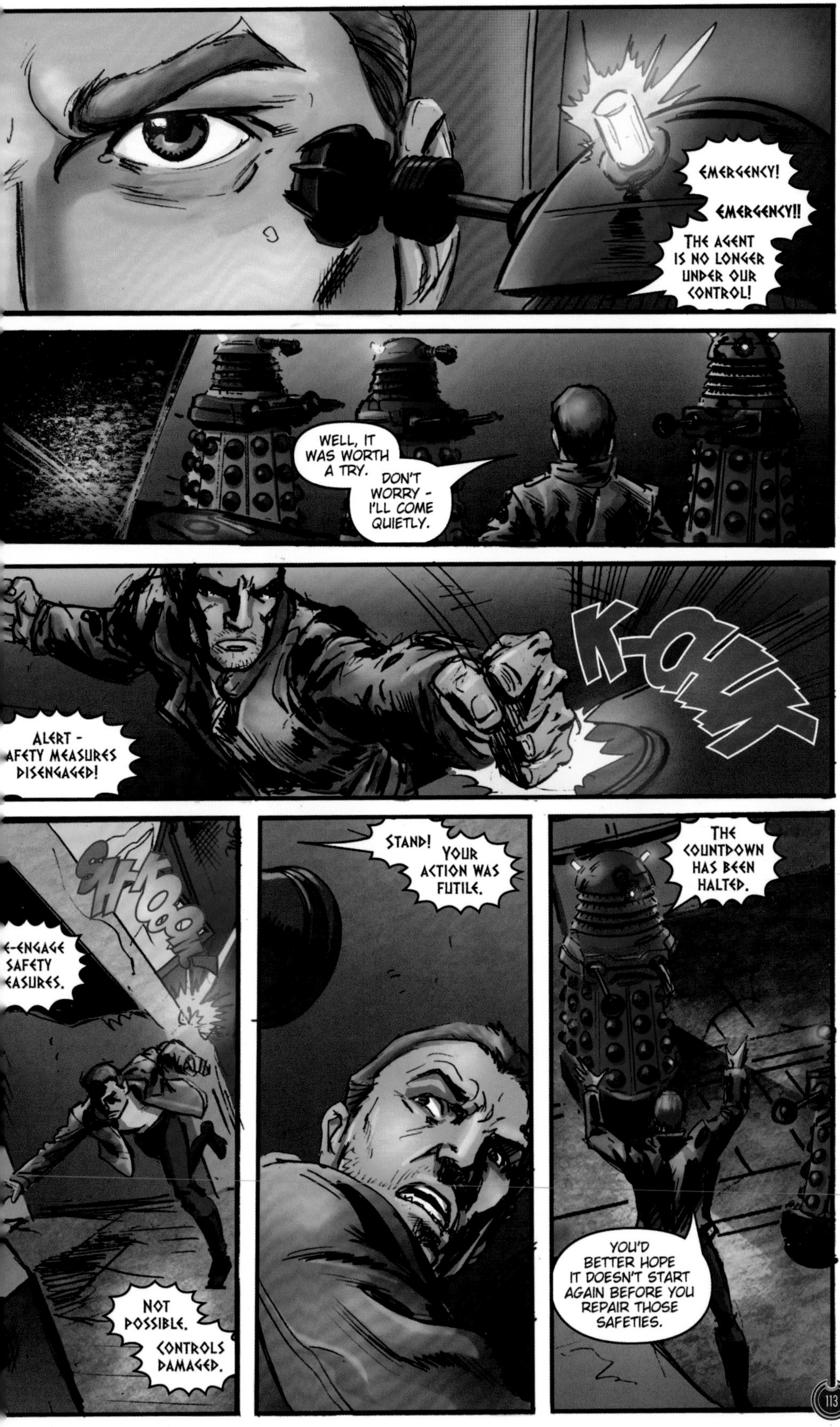
EMERGENCY!
EMERGENCY!!
THE AGENT IS NO LONGER UNDER OUR CONTROL!
WELL, IT WAS WORTH A TRY.
DON'T WORRY - I'LL COME QUIETLY.
K-CHUK
ALERT - AFETY MEASURES DISENGAGED!
E-ENGAGE SAFETY EASURES.
NOT POSSIBLE.
CONTROLS DAMAGED.
STAND!
YOUR ACTION WAS FUTILE.
THE COUNTDOWN HAS BEEN HALTED.
YOU'D BETTER HOPE IT DOESN'T START AGAIN BEFORE YOU REPAIR THOSE SAFETIES.

REACTOR SAFETY MEASURES DISABLED

0:03

THE ABOMINATION IS BECOMING RESTLESS.

CAUTION! NUTRIENT TANK BECOMING UNSTABLE.

INTEGRITY OF CONTAINMENT VESSEL NOT GUARANTEED.

TANK BREAKING.

ALERT.

SMASH!

THE ABOMINATION IS RELEASED.

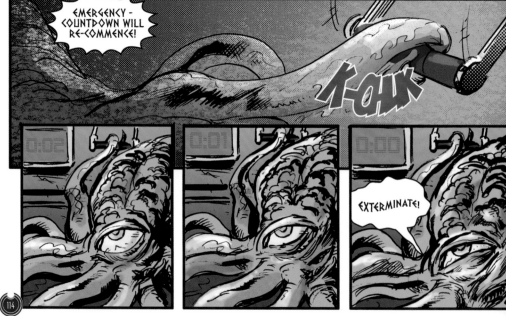

EMERGENCY – COUNTDOWN WILL RE-COMMENCE!

K-CHK

0:02

0:01

0:00

EXTERMINATE!

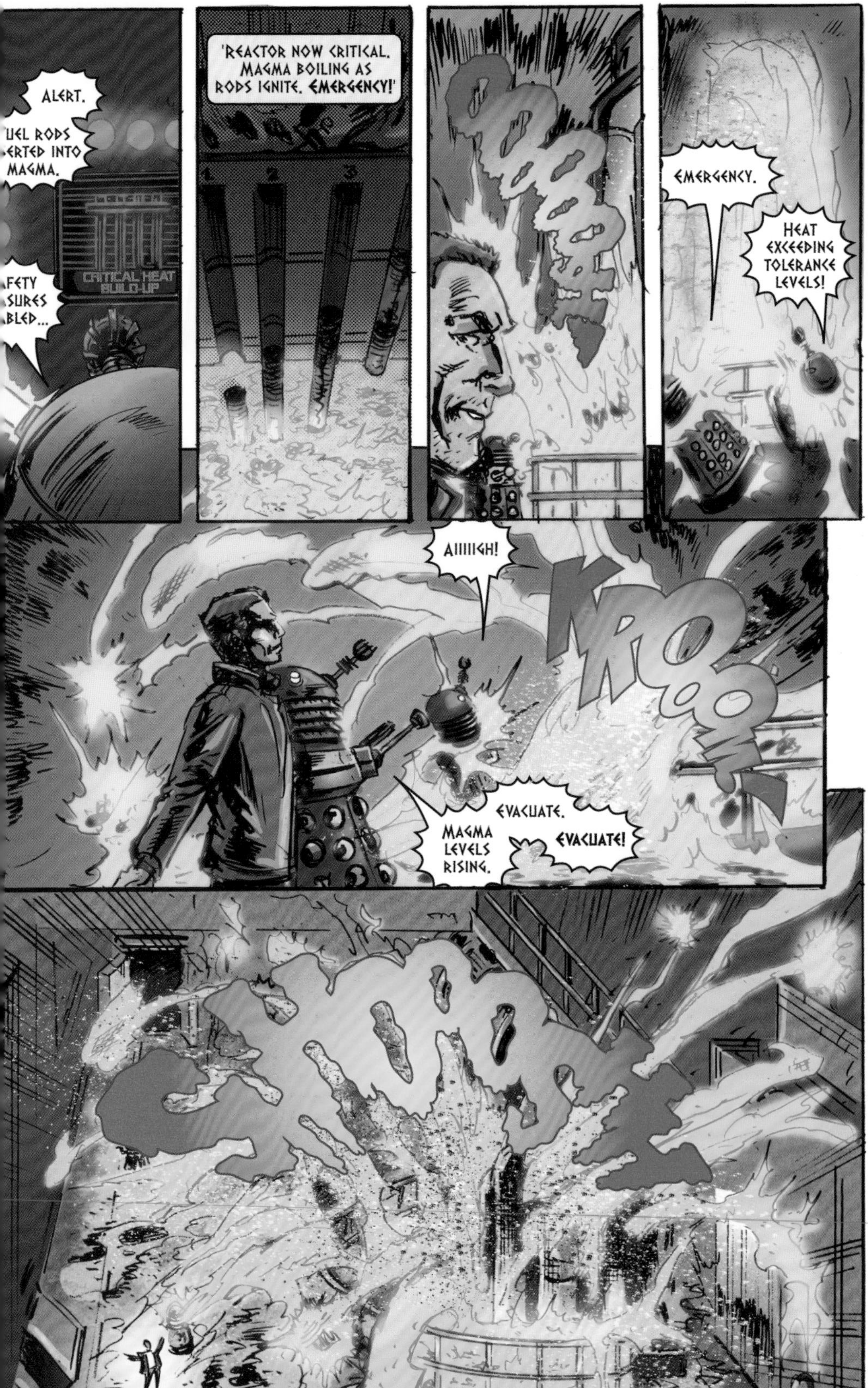

ALERT.
UEL RODS
ERTED INTO
MAGMA.
CRITICAL HEAT
BUILD-UP
FETY
SURES
BLED...
'REACTOR NOW CRITICAL. MAGMA BOILING AS RODS IGNITE. EMERGENCY!'
1
2
3
EMERGENCY.
HEAT EXCEEDING TOLERANCE LEVELS!
AIIIIGH!
EVACUATE.
EVACUATE!
MAGMA LEVELS RISING.

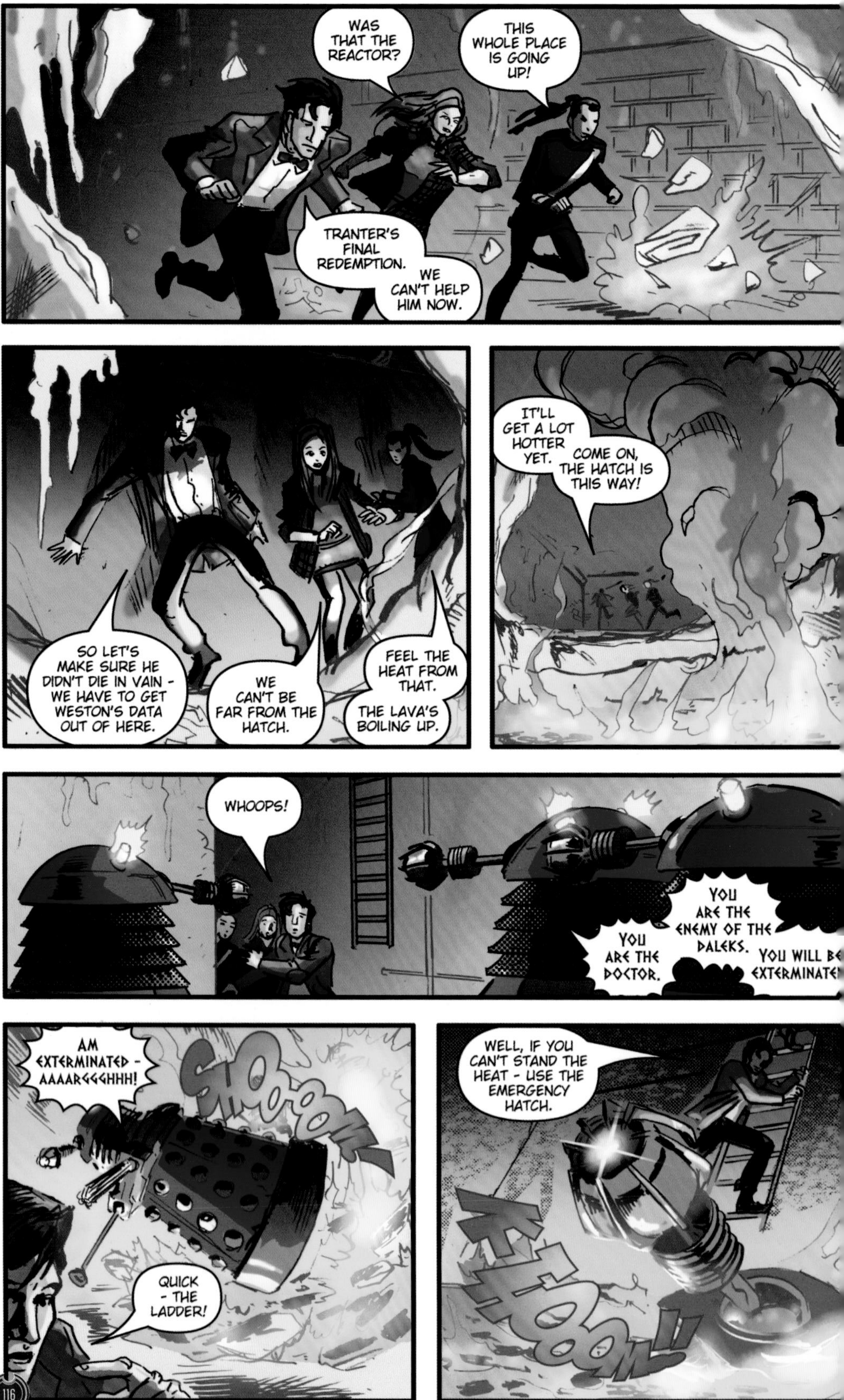
WAS THAT THE REACTOR?
THIS WHOLE PLACE IS GOING UP!
TRANTER'S FINAL REDEMPTION.
WE CAN'T HELP HIM NOW.
SO LET'S MAKE SURE HE DIDN'T DIE IN VAIN - WE HAVE TO GET WESTON'S DATA OUT OF HERE.
WE CAN'T BE FAR FROM THE HATCH.
FEEL THE HEAT FROM THAT.
THE LAVA'S BOILING UP.
IT'LL GET A LOT HOTTER YET.
COME ON, THE HATCH IS THIS WAY!
WHOOPS!
YOU ARE THE DOCTOR.
YOU ARE THE ENEMY OF THE DALEKS.
YOU WILL BE EXTERMINATE
AM EXTERMINATED - AAAARGGGHHH!
SHOOOOM
QUICK - THE LADDER!
WELL, IF YOU CAN'T STAND THE HEAT - USE THE EMERGENCY HATCH.
KA-BOOM!!

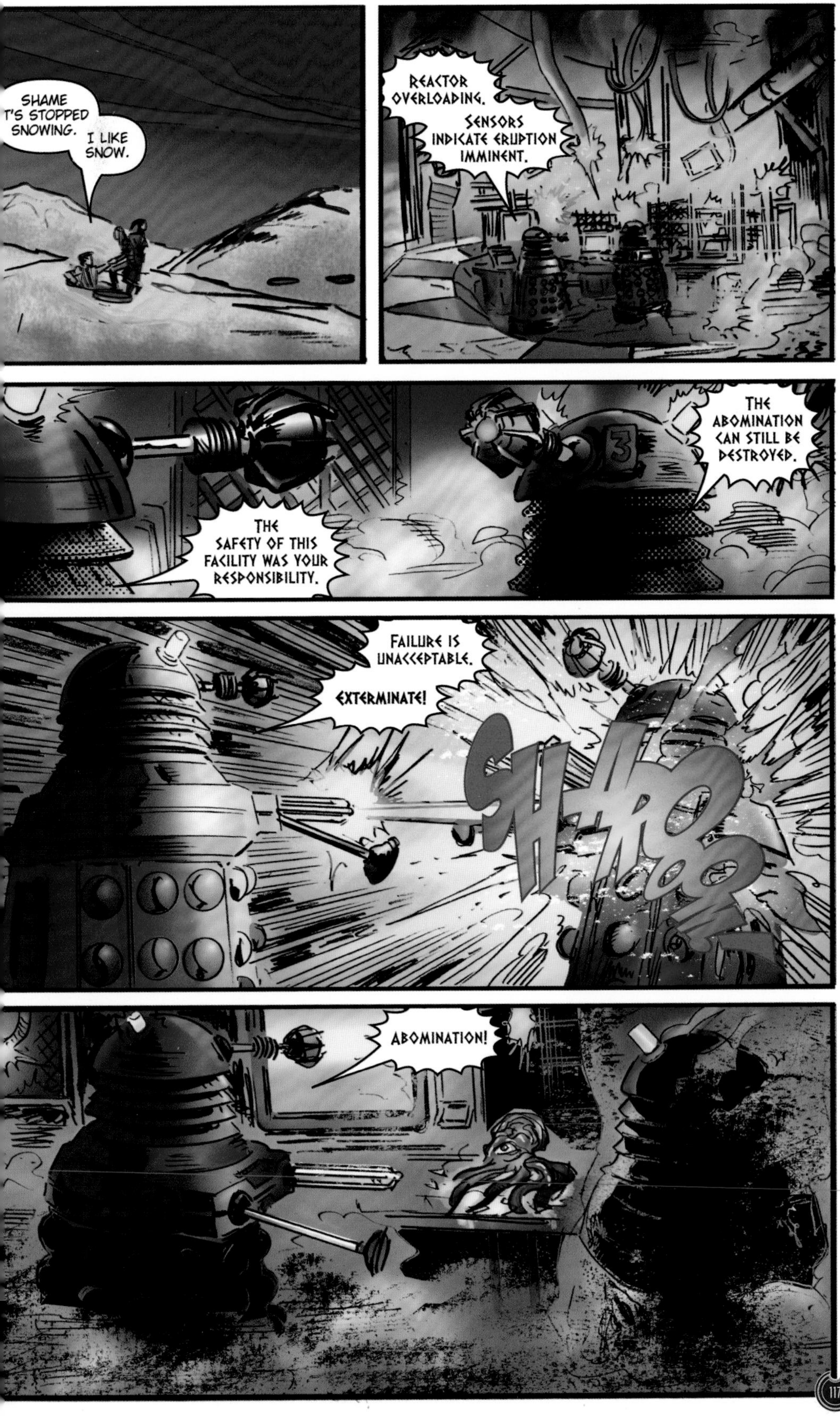

SHAME
T'S STOPPED
SNOWING.
I LIKE SNOW.
REACTOR OVERLOADING.
SENSORS INDICATE ERUPTION IMMINENT.
THE ABOMINATION CAN STILL BE DESTROYED.
THE SAFETY OF THIS FACILITY WAS YOUR RESPONSIBILITY.
FAILURE IS UNACCEPTABLE.
EXTERMINATE!
ABOMINATION!

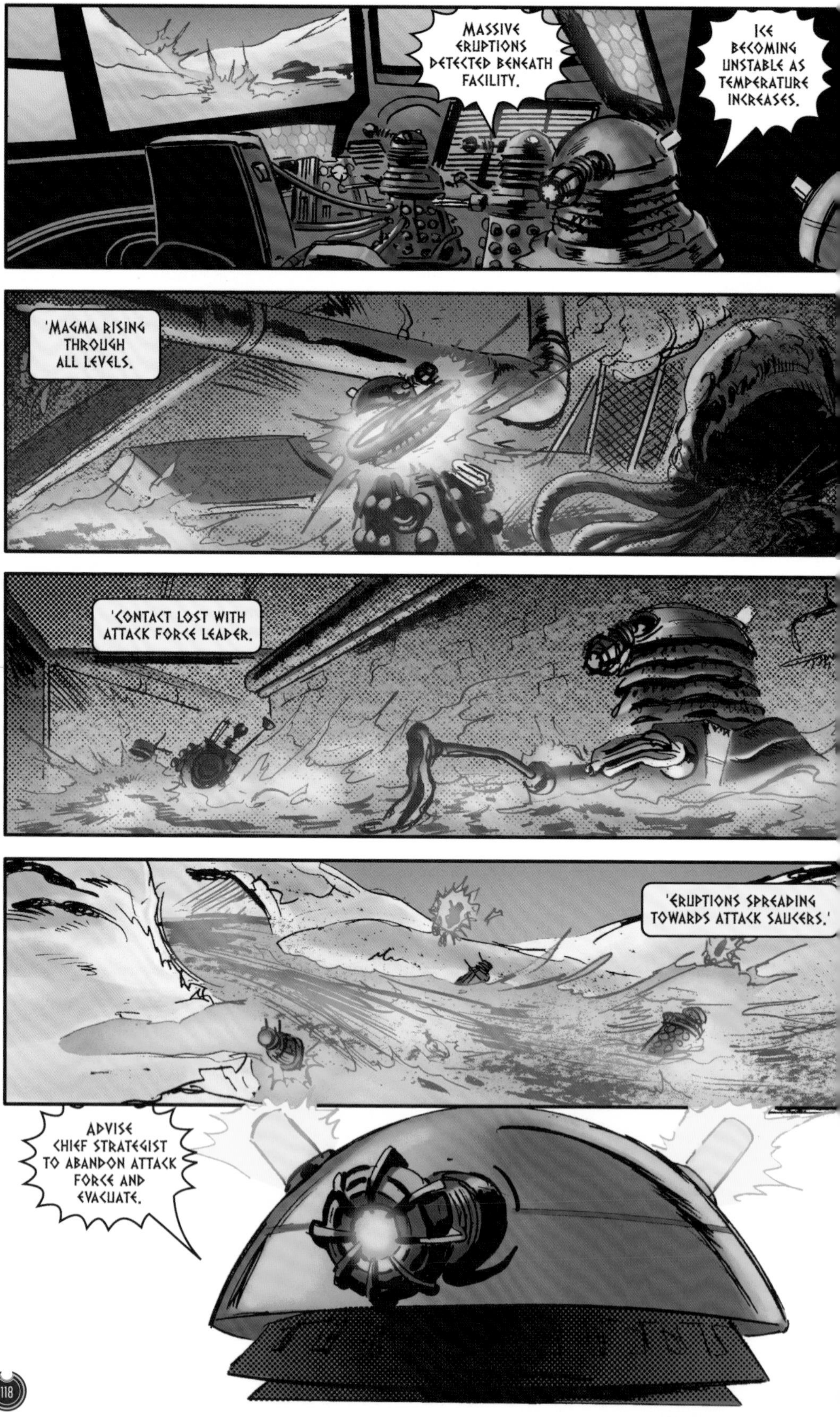
MASSIVE ERUPTIONS DETECTED BENEATH FACILITY.
ICE BECOMING UNSTABLE AS TEMPERATURE INCREASES.
'MAGMA RISING THROUGH ALL LEVELS.
'CONTACT LOST WITH ATTACK FORCE LEADER.
'ERUPTIONS SPREADING TOWARDS ATTACK SAUCERS.'
ADVISE CHIEF STRATEGIST TO ABANDON ATTACK FORCE AND EVACUATE.

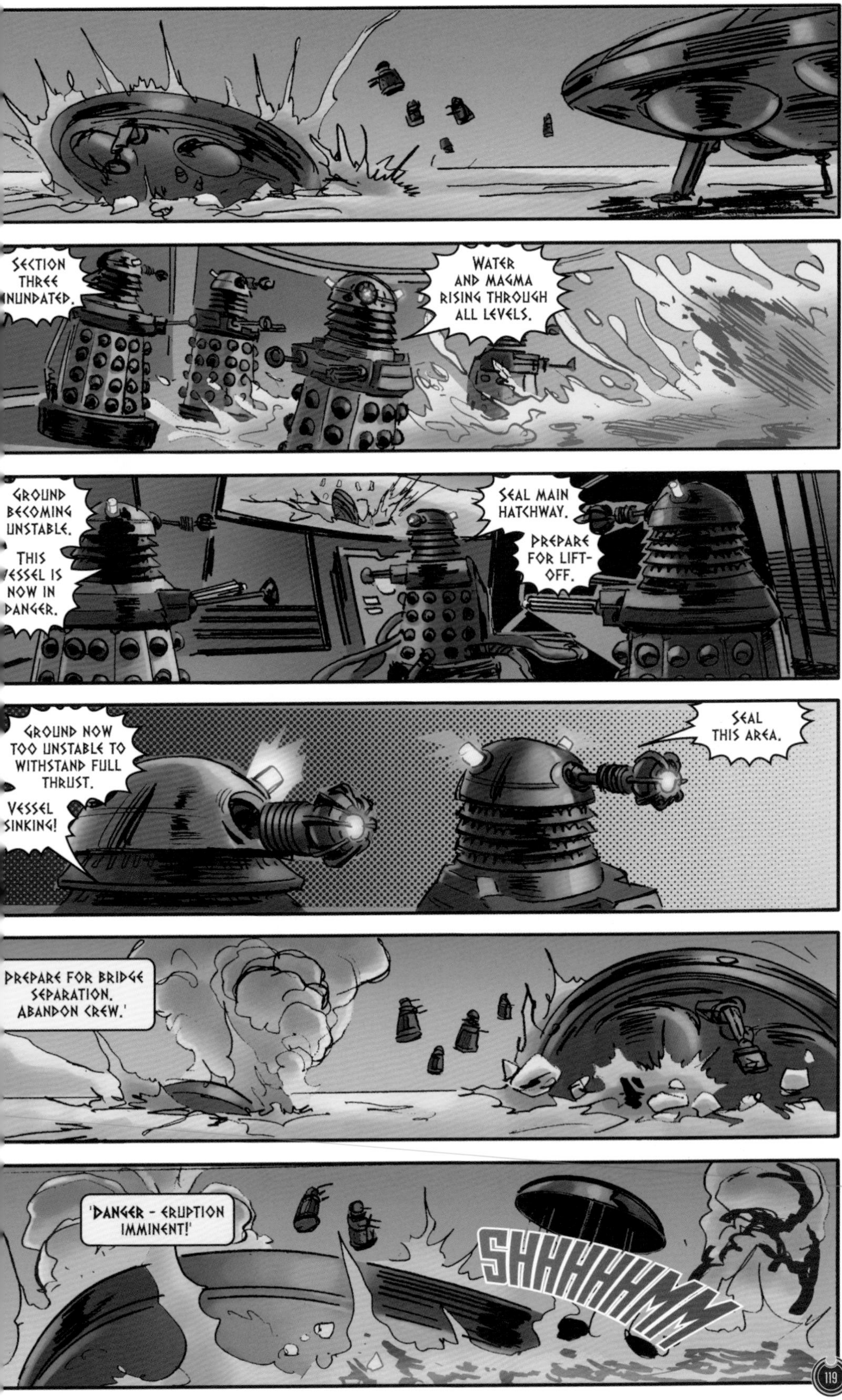

SECTION THREE INUNDATED.
WATER AND MAGMA RISING THROUGH ALL LEVELS.
GROUND BECOMING UNSTABLE.
THIS VESSEL IS NOW IN DANGER.
SEAL MAIN HATCHWAY.
PREPARE FOR LIFT-OFF.
GROUND NOW TOO UNSTABLE TO WITHSTAND FULL THRUST.
VESSEL SINKING!
SEAL THIS AREA.
PREPARE FOR BRIDGE SEPARATION. ABANDON CREW.'
'DANGER - ERUPTION IMMINENT!'
SHHHHHMM

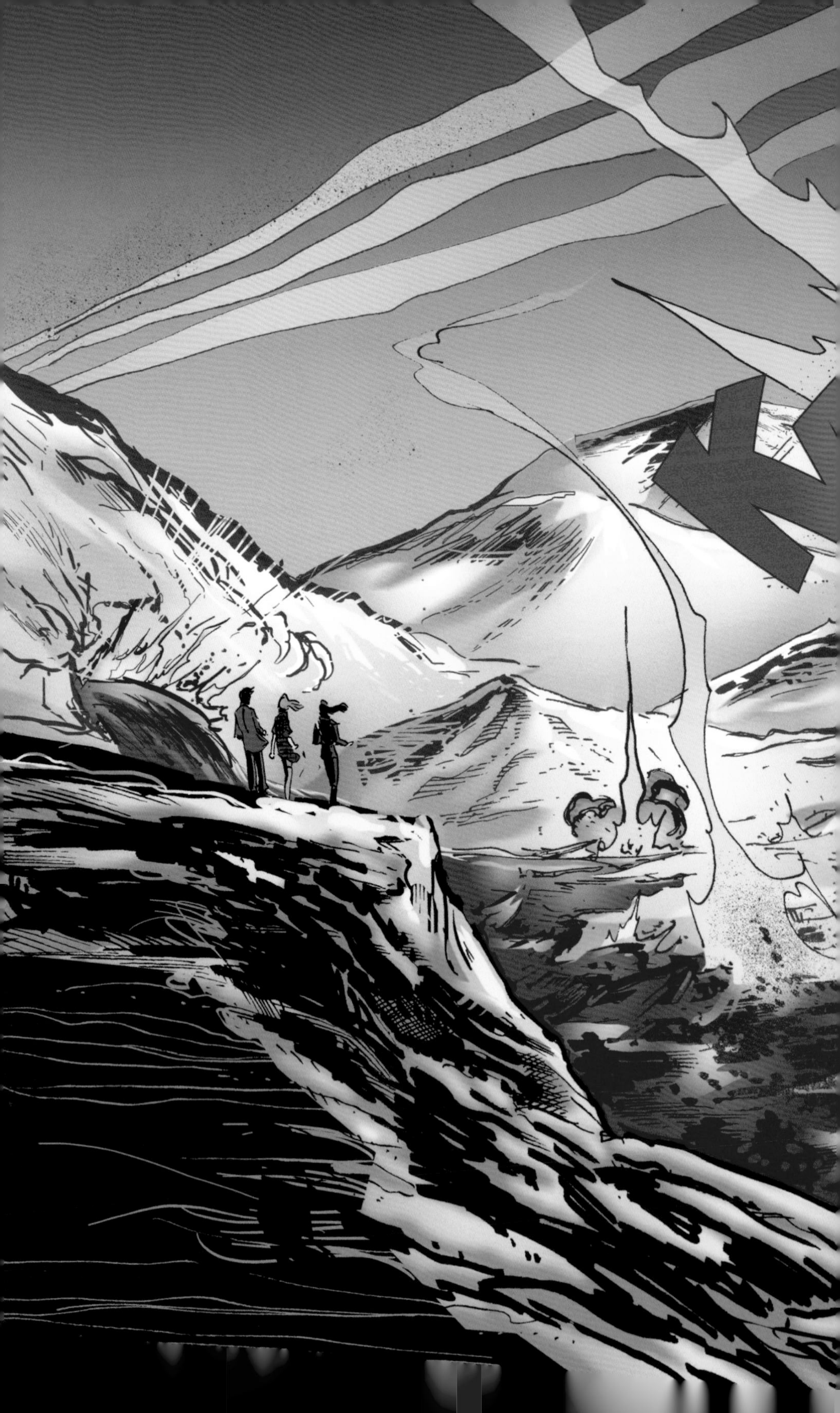

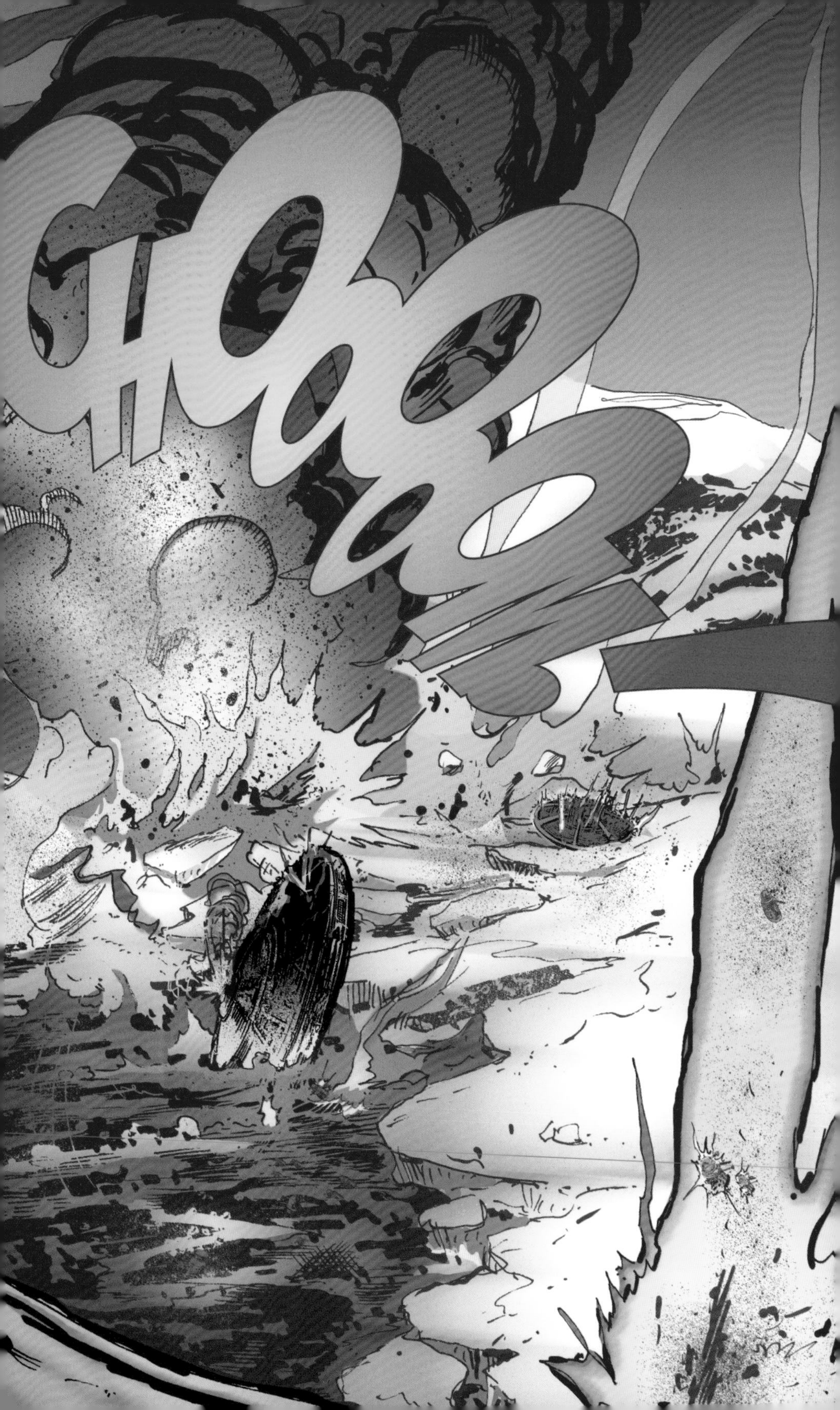

I'M GLAD YOU PARKED A GOOD WAY AWAY.

MAKES FOR A LONG WALK, THOUGH.

WESTON'S LIFE'S WORK.

HE DIED FOR IT.

I WONDER HOW USEFUL IT WILL REALLY BE.

JUST MAKE SURE THE DALEKS DON'T GET HOLD OF THAT.

IF THEY DO, THEY COUL[D] GENETICALLY MOD[IFY] THEMSELVES TO BE RESISTANT.

YOU THINK YOU CAN GET THAT THING TO FLY?

EVEN WITHOUT A TAME DALEK?

I CAN MAKE ANYTHING FLY.

WITH OR WITHOUT DALEKS.

PREFERABLY WITHOUT.

THERE YOU ARE - GOOD AS NEW.

ALMOST.

I GUESS YOU'RE NOT COMING WITH ME.

THANKS - YOU KNOW, FOR EVERYTHING.

GOODBYE, JAY.

GOODBYE, AMY. YOU LOOK AFTER HIM, WON'T YOU.

JUST ONE THING, DOCTOR - ALL THOSE DEATHS.

TRANTER, WESTON, EVERYONE. IT WAS WORTH IT, WASN'T IT?

OF COURSE IT WAS.

THE DALEKS DIDN'T GET WHAT THEY CAME FOR.

YOU HAVE WESTON'S WORK - THA[T'S] SURE TO B[E] USEFUL.

A TERRIBLE COST, BUT YES IT WAS WORTH IT.

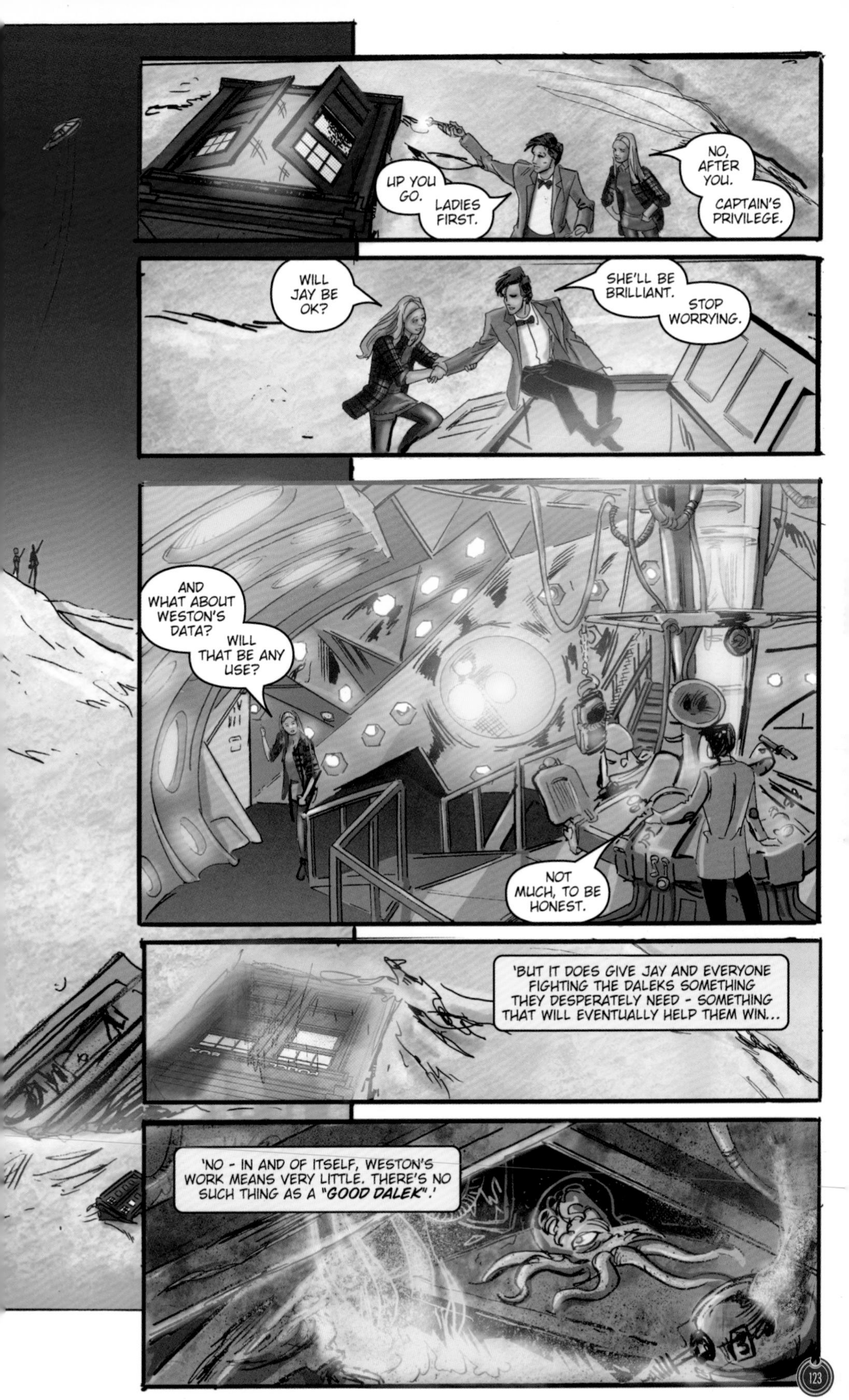

UP YOU GO. LADIES FIRST.
NO, AFTER YOU. CAPTAIN'S PRIVILEGE.
WILL JAY BE OK?
SHE'LL BE BRILLIANT. STOP WORRYING.
AND WHAT ABOUT WESTON'S DATA? WILL THAT BE ANY USE?
NOT MUCH, TO BE HONEST.
'BUT IT DOES GIVE JAY AND EVERYONE FIGHTING THE DALEKS SOMETHING THEY DESPERATELY NEED - SOMETHING THAT WILL EVENTUALLY HELP THEM WIN...
'NO - IN AND OF ITSELF, WESTON'S WORK MEANS VERY LITTLE. THERE'S NO SUCH THING AS A "GOOD DALEK".'

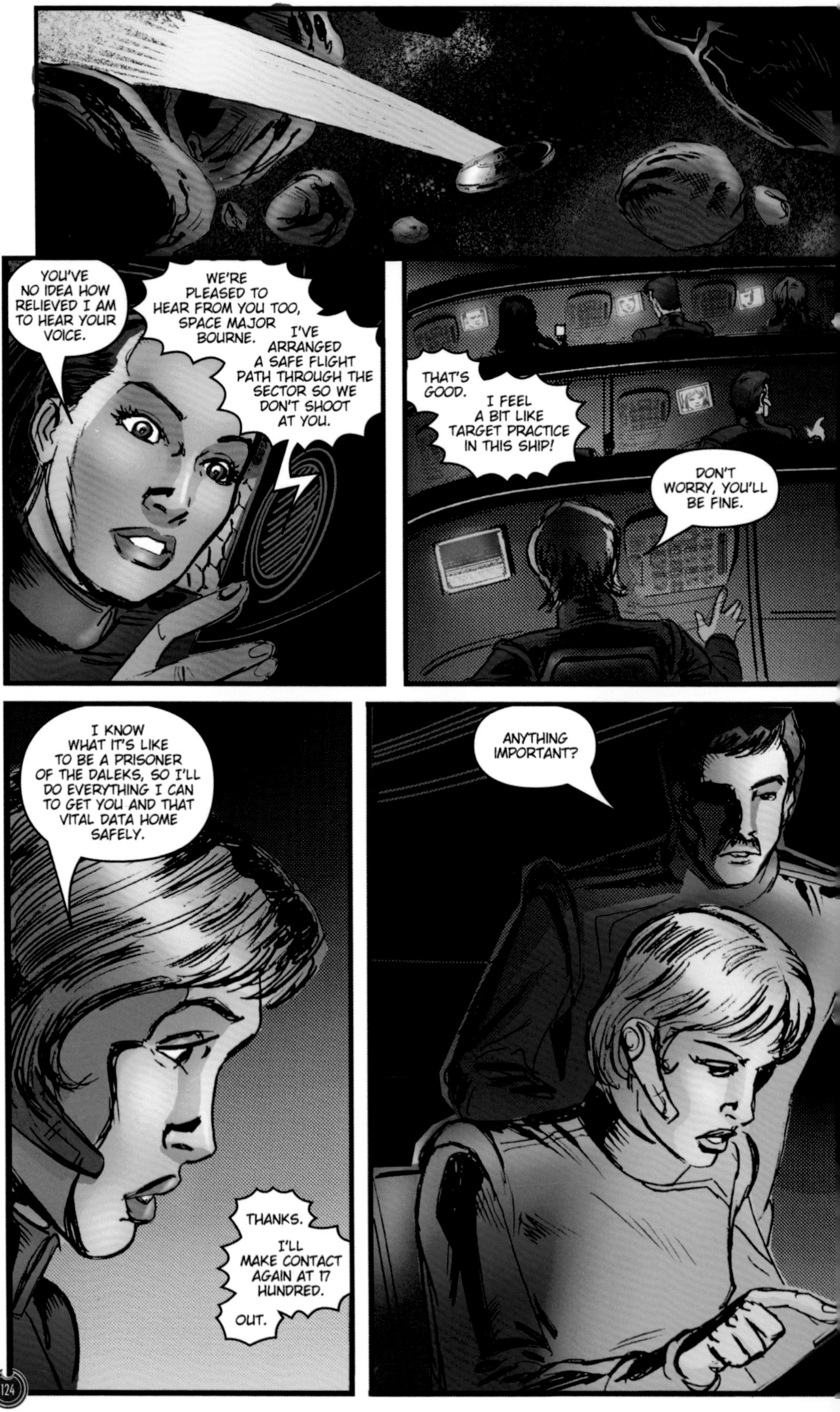

YOU'VE NO IDEA HOW RELIEVED I AM TO HEAR YOUR VOICE.
WE'RE PLEASED TO HEAR FROM YOU TOO, SPACE MAJOR BOURNE.
I'VE ARRANGED A SAFE FLIGHT PATH THROUGH THE SECTOR SO WE DON'T SHOOT AT YOU.
THAT'S GOOD.
I FEEL A BIT LIKE TARGET PRACTICE IN THIS SHIP!
DON'T WORRY, YOU'LL BE FINE.
I KNOW WHAT IT'S LIKE TO BE A PRISONER OF THE DALEKS, SO I'LL DO EVERYTHING I CAN TO GET YOU AND THAT VITAL DATA HOME SAFELY.
THANKS.
I'LL MAKE CONTACT AGAIN AT 17 HUNDRED.
OUT.
ANYTHING IMPORTANT?

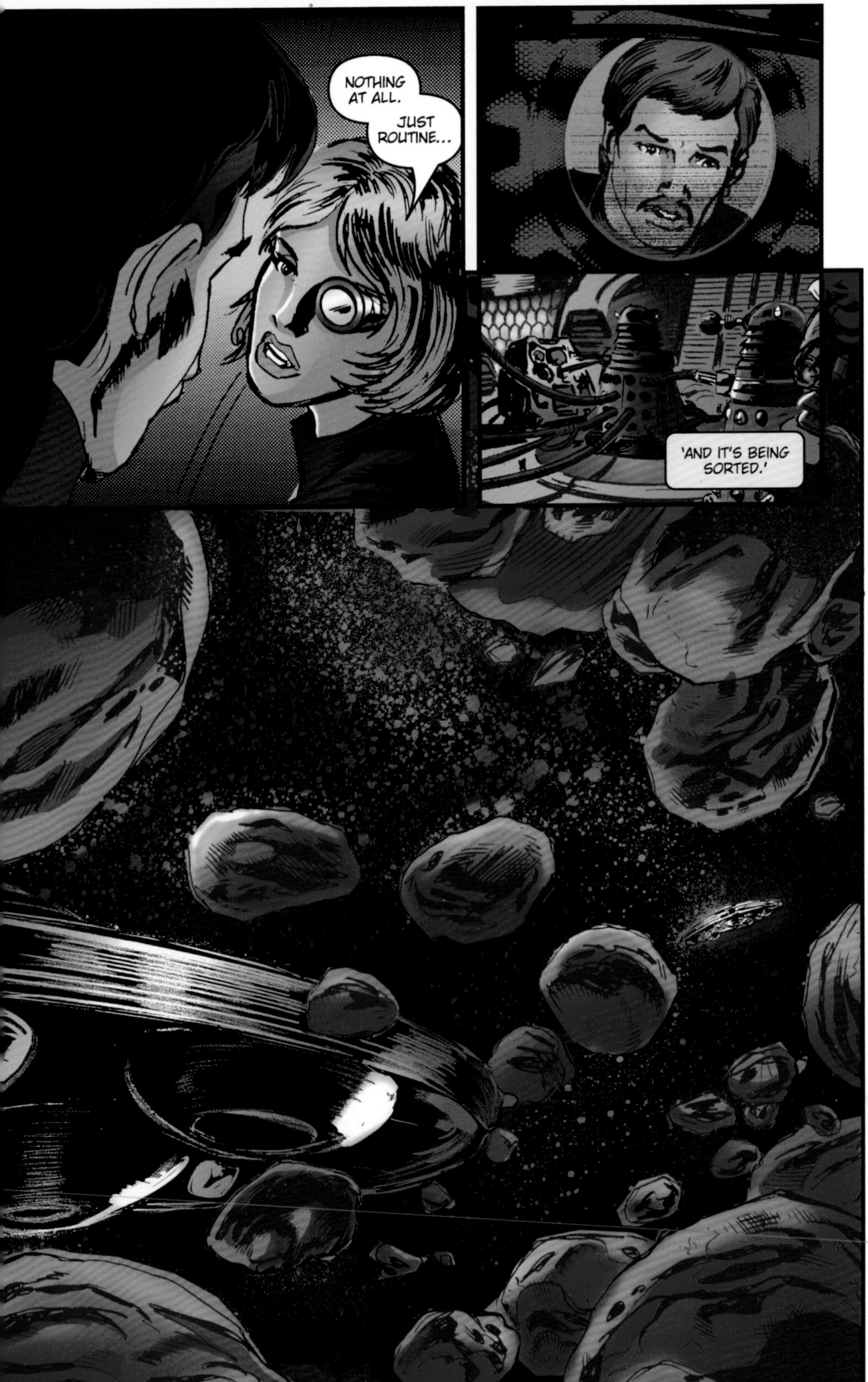
NOTHING AT ALL.
JUST ROUTINE...
'AND IT'S BEING SORTED.'

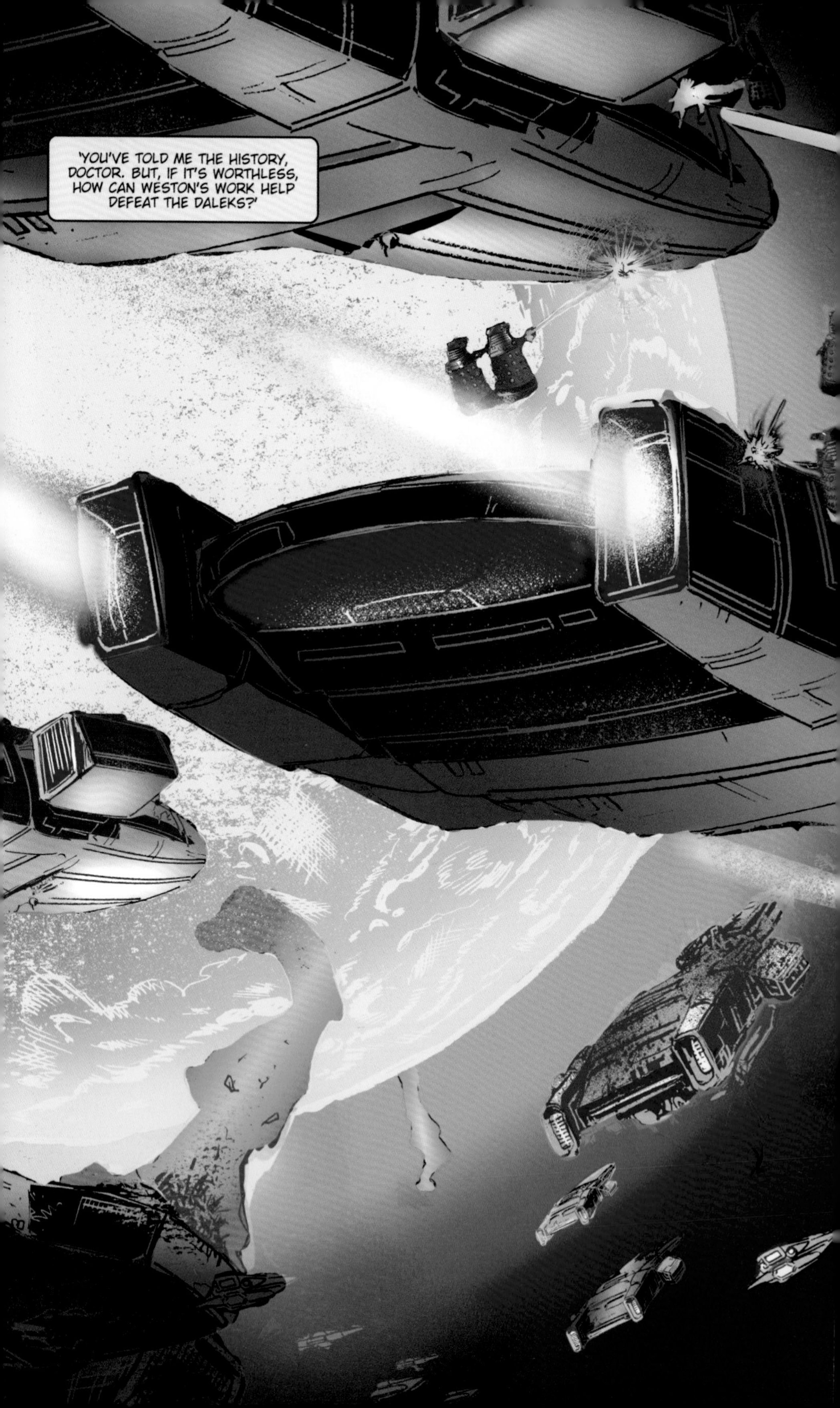
'YOU'VE TOLD ME THE HISTORY, DOCTOR. BUT, IF IT'S WORTHLESS, HOW CAN WESTON'S WORK HELP DEFEAT THE DALEKS?'

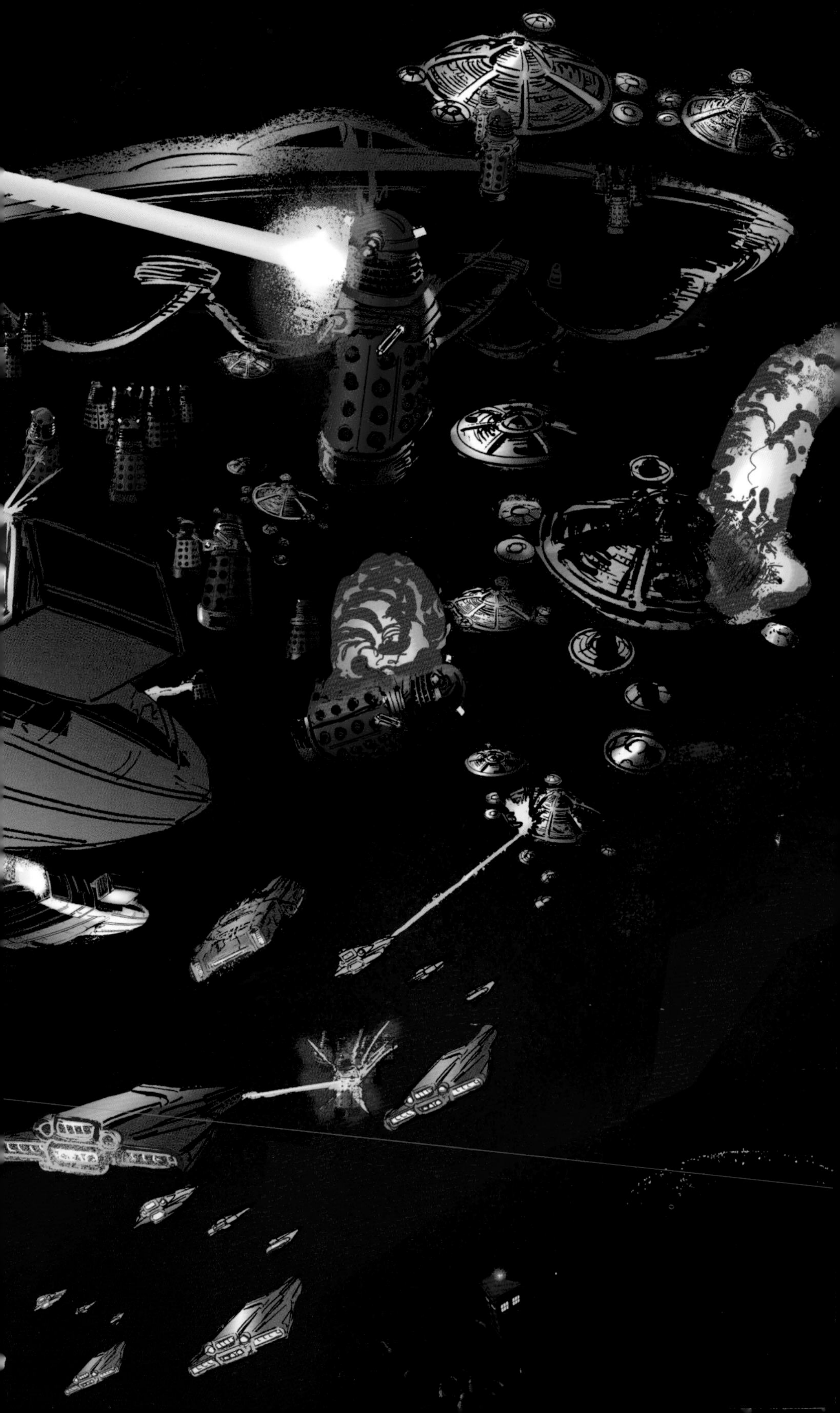

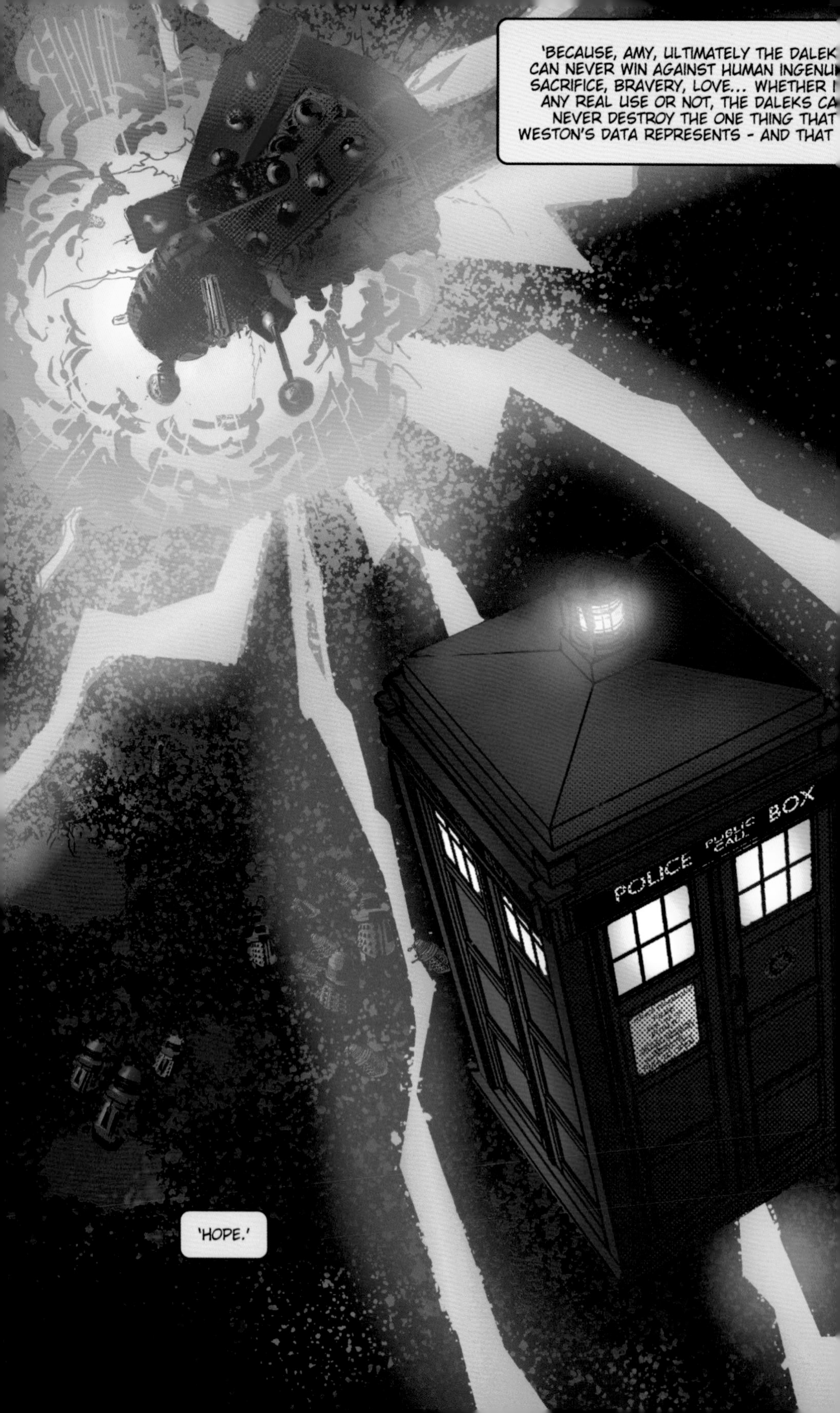
'BECAUSE, AMY, ULTIMATELY THE DALEK
CAN NEVER WIN AGAINST HUMAN INGENU
SACRIFICE, BRAVERY, LOVE... WHETHER I
ANY REAL USE OR NOT, THE DALEKS CA
NEVER DESTROY THE ONE THING THAT
WESTON'S DATA REPRESENTS - AND THAT
POLICE PUBLIC CALL BOX
'HOPE.'

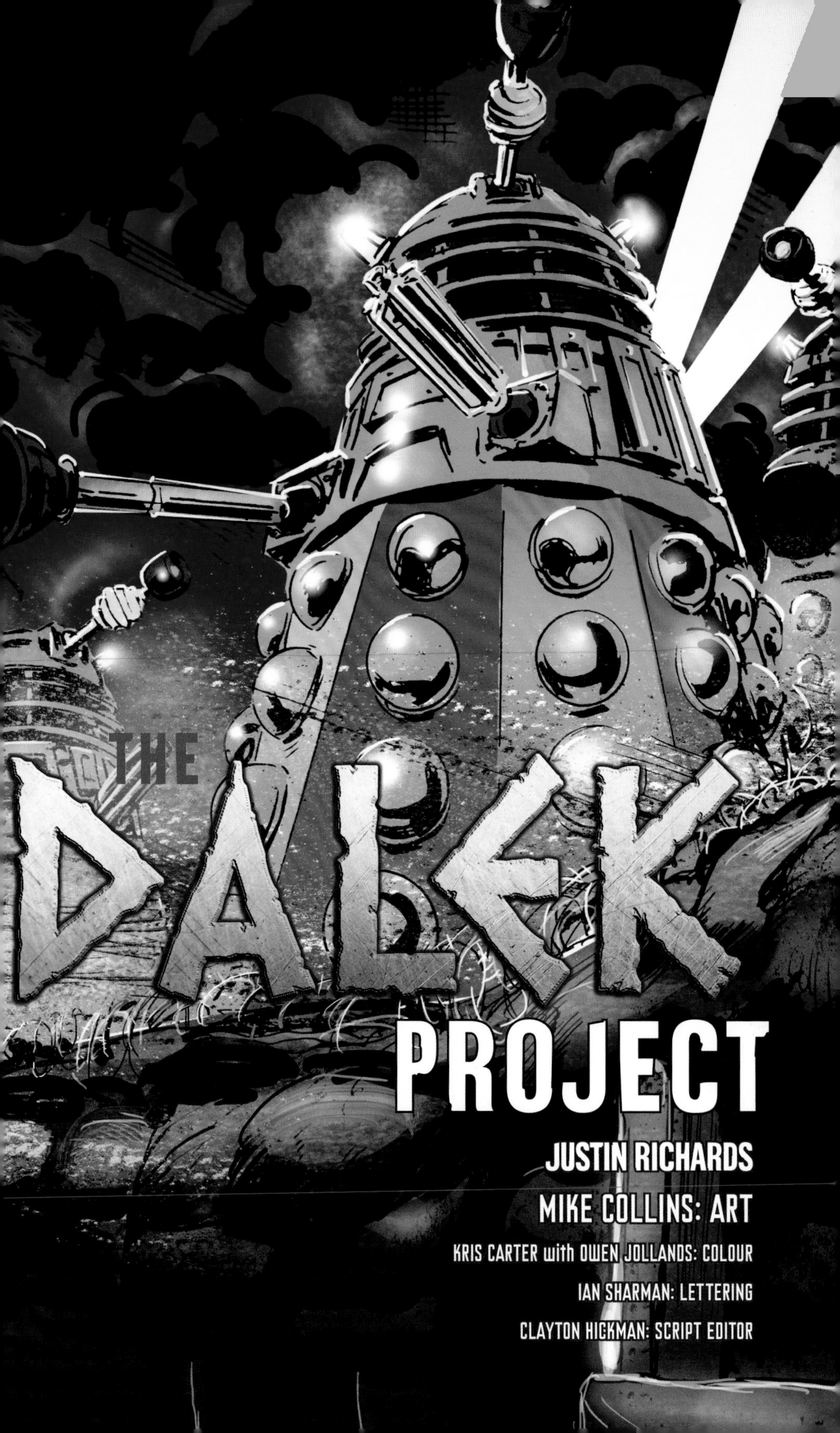
THE DALEK PROJECT
JUSTIN RICHARDS
MIKE COLLINS: ART
KRIS CARTER with OWEN JOLLANDS: COLOUR
IAN SHARMAN: LETTERING
CLAYTON HICKMAN: SCRIPT EDITOR

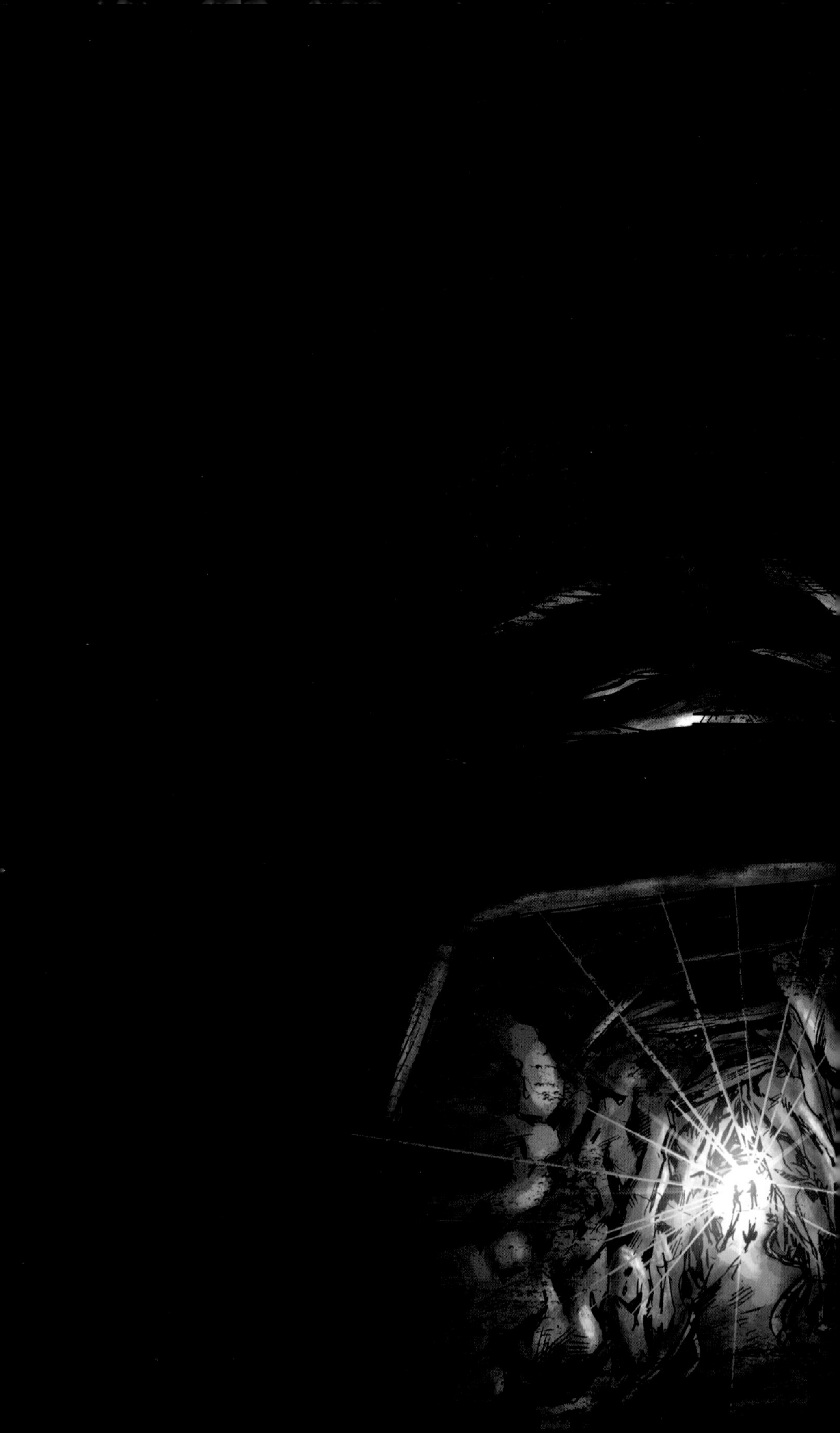

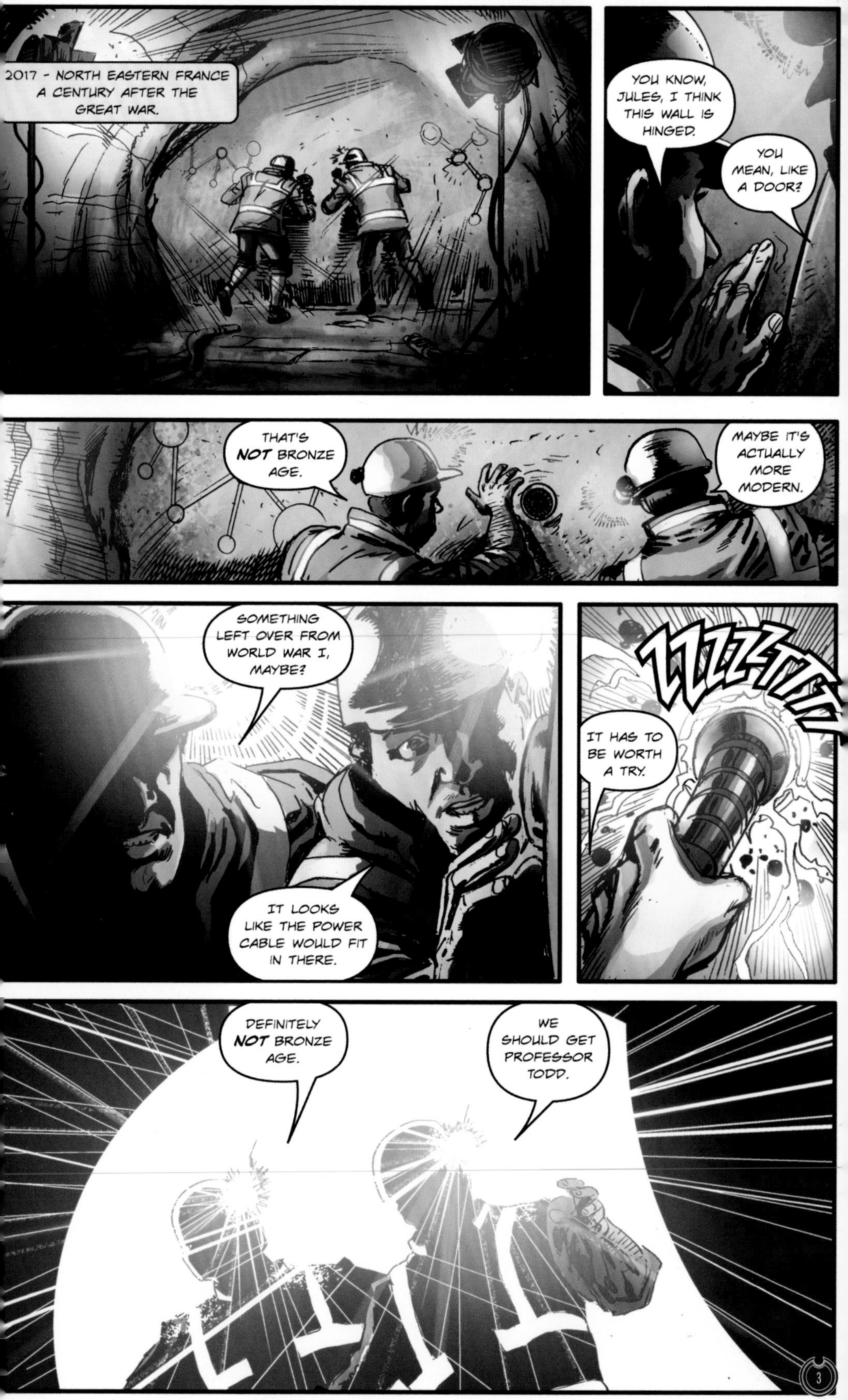

2017 - NORTH EASTERN FRANCE A CENTURY AFTER THE GREAT WAR.
YOU KNOW, JULES, I THINK THIS WALL IS HINGED.
YOU MEAN, LIKE A DOOR?
THAT'S **NOT** BRONZE AGE.
MAYBE IT'S ACTUALLY MORE MODERN.
SOMETHING LEFT OVER FROM WORLD WAR I, MAYBE?
IT LOOKS LIKE THE POWER CABLE WOULD FIT IN THERE.
IT HAS TO BE WORTH A TRY.
DEFINITELY **NOT** BRONZE AGE.
WE SHOULD GET PROFESSOR TODD.

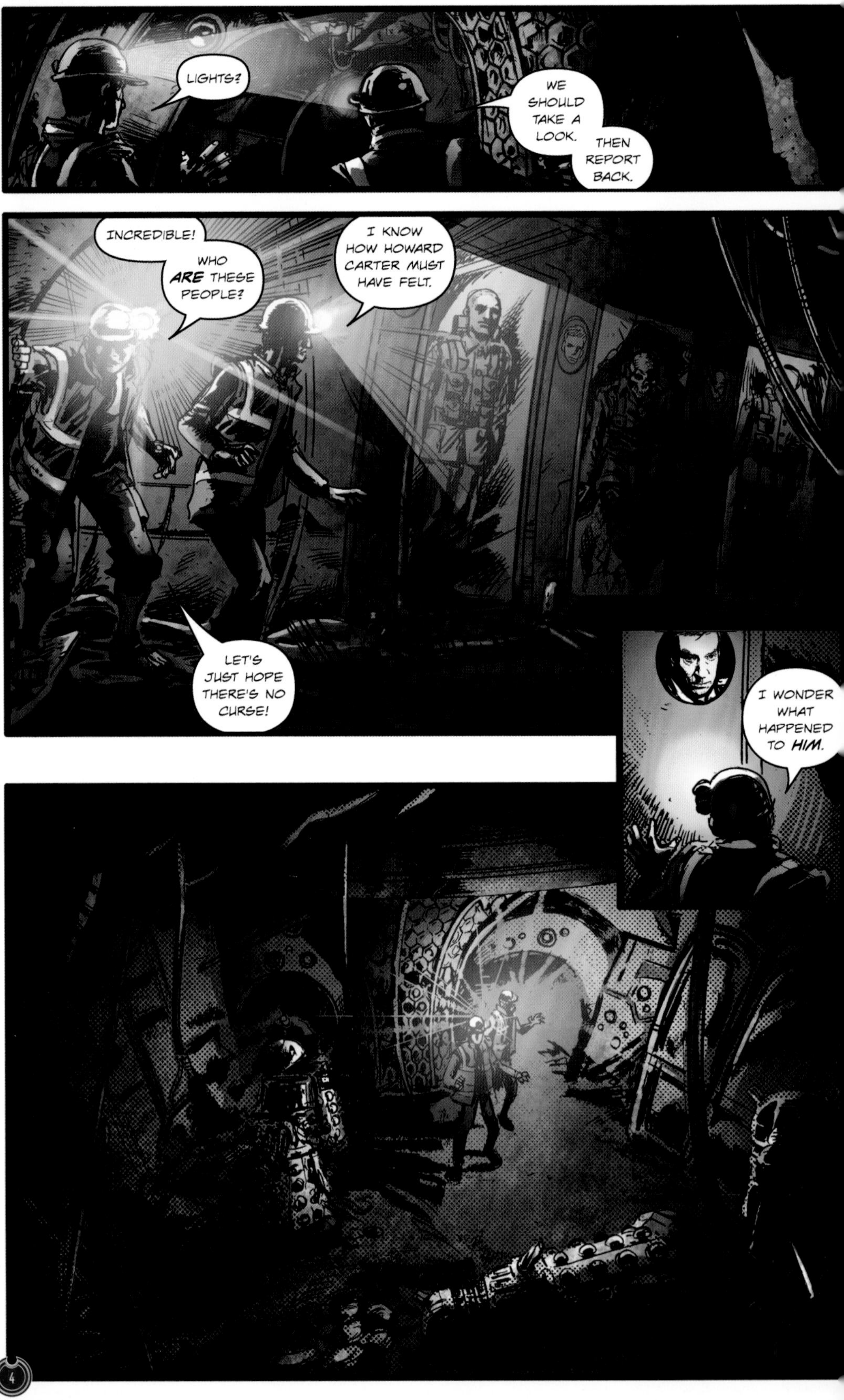
LIGHTS?
WE SHOULD TAKE A LOOK.
THEN REPORT BACK.
INCREDIBLE!
WHO ARE THESE PEOPLE?
I KNOW HOW HOWARD CARTER MUST HAVE FELT.
LET'S JUST HOPE THERE'S NO CURSE!
I WONDER WHAT HAPPENED TO HIM.

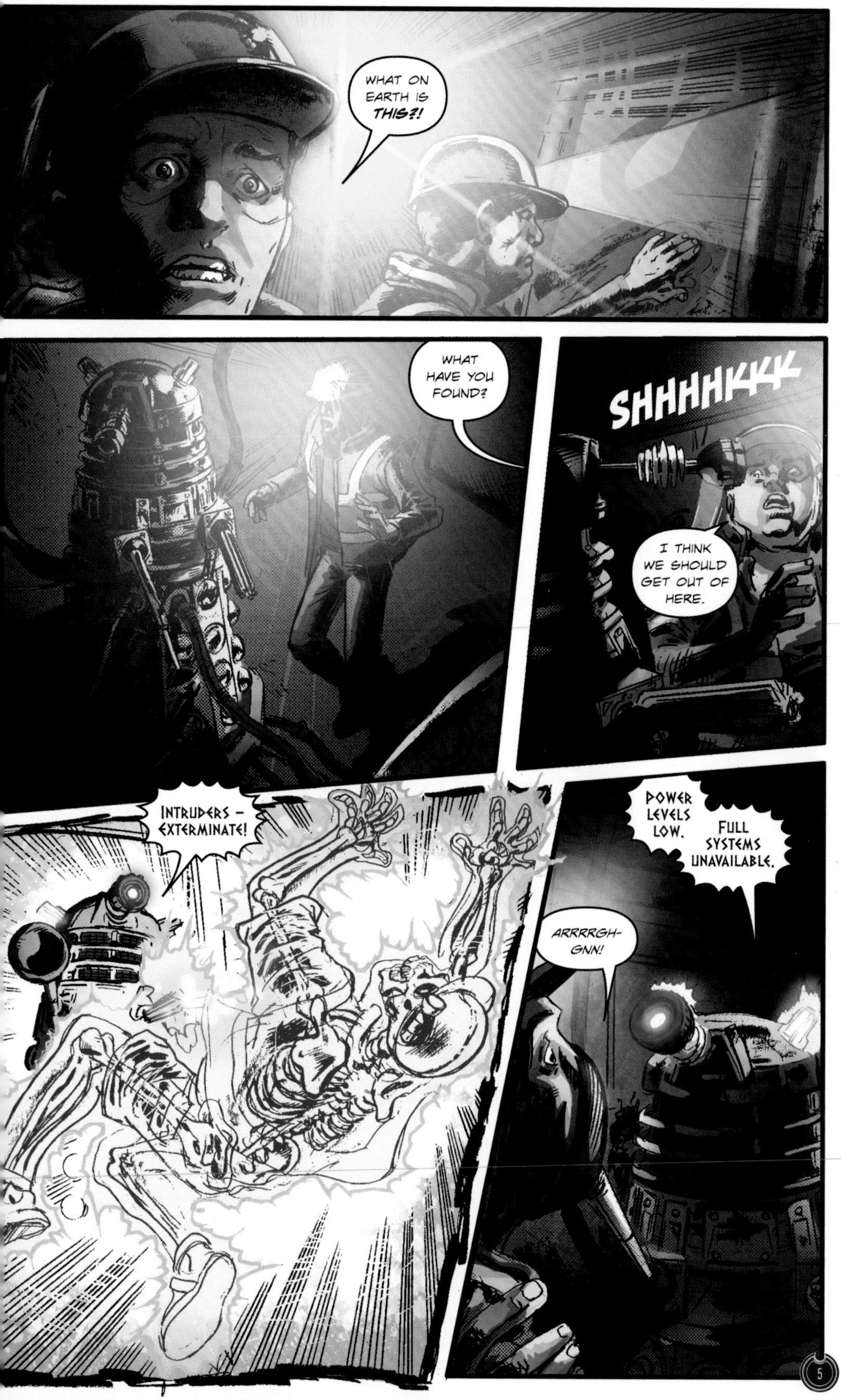
WHAT ON EARTH IS THIS?!
WHAT HAVE YOU FOUND?
SHHHHKKK
I THINK WE SHOULD GET OUT OF HERE.
INTRUDERS – EXTERMINATE!
POWER LEVELS LOW.
FULL SYSTEMS UNAVAILABLE.
ARRRRGH-GNN!

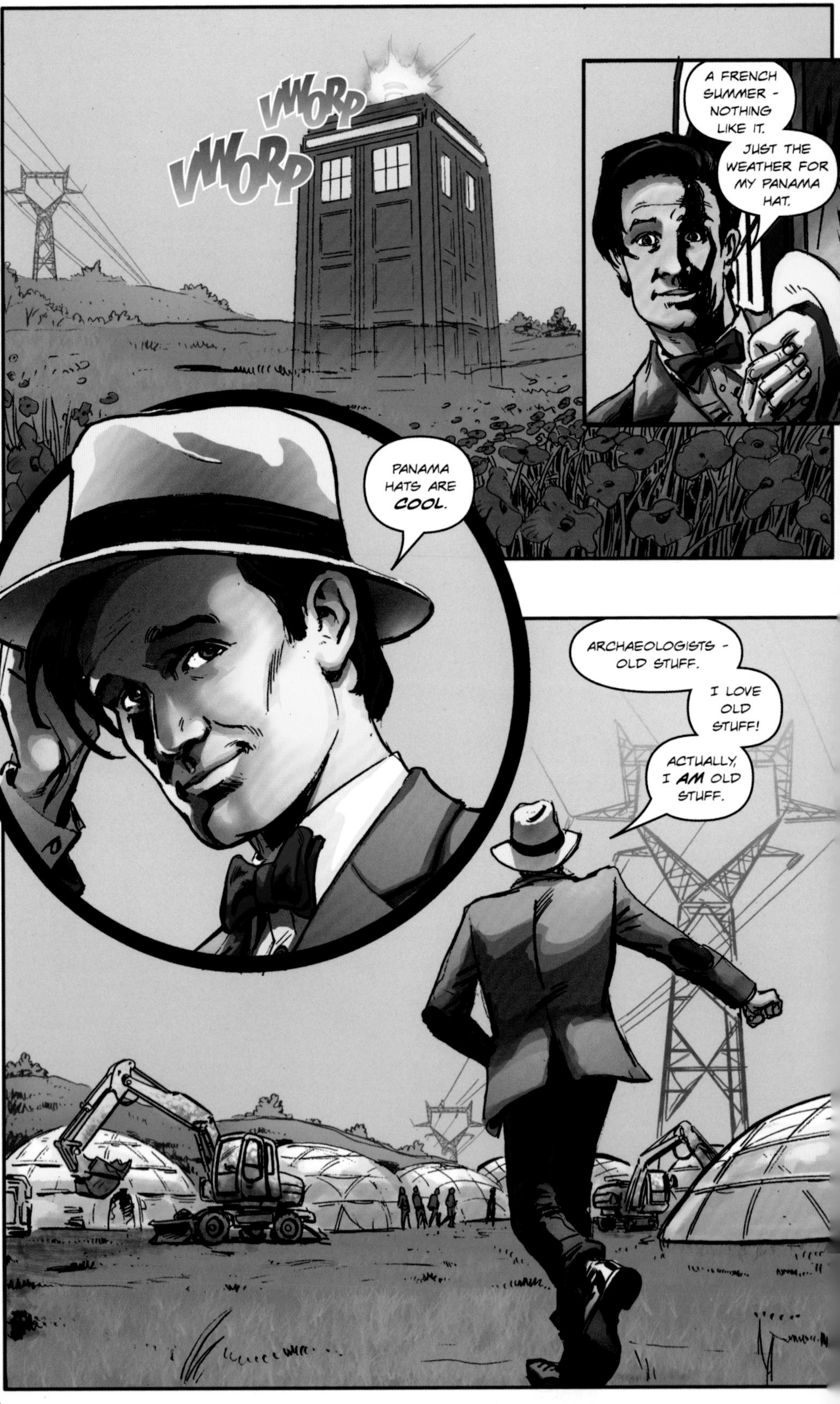
VWORP
VWORP
A FRENCH SUMMER - NOTHING LIKE IT.
JUST THE WEATHER FOR MY PANAMA HAT.
PANAMA HATS ARE COOL.
ARCHAEOLOGISTS - OLD STUFF.
I LOVE OLD STUFF!
ACTUALLY, I AM OLD STUFF.

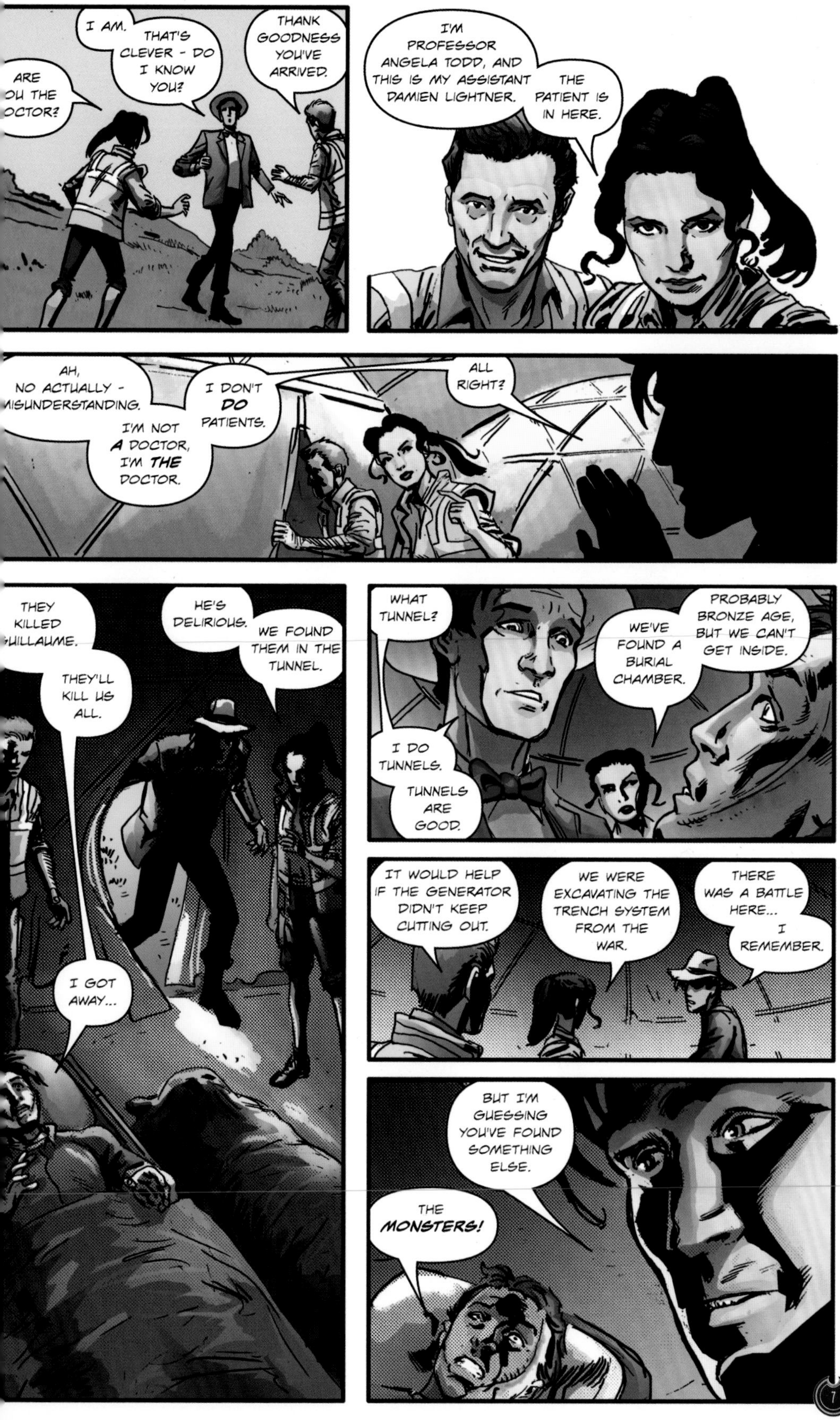
ARE OU THE OCTOR?
I AM.
THAT'S CLEVER - DO I KNOW YOU?
THANK GOODNESS YOU'VE ARRIVED.
I'M PROFESSOR ANGELA TODD, AND THIS IS MY ASSISTANT DAMIEN LIGHTNER.
THE PATIENT IS IN HERE.
AH, NO ACTUALLY - MISUNDERSTANDING.
I'M NOT A DOCTOR, I'M THE DOCTOR.
I DON'T DO PATIENTS.
ALL RIGHT?
THEY KILLED UILLAUME.
THEY'LL KILL US ALL.
HE'S DELIRIOUS.
WE FOUND THEM IN THE TUNNEL.
I GOT AWAY...
WHAT TUNNEL?
I DO TUNNELS.
TUNNELS ARE GOOD.
WE'VE FOUND A BURIAL CHAMBER.
PROBABLY BRONZE AGE, BUT WE CAN'T GET INSIDE.
IT WOULD HELP IF THE GENERATOR DIDN'T KEEP CUTTING OUT.
WE WERE EXCAVATING THE TRENCH SYSTEM FROM THE WAR.
THERE WAS A BATTLE HERE... I REMEMBER.
BUT I'M GUESSING YOU'VE FOUND SOMETHING ELSE.
THE MONSTERS!

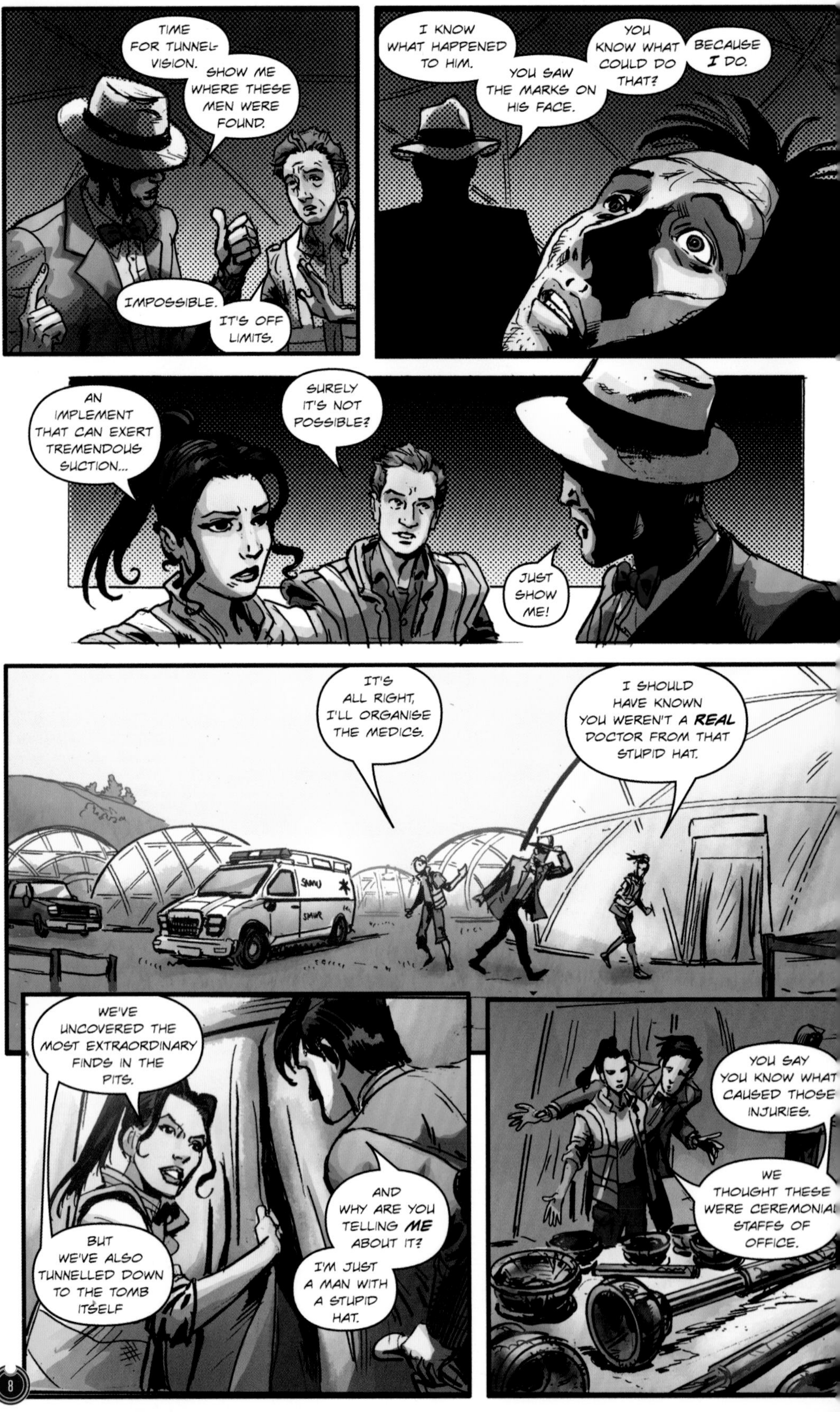
TIME FOR TUNNEL-VISION.
SHOW ME WHERE THESE MEN WERE FOUND.
IMPOSSIBLE.
IT'S OFF LIMITS.
I KNOW WHAT HAPPENED TO HIM.
YOU SAW THE MARKS ON HIS FACE.
YOU KNOW WHAT COULD DO THAT?
BECAUSE I DO.
AN IMPLEMENT THAT CAN EXERT TREMENDOUS SUCTION...
SURELY IT'S NOT POSSIBLE?
JUST SHOW ME!
IT'S ALL RIGHT, I'LL ORGANISE THE MEDICS.
I SHOULD HAVE KNOWN YOU WEREN'T A REAL DOCTOR FROM THAT STUPID HAT.
WE'VE UNCOVERED THE MOST EXTRAORDINARY FINDS IN THE PITS.
BUT WE'VE ALSO TUNNELLED DOWN TO THE TOMB ITSELF
AND WHY ARE YOU TELLING ME ABOUT IT?
I'M JUST A MAN WITH A STUPID HAT.
YOU SAY YOU KNOW WHAT CAUSED THOSE INJURIES.
WE THOUGHT THESE WERE CEREMONIAL STAFFS OF OFFICE.

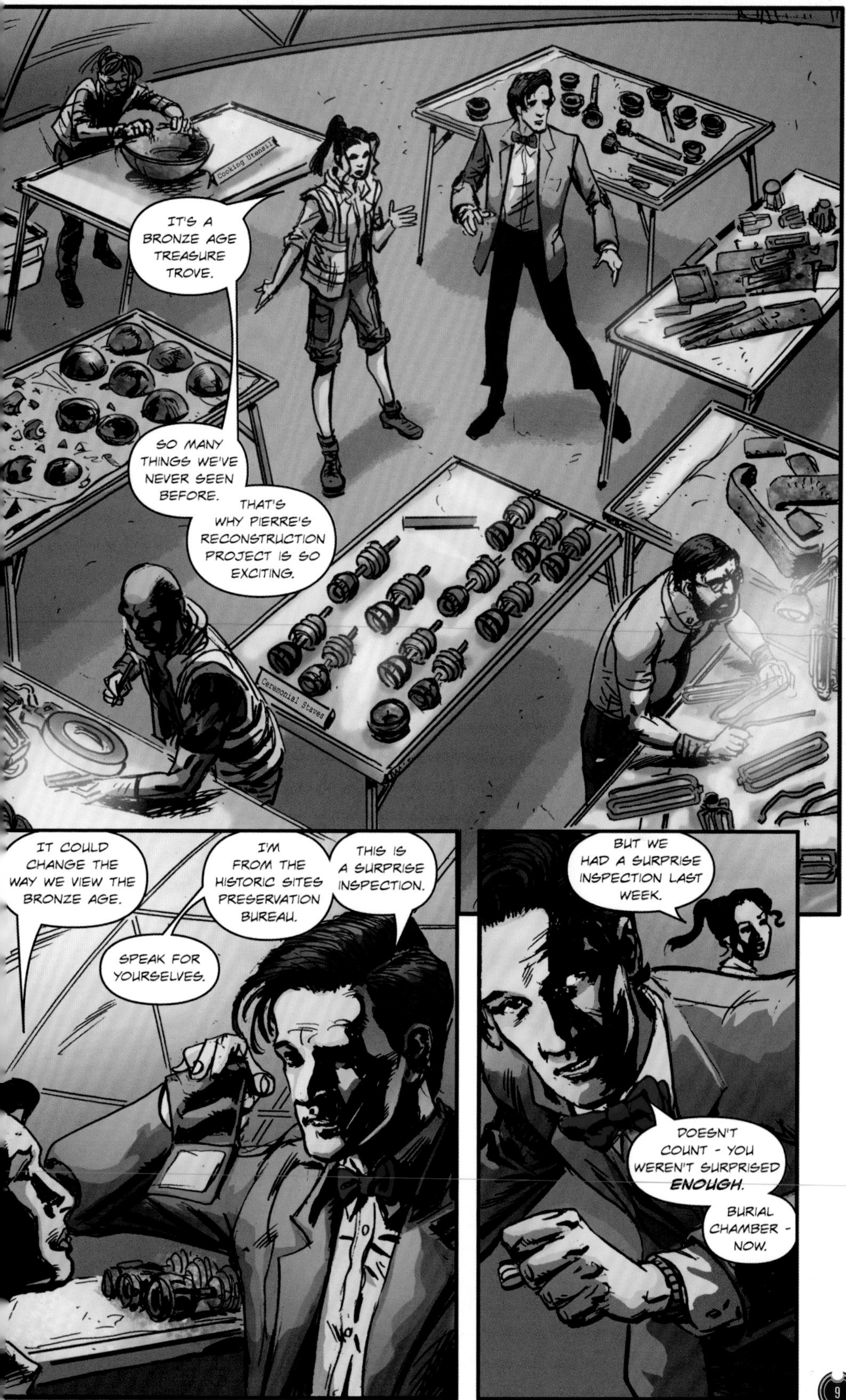
Cooking Utensil
IT'S A BRONZE AGE TREASURE TROVE.
SO MANY THINGS WE'VE NEVER SEEN BEFORE.
THAT'S WHY PIERRE'S RECONSTRUCTION PROJECT IS SO EXCITING.
Ceremonial Staves
IT COULD CHANGE THE WAY WE VIEW THE BRONZE AGE.
SPEAK FOR YOURSELVES.
I'M FROM THE HISTORIC SITES PRESERVATION BUREAU.
THIS IS A SURPRISE INSPECTION.
BUT WE HAD A SURPRISE INSPECTION LAST WEEK.
DOESN'T COUNT - YOU WEREN'T SURPRISED **ENOUGH**.
BURIAL CHAMBER - NOW.

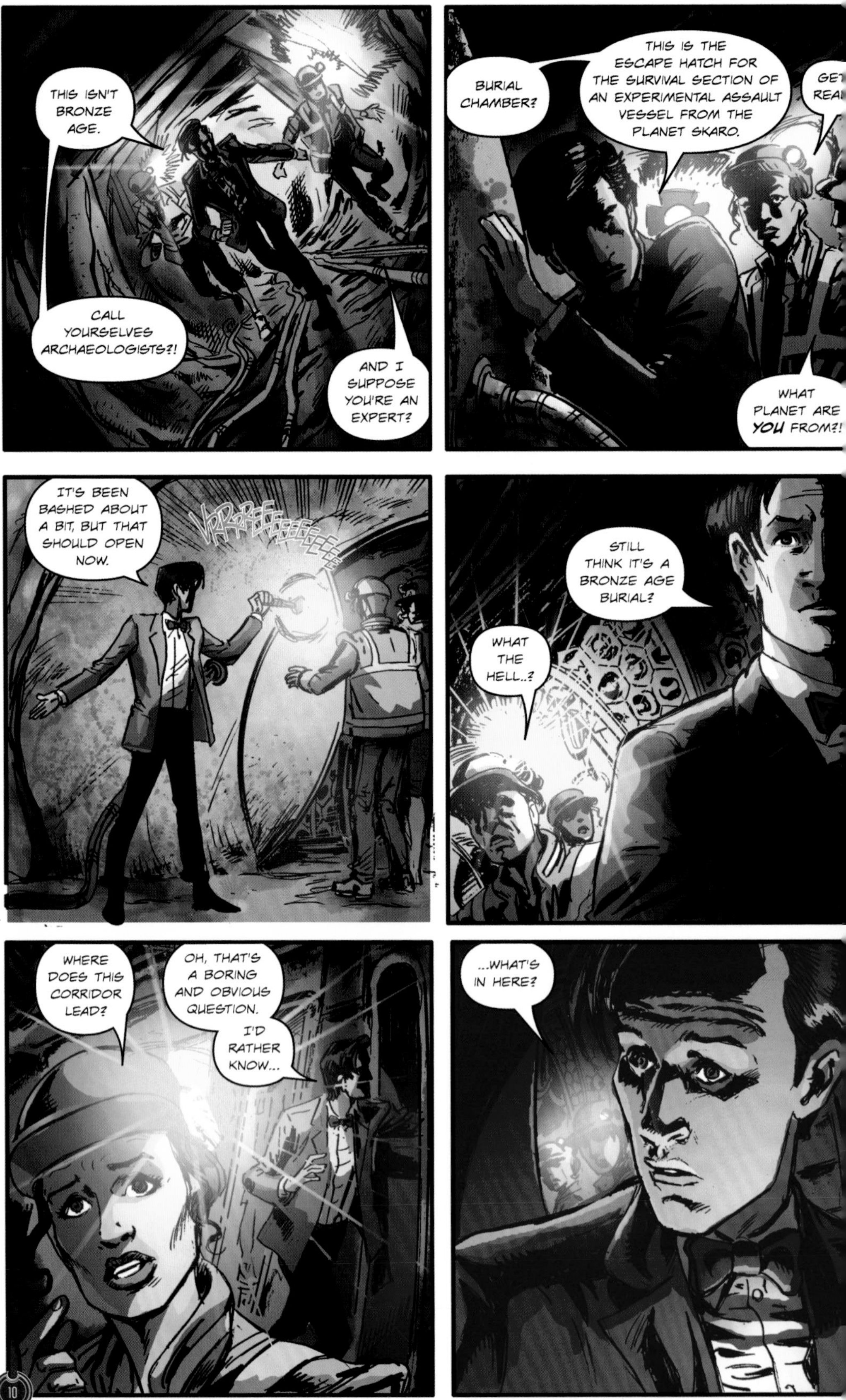
THIS ISN'T BRONZE AGE.
CALL YOURSELVES ARCHAEOLOGISTS?!
AND I SUPPOSE YOU'RE AN EXPERT?
BURIAL CHAMBER?
THIS IS THE ESCAPE HATCH FOR THE SURVIVAL SECTION OF AN EXPERIMENTAL ASSAULT VESSEL FROM THE PLANET SKARO.
WHAT PLANET ARE *YOU* FROM?!
IT'S BEEN BASHED ABOUT A BIT, BUT THAT SHOULD OPEN NOW.
STILL THINK IT'S A BRONZE AGE BURIAL?
WHAT THE HELL..?
WHERE DOES THIS CORRIDOR LEAD?
OH, THAT'S A BORING AND OBVIOUS QUESTION.
I'D RATHER KNOW...
...WHAT'S IN HERE?

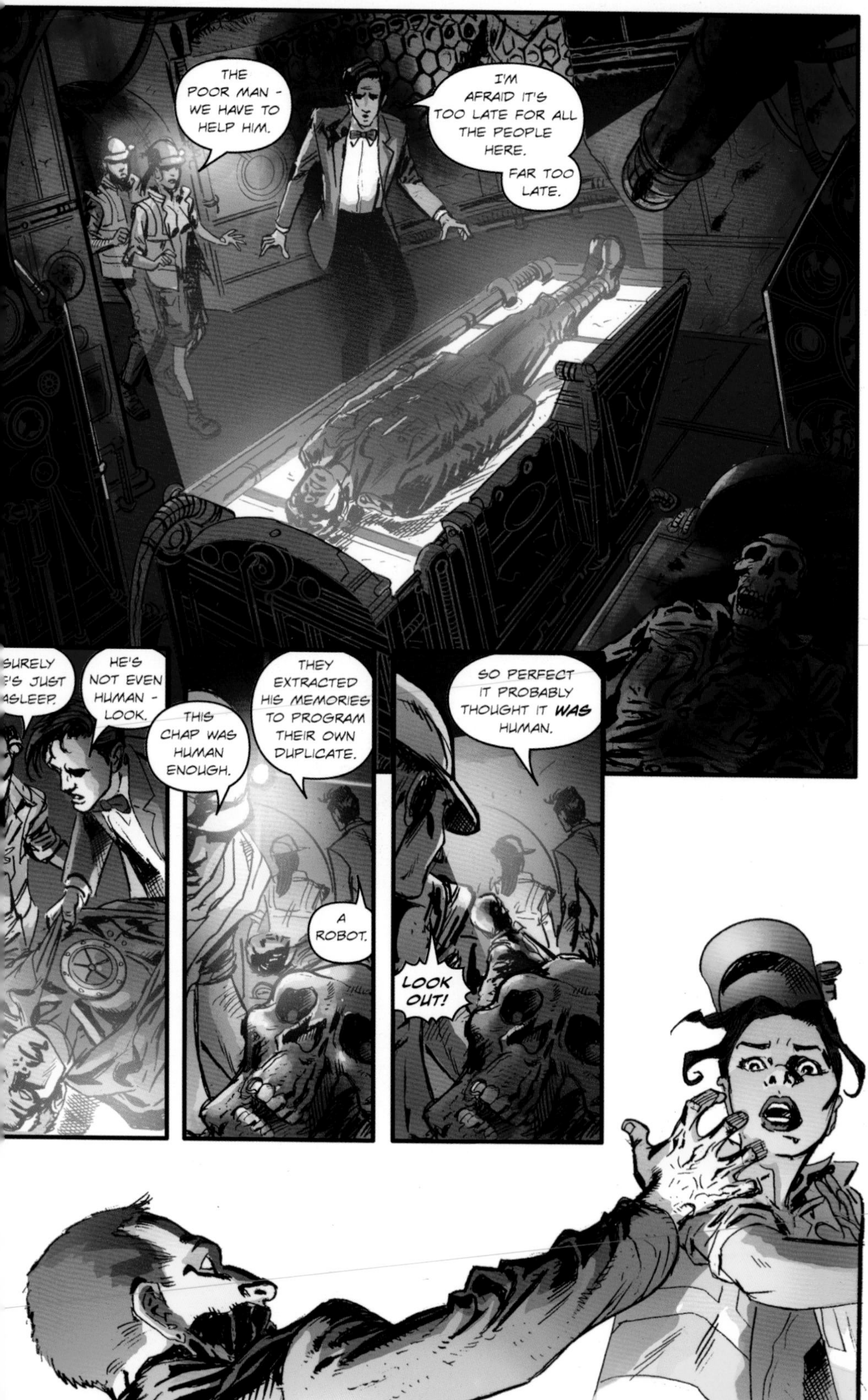
THE POOR MAN - WE HAVE TO HELP HIM.
I'M AFRAID IT'S TOO LATE FOR ALL THE PEOPLE HERE.
FAR TOO LATE.
SURELY E'S JUST ASLEEP.
HE'S NOT EVEN HUMAN - LOOK.
THIS CHAP WAS HUMAN ENOUGH.
THEY EXTRACTED HIS MEMORIES TO PROGRAM THEIR OWN DUPLICATE.
A ROBOT.
SO PERFECT IT PROBABLY THOUGHT IT **WAS** HUMAN.
LOOK OUT!

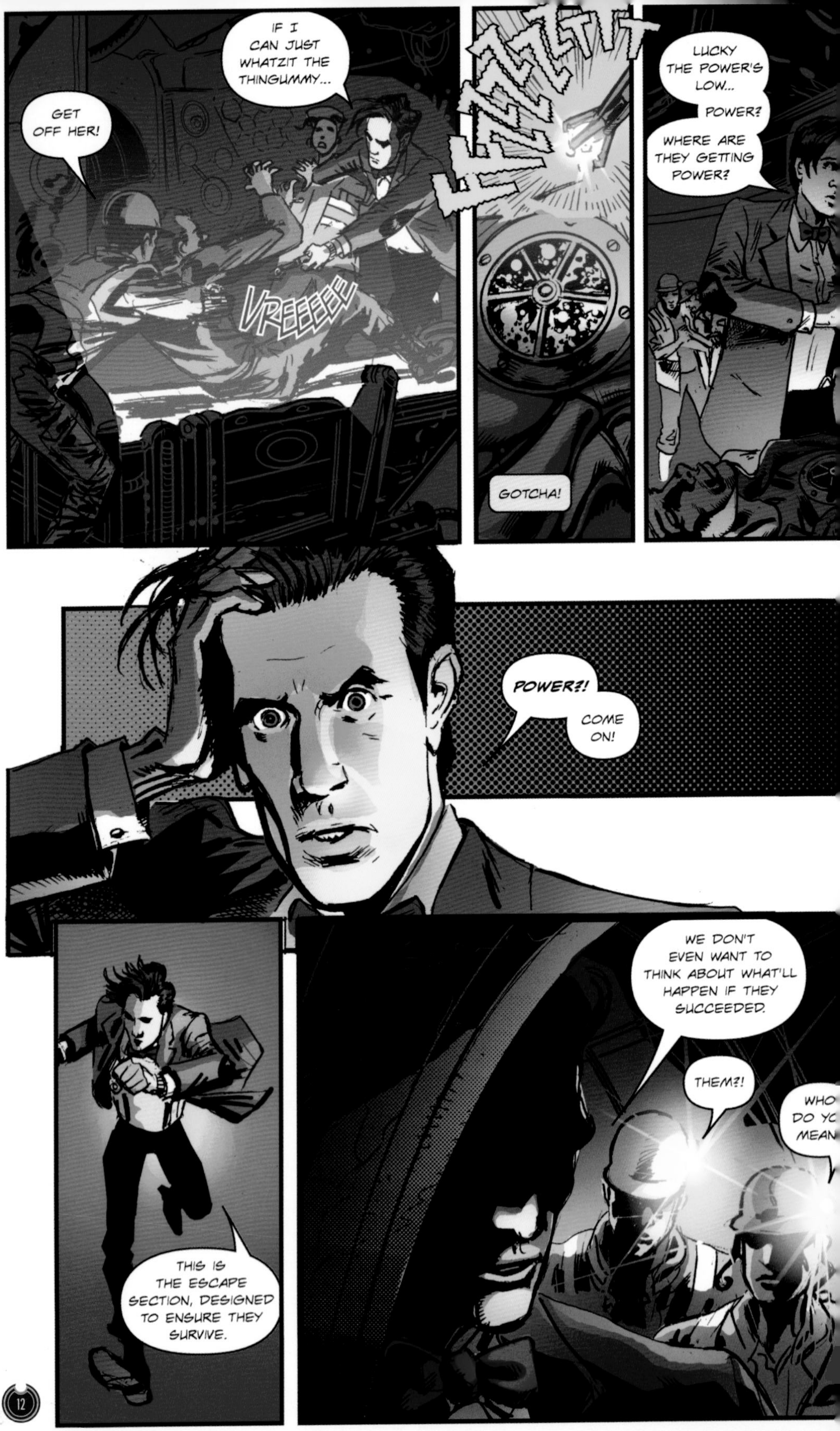
GET OFF HER!
IF I CAN JUST WHATZIT THE THINGUMMY...
VREEEEEE
FZZZZZTTT
GOTCHA!
LUCKY THE POWER'S LOW...
POWER?
WHERE ARE THEY GETTING POWER?
POWER?!
COME ON!
THIS IS THE ESCAPE SECTION, DESIGNED TO ENSURE THEY SURVIVE.
WE DON'T EVEN WANT TO THINK ABOUT WHAT'LL HAPPEN IF THEY SUCCEEDED.
THEM?!

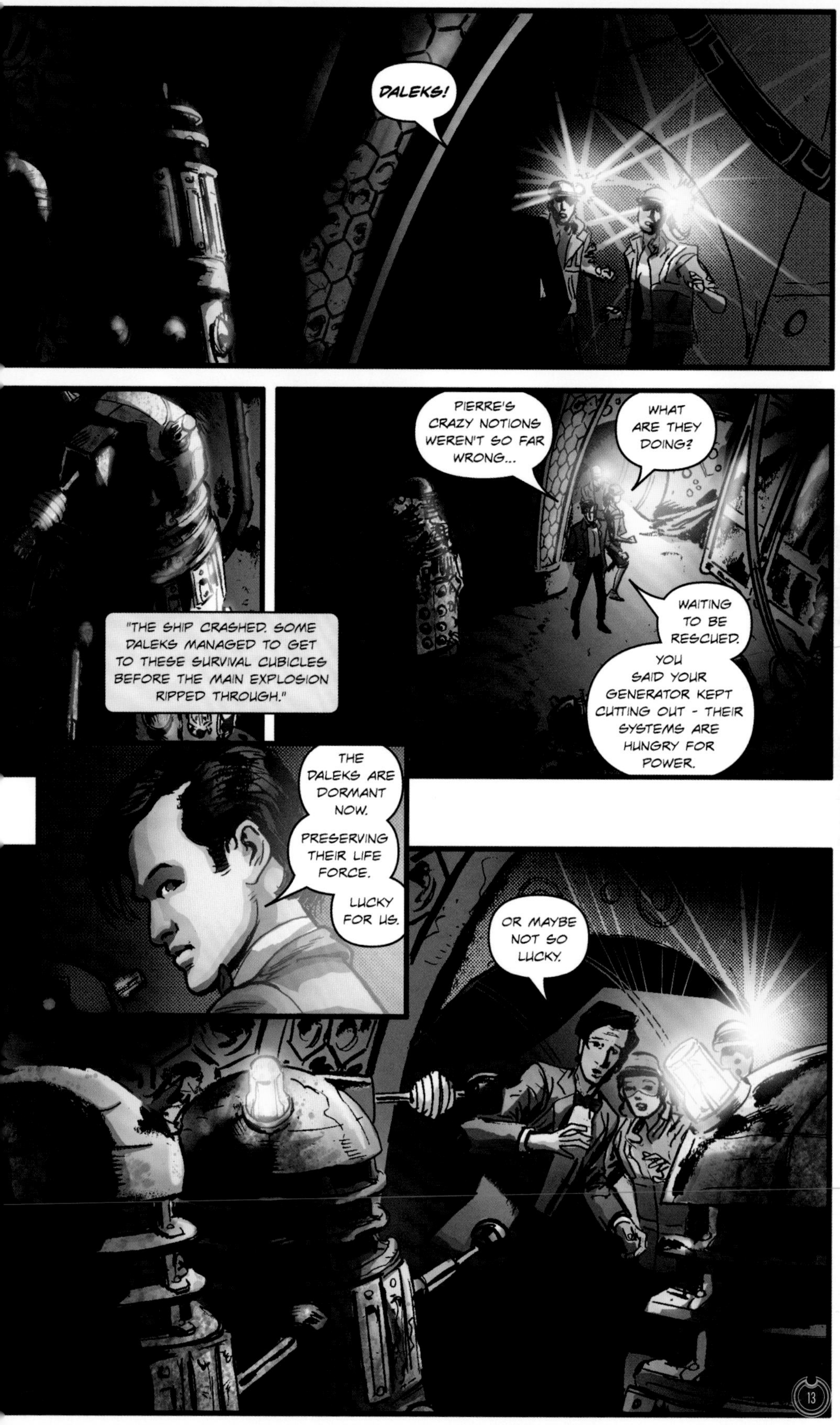
DALEKS!
"THE SHIP CRASHED. SOME DALEKS MANAGED TO GET TO THESE SURVIVAL CUBICLES BEFORE THE MAIN EXPLOSION RIPPED THROUGH."
PIERRE'S CRAZY NOTIONS WEREN'T SO FAR WRONG...
WHAT ARE THEY DOING?
WAITING TO BE RESCUED.
YOU SAID YOUR GENERATOR KEPT CUTTING OUT - THEIR SYSTEMS ARE HUNGRY FOR POWER.
THE DALEKS ARE DORMANT NOW.
PRESERVING THEIR LIFE FORCE.
LUCKY FOR US.
OR MAYBE NOT SO LUCKY.

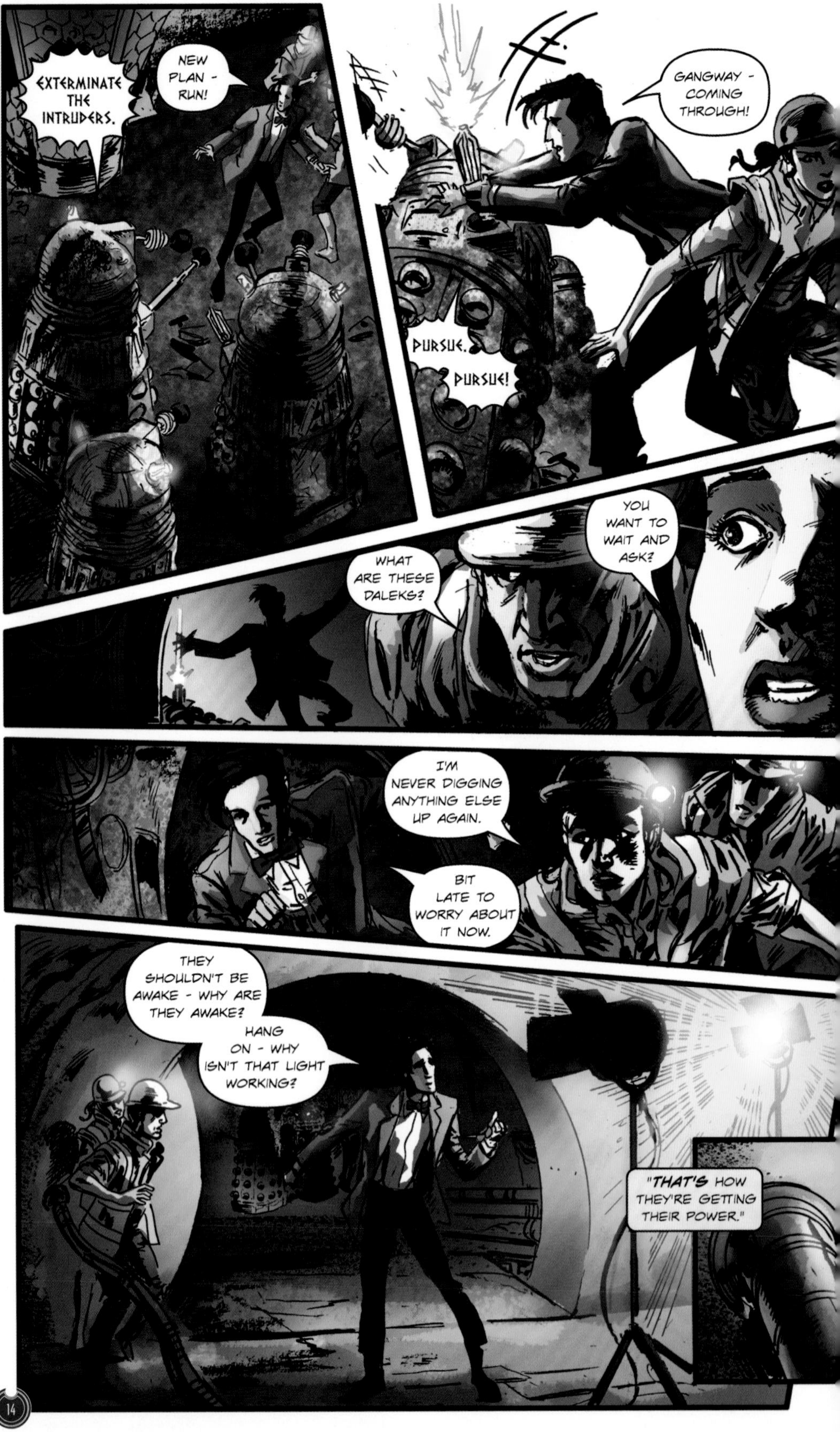
EXTERMINATE THE INTRUDERS.
NEW PLAN - RUN!
GANGWAY - COMING THROUGH!
PURSUE.
PURSUE!
YOU WANT TO WAIT AND ASK?
WHAT ARE THESE DALEKS?
I'M NEVER DIGGING ANYTHING ELSE UP AGAIN.
BIT LATE TO WORRY ABOUT IT NOW.
THEY SHOULDN'T BE AWAKE - WHY ARE THEY AWAKE?
HANG ON - WHY ISN'T THAT LIGHT WORKING?
"THAT'S HOW THEY'RE GETTING THEIR POWER."

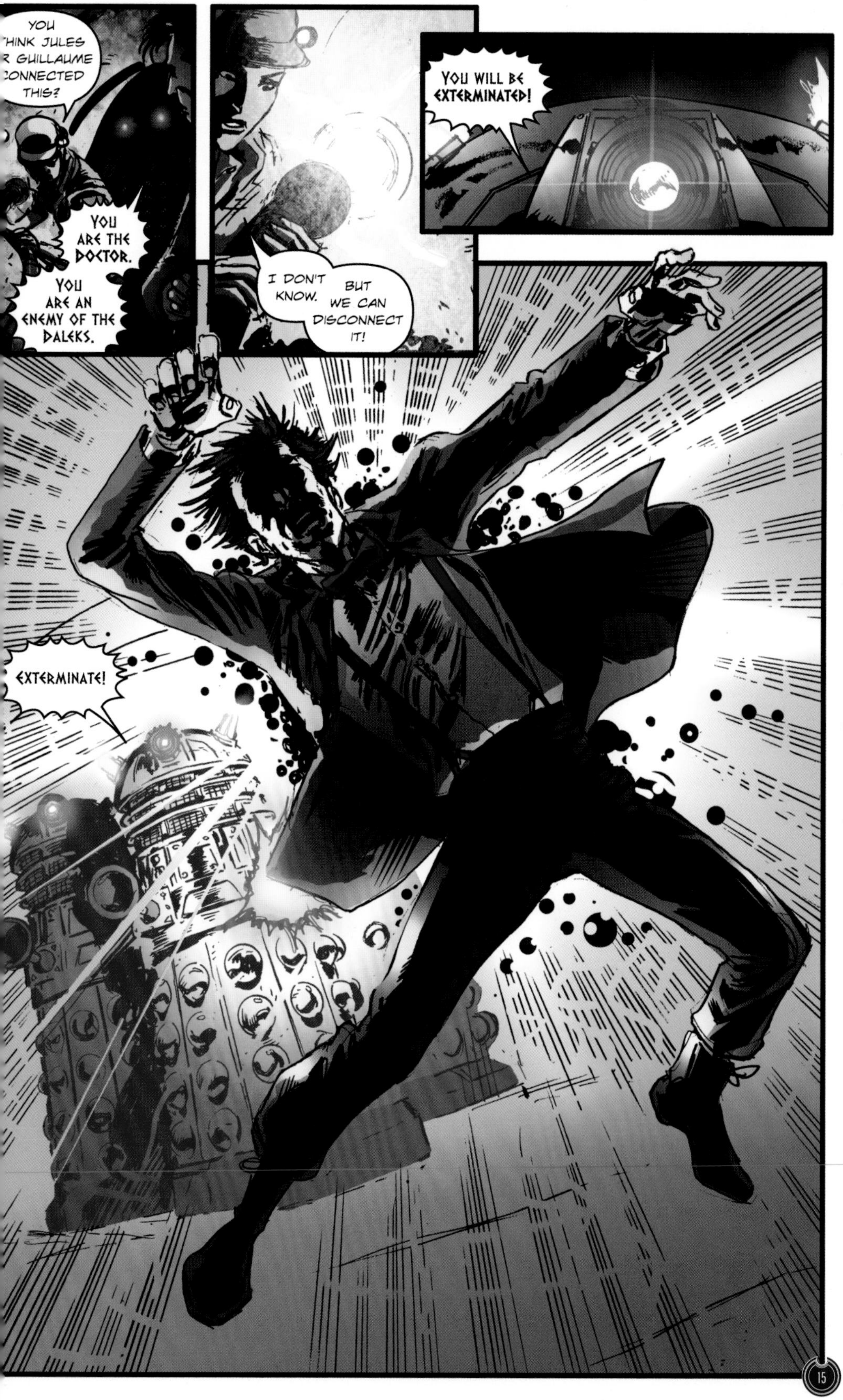
YOU THINK JULES OR GUILLAUME CONNECTED THIS?
YOU ARE THE DOCTOR.
YOU ARE AN ENEMY OF THE DALEKS.
I DON'T KNOW.
BUT WE CAN DISCONNECT IT!
YOU WILL BE EXTERMINATED!
EXTERMINATE!

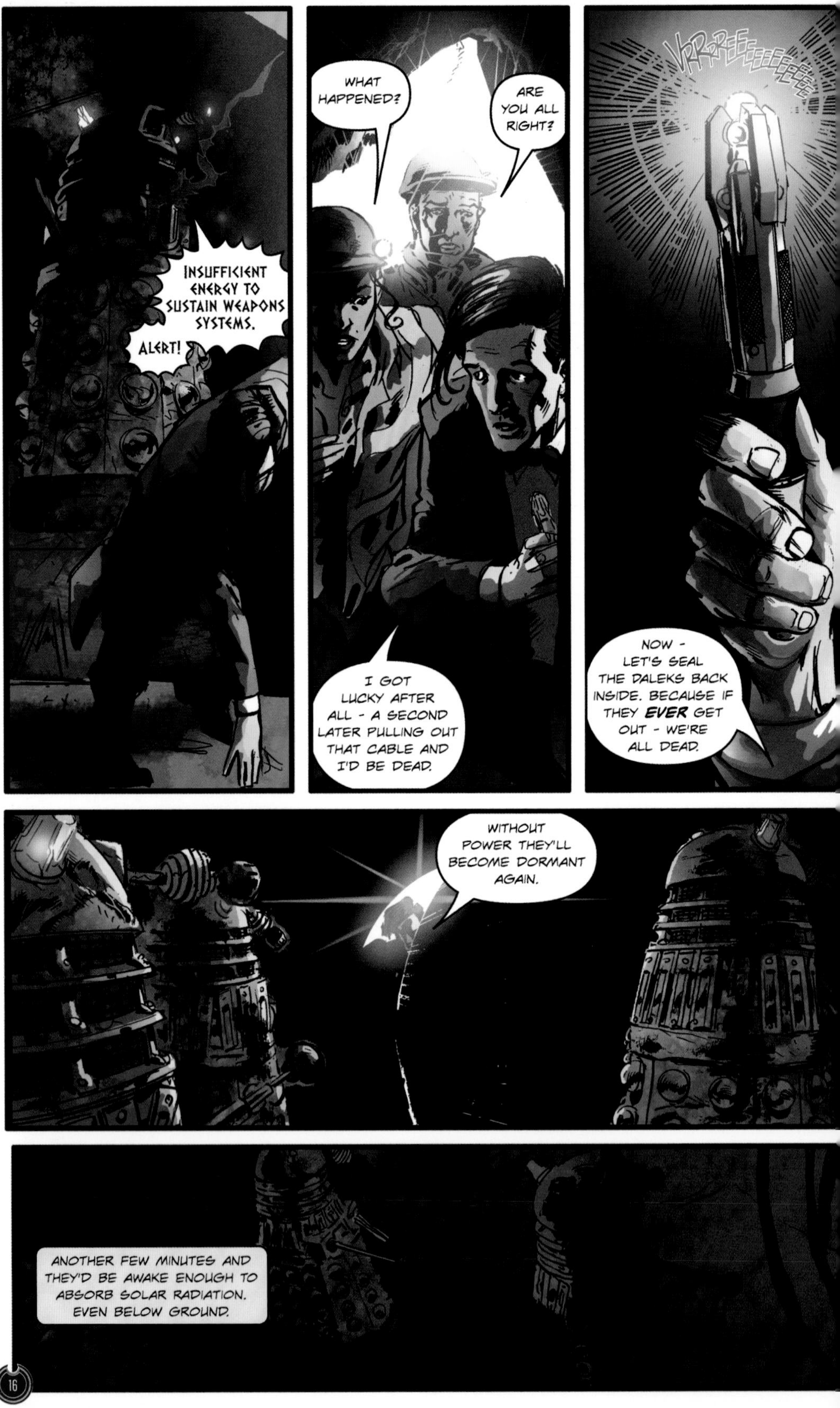
INSUFFICIENT ENERGY TO SUSTAIN WEAPONS SYSTEMS.
ALERT!
WHAT HAPPENED?
ARE YOU ALL RIGHT?
I GOT LUCKY AFTER ALL - A SECOND LATER PULLING OUT THAT CABLE AND I'D BE DEAD.
VRRRREEEEEEEEEEEE
NOW - LET'S SEAL THE DALEKS BACK INSIDE. BECAUSE IF THEY **EVER** GET OUT - WE'RE ALL DEAD.
WITHOUT POWER THEY'LL BECOME DORMANT AGAIN.
ANOTHER FEW MINUTES AND THEY'D BE AWAKE ENOUGH TO ABSORB SOLAR RADIATION. EVEN BELOW GROUND.

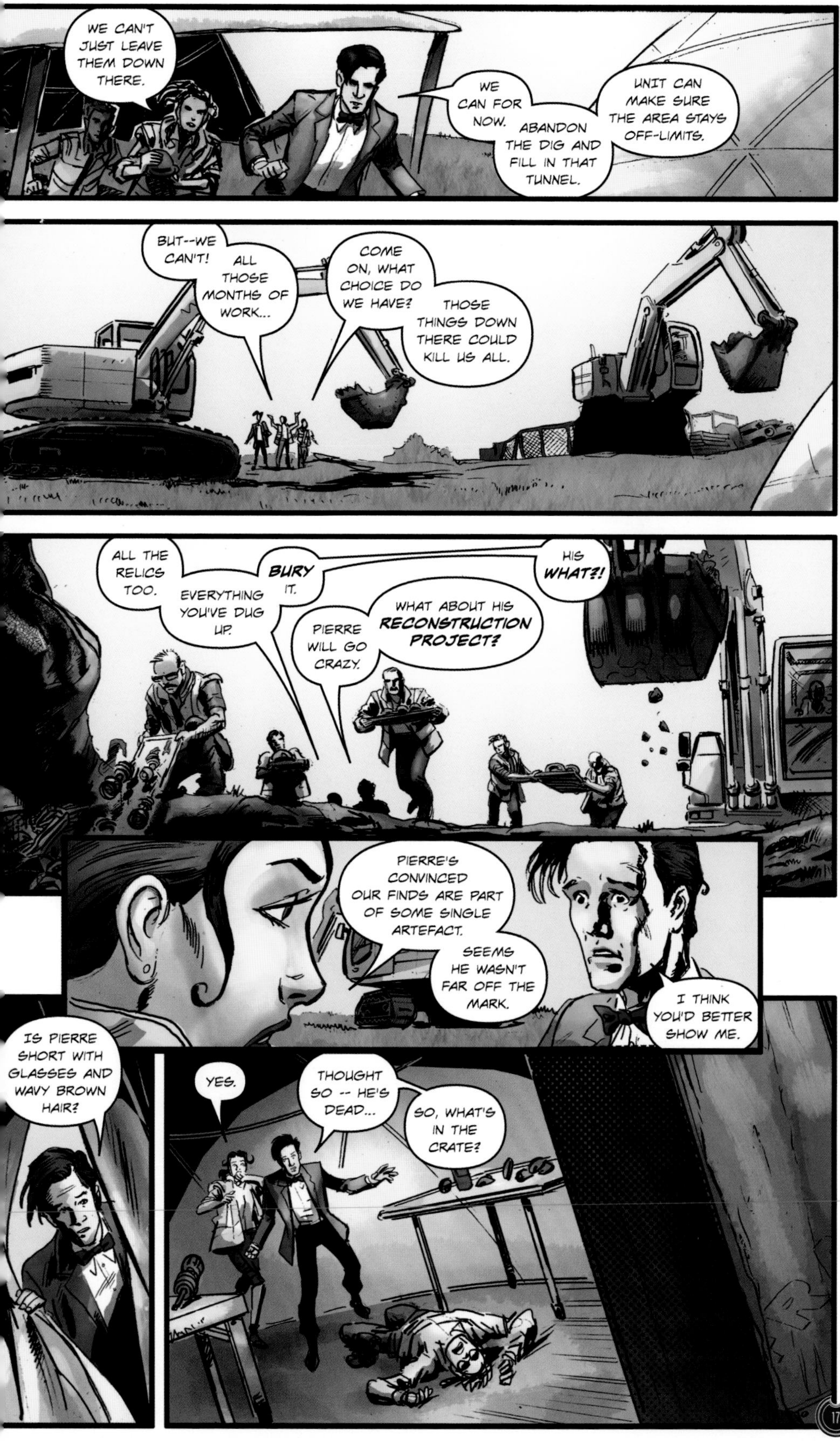

WE CAN'T JUST LEAVE THEM DOWN THERE.
WE CAN FOR NOW.
ABANDON THE DIG AND FILL IN THAT TUNNEL.
UNIT CAN MAKE SURE THE AREA STAYS OFF-LIMITS.
BUT--WE CAN'T!
ALL THOSE MONTHS OF WORK...
COME ON, WHAT CHOICE DO WE HAVE?
THOSE THINGS DOWN THERE COULD KILL US ALL.
ALL THE RELICS TOO.
EVERYTHING YOU'VE DUG UP.
BURY IT.
PIERRE WILL GO CRAZY.
WHAT ABOUT HIS RECONSTRUCTION PROJECT?
HIS WHAT?!
PIERRE'S CONVINCED OUR FINDS ARE PART OF SOME SINGLE ARTEFACT.
SEEMS HE WASN'T FAR OFF THE MARK.
I THINK YOU'D BETTER SHOW ME.
IS PIERRE SHORT WITH GLASSES AND WAVY BROWN HAIR?
YES.
THOUGHT SO -- HE'S DEAD...
SO, WHAT'S IN THE CRATE?

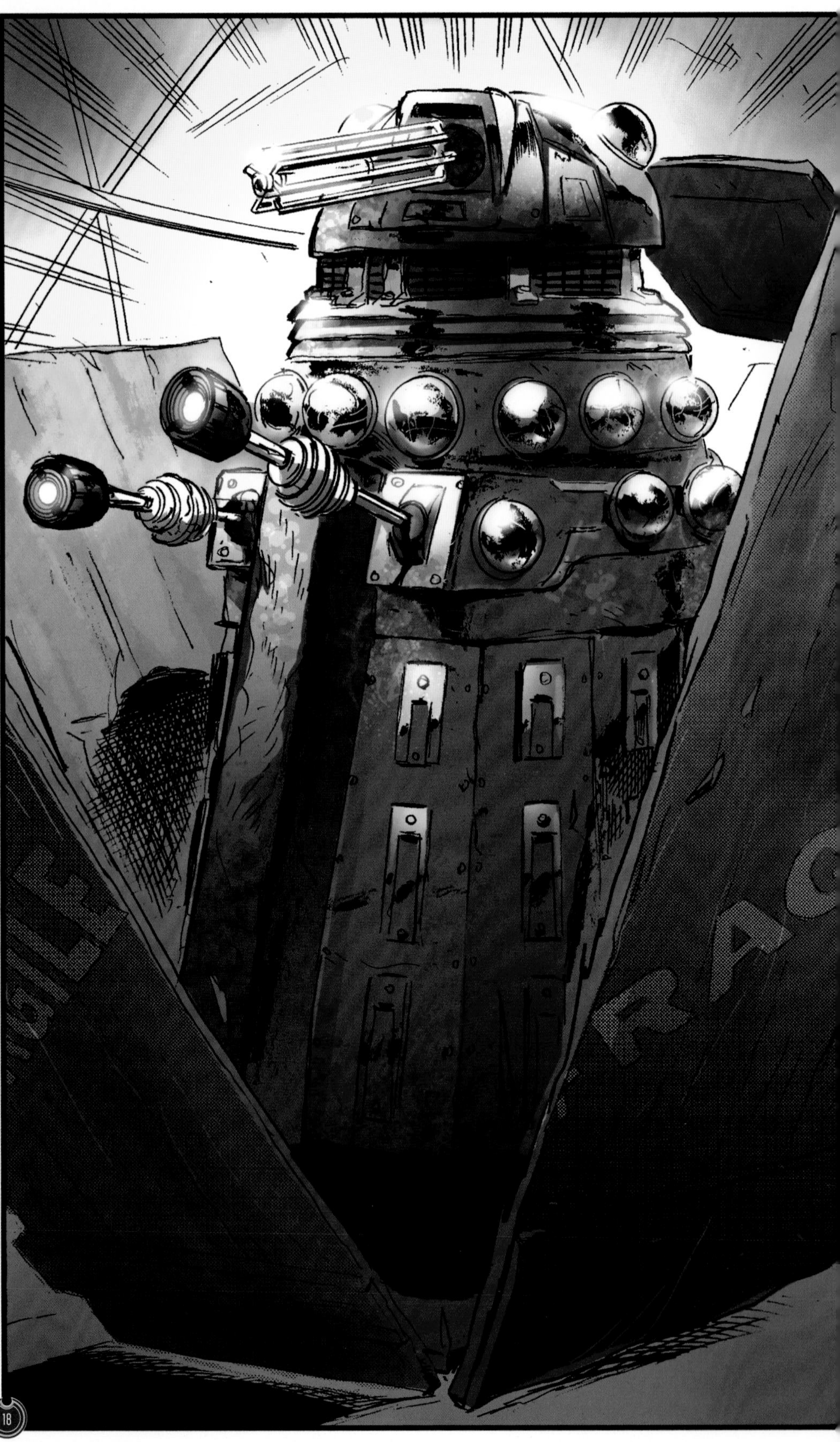

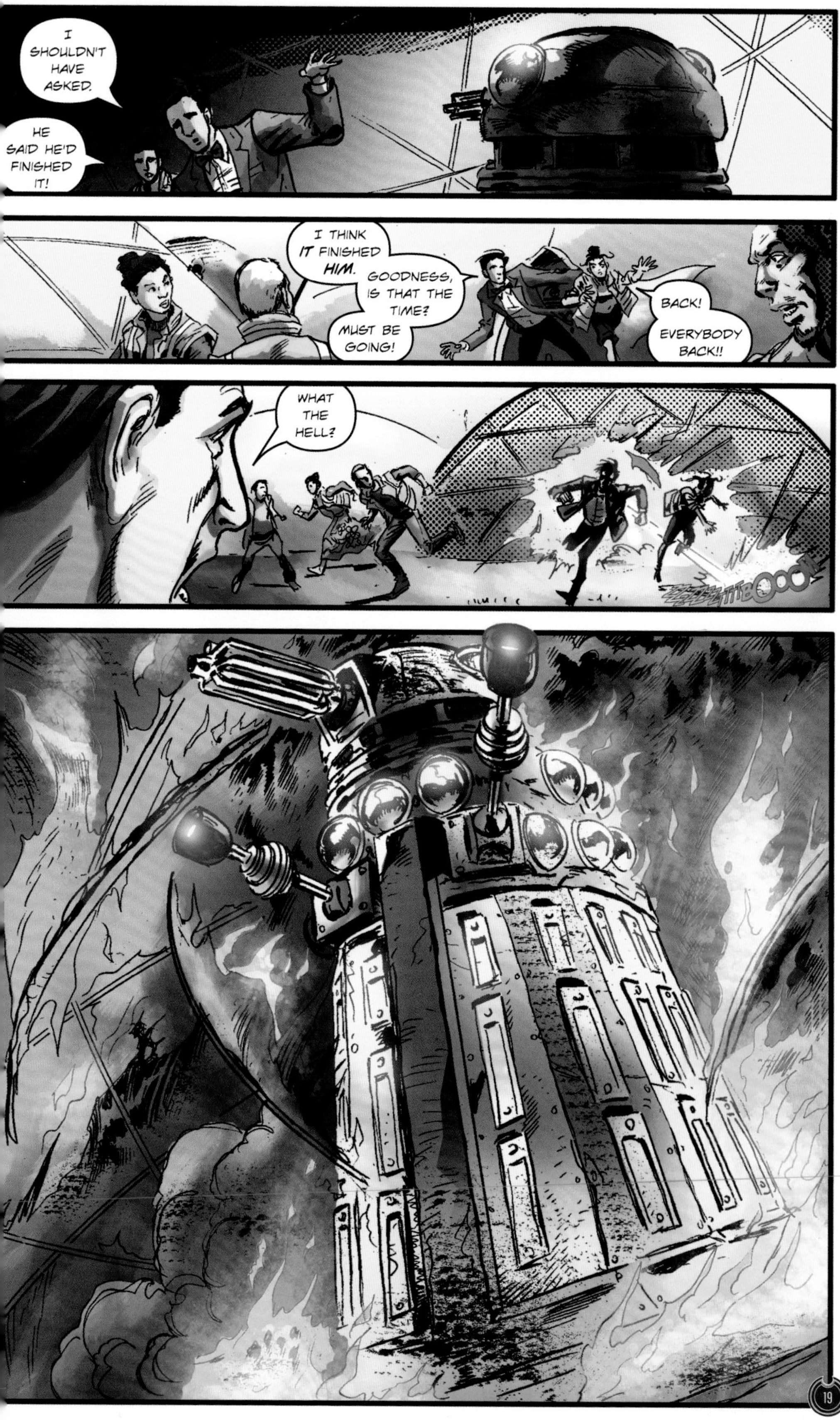

I SHOULDN'T HAVE ASKED.
HE SAID HE'D FINISHED IT!
I THINK *IT* FINISHED ***HIM***.
GOODNESS, IS THAT THE TIME?
MUST BE GOING!
BACK!
EVERYBODY BACK!!
WHAT THE HELL?

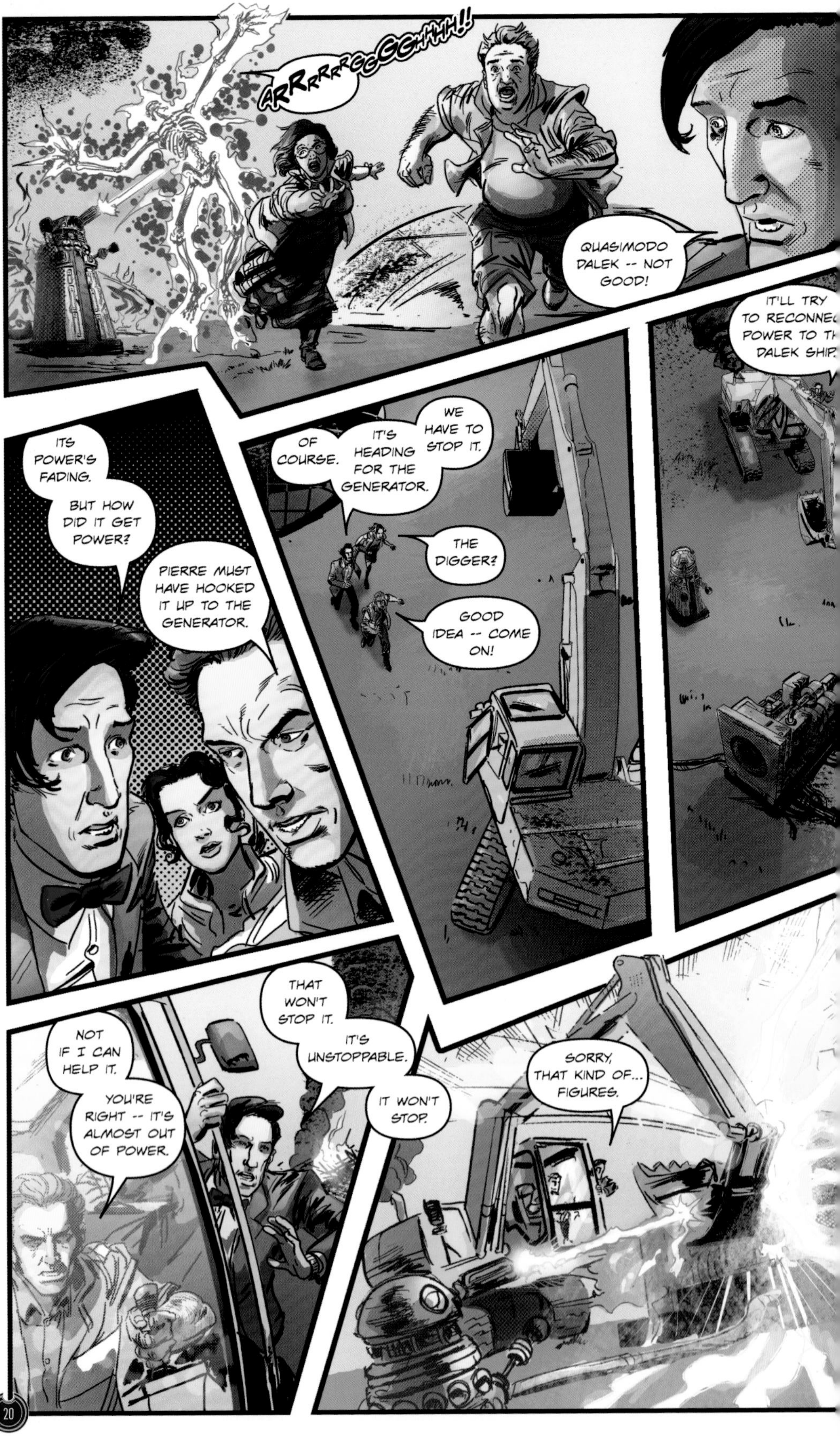
ARRRRRRGGGGHHHH!!
QUASIMODO DALEK -- NOT GOOD!
IT'LL TRY TO RECONNE
POWER TO T
DALEK SHIP.
ITS POWER'S FADING.
BUT HOW DID IT GET POWER?
PIERRE MUST HAVE HOOKED IT UP TO THE GENERATOR.
OF COURSE.
IT'S HEADING FOR THE GENERATOR.
WE HAVE TO STOP IT.
THE DIGGER?
GOOD IDEA -- COME ON!
NOT IF I CAN HELP IT.
YOU'RE RIGHT -- IT'S ALMOST OUT OF POWER.
THAT WON'T STOP IT.
IT'S UNSTOPPABLE.
IT WON'T STOP.
SORRY, THAT KIND OF... FIGURES.

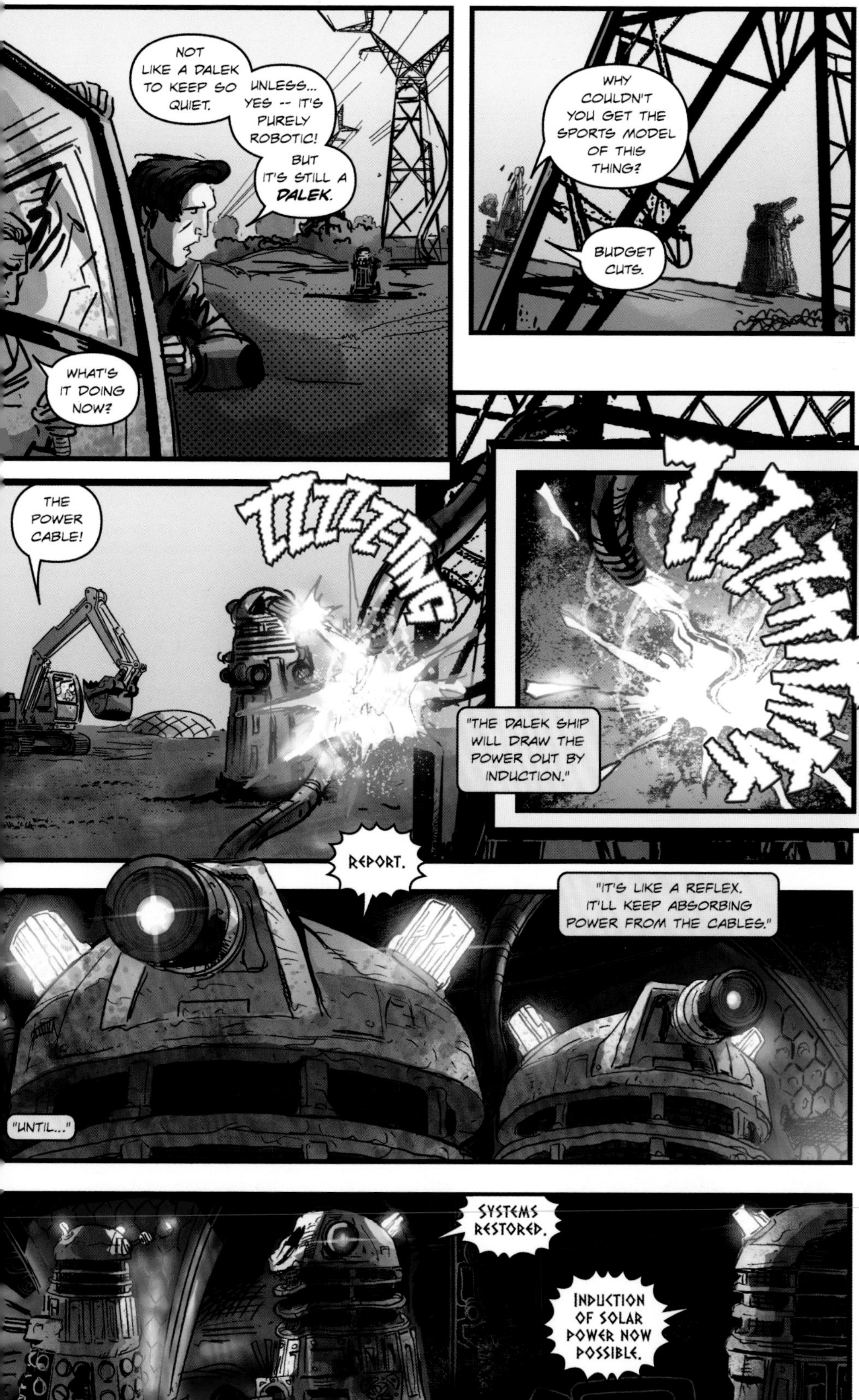

NOT LIKE A DALEK TO KEEP SO QUIET.
UNLESS... YES -- IT'S PURELY ROBOTIC!
BUT IT'S STILL A DALEK.
WHAT'S IT DOING NOW?
WHY COULDN'T YOU GET THE SPORTS MODEL OF THIS THING?
BUDGET CUTS.
THE POWER CABLE!
TZZZZZ-TING
TZZZZTHTHTHTK
"THE DALEK SHIP WILL DRAW THE POWER OUT BY INDUCTION."
REPORT.
"IT'S LIKE A REFLEX. IT'LL KEEP ABSORBING POWER FROM THE CABLES."
"UNTIL..."
SYSTEMS RESTORED.
INDUCTION OF SOLAR POWER NOW POSSIBLE.

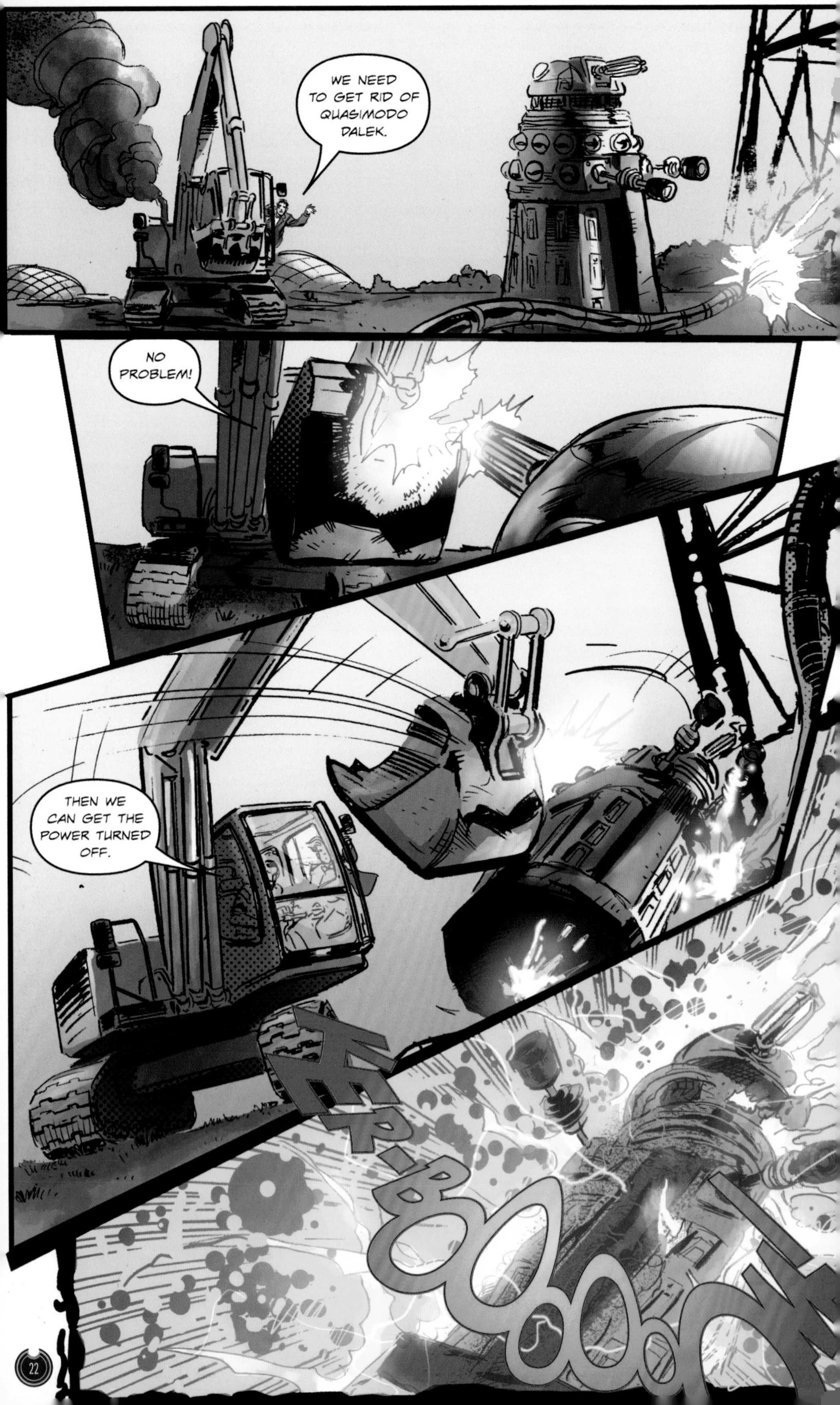
WE NEED TO GET RID OF QUASIMODO DALEK.
NO PROBLEM!
THEN WE CAN GET THE POWER TURNED OFF.
KER-BOOOM!

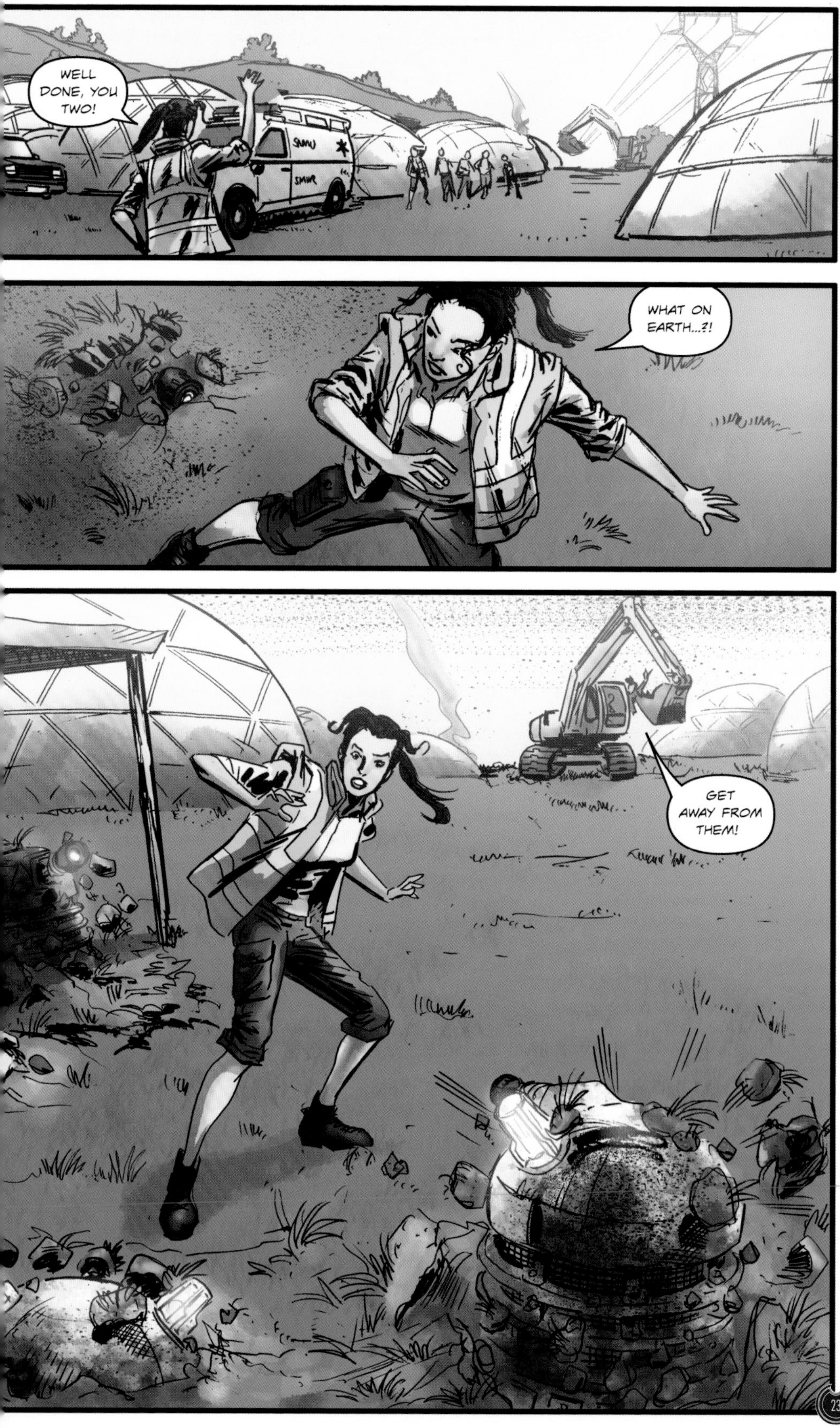

WELL DONE, YOU TWO!
WHAT ON EARTH...?!
GET AWAY FROM THEM!

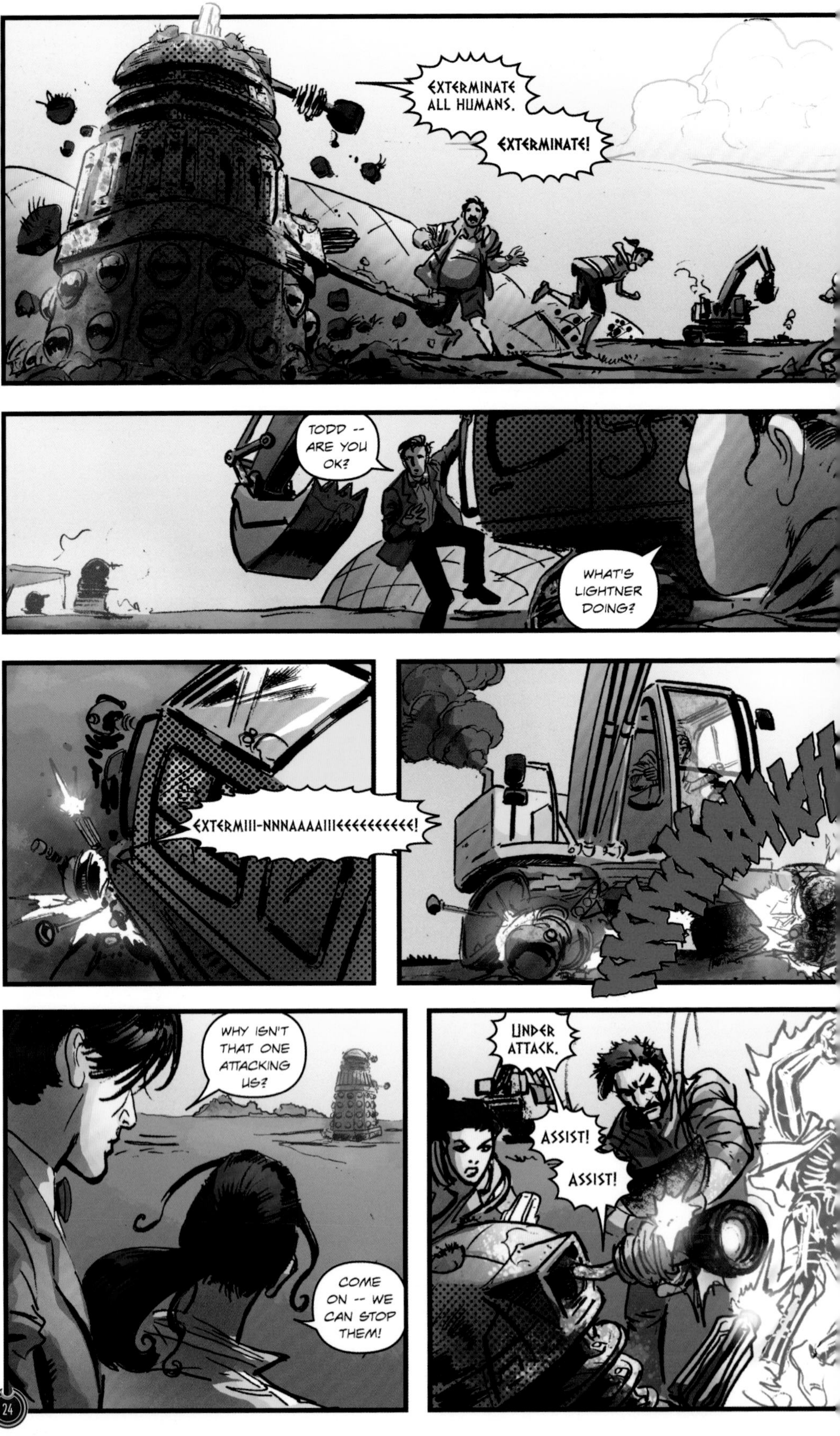
EXTERMINATE ALL HUMANS.
EXTERMINATE!
TODD -- ARE YOU OK?
WHAT'S LIGHTNER DOING?
EXTERMIII-NNNAAAAIIIEEEEEEEEEEE!
WHY ISN'T THAT ONE ATTACKING US?
COME ON -- WE CAN STOP THEM!
UNDER ATTACK.
ASSIST!
ASSIST!

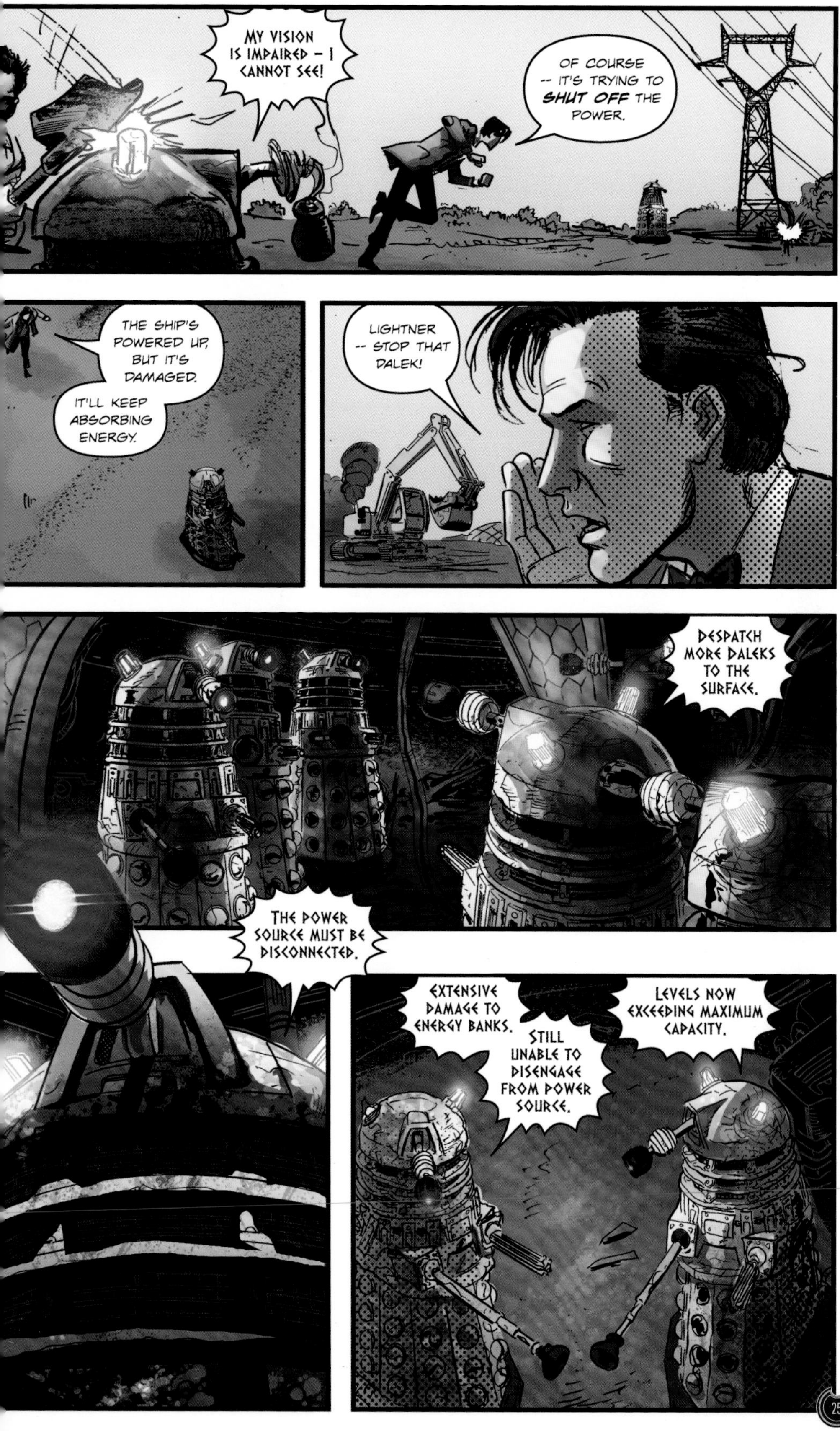
MY VISION IS IMPAIRED – I CANNOT SEE!
OF COURSE -- IT'S TRYING TO SHUT OFF THE POWER.
THE SHIP'S POWERED UP, BUT IT'S DAMAGED.
IT'LL KEEP ABSORBING ENERGY.
LIGHTNER -- STOP THAT DALEK!
DESPATCH MORE DALEKS TO THE SURFACE.
THE POWER SOURCE MUST BE DISCONNECTED.
EXTENSIVE DAMAGE TO ENERGY BANKS.
STILL UNABLE TO DISENGAGE FROM POWER SOURCE.
LEVELS NOW EXCEEDING MAXIMUM CAPACITY.

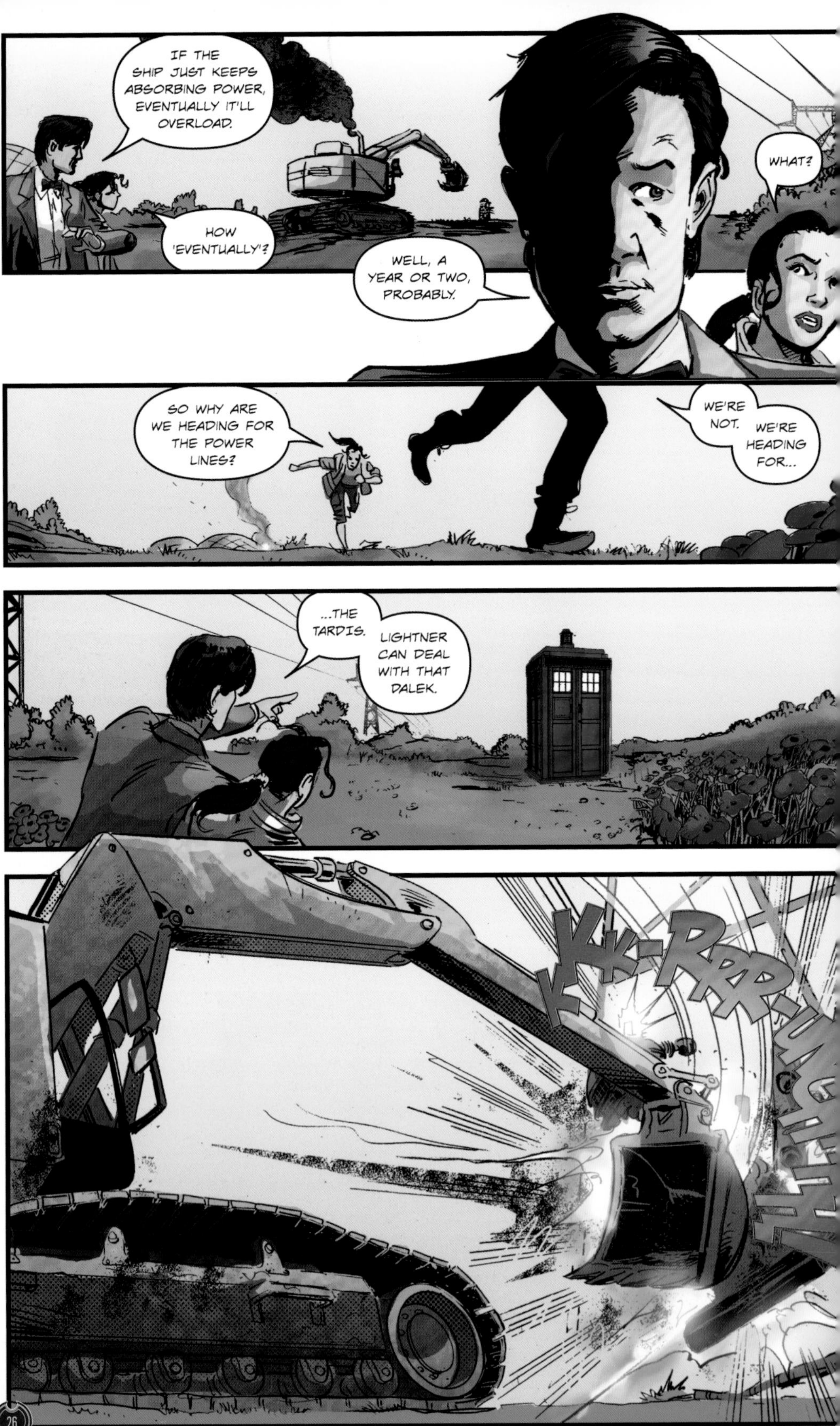
IF THE SHIP JUST KEEPS ABSORBING POWER, EVENTUALLY IT'LL OVERLOAD.
HOW 'EVENTUALLY'?
WELL, A YEAR OR TWO, PROBABLY.
WHAT?
SO WHY ARE WE HEADING FOR THE POWER LINES?
WE'RE NOT.
WE'RE HEADING FOR...
...THE TARDIS.
LIGHTNER CAN DEAL WITH THAT DALEK.
KK-RRR-UNCHH

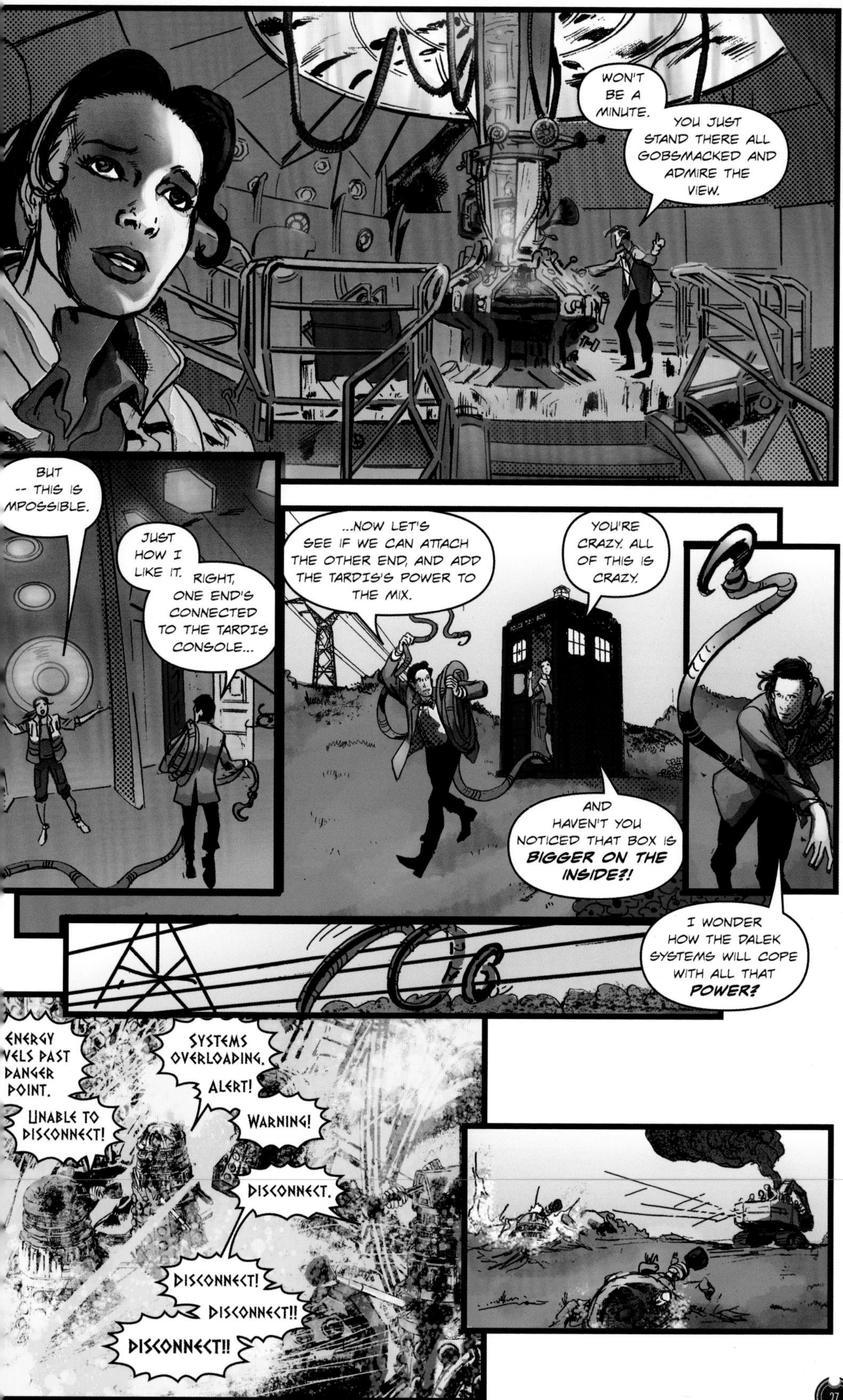
WON'T BE A MINUTE.
YOU JUST STAND THERE ALL GOBSMACKED AND ADMIRE THE VIEW.
BUT -- THIS IS MPOSSIBLE.
JUST HOW I LIKE IT.
RIGHT, ONE END'S CONNECTED TO THE TARDIS CONSOLE...
...NOW LET'S SEE IF WE CAN ATTACH THE OTHER END, AND ADD THE TARDIS'S POWER TO THE MIX.
YOU'RE CRAZY. ALL OF THIS IS CRAZY.
AND HAVEN'T YOU NOTICED THAT BOX IS BIGGER ON THE INSIDE?!
I WONDER HOW THE DALEK SYSTEMS WILL COPE WITH ALL THAT POWER?
ENERGY VELS PAST DANGER POINT.
SYSTEMS OVERLOADING.
ALERT!
UNABLE TO DISCONNECT!
WARNING!
DISCONNECT.
DISCONNECT!
DISCONNECT!!
DISCONNECT!!

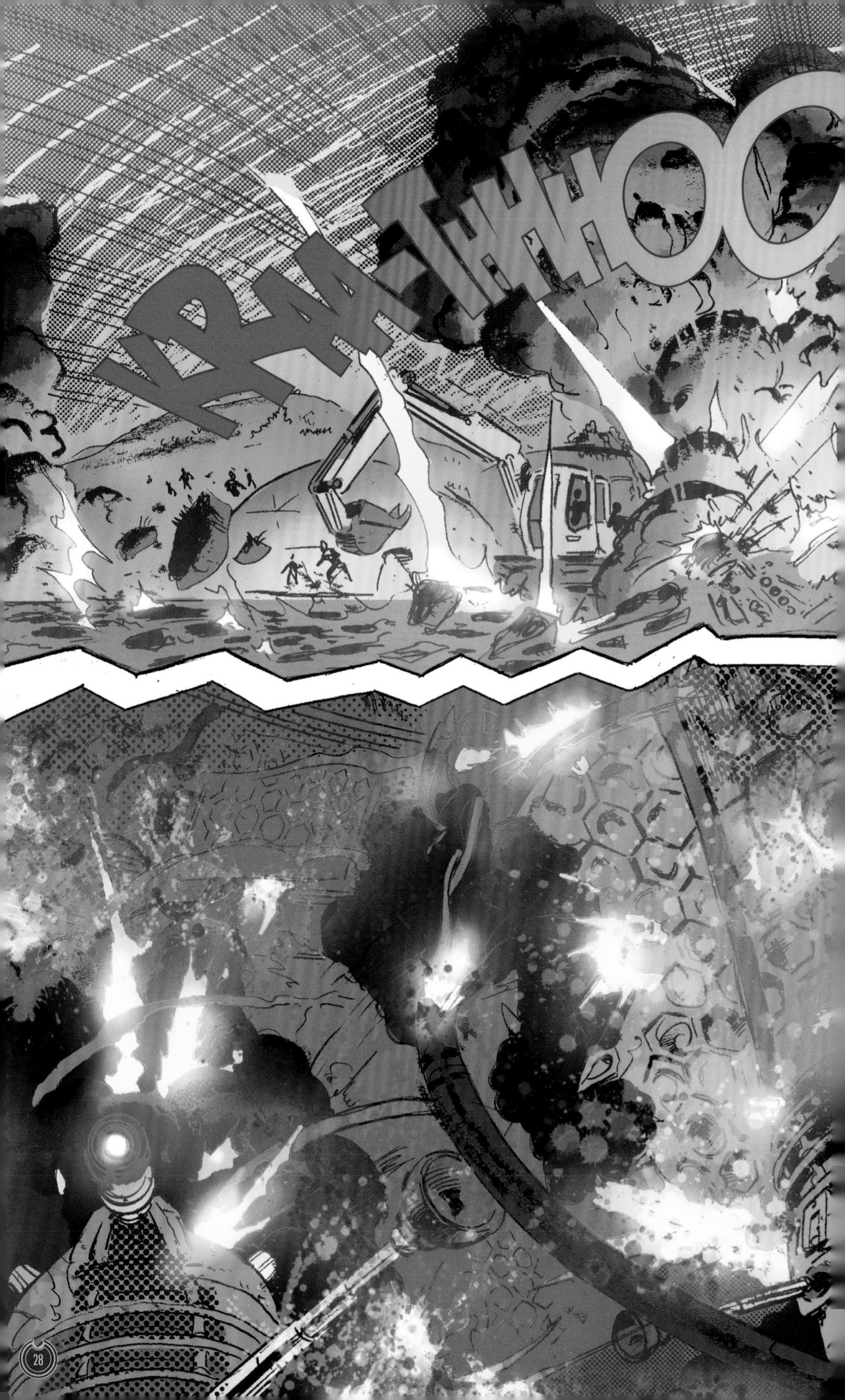
KRAA-THHOO

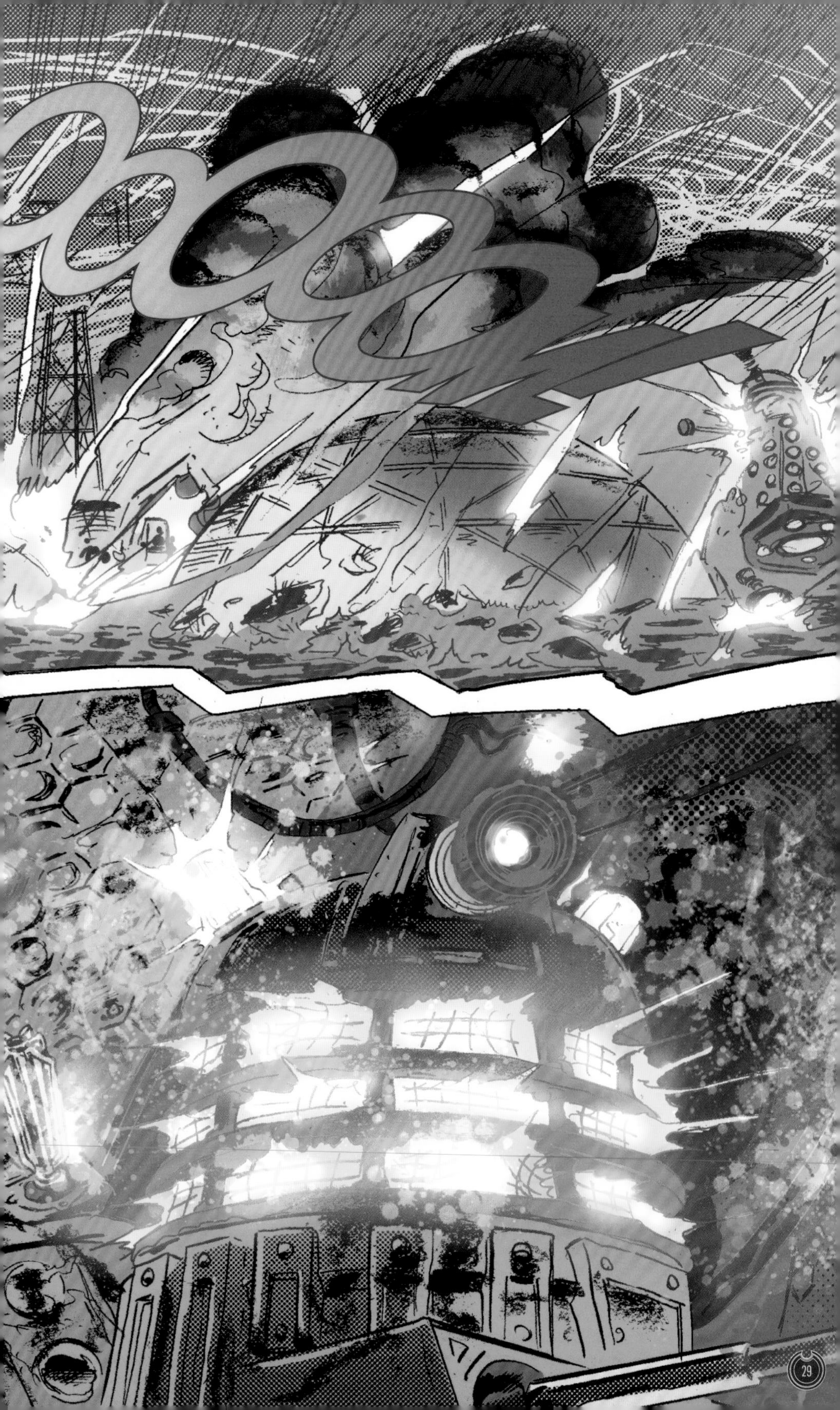

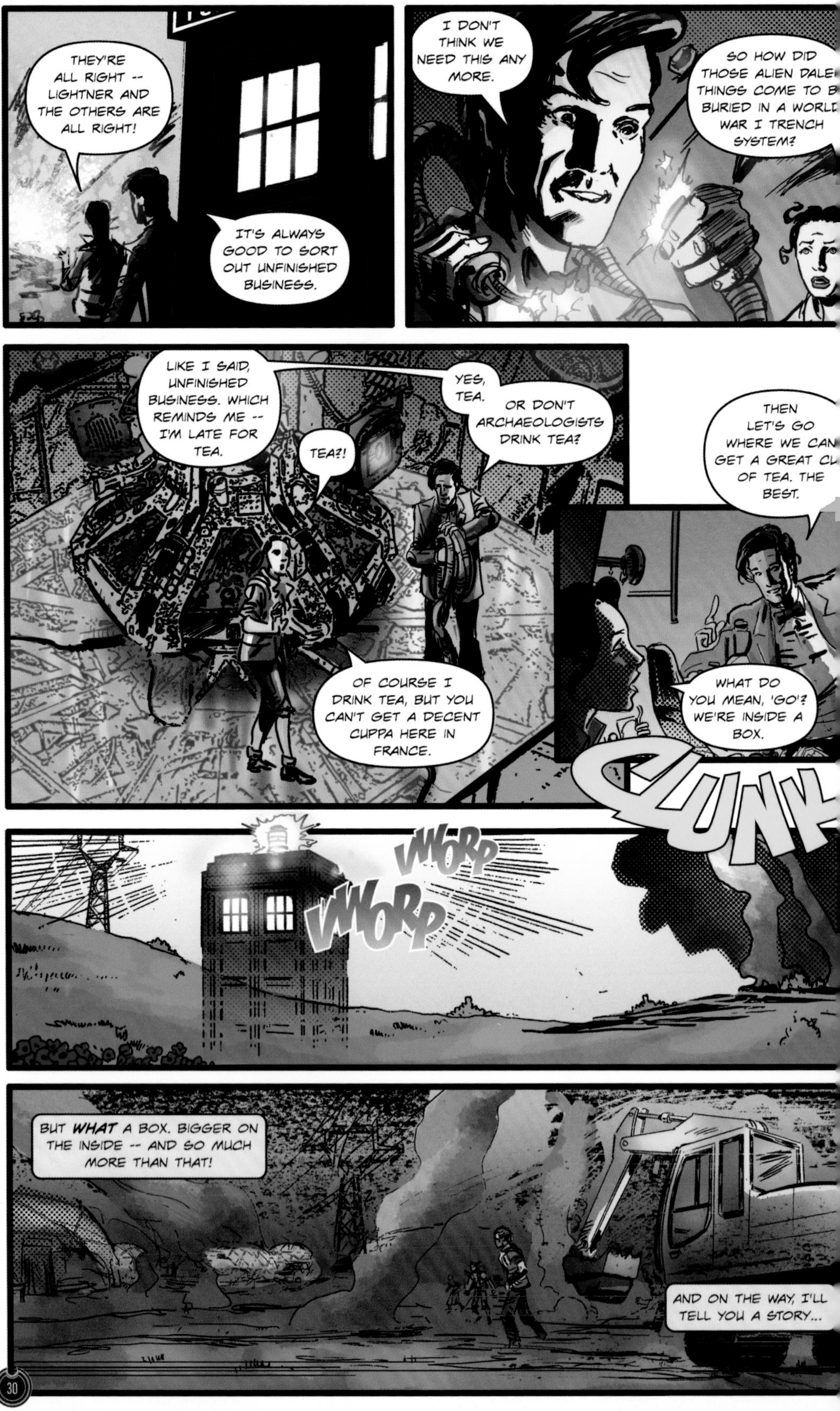

THEY'RE ALL RIGHT -- LIGHTNER AND THE OTHERS ARE ALL RIGHT!
IT'S ALWAYS GOOD TO SORT OUT UNFINISHED BUSINESS.
I DON'T THINK WE NEED THIS ANY MORE.
SO HOW DID THOSE ALIEN DALE THINGS COME TO B BURIED IN A WORLD WAR I TRENCH SYSTEM?
LIKE I SAID, UNFINISHED BUSINESS. WHICH REMINDS ME -- I'M LATE FOR TEA.
TEA?!
YES, TEA.
OR DON'T ARCHAEOLOGISTS DRINK TEA?
OF COURSE I DRINK TEA, BUT YOU CAN'T GET A DECENT CUPPA HERE IN FRANCE.
THEN LET'S GO WHERE WE CAN GET A GREAT CU OF TEA. THE BEST.
WHAT DO YOU MEAN, 'GO'? WE'RE INSIDE A BOX.
CLUNK
VWORP
VWORP
BUT WHAT A BOX. BIGGER ON THE INSIDE -- AND SO MUCH MORE THAN THAT!
AND ON THE WAY, I'LL TELL YOU A STORY...

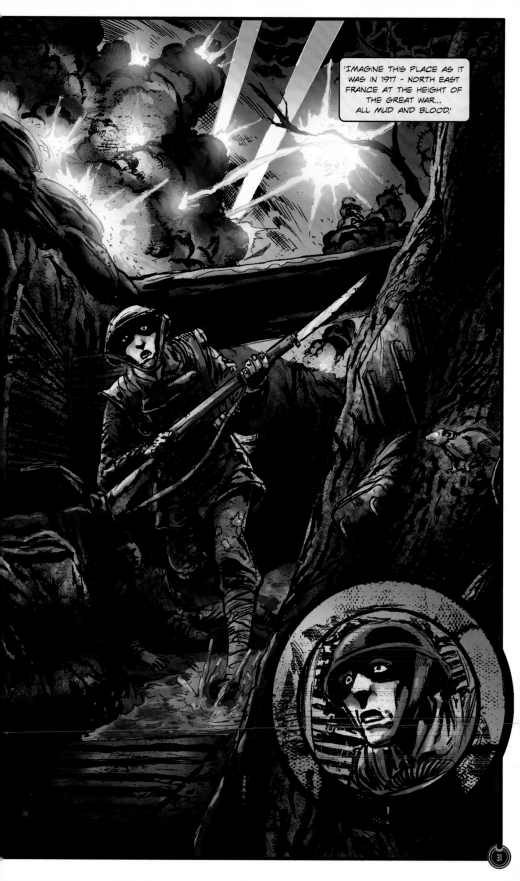

'IMAGINE THIS PLACE AS IT WAS IN 1917 - NORTH EAST FRANCE AT THE HEIGHT OF THE GREAT WAR... ALL MUD AND BLOOD!'

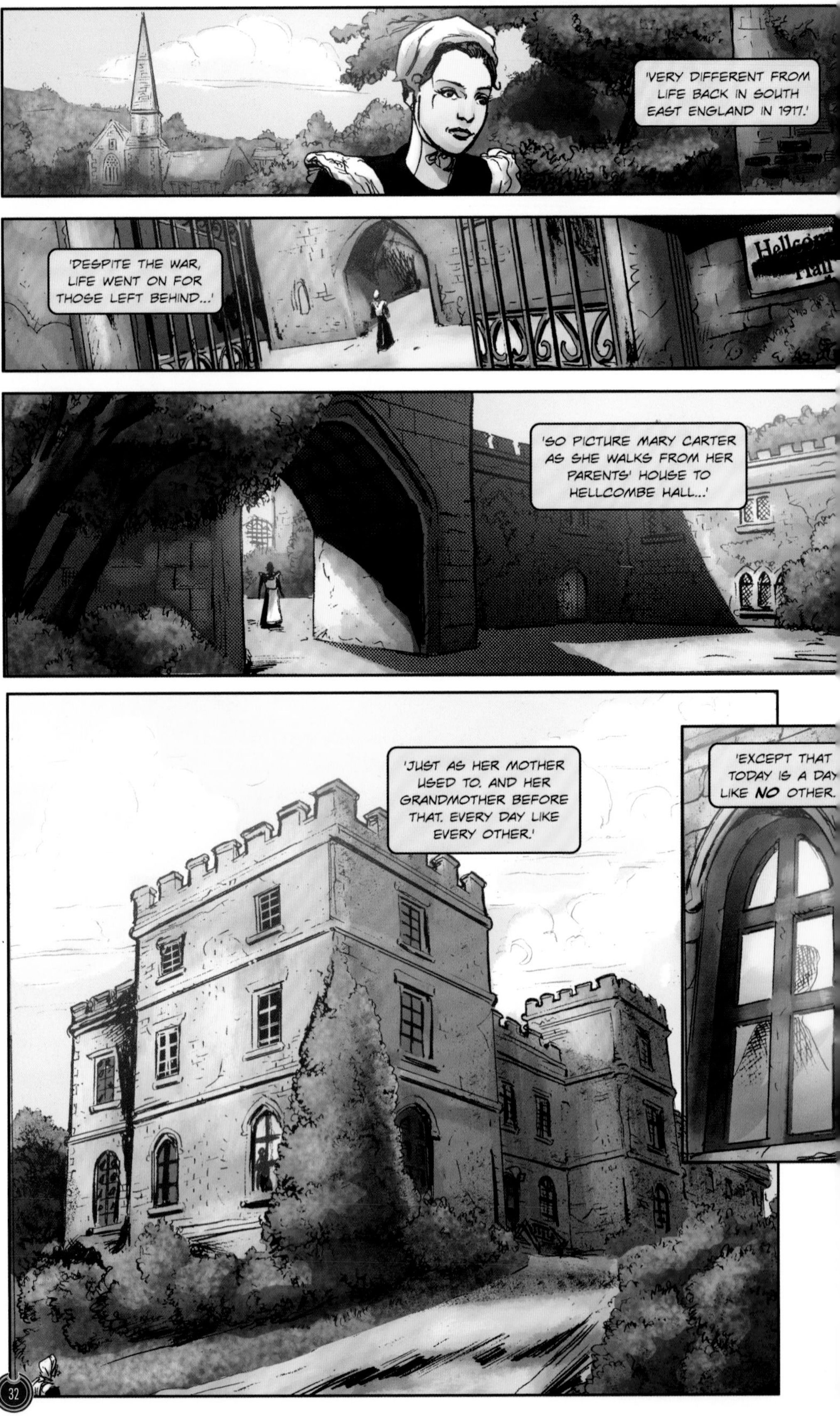
'VERY DIFFERENT FROM LIFE BACK IN SOUTH EAST ENGLAND IN 1917.'
'DESPITE THE WAR, LIFE WENT ON FOR THOSE LEFT BEHIND...'
'SO PICTURE MARY CARTER AS SHE WALKS FROM HER PARENTS' HOUSE TO HELLCOMBE HALL...'
'JUST AS HER MOTHER USED TO. AND HER GRANDMOTHER BEFORE THAT. EVERY DAY LIKE EVERY OTHER.'
'EXCEPT THAT TODAY IS A DAY LIKE **NO** OTHER.

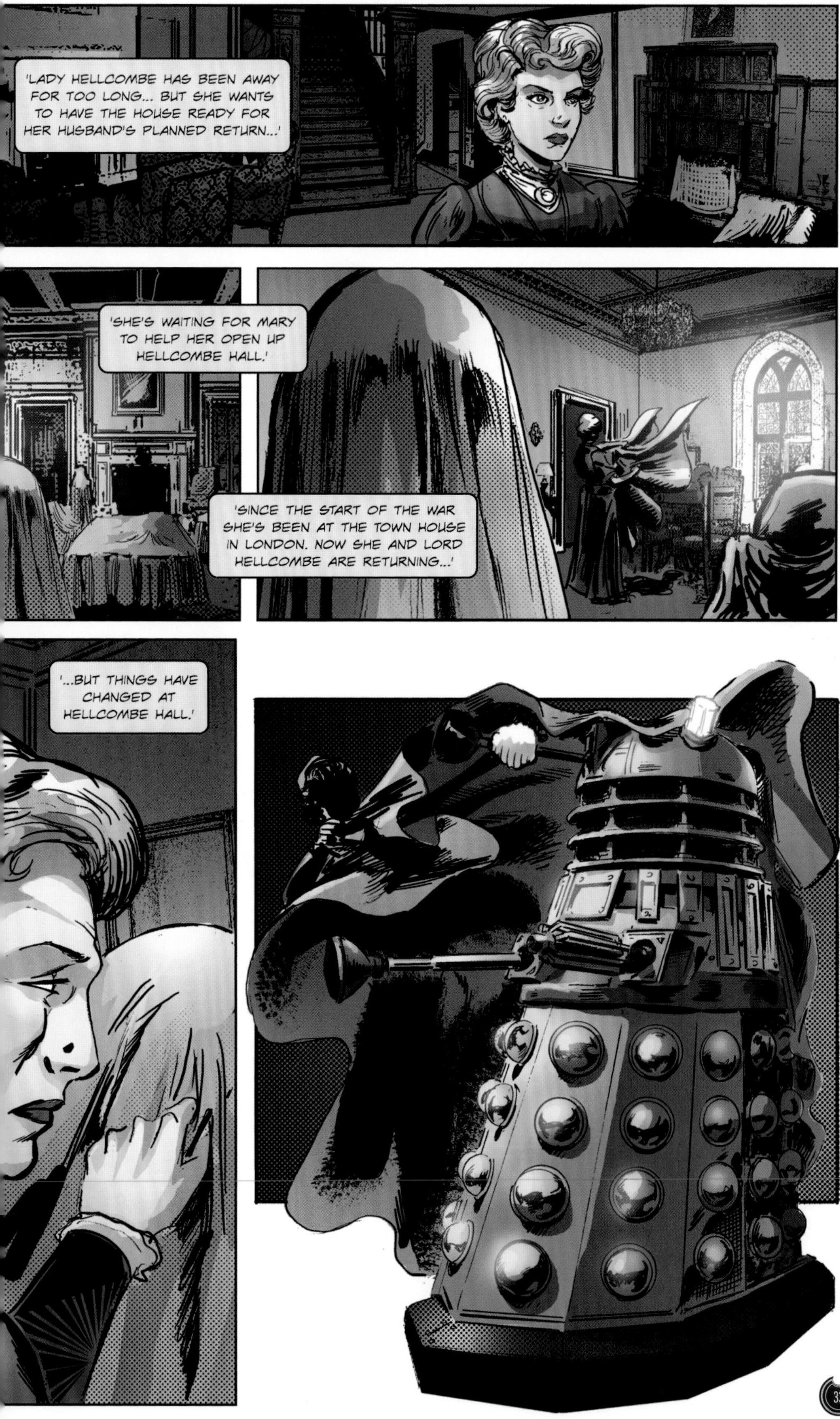
'LADY HELLCOMBE HAS BEEN AWAY FOR TOO LONG... BUT SHE WANTS TO HAVE THE HOUSE READY FOR HER HUSBAND'S PLANNED RETURN...'
'SHE'S WAITING FOR MARY TO HELP HER OPEN UP HELLCOMBE HALL.'
'SINCE THE START OF THE WAR SHE'S BEEN AT THE TOWN HOUSE IN LONDON. NOW SHE AND LORD HELLCOMBE ARE RETURNING...'
'...BUT THINGS HAVE CHANGED AT HELLCOMBE HALL.'

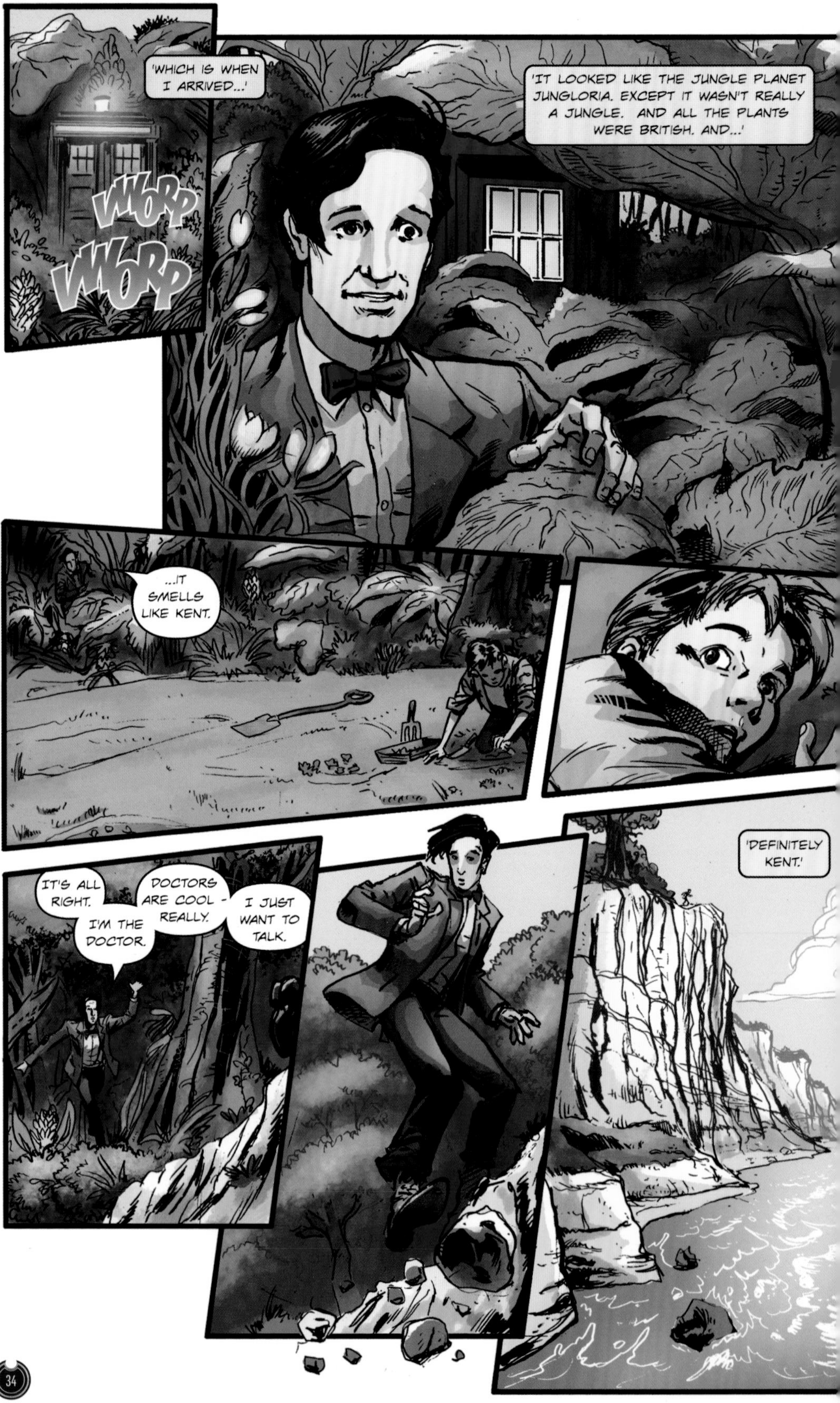
'WHICH IS WHEN I ARRIVED...'
VWORP VWORP
'IT LOOKED LIKE THE JUNGLE PLANET JUNGLORIA. EXCEPT IT WASN'T REALLY A JUNGLE. AND ALL THE PLANTS WERE BRITISH. AND...'
...IT SMELLS LIKE KENT.
IT'S ALL RIGHT.
I'M THE DOCTOR.
DOCTORS ARE COOL - REALLY.
I JUST WANT TO TALK.
'DEFINITELY KENT.'

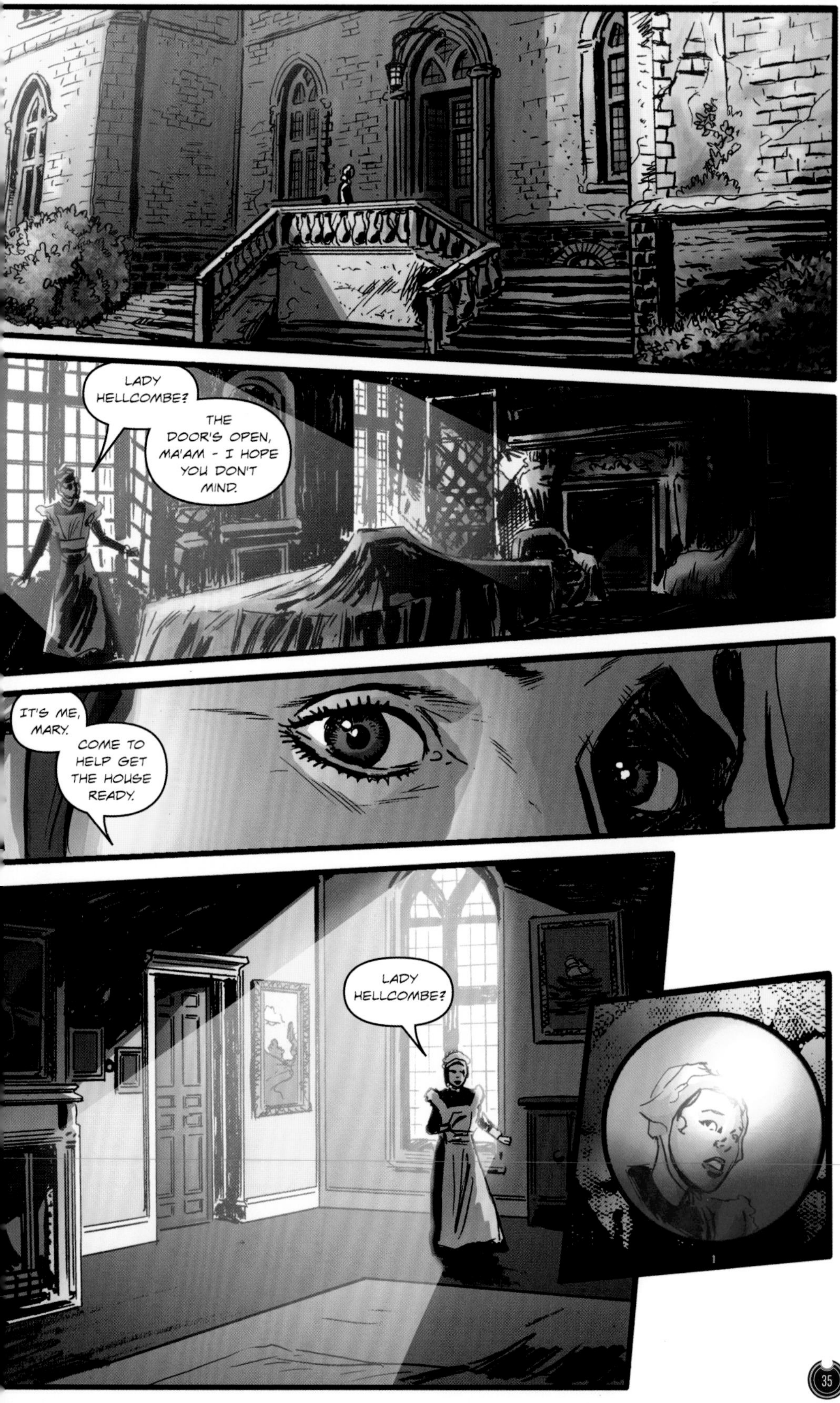
LADY HELLCOMBE?
THE DOOR'S OPEN, MA'AM - I HOPE YOU DON'T MIND.
IT'S ME, MARY.
COME TO HELP GET THE HOUSE READY.
LADY HELLCOMBE?

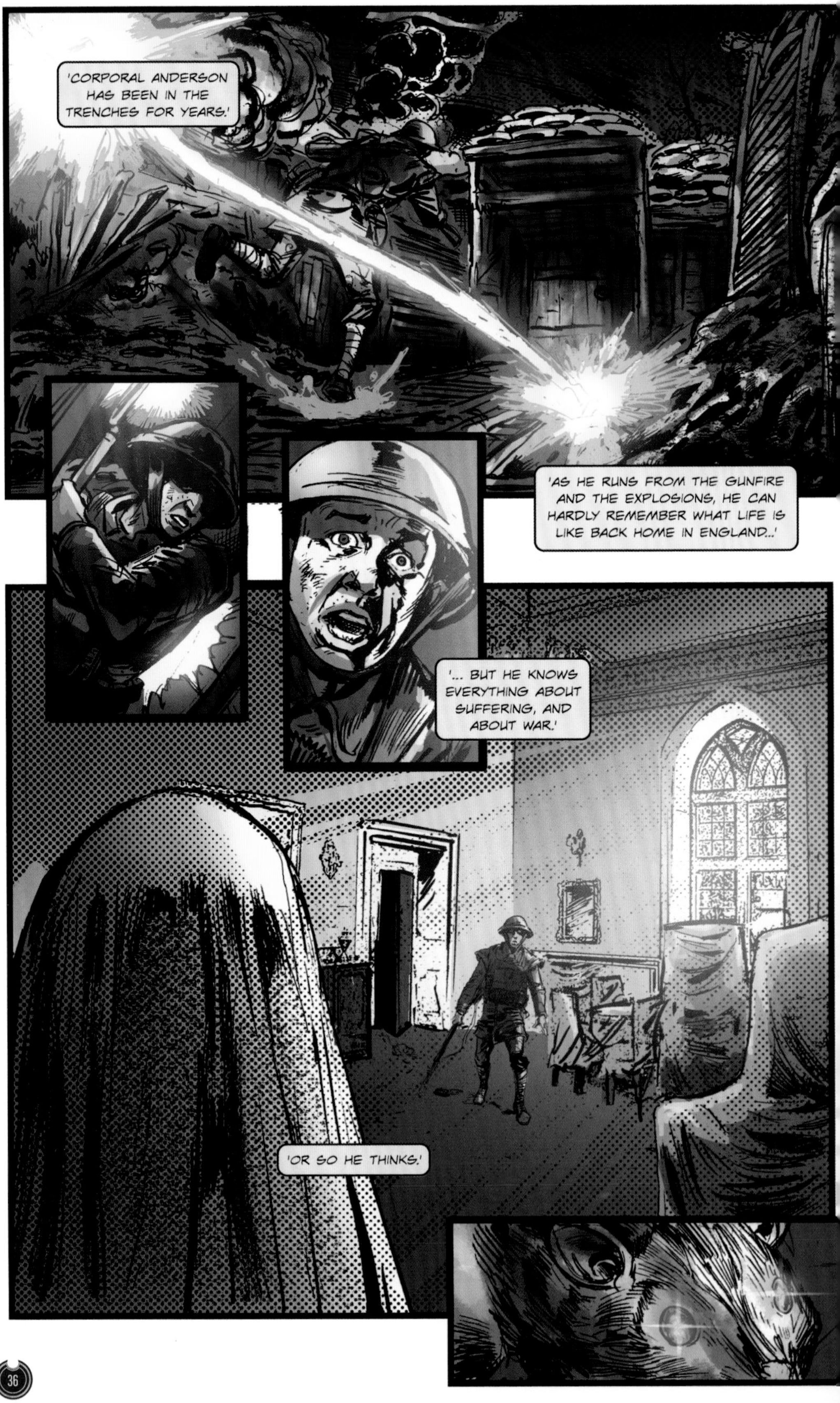

'CORPORAL ANDERSON HAS BEEN IN THE TRENCHES FOR YEARS.'
'AS HE RUNS FROM THE GUNFIRE AND THE EXPLOSIONS, HE CAN HARDLY REMEMBER WHAT LIFE IS LIKE BACK HOME IN ENGLAND...'
'... BUT HE KNOWS EVERYTHING ABOUT SUFFERING, AND ABOUT WAR.'
'OR SO HE THINKS.'

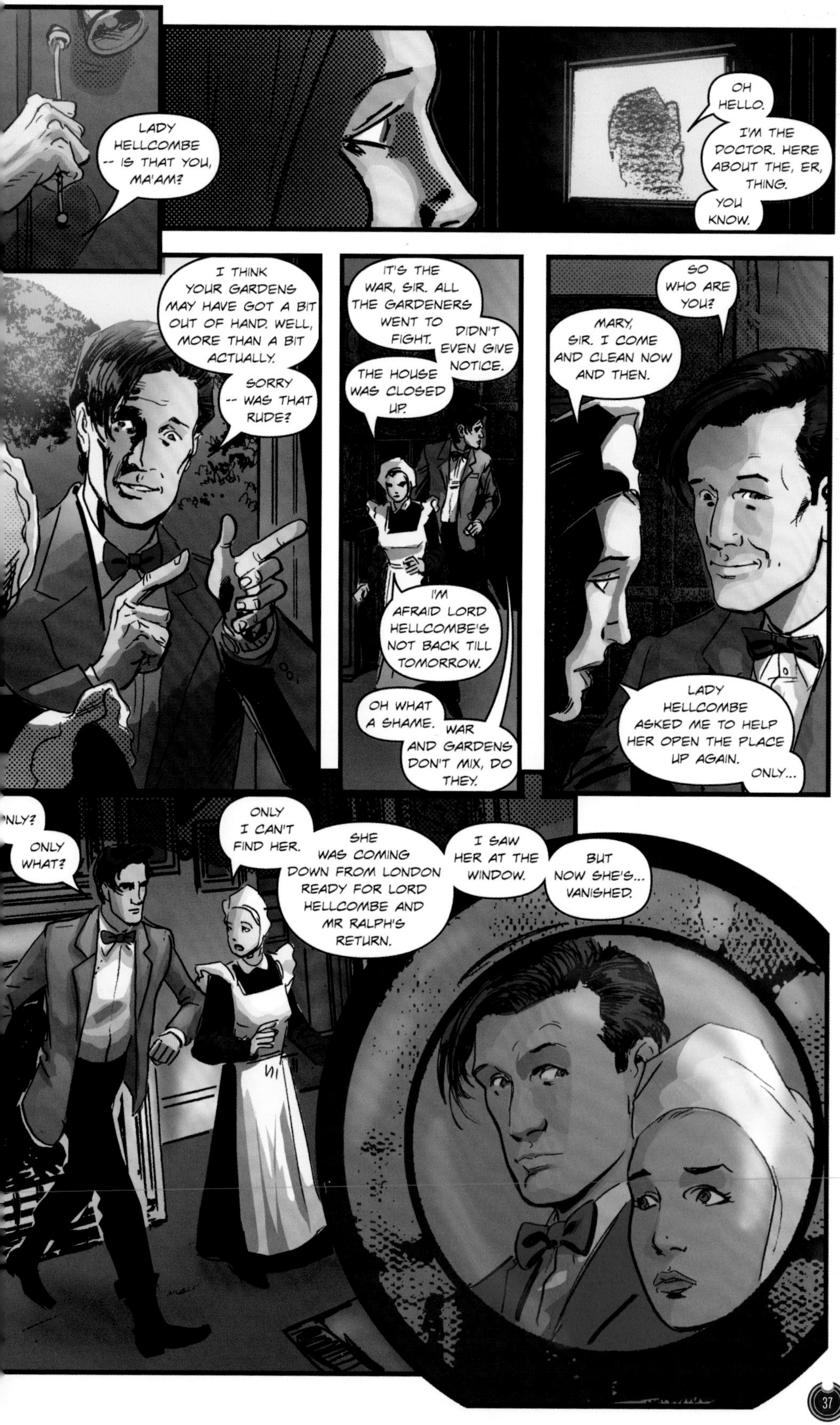
LADY HELLCOMBE -- IS THAT YOU, MA'AM?
OH HELLO.
I'M THE DOCTOR. HERE ABOUT THE, ER, THING.
YOU KNOW.
I THINK YOUR GARDENS MAY HAVE GOT A BIT OUT OF HAND. WELL, MORE THAN A BIT ACTUALLY.
SORRY -- WAS THAT RUDE?
IT'S THE WAR, SIR. ALL THE GARDENERS WENT TO FIGHT.
DIDN'T EVEN GIVE NOTICE.
THE HOUSE WAS CLOSED UP.
I'M AFRAID LORD HELLCOMBE'S NOT BACK TILL TOMORROW.
OH WHAT A SHAME.
WAR AND GARDENS DON'T MIX, DO THEY.
SO WHO ARE YOU?
MARY, SIR. I COME AND CLEAN NOW AND THEN.
LADY HELLCOMBE ASKED ME TO HELP HER OPEN THE PLACE UP AGAIN.
ONLY...
NLY?
ONLY WHAT?
ONLY I CAN'T FIND HER.
SHE WAS COMING DOWN FROM LONDON READY FOR LORD HELLCOMBE AND MR RALPH'S RETURN.
I SAW HER AT THE WINDOW.
BUT NOW SHE'S... VANISHED.

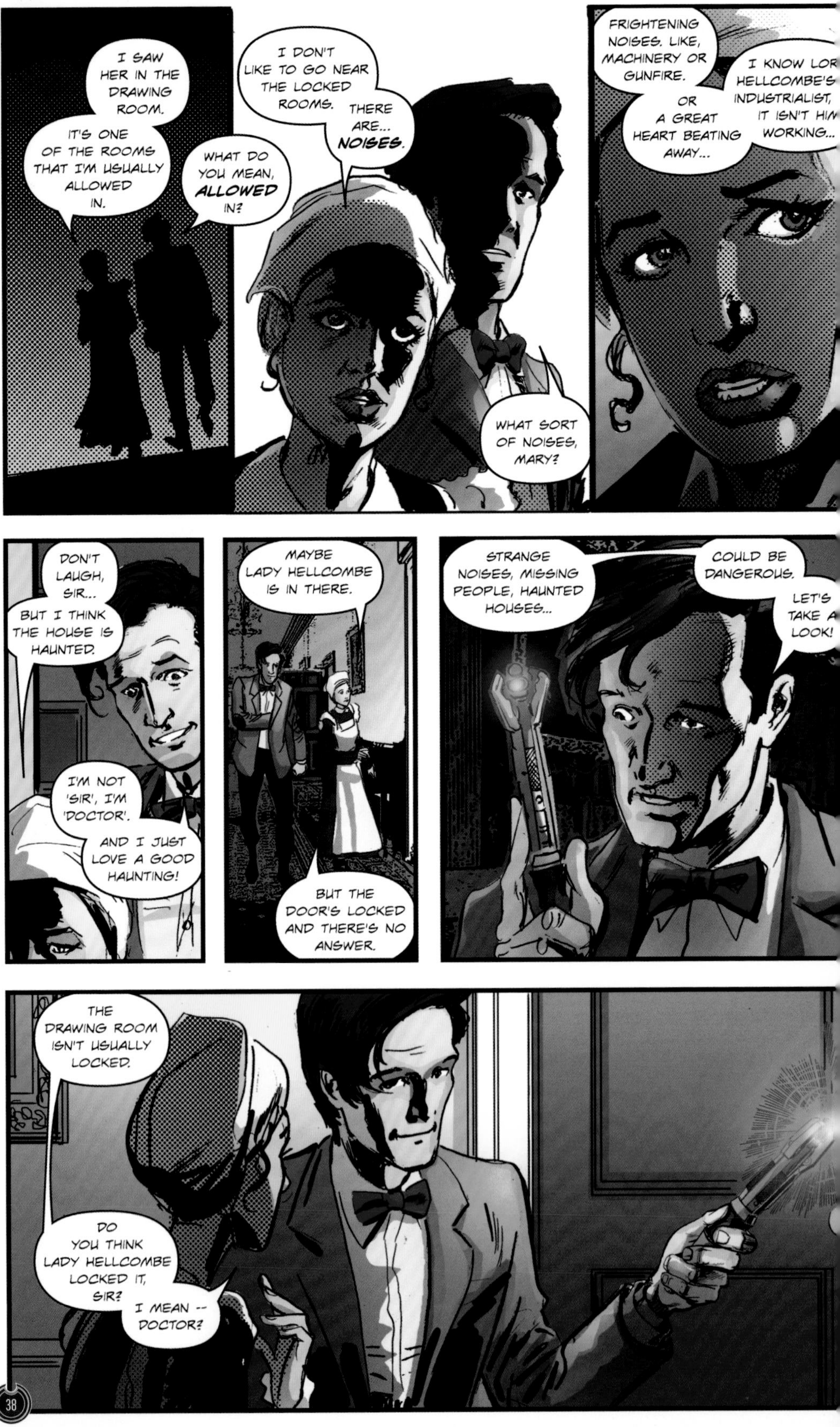
I SAW HER IN THE DRAWING ROOM.
IT'S ONE OF THE ROOMS THAT I'M USUALLY ALLOWED IN.
WHAT DO YOU MEAN, **ALLOWED** IN?
I DON'T LIKE TO GO NEAR THE LOCKED ROOMS.
THERE ARE... **NOISES.**
WHAT SORT OF NOISES, MARY?
FRIGHTENING NOISES. LIKE, MACHINERY OR GUNFIRE.
OR A GREAT HEART BEATING AWAY...
I KNOW LOR HELLCOMBE'S INDUSTRIALIST, IT ISN'T HIM WORKING...
DON'T LAUGH, SIR... BUT I THINK THE HOUSE IS HAUNTED.
I'M NOT 'SIR', I'M 'DOCTOR'.
AND I JUST LOVE A GOOD HAUNTING!
MAYBE LADY HELLCOMBE IS IN THERE.
BUT THE DOOR'S LOCKED AND THERE'S NO ANSWER.
STRANGE NOISES, MISSING PEOPLE, HAUNTED HOUSES...
COULD BE DANGEROUS.
LET'S TAKE A LOOK!
THE DRAWING ROOM ISN'T USUALLY LOCKED.
DO YOU THINK LADY HELLCOMBE LOCKED IT, SIR?
I MEAN -- DOCTOR?

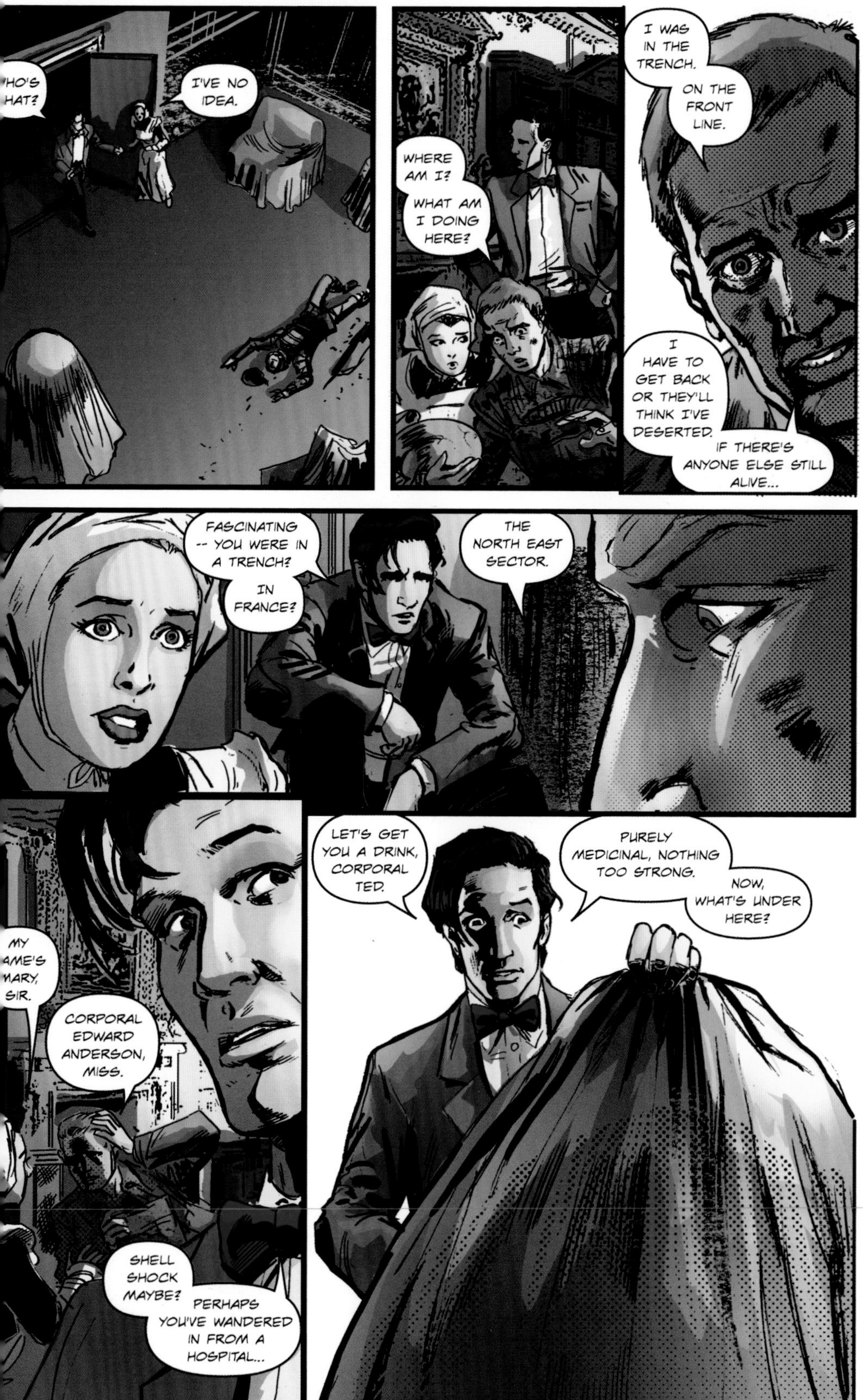
HO'S
HAT?
I'VE NO IDEA.
WHERE AM I?
WHAT AM I DOING HERE?
I WAS IN THE TRENCH.
ON THE FRONT LINE.
I HAVE TO GET BACK OR THEY'LL THINK I'VE DESERTED.
IF THERE'S ANYONE ELSE STILL ALIVE...
FASCINATING -- YOU WERE IN A TRENCH?
IN FRANCE?
THE NORTH EAST SECTOR.
MY
AME'S
MARY,
SIR.
CORPORAL EDWARD ANDERSON, MISS.
SHELL SHOCK MAYBE?
PERHAPS YOU'VE WANDERED IN FROM A HOSPITAL...
LET'S GET YOU A DRINK, CORPORAL TED.
PURELY MEDICINAL, NOTHING TOO STRONG.
NOW, WHAT'S UNDER HERE?

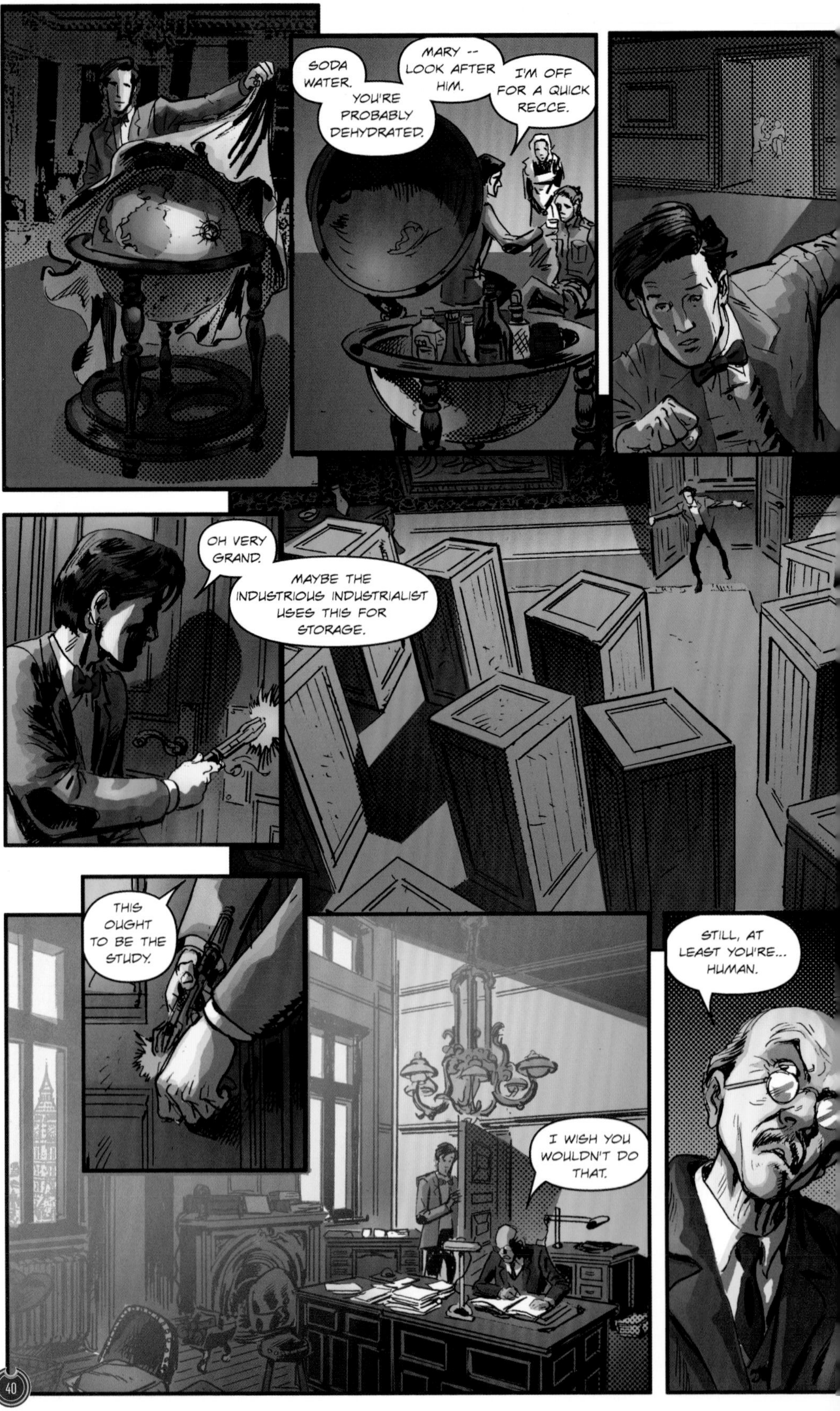
SODA WATER.
YOU'RE PROBABLY DEHYDRATED.
MARY -- LOOK AFTER HIM.
I'M OFF FOR A QUICK RECCE.
OH VERY GRAND.
MAYBE THE INDUSTRIOUS INDUSTRIALIST USES THIS FOR STORAGE.
THIS OUGHT TO BE THE STUDY.
I WISH YOU WOULDN'T DO THAT.
STILL, AT LEAST YOU'RE... HUMAN.

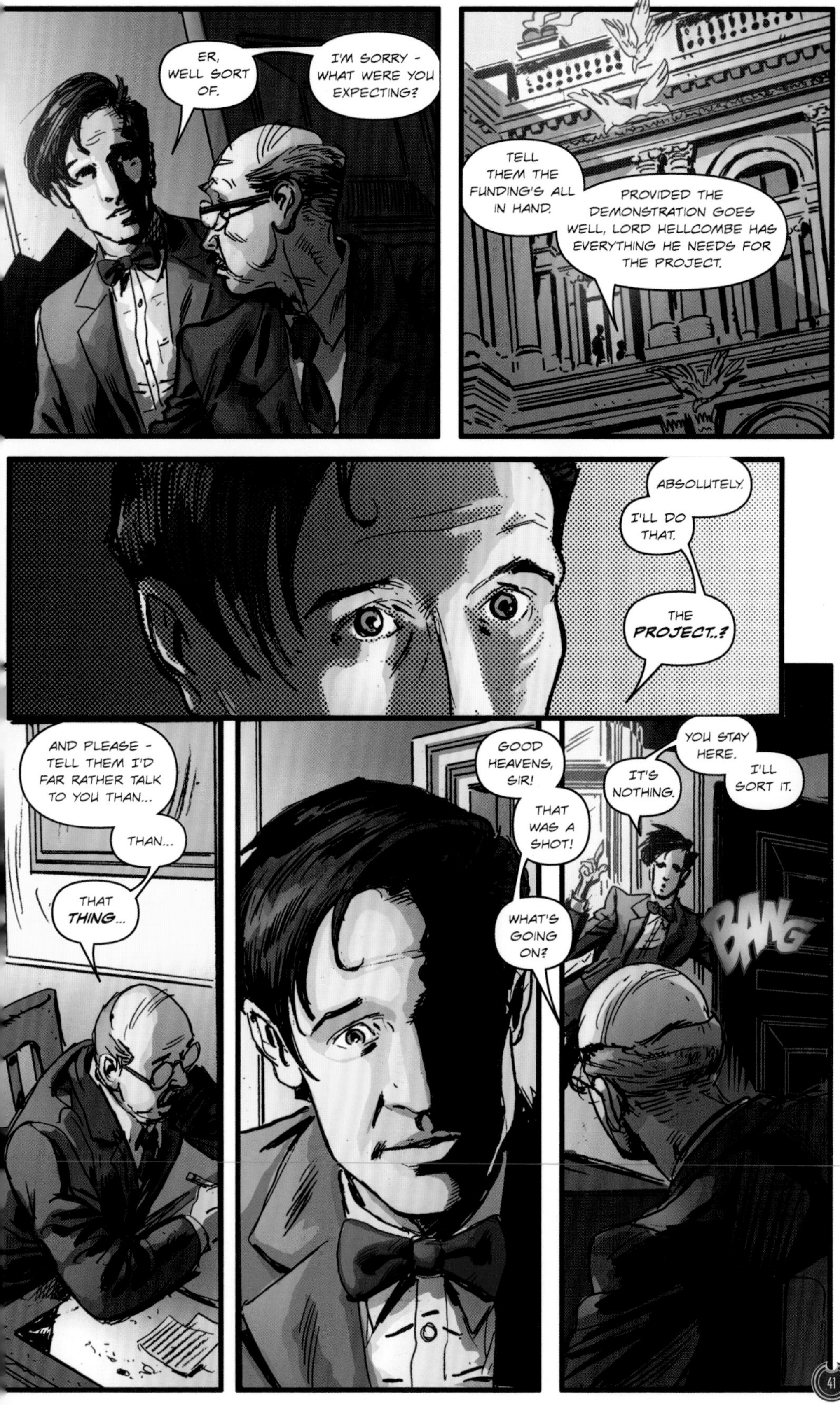

ER, WELL SORT OF.
I'M SORRY - WHAT WERE YOU EXPECTING?
TELL THEM THE FUNDING'S ALL IN HAND.
PROVIDED THE DEMONSTRATION GOES WELL, LORD HELLCOMBE HAS EVERYTHING HE NEEDS FOR THE PROJECT.
ABSOLUTELY.
I'LL DO THAT.
THE *PROJECT..?*
AND PLEASE - TELL THEM I'D FAR RATHER TALK TO YOU THAN...
THAN...
THAT *THING*...
GOOD HEAVENS, SIR!
THAT WAS A SHOT!
WHAT'S GOING ON?
IT'S NOTHING.
YOU STAY HERE.
I'LL SORT IT.
BANG

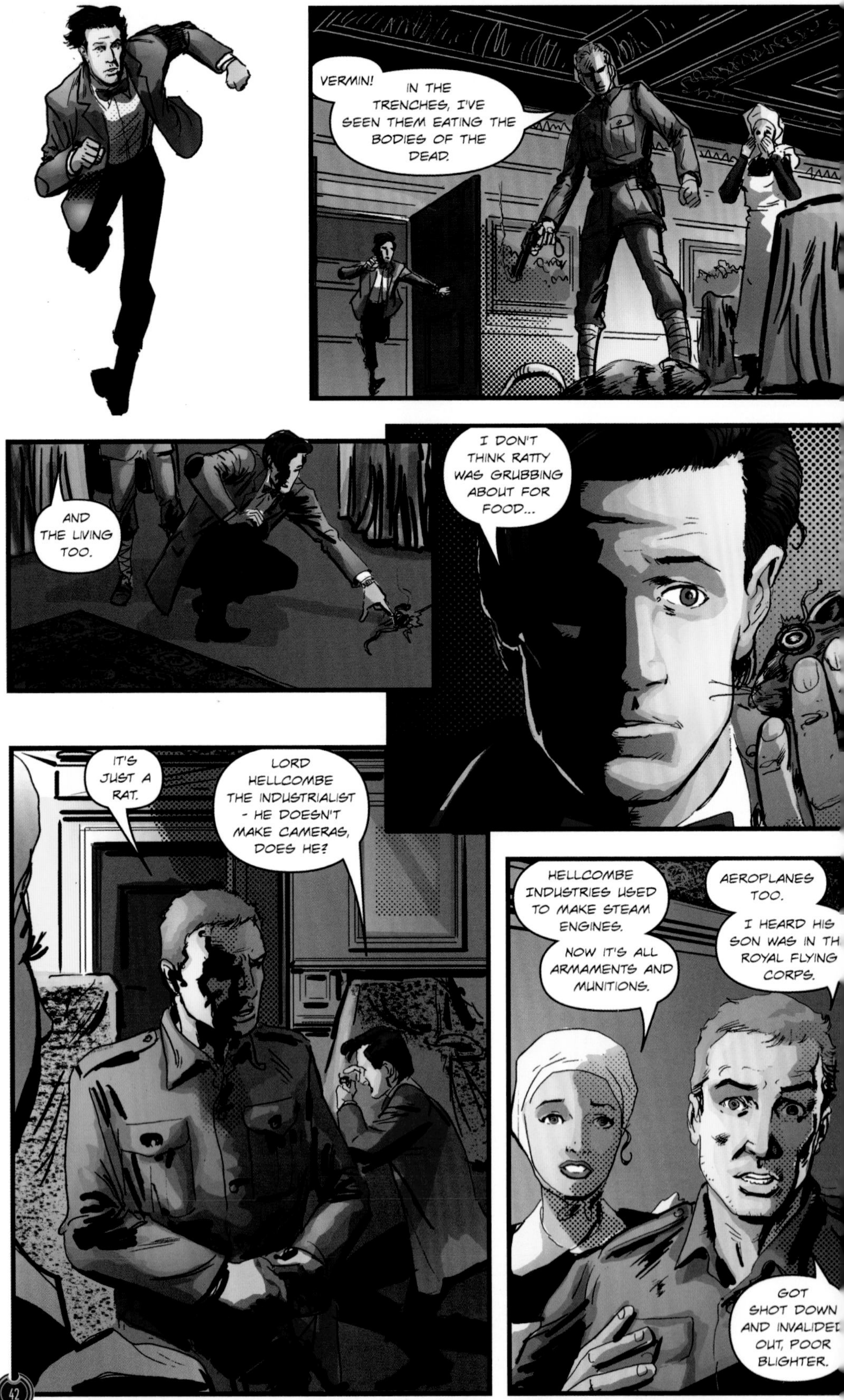

VERMIN!
IN THE TRENCHES, I'VE SEEN THEM EATING THE BODIES OF THE DEAD.
AND THE LIVING TOO.
I DON'T THINK RATTY WAS GRUBBING ABOUT FOR FOOD...
IT'S JUST A RAT.
LORD HELLCOMBE THE INDUSTRIALIST - HE DOESN'T MAKE CAMERAS, DOES HE?
HELLCOMBE INDUSTRIES USED TO MAKE STEAM ENGINES.
NOW IT'S ALL ARMAMENTS AND MUNITIONS.
AEROPLANES TOO.
I HEARD HIS SON WAS IN TH ROYAL FLYING CORPS.
GOT SHOT DOWN AND INVALIDEI OUT, POOR BLIGHTER.

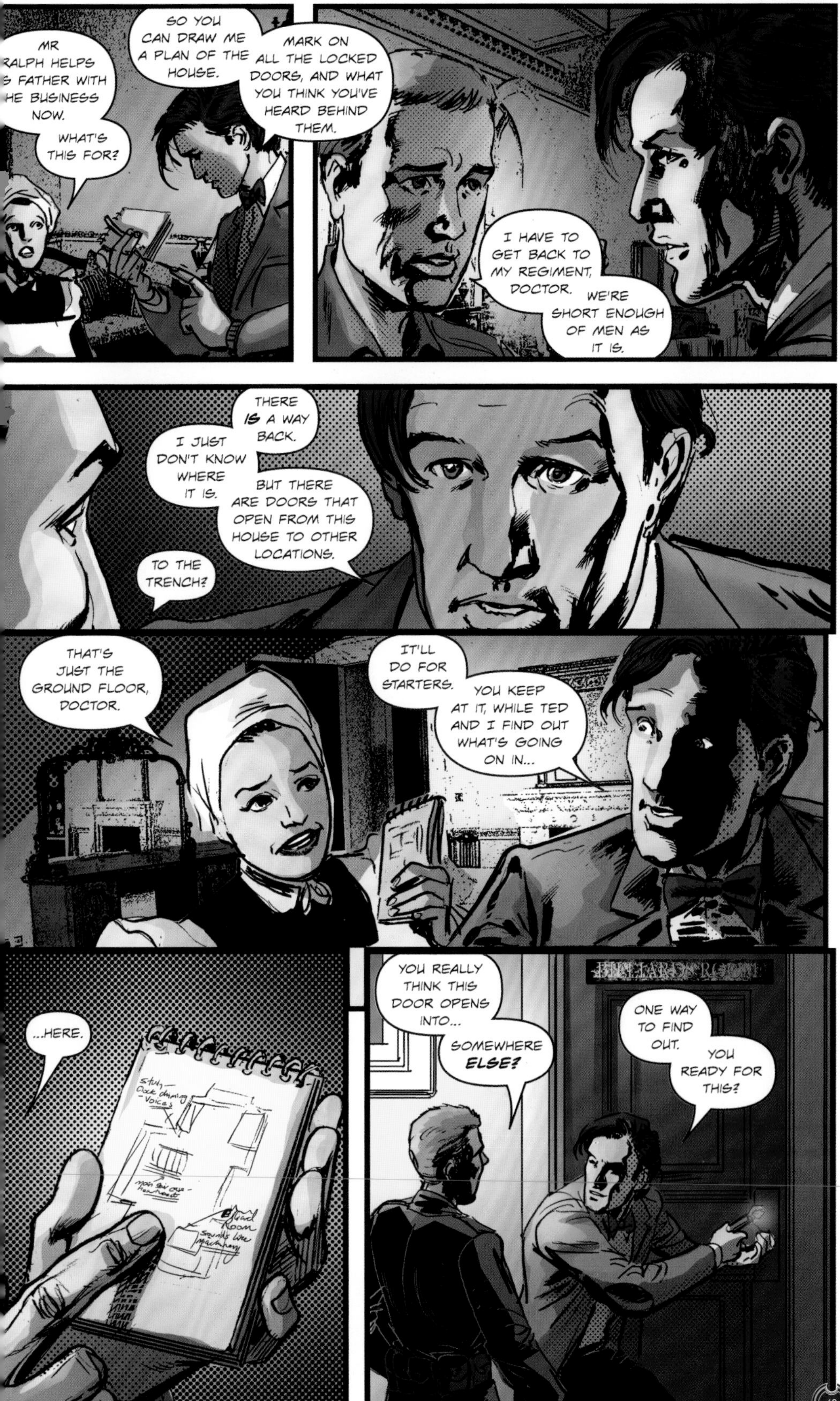
MR RALPH HELPS S FATHER WITH HE BUSINESS NOW.
WHAT'S THIS FOR?
SO YOU CAN DRAW ME A PLAN OF THE HOUSE.
MARK ON ALL THE LOCKED DOORS, AND WHAT YOU THINK YOU'VE HEARD BEHIND THEM.
I HAVE TO GET BACK TO MY REGIMENT, DOCTOR.
WE'RE SHORT ENOUGH OF MEN AS IT IS.
THERE *IS* A WAY BACK.
I JUST DON'T KNOW WHERE IT IS.
BUT THERE ARE DOORS THAT OPEN FROM THIS HOUSE TO OTHER LOCATIONS.
TO THE TRENCH?
THAT'S JUST THE GROUND FLOOR, DOCTOR.
IT'LL DO FOR STARTERS.
YOU KEEP AT IT, WHILE TED AND I FIND OUT WHAT'S GOING ON IN...
...HERE.
YOU REALLY THINK THIS DOOR OPENS INTO...
SOMEWHERE *ELSE?*
ONE WAY TO FIND OUT.
YOU READY FOR THIS?

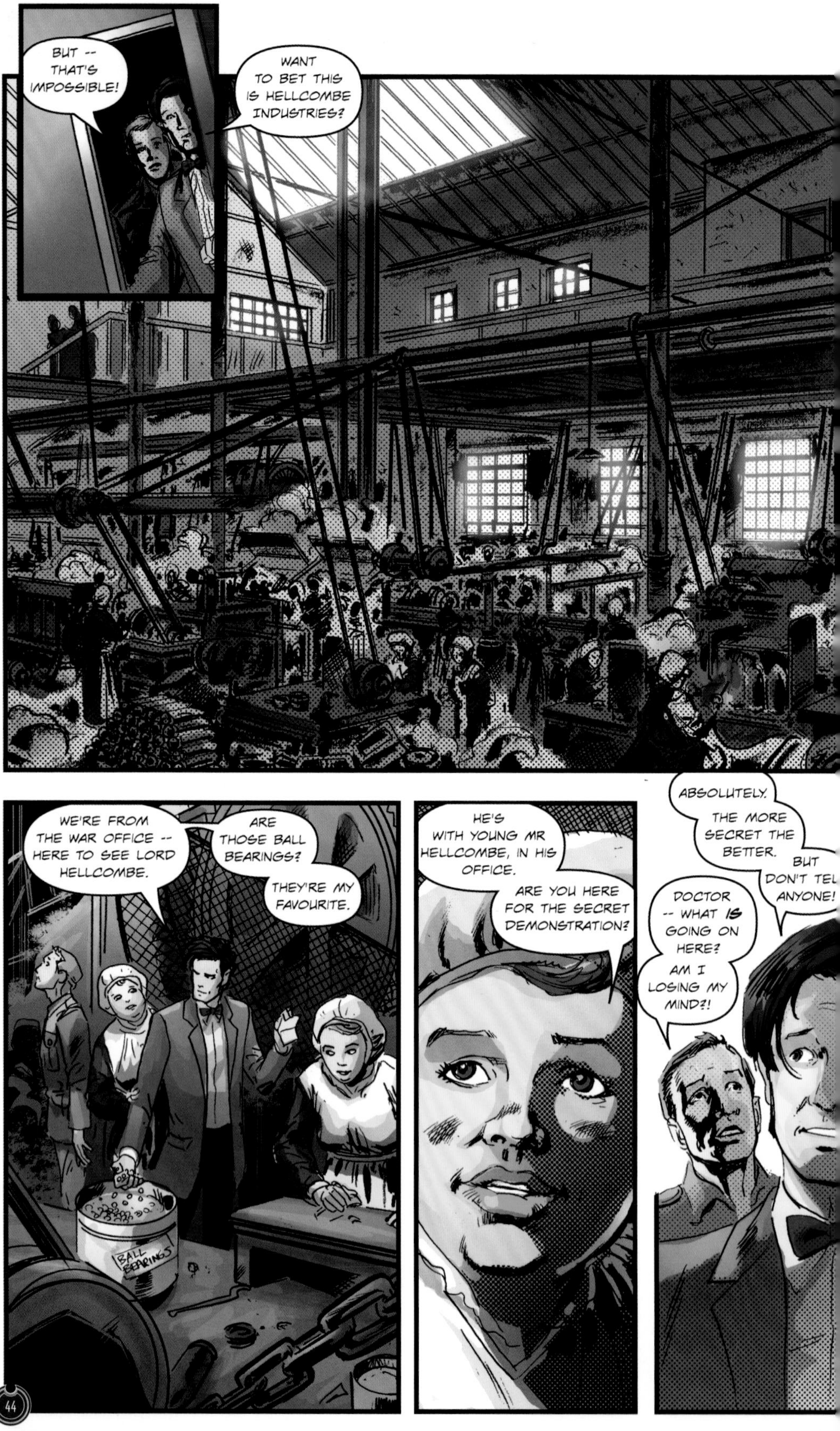
BUT -- THAT'S IMPOSSIBLE!
WANT TO BET THIS IS HELLCOMBE INDUSTRIES?
WE'RE FROM THE WAR OFFICE -- HERE TO SEE LORD HELLCOMBE.
ARE THOSE BALL BEARINGS?
THEY'RE MY FAVOURITE.
BALL BEARINGS
HE'S WITH YOUNG MR HELLCOMBE, IN HIS OFFICE.
ARE YOU HERE FOR THE SECRET DEMONSTRATION?
ABSOLUTELY.
THE MORE SECRET THE BETTER.
BUT DON'T TEL
ANYONE!
DOCTOR -- WHAT IS GOING ON HERE?
AM I LOSING MY MIND?!

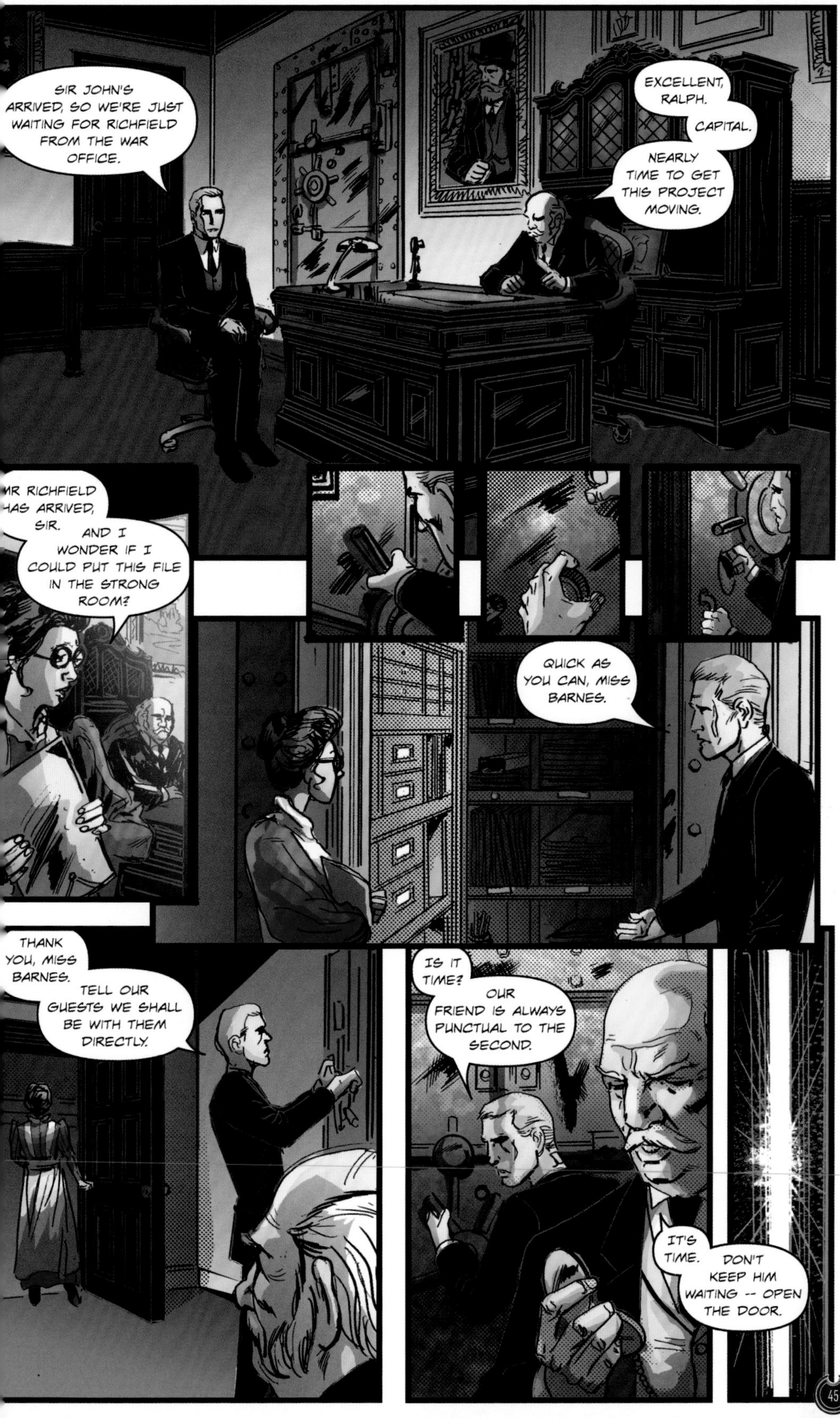
SIR JOHN'S ARRIVED, SO WE'RE JUST WAITING FOR RICHFIELD FROM THE WAR OFFICE.
EXCELLENT, RALPH.
CAPITAL.
NEARLY TIME TO GET THIS PROJECT MOVING.
MR RICHFIELD HAS ARRIVED, SIR.
AND I WONDER IF I COULD PUT THIS FILE IN THE STRONG ROOM?
QUICK AS YOU CAN, MISS BARNES.
THANK YOU, MISS BARNES.
TELL OUR GUESTS WE SHALL BE WITH THEM DIRECTLY.
IS IT TIME?
OUR FRIEND IS ALWAYS PUNCTUAL TO THE SECOND.
IT'S TIME.
DON'T KEEP HIM WAITING -- OPEN THE DOOR.

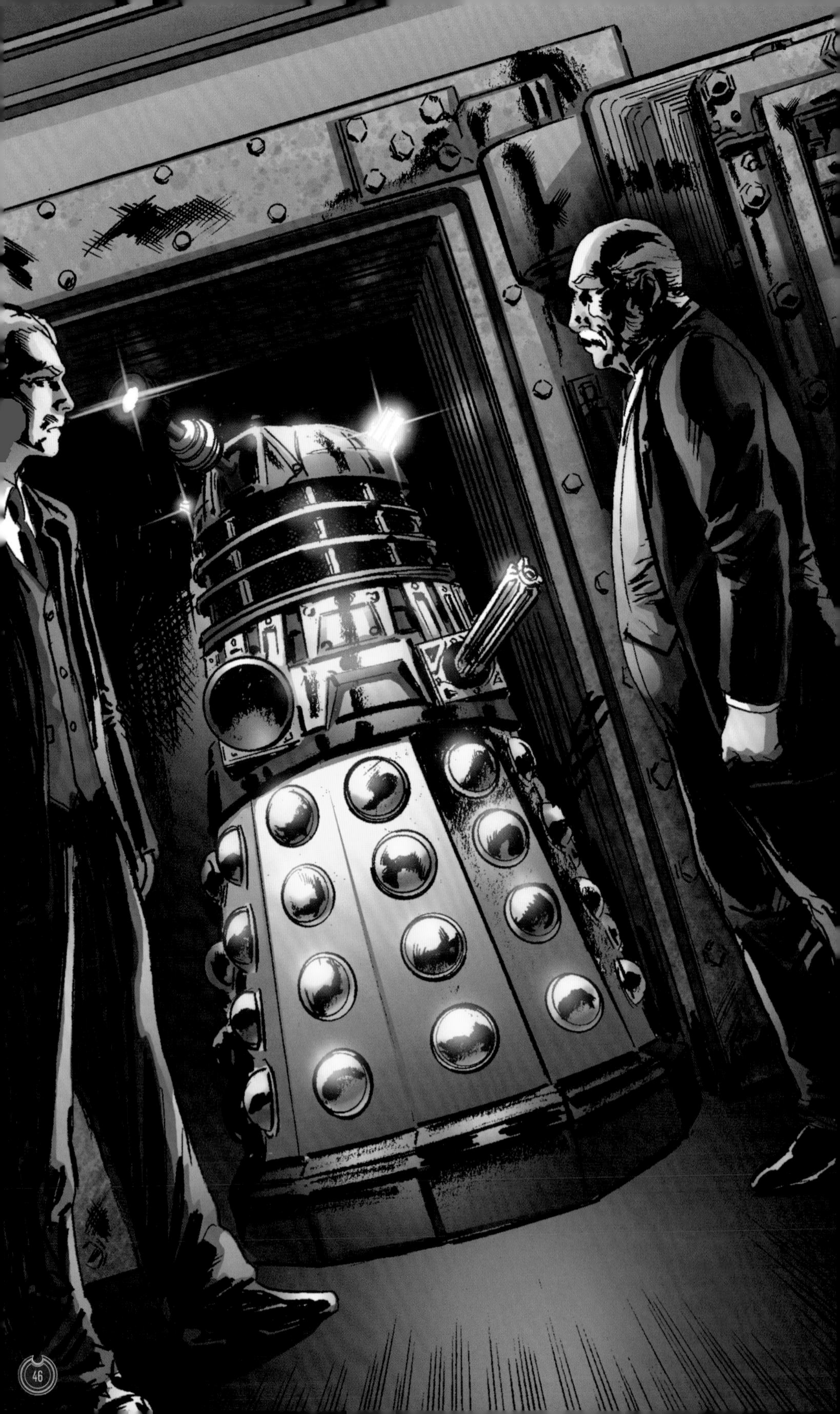

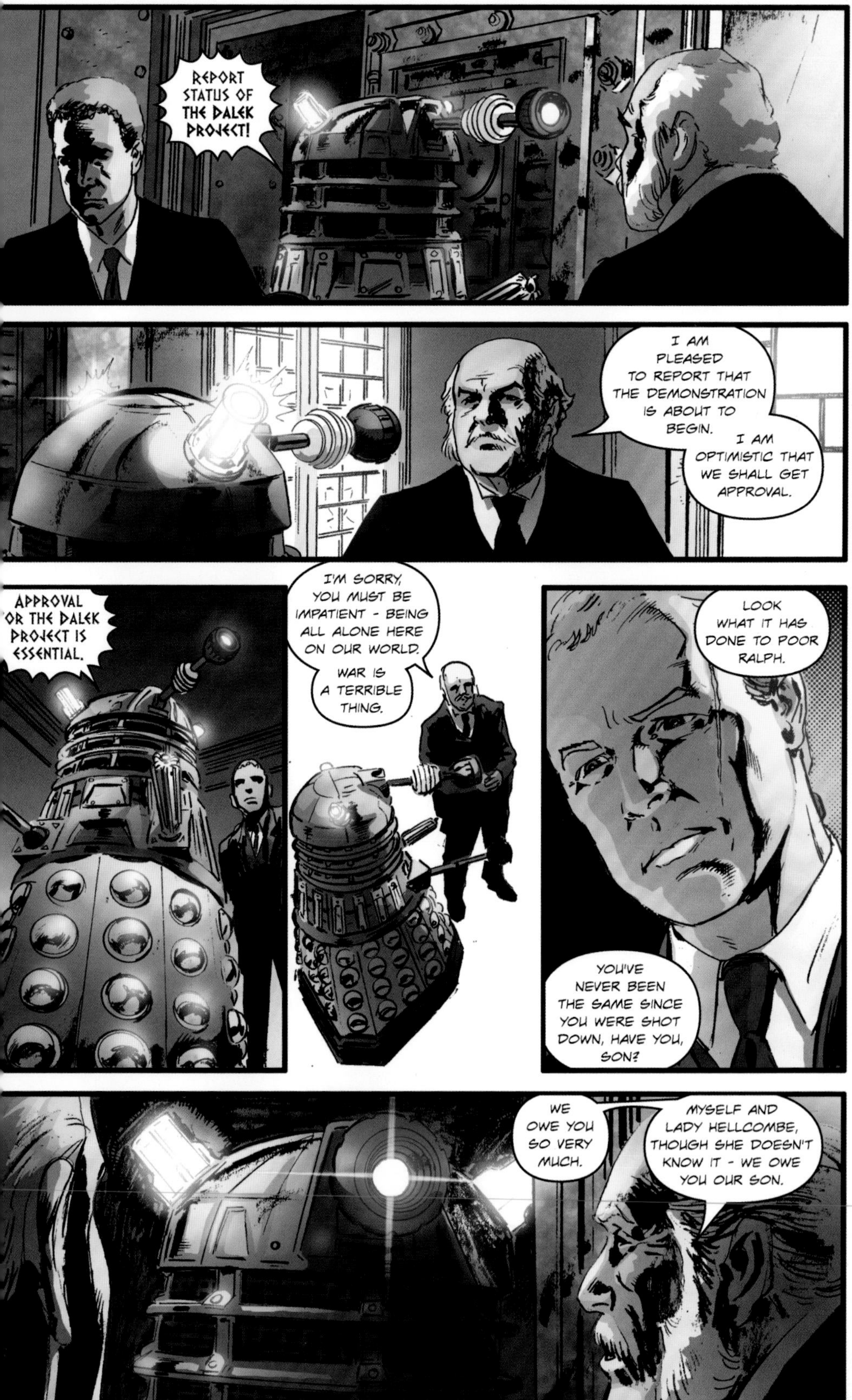
REPORT STATUS OF THE DALEK PROJECT!
I AM PLEASED TO REPORT THAT THE DEMONSTRATION IS ABOUT TO BEGIN.
I AM OPTIMISTIC THAT WE SHALL GET APPROVAL.
APPROVAL OR THE DALEK PROJECT IS ESSENTIAL.
I'M SORRY, YOU MUST BE IMPATIENT - BEING ALL ALONE HERE ON OUR WORLD.
WAR IS A TERRIBLE THING.
LOOK WHAT IT HAS DONE TO POOR RALPH.
YOU'VE NEVER BEEN THE SAME SINCE YOU WERE SHOT DOWN, HAVE YOU, SON?
WE OWE YOU SO VERY MUCH.
MYSELF AND LADY HELLCOMBE, THOUGH SHE DOESN'T KNOW IT - WE OWE YOU OUR SON.

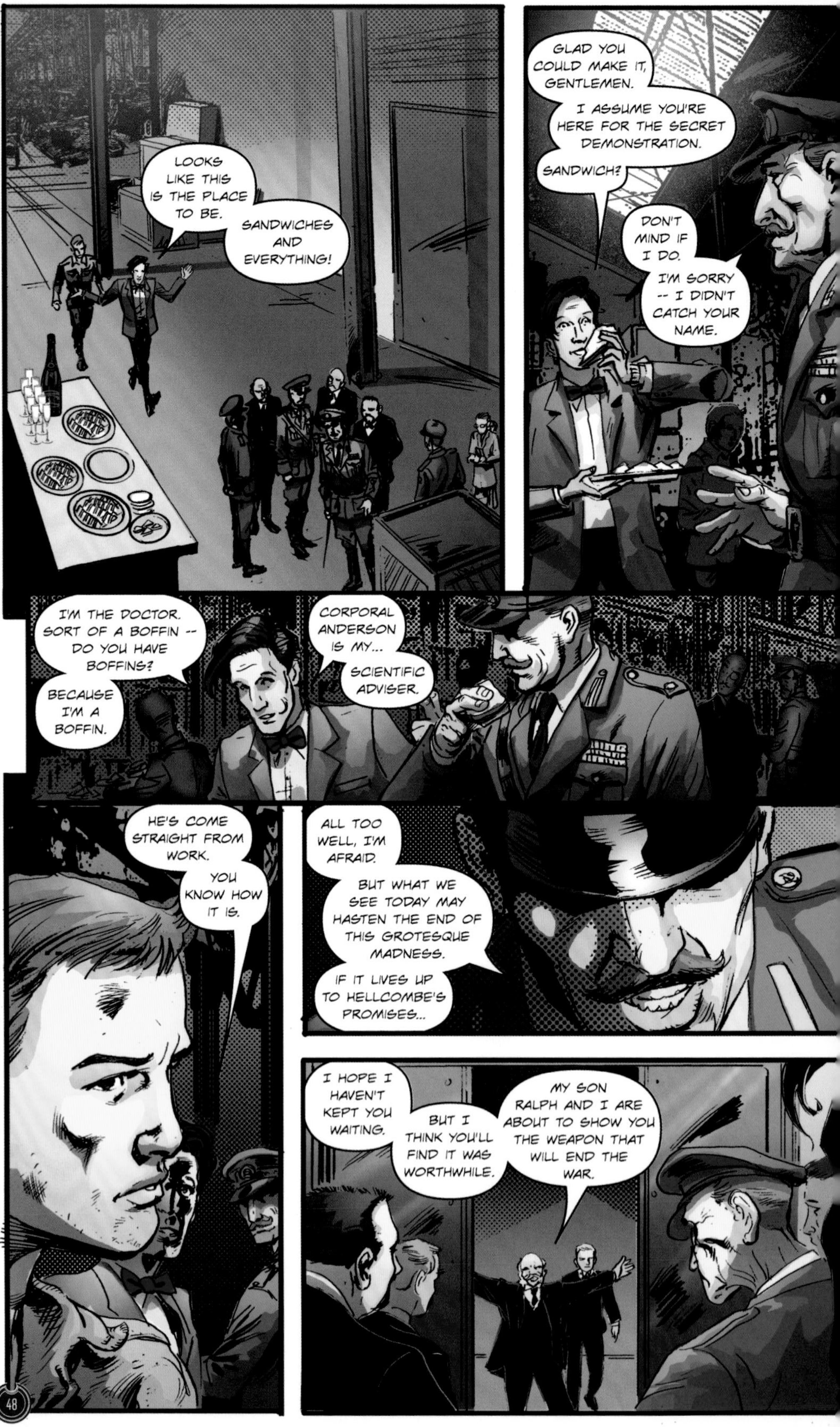
LOOKS LIKE THIS IS THE PLACE TO BE.
SANDWICHES AND EVERYTHING!
GLAD YOU COULD MAKE IT, GENTLEMEN.
I ASSUME YOU'RE HERE FOR THE SECRET DEMONSTRATION.
SANDWICH?
DON'T MIND IF I DO.
I'M SORRY -- I DIDN'T CATCH YOUR NAME.
I'M THE DOCTOR. SORT OF A BOFFIN -- DO YOU HAVE BOFFINS?
BECAUSE I'M A BOFFIN.
CORPORAL ANDERSON IS MY...
SCIENTIFIC ADVISER.
HE'S COME STRAIGHT FROM WORK.
YOU KNOW HOW IT IS.
ALL TOO WELL, I'M AFRAID.
BUT WHAT WE SEE TODAY MAY HASTEN THE END OF THIS GROTESQUE MADNESS.
IF IT LIVES UP TO HELLCOMBE'S PROMISES...
I HOPE I HAVEN'T KEPT YOU WAITING.
BUT I THINK YOU'LL FIND IT WAS WORTHWHILE.
MY SON RALPH AND I ARE ABOUT TO SHOW YOU THE WEAPON THAT WILL END THE WAR.

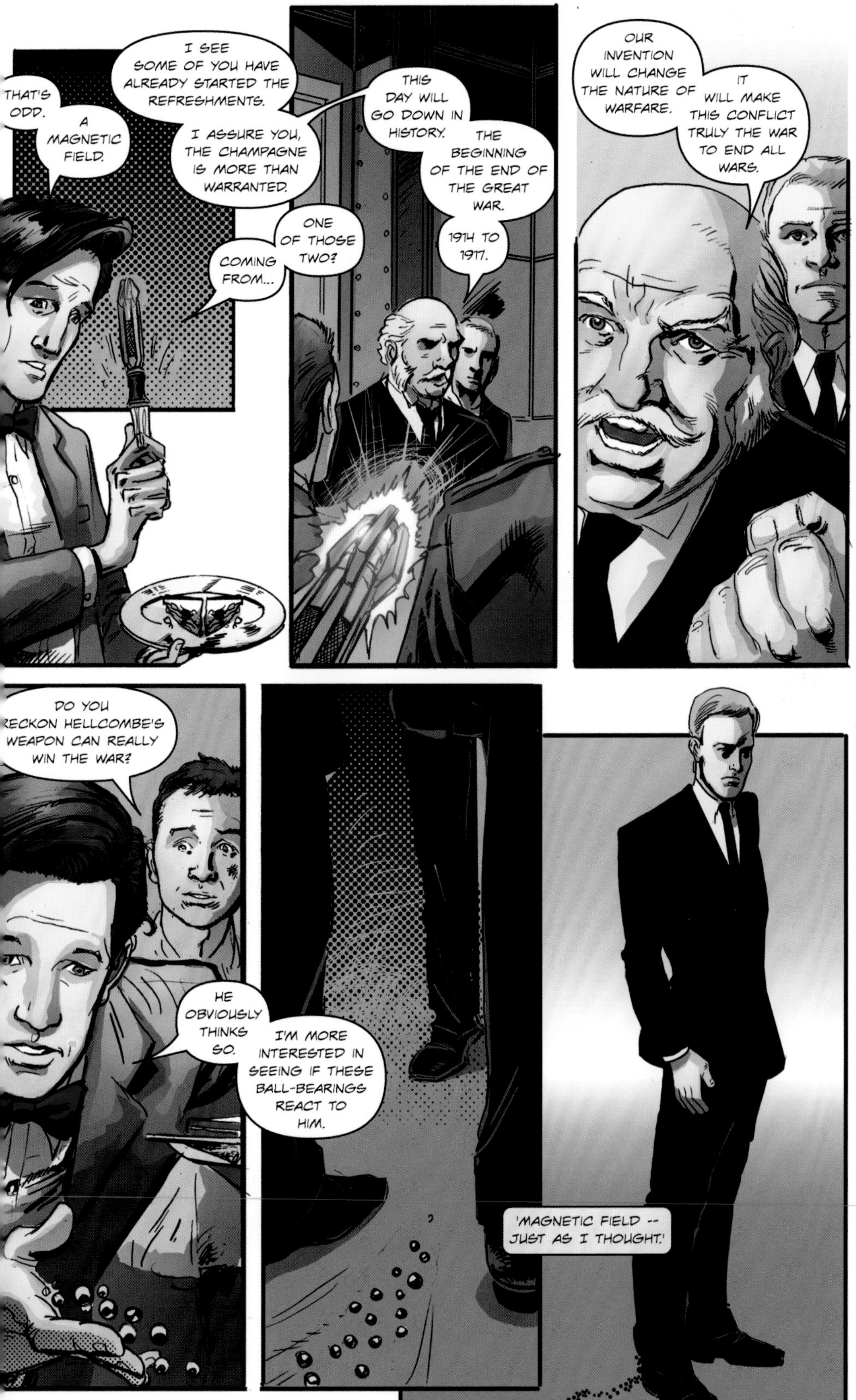

THAT'S ODD.
A MAGNETIC FIELD.
I SEE SOME OF YOU HAVE ALREADY STARTED THE REFRESHMENTS.
I ASSURE YOU, THE CHAMPAGNE IS MORE THAN WARRANTED.
COMING FROM...
ONE OF THOSE TWO?
THIS DAY WILL GO DOWN IN HISTORY.
THE BEGINNING OF THE END OF THE GREAT WAR.
1914 TO 1917.
OUR INVENTION WILL CHANGE THE NATURE OF WARFARE.
IT WILL MAKE THIS CONFLICT TRULY THE WAR TO END ALL WARS.
DO YOU RECKON HELLCOMBE'S WEAPON CAN REALLY WIN THE WAR?
HE OBVIOUSLY THINKS SO.
I'M MORE INTERESTED IN SEEING IF THESE BALL-BEARINGS REACT TO HIM.
'MAGNETIC FIELD -- JUST AS I THOUGHT.'

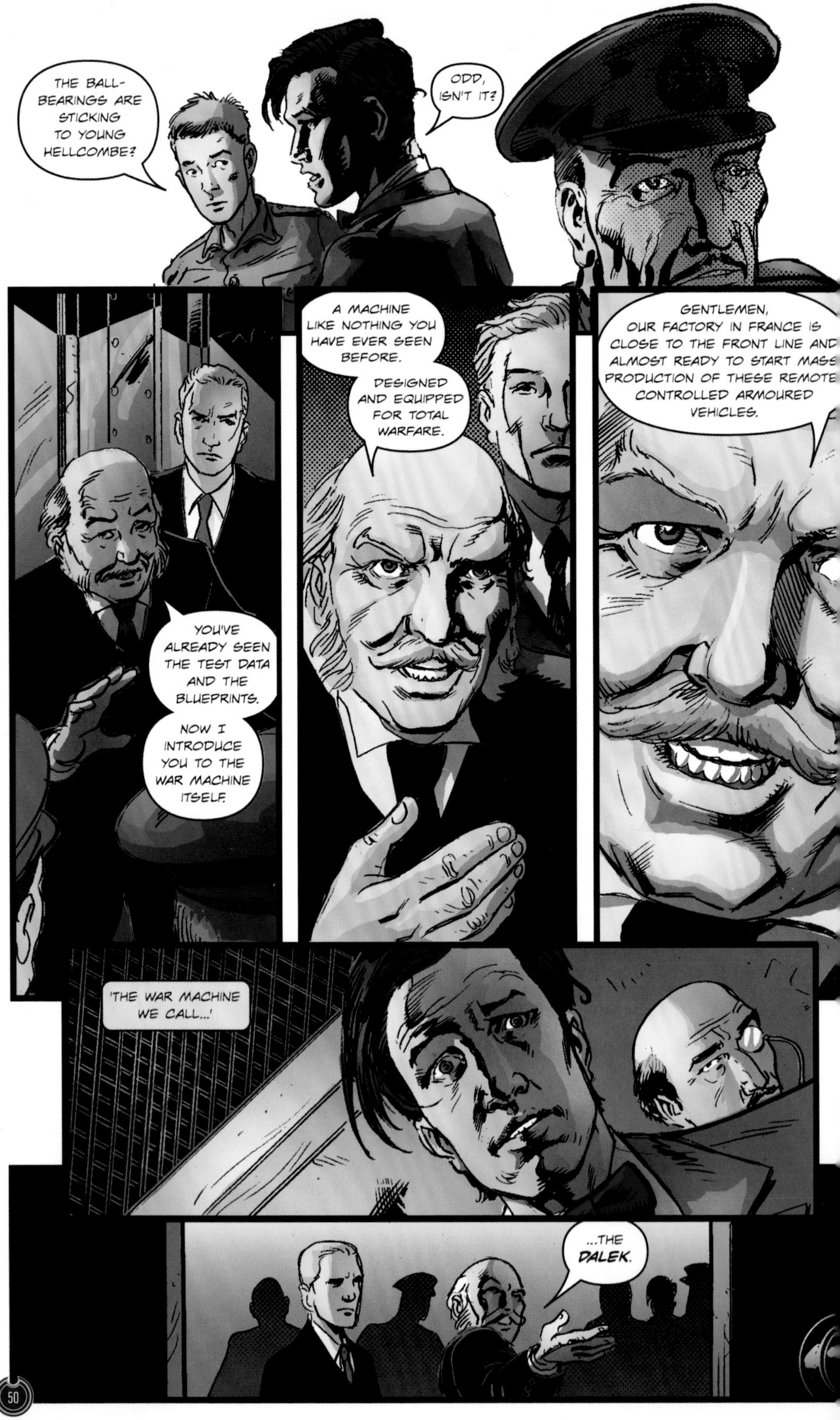

THE BALL-BEARINGS ARE STICKING TO YOUNG HELLCOMBE?
ODD, ISN'T IT?
YOU'VE ALREADY SEEN THE TEST DATA AND THE BLUEPRINTS.
NOW I INTRODUCE YOU TO THE WAR MACHINE ITSELF.
A MACHINE LIKE NOTHING YOU HAVE EVER SEEN BEFORE.
DESIGNED AND EQUIPPED FOR TOTAL WARFARE.
GENTLEMEN, OUR FACTORY IN FRANCE IS CLOSE TO THE FRONT LINE AND ALMOST READY TO START MASS PRODUCTION OF THESE REMOTE CONTROLLED ARMOURED VEHICLES.
'THE WAR MACHINE WE CALL...'
...THE DALEK.

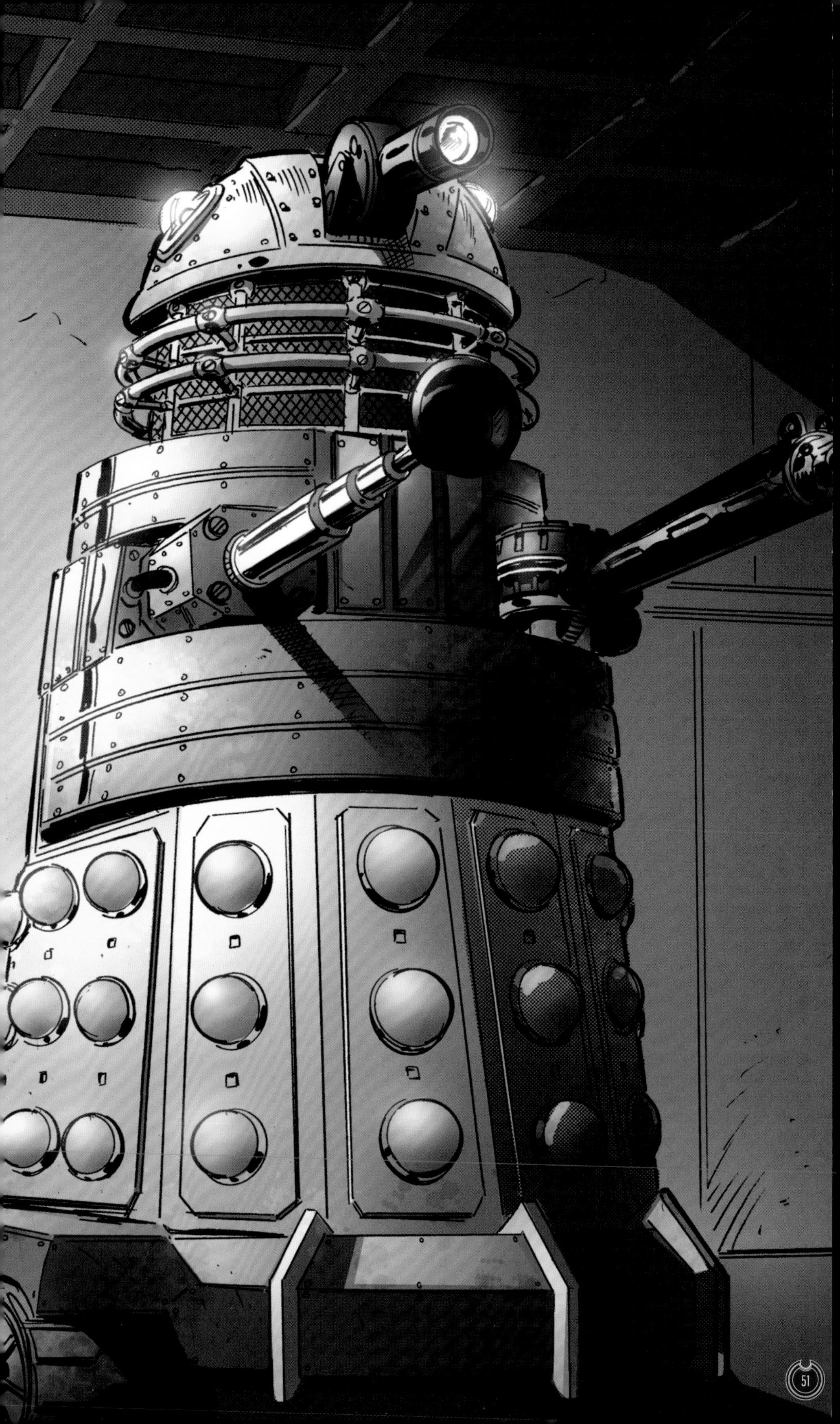

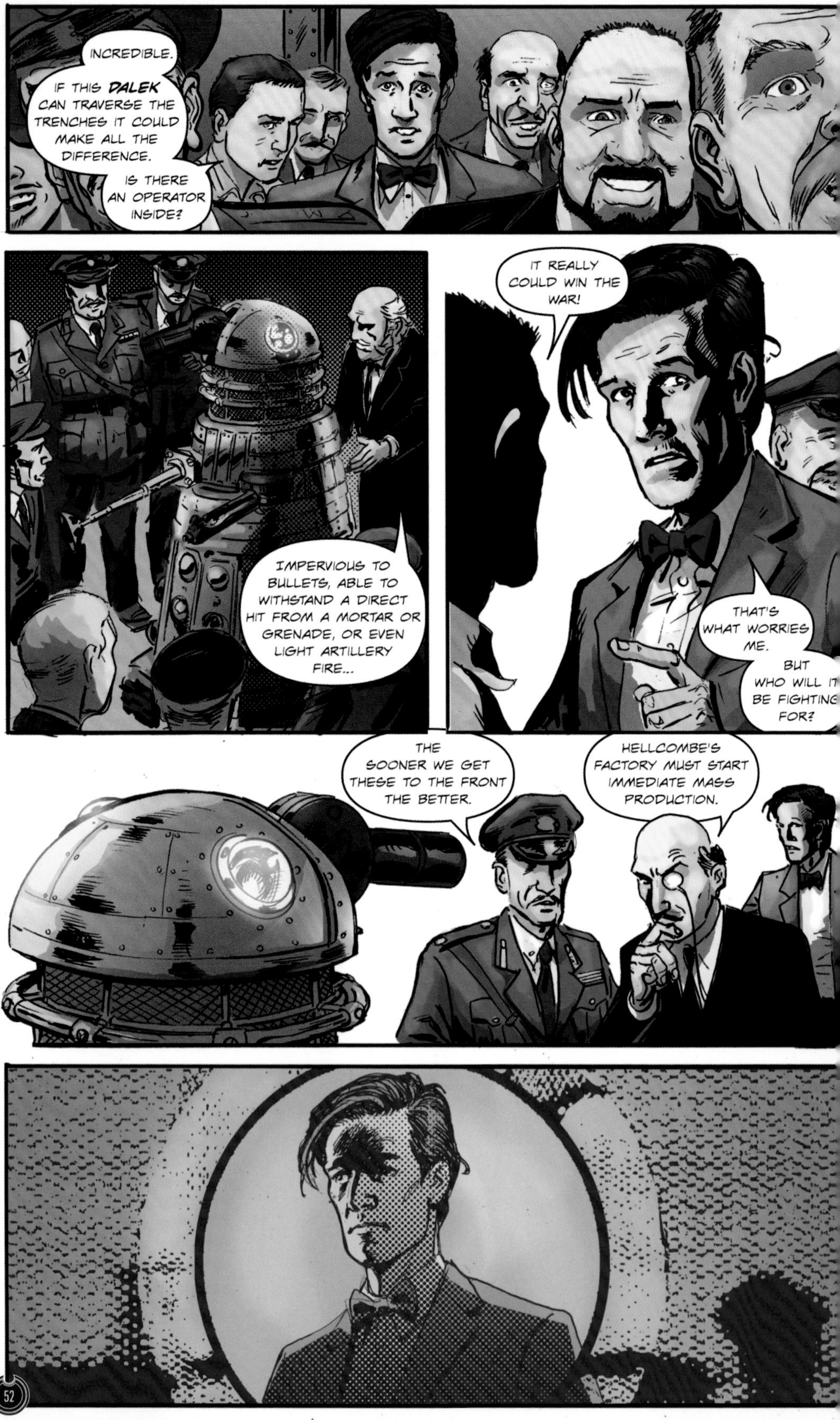
INCREDIBLE.
IF THIS DALEK CAN TRAVERSE THE TRENCHES IT COULD MAKE ALL THE DIFFERENCE.
IS THERE AN OPERATOR INSIDE?
IMPERVIOUS TO BULLETS, ABLE TO WITHSTAND A DIRECT HIT FROM A MORTAR OR GRENADE, OR EVEN LIGHT ARTILLERY FIRE...
IT REALLY COULD WIN THE WAR!
THAT'S WHAT WORRIES ME.
BUT WHO WILL IT BE FIGHTING FOR?
THE SOONER WE GET THESE TO THE FRONT THE BETTER.
HELLCOMBE'S FACTORY MUST START IMMEDIATE MASS PRODUCTION.

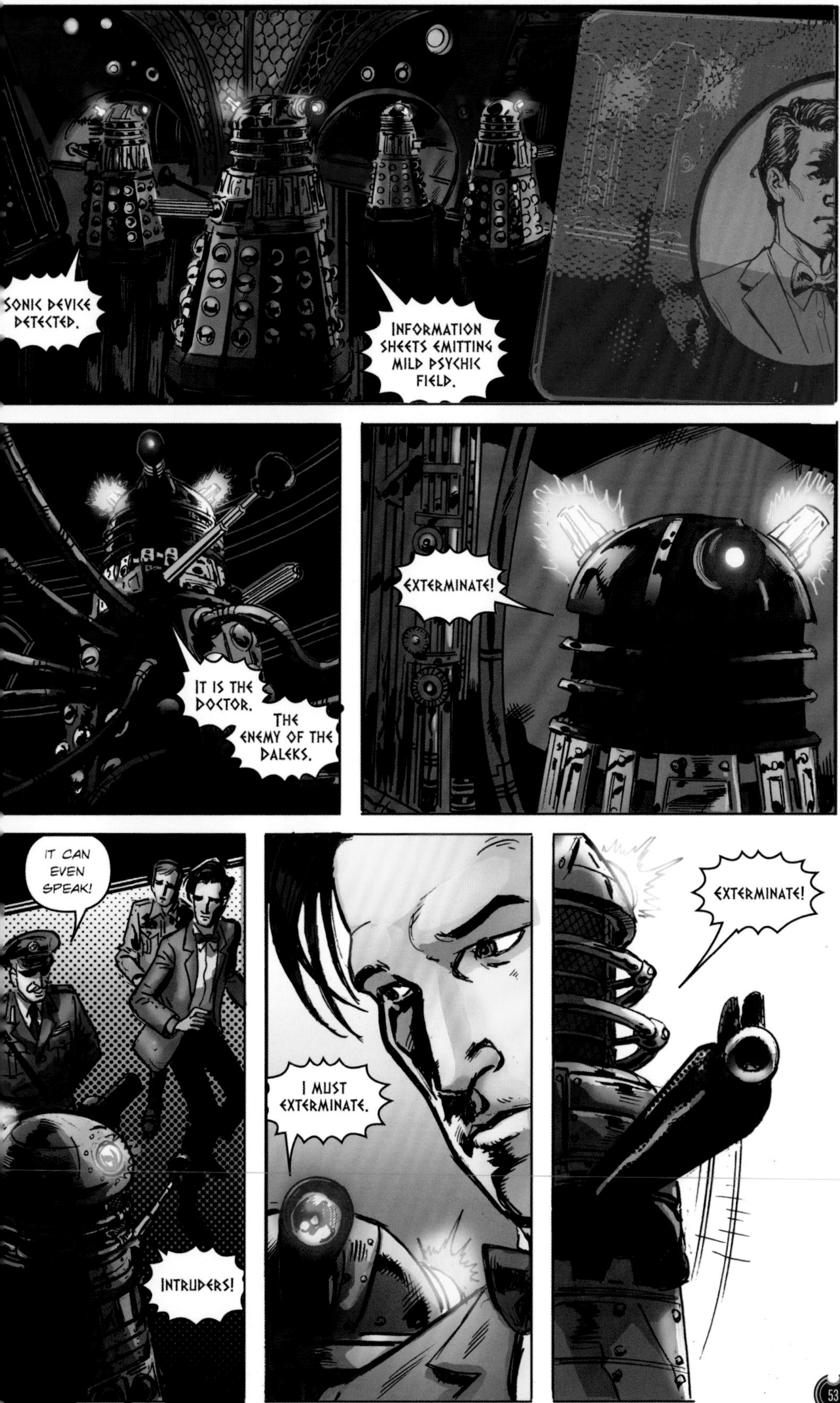
SONIC DEVICE DETECTED.
INFORMATION SHEETS EMITTING MILD PSYCHIC FIELD.
IT IS THE DOCTOR.
THE ENEMY OF THE DALEKS.
EXTERMINATE!
IT CAN EVEN SPEAK!
INTRUDERS!
I MUST EXTERMINATE.
EXTERMINATE!

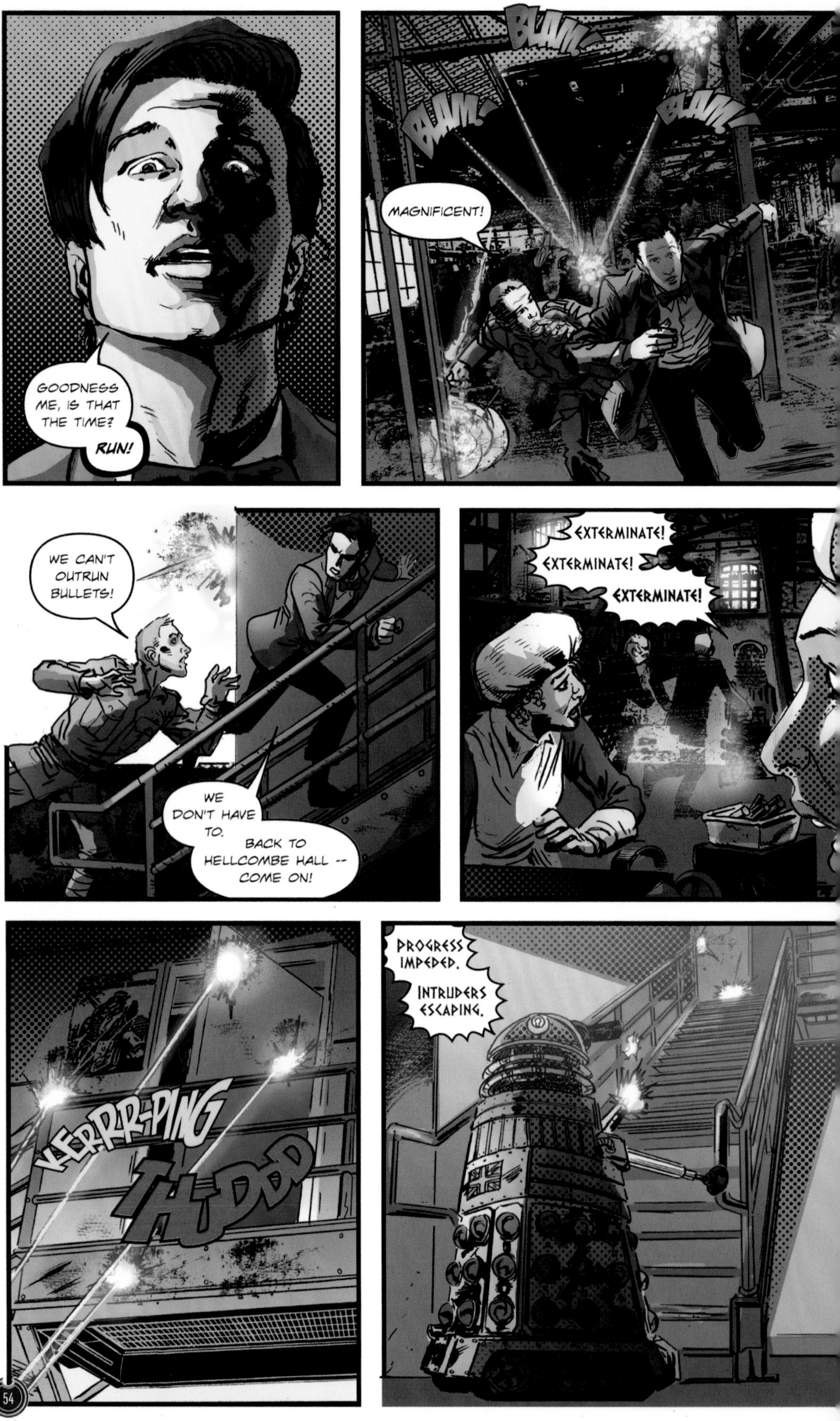
GOODNESS ME, IS THAT THE TIME?
RUN!
BLAM!
BLAM!
BLAM!
MAGNIFICENT!
WE CAN'T OUTRUN BULLETS!
WE DON'T HAVE TO.
BACK TO HELLCOMBE HALL -- COME ON!
EXTERMINATE!
EXTERMINATE!
EXTERMINATE!
KERRR-PING
THUDDD
PROGRESS IMPEDED.
INTRUDERS ESCAPING.

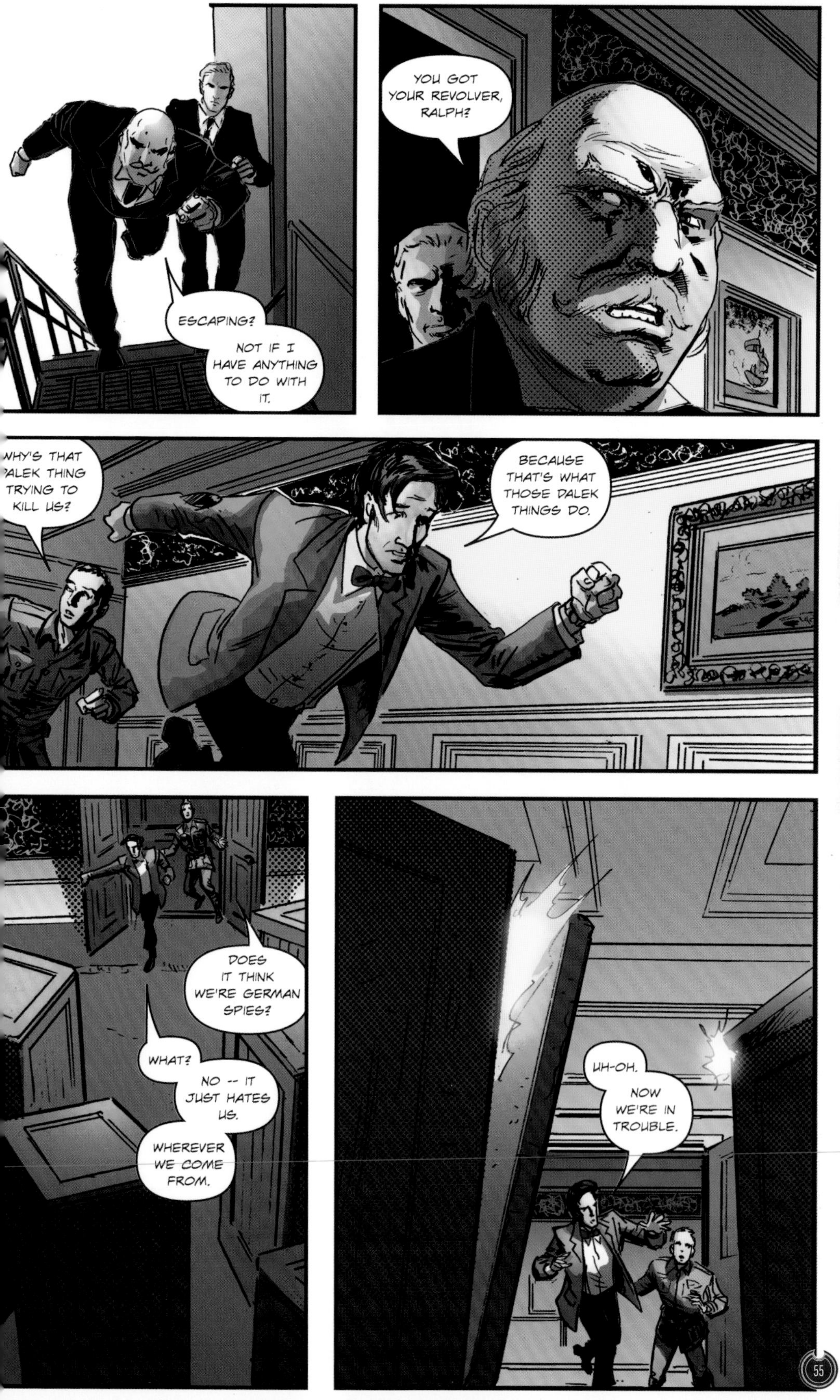
ESCAPING?
NOT IF I HAVE ANYTHING TO DO WITH IT.
YOU GOT YOUR REVOLVER, RALPH?
WHY'S THAT DALEK THING TRYING TO KILL US?
BECAUSE THAT'S WHAT THOSE DALEK THINGS DO.
DOES IT THINK WE'RE GERMAN SPIES?
WHAT?
NO -- IT JUST HATES US.
WHEREVER WE COME FROM.
UH-OH.
NOW WE'RE IN TROUBLE.

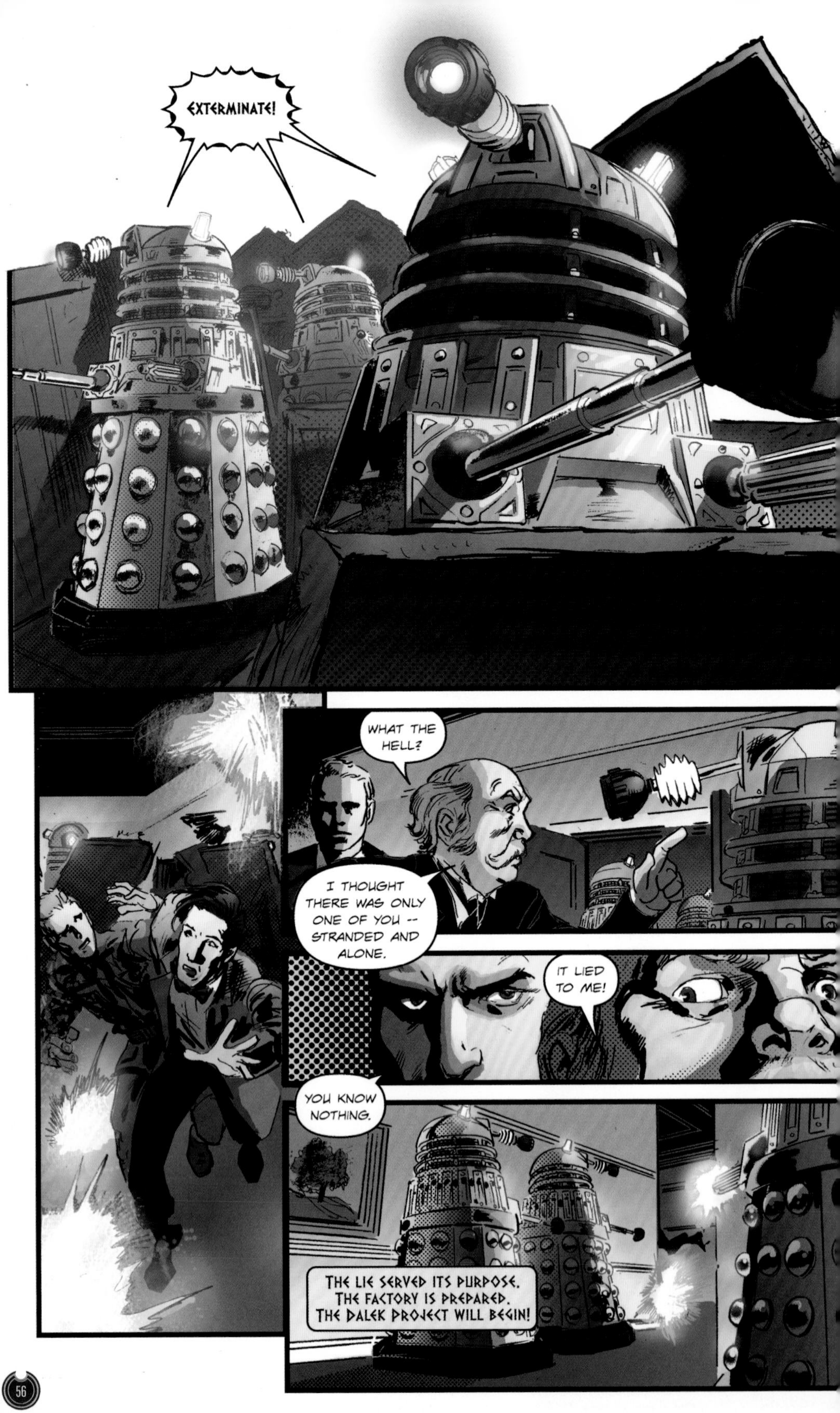
EXTERMINATE!
WHAT THE HELL?
I THOUGHT THERE WAS ONLY ONE OF YOU -- STRANDED AND ALONE.
IT LIED TO ME!
YOU KNOW NOTHING.
THE LIE SERVED ITS PURPOSE. THE FACTORY IS PREPARED. THE DALEK PROJECT WILL BEGIN!

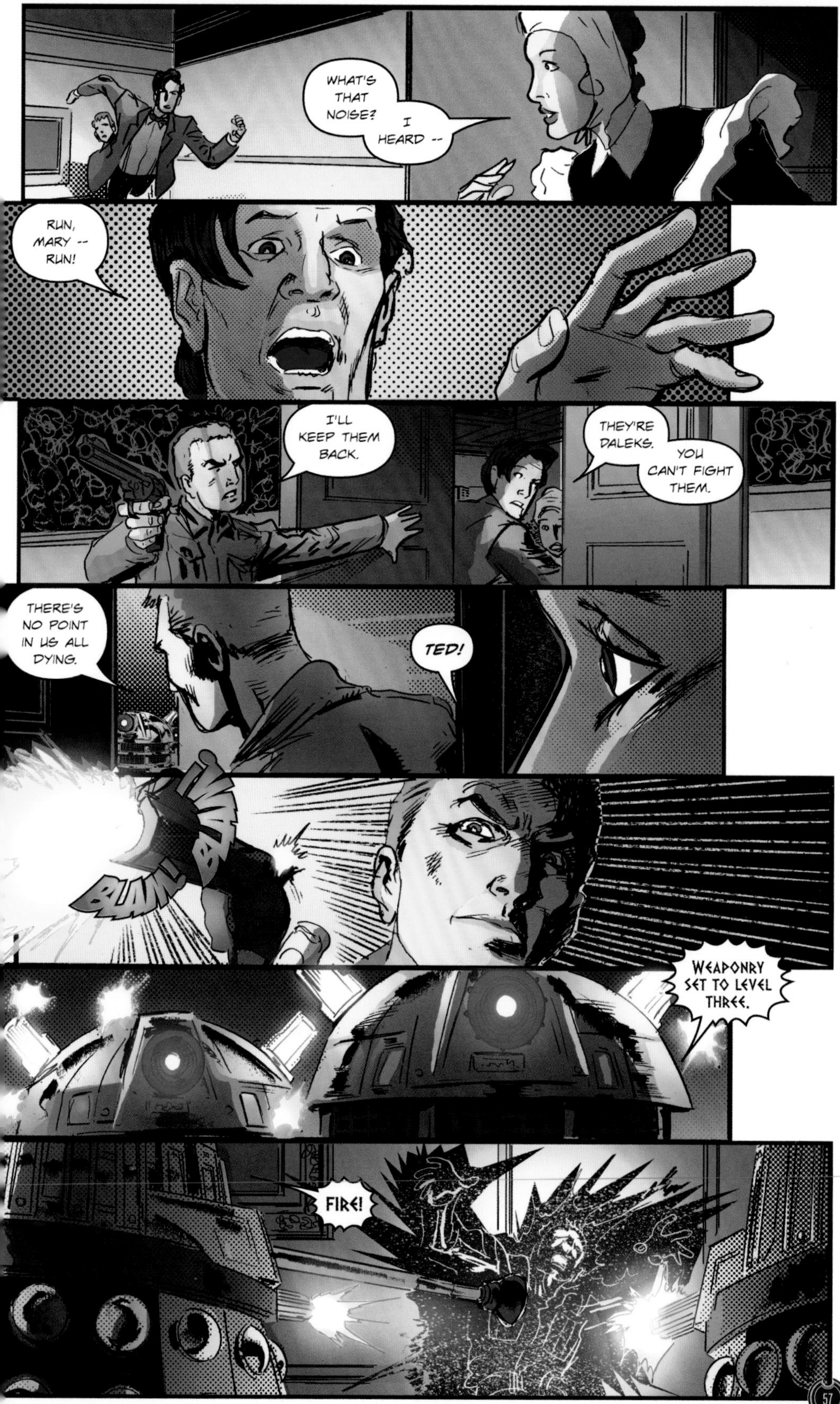
WHAT'S THAT NOISE?
I HEARD --
RUN, MARY -- RUN!
I'LL KEEP THEM BACK.
THEY'RE DALEKS.
YOU CAN'T FIGHT THEM.
THERE'S NO POINT IN US ALL DYING.
TED!
BLAM! BLAM!
WEAPONRY SET TO LEVEL THREE.
FIRE!

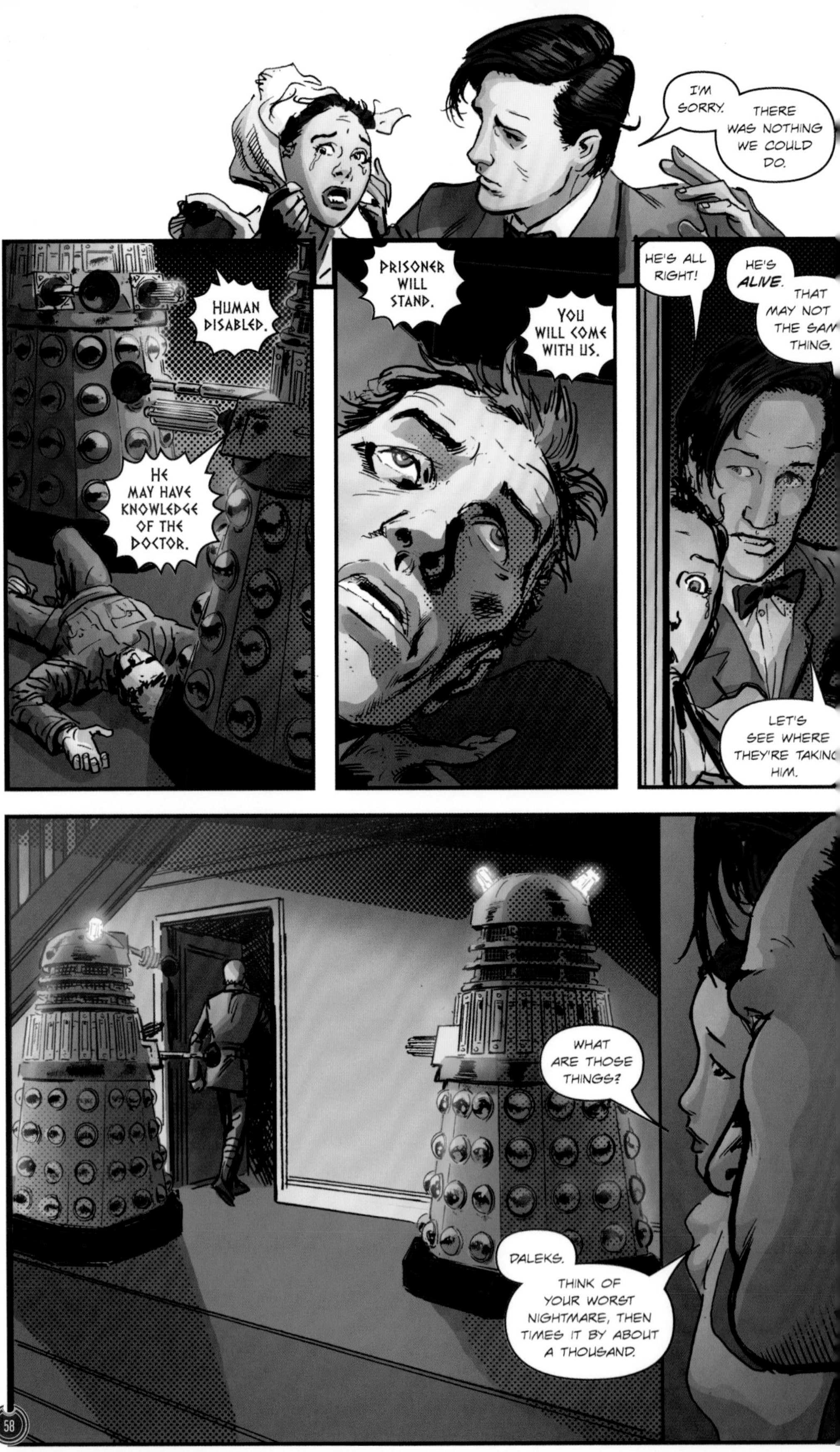
I'M SORRY.
THERE WAS NOTHING WE COULD DO.
HUMAN DISABLED.
HE MAY HAVE KNOWLEDGE OF THE DOCTOR.
PRISONER WILL STAND.
YOU WILL COME WITH US.
HE'S ALL RIGHT!
HE'S ALIVE.
THAT MAY NOT THE SAM THING.
LET'S SEE WHERE THEY'RE TAKING HIM.
WHAT ARE THOSE THINGS?
DALEKS.
THINK OF YOUR WORST NIGHTMARE, THEN TIMES IT BY ABOUT A THOUSAND.

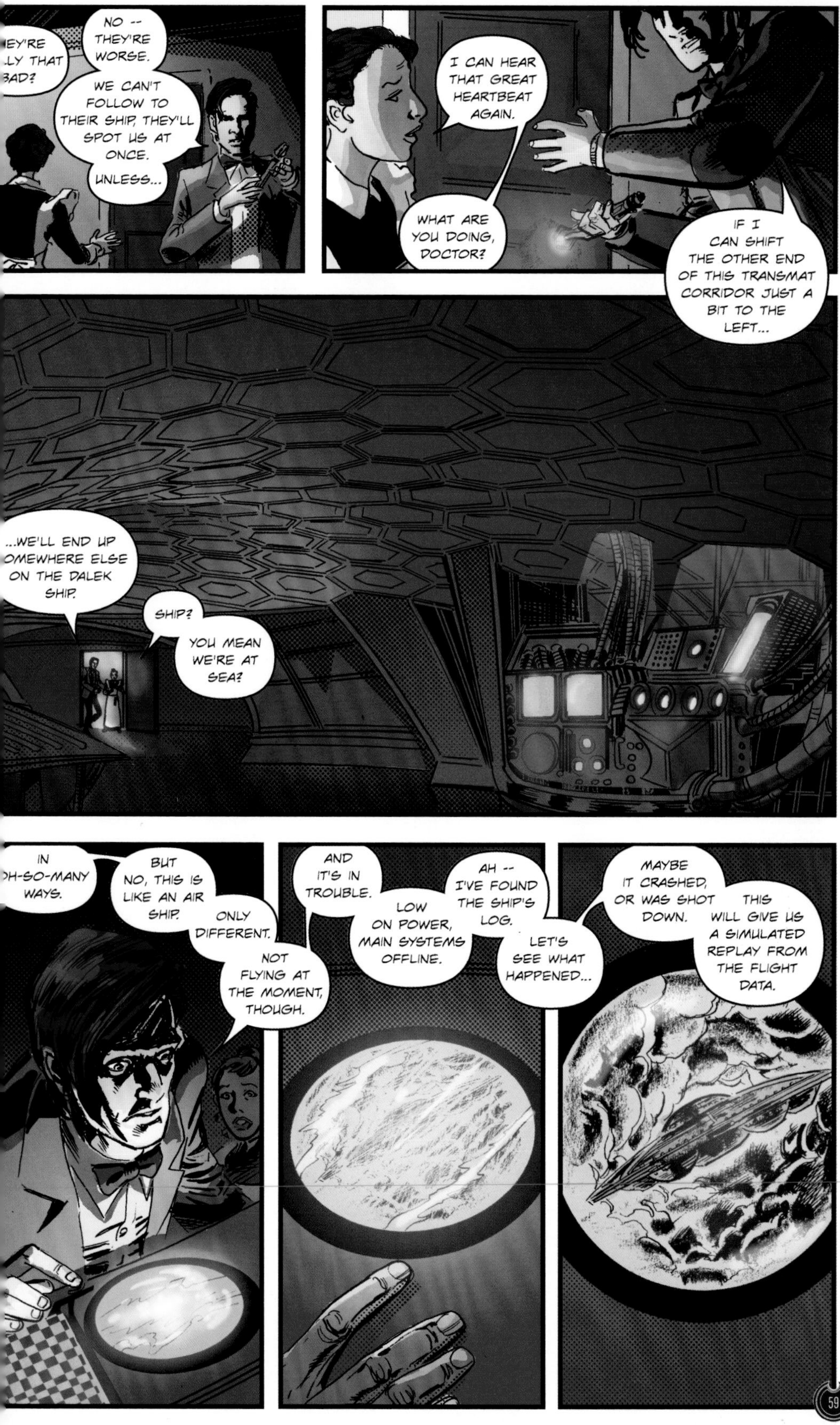

EY'RE LY THAT BAD?
NO -- THEY'RE WORSE.
WE CAN'T FOLLOW TO THEIR SHIP, THEY'LL SPOT US AT ONCE.
UNLESS...
I CAN HEAR THAT GREAT HEARTBEAT AGAIN.
WHAT ARE YOU DOING, DOCTOR?
IF I CAN SHIFT THE OTHER END OF THIS TRANSMAT CORRIDOR JUST A BIT TO THE LEFT...
...WE'LL END UP OMEWHERE ELSE ON THE DALEK SHIP.
SHIP?
YOU MEAN WE'RE AT SEA?
IN H-SO-MANY WAYS.
BUT NO, THIS IS LIKE AN AIR SHIP.
ONLY DIFFERENT.
NOT FLYING AT THE MOMENT, THOUGH.
AND IT'S IN TROUBLE.
LOW ON POWER, MAIN SYSTEMS OFFLINE.
AH -- I'VE FOUND THE SHIP'S LOG.
LET'S SEE WHAT HAPPENED...
MAYBE IT CRASHED, OR WAS SHOT DOWN.
THIS WILL GIVE US A SIMULATED REPLAY FROM THE FLIGHT DATA.

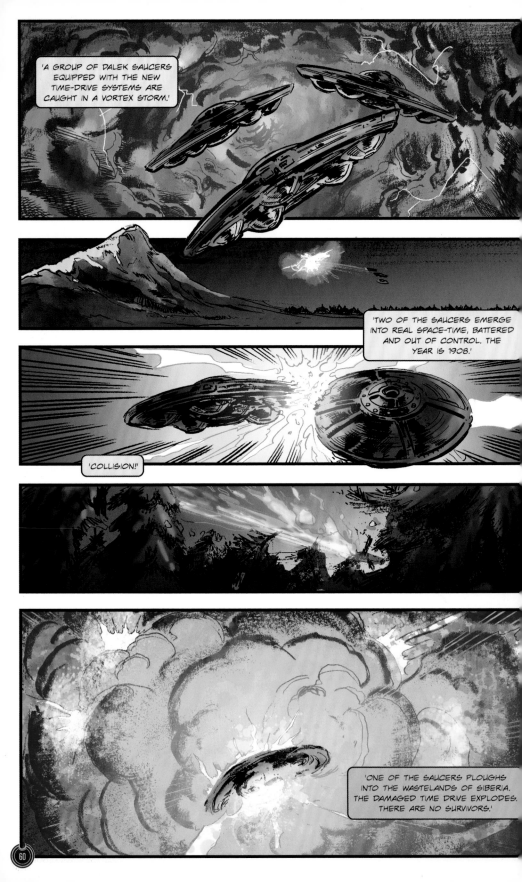

'A GROUP OF DALEK SAUCERS EQUIPPED WITH THE NEW TIME-DRIVE SYSTEMS ARE CAUGHT IN A VORTEX STORM.'

'TWO OF THE SAUCERS EMERGE INTO REAL SPACE-TIME, BATTERED AND OUT OF CONTROL. THE YEAR IS 1908.'

'COLLISION!'

'ONE OF THE SAUCERS PLOUGHS INTO THE WASTELANDS OF SIBERIA. THE DAMAGED TIME DRIVE EXPLODES. THERE ARE NO SURVIVORS.'

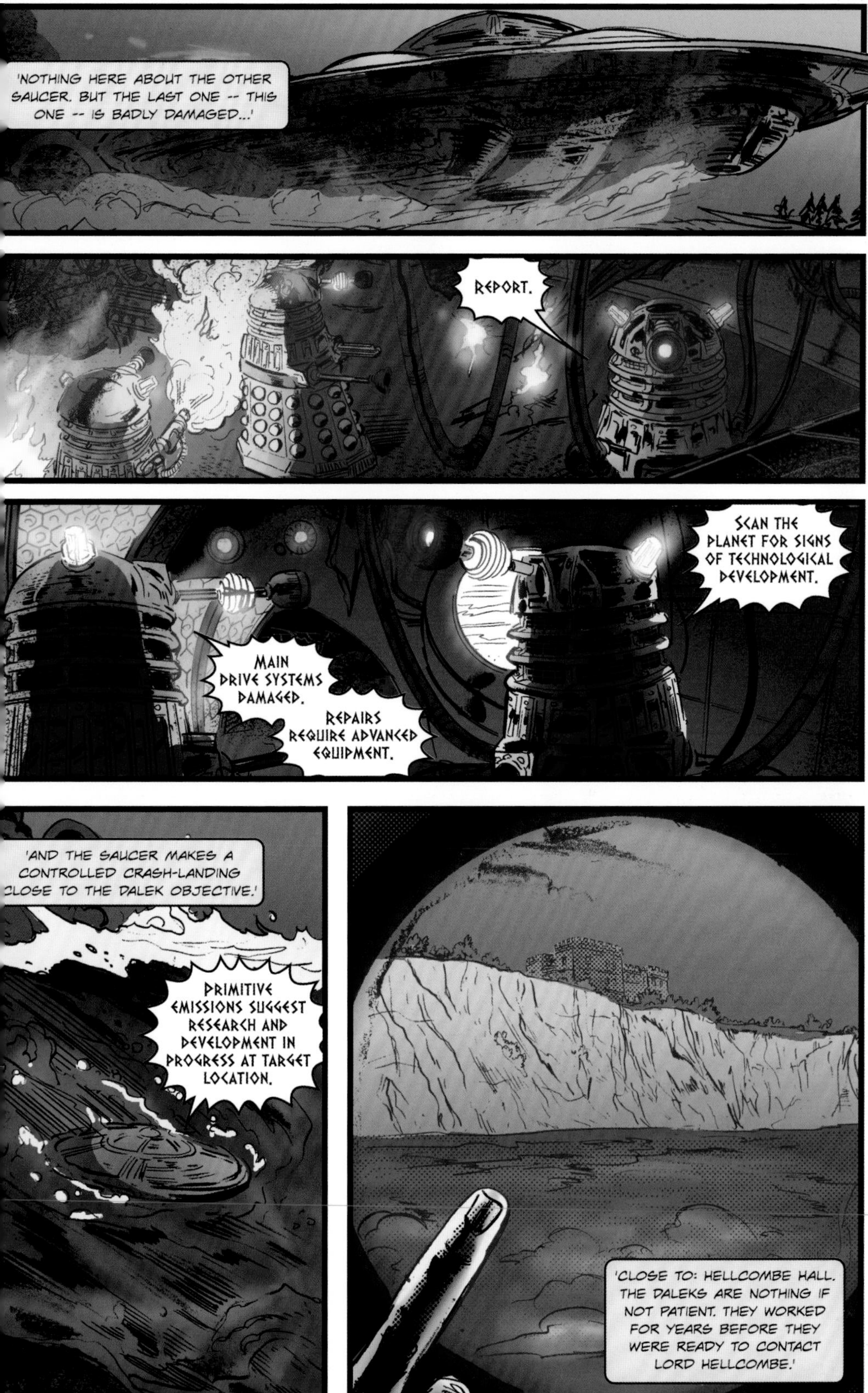
'NOTHING HERE ABOUT THE OTHER SAUCER. BUT THE LAST ONE -- THIS ONE -- IS BADLY DAMAGED...'
REPORT.
SCAN THE PLANET FOR SIGNS OF TECHNOLOGICAL DEVELOPMENT.
MAIN DRIVE SYSTEMS DAMAGED.
REPAIRS REQUIRE ADVANCED EQUIPMENT.
'AND THE SAUCER MAKES A CONTROLLED CRASH-LANDING CLOSE TO THE DALEK OBJECTIVE.'
PRIMITIVE EMISSIONS SUGGEST RESEARCH AND DEVELOPMENT IN PROGRESS AT TARGET LOCATION.
'CLOSE TO: HELLCOMBE HALL. THE DALEKS ARE NOTHING IF NOT PATIENT. THEY WORKED FOR YEARS BEFORE THEY WERE READY TO CONTACT LORD HELLCOMBE.'

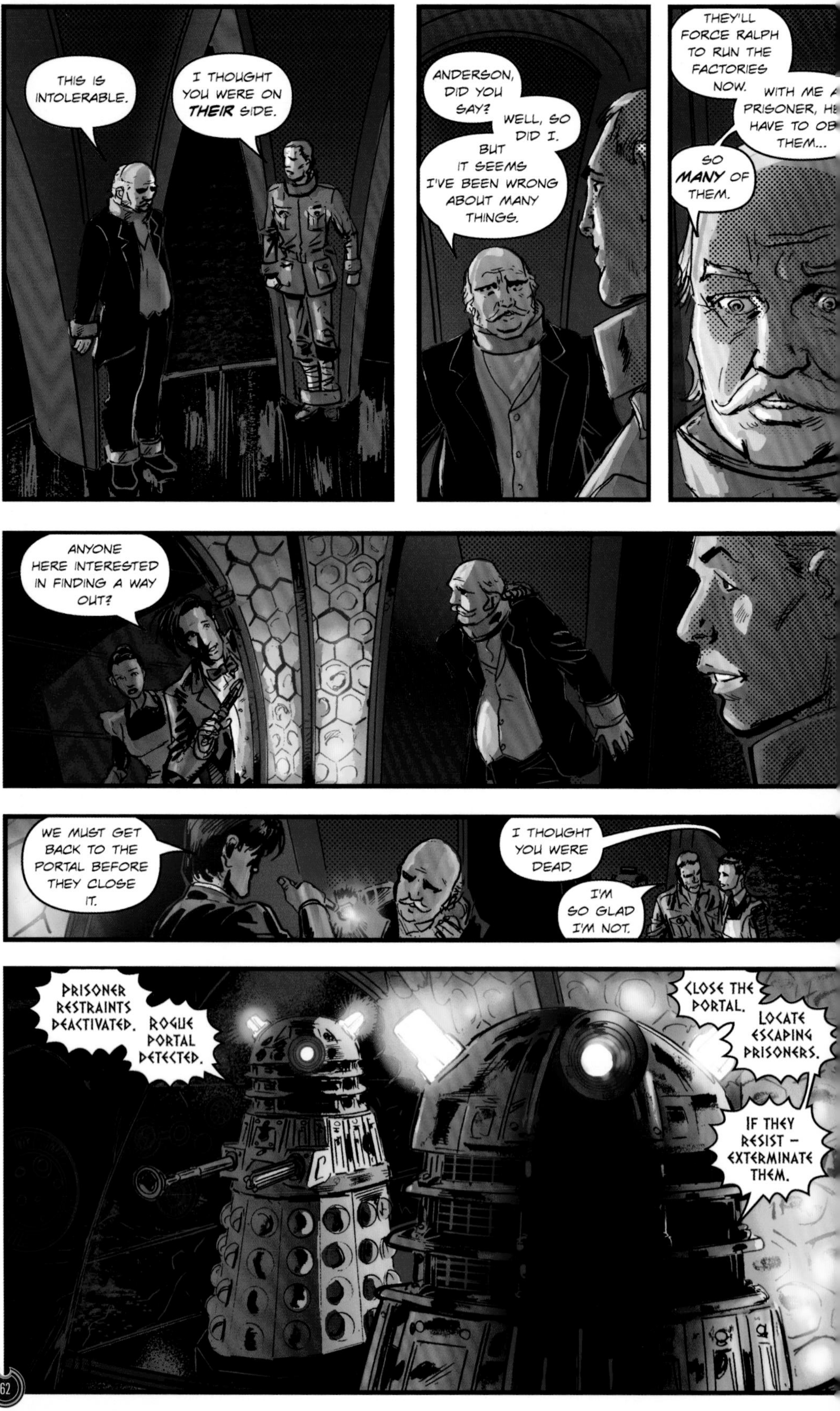

THIS IS INTOLERABLE.
I THOUGHT YOU WERE ON THEIR SIDE.
ANDERSON, DID YOU SAY?
WELL, SO DID I.
BUT IT SEEMS I'VE BEEN WRONG ABOUT MANY THINGS.
THEY'LL FORCE RALPH TO RUN THE FACTORIES NOW.
WITH ME A PRISONER, HE HAVE TO OB THEM...
SO MANY OF THEM.
ANYONE HERE INTERESTED IN FINDING A WAY OUT?
WE MUST GET BACK TO THE PORTAL BEFORE THEY CLOSE IT.
I THOUGHT YOU WERE DEAD.
I'M SO GLAD I'M NOT.
PRISONER RESTRAINTS DEACTIVATED.
ROGUE PORTAL DETECTED.
CLOSE THE PORTAL.
LOCATE ESCAPING PRISONERS.
IF THEY RESIST – EXTERMINATE THEM.

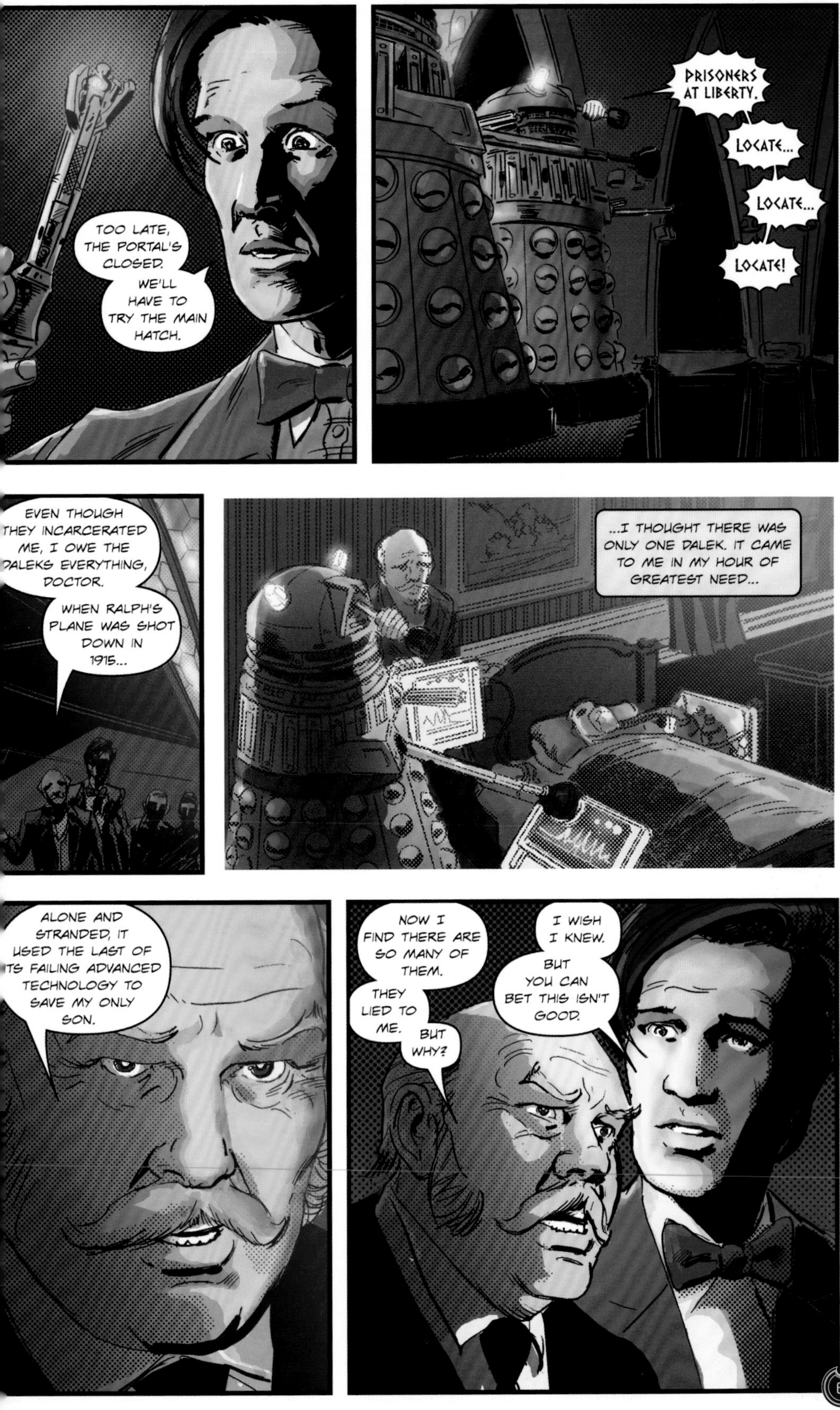
TOO LATE, THE PORTAL'S CLOSED.
WE'LL HAVE TO TRY THE MAIN HATCH.
PRISONERS AT LIBERTY.
LOCATE...
LOCATE...
LOCATE!
EVEN THOUGH THEY INCARCERATED ME, I OWE THE DALEKS EVERYTHING, DOCTOR.
WHEN RALPH'S PLANE WAS SHOT DOWN IN 1915...
...I THOUGHT THERE WAS ONLY ONE DALEK. IT CAME TO ME IN MY HOUR OF GREATEST NEED...
ALONE AND STRANDED, IT USED THE LAST OF ITS FAILING ADVANCED TECHNOLOGY TO SAVE MY ONLY SON.
NOW I FIND THERE ARE SO MANY OF THEM.
THEY LIED TO ME.
BUT WHY?
I WISH I KNEW.
BUT YOU CAN BET THIS ISN'T GOOD.

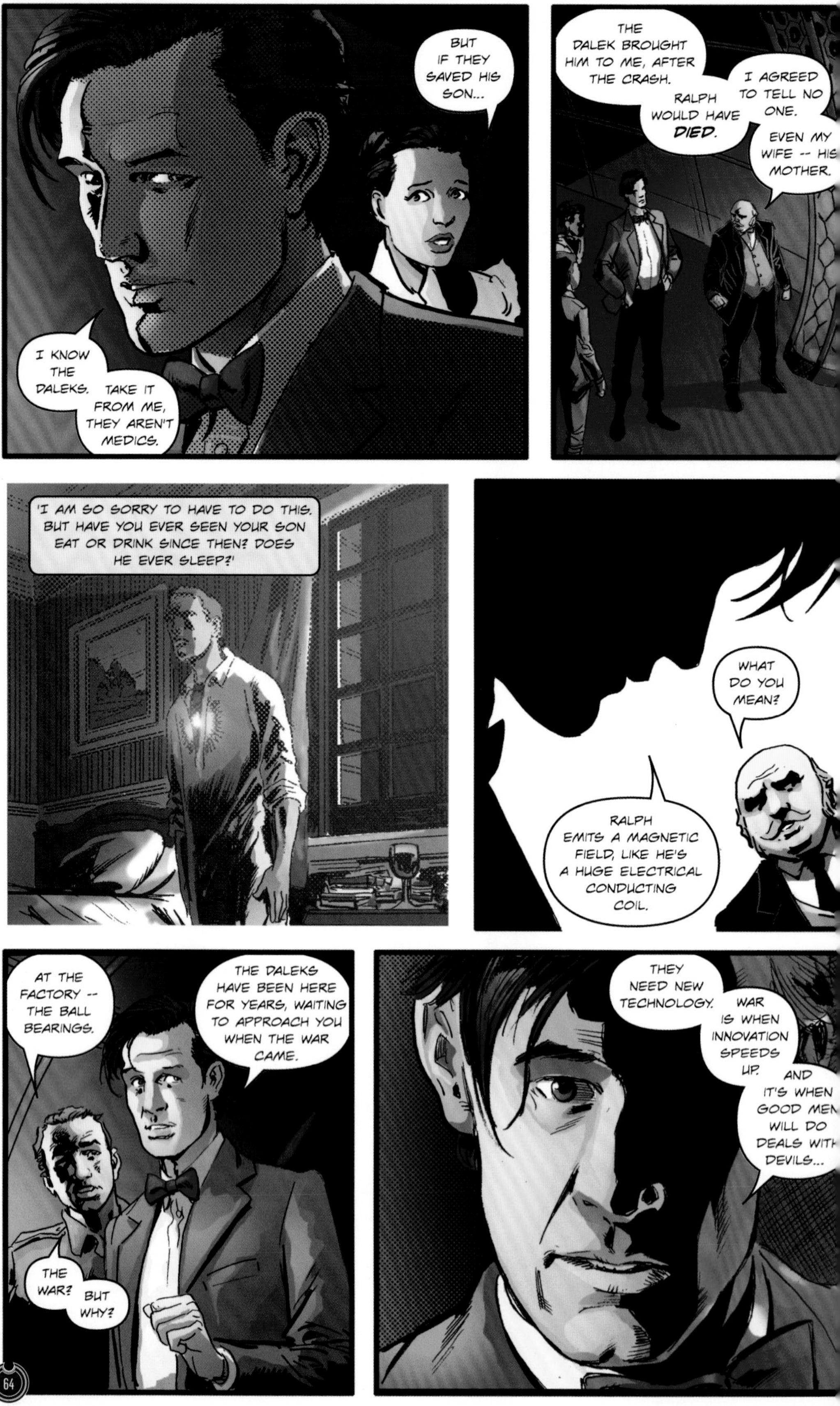
BUT IF THEY SAVED HIS SON...
I KNOW THE DALEKS.
TAKE IT FROM ME, THEY AREN'T MEDICS.
THE DALEK BROUGHT HIM TO ME, AFTER THE CRASH.
RALPH WOULD HAVE DIED.
I AGREED TO TELL NO ONE.
EVEN MY WIFE -- HIS MOTHER.
'I AM SO SORRY TO HAVE TO DO THIS. BUT HAVE YOU EVER SEEN YOUR SON EAT OR DRINK SINCE THEN? DOES HE EVER SLEEP?'
WHAT DO YOU MEAN?
RALPH EMITS A MAGNETIC FIELD, LIKE HE'S A HUGE ELECTRICAL CONDUCTING COIL.
AT THE FACTORY -- THE BALL BEARINGS.
THE DALEKS HAVE BEEN HERE FOR YEARS, WAITING TO APPROACH YOU WHEN THE WAR CAME.
THE WAR?
BUT WHY?
THEY NEED NEW TECHNOLOGY.
WAR IS WHEN INNOVATION SPEEDS UP.
AND IT'S WHEN GOOD MEN WILL DO DEALS WITH DEVILS...

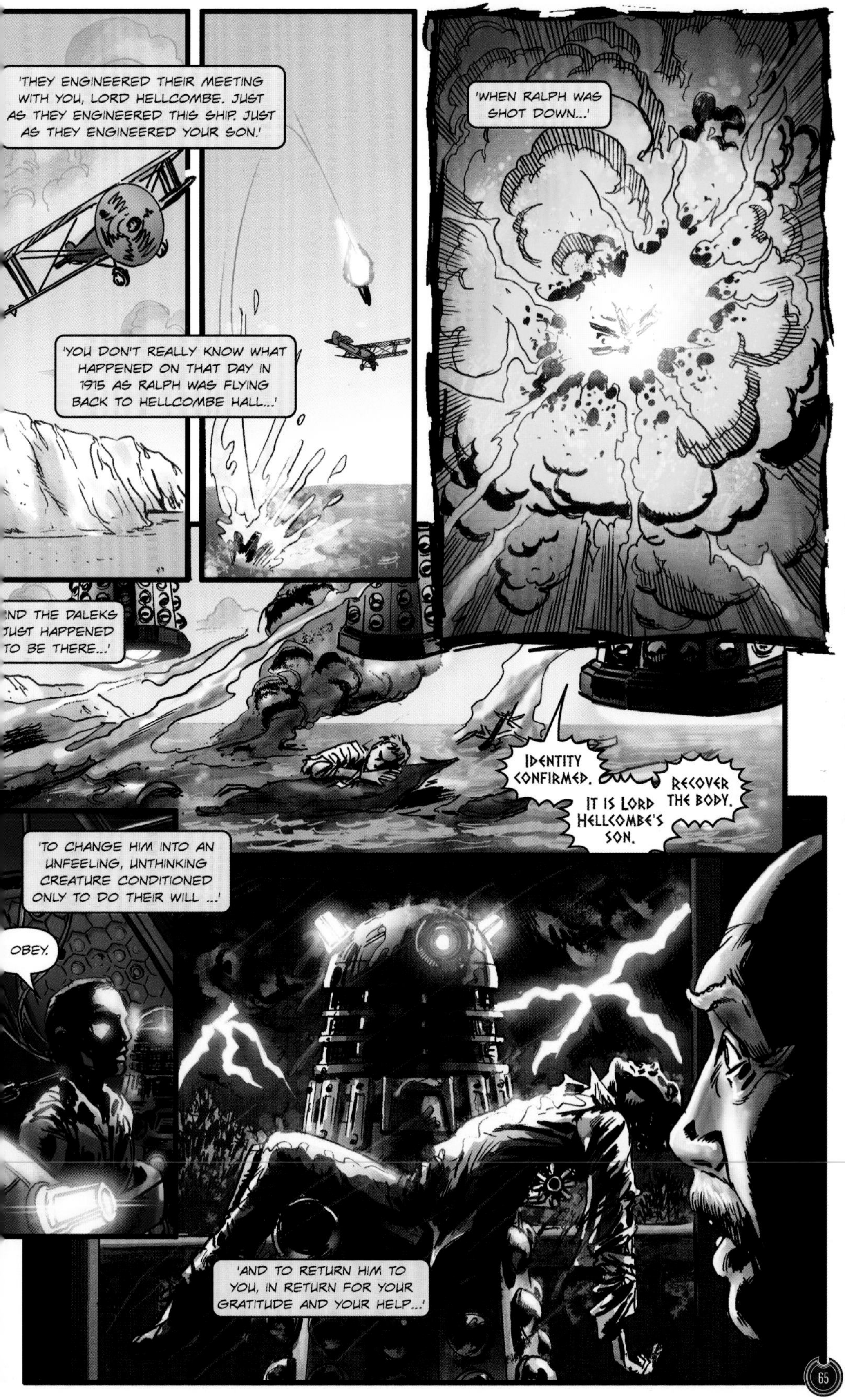
'THEY ENGINEERED THEIR MEETING WITH YOU, LORD HELLCOMBE. JUST AS THEY ENGINEERED THIS SHIP. JUST AS THEY ENGINEERED YOUR SON.'
'YOU DON'T REALLY KNOW WHAT HAPPENED ON THAT DAY IN 1915 AS RALPH WAS FLYING BACK TO HELLCOMBE HALL...'
'WHEN RALPH WAS SHOT DOWN...'
ND THE DALEKS JUST HAPPENED TO BE THERE...'
IDENTITY CONFIRMED.
IT IS LORD HELLCOMBE'S SON.
RECOVER THE BODY.
'TO CHANGE HIM INTO AN UNFEELING, UNTHINKING CREATURE CONDITIONED ONLY TO DO THEIR WILL ...'
OBEY.
'AND TO RETURN HIM TO YOU, IN RETURN FOR YOUR GRATITUDE AND YOUR HELP...'

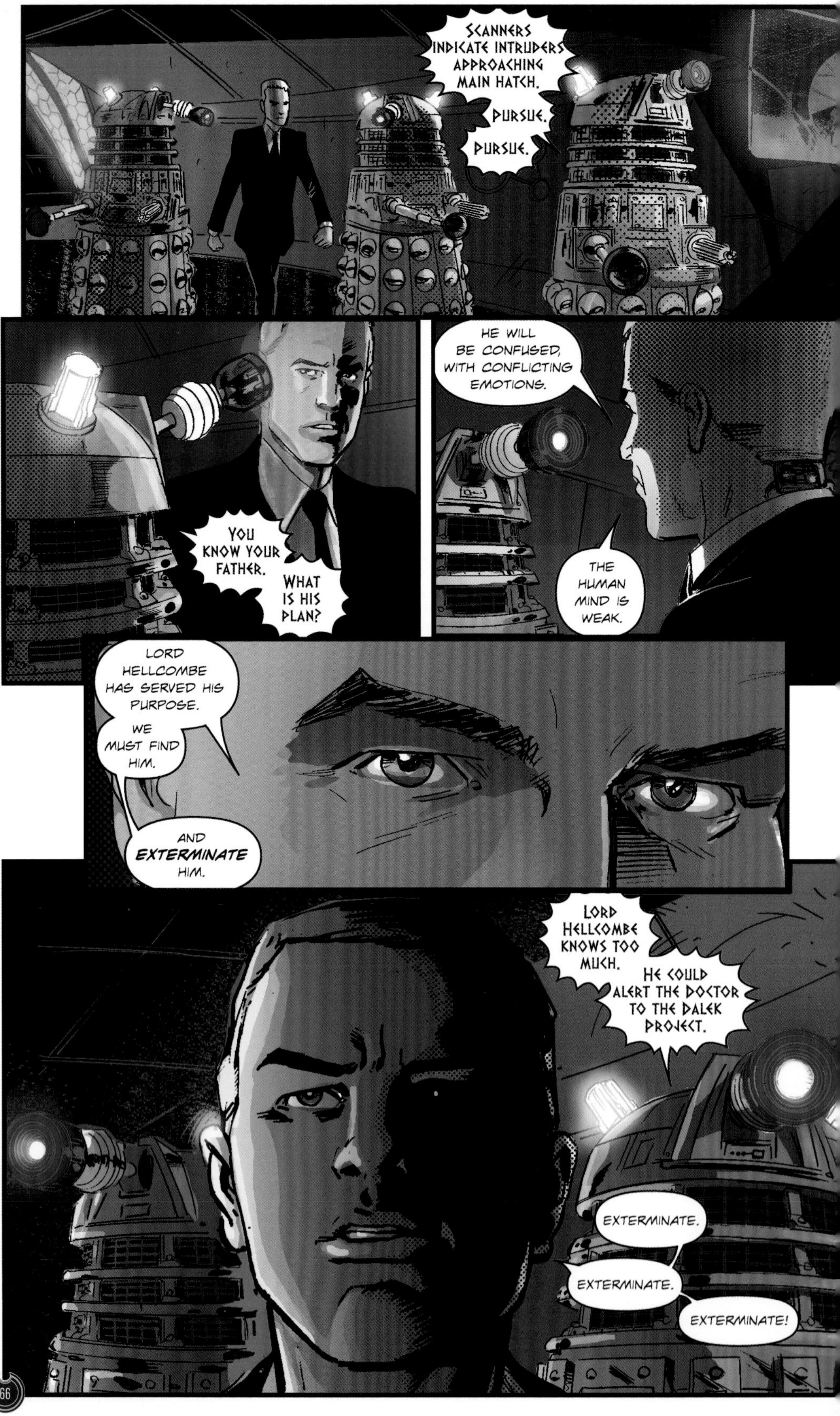
SCANNERS INDICATE INTRUDERS APPROACHING MAIN HATCH.
PURSUE.
PURSUE.
YOU KNOW YOUR FATHER.
WHAT IS HIS PLAN?
HE WILL BE CONFUSED, WITH CONFLICTING EMOTIONS.
THE HUMAN MIND IS WEAK.
LORD HELLCOMBE HAS SERVED HIS PURPOSE.
WE MUST FIND HIM.
AND *EXTERMINATE* HIM.
LORD HELLCOMBE KNOWS TOO MUCH.
HE COULD ALERT THE DOCTOR TO THE DALEK PROJECT.
EXTERMINATE.
EXTERMINATE.
EXTERMINATE!

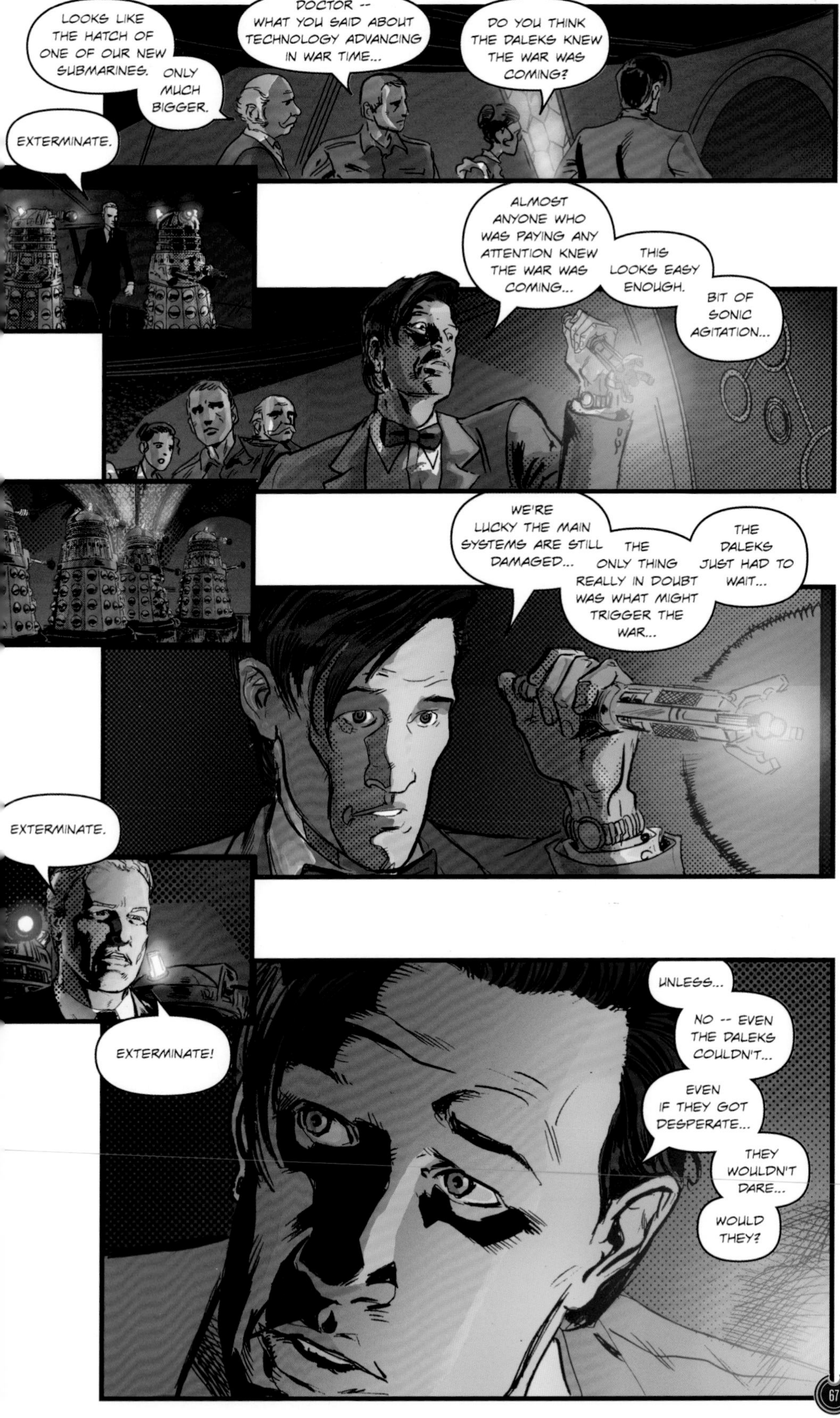
LOOKS LIKE THE HATCH OF ONE OF OUR NEW SUBMARINES.
ONLY MUCH BIGGER.
DOCTOR -- WHAT YOU SAID ABOUT TECHNOLOGY ADVANCING IN WAR TIME...
DO YOU THINK THE DALEKS KNEW THE WAR WAS COMING?
EXTERMINATE.
ALMOST ANYONE WHO WAS PAYING ANY ATTENTION KNEW THE WAR WAS COMING...
THIS LOOKS EASY ENOUGH.
BIT OF SONIC AGITATION...
WE'RE LUCKY THE MAIN SYSTEMS ARE STILL DAMAGED...
THE ONLY THING REALLY IN DOUBT WAS WHAT MIGHT TRIGGER THE WAR...
THE DALEKS JUST HAD TO WAIT...
EXTERMINATE.
EXTERMINATE!
UNLESS...
NO -- EVEN THE DALEKS COULDN'T...
EVEN IF THEY GOT DESPERATE...
THEY WOULDN'T DARE...
WOULD THEY?

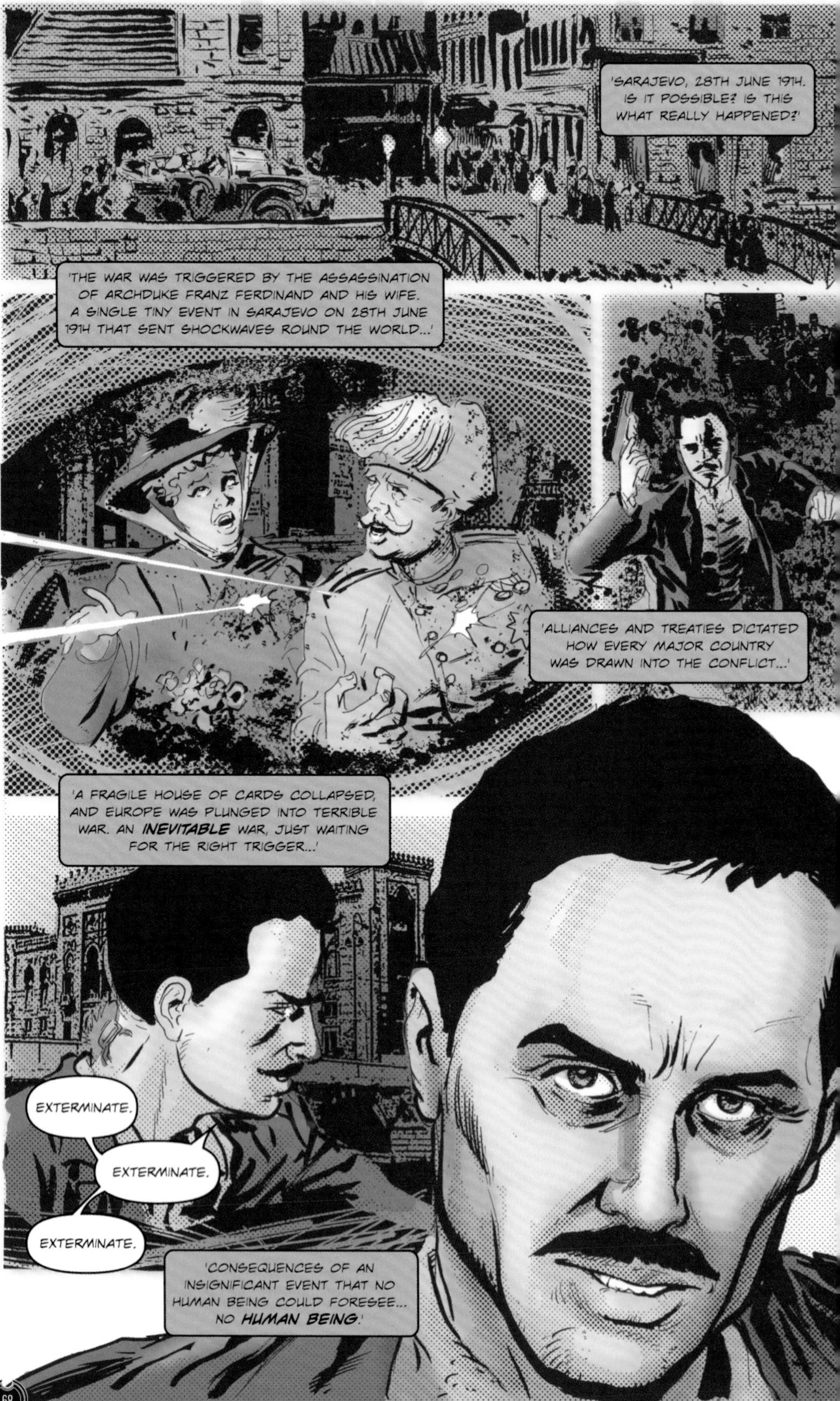
'SARAJEVO, 28TH JUNE 1914. IS IT POSSIBLE? IS THIS WHAT REALLY HAPPENED?'
'THE WAR WAS TRIGGERED BY THE ASSASSINATION OF ARCHDUKE FRANZ FERDINAND AND HIS WIFE. A SINGLE TINY EVENT IN SARAJEVO ON 28TH JUNE 1914 THAT SENT SHOCKWAVES ROUND THE WORLD...'
'ALLIANCES AND TREATIES DICTATED HOW EVERY MAJOR COUNTRY WAS DRAWN INTO THE CONFLICT...'
'A FRAGILE HOUSE OF CARDS COLLAPSED, AND EUROPE WAS PLUNGED INTO TERRIBLE WAR. AN ***INEVITABLE*** WAR, JUST WAITING FOR THE RIGHT TRIGGER...'
EXTERMINATE.
EXTERMINATE.
EXTERMINATE.
'CONSEQUENCES OF AN INSIGNIFICANT EVENT THAT NO HUMAN BEING COULD FORESEE... NO ***HUMAN BEING***.'

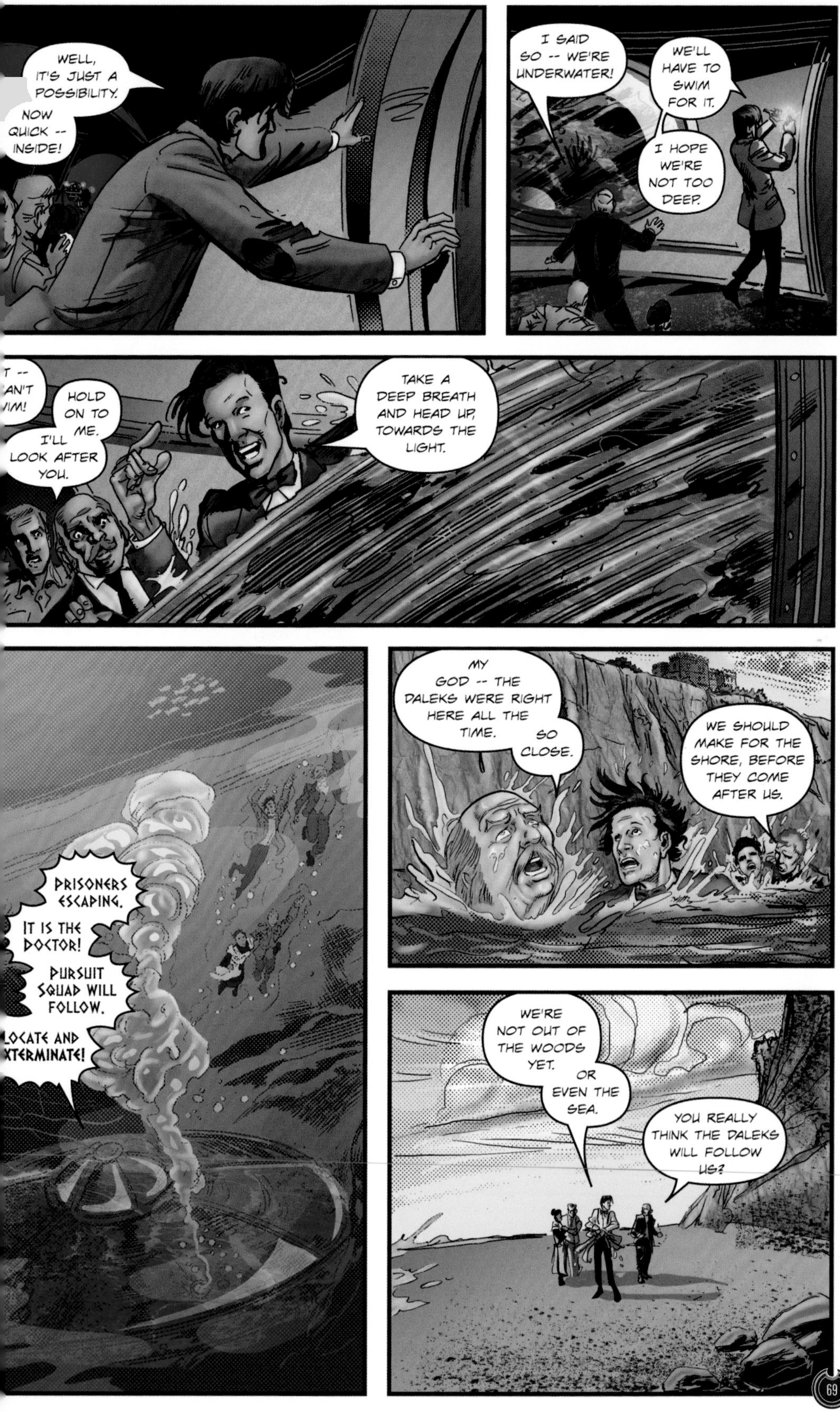
WELL, IT'S JUST A POSSIBILITY.
NOW QUICK -- INSIDE!
I SAID SO -- WE'RE UNDERWATER!
WE'LL HAVE TO SWIM FOR IT.
I HOPE WE'RE NOT TOO DEEP.
T -- AN'T WIM!
HOLD ON TO ME. I'LL LOOK AFTER YOU.
TAKE A DEEP BREATH AND HEAD UP, TOWARDS THE LIGHT.
PRISONERS ESCAPING.
IT IS THE DOCTOR!
PURSUIT SQUAD WILL FOLLOW.
OCATE AND XTERMINATE!
MY GOD -- THE DALEKS WERE RIGHT HERE ALL THE TIME.
SO CLOSE.
WE SHOULD MAKE FOR THE SHORE, BEFORE THEY COME AFTER US.
WE'RE NOT OUT OF THE WOODS YET.
OR EVEN THE SEA.
YOU REALLY THINK THE DALEKS WILL FOLLOW US?

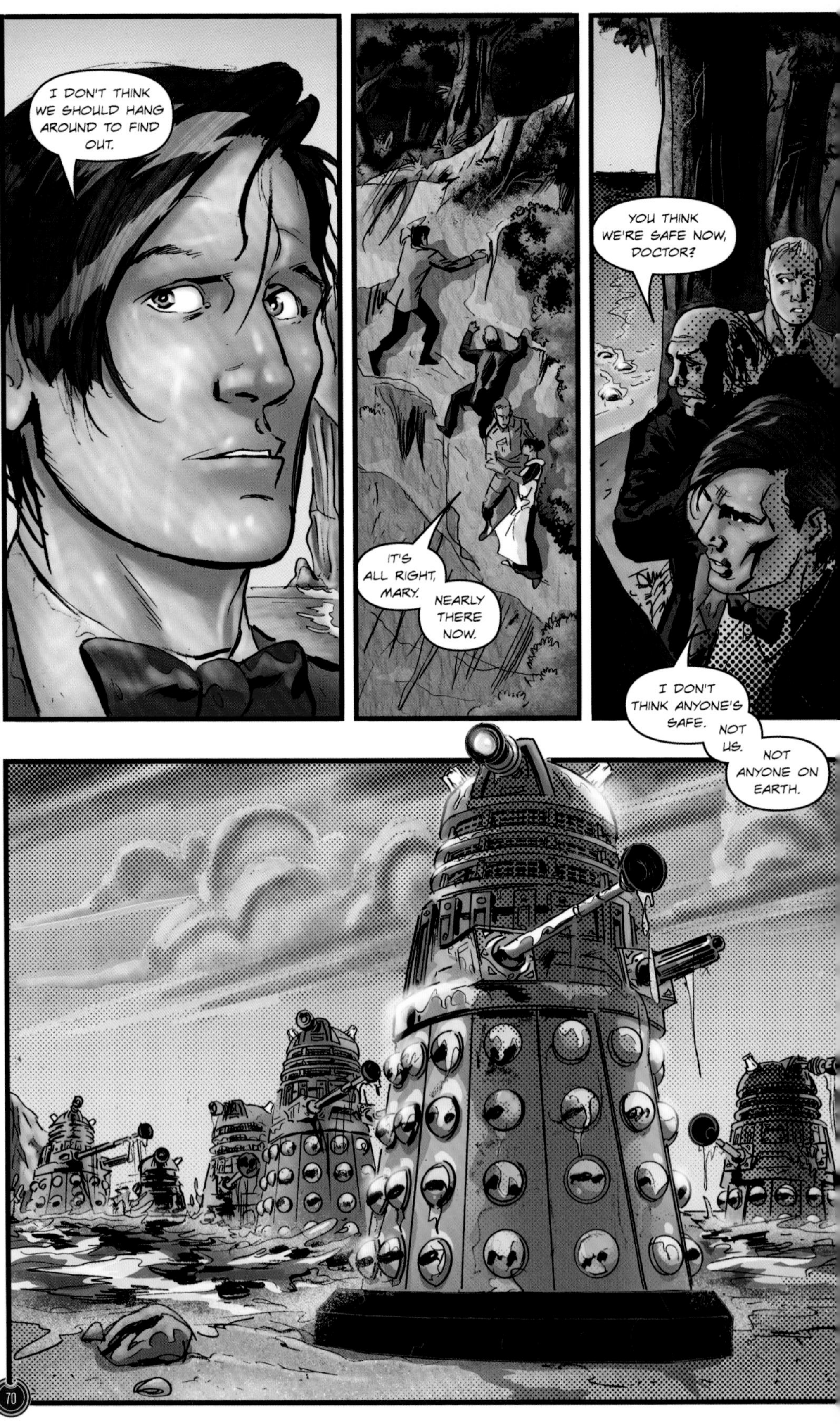
I DON'T THINK WE SHOULD HANG AROUND TO FIND OUT.
IT'S ALL RIGHT, MARY.
NEARLY THERE NOW.
YOU THINK WE'RE SAFE NOW, DOCTOR?
I DON'T THINK ANYONE'S SAFE.
NOT US.
NOT ANYONE ON EARTH.

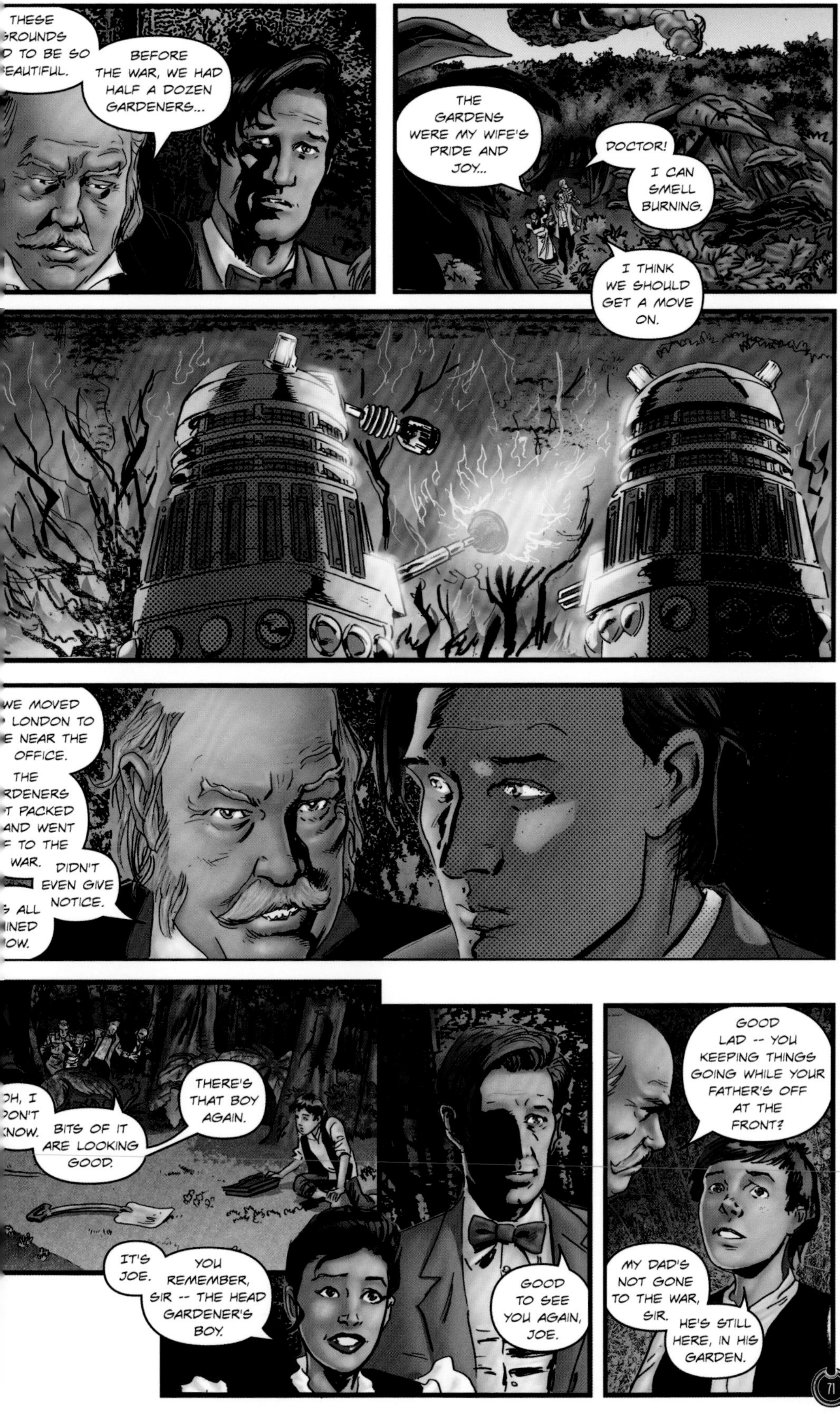

THESE GROUNDS D TO BE SO EAUTIFUL.
BEFORE THE WAR, WE HAD HALF A DOZEN GARDENERS...
THE GARDENS WERE MY WIFE'S PRIDE AND JOY...
DOCTOR!
I CAN SMELL BURNING.
I THINK WE SHOULD GET A MOVE ON.
WE MOVED LONDON TO E NEAR THE OFFICE.
THE RDENERS T PACKED AND WENT F TO THE WAR.
DIDN'T EVEN GIVE NOTICE.
ALL INED OW.
H, I ON'T NOW.
BITS OF IT ARE LOOKING GOOD.
THERE'S THAT BOY AGAIN.
IT'S JOE.
YOU REMEMBER, SIR -- THE HEAD GARDENER'S BOY.
GOOD TO SEE YOU AGAIN, JOE.
GOOD LAD -- YOU KEEPING THINGS GOING WHILE YOUR FATHER'S OFF AT THE FRONT?
MY DAD'S NOT GONE TO THE WAR, SIR.
HE'S STILL HERE, IN HIS GARDEN.

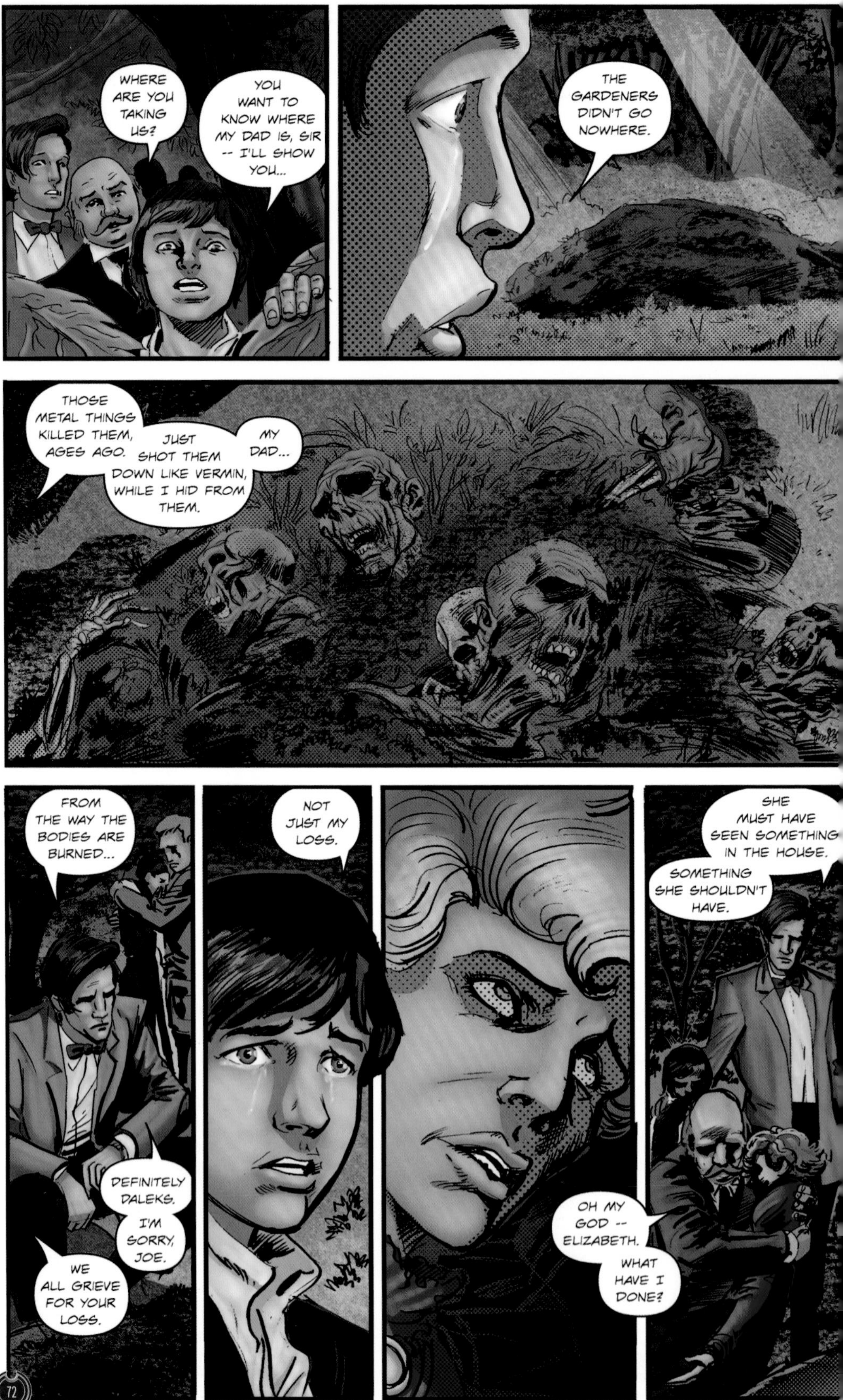
WHERE ARE YOU TAKING US?
YOU WANT TO KNOW WHERE MY DAD IS, SIR -- I'LL SHOW YOU...
THE GARDENERS DIDN'T GO NOWHERE.
THOSE METAL THINGS KILLED THEM, AGES AGO.
JUST SHOT THEM DOWN LIKE VERMIN, WHILE I HID FROM THEM.
MY DAD...
FROM THE WAY THE BODIES ARE BURNED...
DEFINITELY DALEKS.
I'M SORRY, JOE.
WE ALL GRIEVE FOR YOUR LOSS.
NOT JUST MY LOSS.
OH MY GOD -- ELIZABETH.
WHAT HAVE I DONE?
SHE MUST HAVE SEEN SOMETHING IN THE HOUSE.
SOMETHING SHE SHOULDN'T HAVE.

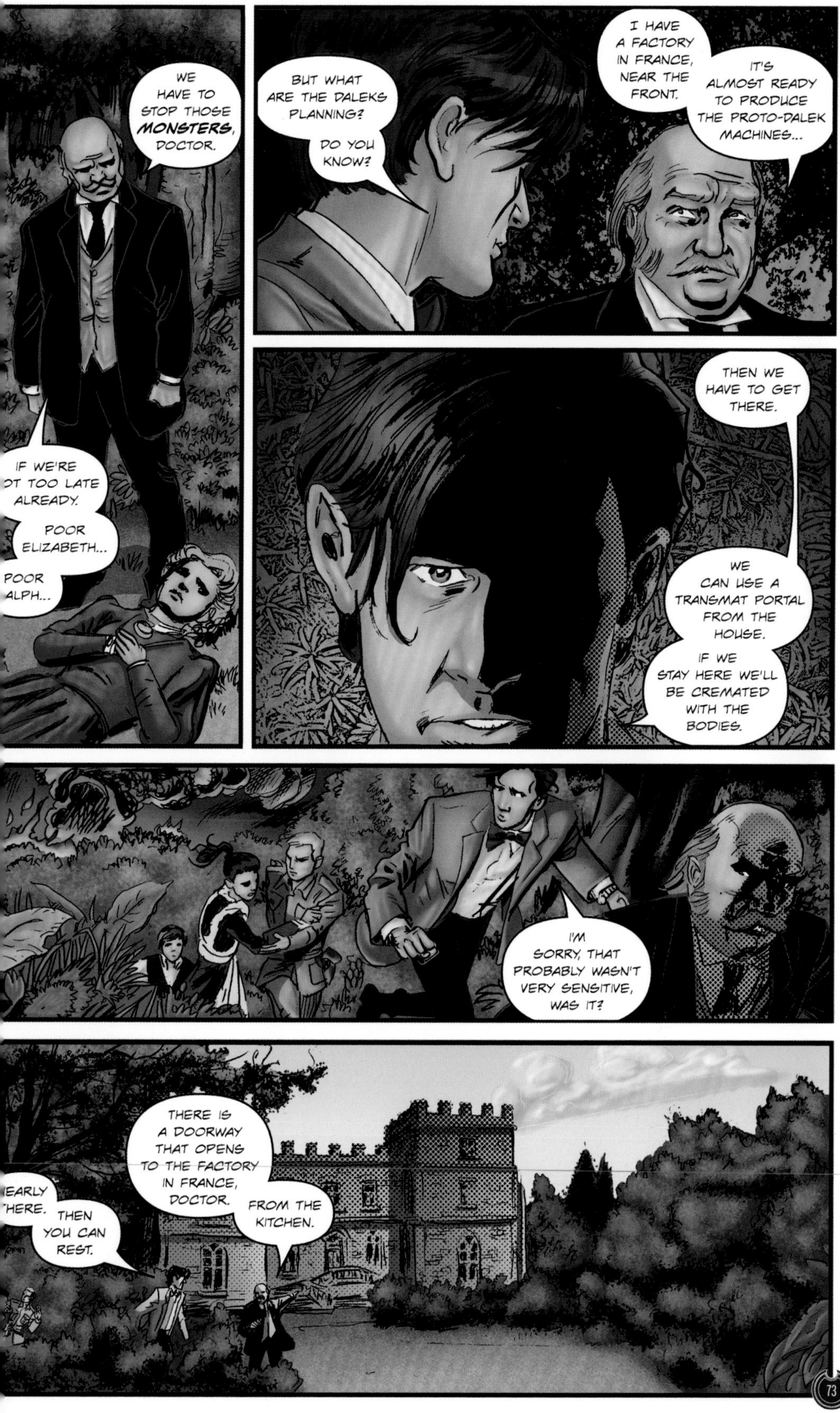

WE HAVE TO STOP THOSE **MONSTERS**, DOCTOR.
BUT WHAT ARE THE DALEKS PLANNING?
DO YOU KNOW?
I HAVE A FACTORY IN FRANCE, NEAR THE FRONT.
IT'S ALMOST READY TO PRODUCE THE PROTO-DALEK MACHINES...
IF WE'RE OT TOO LATE ALREADY.
POOR ELIZABETH...
POOR ALPH...
THEN WE HAVE TO GET THERE.
WE CAN USE A TRANSMAT PORTAL FROM THE HOUSE.
IF WE STAY HERE WE'LL BE CREMATED WITH THE BODIES.
I'M SORRY, THAT PROBABLY WASN'T VERY SENSITIVE, WAS IT?
EARLY HERE.
THEN YOU CAN REST.
THERE IS A DOORWAY THAT OPENS TO THE FACTORY IN FRANCE, DOCTOR.
FROM THE KITCHEN.

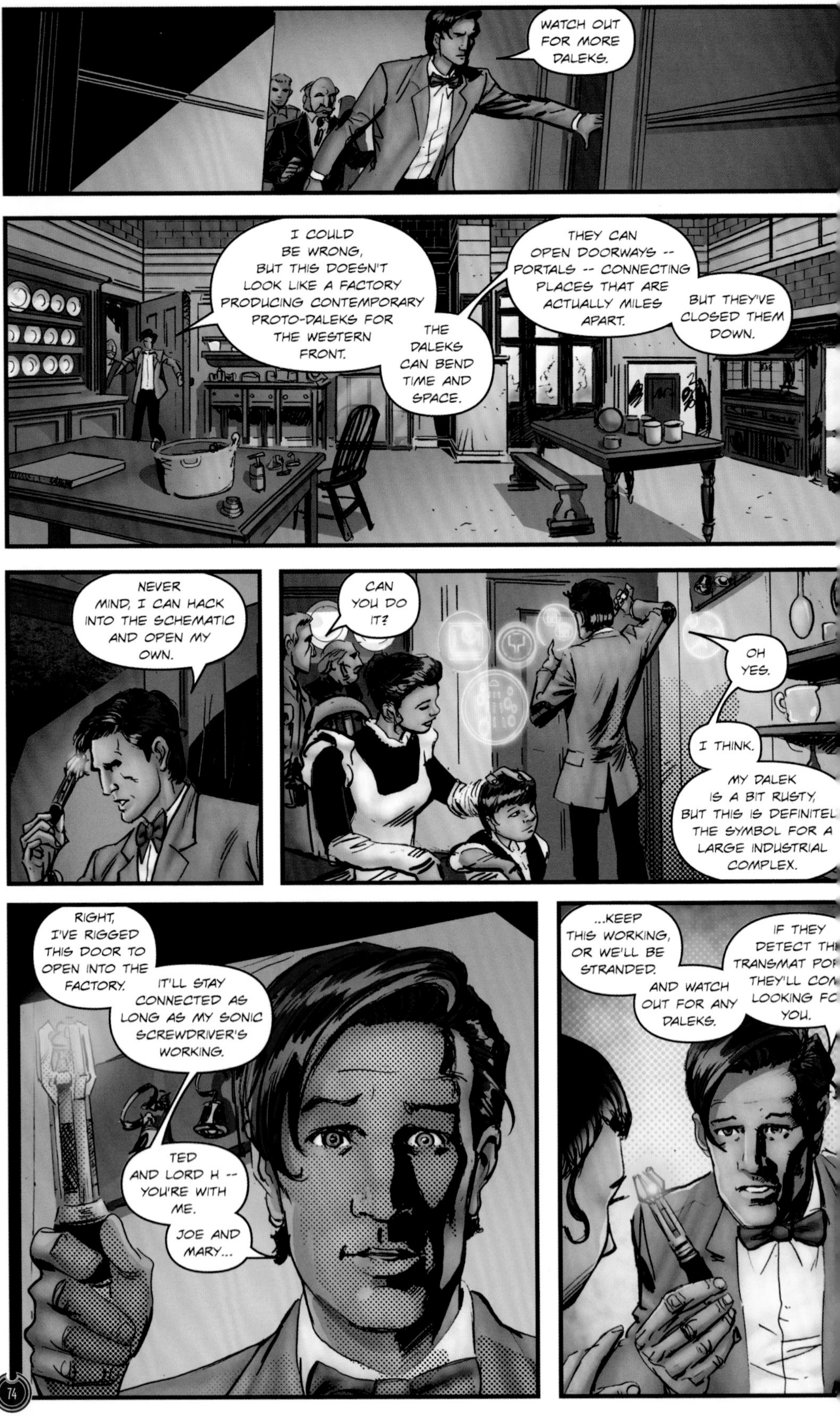
WATCH OUT FOR MORE DALEKS.
I COULD BE WRONG, BUT THIS DOESN'T LOOK LIKE A FACTORY PRODUCING CONTEMPORARY PROTO-DALEKS FOR THE WESTERN FRONT.
THE DALEKS CAN BEND TIME AND SPACE.
THEY CAN OPEN DOORWAYS -- PORTALS -- CONNECTING PLACES THAT ARE ACTUALLY MILES APART.
BUT THEY'VE CLOSED THEM DOWN.
NEVER MIND, I CAN HACK INTO THE SCHEMATIC AND OPEN MY OWN.
CAN YOU DO IT?
OH YES.
I THINK.
MY DALEK IS A BIT RUSTY, BUT THIS IS DEFINITEL
THE SYMBOL FOR A LARGE INDUSTRIAL COMPLEX.
RIGHT, I'VE RIGGED THIS DOOR TO OPEN INTO THE FACTORY.
IT'LL STAY CONNECTED AS LONG AS MY SONIC SCREWDRIVER'S WORKING.
TED AND LORD H -- YOU'RE WITH ME.
JOE AND MARY...
...KEEP THIS WORKING, OR WE'LL BE STRANDED.
AND WATCH OUT FOR ANY DALEKS.
IF THEY DETECT TH
TRANSMAT PO
THEY'LL CO
LOOKING F
YOU.

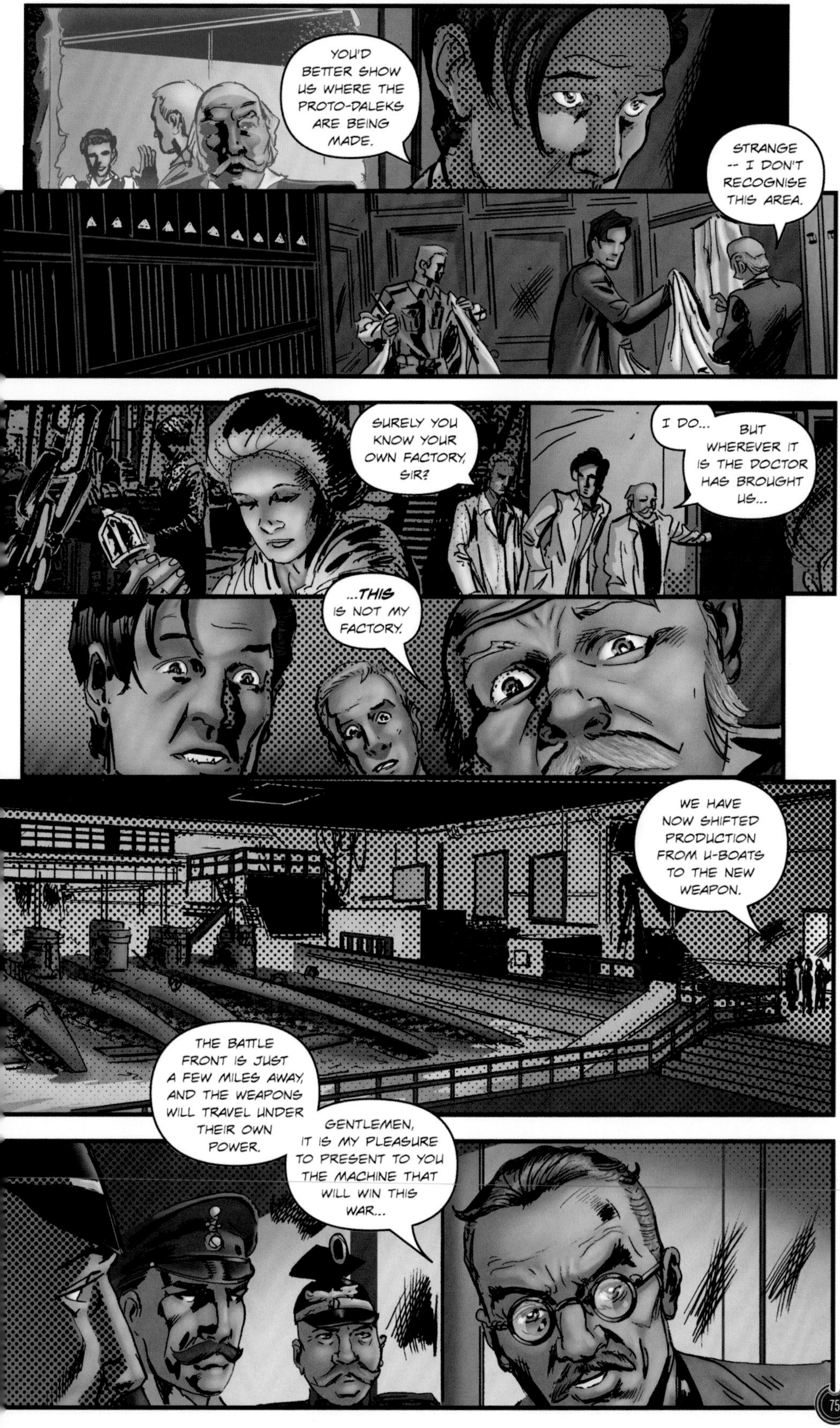
YOU'D BETTER SHOW US WHERE THE PROTO-DALEKS ARE BEING MADE.
STRANGE -- I DON'T RECOGNISE THIS AREA.
SURELY YOU KNOW YOUR OWN FACTORY, SIR?
I DO...
BUT WHEREVER IT IS THE DOCTOR HAS BROUGHT US...
...THIS IS NOT MY FACTORY.
WE HAVE NOW SHIFTED PRODUCTION FROM U-BOATS TO THE NEW WEAPON.
THE BATTLE FRONT IS JUST A FEW MILES AWAY, AND THE WEAPONS WILL TRAVEL UNDER THEIR OWN POWER.
GENTLEMEN, IT IS MY PLEASURE TO PRESENT TO YOU THE MACHINE THAT WILL WIN THIS WAR...

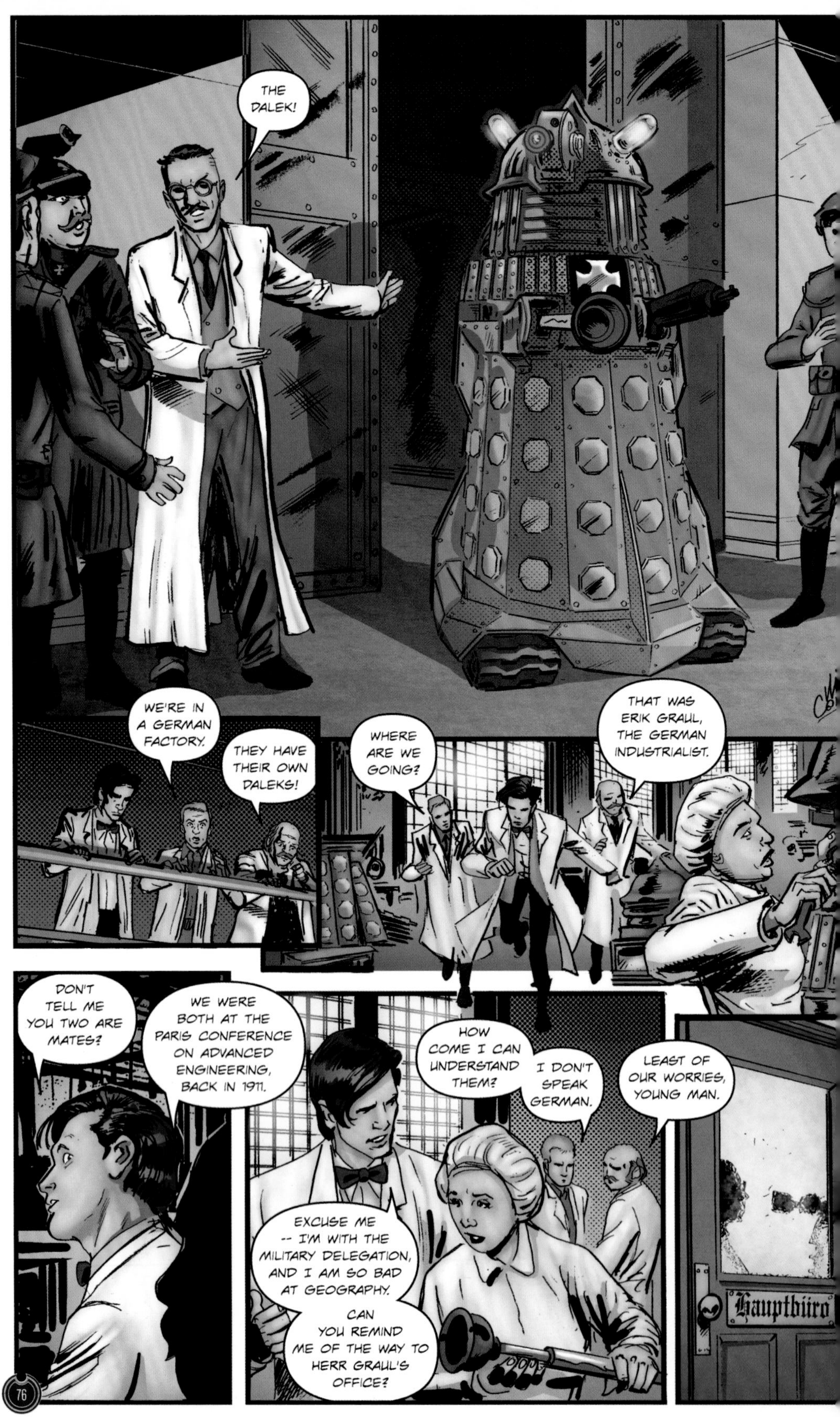
THE DALEK!
WE'RE IN A GERMAN FACTORY.
THEY HAVE THEIR OWN DALEKS!
WHERE ARE WE GOING?
THAT WAS ERIK GRAUL, THE GERMAN INDUSTRIALIST.
DON'T TELL ME YOU TWO ARE MATES?
WE WERE BOTH AT THE PARIS CONFERENCE ON ADVANCED ENGINEERING, BACK IN 1911.
HOW COME I CAN UNDERSTAND THEM?
I DON'T SPEAK GERMAN.
LEAST OF OUR WORRIES, YOUNG MAN.
EXCUSE ME -- I'M WITH THE MILITARY DELEGATION, AND I AM SO BAD AT GEOGRAPHY.
CAN YOU REMIND ME OF THE WAY TO HERR GRAUL'S OFFICE?
Hauptbüro

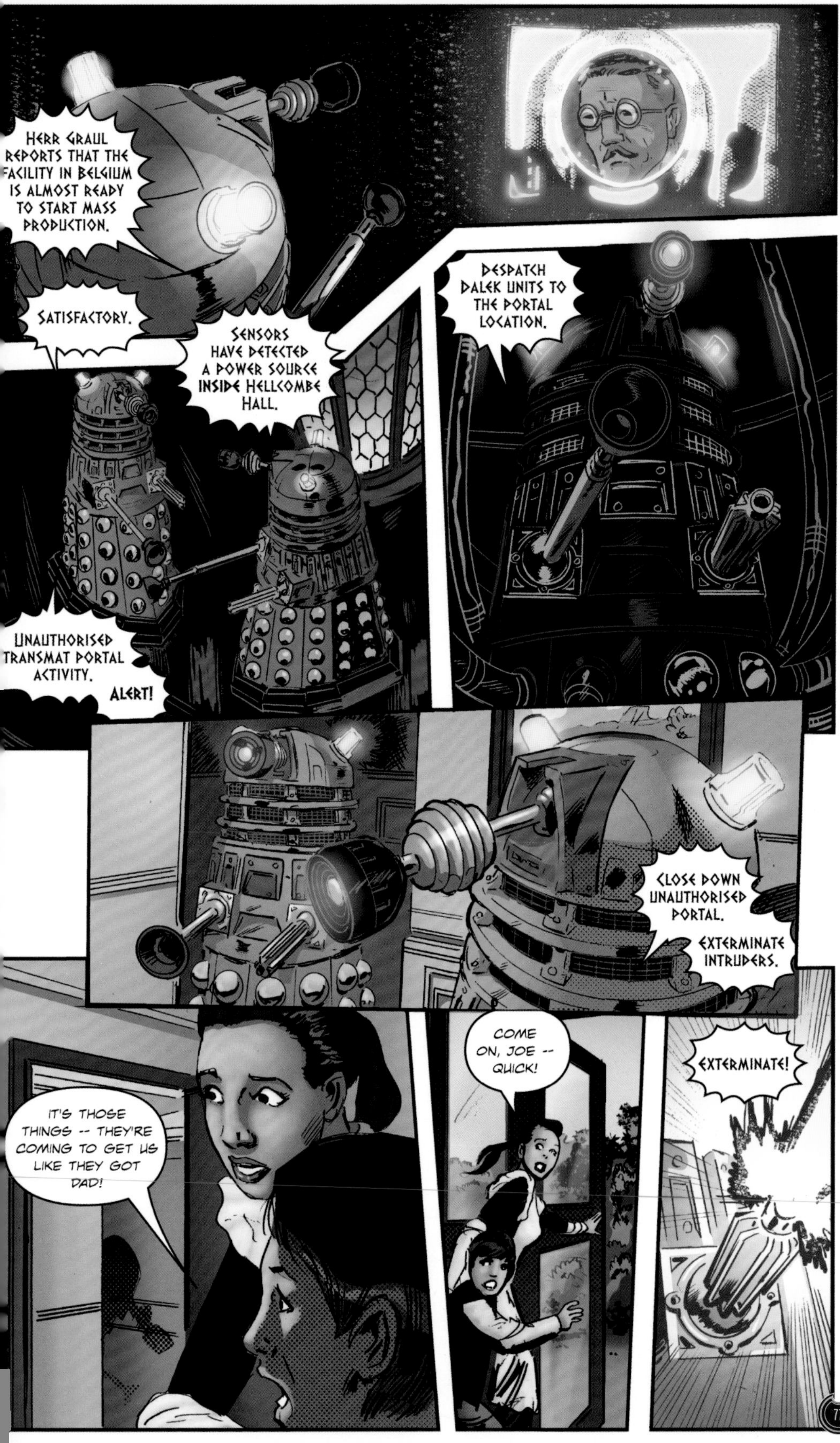
HERR GRAUL REPORTS THAT THE FACILITY IN BELGIUM IS ALMOST READY TO START MASS PRODUCTION.
SATISFACTORY.
SENSORS HAVE DETECTED A POWER SOURCE INSIDE HELLCOMBE HALL.
UNAUTHORISED TRANSMAT PORTAL ACTIVITY.
ALERT!
DESPATCH DALEK UNITS TO THE PORTAL LOCATION.
CLOSE DOWN UNAUTHORISED PORTAL.
EXTERMINATE INTRUDERS.
IT'S THOSE THINGS -- THEY'RE COMING TO GET US LIKE THEY GOT DAD!
COME ON, JOE -- QUICK!
EXTERMINATE!

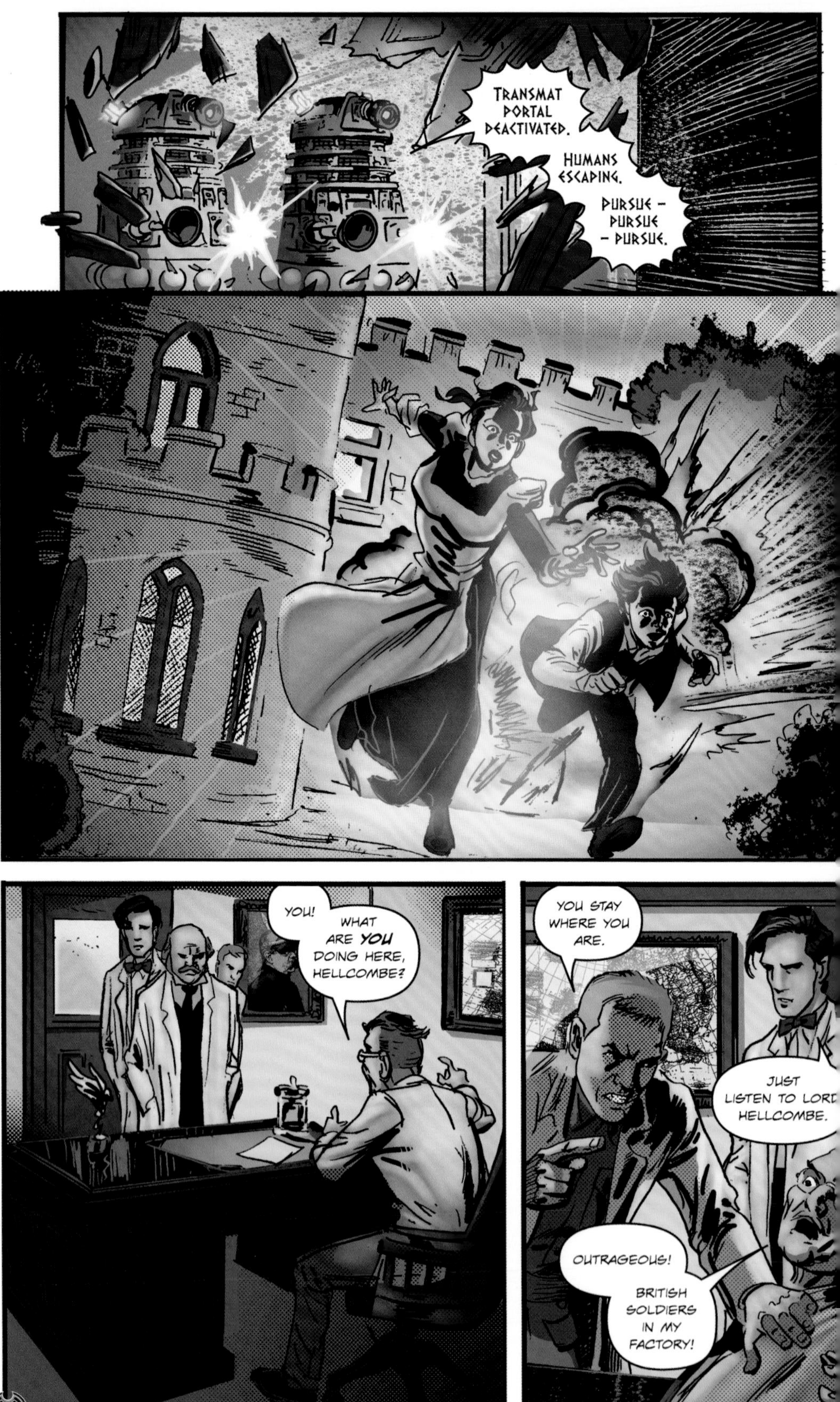
TRANSMAT PORTAL DEACTIVATED.
HUMANS ESCAPING.
PURSUE – PURSUE – PURSUE.
YOU!
WHAT ARE YOU DOING HERE, HELLCOMBE?
YOU STAY WHERE YOU ARE.
JUST LISTEN TO LORD HELLCOMBE.
OUTRAGEOUS!
BRITISH SOLDIERS IN MY FACTORY!

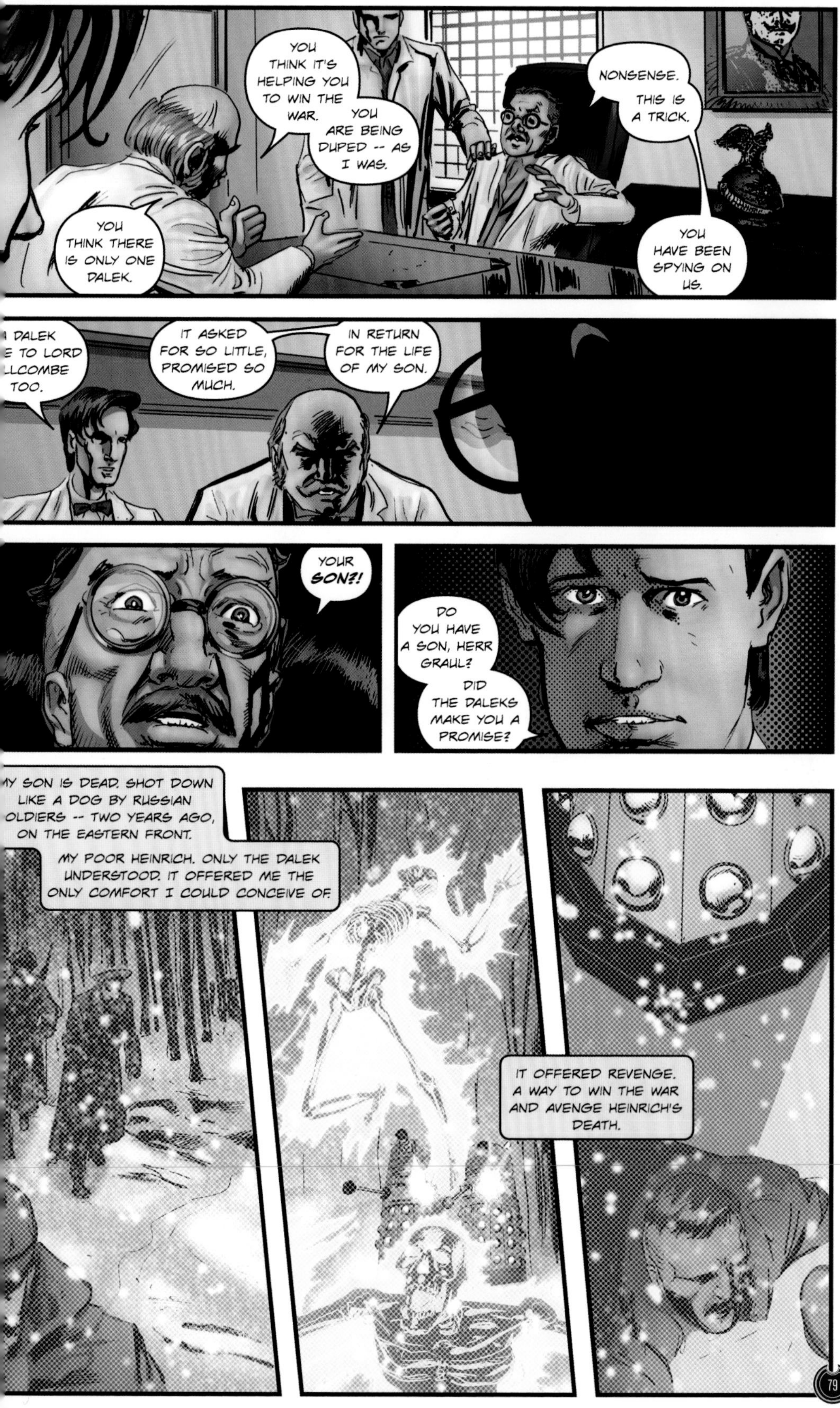
YOU THINK THERE IS ONLY ONE DALEK.
YOU THINK IT'S HELPING YOU TO WIN THE WAR.
YOU ARE BEING DUPED -- AS I WAS.
NONSENSE.
THIS IS A TRICK.
YOU HAVE BEEN SPYING ON US.
DALEK
TO LORD
LLCOMBE TOO.
IT ASKED FOR SO LITTLE, PROMISED SO MUCH.
IN RETURN FOR THE LIFE OF MY SON.
YOUR SON?!
DO YOU HAVE A SON, HERR GRAUL?
DID THE DALEKS MAKE YOU A PROMISE?
MY SON IS DEAD. SHOT DOWN LIKE A DOG BY RUSSIAN OLDIERS -- TWO YEARS AGO, ON THE EASTERN FRONT.
MY POOR HEINRICH. ONLY THE DALEK UNDERSTOOD. IT OFFERED ME THE ONLY COMFORT I COULD CONCEIVE OF.
IT OFFERED REVENGE. A WAY TO WIN THE WAR AND AVENGE HEINRICH'S DEATH.

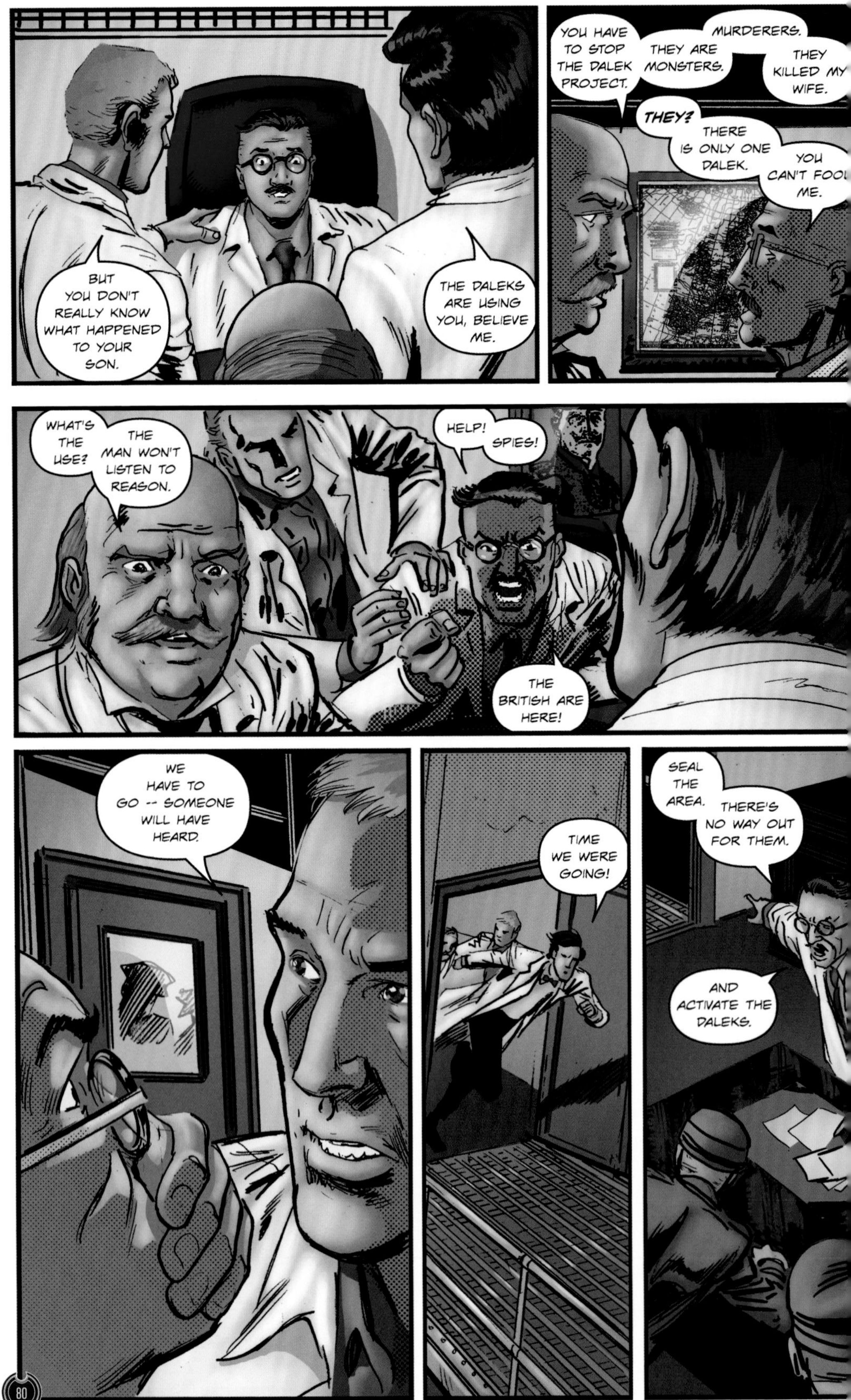
BUT YOU DON'T REALLY KNOW WHAT HAPPENED TO YOUR SON.
THE DALEKS ARE USING YOU, BELIEVE ME.
YOU HAVE TO STOP THE DALEK PROJECT.
THEY ARE MONSTERS.
MURDERERS.
THEY KILLED MY WIFE.
THEY?
THERE IS ONLY ONE DALEK.
YOU CAN'T FOOL ME.
WHAT'S THE USE?
THE MAN WON'T LISTEN TO REASON.
HELP!
SPIES!
THE BRITISH ARE HERE!
WE HAVE TO GO -- SOMEONE WILL HAVE HEARD.
TIME WE WERE GOING!
SEAL THE AREA.
THERE'S NO WAY OUT FOR THEM.
AND ACTIVATE THE DALEKS.

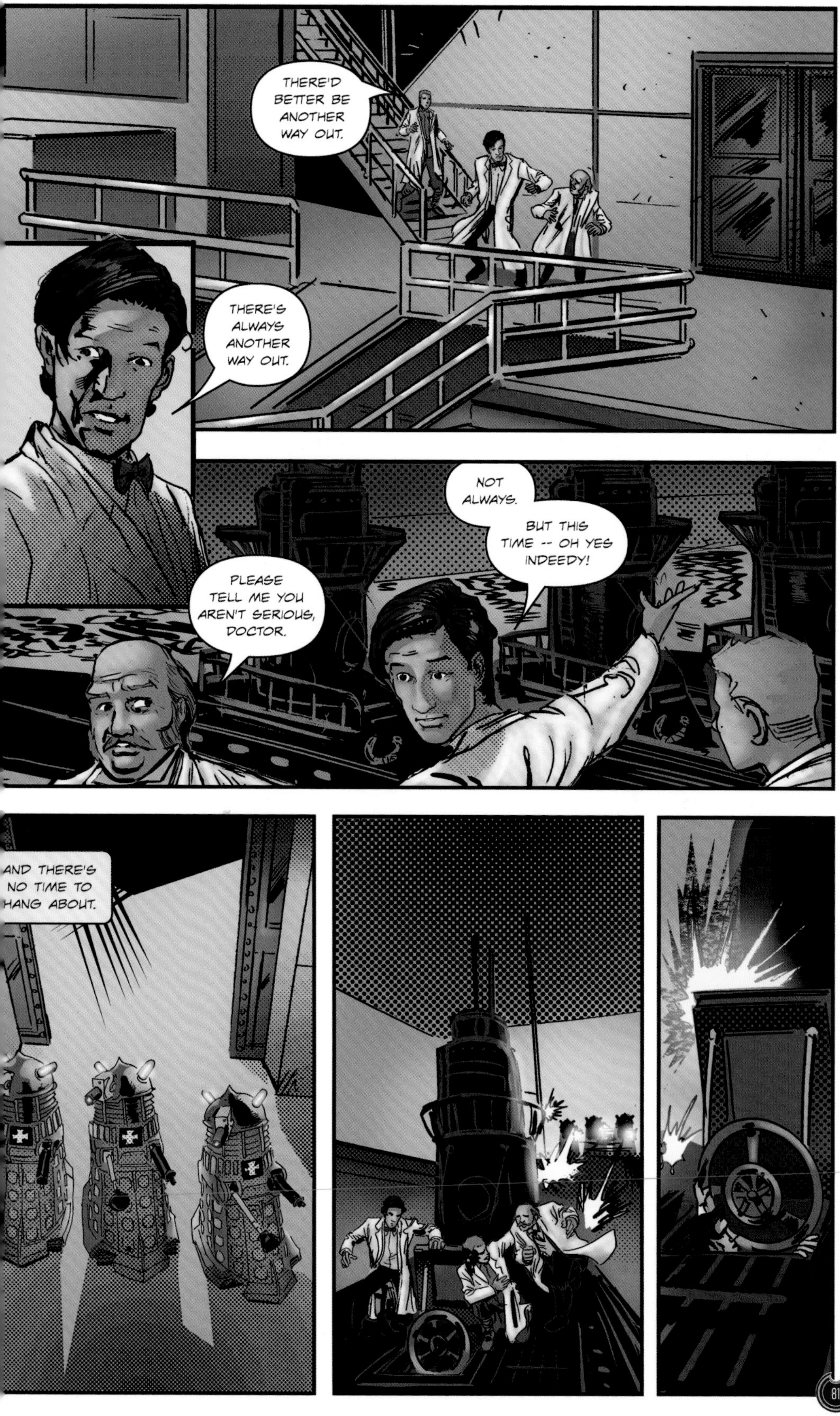
THERE'D BETTER BE ANOTHER WAY OUT.
THERE'S ALWAYS ANOTHER WAY OUT.
NOT ALWAYS.
BUT THIS TIME -- OH YES INDEEDY!
PLEASE TELL ME YOU AREN'T SERIOUS, DOCTOR.
AND THERE'S NO TIME TO HANG ABOUT.

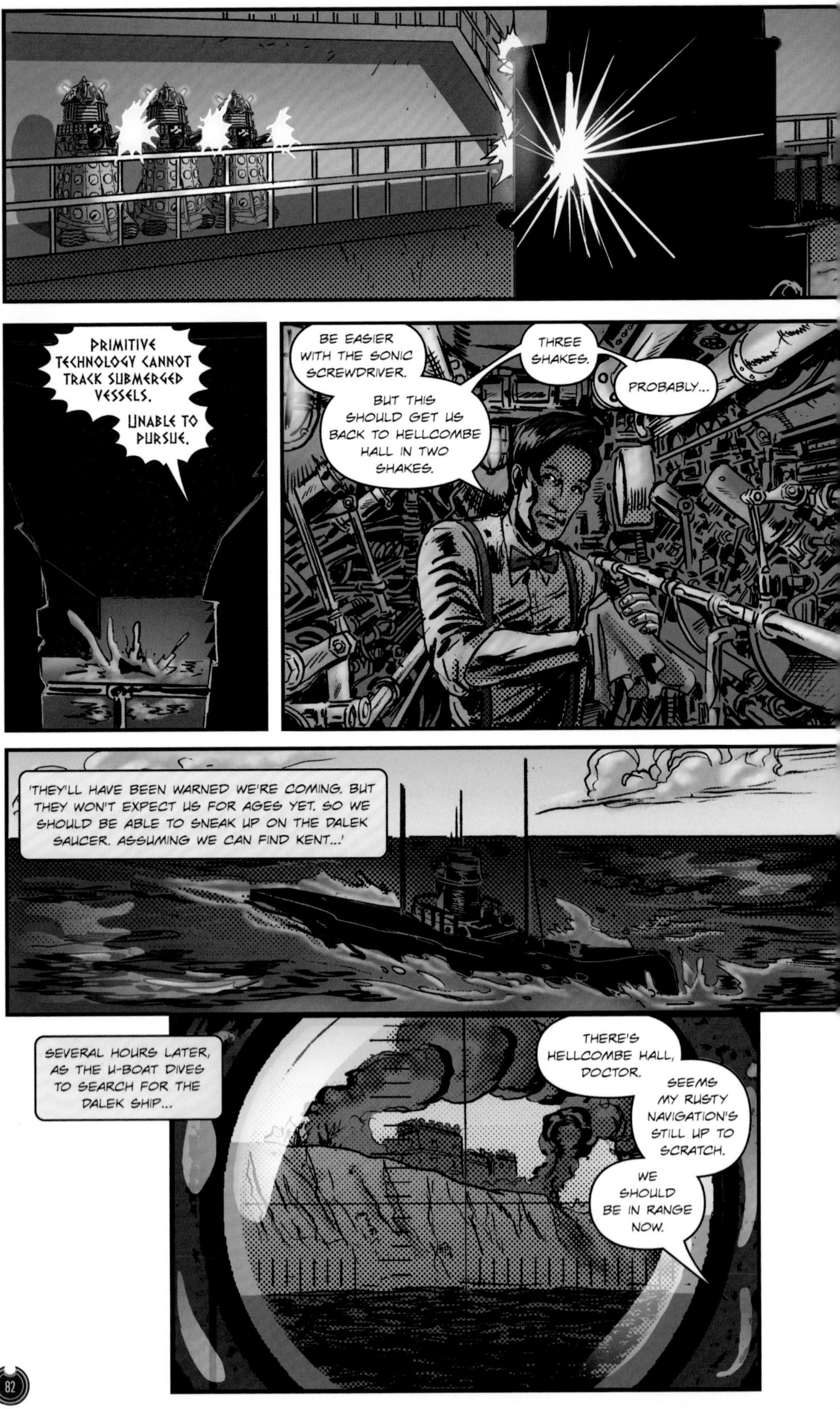
PRIMITIVE TECHNOLOGY CANNOT TRACK SUBMERGED VESSELS.
UNABLE TO PURSUE.
BE EASIER WITH THE SONIC SCREWDRIVER.
BUT THIS SHOULD GET US BACK TO HELLCOMBE HALL IN TWO SHAKES.
THREE SHAKES.
PROBABLY...
'THEY'LL HAVE BEEN WARNED WE'RE COMING. BUT THEY WON'T EXPECT US FOR AGES YET. SO WE SHOULD BE ABLE TO SNEAK UP ON THE DALEK SAUCER. ASSUMING WE CAN FIND KENT...'
SEVERAL HOURS LATER, AS THE U-BOAT DIVES TO SEARCH FOR THE DALEK SHIP...
THERE'S HELLCOMBE HALL, DOCTOR.
SEEMS MY RUSTY NAVIGATION'S STILL UP TO SCRATCH.
WE SHOULD BE IN RANGE NOW.

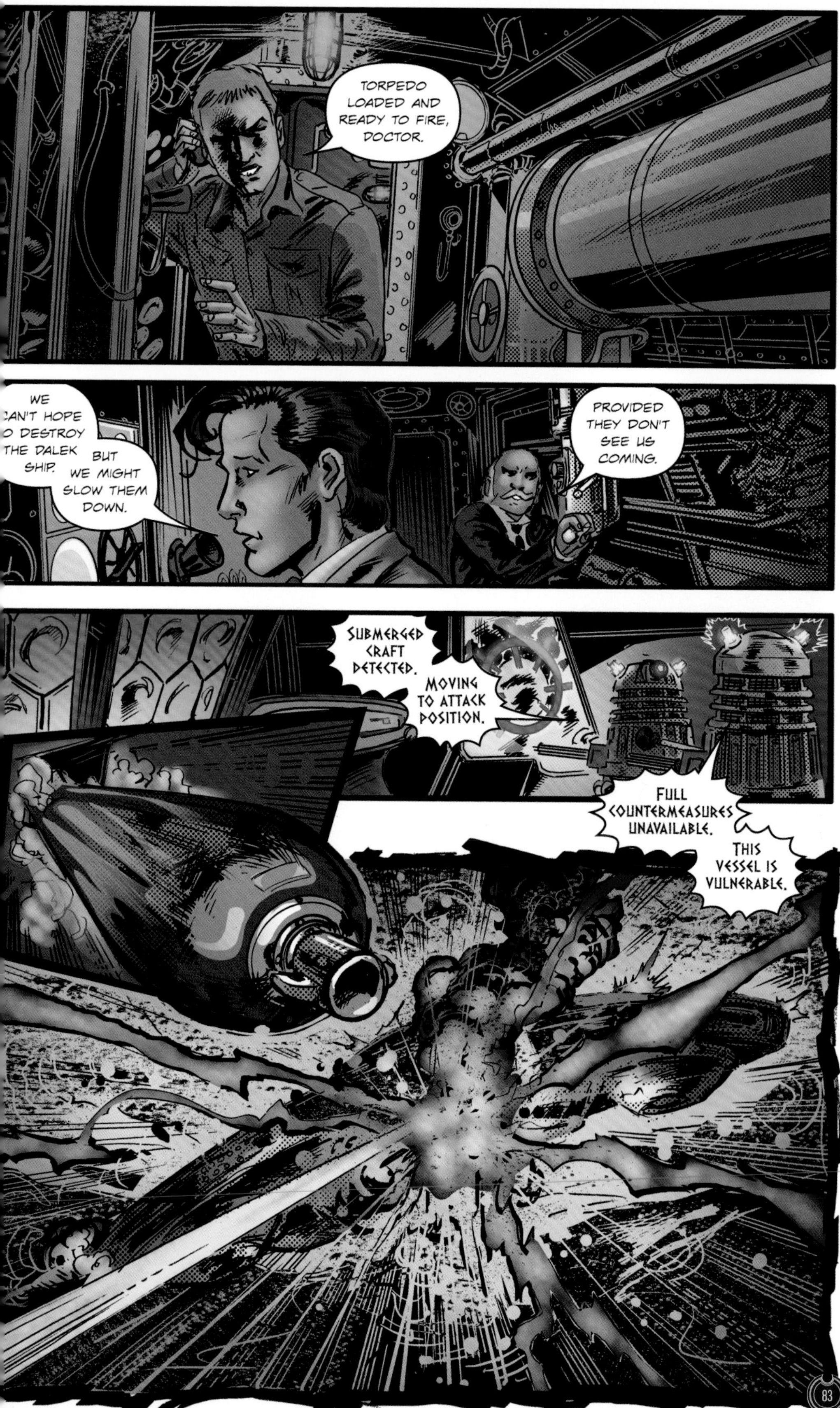
TORPEDO LOADED AND READY TO FIRE, DOCTOR.
WE CAN'T HOPE TO DESTROY THE DALEK SHIP.
BUT WE MIGHT SLOW THEM DOWN.
PROVIDED THEY DON'T SEE US COMING.
SUBMERGED CRAFT DETECTED.
MOVING TO ATTACK POSITION.
FULL COUNTERMEASURES UNAVAILABLE.
THIS VESSEL IS VULNERABLE.

HULL BREACHED.
DRIVE SYSTEMS DAMAGED.
WEAPONRY OFFLINE.
WATER RISING THROUGH ALL SECTIONS.
SEAL ALL AFFECTED SECTIONS.
OPERATE EMERGENCY PUMPS.
REACTIVATE WEAPONS SYSTEMS.
ASSESS DAMAGE AND REPORT.
DEPLOY AQUA-DALEK UNITS TO DESTRO THE ATTACKING VESSEL.
ENEMY VESSEL TARGETED.
EXTERMINATE!

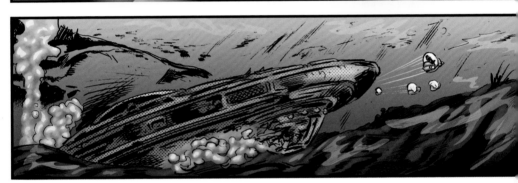

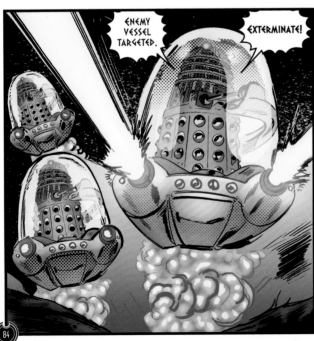

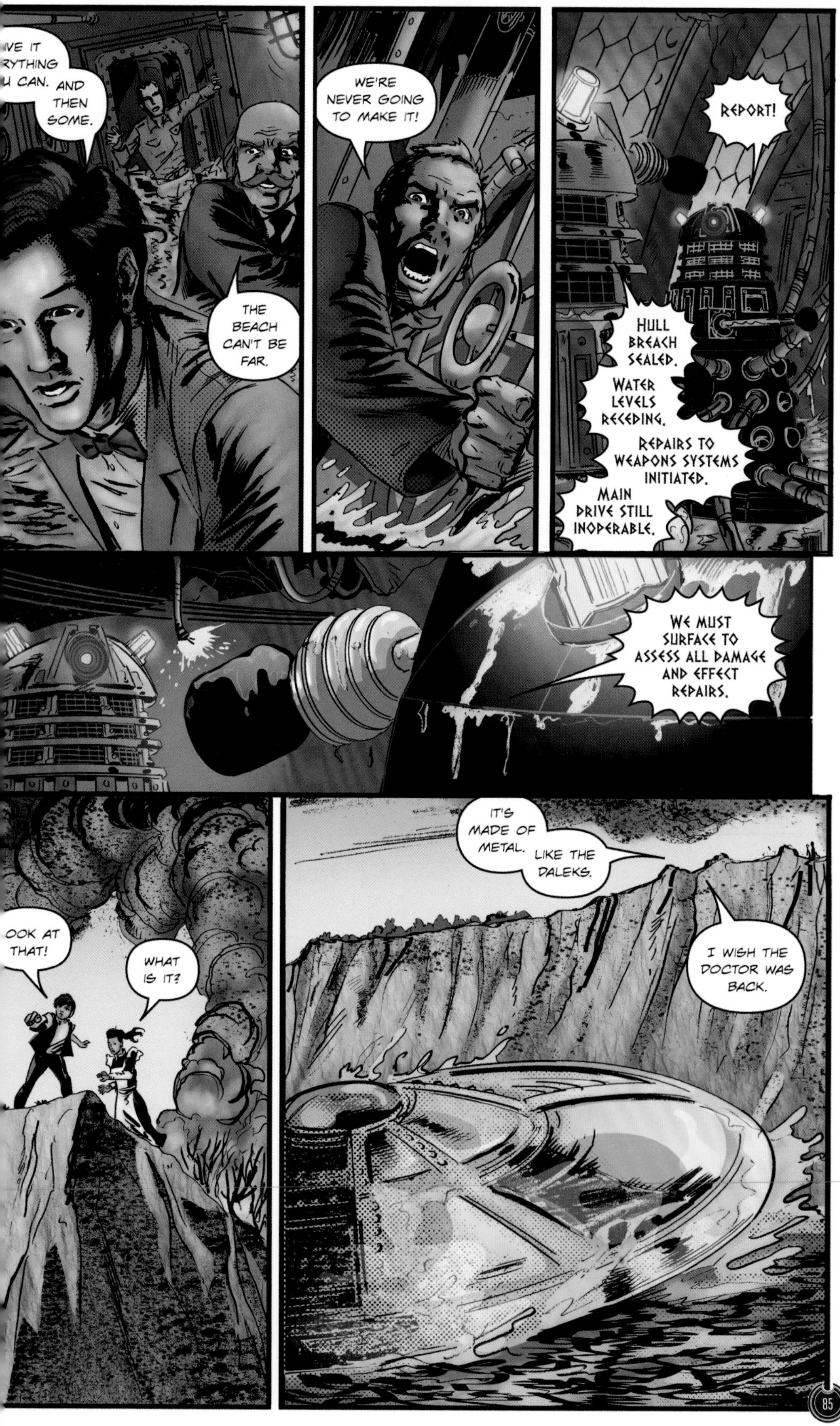

VE IT
RYTHING
U CAN. AND THEN SOME.
THE BEACH CAN'T BE FAR.
WE'RE NEVER GOING TO MAKE IT!
REPORT!
HULL BREACH SEALED.
WATER LEVELS RECEDING.
REPAIRS TO WEAPONS SYSTEMS INITIATED.
MAIN DRIVE STILL INOPERABLE.
WE MUST SURFACE TO ASSESS ALL DAMAGE AND EFFECT REPAIRS.
OOK AT THAT!
WHAT IS IT?
IT'S MADE OF METAL.
LIKE THE DALEKS.
I WISH THE DOCTOR WAS BACK.

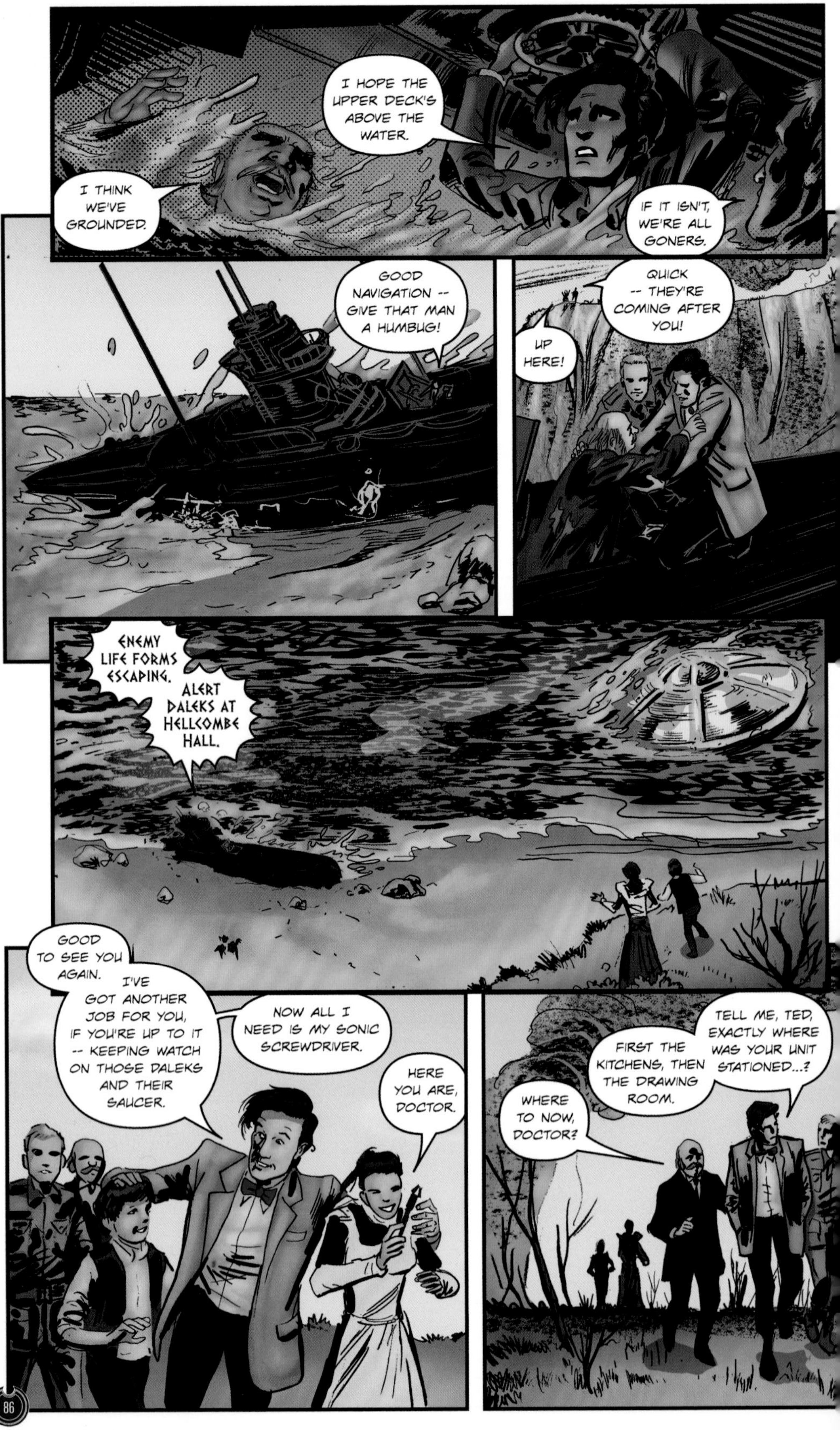
I HOPE THE UPPER DECK'S ABOVE THE WATER.
I THINK WE'VE GROUNDED.
IF IT ISN'T, WE'RE ALL GONERS.
GOOD NAVIGATION -- GIVE THAT MAN A HUMBUG!
QUICK -- THEY'RE COMING AFTER YOU!
UP HERE!
ENEMY LIFE FORMS ESCAPING.
ALERT DALEKS AT HELLCOMBE HALL.
GOOD TO SEE YOU AGAIN.
I'VE GOT ANOTHER JOB FOR YOU, IF YOU'RE UP TO IT -- KEEPING WATCH ON THOSE DALEKS AND THEIR SAUCER.
NOW ALL I NEED IS MY SONIC SCREWDRIVER.
HERE YOU ARE, DOCTOR.
TELL ME, TED, EXACTLY WHERE WAS YOUR UNIT STATIONED...?
FIRST THE KITCHENS, THEN THE DRAWING ROOM.
WHERE TO NOW, DOCTOR?

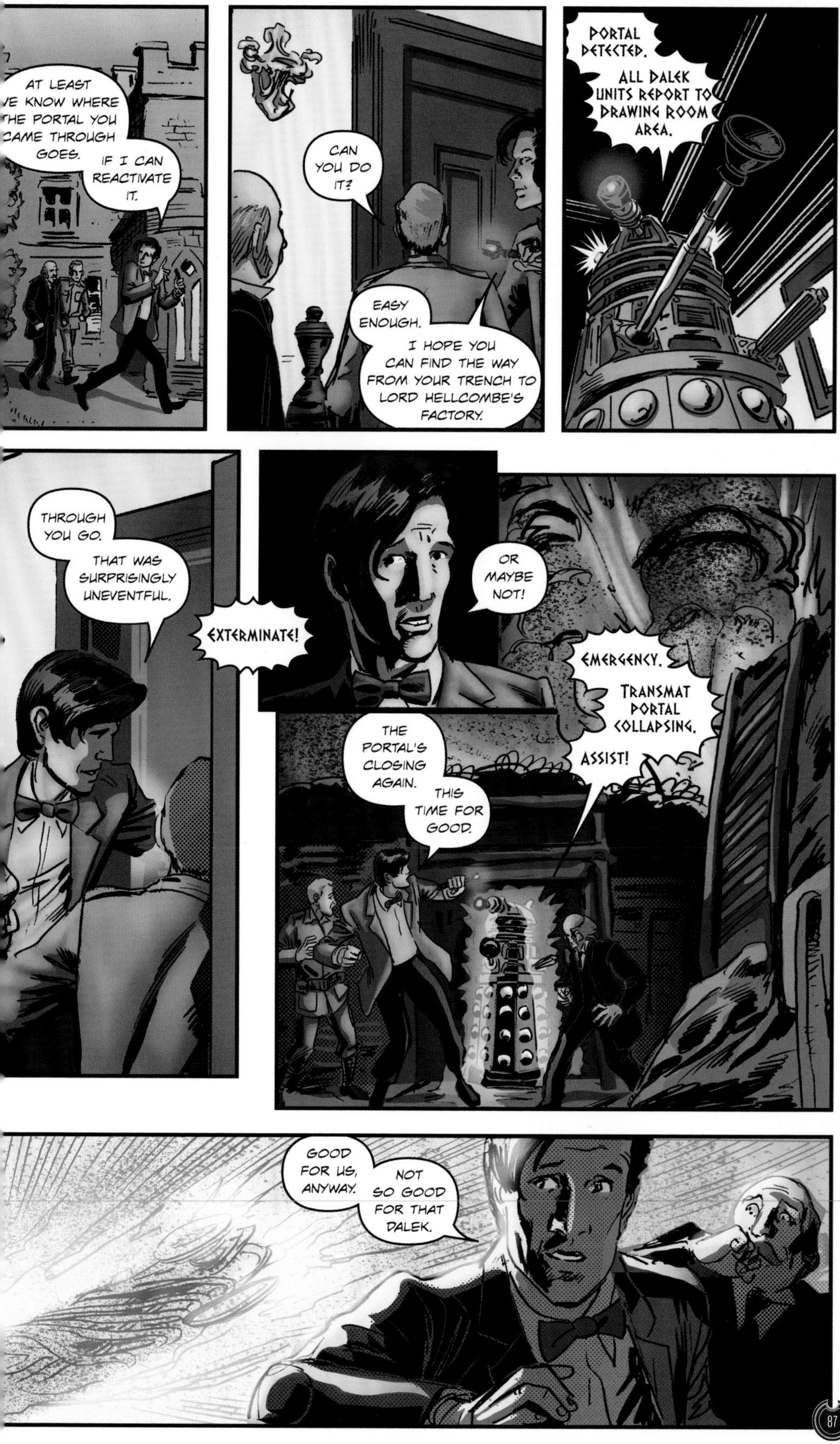

AT LEAST WE KNOW WHERE THE PORTAL YOU CAME THROUGH GOES.
IF I CAN REACTIVATE IT.
CAN YOU DO IT?
EASY ENOUGH.
I HOPE YOU CAN FIND THE WAY FROM YOUR TRENCH TO LORD HELLCOMBE'S FACTORY.
PORTAL DETECTED.
ALL DALEK UNITS REPORT TO DRAWING ROOM AREA.
THROUGH YOU GO.
THAT WAS SURPRISINGLY UNEVENTFUL.
EXTERMINATE!
OR MAYBE NOT!
EMERGENCY.
TRANSMAT PORTAL COLLAPSING.
ASSIST!
THE PORTAL'S CLOSING AGAIN.
THIS TIME FOR GOOD.
GOOD FOR US, ANYWAY.
NOT SO GOOD FOR THAT DALEK.

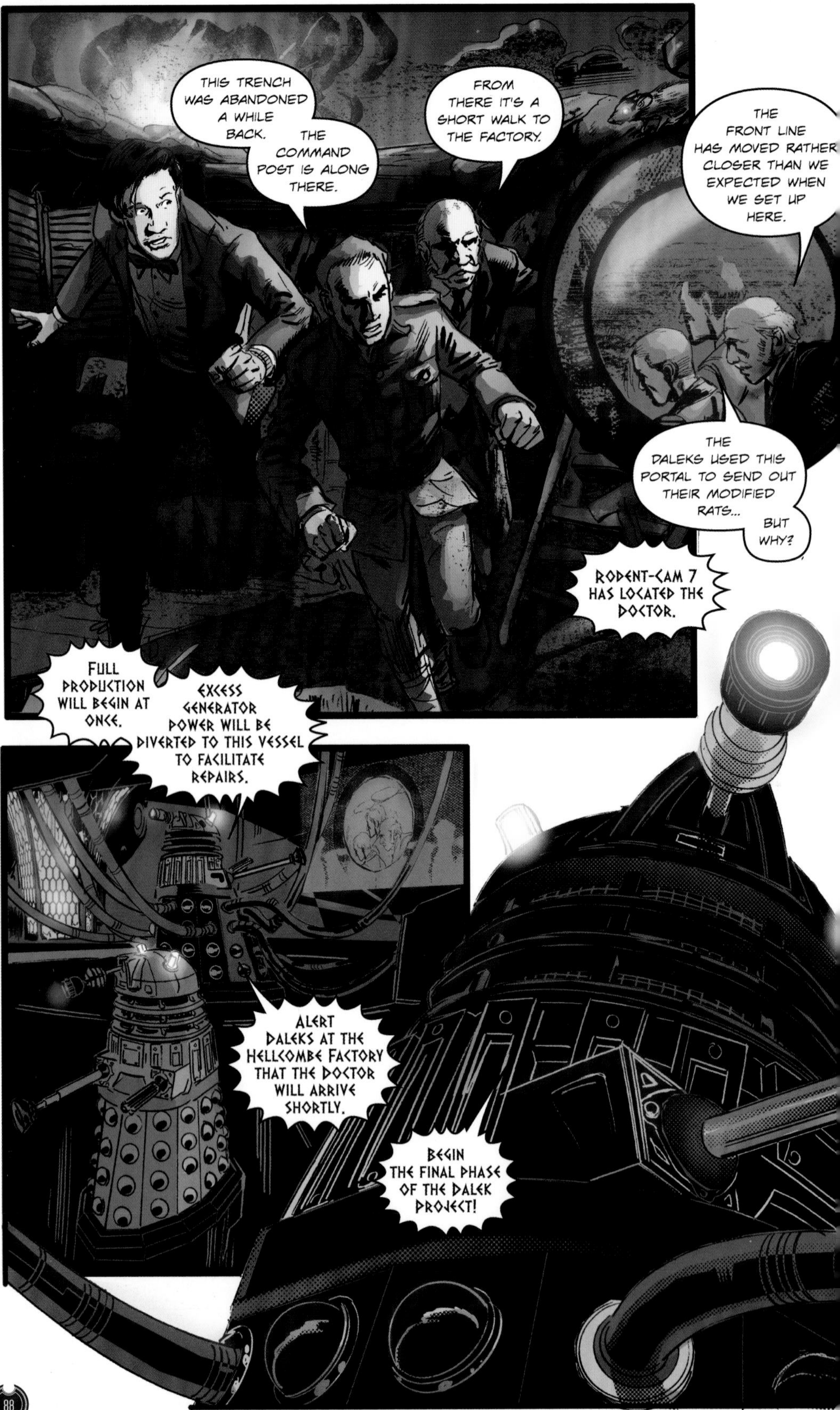

THIS TRENCH WAS ABANDONED A WHILE BACK.
THE COMMAND POST IS ALONG THERE.
FROM THERE IT'S A SHORT WALK TO THE FACTORY.
THE FRONT LINE HAS MOVED RATHER CLOSER THAN WE EXPECTED WHEN WE SET UP HERE.
THE DALEKS USED THIS PORTAL TO SEND OUT THEIR MODIFIED RATS...
BUT WHY?
RODENT-CAM 7 HAS LOCATED THE DOCTOR.
FULL PRODUCTION WILL BEGIN AT ONCE.
EXCESS GENERATOR POWER WILL BE DIVERTED TO THIS VESSEL TO FACILITATE REPAIRS.
ALERT DALEKS AT THE HELLCOMBE FACTORY THAT THE DOCTOR WILL ARRIVE SHORTLY.
BEGIN THE FINAL PHASE OF THE DALEK PROJECT!

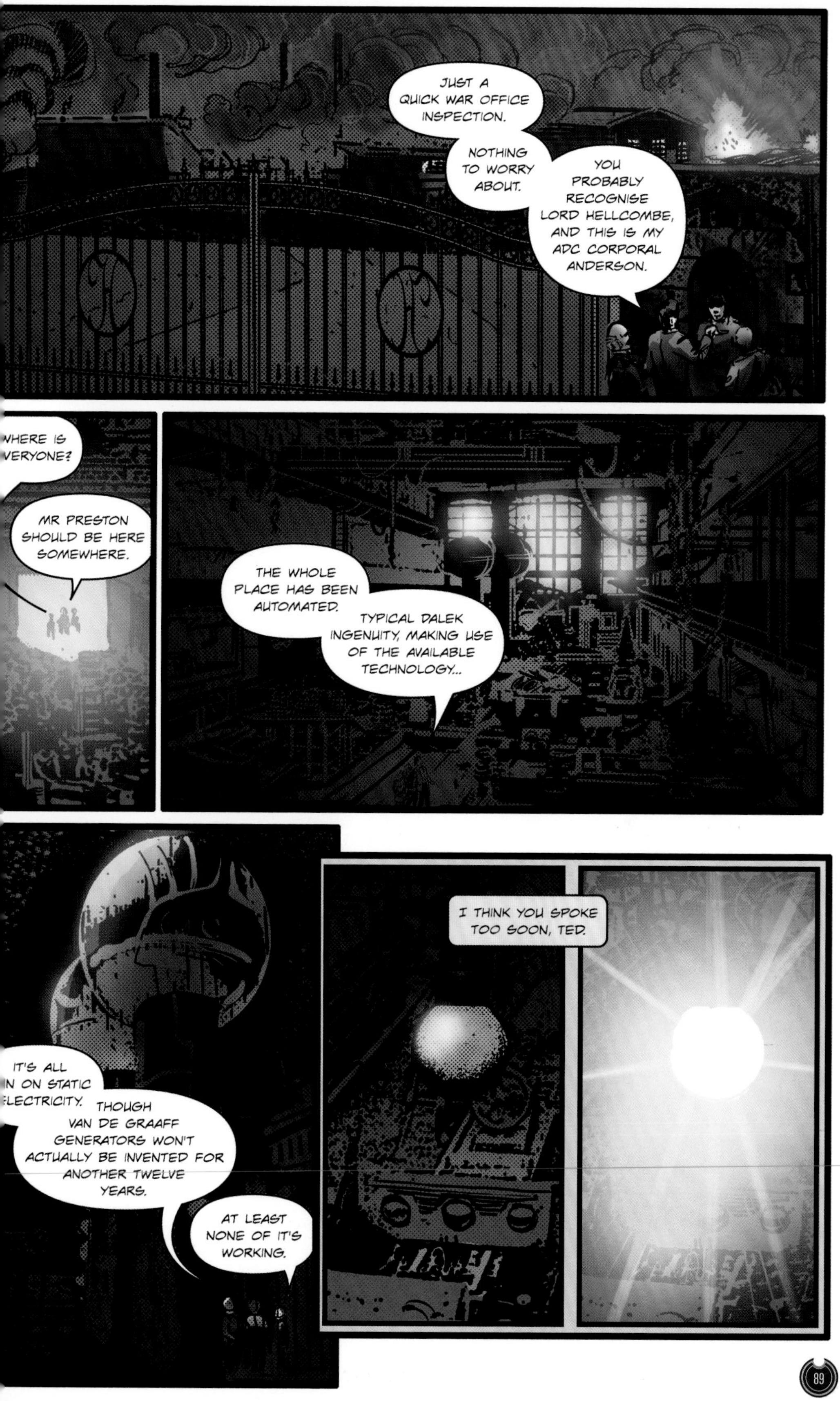
JUST A QUICK WAR OFFICE INSPECTION.
NOTHING TO WORRY ABOUT.
YOU PROBABLY RECOGNISE LORD HELLCOMBE, AND THIS IS MY ADC CORPORAL ANDERSON.
WHERE IS VERYONE?
MR PRESTON SHOULD BE HERE SOMEWHERE.
THE WHOLE PLACE HAS BEEN AUTOMATED.
TYPICAL DALEK INGENUITY, MAKING USE OF THE AVAILABLE TECHNOLOGY...
IT'S ALL N ON STATIC LECTRICITY.
THOUGH VAN DE GRAAFF GENERATORS WON'T ACTUALLY BE INVENTED FOR ANOTHER TWELVE YEARS.
AT LEAST NONE OF IT'S WORKING.
I THINK YOU SPOKE TOO SOON, TED.

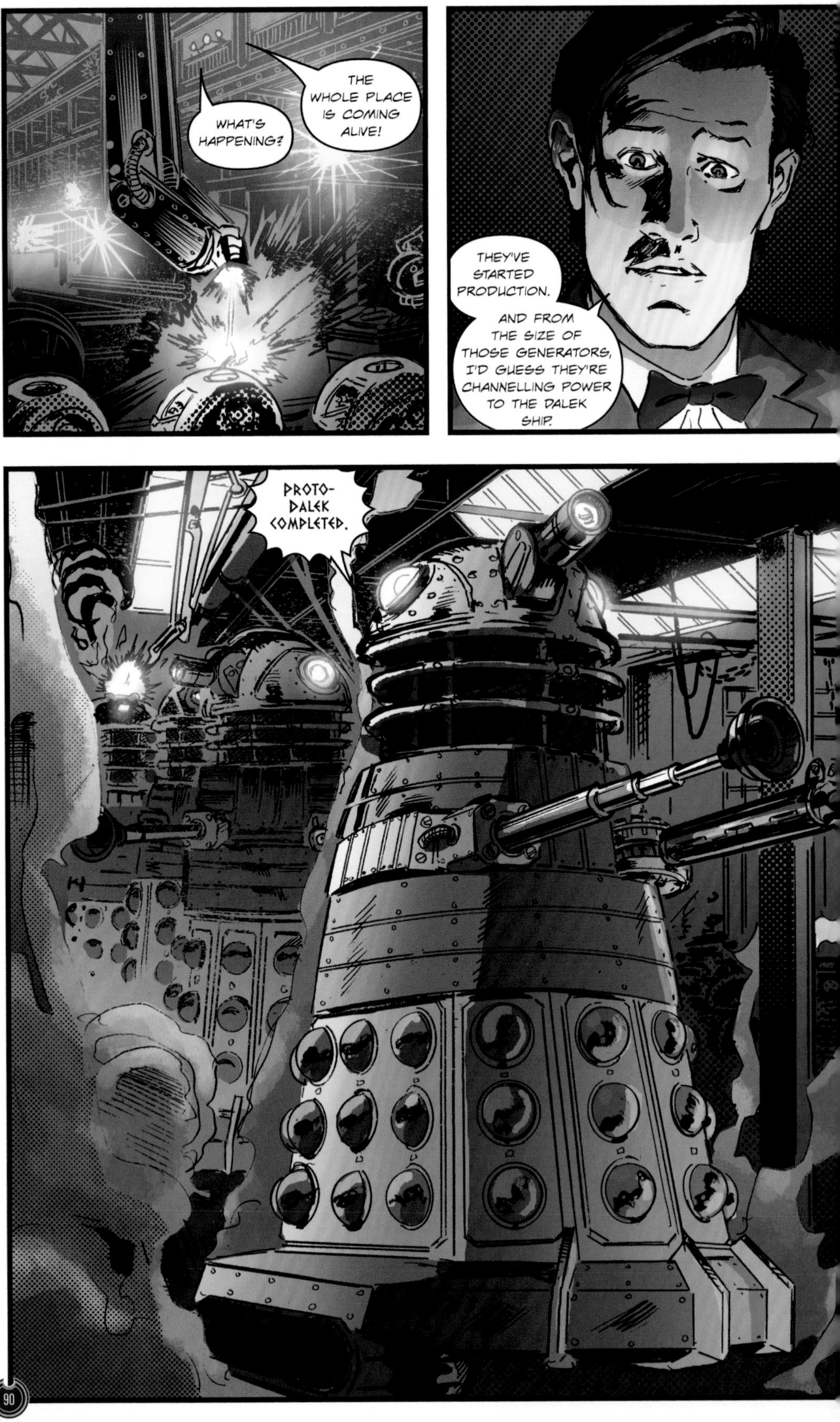
WHAT'S HAPPENING?
THE WHOLE PLACE IS COMING ALIVE!
THEY'VE STARTED PRODUCTION.
AND FROM THE SIZE OF THOSE GENERATORS, I'D GUESS THEY'RE CHANNELLING POWER TO THE DALEK SHIP.
PROTO-DALEK COMPLETED.

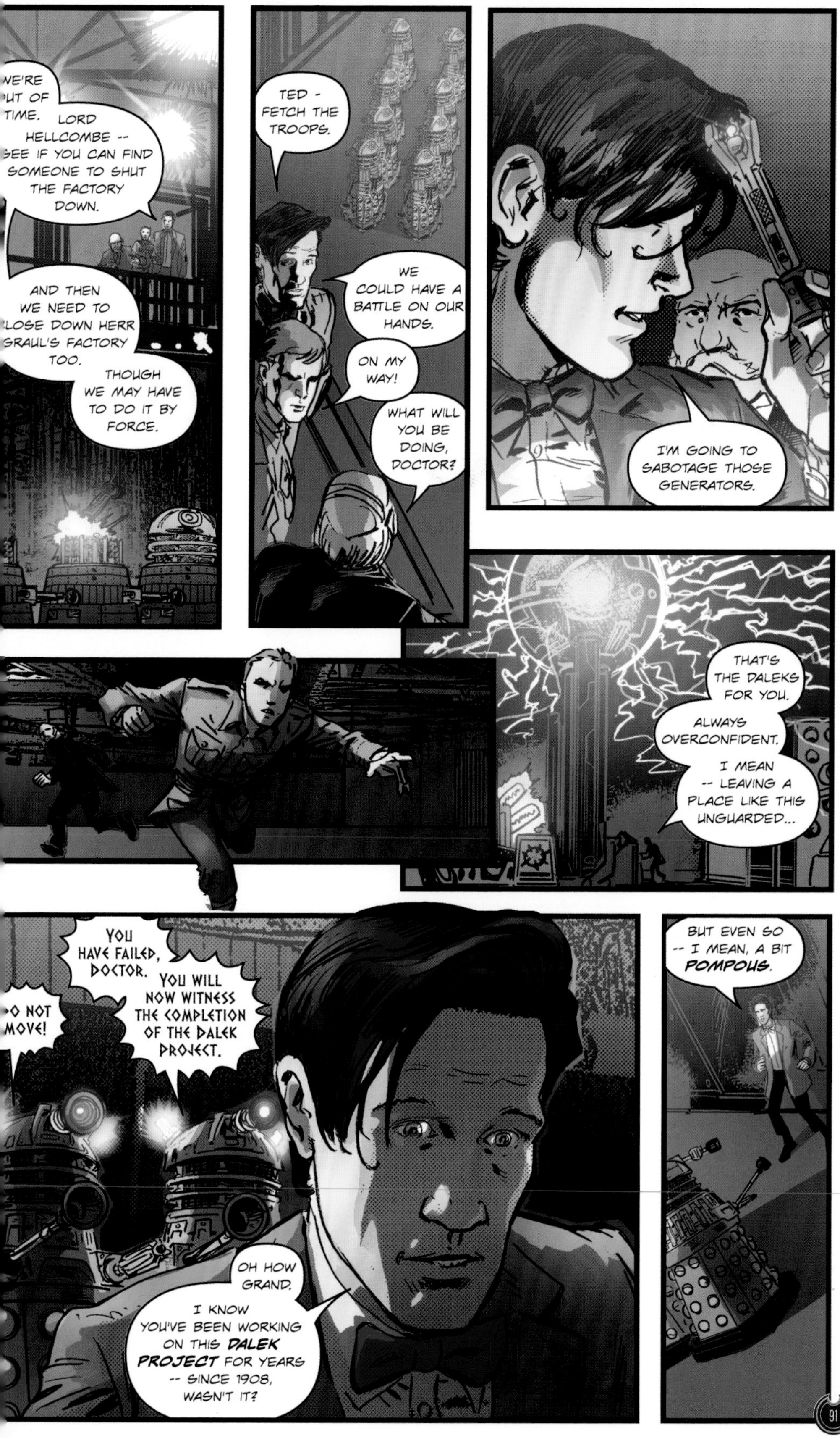
WE'RE
UT OF
TIME.
LORD HELLCOMBE -- SEE IF YOU CAN FIND SOMEONE TO SHUT THE FACTORY DOWN.
AND THEN WE NEED TO CLOSE DOWN HERR GRAUL'S FACTORY TOO.
THOUGH WE MAY HAVE TO DO IT BY FORCE.
TED - FETCH THE TROOPS.
WE COULD HAVE A BATTLE ON OUR HANDS.
ON MY WAY!
WHAT WILL YOU BE DOING, DOCTOR?
I'M GOING TO SABOTAGE THOSE GENERATORS.
THAT'S THE DALEKS FOR YOU.
ALWAYS OVERCONFIDENT.
I MEAN -- LEAVING A PLACE LIKE THIS UNGUARDED...
YOU HAVE FAILED, DOCTOR.
YOU WILL NOW WITNESS THE COMPLETION OF THE DALEK PROJECT.
O NOT MOVE!
OH HOW GRAND.
I KNOW YOU'VE BEEN WORKING ON THIS DALEK PROJECT FOR YEARS -- SINCE 1908, WASN'T IT?
BUT EVEN SO -- I MEAN, A BIT POMPOUS.

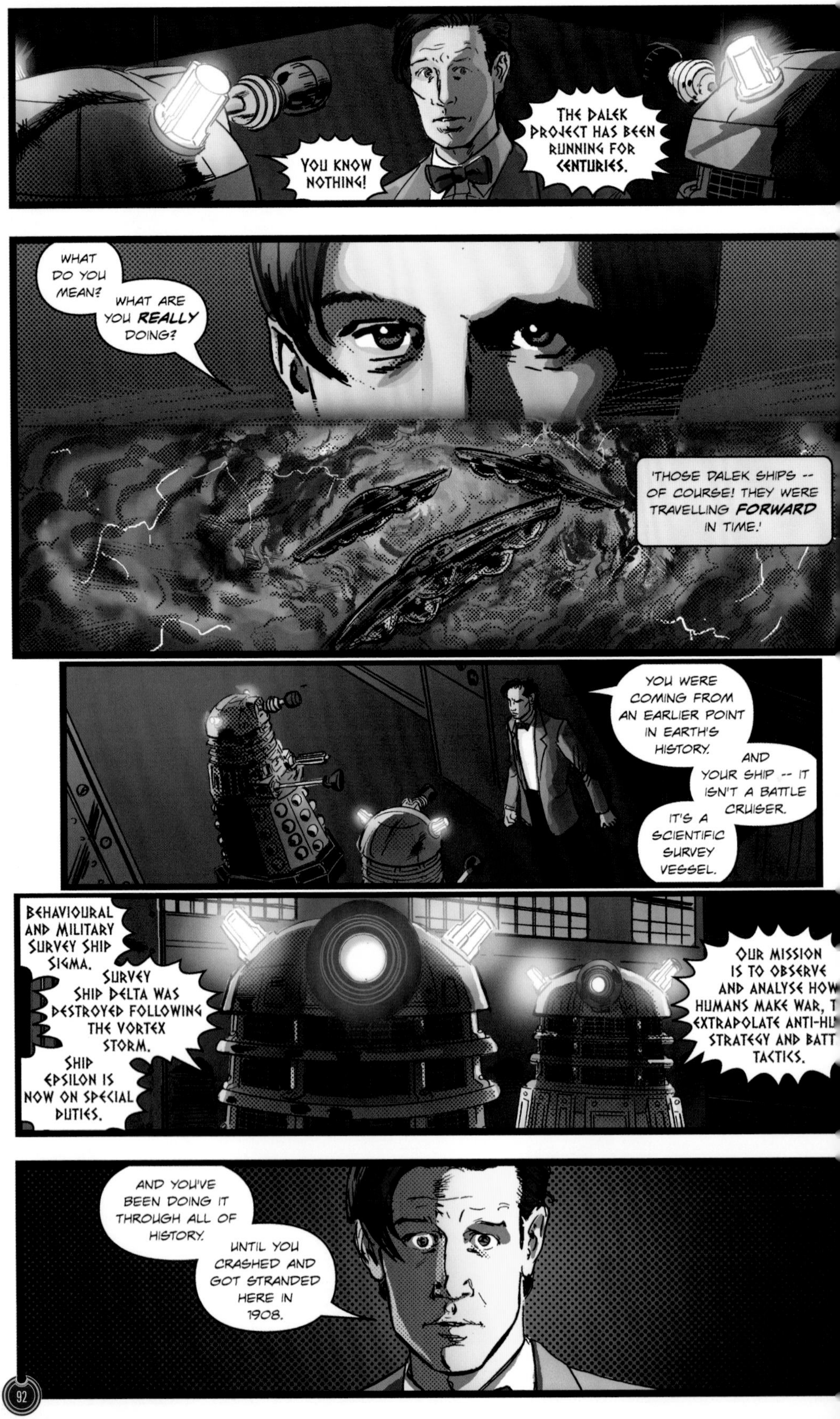
YOU KNOW NOTHING!
THE DALEK PROJECT HAS BEEN RUNNING FOR CENTURIES.
WHAT DO YOU MEAN?
WHAT ARE YOU REALLY DOING?
'THOSE DALEK SHIPS -- OF COURSE! THEY WERE TRAVELLING FORWARD IN TIME.'
YOU WERE COMING FROM AN EARLIER POINT IN EARTH'S HISTORY.
AND YOUR SHIP -- IT ISN'T A BATTLE CRUISER.
IT'S A SCIENTIFIC SURVEY VESSEL.
BEHAVIOURAL AND MILITARY SURVEY SHIP SIGMA.
SURVEY SHIP DELTA WAS DESTROYED FOLLOWING THE VORTEX STORM.
SHIP EPSILON IS NOW ON SPECIAL DUTIES.
OUR MISSION IS TO OBSERVE AND ANALYSE HOW HUMANS MAKE WAR, T EXTRAPOLATE ANTI-HU STRATEGY AND BATT TACTICS.
AND YOU'VE BEEN DOING IT THROUGH ALL OF HISTORY.
UNTIL YOU CRASHED AND GOT STRANDED HERE IN 1908.

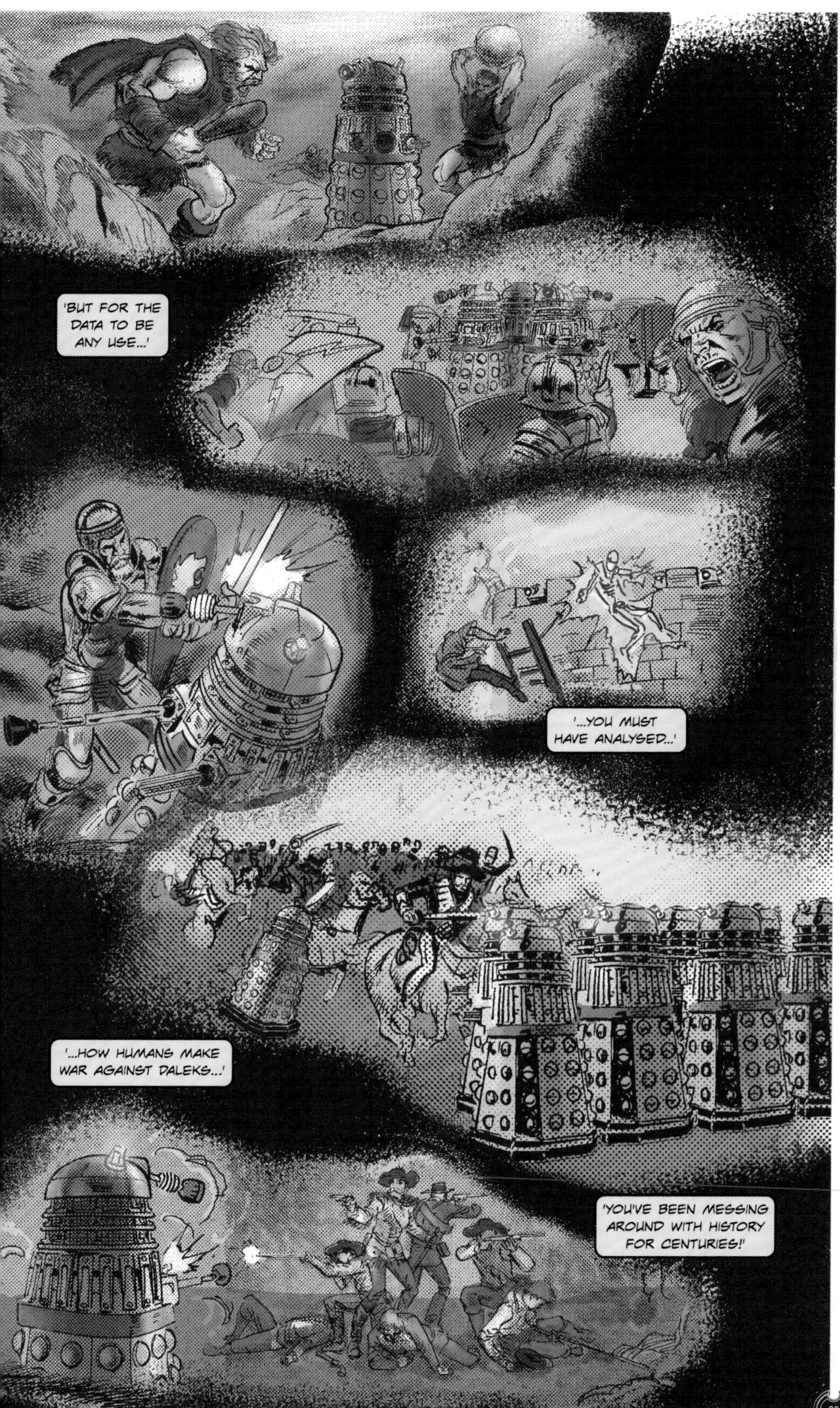
'BUT FOR THE DATA TO BE ANY USE...'
'...YOU MUST HAVE ANALYSED...'
'...HOW HUMANS MAKE WAR AGAINST DALEKS...'
'YOU'VE BEEN MESSING AROUND WITH HISTORY FOR CENTURIES!'

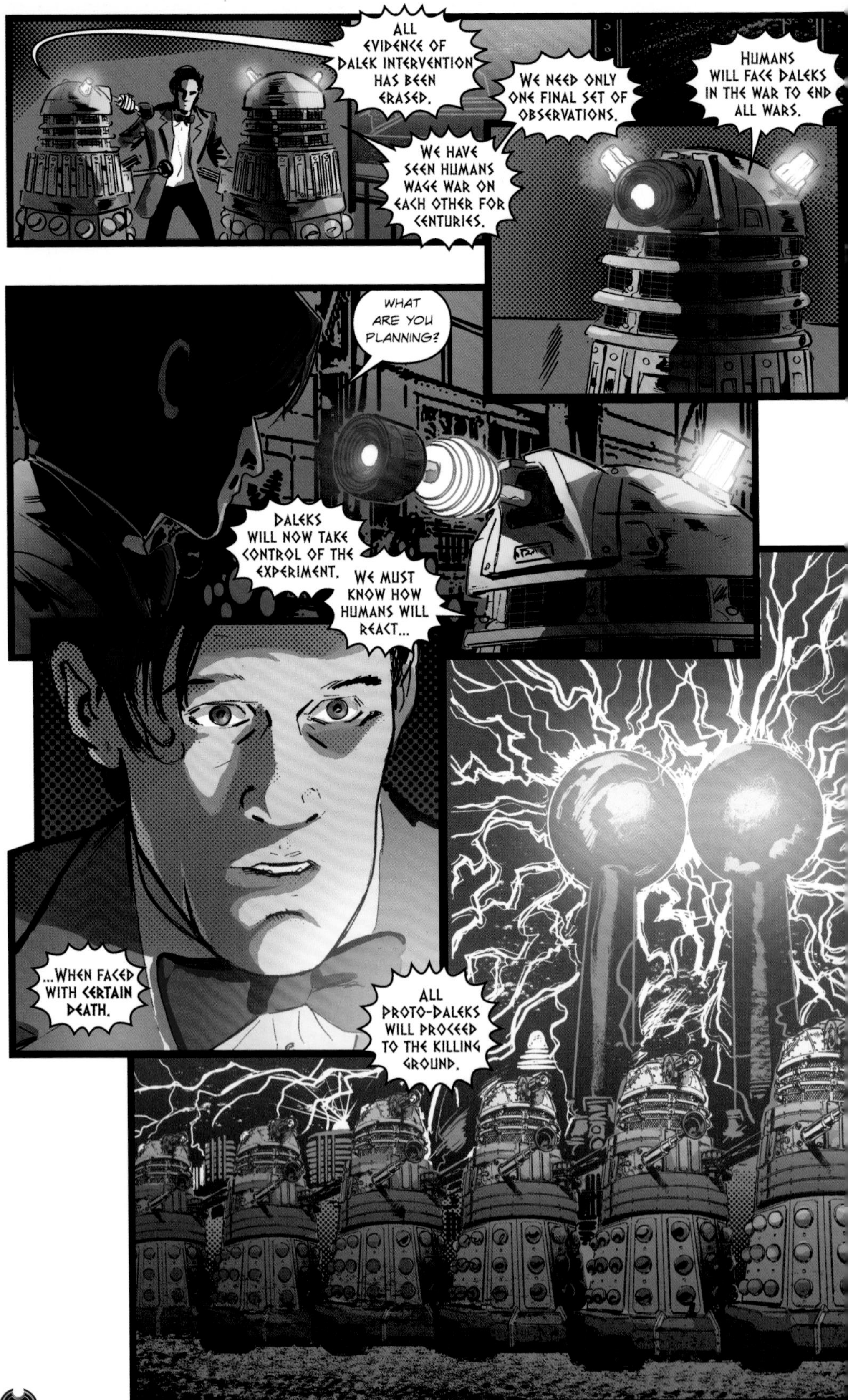
ALL EVIDENCE OF DALEK INTERVENTION HAS BEEN ERASED.
WE HAVE SEEN HUMANS WAGE WAR ON EACH OTHER FOR CENTURIES.
WE NEED ONLY ONE FINAL SET OF OBSERVATIONS.
HUMANS WILL FACE DALEKS IN THE WAR TO END ALL WARS.
WHAT ARE YOU PLANNING?
DALEKS WILL NOW TAKE CONTROL OF THE EXPERIMENT.
WE MUST KNOW HOW HUMANS WILL REACT...
...WHEN FACED WITH CERTAIN DEATH.
ALL PROTO-DALEKS WILL PROCEED TO THE KILLING GROUND.

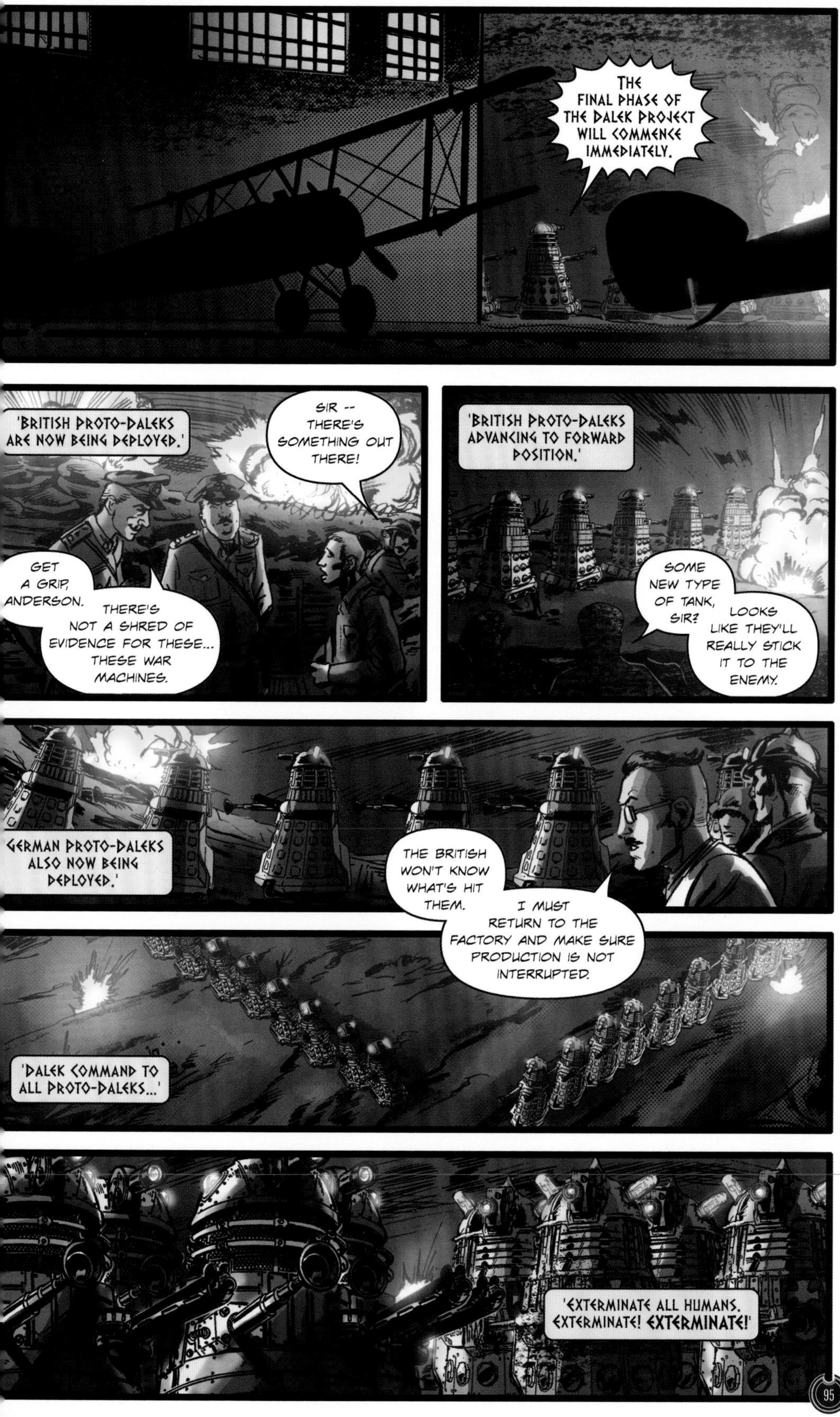

THE FINAL PHASE OF THE DALEK PROJECT WILL COMMENCE IMMEDIATELY.
'BRITISH PROTO-DALEKS ARE NOW BEING DEPLOYED.'
SIR -- THERE'S SOMETHING OUT THERE!
GET A GRIP, ANDERSON.
THERE'S NOT A SHRED OF EVIDENCE FOR THESE... THESE WAR MACHINES.
'BRITISH PROTO-DALEKS ADVANCING TO FORWARD POSITION.'
SOME NEW TYPE OF TANK, SIR?
LOOKS LIKE THEY'LL REALLY STICK IT TO THE ENEMY.
'GERMAN PROTO-DALEKS ALSO NOW BEING DEPLOYED.'
THE BRITISH WON'T KNOW WHAT'S HIT THEM.
I MUST RETURN TO THE FACTORY AND MAKE SURE PRODUCTION IS NOT INTERRUPTED.
'DALEK COMMAND TO ALL PROTO-DALEKS...'
'EXTERMINATE ALL HUMANS. EXTERMINATE! **EXTERMINATE!**'

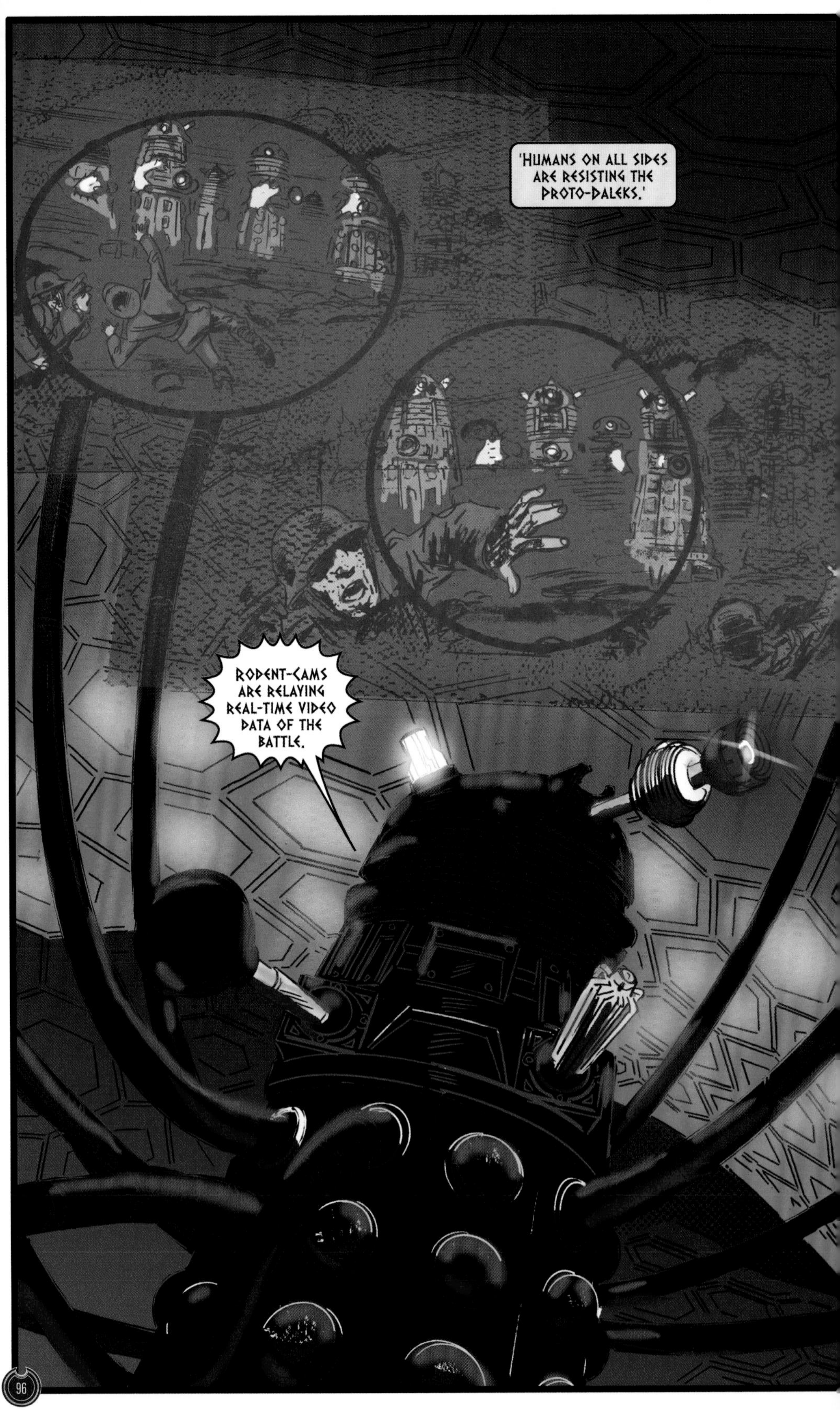
'HUMANS ON ALL SIDES ARE RESISTING THE PROTO-DALEKS.'
RODENT-CAMS ARE RELAYING REAL-TIME VIDEO DATA OF THE BATTLE.

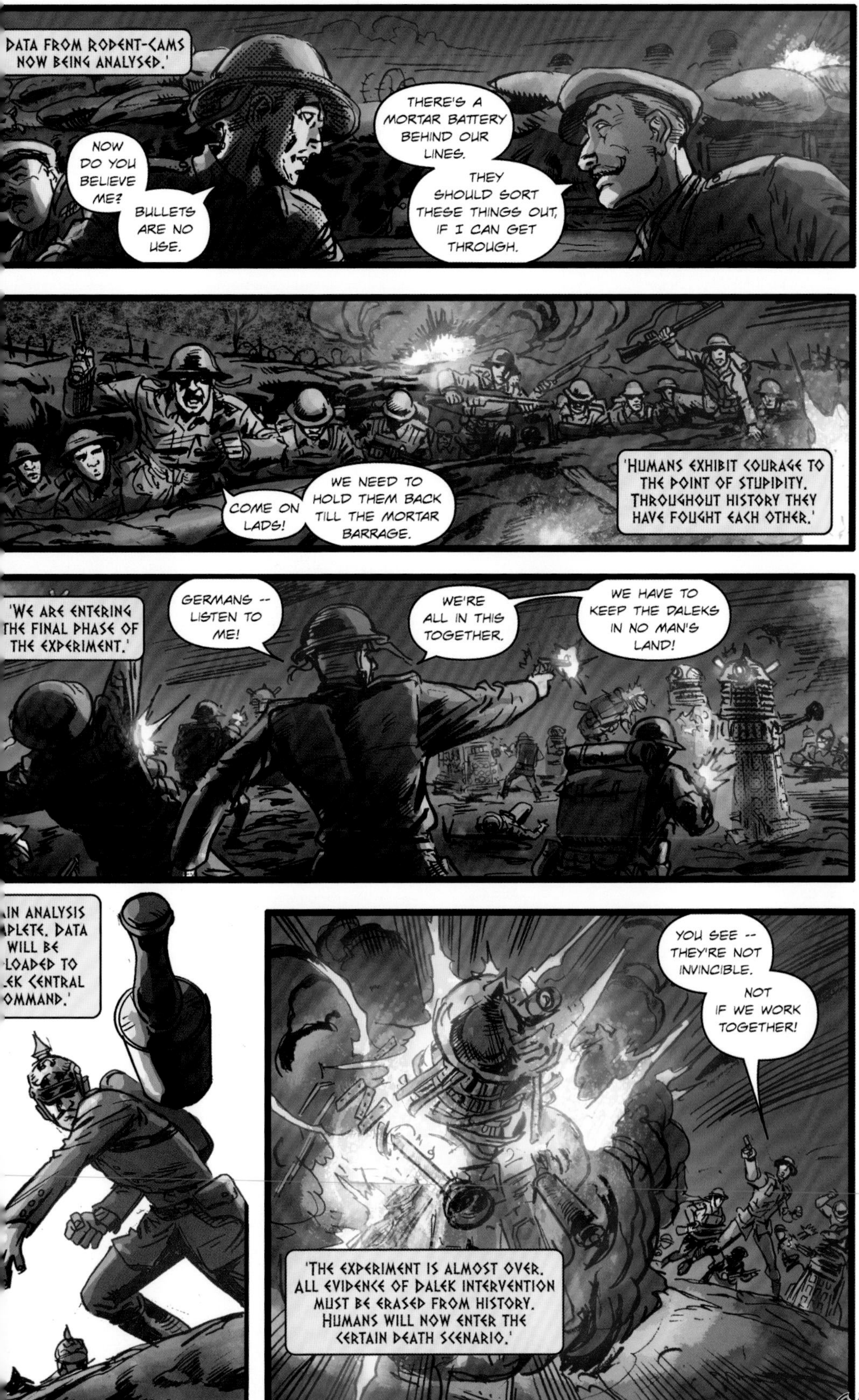

DATA FROM RODENT-CAMS NOW BEING ANALYSED.'
NOW DO YOU BELIEVE ME?
BULLETS ARE NO USE.
THERE'S A MORTAR BATTERY BEHIND OUR LINES.
THEY SHOULD SORT THESE THINGS OUT, IF I CAN GET THROUGH.
COME ON LADS!
WE NEED TO HOLD THEM BACK TILL THE MORTAR BARRAGE.
'HUMANS EXHIBIT COURAGE TO THE POINT OF STUPIDITY. THROUGHOUT HISTORY THEY HAVE FOUGHT EACH OTHER.'
'WE ARE ENTERING THE FINAL PHASE OF THE EXPERIMENT.'
GERMANS -- LISTEN TO ME!
WE'RE ALL IN THIS TOGETHER.
WE HAVE TO KEEP THE DALEKS IN NO MAN'S LAND!
IN ANALYSIS MPLETE. DATA WILL BE LOADED TO EK CENTRAL OMMAND.'
YOU SEE -- THEY'RE NOT INVINCIBLE.
NOT IF WE WORK TOGETHER!
'THE EXPERIMENT IS ALMOST OVER. ALL EVIDENCE OF DALEK INTERVENTION MUST BE ERASED FROM HISTORY. HUMANS WILL NOW ENTER THE CERTAIN DEATH SCENARIO.'

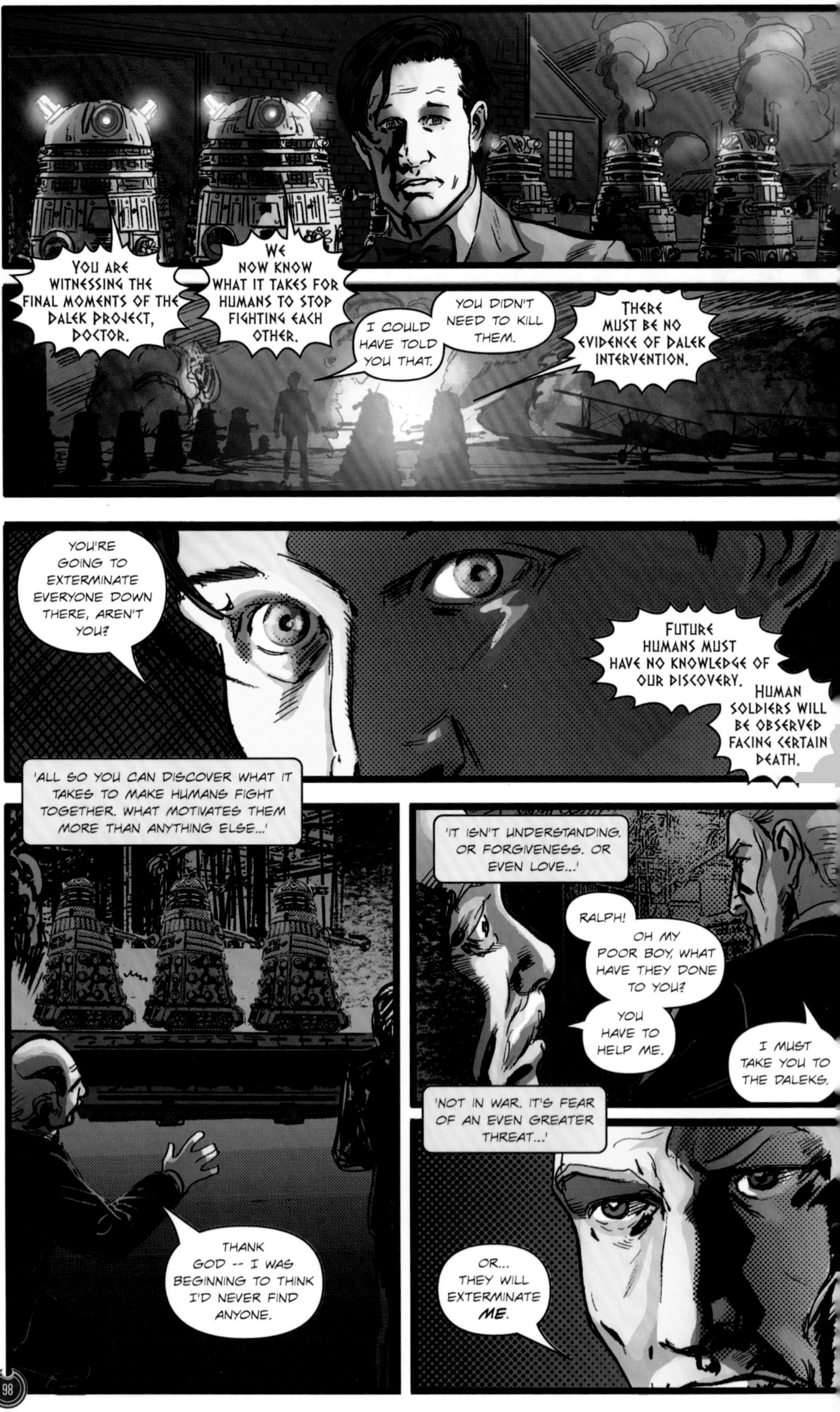
YOU ARE WITNESSING THE FINAL MOMENTS OF THE DALEK PROJECT, DOCTOR.
WE NOW KNOW WHAT IT TAKES FOR HUMANS TO STOP FIGHTING EACH OTHER.
I COULD HAVE TOLD YOU THAT.
YOU DIDN'T NEED TO KILL THEM.
THERE MUST BE NO EVIDENCE OF DALEK INTERVENTION.
YOU'RE GOING TO EXTERMINATE EVERYONE DOWN THERE, AREN'T YOU?
FUTURE HUMANS MUST HAVE NO KNOWLEDGE OF OUR DISCOVERY.
HUMAN SOLDIERS WILL BE OBSERVED FACING CERTAIN DEATH.
'ALL SO YOU CAN DISCOVER WHAT IT TAKES TO MAKE HUMANS FIGHT TOGETHER. WHAT MOTIVATES THEM MORE THAN ANYTHING ELSE...'
THANK GOD -- I WAS BEGINNING TO THINK I'D NEVER FIND ANYONE.
'IT ISN'T UNDERSTANDING. OR FORGIVENESS. OR EVEN LOVE...'
RALPH!
OH MY POOR BOY, WHAT HAVE THEY DONE TO YOU?
YOU HAVE TO HELP ME.
I MUST TAKE YOU TO THE DALEKS.
'NOT IN WAR. IT'S FEAR OF AN EVEN GREATER THREAT...'
OR... THEY WILL EXTERMINATE ME.

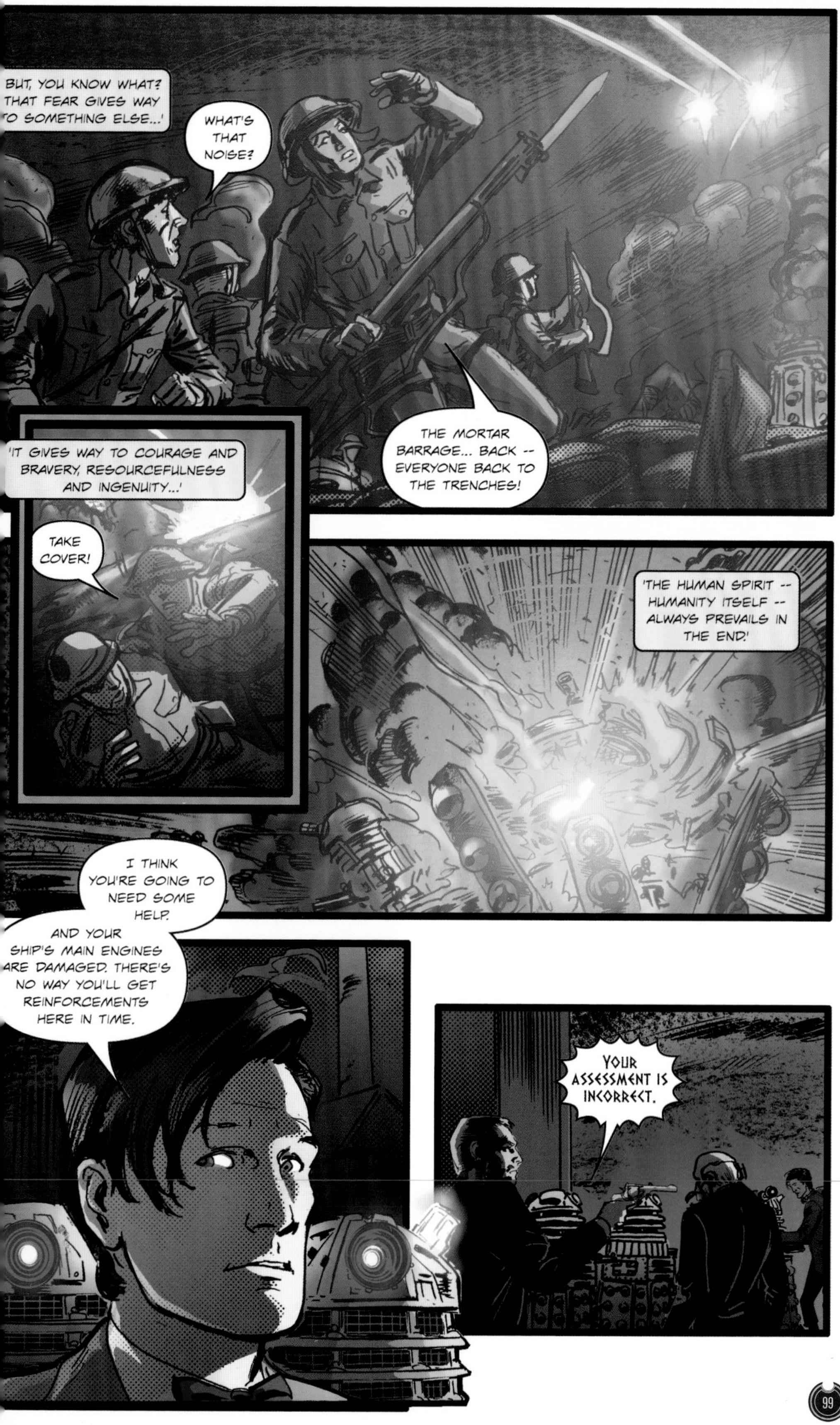
BUT, YOU KNOW WHAT? THAT FEAR GIVES WAY TO SOMETHING ELSE...'
WHAT'S THAT NOISE?
THE MORTAR BARRAGE... BACK -- EVERYONE BACK TO THE TRENCHES!
'IT GIVES WAY TO COURAGE AND BRAVERY, RESOURCEFULNESS AND INGENUITY...'
TAKE COVER!
'THE HUMAN SPIRIT -- HUMANITY ITSELF -- ALWAYS PREVAILS IN THE END.'
I THINK YOU'RE GOING TO NEED SOME HELP.
AND YOUR SHIP'S MAIN ENGINES ARE DAMAGED. THERE'S NO WAY YOU'LL GET REINFORCEMENTS HERE IN TIME.
YOUR ASSESSMENT IS INCORRECT.

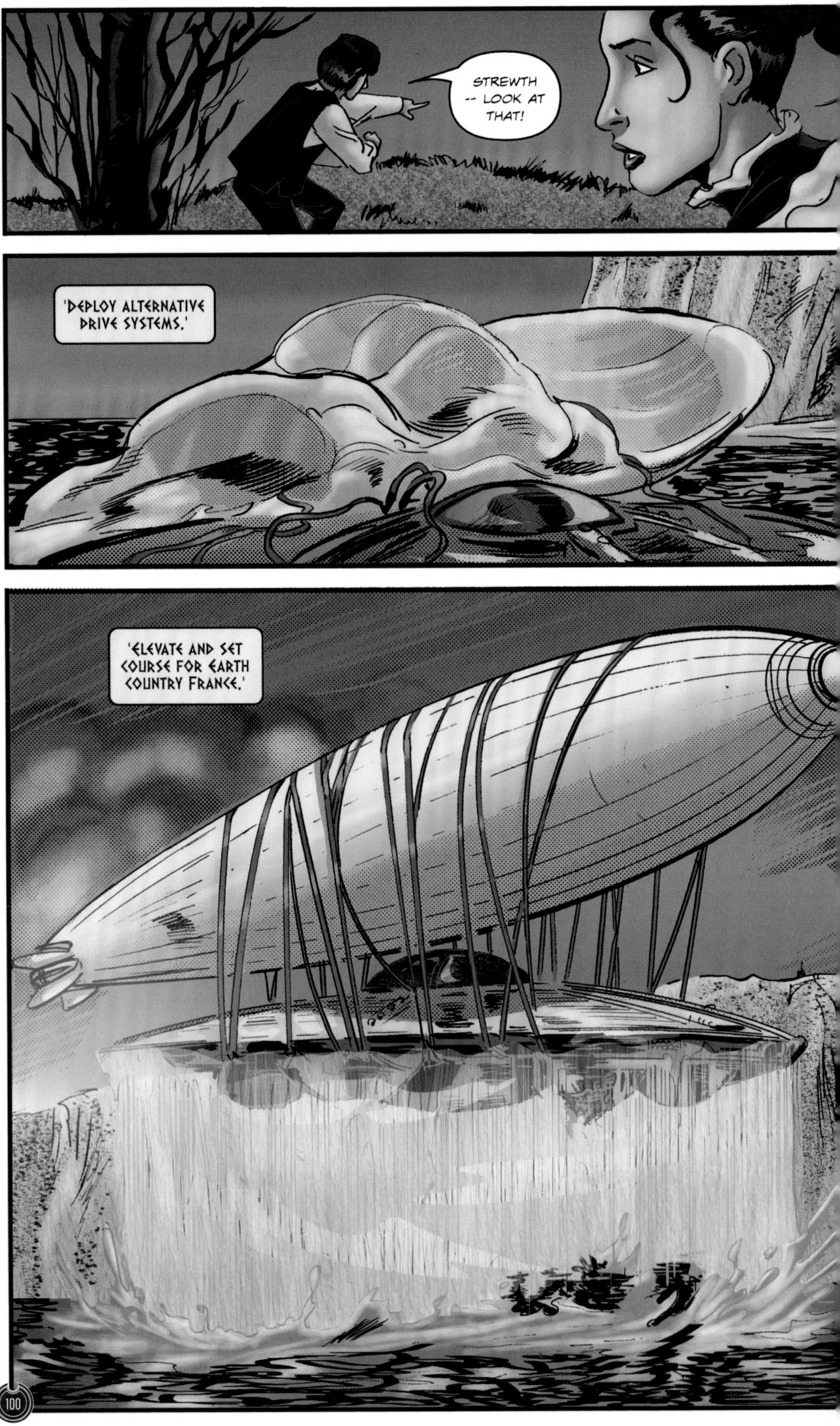
STREWTH -- LOOK AT THAT!
'DEPLOY ALTERNATIVE DRIVE SYSTEMS.'
'ELEVATE AND SET COURSE FOR EARTH COUNTRY FRANCE.'

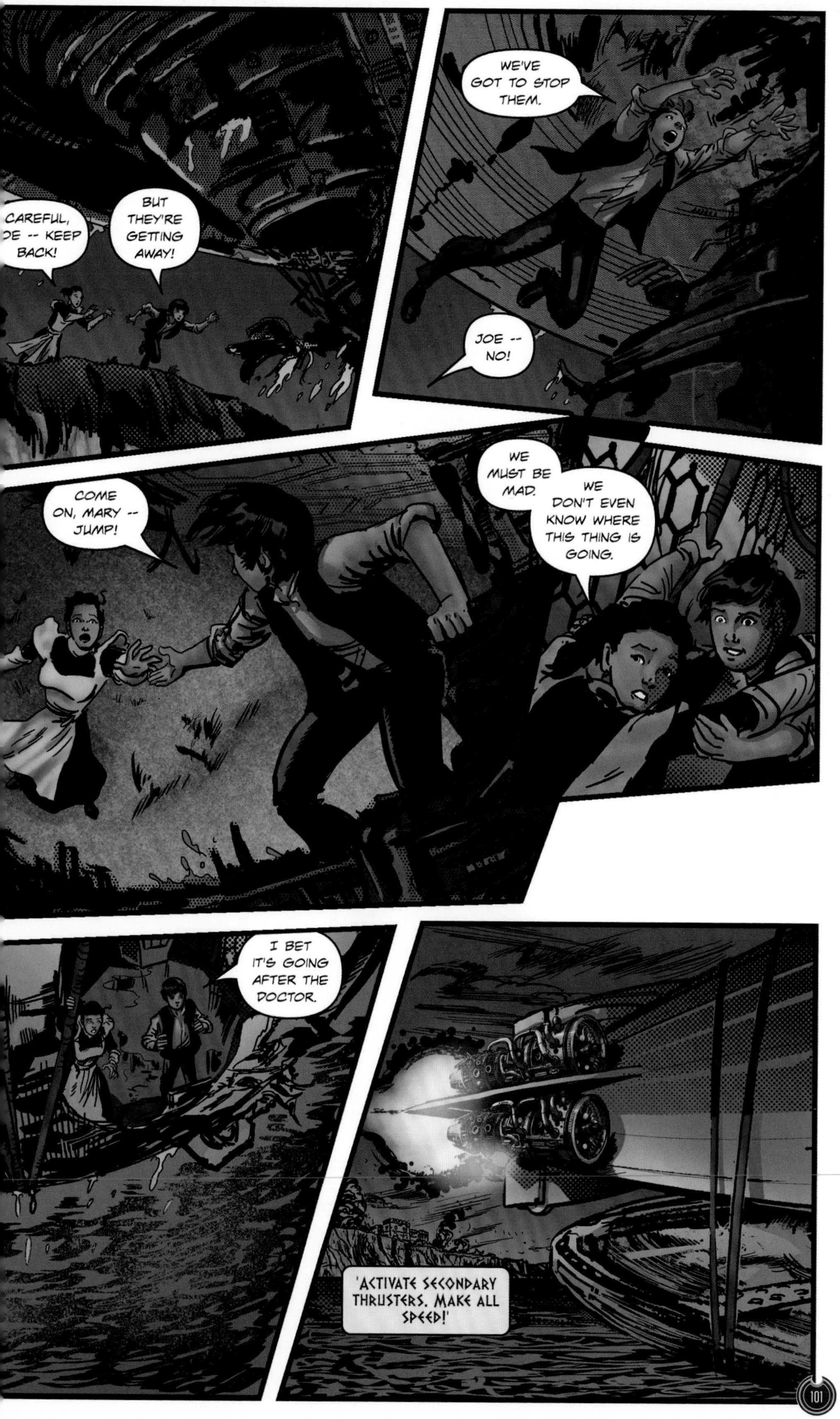
CAREFUL, JOE -- KEEP BACK!
BUT THEY'RE GETTING AWAY!
WE'VE GOT TO STOP THEM.
JOE -- NO!
COME ON, MARY -- JUMP!
WE MUST BE MAD.
WE DON'T EVEN KNOW WHERE THIS THING IS GOING.
I BET IT'S GOING AFTER THE DOCTOR.
'ACTIVATE SECONDARY THRUSTERS. MAKE ALL SPEED!'

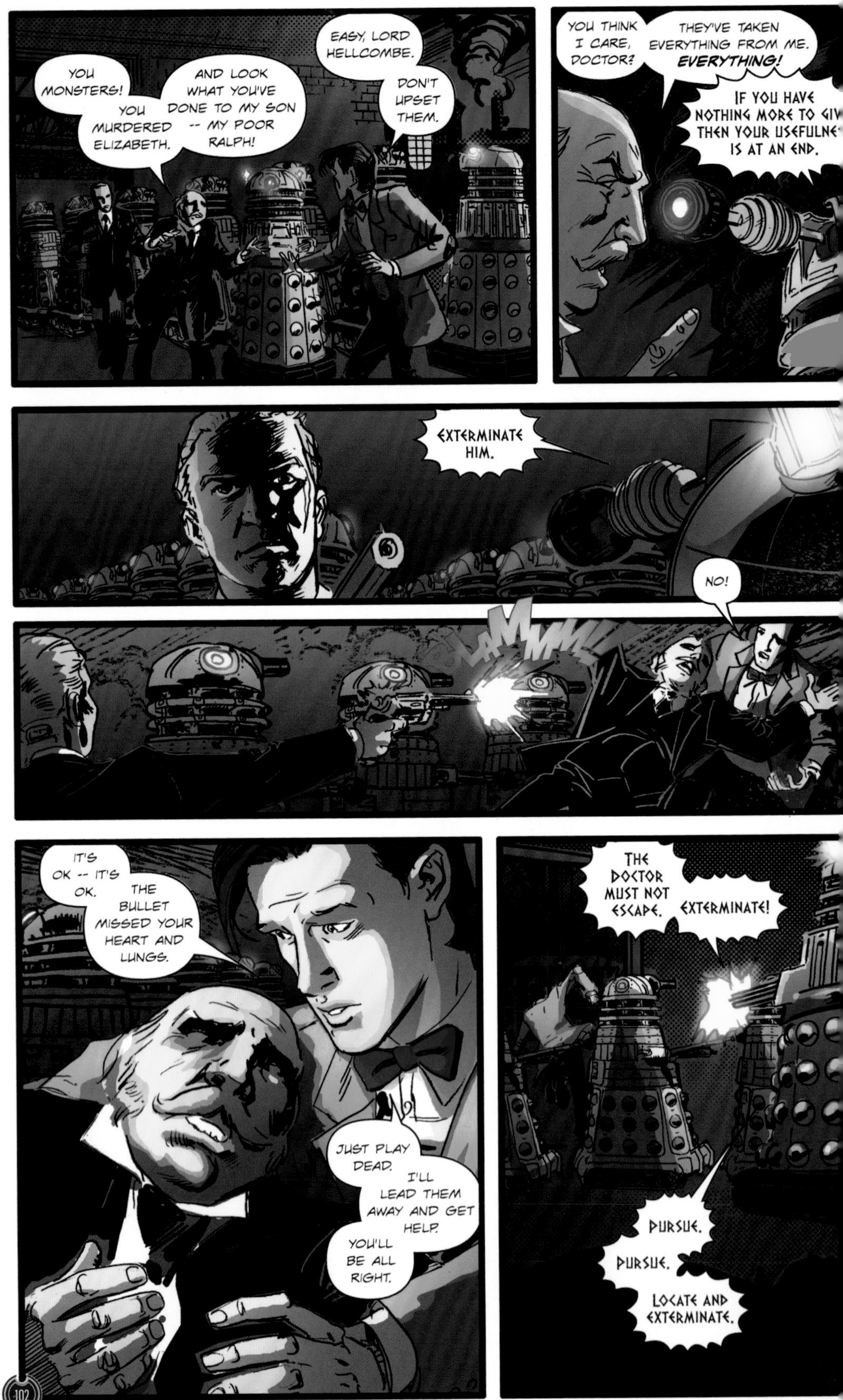
YOU MONSTERS!
YOU MURDERED ELIZABETH.
AND LOOK WHAT YOU'VE DONE TO MY SON -- MY POOR RALPH!
EASY, LORD HELLCOMBE.
DON'T UPSET THEM.
YOU THINK I CARE, DOCTOR?
THEY'VE TAKEN EVERYTHING FROM ME. EVERYTHING!
IF YOU HAVE NOTHING MORE TO GIV
THEN YOUR USEFULNE
IS AT AN END.
EXTERMINATE HIM.
NO!
IT'S OK -- IT'S OK.
THE BULLET MISSED YOUR HEART AND LUNGS.
JUST PLAY DEAD.
I'LL LEAD THEM AWAY AND GET HELP.
YOU'LL BE ALL RIGHT.
THE DOCTOR MUST NOT ESCAPE.
EXTERMINATE!
PURSUE.
PURSUE.
LOCATE AND EXTERMINATE.

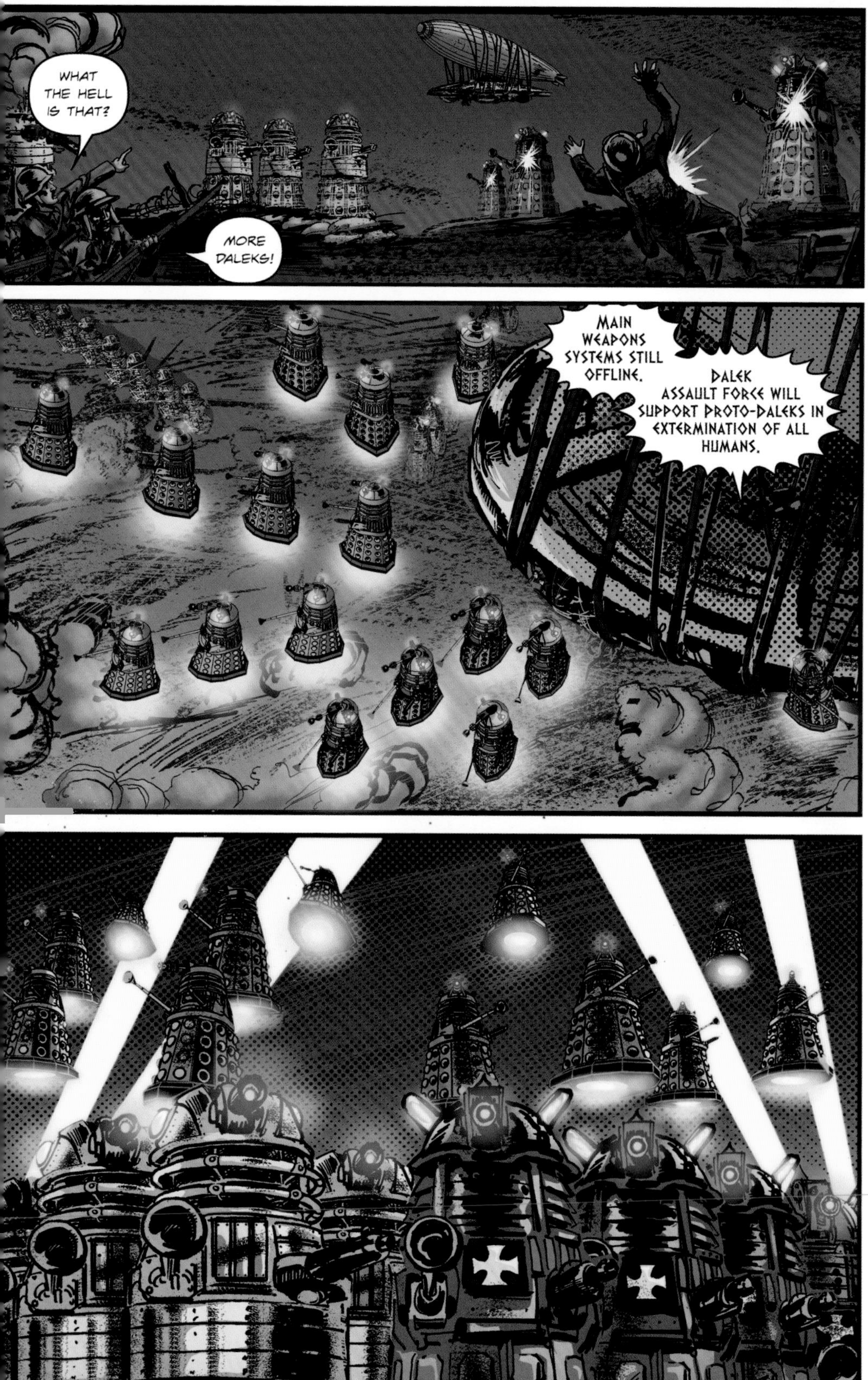
WHAT THE HELL IS THAT?
MORE DALEKS!
MAIN WEAPONS SYSTEMS STILL OFFLINE.
DALEK ASSAULT FORCE WILL SUPPORT PROTO-DALEKS IN EXTERMINATION OF ALL HUMANS.

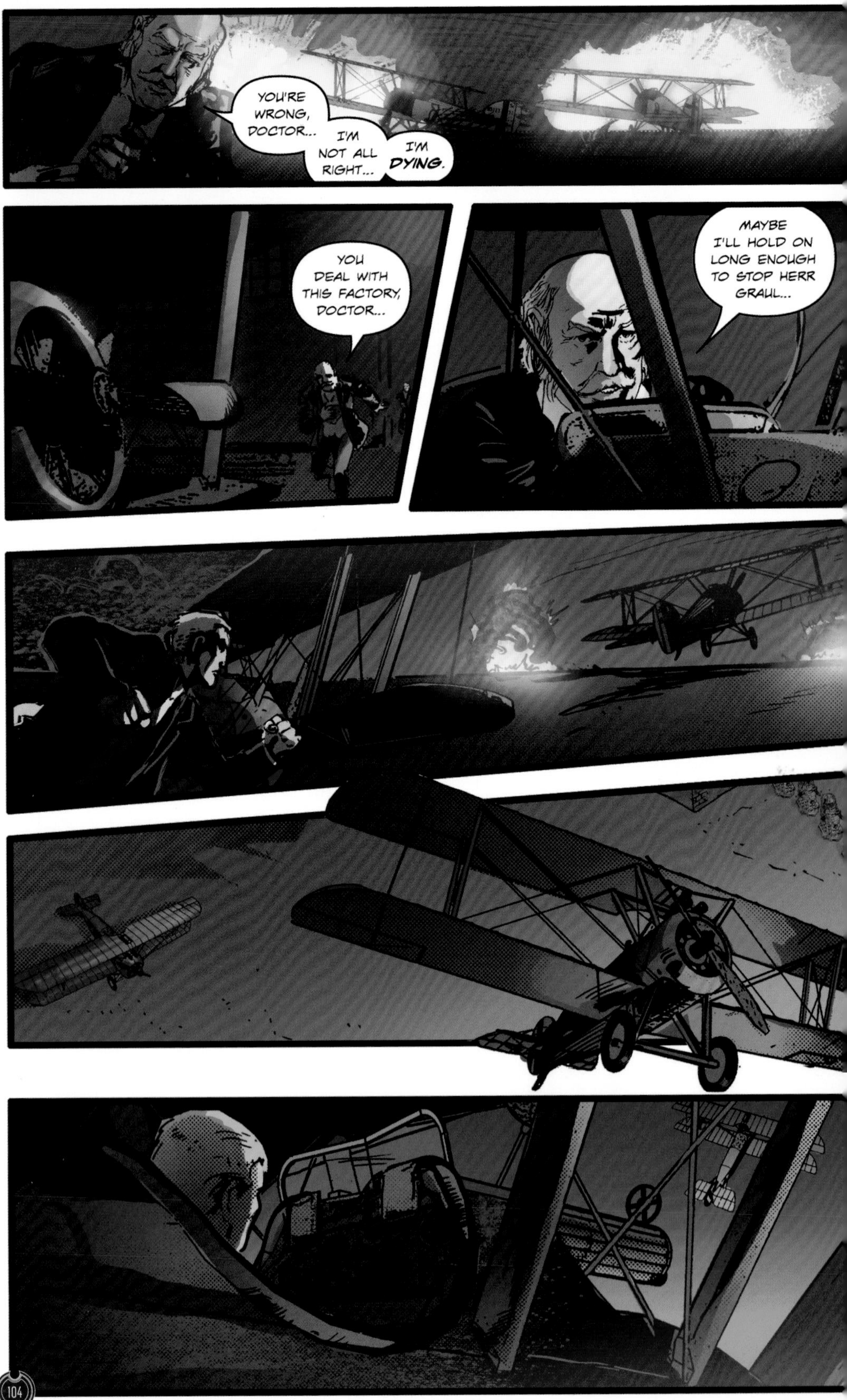
YOU'RE WRONG, DOCTOR...
I'M NOT ALL RIGHT...
I'M DYING.
YOU DEAL WITH THIS FACTORY, DOCTOR...
MAYBE I'LL HOLD ON LONG ENOUGH TO STOP HERR GRAUL...

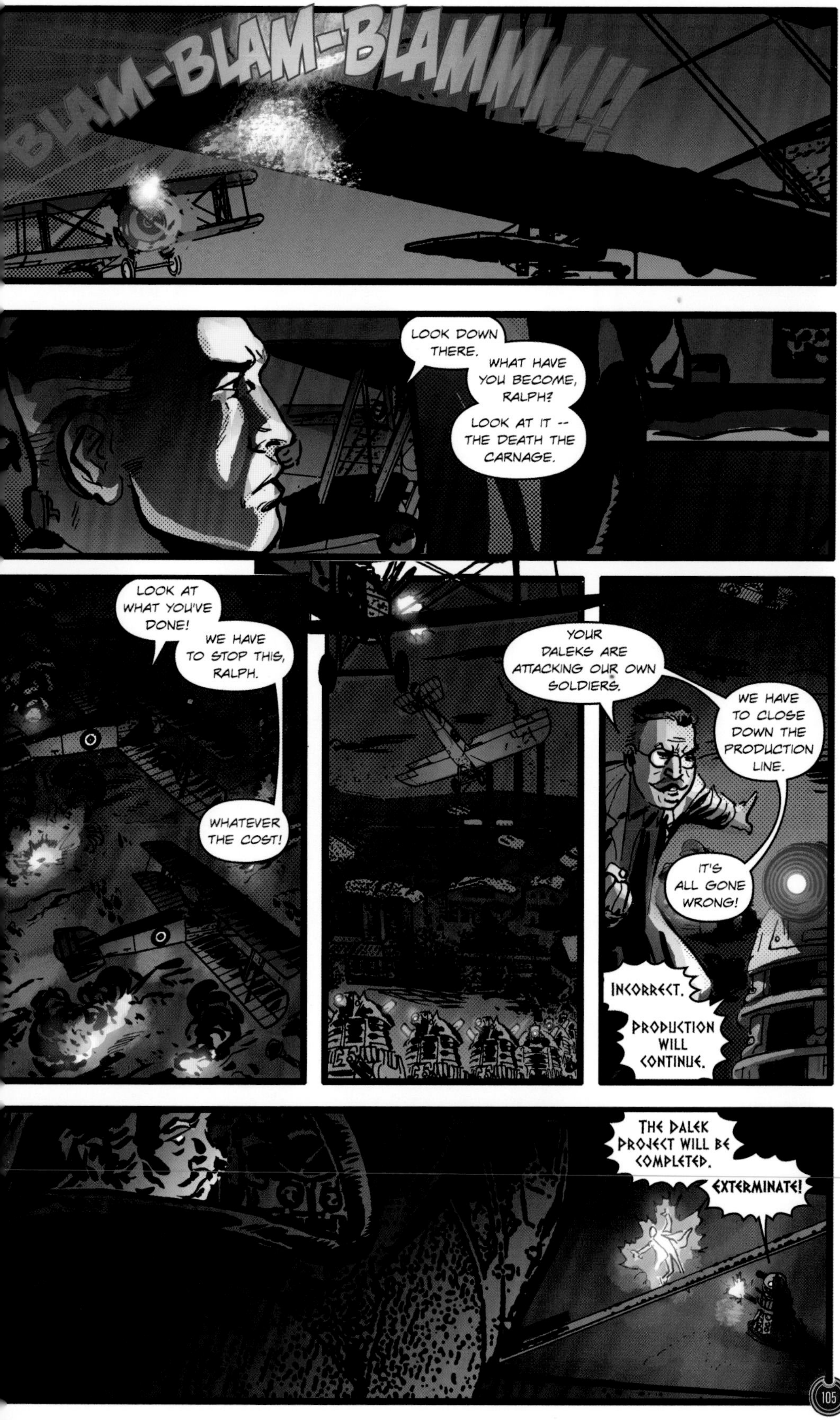
BLAM-BLAM-BLAMMMM!!
LOOK DOWN THERE.
WHAT HAVE YOU BECOME, RALPH?
LOOK AT IT -- THE DEATH THE CARNAGE.
LOOK AT WHAT YOU'VE DONE!
WE HAVE TO STOP THIS, RALPH.
WHATEVER THE COST!
YOUR DALEKS ARE ATTACKING OUR OWN SOLDIERS.
WE HAVE TO CLOSE DOWN THE PRODUCTION LINE.
IT'S ALL GONE WRONG!
INCORRECT.
PRODUCTION WILL CONTINUE.
THE DALEK PROJECT WILL BE COMPLETED.
EXTERMINATE!

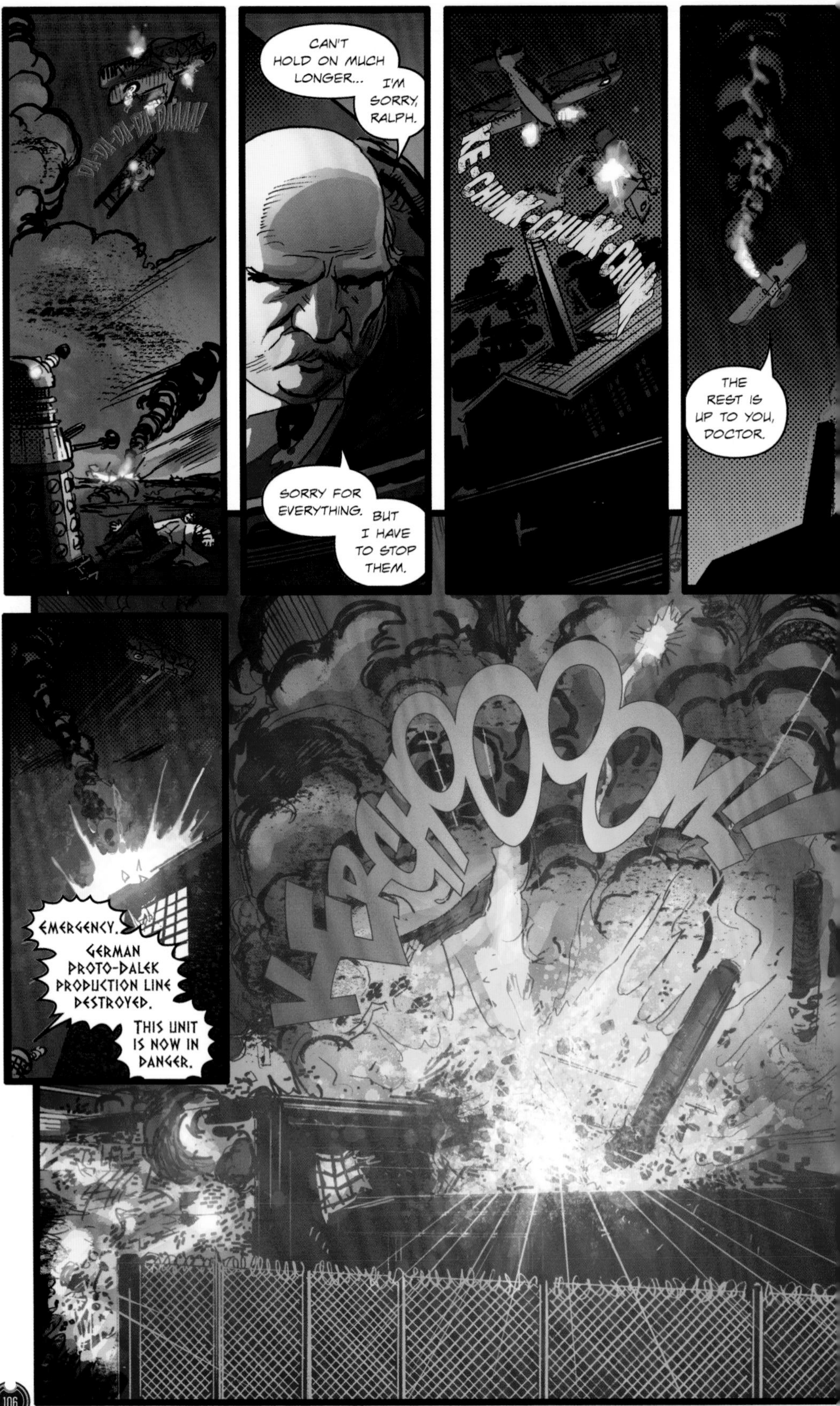
DA-DA-DA-DA-DAAAA!
CAN'T HOLD ON MUCH LONGER...
I'M SORRY, RALPH.
SORRY FOR EVERYTHING.
BUT I HAVE TO STOP THEM.
KE-CHUNK-CHUNK-CHUNK-CHUNK
THE REST IS UP TO YOU, DOCTOR.
EMERGENCY.
GERMAN PROTO-DALEK PRODUCTION LINE DESTROYED.
THIS UNIT IS NOW IN DANGER.

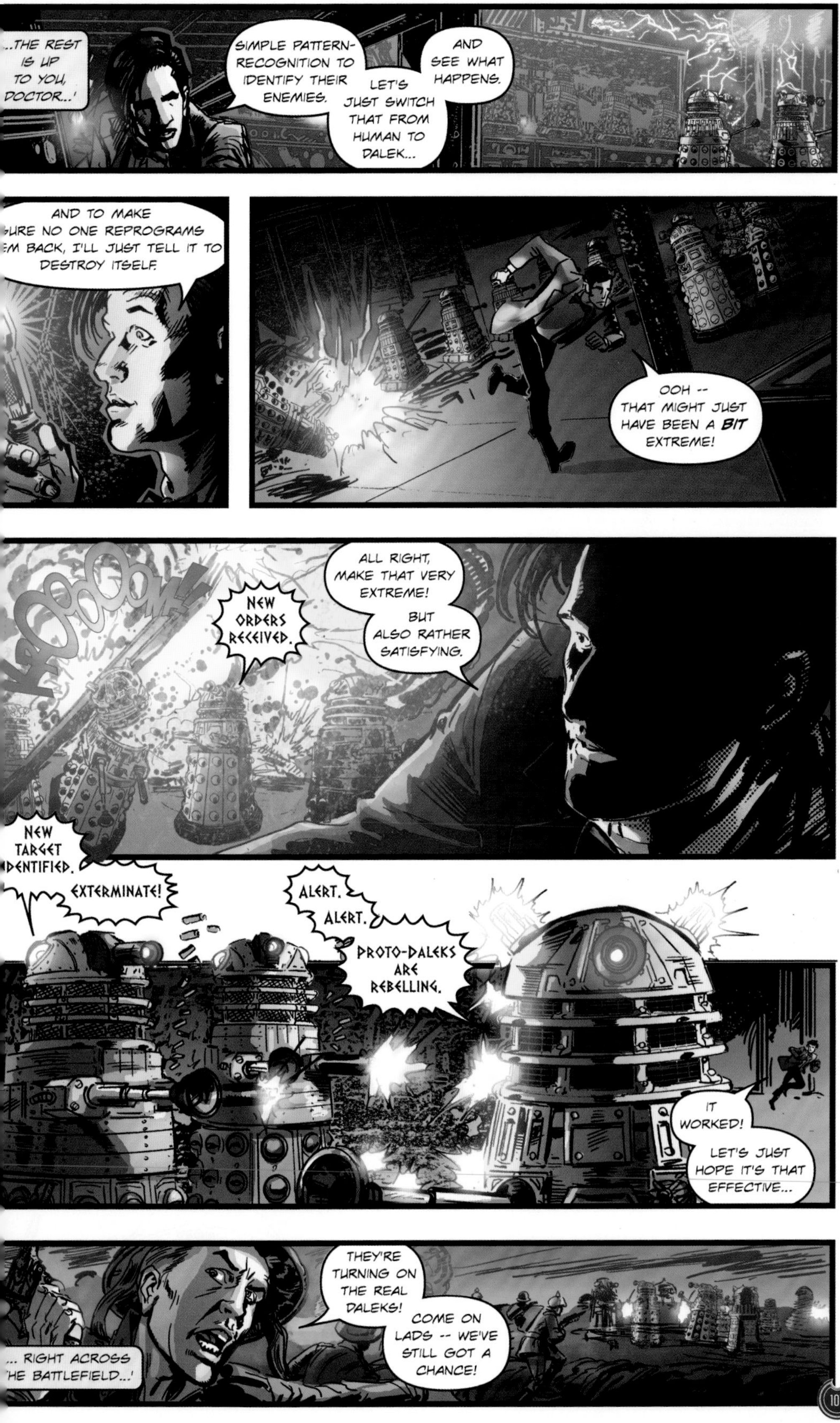
...THE REST IS UP TO YOU, DOCTOR...'
SIMPLE PATTERN-RECOGNITION TO IDENTIFY THEIR ENEMIES.
LET'S JUST SWITCH THAT FROM HUMAN TO DALEK...
AND SEE WHAT HAPPENS.
AND TO MAKE SURE NO ONE REPROGRAMS 'EM BACK, I'LL JUST TELL IT TO DESTROY ITSELF.
OOH -- THAT MIGHT JUST HAVE BEEN A **BIT** EXTREME!
KABOOOOM!
NEW ORDERS RECEIVED.
ALL RIGHT, MAKE THAT VERY EXTREME!
BUT ALSO RATHER SATISFYING.
NEW TARGET IDENTIFIED.
EXTERMINATE!
ALERT.
ALERT.
PROTO-DALEKS ARE REBELLING.
IT WORKED!
LET'S JUST HOPE IT'S THAT EFFECTIVE...
... RIGHT ACROSS THE BATTLEFIELD...'
THEY'RE TURNING ON THE REAL DALEKS!
COME ON LADS -- WE'VE STILL GOT A CHANCE!

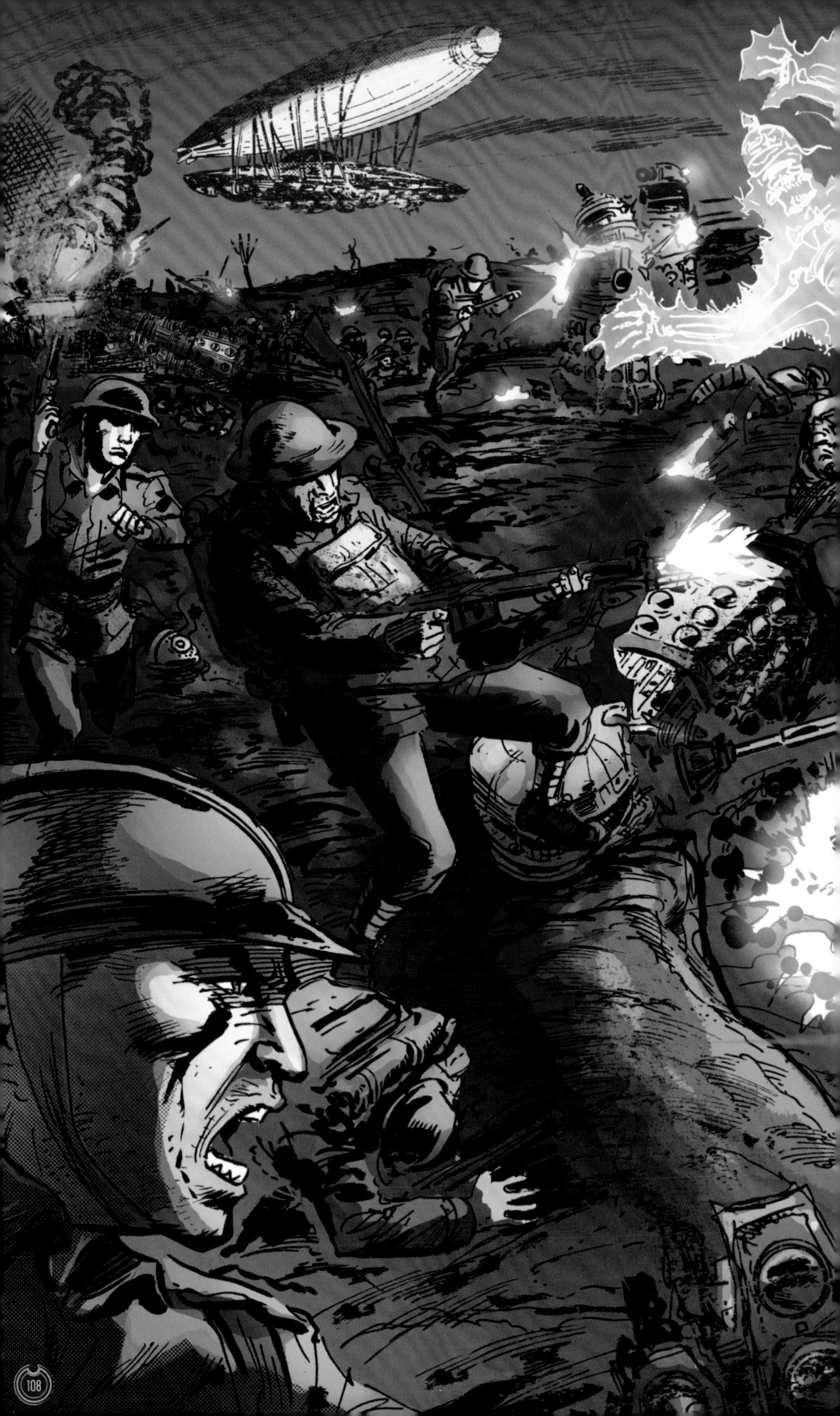

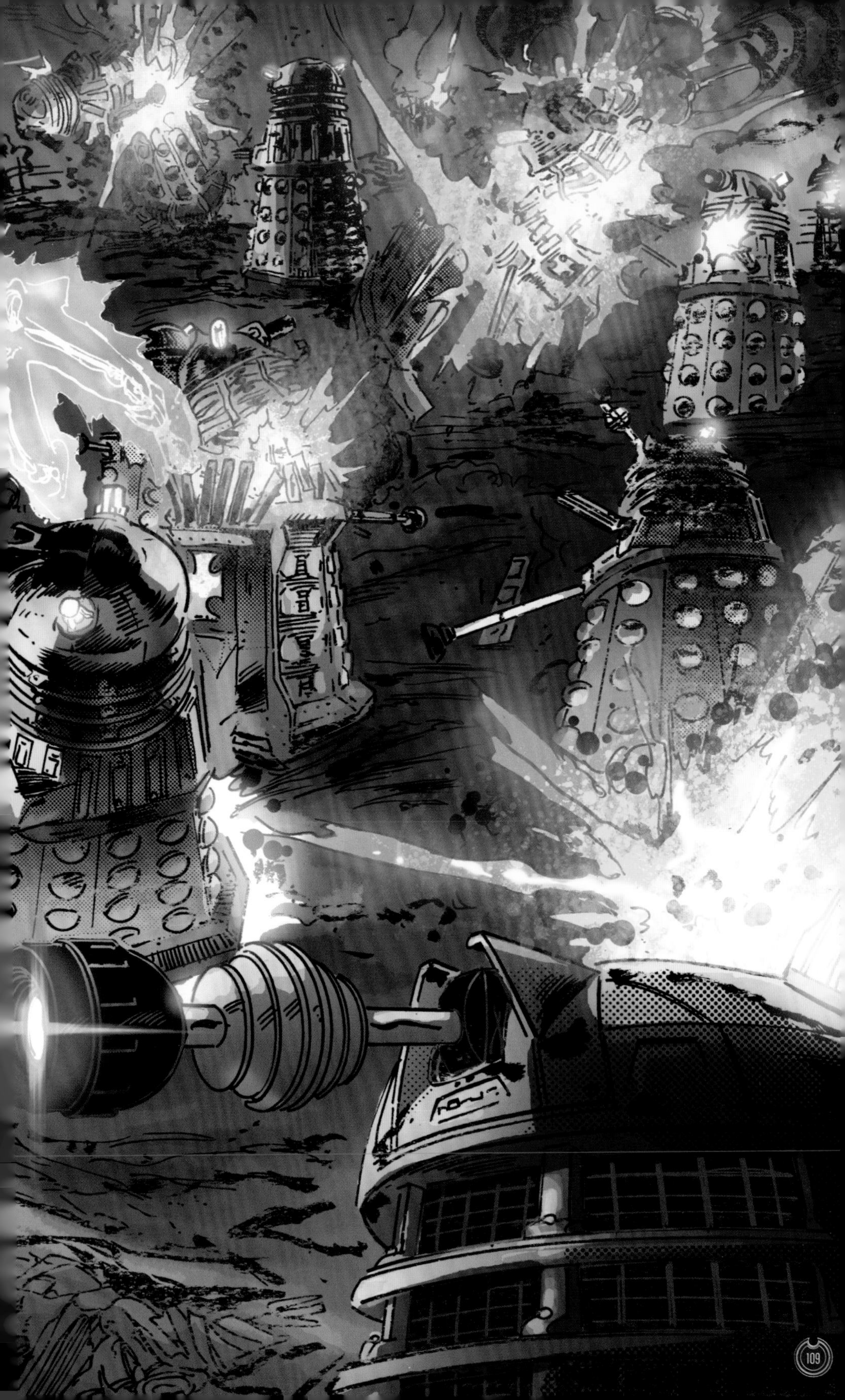

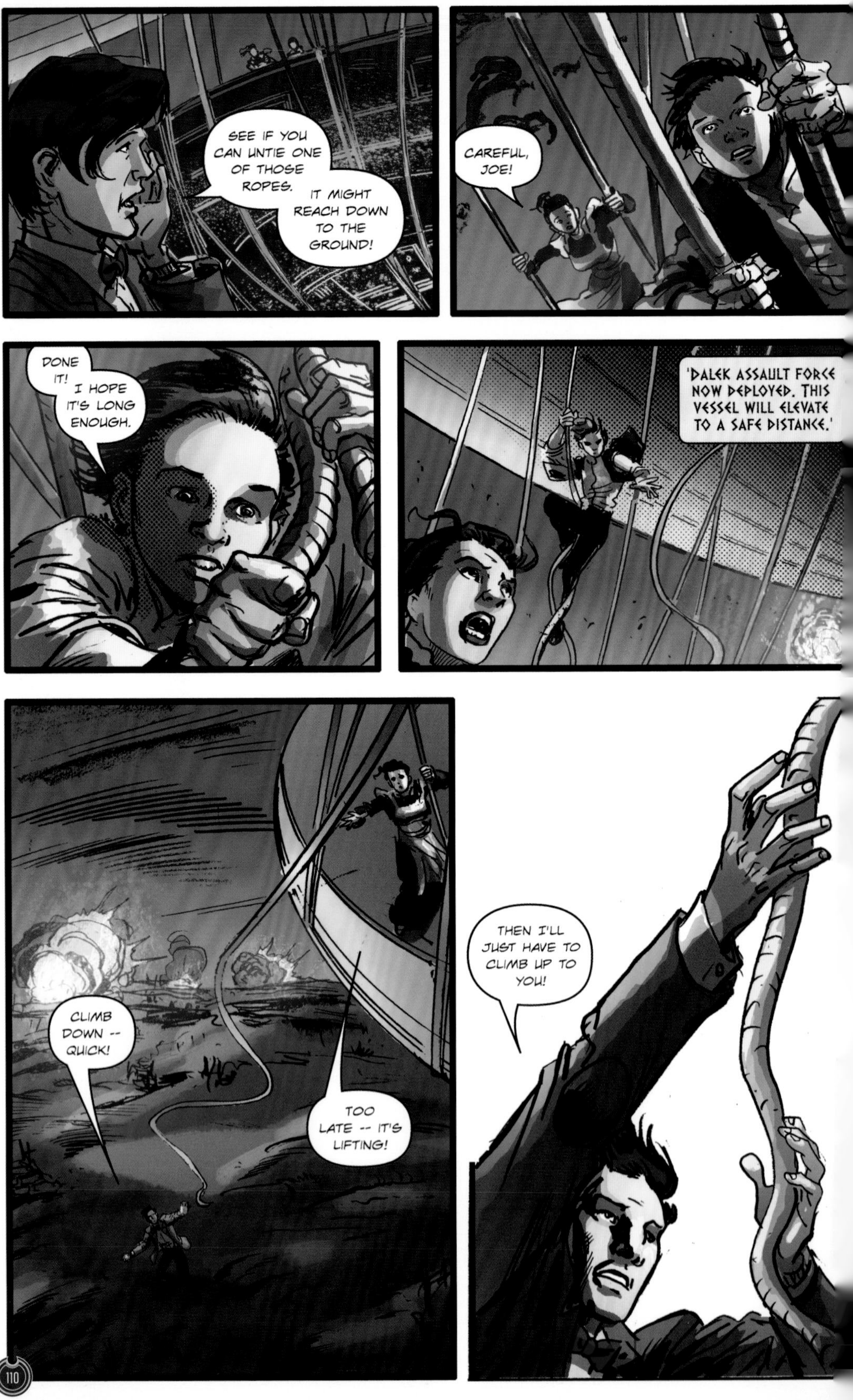
SEE IF YOU CAN UNTIE ONE OF THOSE ROPES.
IT MIGHT REACH DOWN TO THE GROUND!
CAREFUL, JOE!
DONE IT!
I HOPE IT'S LONG ENOUGH.
'DALEK ASSAULT FORCE NOW DEPLOYED. THIS VESSEL WILL ELEVATE TO A SAFE DISTANCE.'
CLIMB DOWN -- QUICK!
TOO LATE -- IT'S LIFTING!
THEN I'LL JUST HAVE TO CLIMB UP TO YOU!

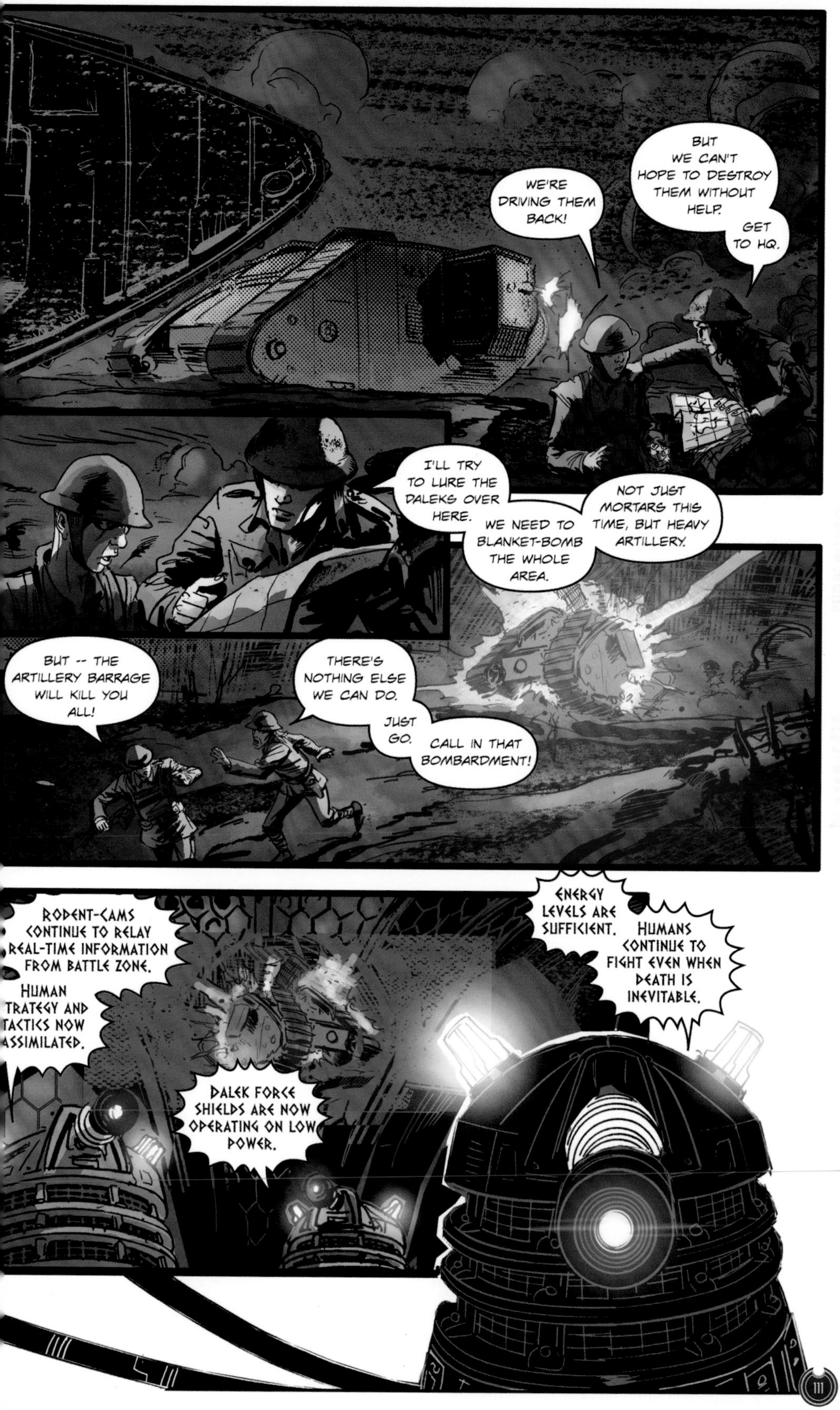
WE'RE DRIVING THEM BACK!
BUT WE CAN'T HOPE TO DESTROY THEM WITHOUT HELP.
GET TO HQ.
I'LL TRY TO LURE THE DALEKS OVER HERE.
WE NEED TO BLANKET-BOMB THE WHOLE AREA.
NOT JUST MORTARS THIS TIME, BUT HEAVY ARTILLERY.
BUT -- THE ARTILLERY BARRAGE WILL KILL YOU ALL!
THERE'S NOTHING ELSE WE CAN DO.
JUST GO.
CALL IN THAT BOMBARDMENT!
RODENT-CAMS CONTINUE TO RELAY REAL-TIME INFORMATION FROM BATTLE ZONE.
HUMAN TRATEGY AND TACTICS NOW ASSIMILATED.
DALEK FORCE SHIELDS ARE NOW OPERATING ON LOW POWER.
ENERGY LEVELS ARE SUFFICIENT.
HUMANS CONTINUE TO FIGHT EVEN WHEN DEATH IS INEVITABLE.

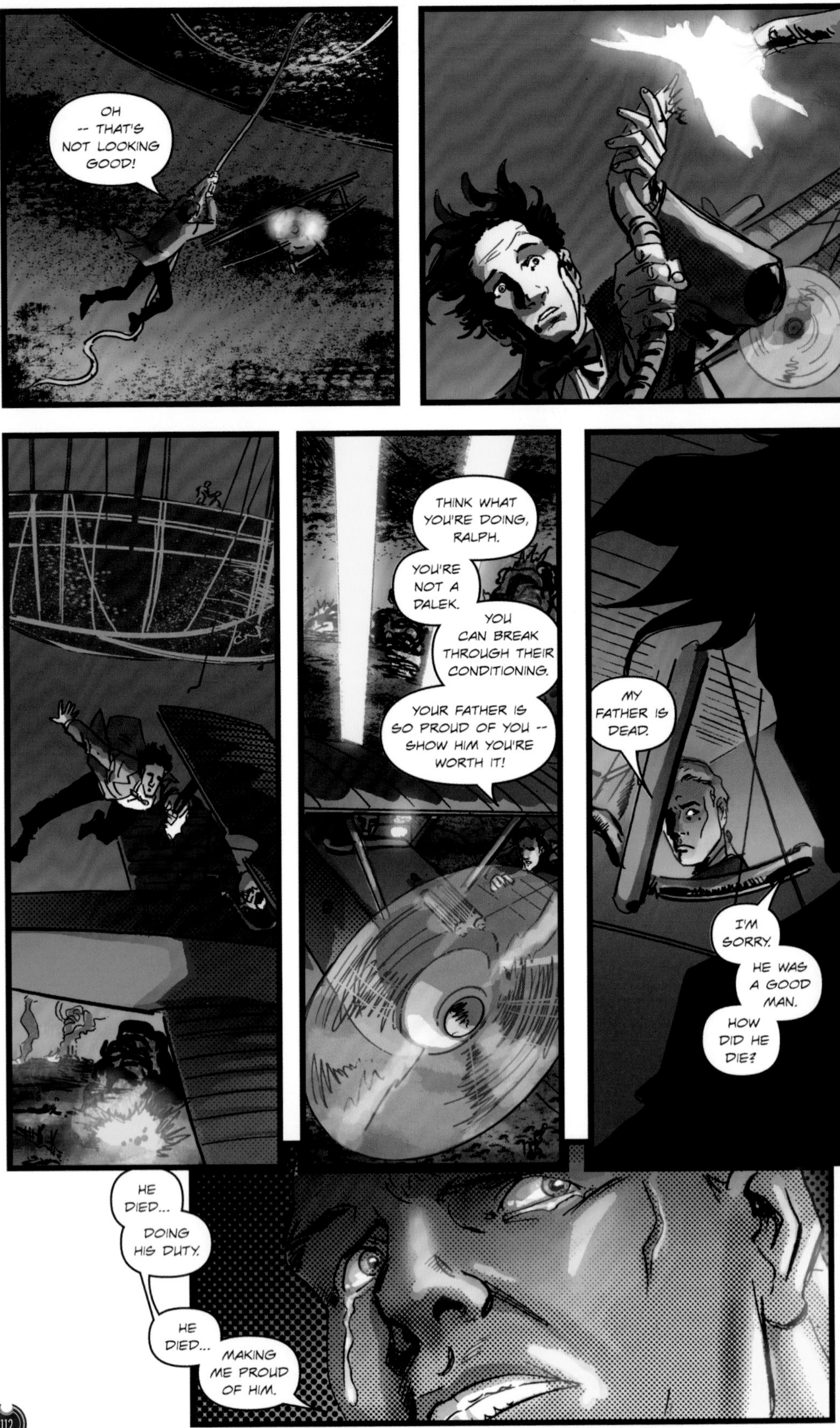

OH -- THAT'S NOT LOOKING GOOD!
THINK WHAT YOU'RE DOING, RALPH.
YOU'RE NOT A DALEK.
YOU CAN BREAK THROUGH THEIR CONDITIONING.
YOUR FATHER IS SO PROUD OF YOU -- SHOW HIM YOU'RE WORTH IT!
MY FATHER IS DEAD.
I'M SORRY.
HE WAS A GOOD MAN.
HOW DID HE DIE?
HE DIED...
DOING HIS DUTY.
HE DIED...
MAKING ME PROUD OF HIM.

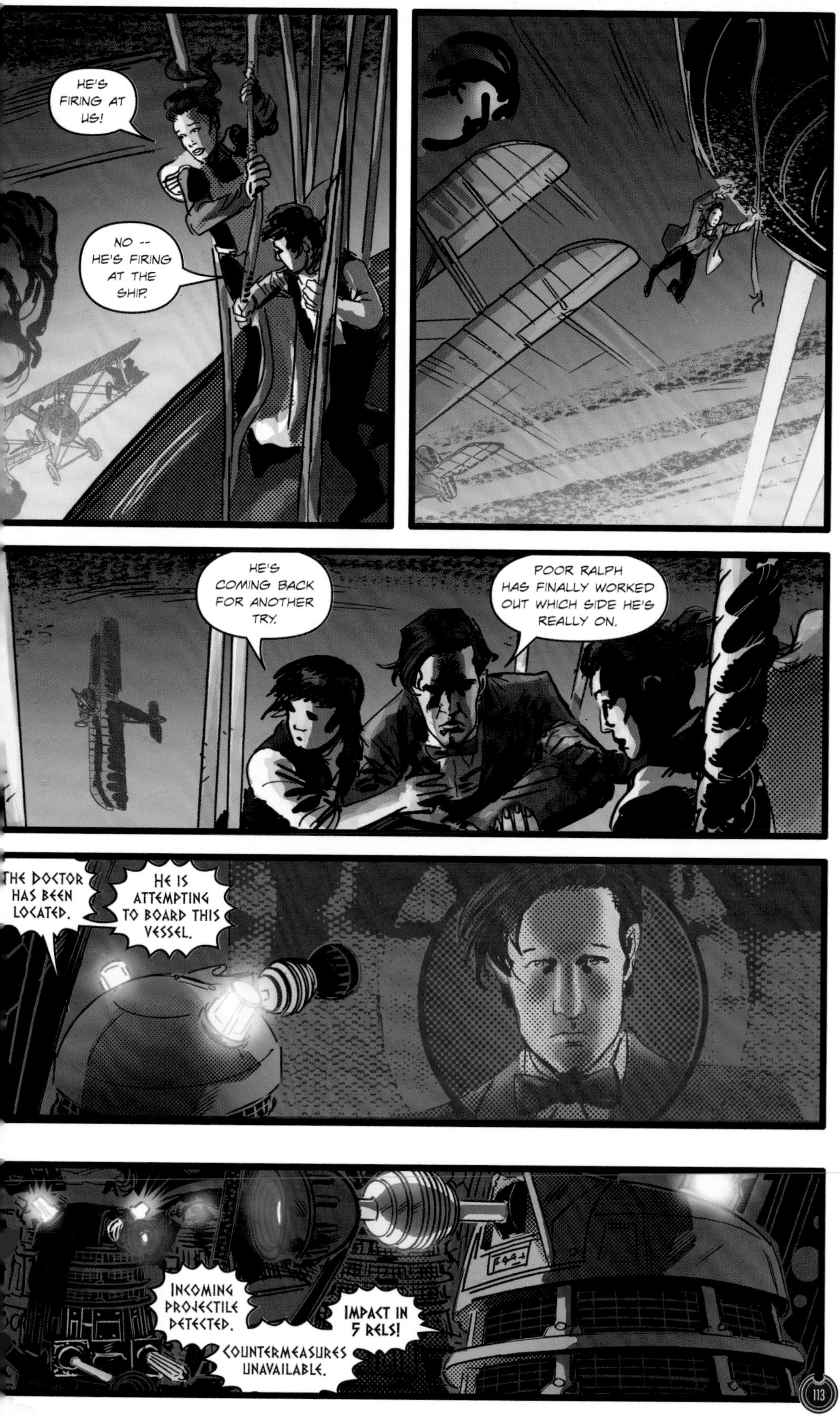
HE'S FIRING AT US!
NO -- HE'S FIRING AT THE SHIP.
HE'S COMING BACK FOR ANOTHER TRY.
POOR RALPH HAS FINALLY WORKED OUT WHICH SIDE HE'S REALLY ON.
THE DOCTOR HAS BEEN LOCATED.
HE IS ATTEMPTING TO BOARD THIS VESSEL.
INCOMING PROJECTILE DETECTED.
COUNTERMEASURES UNAVAILABLE.
IMPACT IN 5 RELS!

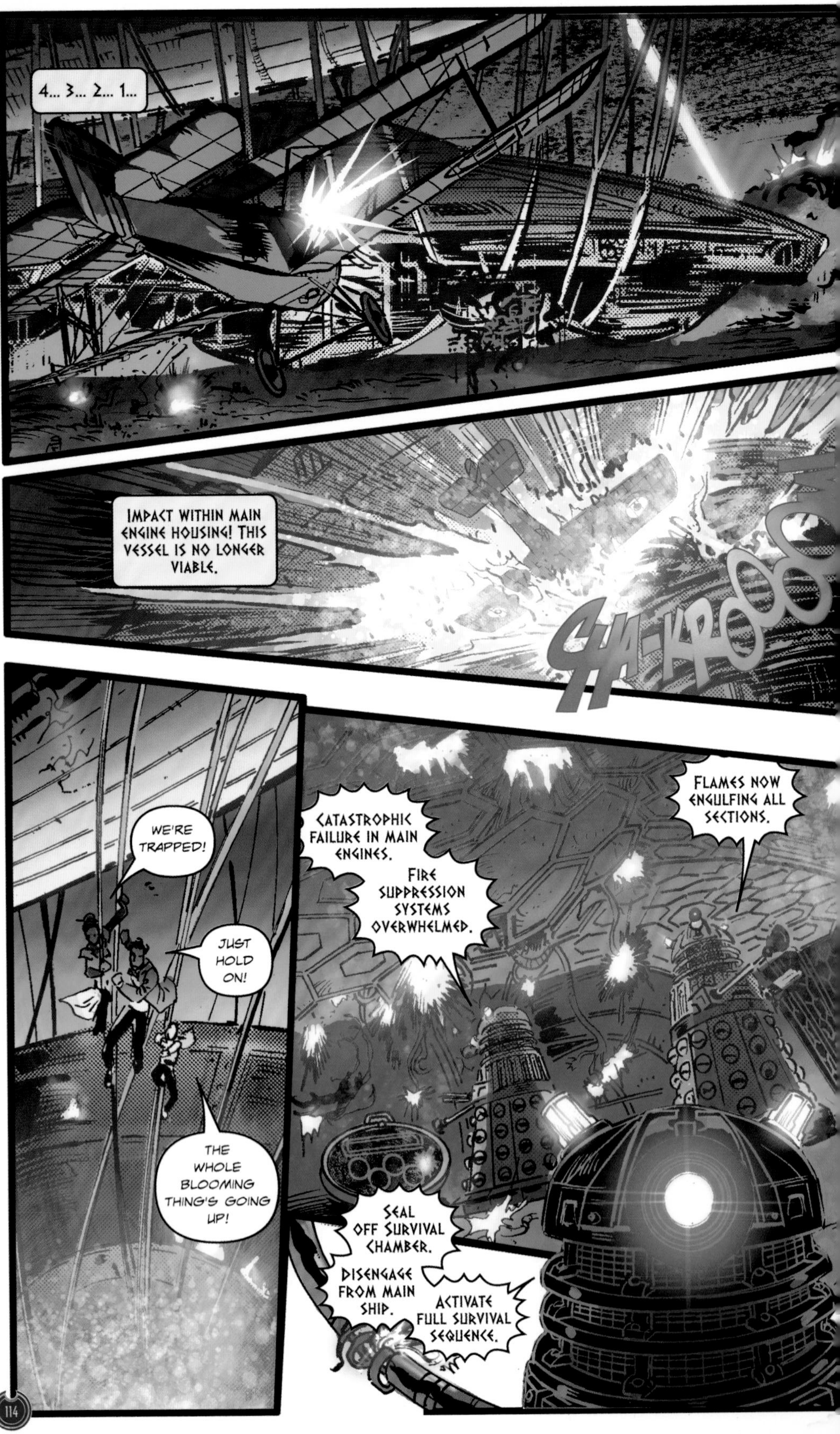
4... 3... 2... 1...
IMPACT WITHIN MAIN ENGINE HOUSING! THIS VESSEL IS NO LONGER VIABLE.
CHA-KROOOOOM
WE'RE TRAPPED!
JUST HOLD ON!
THE WHOLE BLOOMING THING'S GOING UP!
CATASTROPHIC FAILURE IN MAIN ENGINES.
FIRE SUPPRESSION SYSTEMS OVERWHELMED.
FLAMES NOW ENGULFING ALL SECTIONS.
SEAL OFF SURVIVAL CHAMBER.
DISENGAGE FROM MAIN SHIP.
ACTIVATE FULL SURVIVAL SEQUENCE.

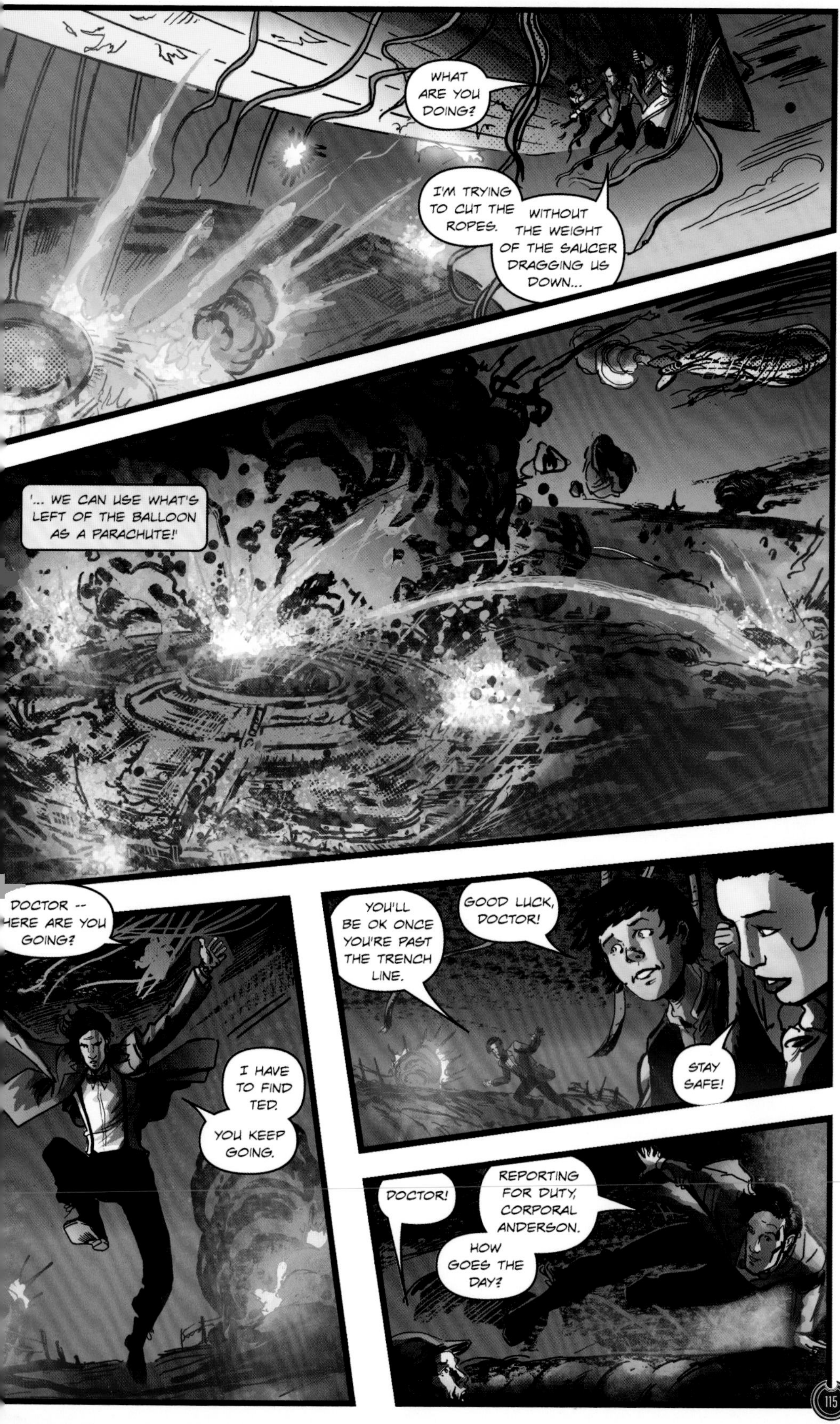
WHAT ARE YOU DOING?
I'M TRYING TO CUT THE ROPES.
WITHOUT THE WEIGHT OF THE SAUCER DRAGGING US DOWN...
'... WE CAN USE WHAT'S LEFT OF THE BALLOON AS A PARACHUTE!'
DOCTOR -- HERE ARE YOU GOING?
I HAVE TO FIND TED.
YOU KEEP GOING.
YOU'LL BE OK ONCE YOU'RE PAST THE TRENCH LINE.
GOOD LUCK, DOCTOR!
STAY SAFE!
DOCTOR!
REPORTING FOR DUTY, CORPORAL ANDERSON.
HOW GOES THE DAY?

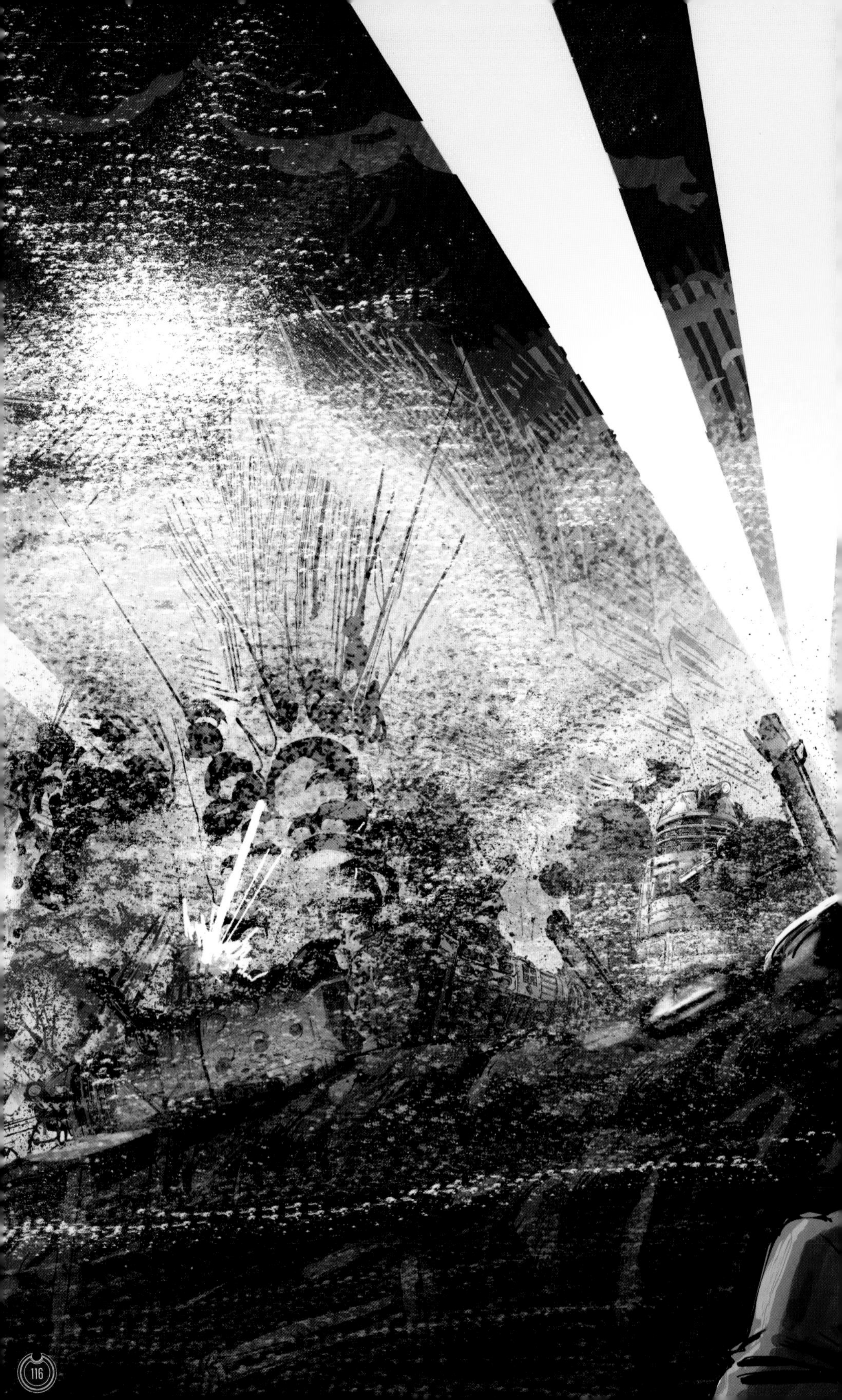

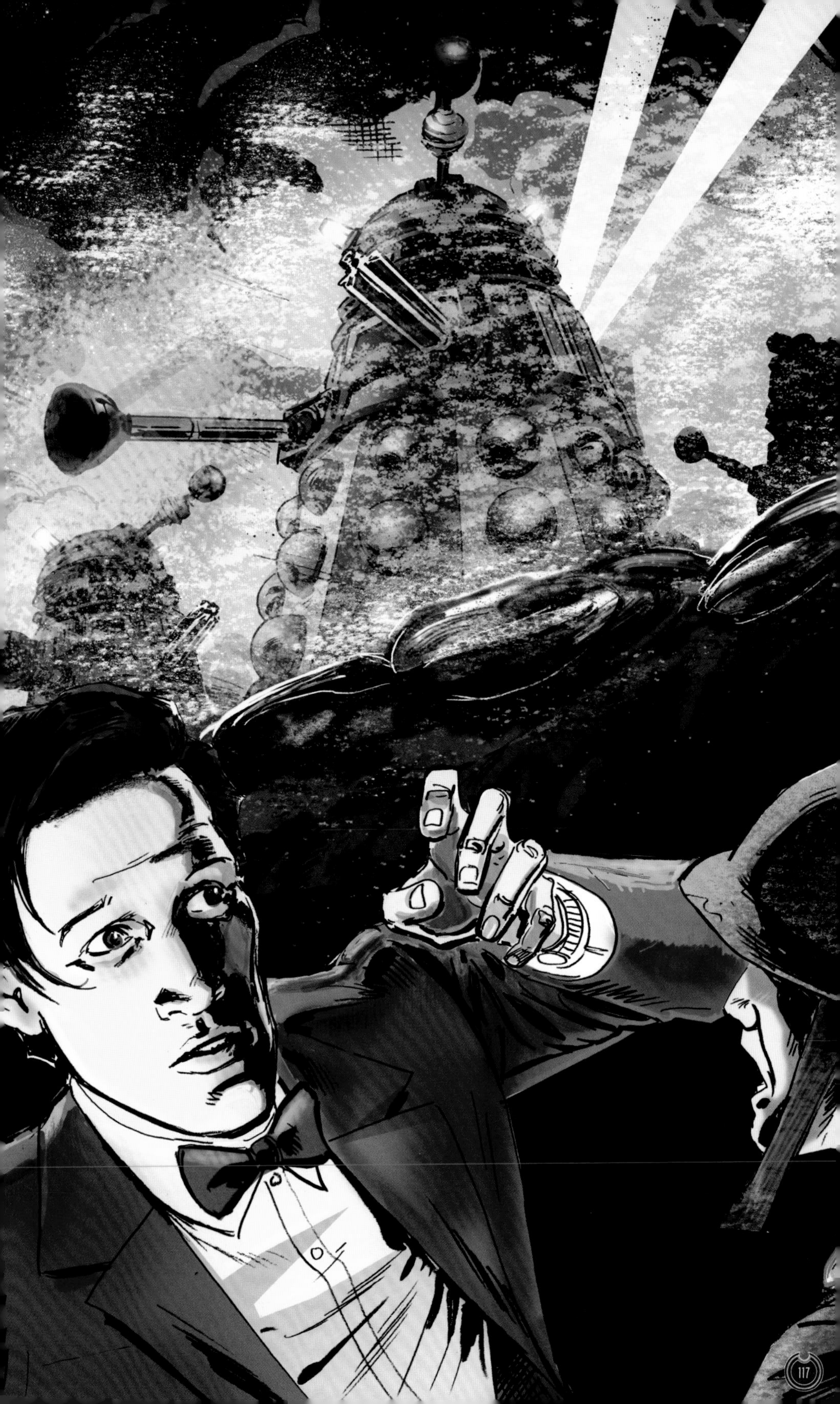

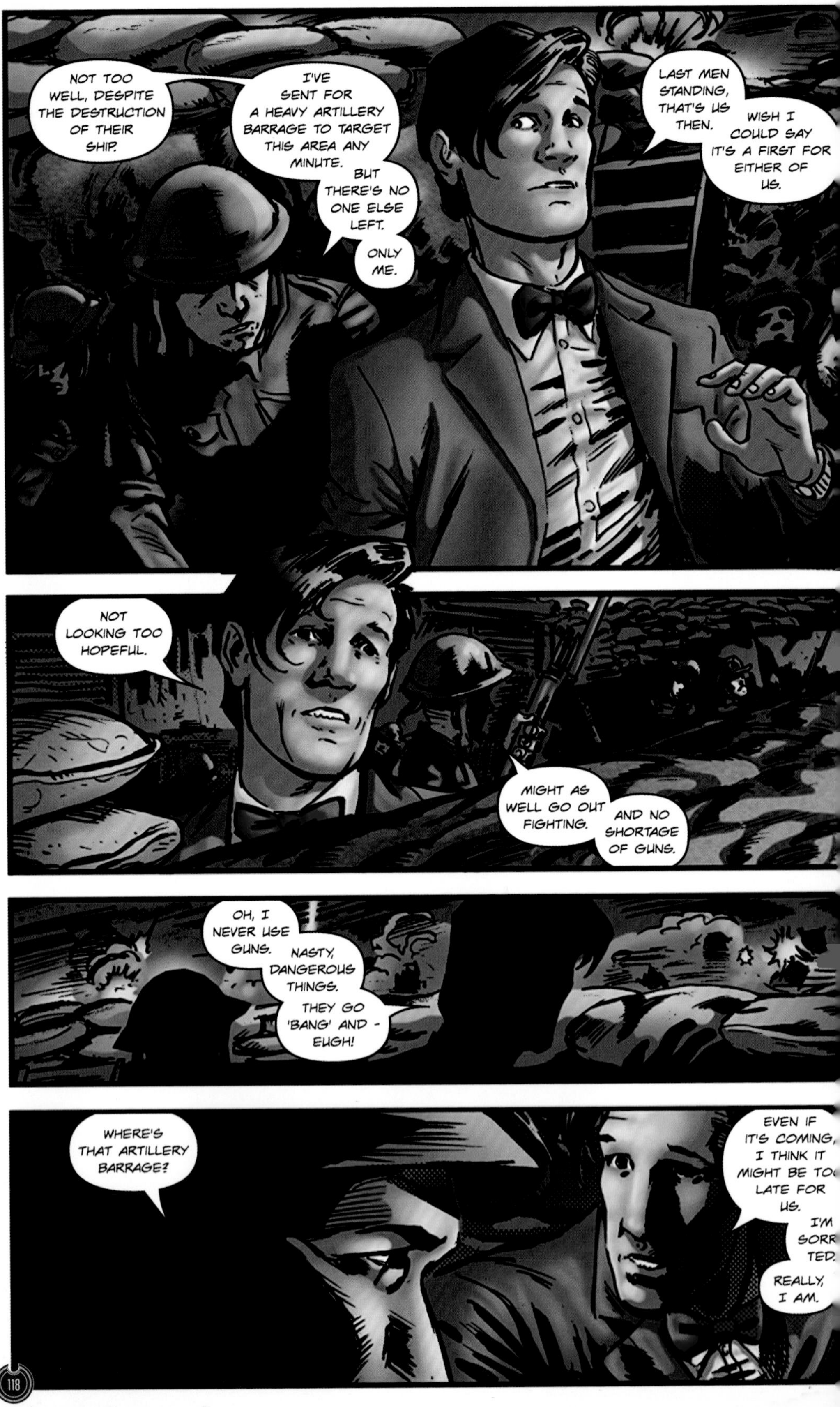
NOT TOO WELL, DESPITE THE DESTRUCTION OF THEIR SHIP.
I'VE SENT FOR A HEAVY ARTILLERY BARRAGE TO TARGET THIS AREA ANY MINUTE.
BUT THERE'S NO ONE ELSE LEFT.
ONLY ME.
LAST MEN STANDING, THAT'S US THEN.
WISH I COULD SAY IT'S A FIRST FOR EITHER OF US.
NOT LOOKING TOO HOPEFUL.
MIGHT AS WELL GO OUT FIGHTING.
AND NO SHORTAGE OF GUNS.
OH, I NEVER USE GUNS.
NASTY, DANGEROUS THINGS.
THEY GO 'BANG' AND - EUGH!
WHERE'S THAT ARTILLERY BARRAGE?
EVEN IF IT'S COMING, I THINK IT MIGHT BE TO
LATE FOR US.
I'M SORR TED.
REALLY, I AM.

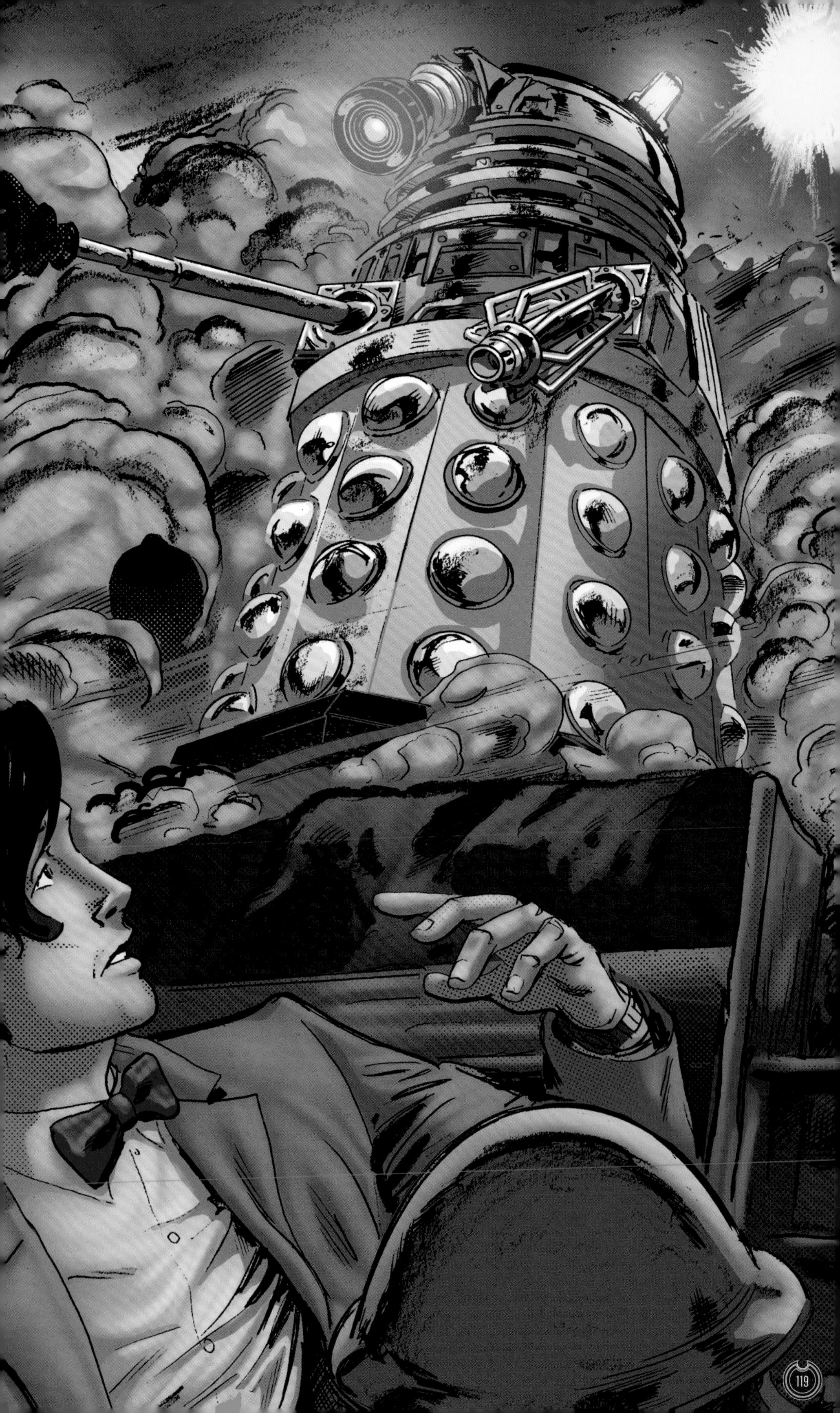

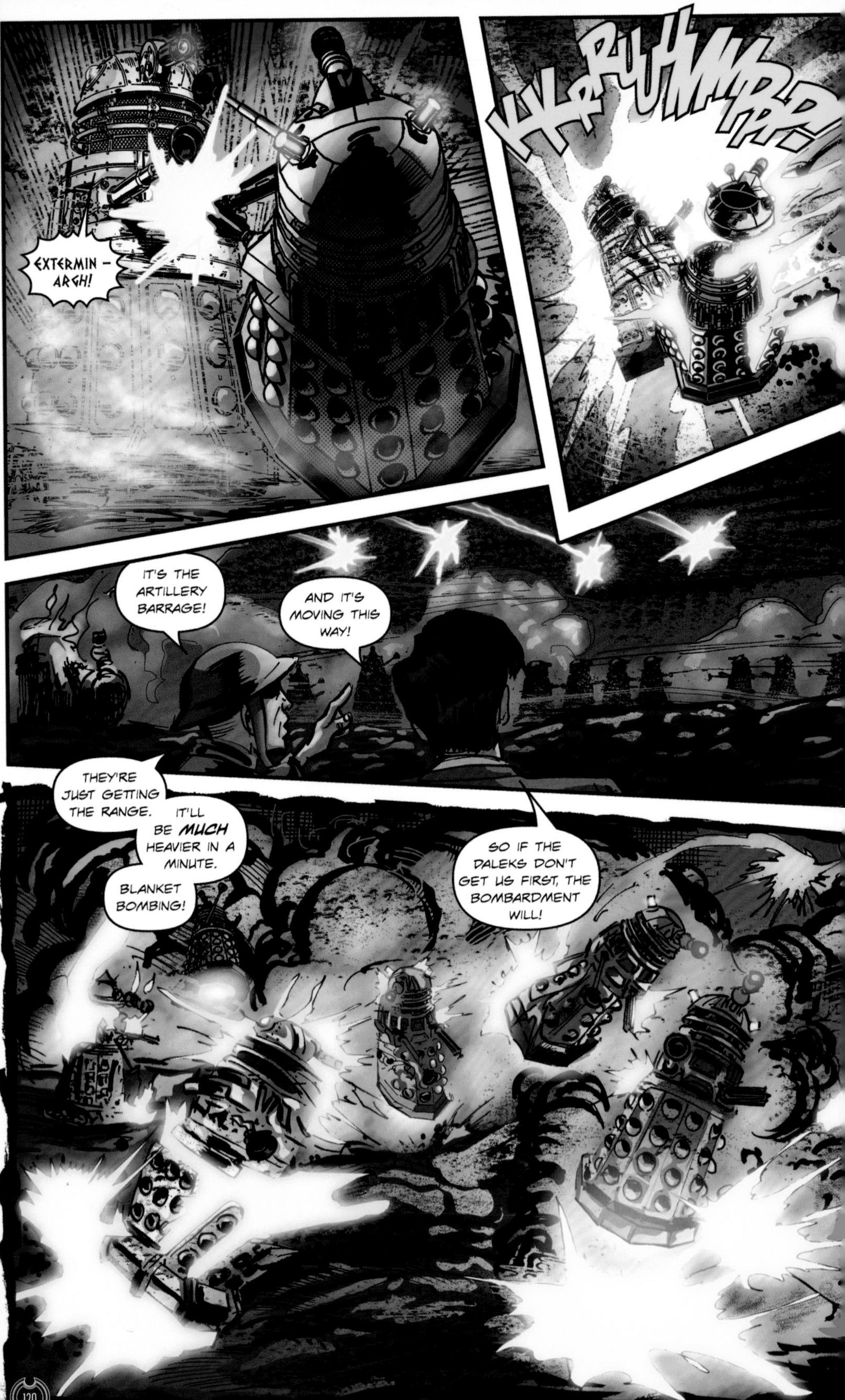
EXTERMIN - ARGH!
IT'S THE ARTILLERY BARRAGE!
AND IT'S MOVING THIS WAY!
THEY'RE JUST GETTING THE RANGE.
IT'LL BE MUCH HEAVIER IN A MINUTE.
BLANKET BOMBING!
SO IF THE DALEKS DON'T GET US FIRST, THE BOMBARDMENT WILL!

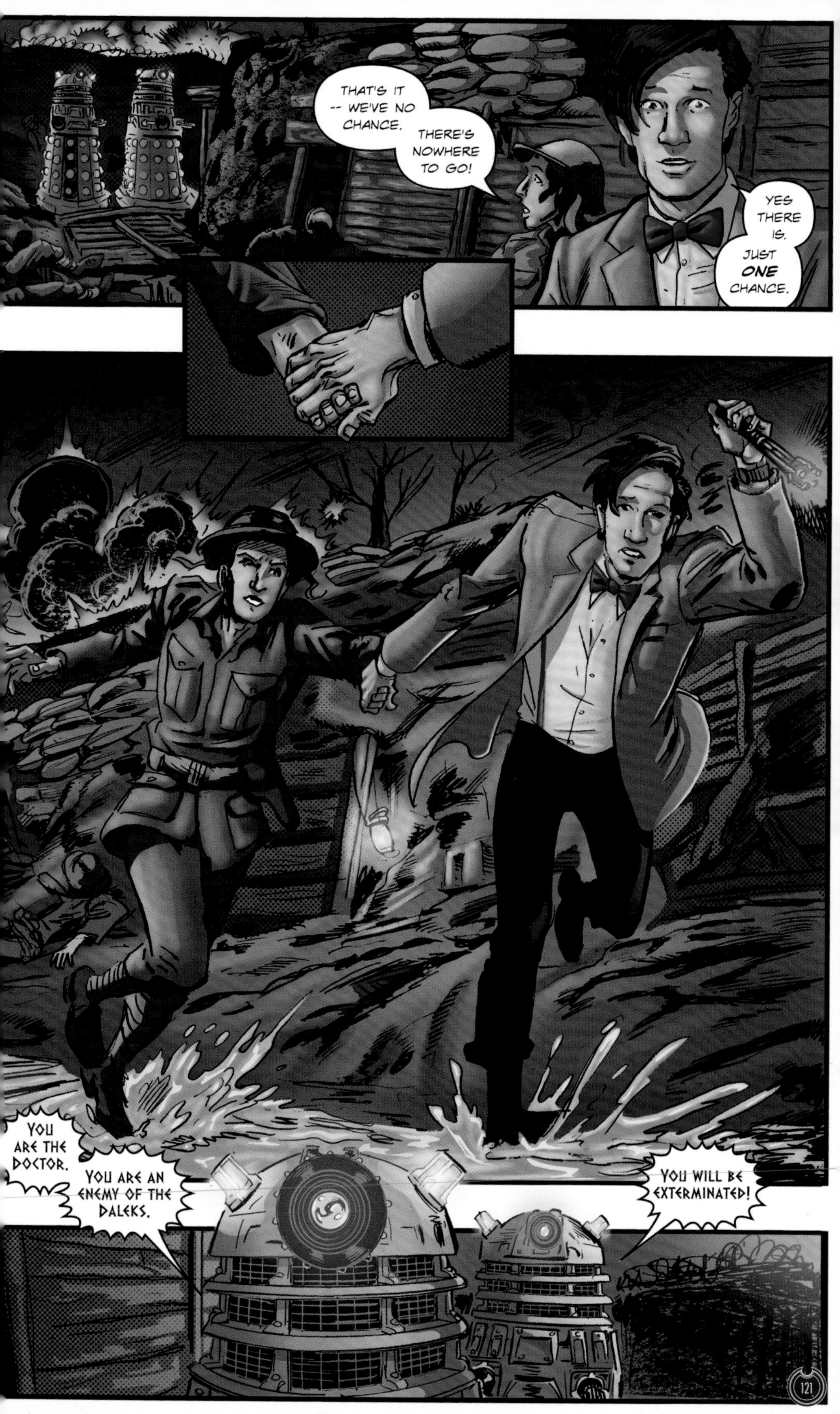
THAT'S IT -- WE'VE NO CHANCE.
THERE'S NOWHERE TO GO!
YES THERE IS.
JUST ONE CHANCE.
YOU ARE THE DOCTOR.
YOU ARE AN ENEMY OF THE DALEKS.
YOU WILL BE EXTERMINATED!

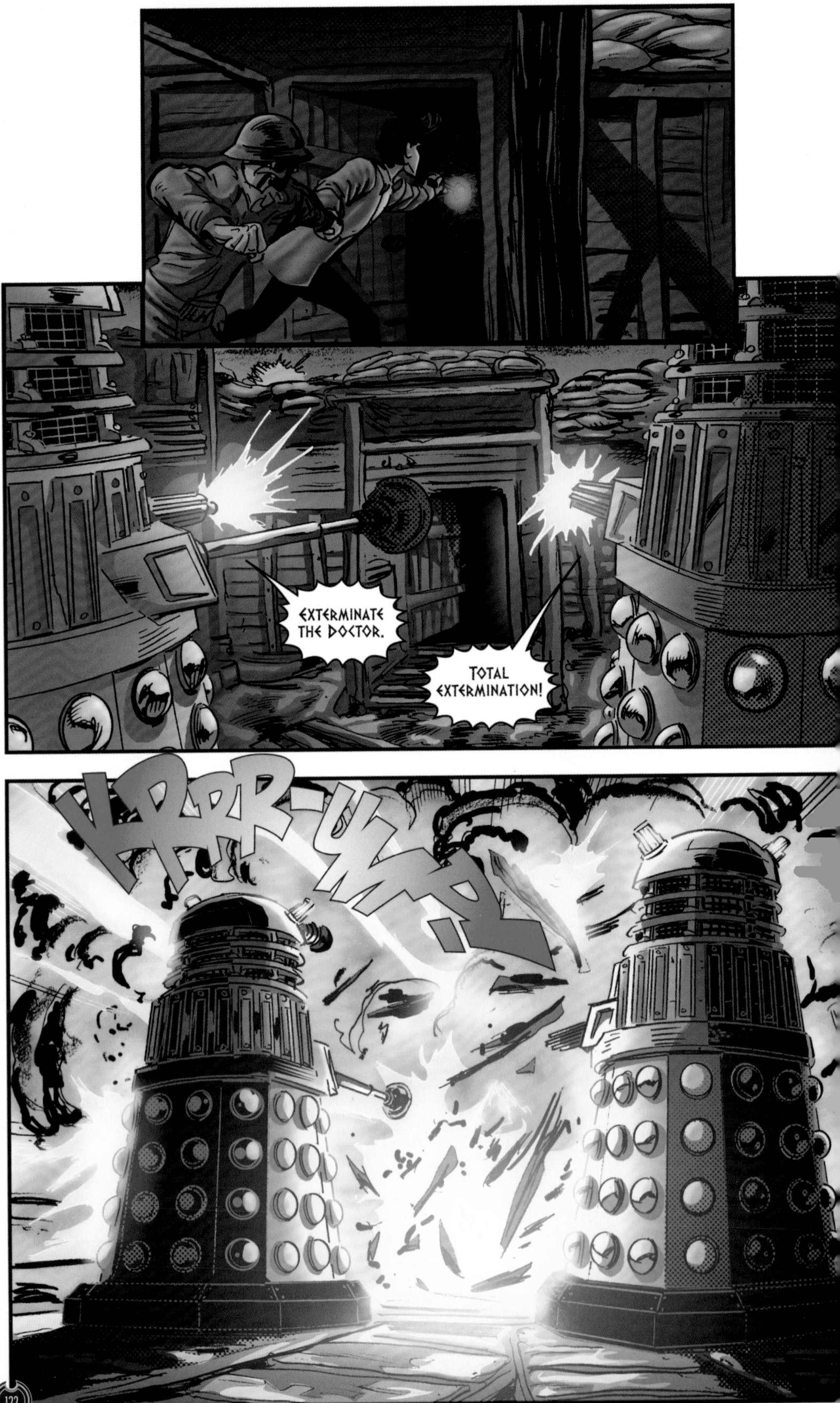
EXTERMINATE THE DOCTOR.
TOTAL EXTERMINATION!
KRR-UMP!

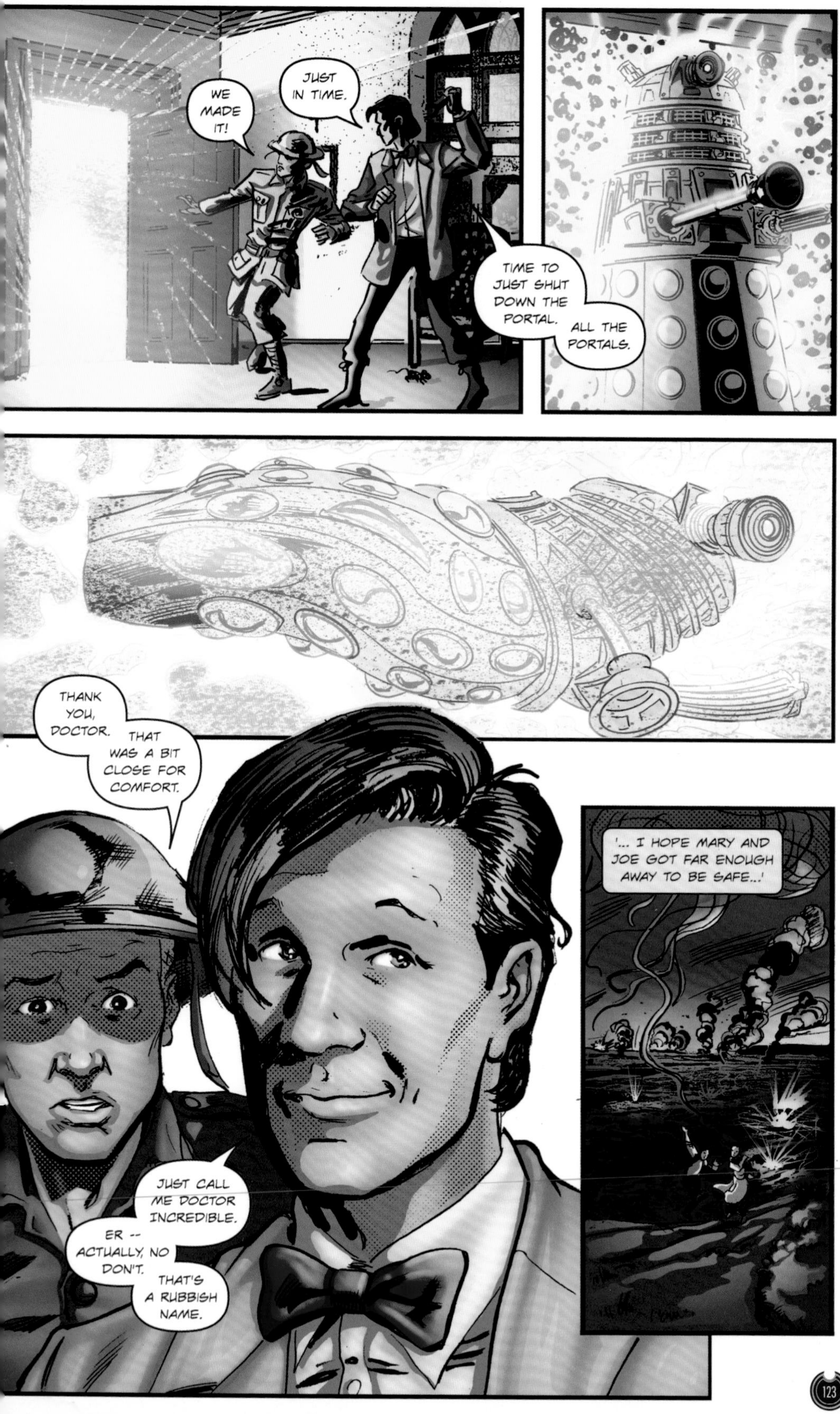

WE MADE IT!
JUST IN TIME.
TIME TO JUST SHUT DOWN THE PORTAL.
ALL THE PORTALS.
THANK YOU, DOCTOR.
THAT WAS A BIT CLOSE FOR COMFORT.
JUST CALL ME DOCTOR INCREDIBLE.
ER -- ACTUALLY, NO DON'T.
THAT'S A RUBBISH NAME.
'... I HOPE MARY AND JOE GOT FAR ENOUGH AWAY TO BE SAFE...'

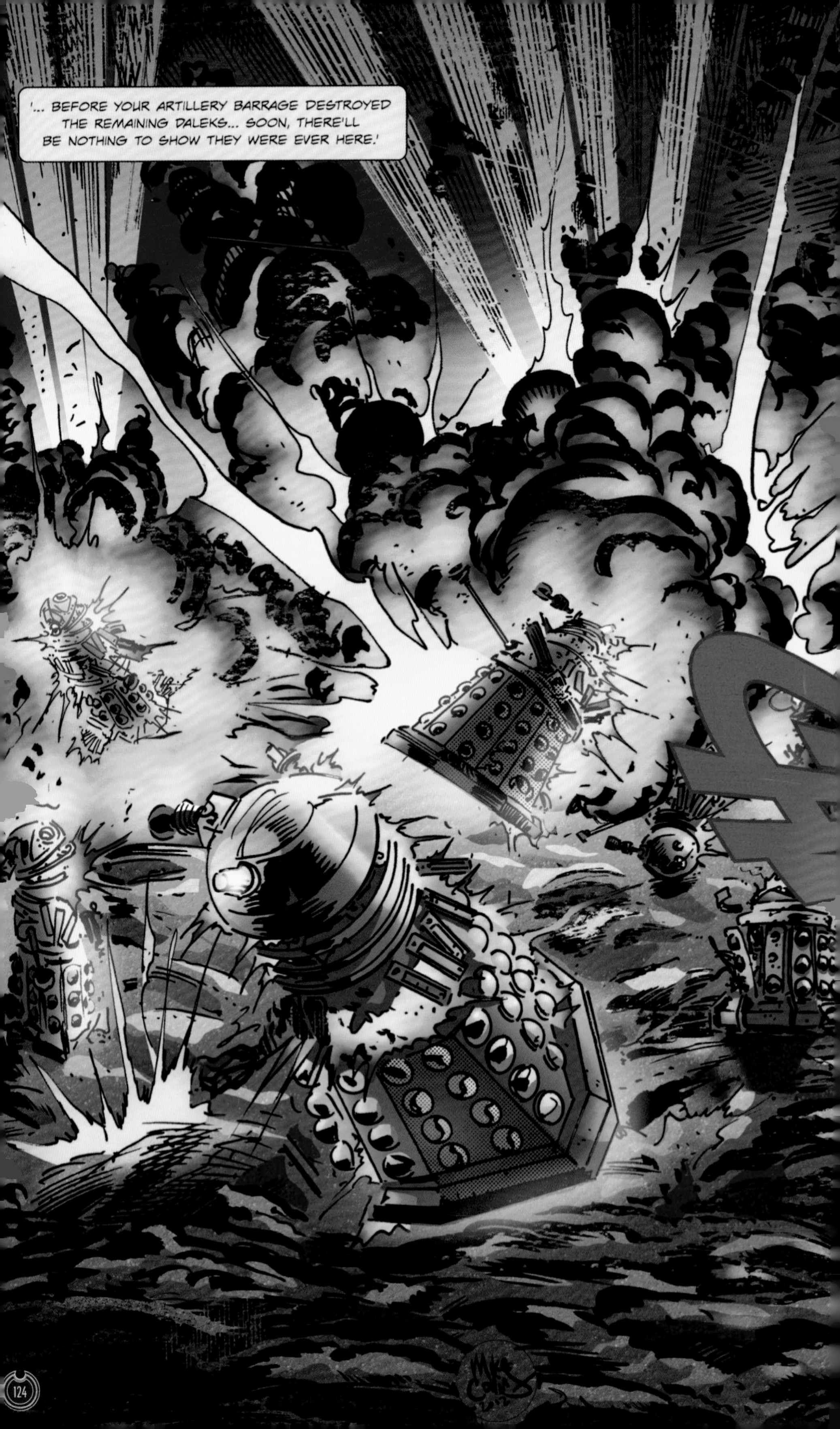
'... BEFORE YOUR ARTILLERY BARRAGE DESTROYED THE REMAINING DALEKS... SOON, THERE'LL BE NOTHING TO SHOW THEY WERE EVER HERE.'

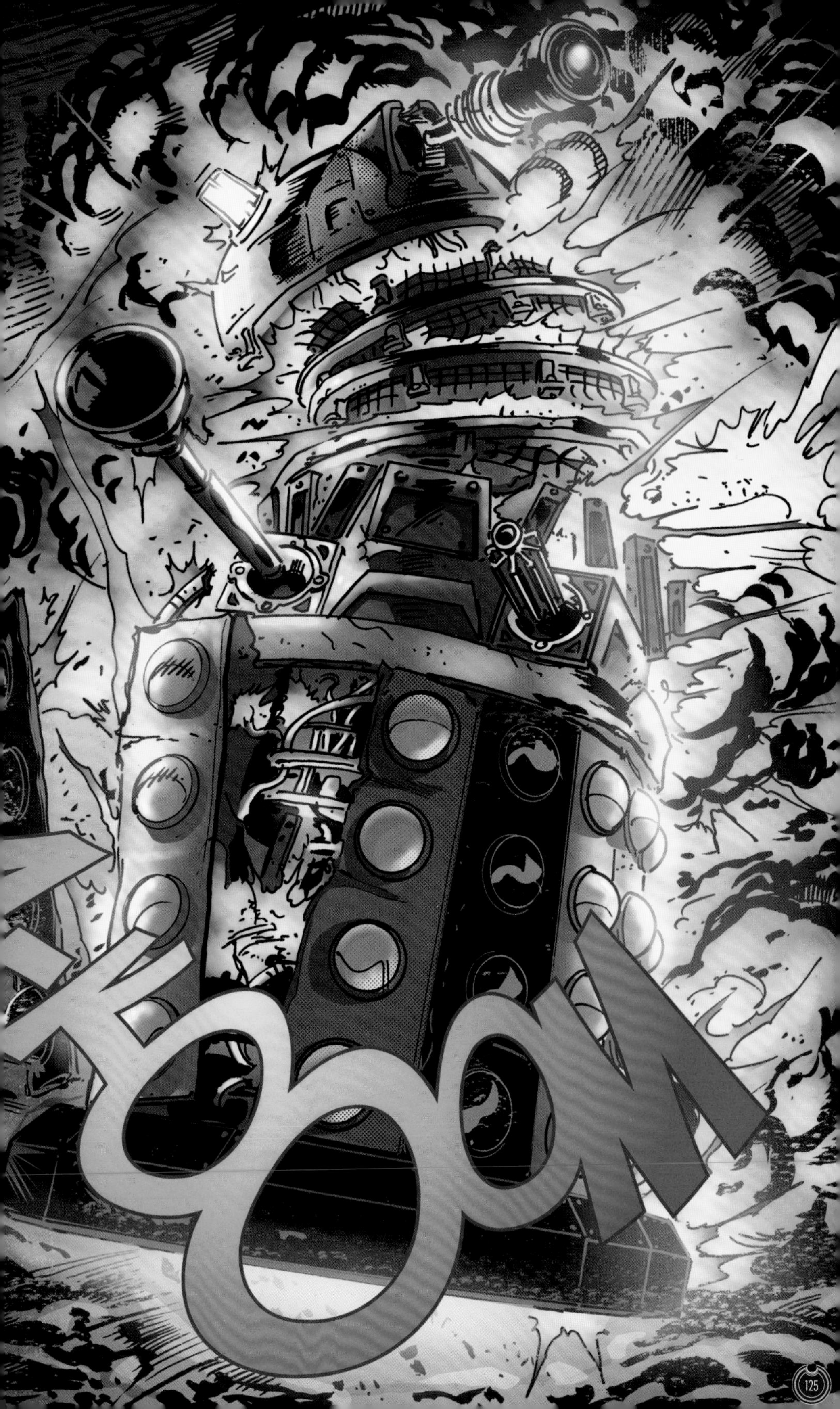

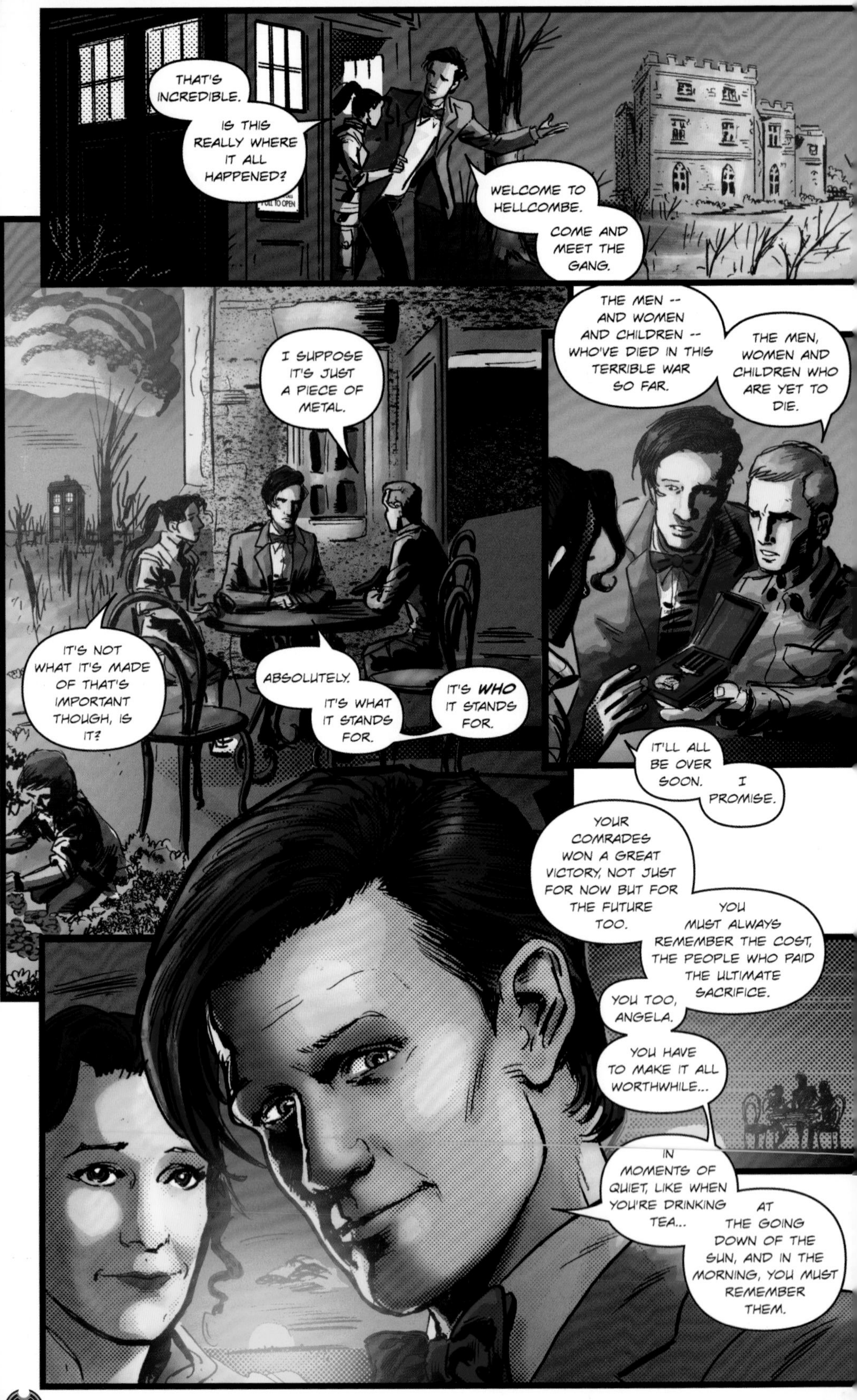
THAT'S INCREDIBLE.
IS THIS REALLY WHERE IT ALL HAPPENED?
PULL TO OPEN
WELCOME TO HELLCOMBE.
COME AND MEET THE GANG.
I SUPPOSE IT'S JUST A PIECE OF METAL.
IT'S NOT WHAT IT'S MADE OF THAT'S IMPORTANT THOUGH, IS IT?
ABSOLUTELY.
IT'S WHAT IT STANDS FOR.
IT'S **WHO** IT STANDS FOR.
THE MEN -- AND WOMEN AND CHILDREN -- WHO'VE DIED IN THIS TERRIBLE WAR SO FAR.
THE MEN, WOMEN AND CHILDREN WHO ARE YET TO DIE.
IT'LL ALL BE OVER SOON.
I PROMISE.
YOUR COMRADES WON A GREAT VICTORY, NOT JUST FOR NOW BUT FOR THE FUTURE TOO.
YOU MUST ALWAYS REMEMBER THE COST, THE PEOPLE WHO PAID THE ULTIMATE SACRIFICE.
YOU TOO, ANGELA.
YOU HAVE TO MAKE IT ALL WORTHWHILE...
IN MOMENTS OF QUIET, LIKE WHEN YOU'RE DRINKING TEA...
AT THE GOING DOWN OF THE SUN, AND IN THE MORNING, YOU MUST REMEMBER THEM.

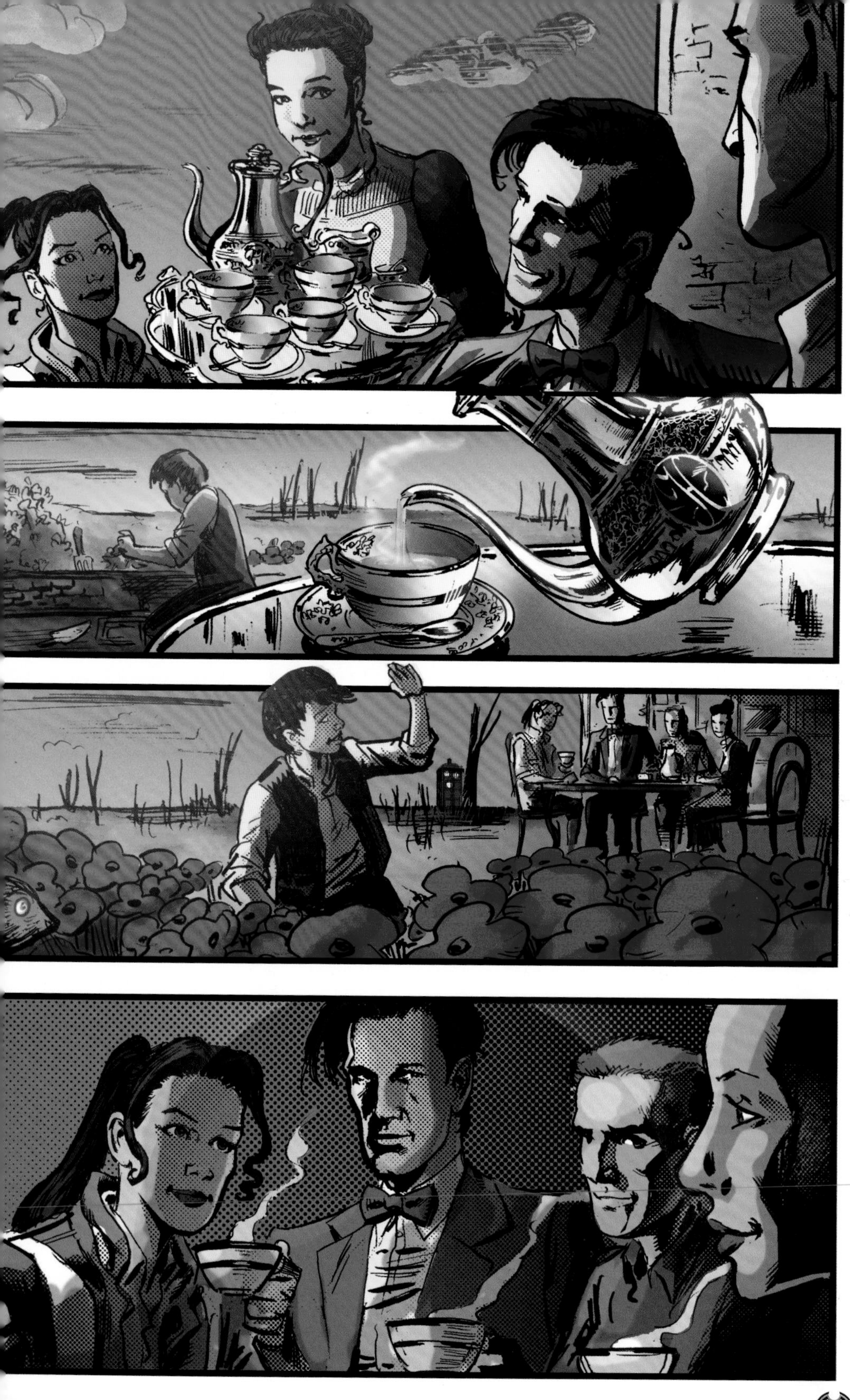

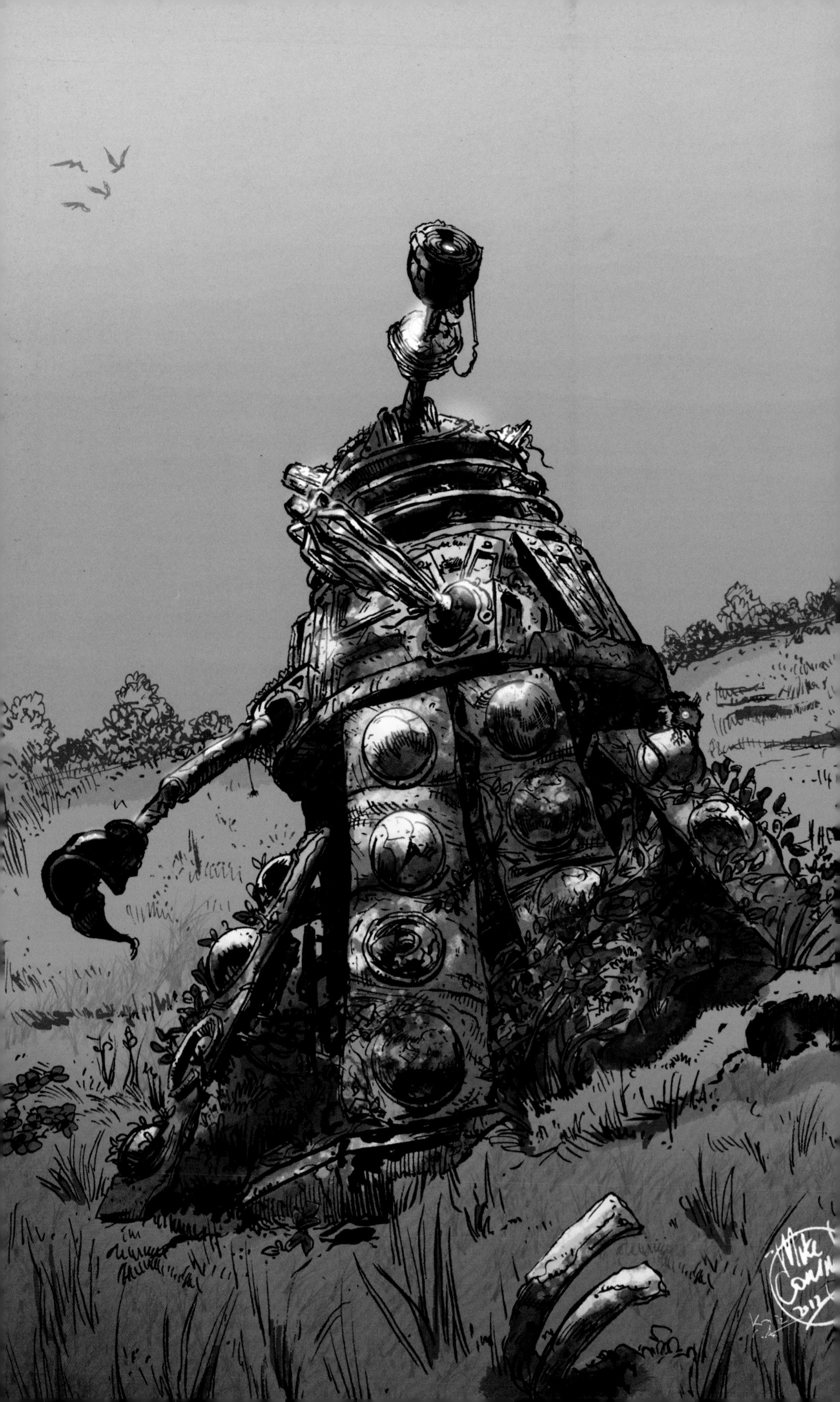